LADY WITH A MEAD CUP

Lady with a Mead Cup

*Ritual, Prophecy and Lordship
in the European Warband
from La Tène to the Viking Age*

Michael J. Enright

Set in 11 on 12.5 point Ehrhardt for
FOUR COURTS PRESS
Kill Lane, Blackrock, Co. Dublin, Ireland
and in North America
FOUR COURTS PRESS
c/o ISBS, 5804 N.E. Hassalo Street, Portland, OR 97213.

A catalogue record for this title
is available from the British Library.

ISBN 1-85182-188-0

Printed in Great Britain
by Antony Rowe Ltd, Chippenham, Wilts.

CONTENTS

For my parents, Michael and Esther Enright.
And in loving memory of "gran", Patrick Kenneally,
and of "daw", Madge Mac Mahon,
in her wonderful "little house under the hill".

ABBREVIATIONS

AAH	Acta Archaeologica Hungaricae
AESC	Annales: Economies, Sociétés, Civilisations
AF	Ausgrabungen und Funde
AG	Archaeologia Geographica
AHR	American Historical Review
AIBL	Academie des Inscriptions et Belles Lettres (Comptes Rendus)
AJAH	American Journal of Ancient History
AK	Archäologisches Korrespondenzblatt
AM	Annuale Medievale
ANB	Archäologische Nachrichten aus Baden
ANF	Arkiv for nordisk Filologi
ANRW	Aufstieg und Niedergang der römischen Welt
ANS	Proceedings of the Battle Conference on Anglo-Norman Studies
ASE	Anglo-Saxon England
BBCS	Bulletin of the Board of Celtic Studies
BIA	Bulletin of the Institute of Archaeology (University of London)
BJ	Bonner Jahrbücher
BJS	British Journal of Sociology
BLAFAM	Bulletin de Liason de l'Association Française d'Archéologie Merovingienne
CHJ	Cambridge Historical Journal
CMCS	Cambridge Medieval Celtic Studies
DA	Deutsches Archiv für die Erforschung des Mittelalters
EC	Études Celtiques
ELN	English Language Notes
ES	English Studies
ES	Epigraphische Studien
FM St.	Frühmittelalterliche Studien
HA	Historisk Arkiv
HdR	Handwörterbuch zur deutschen Rechtsgeschichte
HJ	Historisches Jahrbuch
HZ	Historische Zeitschrift
IF	Indogermanische Forschungen
JAF	Journal of American Folklore
JDAI	Journal des deutschen archäologischen Instituts
JEGP	Journal of English and Germanic Philology
JFH	Journal of Family History
JIES	Journal of Indo-European Studies
JMH	Journal of Medieval History
JMV	Jahresschrift für mitteldeutsche Vorgeschichte

JRGZ	Jahrbuch des römisch-germanischen Zentralmuseums Mainz
JRSAI	Journal of the Royal Society of Antiquaries of Ireland
KZS	Kölner Zeitschrift für Soziologie
LSE	Leeds Studies in English
MAGW	Mitteilungen Anthropologische Gesellschaft in Wien
MGH	Monumenta Germania Historica
MGH AA	Auctores antiquissimi
MGH SS	Scriptores
MGH SS rer. Germ.	Scriptores rerum Germanicarum
MGH SS rer. Lang.	Scriptores rerum Langobardorum et Italicarum saec. VI-IX.
MGH SS rer. Merov.	Scriptores rerum Merovingicarum
MLR	Modern Language Review
MQ	Mankind Quarterly
MP	Modern Philology
MS	Medieval Scandinavia
NAR	Norwegian Archaeological Review
NM	Neophilologische Mitteilungen
NMS	Nottingham Medieval Studies
PBA	Proceedings of the British Academy
PP	Past and Present
PRCA	Paulys Realencyclopädie der klassischen Altertumswissenschaft
PRIA	Proceedings of the Royal Irish Academy
PZ	Prähistorische Zeitschrift
RA	Revue archaeologique
RC	Revue Celtique
RHDFE	Revue historique de droit français et étranger
RSJB	Recueils de la Société Jean Bodin
SBVS	Saga-Book of the Viking Society
SCH	Studies in Church History
SG	Studium Generale
SHR	Scottish Historical Review
SMC	Studies in Medieval Culture
SMRH	Studies in Medieval and Renaissance History
SN	Studia Neophilologica
SP	Studies in Philology
SS	Scandinavian Studies
SSCI	Settimane di studio del centro italiano di studi sull'alto medioevo
St. S	Studien zur Sachsenforschung
TRHS	Transactions of the Royal Historical Society
TZ	Trierer Zeitschrift
VA	Varia Archaeologica
WZ	Westfalische Zeitschrift
ZBL	Zeitschrift für bayerische Landesgeschichte
ZcP	Zeitschrift für celtische Philologie
ZdP	Zeitschrift für deutsche Philologie
Zf.A	Zeitschrift für Archäologie
Zf.DA	Zeitschrift für deutsches Altertum und Literatur
ZSSR (GA)	Zeitschrift der Savigny-Stiftung für Rechtsgeschichte. Germanische Abteilung
ZSSR (RA)	Zeitschrift der Savigny-Stiftung für Rechtsgeschichte. Romanische Abteilung

PREFACE

This book grew slowly, *nolens volens*, because I set out to write a different one. Several years ago, in the midst of research for a socio-institutional history of the Germanic *comitatus*, I composed an article on the cup-offering ritual in *Beowulf* and the *Historia Langobardorum*. It was published in *Frühmittelalterliche Studien* in 1988 (and reappears here as chapter one with only slight modification).* Upon returning to my original project, however, I was continually irked by the nettlesome sense of having excluded too much relevant matter from the article, of not having sufficiently explored the background of the ritual offering to fully explain it in an intellectually satisfying way. Curiosity and self-criticism eventually obliged me to indulge again the lady with a mead cup.

Once decided that a more thorough analysis was needed, two probative essays followed fairly rapidly. These were read and commented upon by Karl Hauck of Münster who suggested that a broader discussion and an additional chapter might make a useful book. That chapter (appearing here as chapter five on warband religion and the Celtic world) became far more extensive than originally planned. Although an avalanche of literature was available to draw upon, many of the assumptions made therein seemed questionable. Archaeologists and historians differed considerably in their approach to cultural change during the Roman period in Central Europe, for example, while two other groups of specialists, Germanists and Celticists, frequently seemed to blithely go their own ways without paying a great deal of attention to their colleague's results. Much can be learned by a comparison of their findings and I hope to have made some progress in the present work. But "some progress" is the operative phrase. An attempt to assess a cross-section of this disparate material in light of conclusions reached or suspected led to exploratory forays in fields in which I am very conscious of being an amateur—archaeology, runology, linguistics, epigraphy, place-names, to name only a few. I have taken some consolation from the fact that a full study of these subjects would be beyond the capability of any one writer although that has been cold comfort on many occasions. Undoubtedly, therefore, experts in these areas will find errors although much effort has been expended to keep them to a minimum. I remain nonetheless convinced that some venture must be made to

* I have also drawn several pages from an article which appeared in Jörg Jarnut, Ulrich Nonn und Michael Richter, eds., *Karl Martell in seiner Zeit* (Sigmaringen, 1994) pp. 367–380.

draw together the myriad strands of evidence in order to eventually develop a coherent picture of cultural interaction in early Europe.

In some ways the present study is an experiment. It is an attempt to isolate the cup-offering ritual of some Germanic peoples of the Early Middle Ages, to establish its function within the institution in which it appears, to seek to explain its cultural and religious sources and to suggest that an analysis of the ritual provides a case study which demonstrates that considerably more continuity existed in European history from La Tène through the Viking period than is commonly supposed. The presence of the cup-offering ritual among diverse peoples over many centuries indicates great social significance.

Since the ritual is best described in the *Beowulf* poem, a work which seems to provide a fairly reliable description of the warband lifestyle, it is *Beowulf* that forms the starting point for the analysis that follows. It is not a study of the poem in the narrow sense for I am not interested in its literary value but rather in certain aspects of the institution to which it frequently alludes and always takes for granted. Chapter one describes the cup-offering ritual and relates it to kingship and the maintenance of cohesion within the warband. The crucial figure is Wealhtheow, the lady with the mead cup, who first presents it to the ruler and then distributes liquor to his followers. Chapter two examines some elements of prophecy and provocation which seem to accompany the distribution and to be especially associated with Hrothgar's queen. These are interpreted as institution-ally functional characteristics of Wealhtheow and not, as one might otherwise suppose, merely personal quirks. Prophecy and provocation appear to have been typical behaviors of women amongst warrior groups in Germanic cultures and a connection with the sibyls who sometimes accompanied early Germanic leaders seems demonstrable. This interpretation then leads naturally to an initial discussion of Julius Civilis of the Batavi and Veleda, a prophetess of the Bructeri, since they are the earliest leader/prophetess team that can also be linked to warband organization.

Chapter three seeks to elucidate a perceived association between entry into lordship, entry into marriage and the distribution of drink among retainers. The idea of the creation of a fictive family, it is argued, is central to this complex pattern of thought. A number of clues indicate that a similar concept and a distribution of drink also played a role in the creation of Civilis as leader of the Batavian revolt in AD 69.

The purpose of chapter four is entirely different, in part because I now seek to examine documents of a different genre. Several problems are dealt with. On one hand, the existence of the motif and ritual in question needs to be more securely demonstrated for the early Germanic milieu. On the other, the eviden-tiary gap between the ages of Civilis and Beowulf requires bridging since little material is available for the former period and only slightly more for the centuries that intervene. The only approach capable of eliciting significant new information is that of archaeology. Hence, chapter four is devoted to the archaeology of intoxication in Central Europe from the Iron Age to that of the Vikings and also adds a brief discussion of the contemporary oral culture in order to clarify the reasons for continuity of the mead cup complex among some peoples of the Early Middle Ages and its disappearance or near disappearance from the literary records of others.

Chapter five provides the most complicated exposition of the book. Despite a large gap of some seven to nine centuries, the figures of Veleda and Wealhtheow seem to be joined by a surprising number of salient characteristics—prophecy, mediation, a religious aura and a link with kingship and a warband. Both names have Celtic connections and so does the *comitatus* itself. This being the case, a further and more complete exploration of the cultural background of the *comitatus* and the origins of warband religion seemed necessary. Investigation of the liquor ritual thus leads to another level of questioning and becomes part of a broader context. In addition, the nature of the hypothesis offered seemed to require a shift to a more novel approach. If, as will be argued, the key relationship in the Germanic *comitatus* was not simply the lord/follower duality (although that is the dominant one) but rather the far more intricate pattern of lord/prophetess/follower, then a new level of complexity has been added and a new attempt at an interpretation makes sense. As far as I know, no other work deals specifically with the variety of problems thus raised although, needless to say, the fine studies of scholars like Reinhard Wenskus, Walter Schlesinger, Hans Kuhn, Christoph Rüger, Karl Paschel and others have been indispensable guides as can easily be read from the footnotes.

Perhaps one should also say what this book is not: it is not a history of the *comitatus*. As I now (reluctantly) accept, a true history of that institution is impossible to write because of the scarcity of the sources and the ambiguity of scattered reference. On the other hand, it is possible, in broad strokes, to analyze the nature of a number of aspects of its organizational development and behavioral pattern; some of these are discussed here although I hope to do more in a subsequent volume. The present focus is on ritual and religiosity. The aim is to demonstrate and document the existence of the lord/prophetess dynamic within the *comitatus* and its continuity over time. By *comitatus* (or warband or *Gefolgschaft*) I mean an organization of free men both within and without tribal structures who swear an oath of allegiance and military support to a leader in return for maintenance, gifts and plunder, but whose oath is not necessarily conditional on balanced reciprocity although a high degree of mutual devotion is intended and expected. In an early stage of development, warband members live in or near the leader's hall but eventually live elsewhere on land gifted or gained where they may also recruit a following of their own. Under certain conditions, the partly free or unfree may play a role in the organization. That is the framework for the following discussion.

A number of debts require acknowledgment. First and foremost, I wish to thank Karl Hauck for his encouragement, advice and frequent hospitality over the years, all of this despite onerous editorial duties and his own daunting research program of singular importance. His solicitude gives meaning to the term "community of scholars". Special thanks also to Forrest McDonald (a teacher who has left his mark) for his typically generous support at an early stage of my research and to the Earhart Foundation for a grant which financed a trip that made this book much easier to write. I also remember with pleasure Edwin Hall who first introduced me to the works of Ernst Kantorowicz. An earlier version of this study (excluding chapter four) was read by Winfred Lehmann who made many helpful suggestions and comments; so did Padraig O'Neill. I am sure that past conversations with friends and colleagues, Edwin Hall, Michael Richter, Robert Walton, Anthony Papalas, also made a difference although I can no longer be specific since most comments have long since been absorbed at various stages of the work. None of the above are responsible for any errors of fact or interpretation. My thanks to Brian Edwards for his typing and attention to the bibliography and to Mrs. Patricia Guyette of Interlibrary Loan at East Carolina University for her kindness and unflagging efforts in chasing the elusive essays of medievalists.[*]

In addition, I am very proud of my son Edward who continues to overlook my numerous faults and who for several years now has navigated his way around tumbling shoals of papers and manuscripts. Likewise my daughter, Anne-Kristin. Even though far away she is constantly in my thoughts. Finally, a special mention for my friends at Happy's Pool Hall (especially Lavonda "Duke" Kelly, Paul Chittum and Joe Meski) who greatly improved my game while also demonstrating a clear, albeit little known, relationship between straight pool and academic research.

Michael J. Enright
Greenville, North Carolina

---

[*] A number of very recent works appear in the bibliography but are cited infrequently in the notes. I learned of these during the last stages of manuscript preparation and was, regrettably, unable to make full use of them. They include Lotte Hedeager on Iron Age societies, Rolf Hachmann on the Gundestrup cauldron, as well as conference proceedings by Karl Hauck on bracteates; Heinrich Beck, Detlev Ellmers, Kurt Schier on the sources of Germanic religion and Günter Neumann and Henning Seemann on aspects of the *Germania* of Tacitus.

RITUAL, GROUP COHESION AND HIERARCHY
IN THE GERMANIC WARBAND

Both the political activities of Germanic queens and the lifestyle of the Germanic warband or *comitatus* are subjects which have often attracted scholarly attention. Interest in the former in particular is now flourishing in the English speaking world and has already eclipsed the latter which belongs to a more traditional category of historiography.[1] In one sense this pattern of inquiry represents a long overdue reexamination of the sources just as it also reflects the social and philosophical ferment characterizing the last generation of Western society. Not surprisingly, a reading of the recent literature tells us almost as much about ourselves as it does of the distant past especially since so much attention has been focused on the degree of independence to which the Germanic queen could aspire or anticipate. Such a question is certainly worth asking but the sources can seldom provide a satisfactory answer since it is so extraordinarily difficult to establish when the queen or royal widow is acting independently or when it is that she is simply functioning as the proxy for someone else, be it a husband, son, a faction of the nobility or the *comitatus*. Moreover, since so little is known about the actual enterprises of royal wives in general, much of what has been written has dealt with a few outstanding figures whose character and virtues, it is sometimes suggested, were fully as "virile" as their male counterparts and would undoubtedly be widely sung did we only know more about them. But this type of conjecture is unlikely to really advance historical knowledge since it actually

---

1 See, for example, Janet Nelson, "Queens as Jezebels: The Careers of Brunhild and Balthild in Merovingian History" (1978); Pauline Stafford, *Queens, Concubines and Dowagers: the King's Wife in the Early Middle Ages* (1983); Suzanne Fonay Wemple, *Women in Frankish Society: Marriage and the Cloister 500–900* (1981); Miles Campbell, "Queen Emma and Aelfgifu of Northampton: Canute the Great's Women" (1971); Helen Damico, *Beowulf's Wealhtheow and the Valkyrie Tradition* (1984); Jenny Jochens, "The Politics of Reproduction: Medieval Norwegian Kingship" (1987). These are only a few of the large number of studies written on this topic in the past two decades. In contrast, works in English on the history of the *comitatus* are scarce on the ground. But see David Green, *The Carolingian Lord: Semantic Studies on Four Old High German Words. Balder, Fro, Truhtin, Herro* (1965); Hector Munro Chadwick, *Studies on Anglo-Saxon Institutions* (1963[2]), pp. 308–354; John Lindow, *Comitatus, Individual and Honor. Studies in North Germanic Institutional Vocabulary* (1975). Not dealing specifically with the warband but often of relevance is Alexander Callender Murray, *Germanic Kinship Structure: Studies in Law and Society in Antiquity and the Early Middle Ages* (1983).

diverts attention from the crucial problem of interaction between king, queen and *comitatus* and it is only through the integrated study of the social exchanges between the three that we can hope to recognize the internal organizational design which often effected external political action.[2]

At first glance this formulation may well strike scholars as somewhat peculiar. Except in the case of female regencies, all studies of the Germanic warband have dealt nearly exclusively with the relations between lord and follower in the arena of the *aula regis* and have rarely taken account of the queen who, aside from her domestic activities and influence on the usual plots and machinations of the court, has never been thought to have had much to do with the *comitatus*. In my opinion this view should be modified to allow for the occasional subtle influence of a third party whose interests usually but not always coincide with those of the leader. What follows here, however, is not an attempt to list all of the possible ways in which a concerned or ambitious wife might influence her husband and his retainers. Such an exercise would have little meaning. Rather, it is a description and analysis of a perceived institutional arrangement. The present chapter seeks to investigate an hypothesized triangular pattern of political intercourse and to show that, contrary to common assumption, the royal consort normally played a significant if subordinate role in the establishment of order and hierarchy among the members of the warband and that, just as women in the wider world were used to bind families in alliances, so did the queen act to help achieve cohesion and unity of purpose between lord and follower in the royal hall. The significant point here is not that she was ever able to direct policy but rather that the queen, acting as her husband's delegate, exercised a number of important functions which, although only vaguely noticed in the literature, have noteworthy implications for the study of early European political organization and its ritual affirmation. In the following pages, using the *Beowulf* poem as a point of departure for social analysis, I shall try to sketch some of the notable ways in which royal (and noble) consorts routinely contributed to the enhancement of stability within a volatile warrior society and then how they helped to maintain continuity in times of stress and transition.

Shortly after his arrival at Heorot, king Hrothgar's great hall, Beowulf is given an honorable seat between the king's sons and witnesses the entrance of Wealhtheow whose formal proffering of the ceremonial cup of liquor to the Danish king signals the true beginning of the feast. Although lengthy, this description of the queen's actions deserves careful attention and must be cited in full since reference will subsequently be made to various aspects throughout the following study:

2 I know of no study dealing specifically with this relationship but many perceptive observations are made in Nelson, "Queens as Jezebels", p. 38f.

607 *Þa wæs on salum   sinces brytta*
    It was then a fine moment for the bestower of treasure,

608 *gamolfeax ond gudrof;   geoce gelyfde*
    grey of hair, good at fight, he had confidence in that help,

609 *brego Beorht-Dena;   gehyrde on Beowulfe*
    the prince of the Bright Danes, [when]

610 *folces hyrde   fæstrædne geþoht*
    the folk's shepherd, heard the firm resolve from Beowulf.

611 *Dær wæs hæleþahleahtor,   hlyn swynsode*
    There was laughter among the warriors, merry noise arose,

612 *word wæron wynsume.   Eode Wealhþeow forð,* ~~for~~th
    words were cheerful. Stepped forth Wealhtheow,

613 *cwen Hroðgares   cynna gemyndig,*
    Hrothgar's Queen, careful of noble usage.

614 *grette goldhroden   guman on healle*
    Gold-adorned she greeted the men in hall.

615 *ond þa freolic wif   ful gesealde*
    And then the gracious woman offered the cup

616 *ærest East-Dena   eþelwearde*
    first to the East-Danes' king, the guardian of their land,

617 *bæd hine bliðne   æt þære beorþege*
    bade him be happy in partaking of this beer-assembly,

618 *leodum leofne;   he on lust geþeah*
    be amiable to the people. He took part eagerly

619 *symbel ond seleful,   sigerof kyning*
    in the feast and formal cup, fully victorious king.

620 *Ymbeode þa   ides Helminga*
    Then her steps led here and there the lady of the Helmings,

621 *duguþe ond geogoþe   dæl æghwylcne*
    to veterans and youths, to each group of them,

622 *sincfato sealde,   oþ þæt sæl alamp*
    she offered from the treasure-vessel. Until the moment came

623 *þæt hio Beowulfe, beaghroden cwen*
    when to Beowulf the ring-adorned queen,

624 *mode geþungen   medoful ætbær;*
    gratified in her heart, brought the cup of mead.

625 *grette Geata leod,   Gode þancode* ~~thanked~~
    She greeted the chief of the Geats, gave thanks to God,

626 *wisfæst wordum   þæs ðe hire se willa gelamp,*
    wise as she was in her words, that her wish had come to good

627 *þæt heo on ænigne   eorl gelyfde*
    that she might have confidence in some hero,

628 *fyrena frofre. He þæt ful geþeah*
    a comforter in her woes. He partook of the cup,

629 *wælreow wiga   æt Wealhþeon,*
    the fierce slayer, from Wealhtheow's hands.
630 *ond þa gyddode   guþe gefysed*
    And then chanted his eagerness to fight.
631 *Beowulf maþelode,   bearn Ecgþeowes.*
    Thus spoke Beowulf, the son of Ecqtheow
632 *"Ic þæt hogode,   þa ic on holm gestah,*
    "I for one had this resolve in mind when I put to sea.
633 *sæbat gesæt   mid minra secga gedriht*
    I embarked on the long ship with my band of men
634 *þæt ic anunga   eowra leoda*
    that I once for all the wish of your people
635 *willan geworhte,   oþðe on wæl crunge.*
    I would accomplish or else fall in the fray.
636 *feondgrapum fæst.   Ic gefremman sceal*
    Fast in hostile grips I must perform
637 *eorlic ellen,   oþðe endedæg*
    heroic deeds or else my last day
638 *on þisse meoduhealle   minne gebidan!"*
    in this mead-hall must meet".
639 *Ðam wife þa word   wel licodon,*
    The woman enjoyed those words,
640 *gilpcwide Geates;   eode goldhroden.*
    the Geat's daring say. She resumed her steps, the gold-adorned.
641 *freolicu folccwen   to hire frean sittan.*
    gracious sovereign to sit by her suzerain.[3]

The stages of Wealhtheow's progress are as follows: she enters with a cup and greets the warriors, offers the cup first to the king, bids him enjoy the drinking and be happy with his people. Hrothgar partakes eagerly. Thereupon, Wealhtheow serves the retainers (it looks as if the same ceremonial vessel was used on each occasion)[4] moving first to the veteran warriors and then to the younger men among whom sits Beowulf. She honors him with a speech before giving him the drink while he proclaims his eagerness to fight and promises to perform heroic deeds. Wealhtheow is pleased by his reply and returns to take her seat beside the king. Let us now seek to unravel the elements in order to fully understand the rationale underlying the queen's behavior.

To begin with, it must be emphasized that the *Beowulf* poet is here using all

---

3 Fr. Klaeber, ed. *Beowulf and the Fight at Finnsburg* (1950[3]), p. 23f. The translation is that of Andre Crépin, "Wealhtheow's Offering of the Cup to Beowulf: A Study in Literary Structure" (1979), pp. 44–58.
4 This is also Crépin's view, "Wealhtheow's Offering", p. 52.

of his powers to describe the idealized archetypical image of aristocratic Germanic life—a way of thinking and doing which, by the late eight or ninth century when the poem (arguably) may have been first declaimed,[5] was already fading into the primordial past but which still maintained a powerful hold on the emotions of the Anglo–Saxon aristocracy who continued to recognize the essential rightness and congruity of the statement.[6] As scholars have constantly noted, Heorot is not just any royal hall; it is "the most famous of buildings under heaven", the "bright dwelling of brave men" whose walls symbolize the realm of warmth, protection and honor standing true against the wintry waste and chaos of the stormy world outside.[7] The mighty Hrothgar had built it at the zenith of his power to furnish the best of all frameworks for the communal life of the warband which he had attracted to his side after years of successful warfare. It is, then, the ideal hall for a model retinue. From the potent *gifstol* at its center,[8] the place of majesty where Hrothgar sits and near where the queen takes her place, flows all the treasure and public recognition which constitute the fundamental cultural values of the archaic world view. From this primary site the kingliness of the king radiates and is most palpably made manifest. It is here that the essential gestures of the society take place—the giving of gifts, the bestowal of honors, the granting of land. It is both the starting point and culmination of the most significant communal rituals, judgements, deliberations and celebrations and thus is a special, even holy, place which the unworthy dare not approach.

These remarks form the necessary introduction to Wealhtheow's ritual and must dispel any notion that the drinking procedure she initiates and which brings her into immediate contact with the high-seat is anything like a commonplace act of service. Most scholars have traditionally underrated the significance of the scene. According to Schücking, we are here "dealing only with a subsidiary figure who was not of central significance to the author", and Müllenhoff dismisses the entire passage as "a pretty interpellation".[9] Recent work has tended to modify

5 The question of dating has recently been discussed but not solved in Colin Chase, ed. *The Dating of Beowulf* (1981). See further Dorothy Whitelock, *The Audience of Beowulf* (1951); and for an excellent study of the context with remarks on possible dates, Patrick Wormald, "Bede, *Beowulf* and the Conversion of the Anglo-Saxon Aristocracy" (1978).

6 The appeal of *Beowulf* to both Christian aristocrats and clerics is rightly emphasized in Wormald, "Bede".

7 Among many studies of the Anglo-Saxon hall concept, see Kathryn Hume, "The Concept of the Hall in Old English Poetry" (1974); Alvin Lee, *The Guest Hall of Eden* (1972); William Chaney, *The Cult of Kingship in Anglo-Saxon England* (1970), pp. 135–136. These might profitably be compared with Pierre Riché, "Les représentations du palais dans les textes litteraires du Haut Moyen Age" (1981); Heinrich Wagner, "Der königliche Palast in keltischer Tradition" (1974).

8 Essential studies on the Germanic throne are now Karl Hauck, "Formenkunde der Götterthrone des heidnischen Nordens" (1984); Hans Drescher and Karl Hauck, "Götterthrone des heidnischen Nordens" (1982), pp. 237–244 (Drescher); 244–301 (Hauck).

9 Levin Schücking, *Heldenstolz und Würde im Angelsächsischen* (1934), p. 40; Karl Müllenhoff, "Die innere Geschichte des Beovulfs", in his *Beovulf. Untersuchungen über das angelsächsische Epos und die älteste Geschichte der germanischen Seevölker* (1889), p. 117.

this view[10] but the scholar who probably came closest to appreciating its importance was Wilhelm Grönbech, the great savant of medieval Germanic culture, for he refers to it in ways which suggest that he was cognizant of Wealhtheow's movements as a ritual, a solemn occasion in which the hierarchial order within the *comitatus* was established and renewed.[11] But even Grönbech did not see to the heart of the rite. In recent times, however, Andre Crépin, whose excellent translation I have borrowed above,[12] has advanced our understanding of the significance of the queen if not of the ritual.

Crépin points out that the poet is very careful to identify the birth, character and queenly attributes of Wealhtheow.[13] She is gold-adorned, *goldhroden*, and ring-adorned, *beaghroden*, and elsewhere we are told that she wore a golden diadem, *gyldnum beage*. These references clearly express her royal status which is further emphasized by descriptions like *ides helminga*, lady of the Helmings, *cwen hroðgares*, Hrothgar's queen, and *freolicu folccwen*, gracious sovereign. In this aspect at least she is the ideal queen and her dress, gestures, words and movements are all noted to underline her stately presence and archetypical status. Just as clearly she is also Hrothgar's delegate, an extension of his authority: She sits by him, expresses his thoughts (ll. 608, 627) and is identified as his queen. Most significantly, she is wise in her words, *wisfæst wordum*, and careful of noble usage, *cynna gemyndig*. In this she is like the distinguished chieftain Wulfgar, Hrothgar's herald, who is "known to many" for his wisdom and who was also described as "knowing the usage of a court" (l. 358) when he advanced to the high-seat and stood waiting to formally announce Beowulf. Wealhtheow's movements are imbued with the same formality. As Crépin points out, the passage cited above owes its unity "to its internal consistency based on repetition. The repetition of the verbs *eode* and *grette* emphasizes the various stages in the stately progress of the queen. She appears (*forð*, l. 612b), walks among the warriors (*ymb*, l. 620a), and finally goes and sits down beside her lord."[14]

10 See especially Crépin, "Wealhtheow's Offering", p. 51f. Damico (*Wealhtheow*) goes too far in the other direction, however, by seeking to make Wealhtheow more important in the poem than she actually is.
11 This work is available in English: Wilhelm Grönbech, *The Culture of the Teutons* (1931), p. 160f.
12 Crépin, "Wealhtheow's Offering". He misses much of the significance of the cup-offering, however, because he leaves aside the ritual itself "to focus on the writing".
13 Crépin, "Wealhtheow's Offering", p. 51f. He is exactly right to point out that "none of her [Wealhtheow] gestures, words or features is idiosyncratic". Unfortunately, he does not follow up the perceptive observation that "the role of the queen is to promote peace among the warriors in the hall by offering them the cup of mead". Although he regards Wealhtheow as a "Nebenfigur", Schücking, (*Heldenstolz*, p. 40) did point out that what she did is characteristic of the behavior of noblewomen in the hall: "Trotzdem erhält ihr Bild durch das, was sie sagt, und wie sie es sagt, einige ganz charakteristische Züge . . . Soweit spiegelt sich in ihren Worten nur das Bild der angelsächsischen Fürstin, das wir auch anderswo finden."
14 Crépin, "Wealhtheow's Offering", p. 51f.

The queen's movements are solemn in nature. They are prescribed acts which pertain to her status and role in the hall. Beyond this, I would suggest that Wealhtheow's progress, at least her offering of the cup to the king, is part of an archaic ritual of lordship which she must act out when the occasion warrants. The arrival of Beowulf and his companions evidently constitutes such an occasion and thus Wealhtheow quickly moves to assert her lord's superior dignity in the company of strangers from across the sea. Fortunately, we need not rely on *Beowulf* alone to establish this pattern, for another Old English work, the gnomic poem *Maxims I*, provides exemplary confirmation of the traditional ceremonial nature of the rite:

> The nobleman must have fighting spirit, his courage must grow, and his wife be a success, liked by her people; she must be cheerful, keep secrets, be generous with horses and precious things; *at mead drinking she must at all times and places approach the protector of princes first, in front of the companions, quickly pass the first cup to her lord's hand*, and know what advice to give him as joint master and mistress of the house together.[15]

These lines make it rather certain that Wealhtheow's cup offering is simply a specific instance of a general behavioral prescription which applies to all noblemen's wives. Aside from the poetic statement, the genre in which this appears suggests the same conclusion. *Maxims I* belongs to that type of Old English verse which is called "wisdom literature".[16] Such, in Bloomfield's words, is "devoted, in one way or another, to rules for conduct or control of the environment or to information about nature and man and designed to suggest a scheme of life, . . .

---

15 Original text and translation are printed in T.A. Shippey, *Poems of Wisdom and Learning in Old English* (1976), pp. 68–69. Precise dating of *Maxims I* is impossible. It may belong to the eighth or ninth century but George Philip Krapp and Eliot van Kirk Dobbie (*Anglo-Saxon Records* 4, [1954]), p. xlvii. are also comfortable with the idea of an early tenth century date.

     Cyning sceal mid ceape   cwene gebicgan,
bunum ond beagum;   Bu sceolon ærest
geofum god wesan.   Guð sceal in eorle,
wig geweaxan, ond wif geþeon,
leof mid hyre leodum,   leohtmod wesan,
rune healdan,   rumheort beon
mearum ond maþmum,   meodorucædenne
for gesiðmægen   symle æghwær
eodor æþelinga   ærest gegretan,
forman fulle   to frean hond
ricene geræcan,   ond him ræd witan
boldagendum   bæm ætsomne.

[handwritten margin note: loved by her people?]

16 See the introduction to Shippey, *Poems of Wisdom and Learning.*

to ensure its continuance, . . . to control life by some kind of order."[17] Wealhtheow's actions fall within this definition for she is clearly imposing an order in the hall and *Maxims I* makes it certain that she must perform in this way.

There are two other reasons for holding that Wealhtheow's movements are part of a specialized ritual which others cannot perform in the same way—the first having to do with formal declaration of Hrothgar's title and the second with its formal acknowledgement. When Wealhtheow offered the cup to Hrothgar, she bade him be happy in partaking of the feast and amiable to the people. But it is important to note that this is a poetic summary of what she said and not her exact words. The poet feels no compulsion to be precise at this point for the ritual which we need to examine in detail was for him, we now know, an aristocratic commonplace and subordinate to his main purpose which was the setting of a scene and the description of a feast. There are six such descriptions in *Beowulf* and, as Crépin remarks, allusions to banquets "are inserted into the narrations in the manner of Chinese boxes: a banquet at Ingeld's court is referred to by Beowulf (l. 2041) while narrating the one at Hrothgar's (l. 2029), while he himself is at that moment being entertained at his uncle's banquet"![18] The length of these narrations varies greatly and depends on the poet's desire to develop their constituent elements. The queen's offering of drink is only one such element which, in poetry but not in fact, can be omitted or elaborated at need although the basic ritual, as shown by *Maxims I*, will always remain the same. When Beowulf later describes the queen's circuit of the hall for his uncle, for example, he uses different terms to describe her and speaks of her offering gifts and greetings but not drink (ll. 2017–2019).

Although the exact words which Wealhtheow spoke when offering the cup are lost, it does seem possible, using lines 616–618 of the poem as a partial control, to reconstruct some specific aspects of what, under the circumstances, she must have said. Since we know that Wealhtheow was "careful of noble usage" and "wise in her words" and since we also know that she was required to greet the king while presenting the mead cup, it seems highly probable that her address would not vary very much from one ritual occasion to another. After all, the essence of ritual is repetition and a public greeting before the high-seat must always be a solemn one. Lines 1163–1175, interspersed with commentary record a second cup-offering. The crucial words are these:

---

17 Morton Bloomfield, "Understanding Old English Poetry" (1968), p. 17. The following works are also suggestive: Barbara Nolan and Morton Bloomfield, "*Beotword, Gilpcwides*, and the *Gilphlaeden* Scop of *Beowulf*" (1980); Elaine Tuttle Hansen, "Hrothgar's 'Sermon' in *Beowulf* as Parental Wisdom" (1982); Eadem, "*Precepts*: An Old English Instruction" (1981); Geoffrey Russom, "A Germanic Concept of Nobility in *The Gifts of Men* and *Beowulf*" (1978).
18 Crépin, "Wealhtheow's Offering", p. 52.

Then came Wealhtheow forth,
walking under a golden diadem to where
the two good cousins sat. . .
Spake then the Scyldings' dame:
accept this cup, my beloved lord,
dispenser of treasure! Be thou happy,
gold-friend of men, and to the Geats
speak with kind words, as one should do!
Be cheerful towards the Geats, mindful of
gifts, near and far.[19]

In the first line attention is called again to the queen's golden diadem and in a few lines later to her noble status as lady of the Scyldings. This epitomizes her queenly character when she proffers the cup and greets the king. Her words are now quoted exactly and it is most significant that she immediately proclaims Hrothgar as lord and king, *freadrihten*, and metaphorically emphasizes the point by proclaiming him bestower of treasure, *sinces brytta, goldwine gumena*.[20] Standing before the high-seat and delivering an address which pertains to her duty as queen, this oration can only be construed as a formal statement of Hrothar's status as ruler. It closely parallels the poet's language in the lines immediately before the first appearance of Wealhtheow (ll. 607–610) when Hrothgar is characterized as bestower of treasure, *sinces brytta*, princes of the Bright-Danes, *brego Beorht-Dena*, and the folk's shepherd, *folces hyrde*. At the precise moment

---

19 The translation is essentially that of Benjamin Thorpe, *Beowulf Togetherth Widsith and the Fight at Finnesburg* (1962²). In Klaeber's edition, the original reads as follows:

Þa cwom Wealhþeo forð

gan under gyldnum beage   *þær þa godan twegen*
sæton suhtergefæderan;   *þa gyt wæs hiera sib ætgædere,*
æghwylc oðrum trywe.   Swylce *þær Unferþ þyle*
æ fotum sæt frean Scyldinga;   *gehwylc hiora his ferhþe treowde,*
þæt he hæfde mod micel,   *þeah þe he his magum nære*
arfæst æt ecga gelacum.   *Spræc ða ides Scyldinga:*
'Onfoh *þissum fulle,*   *freodrihten min,*
sinces brytta!   Þu on sælum wes,*
goldwine gumena,   *ond to Geatum spæc,*
mildum wordum,   *swa sceal man don!*
Beo wid Geatas glæd,   *geofena gemyndig,*
nean on feorran   *þu nu hafast.*

20 For the significance of the diadem as a sign of high social rank, see Nikolaus Gussone and Heiko Steuer, "Diadem" (1984). And for the relationship between queen, treasure and kingship, see Reinhard Schneider, *Königswahl und Königserhebung im Frühmittelalter. Untersuchungen zur Herrschaftsnachfolge bei den Langobarden und Merowingern* (1972), pp. 242–8. An important interpretation is presented by Karl Hauck, "Von einer spätantiken Randkulter zum karolingischen Europa" (1967), esp. p. 34f. See also the comments of Stafford, *Queens, Concubines and Dowagers*, p. 108f.

offering he is called East-Danes king, the guardian of their land, *East-Dena eþ elwearde*, and fully victorious king, *sigerof kyning*. Wealhtheow then goes on to speak of kingly qualities when she refers to *mildum wordum* and *geofena gemyndig*. This public naming of the ruler is extremely significant and, quite apart from references to the *nomen regis* in the works of Isidore of Seville, the Irish *Twelve Abuses* and the Frankish *Royal Annals*,[21] it was a feature of royal inaugurations among the North Germans. Olivecrona demonstrated that it was the essence of the *döma*, "judgement" of the king by the law-speaker of the Svear, and that the subsequent giving of the royal name by each assembly along the route of the king's circuit was central to the election rite.[22] Hoffmann believes that the Norwegians and Danes had a similar practice.[23] In the Anglo-Saxon offering rite, of course, the element of primacy and precedence stands out most clearly. Wealhtheow served the king first and the gnomic poem shows her ministration to be a traditional and necessary custom. The followers then acknowledge and assent to the ruler's precedence by each accepting a drink of liquor from the hands of the queen after the first offering. As will be shown below their acceptance of the liquor had legal and religious significance. It is quite certain, therefore, that the queen's service was not, as might otherwise be supposed,[24] just a communal bonding rite which made the *comitatus* a band of brothers, although it did that too; its primary purpose was to establish the lordship of the individual first served and named and the subordinate status of those served afterwards. This novel finding carries a number of important implications which can now be discussed and analyzed in detail for the light it throws on the structure of the warband and the role of the queen within it.

The Germanic ritual feast, the *symbel*, of which the Wealhtheow episode is often taken as a particularly good example, has been described as a situation in which the participants "significantly" sit down.[25] As Bauschatz recently emphasized, sitting down does not occur as a significant action very often in Germanic literature and when it does the occasion is a special one. When leaders sit down,

21 Hans Hubert Anton, *Fürstenspiegel und Herrscherethos in der Karolingereit* (1968), p. 66f.; Helmut Beumann, "Nomen imperatoris. Studien zur Kaiseridee Karls des Grossen" (1972); Arno Borst, "Kaisertum und Nomentheorie im Jahre 800" (1972); Michael John Enright, *Iona, Tara and Soissons. The Origin of the Royal Anointing Ritual* (1985), p. 85f.
22 Karl Olivecrona, *Das Werden eines Königs nach schwedischem Recht* (1947).
23 Erich Hoffmann, *Königserhebung und Thronfolgeordnung in Dänemark bis zum Ausgang des Mittelalters* (1976).
24 That is generally the way in which the ritual has hitherto been interpreted. Crépin assumes it to be the case, for example.
25 Paul Bauschatz, "The Germanic Ritual Feast" (1978), p. 290f. See, among many other studies, Karl Hauck, "Rituelle Speisegemeinschaft im 10. und 11. Jahrhundert" (1950); Walter Janssen, "Essen und Trinken in frühen und hohen Mittelalter aus archäologischer Sicht" (1981); Ottar Gronvik, *The Word for 'Heir,' 'Inheritance' and 'Funeral Feast' in Early Germanic* (1982); Hugh Magennis, "The Cup as Symbol and Metaphor in Old English Literature" (1985).

for example, retainers often remain standing and that is an appropriate sign of status. Otherwise, men sit to eat or drink and a guest is invited to sit.[26] But the manner and place of sitting is especially noteworthy for it suggests a certain recognized order within a group and also suggests an apportioning of positions corresponding to rank. This type of arrangement seems demonstrable in *Beowulf* for it is logical to suppose that a serving ritual which must begin with the establishment of precedence will continue in the same way, that is, according to the hierarchy made manifest by the seating order. Unfortunately, the exact seating arrangements around the high-seat, the place of greatest honor, are impossible to deduce from the poem itself. Nevertheless, certain remarks by the poet do seem to affirm that places were assigned according to rank. We know that a major division existed in the hall between the *duguð*, veterans, and *geoguð*, youths.[27] Each area was an honorable one and reflected, aside from age and experience, the reputation of the fighter and the ruler's knowledge of his forbears. It is the ruler who directs each individual to his place. Thus, when Beowulf arrived at Heorot and identified himself as a son of Hrothgar's friend who had come to fight Grendel, Hrothgar assigned him a seat of honor between his two sons who sat among the youths (ll. 1191, 2013). This cannot have been a hasty directive—on the contrary, much that had gone before is a prelude to its realization—for it settles the touchy matter of a guest's status and proclaims the lord's precise level of regard for his qualities. The importance of the act, together with a hint of its perennial potential for disruption, is indicated by the second strophe of *Hávamál*:

> Hail to the giver! a guest has come;
> Where shall the stranger sit?[28]

Later, when Beowulf had vanquished Grendel and had returned to his own land after proving his mettle, king Hygelac, his father's brother, gave him a seat at his side (l. 1077). Significantly, this corresponds exactly to the place held by Hrothulf, king Hrothgar's nephew, at Heorot (ll. 1017, 1164). Nearness to royalty was the key criterion of rank and the king's nephew, after being appropriately tested as a warrior, probably always sat beside his uncle. At this point, Hygelac's

---

26 The most recent work is Leopold Hellmuth, *Gastfreundschaft und Gastrecht bei den Germanen* (1984). This is a useful and competent study but breaks no new ground. An opportunity may have been missed to cast additional light on an important topic.

27 The most recent discussion is J.A. Burrow, *The Ages of Man. A Study of Medieval Writing and Thought* (1986), pp. 123–134. Especially useful are Hilding Bäck, *The Synonyms for 'Child,' 'Boy' and 'Girl' in Old English* (1934); Hildegard Stibbe, *'Herr' und 'Frau' und verwandte Begriffe in ihren altenglischen Äquivalenten* (1935). See also George Engelhardt, "On the Sequence of Beowulf's *Geogod*" (1953). A magisterial study is that of Caroline Brady, " 'Warriors' in *Beowulf*: An Analysis of the Nominal Compounds and an Evaluation of the Poet's Use of Them" (1983).

28 Henry Adams Bellows. *The Poetic Edda* (1923), p. 29.

queen is also described as serving liquor to her husband and his followers. As Beowulf sat next to him she must have served him second since she would hardly have skipped a place only to serve someone else and return to Beowulf. Almost certainly, then, the queen's order of service proceeded according to the grades of rank and honor within the *comitatus*.

Other evidence confirms this exceptionally significant pattern. In the year 588, after his betrothal to the sister of the Frankish king Childebert II fell through, the recently elected king Authari of the Lombards sought the daughter of the Bavarian ruler Garibald, for his wife. The story of how he won her is contained in Paul the Deacon's *Historia Langobardorum* (compiled during the last decade of the eighth century and thus perhaps roughly contemporary with *Beowulf*) which contains a number of motifs comparable to those we have been discussing.[29] Paul relates that Authari first sent envoys to Garibald to ask for his daughter's hand. They were given a favorable reply and, upon their return, the king conceived the idea of visiting Bavaria in order to assess for himself the beauty of Theudelinda. Disguised as an ambassador he asked Garibald for permission to interview his daughter so that he might accurately report to his master on her appearance. Garibald acceded to the request and Theudelinda turned out to be so pleasing that Authari said to him:

> "Since we see that the person of your daughter is such that we may properly wish her to become our queen, we would like if it please your mightiness, to take a cup of wine from her hand, *as she will offer it to us hereafter*." And when the king (Garibald) had assented to this that it should be done, she took the cup of wine and *gave it first to him who appeared to be the chief.* Then . . . she offered it to Authari, whom she did not know was her affianced bridegroom . . .[30]

This passage is important because it shows that the queen's serving of her husband's followers is not a practice confined to the Anglo-Saxons but extends to other Germanic peoples. It also demonstrates that in any group the drink offering will proceed strictly according to rank. Although the setting is different, the overall approach is the same in the poem called the *Waltharius* whose newest

---

29 Georg Waitz, ed. *Pauli Historia Langobardorum* (1878), p. 133f. For analysis, see Hermann Fröhlich, *Studien zur langobardischen Thronfolge von den Anfängen bis zur Eroberung des italienischen Reiches durch Karl den Grossen (774)* I (1980), p. 97f.; Schneider, *Königswahl*, p. 25f.

30 Waitz, *Historia Langobardorum*, p. 134: 'Quia talem filiae vestrae personam cernimus, ut eam merito nostram reginam fieri optemus, si placet vestrae potestati, de eius manu, sicut nobis postea factura est, vini poculum sumere praeoptamus.' Cumque rex id, ut fieri deberet, annuisset, illa, accepto vini poculo, ei prius qui senior esse videbatur propinavit. Deinde cum Authari, quem suum esse sponsum nesciebat . . . . The translation is that of William Dudley Foulke, *Paul the Deacon. History of the Lombards* (1974²).

editor joins those arguing for a ninth century date.[31] During the famous scene where Walter, Hagen and Gunther are resting after battle (ll. 1409–1416) Walter tells his betrothed to mix wine. She is to serve Hagen first because he is a worthy champion (*athleta bonus*) and then Walter. Gunther is to be served last for, although he is a king, he is also sluggish in battle. In the hall, of course, Gunther would have been served first but Walter is not his follower and assigns him a rank and service appropriate to his showing on the battlefield. While the reversal of precedence is appropriate because the king is a coward, the explanation for the peculiar sequence shows that it is in conflict with the normal requirements of hierarchical recognition. Actually, any variation of this type will always require an explanation for it constitutes a grave insult to the person passed over; any other procedure would be quite surprising. The Icelandic sagas, some parts of which many scholars have thought to accurately depict an earlier stage in Germanic development, make it quite clear that it was a prerogative of kings to be greeted first and also contain scores of references to serious quarrels about precedence in the hall which are nearly invariably related to the seating arrangement and hence also to the sequence of service (a similar conflict is mentioned in *Beowulf* [ll. 1085–1096]).[32] Whether the queen's serving rite continued to exist as such in

31 Dennis Kratz, ed. *Waltharius and Ruodlieb* (1984), p. 68:
    "*Iam misceto merum Haganoni et porrige primum.*
    Est athleta bonus, fidei si iura reservet.
    Tum praebeto mihi, reliquis qui plus toleravi.
    Postremum volo Guntharius bibat utpote segnis
    inter magnamimum qui paruit arma virorum
    et qui Martis opus tepide atque enerviter egit."
    Obsequitur cunctis Heririci filia verbis.
    Francus at oblato licet arens pectore vino
    "*Defer*" *ait* "*prius Alpharidi sponso ac seniori,*
    virgo, tuo, quoniam, fateor, me fortior ille
    nec solum me, sed cunctos supereminet armis."
32 See, for example, Hellmuth, *Gastfreundschaft*, pp. 54–68 et passim. As the author rightly notes (p. 55): "In der altnordischen Literatur wird dem Platz des Gastes grosse Aufmerksamkeit geschenkt: Es wird nicht nur verhältnismassig oft erwähnt, dass ein Gastgeber nach der Frage nach dem Namen und der Herkunft eines Fremden diesem einen Platz in seiner Halle anbot, sondern es wird dabei stets gesagt, um *welchen* Platz es sich handelt." There are some intriguing similarities here between Celts and Germans and I hope to discuss this question in greater detail below. See the acute observations of Philip O'Leary, "Contention at Feasts in Early Irish Literature" (1984). Much can be learned from a study of early Greek concepts as well. See, especially, Gerard Baudy, "Hierarchie oder: Die Verteilung des Fleisches. Eine ethnologische Studie über die Tischordnung als Wurzel sozialer Organisation" (1983); Walter Burkert, "Opfertypen und antike Gesellschaftsstruktur" (1976). Attention should also be called to the "Opfer"—Kolloquium held at Münster in 1983. The papers are published in *Frühmittelalter-liche Studien* 18, 1984, and many are relevant to this discussion. One thinks especially of Otto Gerhard Oexle, "Mahl und Spende im mittelalterlichen Totenkult" (pp. 401–420).

later centuries is difficult to say but,[33] given what we know of the Germanic mentality of the eight century, it seems quite clear that any such formal procedure would be closely bound to the status hierarchy within the warband. The close connection which existed between the seat taken and the authority or status which one might legitimately claim is further demonstrated by OE *frumstol*, a word which means "original or principle dwelling place" but can be literally translated as "first seat".[34] The seventh century laws of Ine of Wessex refer to a son's right to his *frumstol*.[35] Regardless of the late date of some of the sources, therefore, it seems very likely that the hierarchical seating arrangement and the associated ritual are extremely old.

What, then, have we learned of the lord-queen-follower relationship through our analysis of Wealhtheow's progress? There have been a number of intriguing results. It is now clear that the lady of the hall is an instrument of her husband used to express his lordship and maintain order among his *Gefolgschaft*. This purpose becomes more obvious if we compare Wealhtheow for a moment to that other most fascinating figure, Unferth the *þyle*,[36] who occupies an ambiguous place at the king's feet and whose chief purpose in the poem is to act as a foil to Beowulf. Actually, the role of both figures is complimentary although only that of the latter has been properly explained. When Beowulf enters the hall he is welcomed by Hrothgar and invited to tell of his past exploits. Unferth now intervenes in a sharply hostile and aggressive manner (ll. 499–529); he unbound war-words, *onband beadu-rune*, in an attempt to show that Beowulf is a fool and a simpleminded adventurer. But the hero calmly replies, defends his deeds and turns the tables by sarcastically recalling Unferth's past. There could hardly be a more puzzling contrast than that between the obliging and decorous welcome of the lord and the stinging rebukes of his follower who, however, seems to hold a privileged position and whose behavior is clearly tolerated, even perhaps expected. The truth is that it was actually awaited behavior. As Clover has recently argued, Hrothgar's silence during this episode is not really puzzling for it "must indicate sponsorship" of Unferth.[37] This is shown by the mocker's place in the hall which presumes a special relationship with the king. Unferth is his extension, his agent in any encounter which calls for hard questioning or close assessment.

---

33 The clergy, of course, promoted different rituals and the bishops especially inveighed against feasting practices in which the lower clergy often took part. Much that was of pagan origin continued to find expression on these occasions. Some examples are discussed by Hauck, *Rituelle Speisegemeinschaft*.

34 See Jaqueline Simpson, "A Note on the Word *Fridstoll*" (1955), esp. p. 201.

35 F.L. Attenborough, ed. *The Laws of the Earliest English Kings* (1922), p. 48, n. 38.

36 Norman Eliason, "The *þyle* and Scop in *Beowulf*" (1963); Ida Masters Hollowell, "Unferth the *þyle* in *Beowulf*" (1976).

37 Carol Clover makes this brilliant argument in "The Germanic Context of the Unferth Episode" (1980), p. 460.

Hrothgar can afford to play the gracious host who is above the fray because he knows that Unferth will "put the alien through the necessary paces".[38] Once the stranger's character has been tested, the queen can then enter, as Wealhtheow does, and restore harmony by renewing formality, bidding the king be amiable and speaking cheerfully to the retainers, including Beowulf whom she greets effusively shortly thereafter. In this, she acts very much like Sif, the queenly wife of Thor, who offers drink to Loki in the concluding stanzas of *Lokasenna* after he has insulted the gods: "Hail to thee, Loki, and take thou here/The crystal cup of old mead". The same motif also recurs in the sagas. In fact, then, both Unferth and Wealhtheow are governmental tools of Hrothgar, delegates who help him dominate the hall. They are, in the idiom of police interrogators all over the world, "Mr. Nice Guy and Mr. Tough Guy" who, by alternate bouts of harsh and tender questioning, compel the suspect to revel his motives and qualities, his strengths and weaknesses.

If it is Unferth's role to stir up strife (and he has justly been called an originally "Wodanistic figure")[40] then it is Wealhtheow's to mend relations. The full depth and complexity of her behavior will not become apparent, however, until we also understand something more about the organization of the warband and the role of lordly wives in its confirmation and continuity. The fact is that the *comitatus* has often been unduly and unrealistically eulogized by scholars who have argued that its basis lay primarily in a reciprocal relationship between lord and follower in which the former was little more than *primus inter pares*.[41] But the present

38 Ibid.
39 Ibid. p. 465, n. 72. She notes that Magnus Olsen called attention to this link and adds that the *Morskinskinna* version of *Magnussona saga* depicts a similar intervention of the queen.
40 Joseph Baird, "Unferth the *þyle*" (1970), p. 9. The cultic background is explained in Karl Hauck, "Carmina Antiqua. Abstammungsglaube und Stammesbewusssein" (1964); Idem, "Lebensnormen und Kultmythen in germanischen Stammes-und Herrschergenealogien" (1955). See also Hermann Moisl, "Kingship and Orally Transmitted Stammestradition Among the Lombards and Franks" (1985).
41 The ideal of reciprocity is much more heavily stressed in older works. In recent times modifications have been made but the concept of mutually contingent loyalty among free men continues to be regularly opposed to that of obedience among dependents. The conflicting approaches are well illustrated by the following two studies: Walter Schlesinger, "Herrschaft und Gefolgschaft in der germanisch-deutschen Verfassungsgeschichte" (1963); Hans Kuhn, "Die Grenzen der germanischen Gefolgschaft" (1956). See further, Reinhard Wenskus, *Stammesbildung und Verfassung. Das Werden der frühmittelalterlichen gentes* (1977²), pp. 346–374; Ruth Schmidt-Wiegand, *Fränkische und frankolateinische Bezeichnungen für soziale Schichten und Gruppen in der Lex Salica* (1972); Gabriele von Olberg, *Freie, Nachbarn und Gefolgsleute. Volkssprachige Bezeichnungen aus dem sozialen Bereich in den frühmittelalterlichen Leges* (1983); Karl Kroeschell, *Haus und Herrschaft im frühen deutschen Recht* (1968); Ernst Dick, *Ae. Dryht und seine Sippe. Eine wortkundliche, kultur-und religionsgeschichtliche Betrachtung zur altgermanischen Glaubensvorstellung vom washstümlichen Heil* (1965); Jürgen Hannig, *Consensus Fidelium. Fruhfeudale Interpretationen des Verhältnisses von Königtum und Adel am Beispiel des Frankenreiches* (1982). See also Green, *Carolingian Lord*, Chadwick, *Anglo-Saxon Institutions*, and Murray, *Germanic Kingship Structure*.

analysis shows that this interpretation cannot be correct for the ritual feast, long taken to be the purest expression of a communal bonding rite, is simultaneously an expression of lordship, hierarchy and disparity of rank. One must not forget that it is the lord who provides the feast, who tests the worth of newcomers, who assigns them to seats—which is in fact a public statement of their status—and who, finally, directs his wife to serve them in a ritual which forces them to accept the superiority of every individual who is served before them. These warrior societies cannot have been other than deeply status-conscious for the crucial mechanism which creates their coherence simultaneously establishes subordination. It is not surprising, therefore, that many of the problems and contradictions which plagued this society are reflected in the relationships of the mead-hall, a name which is revealing in itself.

Having analyzed the significance of the distribution of drink we may now discuss the meaning of its mutual consumption for that too will help us to appreciate the role of the lord's wife in her function as delegate. Communal feasting was the outward sign of mutual dedication demanded by the archaic mind-set. Fundamental to barbarian society was the belief that the only man one could trust was a relative and the only man one could truly call "friend" was a kinsman. Hence, the persons who collectively form the kingroup are referred to as *propinqui* or *parentes* but they can also be called *amici*;[42] the two concepts interlock. Like the members of a kindred, the retainers of a lord are bound to him and to each other by ties expressed in terms of blood kinship. In *Beowulf*, they can be called young kin retainer, *maguþegnas*, kinsmen, *magas*, and the group as a whole can be called a band of kinsmen, *sibbegedryht*.[43] Of course this is fictive kinship created through a convivial communion at the feast, a drinking which serves as a substitute for blood. As such it needed a strong religious sanction and we get some idea of its nature by the horror it inspired among hagiographers. In his *Vita Columbani*, written by Jonas of Bobbio, the author mentions that the holy man encountered a group of heathens with a vessel of beer in their midst called a *cupa* while on his way to Swabia. They were about to make an offering to their god Wodan. Columbanus destroyed the vessel for, as Jonas says, it was clear that the devil was hidden in the cask and that through earthly drink he had proposed to capture the souls of the participants.[44] Similarly, in the *Vita Vedastis* it is told how the saint and the king were invited to a feast at which both pagans and Christians were present. Because of the mixed character of the company the

42 Donald Bullough, "Early Medieval Social Groupings: The Terminology of Kinship" (1969), p. 12 with n. 21 where many examples are cited.
43 Schlesinger, "Herrschaft und Gefolgschaft", p. 19f.; Brady, " 'Warriors' in *Beowulf*", p. 214f.
44 Bruno Krusch, ed. *Ionas. Vita Columbani abbatis* (1902), p. 102. See commentary in Karl Hauck, "Zur Ikonologie der Goldbrakteaten XV: Die Arztfunktion des seegermanischen Götterkönigs, erhellt mit der Rolle der Vögel auf den goldenen Amulettbildern" (1977).

liquor had been placed in separate vessels, one of which was "consecrated in the heathen manner".[45] The saint destroyed it with the sign of the cross. In view of these examples, communal drinking, which had the purpose of creating fictive kinship, must also be viewed as having some of the aspects of a cultic act.[46] It aimed at creating a non-natural bond of loyalty, and liquor was used because liquor was the medium through which one achieved ecstacy and thus communion with the supernatural.[47] For the present it is enough to say that this conception was a widespread one among Indo-European peoples and seems to have been closely related to the earliest rites of royal inauguration. In view of the religious significance of communal drinking it is only to be expected that oaths would commonly be made over liquor at the *convivia*.[48] When Wealhtheow served Beowulf in the hall he drank what she poured and then proclaimed that he would kill the monster Grendel or die trying. Words spoken in this way had a powerful social significance. The poet calls it a *gilpspræc* and a *gilpwide* (l. 640). As Nolan and Bloomfield point out, this manner of speaking cannot be construed as "boasting" in the modern sense of the word: "The hero's speech as it is matched by subsequent deeds appears to serve a ritual function not unlike that of incantation, bolstering the sense of his own ability and fortifying his will to fulfill the tribal definition of heroism by facing death for the community's sake."[49] Such strengthening of will was often needed. Hrothgar had already explained that his men had made vows over their cups to stop Grendel but repeatedly failed (ll. 480–487). In later years, when Beowulf battled the dragon, Wiglaf also reminded the retainers of how often they had sworn their bravery and dedication in the mead-hall (ll. 2632–2635). In the *Battle of Maldon* Aelfwine bids his comrades to remember the words spoken over mead, and the more sensible if also more melancholy *Wanderer* cautions warriors to wait until they are sober before taking oaths.[50] In his now classic article, Einarsson took careful note of the solemn

45 Bruno Krusch, ed. *Ionas. Vita Vedastis episcopi* (1905), p. 314f. On Merovingian saints lives in general, see Frantisek Graus, *Volk, Herrscher und Heiliger im Reich der Merowinger* (1965).

46 The studies cited in note 32 all emphasize this point. For the Indo-European background, see Emile Benveniste, *Indo-European Language and Society* (1973), pp. 470–480. This important work, translated from the French edition of 1969 by Elizabeth Palmer, deserves far more attention by medievalists than it has hitherto received. See also Maurice Cahén, *Études sur le vocabulaire religieux du Vieux-Scandinave. La Libation* (1921); Renate Doht, *Der Rauschtrank im germanischen Mythos* (1974); Stefan Einarsson, "Old English *Beot* and Old Icelandic *Heitstrenging*" (1968).

47 See the discussion of *Germania* 22 in Rudolf Much, Herbert Jankuhn and Wolfgang Lange, *Die Germania des Tacitus* (1967), p. 307f.; Doht, "Rauschtrank", p. 168f.; Nolan and Bloomfield, "*Beotword*".

48 Einarsson, "Old English *Beot*"; Nolan and Bloomfield, "*Beotword*".

49 Nolan and Bloomfield, "*Beotword*", p. 502.

50 Text and discussion in Einarsson "Old English *Beot*", p. 102f.

nature of such promises in the mead-hall and also pointed out that liquor usually fortified important bargains such as the buying of a bride or even of lesser commercial transactions.[51] If liquor was not a necessary concomitant of the *gilp* or *beot* it is clear that *gilpcwidas* over liquor were extremely common. But the fact that it is invariably the lord's wife who bears the liquor during solemn ritual occasions has never been adequately noted. Upon considering the full context, however,—the importance of fictive kinship, the cultic implications of the act, the "incantatory" nature of the words spoken over liquor—it now seems probable that she too was perceived as being in some pivotal way connected to the rite. Her person might also be thought of as *gilphlaeden* as is that of the *scop* who remembers heroic deeds and sings of them (and who is really the third delegate of the king in the hall).[52] At the very least, she must have been viewed as especially worthy of trust. She is the bearer of the consecrated liquor and, in the case of Beowulf, seems to incite his *gilp*.

But how often were such oaths kept? The foregoing remarks on fictive kinship and liquor consecration were designed in part to delineate the ideal warband relationship praised by Germanic poets and many modern scholars as well. Reality was far more brutal. To the extent that the ideal helped foster group loyalty and reciprocity between lord and follower it was a noble one. But both the elements of mutual aid and friendship in the kingroup and *comitatus* have been exaggerated. In the fifth century, for example, Clovis sought out his kinsmen only to butcher them. He manipulated the values of his society to further a savage ambition—in one case persuading a son to plot his father's death and in another to bribe a king's followers to desert their lord for gilded copper rings.[53]

Where is the ideal of dying with one's lord or even of living to avenge the death of one's lord?[54] Ragnachar, the betrayed king, was killed by Clovis in front of his followers who, on discovering the fraud of the rings, yet begged for peace and declared themselves satisfied at being allowed to live. True consanguinity was insufficient to restrain murder in these episodes and fictive kinship was an even less effective control. The pages of Gregory's *Historia Francorum* are strewn with the remains of broken oaths, as well as those who believed them.[55]

51 Ibid., p. 103.

52 Since it is the ruler who rewards the poet and, in the final analysis, controls his singing, one must suppose this relationship to be vertical and only vaguely reciprocal. Theoretically, this need not be the case but one is entitled to doubt that many scops acted against the will of the *hlaford*.

53 These famous examples, and others, are discussed in Frantisek Graus, "Über die sogenannte germanische Treue"(1959). His criticism is discussed by Walter Schlesinger, "Randbemerkungen zu drei Aufsätzen uber Sippe, Gefolgschaft und Treue" (1963), p. 316f.; Walter Kienast, "Germanische Treue und Königsheil" (1978).

54 Kuhn, "Grezen", p. 7f.; Rosemary Woolf, "The Ideal of Men Dying With Their Lord in the *Germania* and in *The Battle of Maldon*" (1976); Helmut Gneuss, *Die Battle of Maldon als historisches und literarisches Zeugnis* (1976), p. 15f.

55 Graus, "Sogenannte germanische Treue".

Nor, indeed, does the *comitatus* appear to have been a happy society of friends who dealt with each other on the basis of equality and brotherhood. To the extent that it lasted beyond the migration period at all—and that in itself is a debatable proposition—the horizontally organized *Gefolgschaft* gradually lost the element of rough equality between lord and follower to be replaced by a vertical relationship based on service if, actually, it had ever been otherwise for most peoples.[56] Even in the earliest sources, for example, Germanic terms for "friend" like OHG *wini* and OE *wine* can express a vertical as well as a horizontal relationship.[57] So with the Latin *amicus* which probably influenced them and which already in the imperial period could be used as a technical term for a particular rank. In Merovingian times it could be used to designate an inferior in a lord-vassal relationship.[58] Even in the Tacitean *comitatus* where the principle of reciprocity is held to have predominated, definite elements of precedence and subordination existed. Tacitus explicitly states that the chief's retinue contained different grades of rank determined at his discretion: *gradus quin etiam ipse comitatus habet, indicio eius quem sectantur.*[59] This determination of rank probably led to a great deal of ill-will which may have been as cumulative as the drinking bouts were repetitive and must, in any case, have sorely threatened and often broken the fictive kinship bond established by communal intoxication. According to Tacitus, the drinking bouts of the Germans frequently caused quarrels which were rarely settled by harsh words but commonly by wounds and killing: *crebrae, ut inter vinolentos, rixae raro conviciis, saepius caede et vulneribus transiguntur.*[60] He adds that warriors normally took weapons to feasts: *ad convivia procedunt armati.*[61] Carried to demonstrate free birth and status, no doubt these weapons were also present because of the great rivalry to decide who should have first place with the chief: *magnaque et comitum aemulatio, quibus primus apud principem suum locus.*[62] Conditions by the eighth century had not improved. The *Beowulf* poet says that one of the hero's outstanding qualities was that he never killed his drinking companions —a remark which presupposes that such commonly occurred.[63]

If brotherhood was often absent so too was altruism. Many a sad story is concealed behind the facade of occasional individual success in heroic literature

56 Kuhn, "Grezen", p. 14: "Wo nicht eine starke Oberschicht entwickelt ist, ist kein Raum für die Gefolgschaft." This is a highly significant observation. An immense amount of relevant archaeological material, yet to be digested by historians, is contained in the important study by Heiko Steuer, *Frühgeschichtliche Sozialstrukturen in Mitteleuropa* (1982).
57 Green, *Carolingian Lord*, p. 106f.
58 Ibid., pp. 65f., 107f.
59 M. Hutton, ed. *Tacitus: Agricola, Germania* (1963⁴), p. 283.
60 Ibid., p. 294f.
61 Ibid.
62 Ibid., p. 282.

for a great deal of warband life consisted of one-upmanship and a striving for riches and rank. Early in his career, for example, Beowulf was despised by his comrades. The Geats thought him worthless because he could not win his lord's favor. It was only years later that the hero won compensation for those insults. He did so by coming back rich and giving all of his noble gifts to the man who had once humiliated him, or at least tolerated his humiliation, his uncle, Hygelac.[64] Hygelac then gave him a princely counter-gift of sword, land and dwelling. While this transaction is presented in an essentially positive light, it is also true that Beowulf thereby gained revenge for the many shames and the poet takes pleasure in pointing it out (ll. 2178–2189) for he says that Ecgtheow's son had proved himself and thereby "all the insults were reversed"—just as Beowulf could drink to Hrothgar's gifts because "he did not need to feel ashamed before warriors" (ll. 1024–1026).

Clearly, then, the gift-giving nexus is profoundly complex and redolent of ambiguity.[65] The real atmosphere of the mead-hall, as opposed to its sanitized idealization, often rippled with currents of bitterness and jealousy which gave rise to polemic, vindictiveness and bloodshed. A gift given to one follower could be a taunt to another and a lesser gift could easily damn with faint praise. The warriors in turn had to be careful of their dealings with the primary gift-giver. After Beowulf's victory, for instance, they loudly celebrated his glory and proclaimed that no one in the world was worthier to rule a warband. The poet is quick to add that this was not intended as a slight to Hrothgar and that he took no umbrage (ll. 856–863). Other kings might have. Wealhtheow at least was deeply dismayed. She now began to fear that Hrothgar loved Beowulf so much that he would declare him his successor. What would happen to her children? As we know, they were murdered by a kinsman who sat next to Hrothgar's high-seat.

Of all gifts, food and drink were the most basic. That is why the Anglo-Saxon lord was called *hlaford*, loaf-guardian, and his follower *hlafoeta*, loafeater. A certain mutuality is suggested by these terms and the counter-gift of service in return for food and a share of the plunder need not always be envisioned as onerous. Savage twists can occur in this pattern, however, and prestation has a destructive side not often explained. It could be, and often was, a type of potlatch. Because every gift called for a counter-gift of equal value, a follower could be subordinated or an enemy shamed through bestowal of a present which he could

63 Many examples are cited in Much, Jankuhn and Lange, *Germania*, p. 308f.
64 The classic work is Marcel Mauss, *Essai sur le don. Forme et raison de l'échange dans les sociétés archaïques* (1950²).
65 See Aaron J. Gurevich, "Wealth and Gift-Bestowal Among the Ancient Scandinavians" (1968); Charles Donahue, "Potlatch and Charity: Notes on the Heroic in *Beowulf*" (1975); Marshall Sahlins, *Stone-Age Economics* (1972), pp. 149–183.

not match. Such a gift was that of land, craved by every follower for it sustained rank and permitted marriage. Yet, even when freely and generously given, it was usually a life-gift only or held at the lord's pleasure. As there was only a limited amount of arable land available to be distributed and since lords had many followers to reward, it was also a difficult gift to keep. The poet Deor lamented his deprivation of an estate given him by his lord but then taken back and given to another who had risen in favor.[66] Similarly, *Widsith*, the oldest poem in any Germanic language, records the poet's giving of a valuable arm-ring to his lord Eadgils, king of the Myrgingas, in return for receiving back the same estate which his father had held.[67] But this estate would have to be paid for over and over again for land's enduring value was such that an adequate counter-gift was almost impossible to make. As a gift, then, land acted to permanently subordinate the receiver who became liable for unfailing life-long service—an obligation which could become increasingly debilitating with age. The land might also be lost by lack of suitable sons to do the lord's bidding. Of course, the gift of food and drink called for a lesser return. Nevertheless, the longer one accepted these gifts, the greater the pressure to perform and the tensions between lord and follower (and within the *comitatus* as a whole) would thereby rise proportionately. Paradoxically, it is for that very reason that the dual purpose mead-bond had to be exalted. Without powerful religiously supported and periodically renewed sanctions this society would explode for it is one which almost encourages bloodshed and treachery, all the eulogies to faith and trust notwithstanding. Heroic poetry was needed because so few were really heroic.

Against this background the role of the lord's wife comes into much sharper focus. While many have recognized that she is a *freoðuwebbe*, a peace-weaver, the term is most often applied to women given in marriage in order to secure peace

---

66 George Philip Krapp and Elliot van Kirk Dobbie, eds. *The Exeter Book* (1936), p. 179:

> *Þæt ic bi me sylfum   secgan wille,*
> *þæt ic hwile wæs   Heodeninga scop,*
> *dryhtne dyre.   Me wæs Deor noma.*
> *Ahte ic fela wintra   folgað tilne,*
> *holdne hlaford,   oþþæt Heorrenda nu,*
> *leoðcræftig monn   londryht geþah,*
> *þæt me eorla hleo   ær gesalde.*
> *Þæs ofereode,   þisses swa mag!*

For discussion, see Chadwick, *Anglo-Saxon Institutions*, p. 368f.

67 Krapp and Dobbie, *Exeter Book*, p. 152:

> *þone ic Eadgilse   on æht sealde,*
> *minum hleodryhtne,   þa ic to ham bicwom,*
> *leofum to leane,   þæs þe he me lond forgeaf,*
> *mines fæder eþel,   frea Myrginga.*

See again Chadwick, *Anglo-Saxon Institutions*, p. 368f. Also Eric John, *Land Tenure in Early England. A Discussion of Some Problems* (1964), p. 54f.

among peoples.[68] A few others have recognized that the term might also be applied to lord's wives like Wealhtheow who give jewels to guests, speak *freondlaþu wordum* and thus function as diplomats who "construct bonds of allegiance between the outsider and the king and his court".[69] Our findings above indicate that this is only a partial picture of the queen's significance, the full depth of which is considerable more profound. Wealhtheow is a binder, a "weaver", and may also perhaps be called an oath-carrier. In Hrothgar's hall she is the instrument which sanctifies his status by naming him lord, by serving him before all others and by causing each of the retainers to drink after him. By serving the followers in strict order of precedence she also sanctifies the status of each warrior in relation to his companions. In one sense Wealhtheow makes them all into a band of brothers but, while this formulation is true as far as it goes, it is necessary to add that this is also a perfectly hierarchical family for the true focal point is the "father" in his *gifstol* before whom the liquor rite begins and ends. No doubt the holders of these valued hall-seats will change as aspiring warriors range through the organization, drink to generosity, fashion their oaths, jockey for position and seek to impress the leader; the queen cannot control their circuits although she may well be able to exert a subtle influence. Nevertheless, her presence is essential in the long run because the binding rite she performs is her particular privilege and duty and thus her passage from the high-seat to bench and back again is the spatial trace of a personal commitment which the group recognizes as actually a commitment to its own existence. Her cheering words and gifts help the unsuccessful to accept their lot or to bide their time. From the social viewpoint that is her primary function, to make a harsh life full of conflict and rivalry more bearable. At the same time she is a well-honed tool of her husband's dominance for it is his power that she symbolizes and she acts throughout as his representative. No other outlook is possible within the Germanic *Männerbund*.

If the queen is a stabilizing influence on the *comitatus* during her husband's lifetime, what happens after his death? This question has been much discussed in recent years and it may now be possible, based on our findings above, to add some significant modifications and additions to previous commentary.[70] *Beowulf*

---

68 Bernice Kliman, "Women in Early English Literature, *Beowulf* to the *Ancrene Wisse*" (1977), p. 33. Christine Fell, *Women in Anglo-Saxon England* (1984) offers many improbable feminist readings with regard to female status.

69 Larry H. Sklute, "*Freothuwebbe* in Old English Poetry" (1970), p. 540.

70 See the studies cited in note 1 to which can be added Pauline Stafford, "The King's Wife in Wessex, 800–1066" (1981); and Silvia Konecny, *Die Frauen des karolingischen Königshauses. Die politische Bedeutung der Ehe und die Stellung der Frau in der fränkischen Herrscherfamilie vom 7. bis zum 10. Jahrhundert* (1976); Thilo Vogelsang, *Die Frau als Herrscherin. Studien zur 'consors regni' Formel im Mittelalter* (1954); Susanne Wittern, "Frauen zwischen asketischem Ideal und weltlichem Leben. Zur Darstellung des christlichen Handels der merowingischen Königinnen Radegunde und Balthilde in den hagiographischen Lebensbeschreibungen des 6. und 7. Jahrhunderts" (1986). An especially thoughtful essay is that of Eleanor Searle, "Women and the Legitimization of Succession at the Norman Conquest" (1980).

can be again a convenient starting point. In the prelude to Beowulf's arrival at Heorot and during the speeches which follow his coming, Hrothgar several times reiterates a desire to lavishly reward the hero who survives the task of defeating the monster (ll. 385, 660–661). Thereafter, Hrothgar deepens his purpose and his intentions become far more encompassing than originally intended; he now wants to name Beowulf as his successor.[71] The old king realizes that he must soon die and that his sons are too young to succeed him. Beowulf's behavior, demeanor and superb victory, beyond the ability of any of the Danes, have now convinced the old *hlaford* that the Geatish warrior would be the best protector of his people and he seeks to bind him to his following in the closest way possible by adopting him as his son and by bestowing gifts which suggest a future kingship of the Danes. Hrothgar's original placing of Beowulf between his sons might indicate that he was thinking along these lines from the beginning and it is clear that the retainers now share his opinion and are enthusiastically willing to accept Beowulf's designation for they have sworn that no warrior is more worthy to rule over men (ll. 856–861). If Hrothgar and his *comitatus* are united in purpose, however, Beowulf and Wealhtheow, for different reasons, are opposed—Beowulf because he is bound to Hygelac and the Geats (and perhaps also because he foresees trouble with Hrothgar's sons), and Wealhtheow because she hopes that her sons can survive their minority under Hrothgar's nephew, Hrothulf, and then govern independently. Were Beowulf to become king he would undoubtedly marry and have sons of his own to provide for. Hrothulf, on the other hand, might treat her children better because of their kinship and long acquaintance. Although Wealhtheow knows it to be a gamble, she decides to use her influence on behalf of Hrothulf. And yet, what influence does she have against her husband? All she can do is offer veiled pleadings to Beowulf and mild hints to Hrothgar; she is powerless to counter the implicit offer of kingship, at least while her husband lives. All of this, apparently, is in stark contrast to the power of Hygd, Hygelac's wife, after her husband's death in a battle against the Frisians. Upon Beowulf's return from this war she offers him the throne—more specifically she offers him treasure and kingdom, rings and high-seat, *hord ond rice, beagas ond bregostol* (ll. 2369–2370), and does so despite the fact that Heardred, her son, is willing to become king. According to the poet, she did not trust Heardred to be capable of defending the land against foreign invaders. Although the remaining Geats tried to prevail on Beowulf to accept the offer, he refused to do so out of loyalty to his lord's memory; instead he became Heardred's councilor and gave him his full support. Unfortunately, later events proved the queen's pragmatism better founded

---

71 A convincing analysis is presented by John Hill, "*Beowulf* and the Danish Succession. Gift Giving as an Occasion for Complex Gesture" (1982). Also, Malcolm M. Brennan, "Hrothgar's Government" (1985). I have not seen Stephanie Hollis, "Beowulf and the Succession", which appeared in *Parergon*.

than the hero's faith since Heardred's rashness brought death to himself and defeat to his people. Beowulf then acceded to the throne which he had earlier refused.

These examples of the queen's role in succession decisions present the historian with a curiously contrasting and dubious pattern—the portrait of a consort who is relatively powerless while her husband lives but suddenly appears to inherit decisive influence upon his death. Hygd's startling ability to offer kingship to a retainer is a pointed example but, when carefully considered, it ill accords with Wealhtheow's previously described vulnerability and, presumably, with Hygd's own impotence during Hygelac's reign. Something is surly amiss for if the younger wife of an older lord could expect to later decide the succession, then she should, because of this potential, also grow in authority and stature in proportion to her husband's increasing feebleness. And yet this is not what happened to Wealhtheow whose husband's impending and anticipated death lent her no power to appoint a successor. She offers rich gifts to Beowulf but that is more in the nature of a bribe than a true attempt to reward or to establish friendship and reciprocity.[72] Clearly, she does not want Beowulf as lord or protector for that is a role to be assumed by Hrothulf; she wishes the Geat to be satisfied with his new wealth and reputation, to remain uninvolved in the forthcoming transition and to either depart or else elect to stay as an honored retainer and councilor—but no more than that (ll. 1215–1231). She begs Beowulf to befriend her sons, to be kind to them, and even hints at defiance when she says that the drunken warriors will do her will although that is no more than a worried mother's forlorn parting shot as she ends her speech.[73] The warriors are pledged to Hrothgar not to her and they have already chanted the hero's victory and proclaimed that no man was worthier to rule than this leader of the Geats. Beowulf, a recently arrived guest, appears unsure what to make of this. While presumably flattered by Hrothgar's implicit promise he wants to remain above the fray for he has no real desire to become king of the Danes; his ties to his own lord and people remain too strong. The fact is, however, that he could easily have chosen otherwise and we cannot hope to understand the politics of the lord-queen-retainer relationships until the rationale for the heterogeneous approaches of the two women can be explained. Although the *Beowulf* poem cannot help us further with this problem, other sources do offer a solution and a brief analysis of these will also provide an opportunity to deepen our understanding of the basic conventions and principles accepted by the *comitatus* in crucial times of transition. They can help us to recognize and explain an important technique for the bolstering of group cohesion during the interregnum.

---

72 See Hill, "Danish Succession", p. 188f.
73 The reference to "drunken warriors" is discussed by Hugh Magennis, "The *Beowulf* Poet and his *druncne dryhtguman*" (1985); Idem, "The Treatment of Feasting in the *Heliand*" (1985).

Allusion has been made in another context to the marriage of Authari of the Lombards and Theudelinda, daughter of duke Garibald of the Bavarians, in May of 589. Authari died childless in September 590, however—he was poisoned— and, according to Paul's *Historia Langobardorum*, Theudelinda then assumed a key role in determining the succession.[74] The queen, he said, had so won the respect of the Lombards (the term "Lombards" does not refer to the people as a whole but to the nobles of the kingdom and the members of Authari's retinue) that "they allowed her to remain in her royal dignity, advising her to choose for herself whomever she might wish from all the Lombards" as her husband so long as he was one "who could capably rule the kingdom".[75] After taking council with the prudent, *consilio cum prudentibus habens*,[76] the queen chose Agilulf, the powerful duke of Turin, to be her husband for he was energetic and warlike and suited both in body and mind for the government of the kingdom: *Erat enim idem vir strenuus et bellicosus et tam forma quam animo ad regni gubernacula coaptatus.*[77] She then sent word to Agilulf to meet her at the town Lumello where, after a discussion with the duke which Paul mentions but does not describe, she caused wine to be brought and, taking a drink herself, she then offered the cup to Agilulf who took it from her hands and kissed her.[78] Marriage and kingship were then formally discussed although, from what we now know of the ritual cup offering, it is clear that the basics of the agreement had already been symbolically sealed. Shortly afterwards, with Theudelinda as his wife, Agilulf assumed the *regia dignitas*.

This story has an interesting sequel for, if the Frankish chronicler Fredegar is to be trusted, Gundberga, Theudelinda's daughter, followed her mother's lead in the next generation.[79] Fredegar says that Gundberga was good-natured, generous and universally loved.[80] She was also well disposed to a certain Adalulf who was in her husband's service but he mistook her admiration for something more and asked her to sleep with him. After receiving a contemptuous refusal Adalulf attempted to save his now endangered life by undermining her position with her

---

74 Schneider, *Königswahl*, p. 29f.; Fröhlich, *Langobardischen Thronfolge*, pp. 18f., 97f.
75 Waitz, *Historia Langobardorum*, p. 140: Regina vero Theudelinda quia satis placebat Lango-bardis, permiserunt eam in regia consistere dignitatem, suadentes ei, ut sibi quem ipsa voluisset ex omnibus Langobardis virum eligeret, talem scilicet qui regnum regere utiliter possit.
76 Ibid.
77 Ibid.
78 Ibid., p. 141.
79 Schneider, *Königswahl*, p. 39f., 247; Fröhlich, *Langobardischen Thronfolge*, pp. 104f., 126f.
80 John Michael Wallace-Hadrill, ed. *The Fourth Book of the Chronicle of Fredegar With its Continuations* (1960), p. 41f.: Gundeberga regina, cum esset pulchro aspecto, benigna in cunctis et piaetate plenissema christiana, aelimosinis larga, praecellenti bonitatem eius, diligebatur a cunctis.

husband. He hastened to king Charoald and reported that Gundberga was scheming to poison him and then to place duke Taso of Tuscany on the throne by marrying him.[81] The queen was eventually cleared of all charges. When Fredegar next mentions Gundberga, however, her husband is dead and all of the Lombards have sworn fealty to her: *Gundeberga regina, eo quod omnes Langobardi eidem fidem cum sacramentis firmauerant.*[82] She sent for Rothari, duke of Brescia, and compelled him to abandon his wife in order to marry her. With her support, she said, he would become king. Then, "because the Lombard lords were beguiled by Gundberga", they "did raise Rothari to the throne".[83] Soon afterwards, however, Rothari imprisoned her and contented himself with concubines for the next five years.

The Gundberga episode is less historically certain than that of Theudelinda but the latter's resemblance to Hygd is quite clear.[84] Even the marriage references are probably not an exception since, although the Anglo–Saxon poet does not mention that Beowulf married Hygd when he became king, it is quite likely that such did indeed occur. It is a more than reasonable assumption since the union of royal widow and throne-claimant fits a common traditional Germanic pattern demonstrable for many peoples over a long chronological span.[85] In England, for example, Bede had rough words for Eadbald, son of Aethelberht of Kent, who married his deceased father's second wife in 616 and, in the late ninth century, Asser, the biographer of king Alfred, was equally outraged when Aethelbald of Wessex, Alfred's brother, married his father's widow.[86] This custom, sometimes associated with "levirate marriage" because of similar Old Testament practices, was especially common in the pagan period so that Augustine found it necessary to query its legitimacy in one of his *questiones* to pope Gregory the Great.[87] Despite many biblical *exempla* the church proclaimed the practice to be uncanonical—a recent work maintains that its legal recognition would have limited the

81 Ibid.: Locum acceptum dixit [Adalulf] ad regem: 'Domina mea, regina tua Gundebarga, apud Tasonem ducem secrecius tribus diebus locuta est, ut te uenino interficerit, ipsum coniugatum sublimarit in regnum.'

82 Ibid., p. 59.

83 Ibid.: Gundoberga adtragente omnes Langobardorum primati Crotharium sublimant in regno.

84 Walter Schücking, for example, refuses all credence: *Der Regierungsantritt. Eine rechtsgeschichtliche und staatsrechtliche Untersuchung* (1898), p. 81. Both Schneider, *Königswahl*, p. 40; and Fröhlich, *Langobardischen Thronfolge*, p. 129, are uncertain. In Jörg Jarnut's view, the matter cannot certainly be decided: *Geschichte der Langobarden* (1982), p. 57.

85 Schneider, *Königswahl*, p. 246f.; Dorothy Whitelock, *The Beginnings of English Society* (1977²), p. 150.

86 Bertram Colgrave and R.A.B. Mynors, eds. *Bede's Ecclesiastical History of the English People* (1969), p. 150; Michael John Enright, "Charles the Bald and Aethelwulf of Wessex: The Alliance of 856 and Strategies of Royal Succession" (1979).

87 Colgrave and Mynors, *Bede*, p. 84: Interrogatio Augustine: Vsque ad quotam generationem fideles debeant cum propinquis sibi coniugio copulari; et nouercis et cognatis si liceat copulari coniugio.

number of testamentary bequests to the church[88]—and later ecclesiastics waged a centuries long campaign against these "incestuous" unions which included those to the surviving spouses of near relatives.[89] The monkish poet's lack of reference to Beowulf's nuptials, therefore, can be explained by his reluctance to sully the reputation of his hero who would have to be regarded as a self-condemned sinner if he actually married his uncle's widow.

Beowulf's marriage choice is likely to have been dictated by sound economic and political thinking (of which the poet provides a number of examples). As the widow of the king, Hygd was probably the richest woman in the kingdom. Her family had surely contributed to the union and Hygelac's gifts to her, particularly his "morning gift"[90] which might have included large estates, made her an extremely valuable source of wealth (Gregory of Tours says that Chilperic loved his wife "very dearly for she had brought a large dowry with her").[91] To allow this wealth to leave the royal fisc, or to chance the strengthening of possibly hostile others who might seek out the queen for the sake of it, could not be allowed by any ruler who hoped to maintain a stable government. Medieval sources make frequent allusions to this queen-treasure problem and to its political ramifications.[92] An episode from Gregory's history of the Franks describes a common solution if marriage did not take place. After the death of the polygynous king

88 Jack Goody, *The Development of the Family and Marriage in Europe* (1983).
89 J. Fleury, *Recherches historiques sur les empêchements de parenté dans le mariage canonique des origines aux fausses décretalés* (1933); Korbinian Ritzer, *Formen, Riten und religiöses Brauchtum der Eheschliessung in den christlichen Kirchen des ersten Jahrtausends* (1962), p. 214.
90 King Chilperic gave the Visigothic princess Galswintha five cities, for example: De civitatibus vero, hoc est Burdegala, Lemovecas, Cadurcus, Benarmo et Begorra, quae Gailesuinda, germana domnae Brunichilde, tam in dote quam in morganegyba, hoc est matutinale donum, in Francia veniens certum est adquisisse. . . . Rudolf Buchner, ed. *Gregor von Tours. Zehn Bucher Geschichten* II (1974), p. 262f. There is considerable dispute about the significance of Germanic marriage gifts. For recent commentary, see Diane Owen Hughes, "From Brideprice to Dowry in Mediterranean Europe" (1978), p. 268f.; Wemple, "Women in Frankish Society", pp. 12, 44; Whitelock, *Beginnings of English Society*, p. 150f. Cf. Heinrich Brunner, *Deutsche Rechtsgeschichte* I (1961²), pp. 94f., 391. A helpful discussion of specific examples can be found in Margarete Weidemann, *Kulturgeschichte der Merowingerzeit nach den Werken Gregors von Tours* I (1982), p. 313f. An overly optimistic assessment of wives' control over marriage gifts and the general status of women is argued in Marc Meyer, "Land Charters and the Legal Position of Anglo-Saxon Women" (1980). Michael Hillmann, on the other hand, reaches an opposing and overly pessimistic conclusion in "Geschlecht als Massstab der Rechtsordnung. Überlegungen zur Geschlechterpolarität in den altenglischen Gesetzen" (1986). The most sensible discussion of this topic I have found is Anne Klinck, "Anglo-Saxon Women and the Law" (1982). See also Rosalind Hill, "Marriage in Seventh-Century England" (1979); Margaret Clunies Ross, "Concubinage in Anglo-Saxon England" (1985). Richard L. Schrader, *God's Handiwork: Images of Women in Early Germanic Literature* (1983), is useless.
91 Buchner, *Gregor von Tours* I, p. 232f.
92 Weidemann *Kulturgeschichte* I, p. 20; Dietrich Claude, "Beiträge zur Geschichte der frühmittelalterlichen Königsschätze" (1973); Schneider, *Königswahl*, p. 246f.; Nelson, "Queens as Jezebels", p. 36f.

Charibert, Theudechild, one of his queens, sent messages to her former husband's brother, king Guntram, saying that she would like to offer him her hand in marriage. Guntram replied that "she may come to us and bring her treasure with her." [93] Theudechild was delighted at the news and gathered all her possessions. She clearly wanted to remain a queen. But when he met her Guntram decided "it is better that this treasure should fall into my hands than that it should remain in the control of this woman who was unworthy of my brother's bed". He seized her goods, left her a small portion, and packed her off to a nunnery at Arles where the fasts and vigils were not at all to her taste. A former queen was always a dangerous presence. In fact, at the third Synod of Saragossa, the Visigothic bishops decreed that a royal widow must always enter a convent.[94] The putative grounds for the decision were protection against insult and harm but political concerns probably played a significant role. Except in the case of a particularly secure ruler or dynasty (and these were rare although female regencies were less so) former royal wives were usually faced with the prospects of re-marriage, death, imprisonment or exile. Let us now return to Theudechild, who was nothing if not persistent. She sought desperately to escape her fate: "She sent messengers in secret to a certain Goth, promising him that, if he would carry her off to Spain and marry her there, she would escape from the nunnery with what wealth remained to her and set off with him without the slightest hesitation."[95] Interrupted in her attempt at freedom by the suspicious abbess, Theudechild was beaten mercilessly and locked in a cell where "she remained until her dying day, suffering great anguish". Gundberga's five years pale in comparison.

A number of other associations between queen and treasure are also significant in clarifying the queen-*comitatus* relationship. Recent research makes it seem likely that women of the Thuringians, Anglo-Saxons and Franks, among others, wore a key or a key-like object hanging from their belts as a sign of free, married status.[96] Many have been found in female graves. They are unsuitable for actual use, however, and are probably to be explained as symbols of the right of the women of the house to control the door, storeroom or chest of valuables. Thus, the *friwif locbore* of Aethelberht's laws has recently been explained as the free woman "in charge of the keys".[97] This interpretation makes considerable sense

93 Buchner, *Gregor von Tours* I, p. 230.
94 For commentary, see Walter Laske, *Das Problem der Mönchung in der Völkerwanderungszeit* (1973), p. 48f.; Klaus Sprigade, *Die Einweisung ins Kloster und in den geistlichen Stand als politische Massnahme im frühen Mittelalter* (1964), p. 51f.
95 Buchner, *Gregor von Tours* I, p. 230.
96 Birgit Dubner-Manthey, "Kleingeräte am Gürtelgehänge als Bestandteil eines charakteristischen Elementes der weiblichen Tracht. Archäologische Untersuchungen zu einigen Lebensbereichen und Mentalitäten der Frauen in Spätantike und Frühmittelalter" (1986), p. 150; Hayo Vierck, "Religion, Rang und Herrschaft im Spiegel der Tracht" (1978).
97 Christine Fell, "A *friwif locbore* Revisted" (1984). She is wrong, however, to think that hairstyle did not indicate both marital and social status.

because of the close link between dress, ornament and rank in Germanic culture. Applied to the king's wife, it enables us to further clarify her role. Since queens were generally women of the house writ large and Germanic rulers often divided their kingdoms as they did their farms and made little or no distinction between their own property and that of the royal fisc,[98] it also seems to follow that many Germans will have perceived the rights of the queen in the *aula regis* to be very similar to those of the free wife in her home. Hence, they will have viewed her close association with treasure, the possessions of the house, as something quite natural and proper (the same reasoning applies to her serving ritual) and will have deferred to her in many areas. The *Vita Balthildis*, written soon after her death in 680 or thereabouts, shows the queen, the wife of Clovis II, doing much the same as Wealhtheow in *Beowulf*; she is "nurse to the young men" and she is the distributor of "rich gifts of gold and silver".[99] Even in a later period, according to Hincmar's *De ordine palatii* which incorporates material dating from the reign of Charlemagne,[100] the queen supervises the *camerarius*, the royal treasurer, and is also responsible for distributing yearly gifts to the household followers (we also know that the gifts were graded according to the rank of the recipients).[101] All of this suggests a special intimacy between queen and *comitatus*. In this position of key-holder she was also the guardian of the royal insignia and thus, as Hincmar records, after Charles the Bald's death, his wife, Richildis, handed over to her son the royal raiment, a staff of gold and jewels and "the sword called the sword of St. Peter through which she was to invest him with the kingdom".[102] Finally, it

---

98 I am not convinced by Ian Wood's arguments to the contrary in Peter Sawyer and Ian Wood, eds. *Early Medieval Kingship* (1979), pp. 6–29. The fundamental studies are contained in Eugen Ewig, *Spätantikes und fränkisches Gallien. Gesammelte Schriften (1952–1973)* (1976), pp. 114–230. See also Heinz Joachim Schussler, "Die fränkische Reichsteilung von Vieux-Poitiers (742) und die Reform der Kirche in den Teilreichen Karlmanns und Pippins. Zu den Grenzen der Wirksamkeit des Bonifatius" (1985).

99 Bruno Krusch, ed. *Vita S. Balthildis* (1888), p. 486.; Eugen Ewig, "Das Privileg des Bischofs Berthefried von Amiens fur Corbie von 664 und die Klosterpolitik der Königin Balthild" (1976), p. 577, n. 89.; Nelson, "Queens as Jezebels", p. 47f.

100 Thomas Gross and Rudolf Schieffer, ed. *Hincmarus de ordine palatii* (1980), p. 11.

101 Ibid., p. 72: De honestate vero palatii seu specialiter ornamento regali nec non et de donis annuis militum . . . ad reginam praecipue et sub ipsa ad camerarium pertinebat. For the grading of gifts, see Hans Haefele, ed. *Notker Balbulus. Gesta Karoli Magni Imperatoris* (1962²), p. 92; Timothy Reuter, "Plunder and Tribute in the Carolingian Empire" (1985), p. 81, n. 36; Janet Nelson, "The Church's Military Service in the Ninth Century: A Contemporary Comparative View?" (1983), p. 24.

102 F. Grat, J. Vielliard and S. Clemencet, eds. *Annales de Saint-Bertin* (1964), p. 218f.: Richildis Compendium ad Hlodowicum veniens, missa sancti Andreae attulit et praeceptum, per quod pater suus illi regnum ante mortem suam tradiderat, et spatam quae vocatur sancti Petri, per quam eum de regno revestiret, sed et regium vestimentum et coronam ac fustem ex auro et gemmis. On Richildis, see Karl Werner, "Die Nachkommen Karls des Grossen bis um das Jahr 1000" (1967), p. 411; Enright, "Charles the Bald", p. 299f.; Jane Hyam, "Ermentrude and Richildis" (1981), pp. 153–6.

should also be noted that since a king normally carried his treasure with him on travels to royal residences, a queen might well be the first to lay her hands on it in the event of the king's demise. In sixth century Francia, this occurred at the deaths of kings Charibert, Chilperic and Sigibert.[103] Capture of the queen, then, and especially capture of the queen and royal *thesaurus*, could lend a clear aura of legitimacy to any candidate with a reasonable claim to the throne.[104] As abduction for the purpose of marriage was quite common, a contender who possessed both the queen and treasure was in an excellent position to exploit his advantage and bring any rivals to heel.[105] Early Medieval sources furnish many instances of this type of political configuration. The same principles apply to the thinking of the nobility. Indeed, the idea of expressing a claim to a particular territory through the possession of a woman (usually the wife of a recalcitrant rival or retainer) might also be applied to consecrated nuns. This, apparently, is what earl Swein Godwinson was doing when, on his way home from a campaign against the Welsh in 1046, "he ordered the abbess of Leominster to be brought to him, and kept her for as long as he pleased and afterwards allowed her to go home".[106]

Traversing the passages related to Hygd, Theudelinda, Gundberga and Richildis, the unwary reader might conclude that the barbarian queen exercised a great deal of authority "in her own right". This somewhat nebulous phrase, which bids fair to become an historiographic cliché, is actually misleading for it implies that she could act openly and independent of the wishes of her husband and his *comitatus* and such was hardly ever true even after the death of the lord. In the case of Theudelinda and Gundberga, one might conceive them (as Fröhlich does in his recent dissertation on the Lombards)[107] to have been covered by chapter 182 of the *Edictus Rothari* which decrees that a widow shall have the right to choose another husband provided he be a free man.[108] But a number of conditions are attached to this law in order to protect the rights of the relatives who had originally transferred her *mundium* or guardianship to her first husband and chapter 188 states that if she acts without the consent of her relatives the man who receives her must pay two fines for doing so, the first to compensate for illegal intercourse and the second in order to avert a feud. Widows do have greater

---

103 Weidemann, *Kulturgeschichte* I, p. 20.
104 There now seems to be wide general agreement on this. Even abandoned queens, as Eugen Ewig points out, might still remain in possession of sizable *thesauri*: "Studien zur merowingischen Dynastie" (1974), p. 44.
105 Rupert Köstler, "Raub-, Kauf- und Friedelehe bei den Germanen" (1943); Simon Kalifa, "Singularités matrimoniales chez les anciens germains: le rapt et le droit de la femme a disposer d'elle-méme" (1970); Ferdinand Ganshof, "Le statut de la femme dans la monarchie franque" (1962), p. 44f.
106 John Earle and Charles Plummer, eds. *Two of the Saxon Chronicles Parallel* I (1892), p. 164. See Ross, "Concubinage", p. 30f.
107 Fröhlich, *Langobardischen Thronfolge*, p. 105.
108 Franz Beyerle, ed. *Edictus Rothari* (1962), p. 43.

freedom of choice and movement but their behavior continues to remain subject to external constraints. Royal widows, to whom the challenged interpretation above has recently been applied, seem to have operated under similar controls although with some modification. What appears to have happened is that the ex-husband's *comitatus* assumed the role of *mundium* holder—something which follows naturally from the organization of the warband as a fictive family so that the surviving "sons" laid claim to the guardianship of their widowed "mother". As noted previously, she is normally too important to potential claimants—and thus also to the *comitatus* who will often continue to feel a loyalty to their dead lord—to be allowed a retirement to her own devices. It may be that many widows preferred this arrangement. During years of dealing with the retinue the capable queen will have had plenty of occasions to form personal relationships with the individuals whom she tended and gifted in their youth. She might also have played a role in nurturing factions who would naturally turn to the ruler's bed-mate in order to influence his decisions. The leader, as we have seen, encouraged such activity because it provided a vent for dissatisfaction and kept him in intimate touch with attitudes, personal sentiments and potential plots. A widowed queen, then, if she had accumulated wealth, friends and political acuity, might well prefer to remain at the node of power rather than the periphery. If she had borne a living and suitable son her position becomes stronger for such extends her period of influence, always provided of course that she can keep the boy's uncles at bay.

All these many variables depend to a decisive degree on the attitudes of the retainers, a fact which goes far to explain the differences between Wealhtheow and Hygd. Despite having a son, the former can do little except plead by implication because Hrothgar, although old, continues to command the loyalty of his *comitatus* who in any event are united in wanting Beowulf as king. The move fails solely because of Beowulf's lack of commitment and the queen's years of ministrations to the followers make not an iota of difference. The Hygd episode is more complicated. On the face of it, Hygd is both far seeing and altruistic because she is willing to exclude her son in favor of his cousin Beowulf who can better protect the country. But why could he not protect the kingdom as the boy's chief councillor with the full support of dowager and warband? Confronted with unanimity a young leader has little choice but to do what he is told. The best explanation for this difficulty is that Hygd wished otherwise but had no choice in the matter; she was compelled to act as the emissary of Hygelac's *comitatus* who wanted a veteran warlord to follow instead of an untried boy. True, there is no mention of such pressure but, under the circumstances and especially when one recalls Wealhtheow's worry about the fate of her sons destined to be murdered by their uncle, it seems most likely that Hygd acted under duress. The Anglo-Saxons who listened to the *Beowulf* poem would have well understood the limits on her freedom but the poet avoided explanation for the same reason he excluded reference to her subsequent marriage—in order to demonstrate once again the ideal moral character of his hero. Beowulf's refusal, of course, depends on the same reasoning. In view of this explanation and reconstruction, let us now examine more closely the story of Theudelinda whose actions parallel those of the Geatish queen.

Although a monograph would be needed to properly delineate the queen-*comitatus* relationship in all its details, a brief sketch of the events in Lombardy in 590 will allow us to discuss some of the relevant forces which often come into play at the death of a king. It is necessary to stress at the outset that Paul's story of Agilulf and Theudelinda is too colorful and saga-like to be accepted at face value especially since Agilulf appears as a completely passive character despite his being a duke and thus a man of power and consequence in the kingdom.[109] He was also a relative of the king: *cognatus regis Authari*.[110] Birth and position, then, as well as the fear of an enemy assuming the throne, would all require Agilulf to aggressively intervene in any major political transaction. Paul probably underplays this aspect because he is captivated by the chance to tell a good story with a happy dénouement. Even so there are hints as to what actually occurred. We are told, for example, that Authari was poisoned. The only clue to the possible perpetrator is an earlier reference to a contretemps between Agilulf and a wizard who predicts his future marriage to Theudelinda. Agilulf threatens him with death if he speaks further of the matter and so the implication is that rumor at least had already credited Agilulf with ambitions for the throne.[111] An earlier source, the *Origo gentis Langobardorum*,[112] tends to support the hypothesis of the duke's energetic management. It depicts him as a warlike and decisive figure who seizes the initiative by marrying the queen (*iunxit se Theudelendae reginae*), taking the throne and defeating rebels who oppose him. This source, which is far closer to the events it describes, seems to present the more accurate interpretation; it is Agilulf who wants Theudelinda to wife in order to strengthen his claim to the kingship and not Theudelinda who wants him.

The dead king's *comitatus* plays a crucial role in such succession politics. A close reading of the Deacon's remarks on Theudelinda's freedom to choose a husband actually indicates that she is a stalking-horse for the palace retainers, a messenger on behalf of others who is herself part of the prize. After all, the fact from which all else depends is that Theudelinda does not remain in power by her own will but because the warband allows her to do so: *permiserunt eam in regia*

109 See Fröhlich, *Langobardischen Thronfolge*, p. 99f.
110 Waitz, *Historia Langobardorum*, p. 141.
111 Ibid., P. 135f.
112 Georg Waitz, ed. *Origo gentis Langobardorum* (1878), p. 5: Et exivit Acquo dux Turingus de Thaurinis, et iunxit se Theudelendae reginae, et factus est rex Langobardorum.

consistere dignitatem.[113] It follows that her taking counsel with the *prudentes* is not a voluntary act and neither is the additional requirement that she "choose" someone capable of governing the country. On the contrary, there seems little doubt that Authari's *comitatus* had already opened negotiations with Agilulf (who may have plotted Authari's death) and that they had made plans with him for the transition so that he could confront other possible claimants with a *fait accompli*. To suppose otherwise is to make the very large assumption that the Lombards would actually have been willing to place the affairs of the kingdom in the hands of a young woman of the Bavarians who had lived with them for only about sixteen months from her marriage on 15 May 589 to the death of Authari on 5 September 590. Of course, things might have been otherwise if Theudelinda had borne a throneworthy son and a large enough faction of the *comitatus* and nobility wished to establish a regency and allowed her to become regent. One thinks here of the famous (or notorious) Merovingian queens Brunhild and Fredegund, the former a Visigoth and the latter originally a slave. But even these women, perhaps the most interesting and capable of the sixth century, could only "rule" through their sons with the support of aristocratic factions. It is, then, the palace retainers and the nobles (many of whom are still regarded as members of the *comitatus* even if they are not often present in the hall) who play the key role in dealing with contenders and establishing kings on the throne. Later sources refer to their offer of rule to a candidate with the technical term *invitatio, invitare*,[114] but the basic process can be traced to a far earlier period.

Why then the recurrent pattern of the queen offering the kingship if she does not have a free choice in the matter? There are several reasons which might be cited, all of which have been mentioned or adumbrated above. Of these, the traditional Germanic attitudes of respect for the free married woman who administers the family household and whose widowhood entitles her to a somewhat wider measure of independence are notable for they color the perception of the protagonists. Seen from this angle, the queen's former relationship with the deceased ruler and her association with important affairs in the royal hall imbue her with a certain aura of legitimacy which can be captured and utilized by those who need it. This is an extraordinarily important and perhaps even pivotal quality because the Germans did not posses any clearly defined rules of succession to the throne, a circumstance which often led to open warfare on the king's demise.[115] To all concerned the old king's wife would have appeared as the most promising

---

113 Waitz, *Historia Langobardorum*, p. 140.
114 See Erich Hoffmann, "Die Einladung des Königs bei den skandinavischen Völkern im Mittelalter" (1975). Both Procopius and Gregory of Tours contain examples.
115 This is emphasized in Philip Grierson, "Election and Inheritance in Early Germanic Kingship" (1941); Schneider, *Königswahl*, p. 240f. He refers to "die Dominanz der Macht".

bridge to peaceful possession, a conduit to the justifiable power which she symbolizes but cannot exercise in her own name. At the root of this thinking lies the simple but expressive concept of sexual union which joins man and wife and produces a completely new family which yet shares a blood relationship with two others. The *comitatus*, acting in the role of the queen's *mundium* holder, offers her to a leading contender and thereby creates an association based on the ubiquitous and culturally intrinsic view of women as living links between families and peoples. The queen in turn appears as the symbolic carrier of royal authority. It is further natural to view her in this light since, aside from joining families, she also joins leader and warband in the communal drinking rite and proclaims the lordship of the man served first. This is her traditional, originally religiously sanctioned and probably jealously guarded prerogative which lasts, it seems, until the eighth and ninth centuries when the Christian clergy take over or replace many of the king-making rituals of the Germans.[116] As mediatrix and covenant bearer of the *comitatus* the queen is the appropriate emissary to the new lord and that is why her capture and marriage, voluntary or involuntary, are so important to usurpers, rebels, royal claimants and warband alike. In this simple society she represents the element of continuity between reigns and seems to vaguely foreshadow the idea of the eternal kingship at a time long before the concept developed that the king never dies.[117] Considerably more research will be needed in order to properly verify this latter observation but the important ingredients of hierarchy, legitimacy and especially of a shadowy concept of continuity do seem to be present in her service ritual and suggest the possible existence of a body of Germanic or Indo-European thought about this aspect of kingship which has hitherto been largely overlooked.

Some overall conclusions may now be drawn. The foregoing investigation results in a picture of the *comitatus* which differs considerably from the prevailing view in which reciprocity is deemed more important than hierarchy and in which the lord's wife, when she is mentioned at all, figures primarily as a cup bearer to the retainers or a decorative presence at the welcoming of guests. If I have correctly interpreted the evidence assembled then neither view seems fully warranted. The king's wife or chief wife, the queen if she has been formally recognized as such, is more than just a hostess who dispenses drink; rather, she functions in the hall as women do in society where they act as binders between families who create and embody alliances in order to fashion friendship or restore peace between feuding groups. This brittle equilibrium is achieved through a

---

116 See Janet Nelson, "Inauguration Rituals" (1979), p. 51f. et passim.
117 On which, of course, see the great work of Ernst Kantorowicz, *The King's Two Bodies. A Study in Medieval Political Theology* (1970²).

periodic renewal of the bond between lord and warband which is easily strained because of the inherently subjective judgements involved in the distribution of plunder, treasure and land together with the accompanying tensions and calcu-lations. Conflict is bound to be endemic since rivalry for the lord's favor is constant and normally determines the future of the retainer. The public relig-iously sanctioned assignment of ranks is necessary, therefore, in order to prevent a relentlessly flourishing dissent. On the other hand, a moderate amount of internal tussling is not always disruptive since, if rivalry be inevitable, it can also be harnessed and made to work to the leader's advantage and for the security of the group. Here, in both cases, is where the queen can enter the breach. Although her husband fixes the status gradations she can make his decisions more palatable through subtle non-threatening mediation appropriate to a woman. It is effective because of her sex, because of the religious significance of the ritual and because she shares some of the characteristics of both lord and follower without full membership in either category.[118] The same reasoning tends to increase her value to the *comitatus* when she becomes a widow for, among other possibilities, marriage and service ritual can help cushion the impact of the accession of the new lord with a separate following who may also want to settle scores with some members or factions of the band she now represents. The ritual itself, of course, which we see to be common to peoples as diverse and geographically distant as the Anglo-Saxons and Lombards, gives every sign of great antiquity indicating that its roots must be sought in the domestic activity of the wife in the early Germanic household, the mediatrix between father, sons and dependent *familia*.

Arguably, the most surprising finding concerns the structure of the warband. For obvious reasons (as even the name suggests) historians have always viewed the *comitatus* in unanimously unspoken assumption as a purely male institution with the royal consort operating mainly in the same relation to her husband as do the wives of his followers back on their farms. Neither her activities as hostess, her giving of gifts nor her occasional advice make much of a difference here for they all have a common domestic basis in Germanic culture. Contrarily, the present reading suggests that the queen's activities within the group are too thoroughly integrated, too nicely interwoven, to consider her any longer as an attending but essentially extraneous character comparable, say, to a steward or groom. Although she does not fight, and while her role is undeniably unique, her ritual and ministrations would seem to be too closely tied to the maintenance and thus existence of the group to view her as a total outsider and too functional during successions to describe her as really extraneous. The mortar that cements

118 Approaching the matter from a different perspective, John Michael Wallace-Hadrill seems to reach a somewhat similar conclusion. "A queen," he says "was an honorary man" (*The Frankish Church* [1984], p. 404). So also, for the church at least, was the nun.

the bricks must be regarded as part of the building. That is not to imply that the queen is indispensable; in fact she can be rejected, exiled, demoted or killed like any of the followers but a substitute, another wife, must then be found who will perform the same necessary functions. A liminal figure, the queen belongs to both lord and *comitatus* at different times in her political life-cycle. Under normal circumstances, that is with a competent living ruler, her influence is contained within narrow limits and she cannot devise policy. On the other hand, it is probably not beyond her powers to sometimes influence policy, to nudge it along or to slow it down. Should one speak then, perhaps, of a triune pattern of political dialectic within the warband? On balance, the answer must be a qualified negative —negative because her power is largely borrowed, qualified because the proposed formulation might well apply to three situations of not infrequent recurrence: when counsel is divided and the ruler uncertain, in the case of evenly balanced factions during an interregnum (when contenders will also negotiate) or in the event that a clever dowager can manipulate an inexperienced son. Otherwise, as argued above, the queen is the flexible instrument of the lord and upon his death usually becomes the instrument of the warband which she continues to hold together as an organization since she is the living symbol of continuity and the channel to legitimacy. Her marriage, arranged by the *seniores* of the retinue, is essentially an extension of family politics which will seal the bargain joining new leader and old follower. This design is so pervasive, however, that it seems to have achieved a life of its own—constant references to the capture of queens by throne-claimants are difficult to explain—and hence must also be regarded as an actual aspect of an as yet unexplained barbarian "political theory". It is not one which is written down but that lack is easily explainable on the basis of familiarity accompanied by a typically Germanic reluctance to form abstractions. Nevertheless, at least some parts of the whole are discernable through analysis and the liquor ritual would seem to be the key which can unlock the storeroom.

It is to the sources and socio-cultural meanings of the liquor ritual that we may now turn our attention. As it unfolds in the chapters which follow, the search will eventually range over a long millennium. It will, because of the scattered nature of the evidence and the complexity of the thesis, require numerous digressions and, occasionally, some repetition. The thesis that will be argued is fourfold: first, Wealhtheow's behavior reflects ancient elements in the tradition of the Germanic *comitatus* and has some points in common with the behaviors of women in Germanic society; second, her ritual and organizational relationship with the warlord can be traced to the milieu surrounding Julius Civilis of the Batavians and the prophetess Veleda in the first century AD; third, the practices involved, even the form of warband organization itself, are ultimately derived from contact with Celtic cultures; fourth, analysis of the warlord/prophetess linkage reveals the existence of a frequently overlooked historical current of continuity stretching from the beginnings of La Tène culture to the Carolingian period on the continent and, on the periphery, in Scandinavia and Ireland, for some consider-able time beyond it.

II

WARLORDS, *HETZERINNEN* AND SIBYLS

Chapter one explored selected aspects of the social and political interactions between warlord, wife and followers and maintained the hypothesis that close examination reveals the existence of a triangular pattern of relationships which helps to explain some hitherto confusing patterns in the history of the *comitatus*. I have argued that the queen is a delegate of the lord who fortifies the ties between leader and retainer. The primary mechanism employed for this purpose is the liquor service which joins the members of the warband community in a complex web of duties, loyalties and acknowledgements. All of these are woven into a multi-textured ritual by the lady who carries the mead cup and pours the liquor over which, and accompanying which, the warriors make their oaths. Against this background, several elements which have as yet only been remarked upon in passing now deserve to be isolated and analyzed in greater detail.

The first aspect requiring comment is that the entire procedure is quite thoroughly charged and suffused with a religious aura. Wealhtheow is a liminal figure carrying out, *in prescribed fashion*, a rite which is central to the maintenance of the warband. In a later age, what she does might be termed a state ritual. The cultic component of her actions, moreover, is still further emphasized when she offers the mead to Beowulf and gives thanks to God that her plea for succor has been heard. It is in reaction to her speech and presentation—itself a ritual act— that Beowulf makes his powerful promise to either perform heroically or to die in the process. The poet's description of Wealhtheow as being *wisfæst wordum*, wise in her words, while at the same time she is speaking to the deity and offering drink is still another element which accentuates the religious atmosphere appropriate to the making of vows; it contains a certain subtle hint of the numinosity which surrounds her.

A kind of latent religious atmosphere also vitalizes the queen's speech in the second banquet scene which is declaimed after Hrothgar has expressed an intention to adopt Beowulf and after the queen has entreated him to leave the realm instead to his nephew, Hrothulf. Wealhtheow attempts to bribe Beowulf with gifts and good wishes after he has received another cup of drink:

> Wealhtheow spoke to the warrior host:
> "Take, dear Beowulf, collar and corselet,

Wear these treasures with the right good will!
Thrive and prosper and prove your might!
Befriend my boys with your kindly counsel;
I will remember and I will repay.
You have earned the undying honor of heroes
In regions reaching as far and wide
As the windy walls that the sea encircles.
May fate show favor while life shall last!
I wish you wealth to your heart's content;
In your days of glory be good to my sons!
Here each hero is true to each other,
Gentle of spirit, loyal to lord,
Friendly thanes and a folk united,
Wine-cheered warriors who do my will." [1]

Other scholars, of course, have also detected the religious flavor of these lines. Although Helen Damico's recent interpretation of Wealhtheow (in which she argues that the queen is modeled after the valkyrie figure) may be somewhat strained, she is undoubtedly correct in her view that the tone of much of this speech "resembles that of a benison". [2] Her attribution of a prophetic power to the queen in this instance may seem more debatable but in the final analysis it, too, appears sound since Wealhtheow's exhortation to the hero is to "thrive and prosper" and the wish that fate show him favor in wealth and honor cannot be readily separated from her ritual actions. Her expressed desire is certainly borne out by the long life and fame of king Beowulf. We note also the conspicuous combination of these wishes with the visceral concepts of kin-loyalty and allegiance to lord and folk. The religious and prophetic overtones cannot be overlooked for they are present in the language itself. As Irving said of some of these lines, they have an incantatory quality approaching that of prayer. [3]

The second element requiring explanation is that of Wealhtheow as *agent provocateur* for it cannot be denied that the queen is a dangerous women whose counsel is sometimes poorly thought out and, on one fateful occasion at least, leads to horrible disaster. [4] We note that she has completely misjudged Hrothulf's character, for example. She proclaims that she "knows" his goodness although the poet knows that he is the man who will kill her children for the sake of

---

1 Klaeber, *Beowulf,* ll. 1215–1232. The translation is by Charles W. Kennedy, trans. *Beowulf: The Oldest English Epic* (1940), p. 39f.
2 Damico, *Wealhtheow,* p. 97. Damico persuasively compares this speech to that of the valkyrie in *Helgakviða Hundingsbana* I.
3 Edward B. Irving, *A Reading of Beowulf* (1968), pp. 140–4. See also Nolan and Bloomfield, "Beotword", pp. 499–516.
4 See, for example, Brennan, "Hrothgar's Government", p. 13; Hill, "Danish Succession", pp. 177–97.

ambition. But Wealhtheow's assessment of his qualities is so faulty that she prefers him to Beowulf who, despite his short stay at Heorot, has demonstrated the best of characters judged according to the values of the society to which she belongs. All recognize this except the queen. By desiring her husband to nullify his newly established kinship with Beowulf and retract his offer of kingship, she is introducing a perilous note of dissention into the society of the *comitatus*. Moreover, she is willing to put her prestige on the line by running a foolish bluff. In the last several lines cited above, she obliquely threatens Beowulf by suggesting that the warriors of the hall will do her will against him even though the poet makes clear that both Hrothgar and his retainers are unanimous in wanting Beowulf as king. The hint that she possess autonomous power is not only untrue but also hazardous since she thereby warns her potential ruler of her reservations and possible untrustworthiness. Had Beowulf accepted Hrothgar's offer—which must have seemed likely because of its munificence—and had Wealhtheow's judgement of his character been correct, her words would undoubtedly have made him suspicious and perhaps have created the very situation which she feared so desperately. As with Unferth, however, we may also assume that the queen is accustomed to being provocative on special occasions since, as noted above, her words and actions when presenting mead to the hero are actually calculated to elicit his promise to essay the killing of Grendel. *guþe gefysed* in line 630 can be aptly translated as "incited to battle".[5] Not only is this interpretation of her action supported by the poem itself but numerous studies of Germanic culture confirm the practice as historical; men often make promises in the hall when presented with drink by women and both sexes expect it to be that way.[6]

Finally, one of the most intriguing questions of all centers on the fact that it is a woman, the warlord's wife, who is expected to ritually name and praise the king and then to confirm the warband's system of precedence. As with some other questions raised about Wealhtheow in the present study, this one also seems to have escaped the close scrutiny it deserves. When the context is taken into consideration, however, it all seems paradoxical and noteworthy. The *comitatus* is a band of armed, bellicose, ambitious and often cruel warriors who treasure the virtues of courage and loyalty and exalt the characteristics of physical strength

---

5 Geoffrey Russom, "The Drink of Death in Old English and Germanic Literature" (1988), p. 182f. He notes that "several passages in *Beowulf* show a close association between an offer of drink and an incitement to show one's merit" and cites the following lines:

> Hwilum maeru cwen,
> friousibb folca, flet eall geondhwearf,
> baedde byre geonge.

"At times the famous queen, peace-pledge of nations, went all around the hall, urged on [baedde] the young men." See also Nolan and Bloomfield, "*Beotword*", pp. 499–516.

6 Ibid.; Einarsson, "Old English *Beot*", pp. 99–123. One may refer to analysis in the first chapter from notes 36 to 53. Further analysis in chapter III.

and dexterity. Even if our examination in the previous section shows that a woman might find it easier (and safer) to act as an intermediary within this group, it continues to seem unusual that she should be so closely tied to the aggressive ethos and power structure of the masculine *comitatus*. If one need see nothing unusual in the fact that the warriors are served by a woman, one hardly expects this woman to have highly significant speechmaking rights within the gathering. Nor does the fact that she is the wife of the leader carry much weight in this regard (although it can be important otherwise) since that might help explain occasional speeches at his behest or with his indulgence but cannot explain the traditional and *institutional* demand that she frequently speak. Yet, we are told in *Maxims I*, and have already found it confirmed in *Beowulf* and other Germanic and Latin texts, that the lady of the hall must publicly offer the cup to the leader first and also offer him advice. One finds it difficult to escape the suspicion that something is being overlooked here which is fundamental to the thought-world of the Germanic warband.

We are confronted with a bundle of characteristics centering on Wealhtheow which seem strangely puzzling or even contradictory—a connection with royal power, a religious aura, prophetic ability and a tendency to provoke. Aside from the fact that most modern criticism tends towards the same assessment, we can be quite certain that the poet wished to highlight the contrasts since the very name Wealhtheow, a baffling choice, apparently means "British slave". Commentators over the past several generations are united in the view that this is the most extraordinary name in Old English literature and such unanimous perplexity has only been deepened by studies demonstrating that the Anglo-Saxons took great care in the choosing and bestowal of names which they regarded as keys to character.[7] But how does one reconcile the queenly character of the *ides Helminga* with an appellation which denotes servitude and suggests contempt? So far, no explanation has won universal acceptance and no scholar has sought for an answer within the institutional context of the *comitatus* although the nature of the poem might well seem to suggest that much can be learned by doing so.

Setting, words and actions in the *Beowulf* poem combine to indicate that Wealhtheow is a curiously provocative figure at home in the cultic-ritual field whose speeches are institutionally significant to the *comitatus* and are tinged with religious symbolism. Although I am not suggesting that she is a priestess—she is too clearly depicted as the noble wife and mother for that—the poet has certainly chosen to present her as a guide and key participant in ritual and to endow her with qualities which suggest a subtly hieratic and at least partially oracular character. Why he did so requires some sustained attempt at explanation. We must, therefore, seek to uncover the reasons for the ascription of these distinctive

---

7 Fred C. Robinson, "The Significance of Names in Old English Literature" (1968), pp. 14–58.

oddities to the character of the warlord's wife knowing that the poet would not have chosen them had his model been either incredible or uncommon. It has already been shown that other aspects of her behaviour—cup-offering, royal naming and mediation—are universally expected in this milieu and there is no reason why those now under discussion should be any different.

In the pages which follow, I will seek to show that the depiction of Wealhtheow as provoker of dissension is solidly grounded in the social reality of the behavior of women in Germanic culture while the hint at her apparently premonitory abilities is equally well grounded in the religious reality of oracular belief. What will then strengthen this hypothesis, in my view, is the subsequent demonstration that the qualities mentioned were usually associated with certain women companions who served the earliest known Germanic warlords so that a clearer connection will emerge with Wealhtheow's previously discussed delegatory function and the actual historical context of the developing *comitatus*. It will be argued that female exhortation, status assignment, provocation and prophecy all played a role in the growth of that institution and thus demand analysis from an institutional viewpoint. Wealhtheow's actions are not eccentric and, in the present writer's opinion, have not hitherto been fully understood because they have generally been studied apart from that context which gave them meaning in the culture in which they appear, the network of relations between the warlord and warband.

The immediate problem is methodological. Since the present exercise aims at the explication of the principles underlying an archaic set of attitudes - ones taken for granted by those concerned and not usually expressly voiced in the few sources available—the only way to demonstrate the required chain of associations is through the citation of examples which, unfortunately, themselves require explanation to expose their rationale. Much must be gleaned from context alone and this necessitates what may initially seem to be an unduly circuitous approach. One may hope, however, that such will eventually prove rewarding and enlighten more than it confuses.

Within this scheme, one way to begin to achieve a greater insight into the cultural background to Wealhtheow's incitements is to examine the figure of the *Hetzerin*, the woman who provokes conflict in Icelandic saga, and then draw some parallels with an earlier period which demonstrate continuity. One proceeds from what is better known to what is less understood. The *Hetzerin*, it will be argued, has roots which lie at least as far back as the first century AD and, under certain conditions, also has a peculiar power to influence the opinions of men concerning reputation and status. Some of Wealhtheow's behavior, at last, might well fit this model and, if so, then we are in a much better position to understand her character and the institution in which, as we now know, she plays so notable a role.

In medieval Iceland, as in earlier continental societies, women could not represent themselves in court cases. Neither could they witness, prosecute directly, fight in a dual or speak at *Thing* assemblies.[8] Nevertheless, they exercised a notable degree of indirect influence which they gained through persuasion, exhortation and, most interestingly, through insult. This is a strikingly apparent contradiction; in a society which excluded them from the public sphere, women still contrived to play an inordinate role in decision-making and getting things done. When the problem is closely examined, it becomes clear that in the sagas it is often women who draw attention to the slighted honor of their neighbors and menfolk and they frequently incite, goad and urge the men into action by harping on the perceived deficiency. So common is this motif that it transcends all literary genres and Rolf Heller, in an incomplete count, could list fifty-one saga instances in which women incited men to take vengeance or perform risky deeds—hence the term, *Hetzerin,* female provoker, which he applied in these cases.[9] Heller's monograph appeared thirty years ago and since then the *Hetzerin* has been widely recognized as the dominate female type in the sagas.[10] One group of these *Hetzerin* incidents exhibits pronounced ritual characteristics and is especially worth examining.

A recent outstanding study in this area is that by William Miller who convincingly demonstrated the existence of a gruesome ceremony by which Icelandic women were able to force their reluctant male relatives to take vengeance by taunting them with the head of the slain, with the bloody clothing of the corpse or with the bloody weapon which had wounded the dead man.[11] The moral force of this act *always* caused men to resort to arms *despite* previous unwillingness. A good example which shows how this ritual incitement might work occurs in *Njáls saga.*[12] When Skarphedin Njalsson and his brothers killed Hoskuld Thrainsson, a legal action was immediately started by the dead man's relatives. This was not enough for Hoskuld's widow, Hildigunn, who demanded her uncle Flosi's support. Flosi was a respected chieftain who had given Hildigunn to Hoskuld in marriage and thus had some obligation to support her husband's kin even if the precise boundaries of his duties are uncertain. Although quite ready to advance Hildigunn's case, he did not believe that the matter should come to blood. The widow was well aware of his views and strongly opposed them. When Flosi stopped by the farm on his way to the *Althing* to plead her case, Hildigunn began

---

8 William I. Miller, "Dreams, Prophecy and Socery: Blaming the Secret Offender in Medieval Iceland" (1986), p. 114f.; Jesse L. Byock, "Governmental Order in Early Medieval Iceland" (1986), p. 134f.

9 Rolf Heller, *Die Literarische Darstellung der Frau in den Islandersagas* (1958) pp. 98–122.

10 Jenny M. Jochens, "The Icelandic Heroine: Fact or Fiction?" (1986), pp. 35–50; eadem, "The Female Inciter in the King's Sagas" (1987), pp. 100–19.

11 William Ian Miller, "Choosing the Avenger: Some Aspects of the Bloodfeud in Medieval Iceland and England" (1983), pp. 159–204.

12 Einar Ól. Sveinsson, *Brennu-Njáls saga* chs. 111–16. English citation from Magnusson and Palsson, trans. *Njals Saga,* pp. 238–40.

a campaign to force him to take up weapons. The way in which she did so is profoundly revealing of a whole series of Germanic mores and of the way in which the legally and physically weaker sex could exert pressure on their more powerful male relatives. As we shall see, a close analysis of this passage reveals a decidedly archaic stratum of Germanic custom which tells us much about female provokers and the power they exercised even over the actions of kings. It seems best to cite the passage *in extenso* as detailed analysis will be necessary.

Prior to Flosi's arrival, Hildigunn carefully set the stage for her plans:

"I want all the men to be out here when Flosi rides in," she said. "The women are to clean the house and put up the hangings, and to make ready a high-seat for Flosi."

Soon Flosi came riding into the home-meadow. Hildigunn went to meet him.

"You are welcome, kinsman," she said. "My heart rejoices at your coming."

"We shall eat here and then ride on," said Flosi.

The horses were tethered. Flosi went inside. He sat down, and threw the high-seat away from him on to the dais.

"I am neither king nor earl," he said, "and there is no need to make me a high-seat. There is no need to mock me, either."

Hildigunn was beside him. "It is a pity you are offended," she said. "We did this in all sincerity."

Flosi replied, "If you are being sincere with me and your motives are good they will speak for themselves, and condemn themselves if they are evil."

Hildigunn laughed an icy laugh. "This is nothing," she said. "We shall get closer yet before we part."

She sat down beside Flosi, and they talked in undertones for a long time.

After that the tables were set up, and Flosi and his men washed themselves. Flosi examined the towel; it was full of holes, and one end had been ripped away. He threw it down on the bench and refused to use it; instead he tore a piece off the table-cloth, dried his hands on it, and tossed it to his men. Then he sat down at the table and told his men to eat.

At that moment Hildigunn came into the room and went up to Flosi, pushed her hair back from her eyes, and wept.

Flosi said, "You are sad now, kinswoman, you are weeping. It is only right that you should weep over a good husband."

"What redress will you get me?" she asked. "How much help will you give to me?"

"I shall press your claims to the full extent of the law," said Flosi, "or else conclude a settlement which in the eyes of all good men will satisfy every demand of honour."

Hildigunn said, "Hoskuld would have avenged you with blood if he were in your place now."

"You are a ruthless woman," said Flosi. "It is clear now what you are after."

Hildigunn said, "Arnor Ornolfsson from Forsriverwoods never did your father as grave an injury as this, and yet your brothers Kolbein and Egil killed him at the Skaptafell Assembly."

She walked from the room and unlocked her chest. She took out the cloak, the gift from Flosi, which Hoskuld had been wearing when he was killed, and in which she had preserved all his blood. She came back with the cloak and went up to Flosi without a word; Flosi had finished eating and the table had been cleared. She threw the cloak around his shoulders, and the clotted blood rained down all over him.

"This is the cloak you gave to Hoskuld, Flosi," she said, "and now I give it back to you. He was wearing it when he was killed. I call upon God and all good men to witness that I charge you in the name of all the powers of your Christ and in the name of your courage and your manhood, to avenge every one of the wounds that marked his body—or be an object of contempt to all men."

Flosi threw off the cloak and flung it back into her arms. "Monster," he cried. "You want us to take the course which will turn out the worst for all of us. 'Cold are the counsels of women.'"

He was so agitated that his face changed colour rapidly; one moment it was red as blood, then pale as withering grass, then black as death. He and his men went out to their horses and rode away to Holtsford; here they waited for the Sigfussons and other friends.

The passage is puzzling at a number of points but leaves a powerful impression. Let us look first to the episodes of the bloody garment, the charge of Hildigunn, and then to those of the tablecloth and high-seat. Each can tell us something important about the exhortatory role of women in Germanic society and thus, eventually, also throw new light on the atmosphere surrounding the lord's wife in the liquor ritual.

As Miller points out, in each of the seven instances of the blood-vengeance ritual the aggrieved party who called for the principle of *lex talionis* was a woman.[13] In four cases it was the widow and in three the dead man's mother. While the grievant does not always have to be a woman, women do appear to be the usual initiators. Some real part of the corpse must be present, however, so that, in the biblical phrase, his blood may "cry out" for vengeance. Thus, the woman presents herself as simply carrying out the wishes of the corpse. In *Laxdoela saga* for example, Gudrun shows her sons the preserved blood-stained clothing of their

13 Miller, "Choosing the Avenger", p. 185.

sire saying "these very clothes you see before you here challenge you to avenge your father".[14]

The ritual also has much older antecedents and it is important to note this fact. While Miller does cite some Anglo-Saxon evidence,[15] he does not introduce a partial Frankish parallel which, though not concerning a corpse, clearly recalls the Icelandic practice for here too the grievant is a woman who wishes to force revenge for an injury and does so by sending a bloody token to a relative. Her name was Clotild, daughter of king Clovis of the Franks. Her brother had sent her off to Spain as bride for king Amalric of the Visigoths and she had taken with her a great dowry of treasure. Within a few years her husband began mistreating her because of her refusal to convert (the Visigoths being Arians) and at one point he beat her so severely that she sent a towel stained with her own blood to her brother, Childebert.[16] "Greatly moved", Childebert readied an expedition and caused the death of Amalric when one of his men struck him down with a javelin. Clotild then began the journey home with him but died on the way and was eventually buried in Paris with her father. Although this Frankish incident is not fully comparable to that of the saga, the motif of female grievant provoking revenge with a bloody token is certainly present and indicates the antiquity of the principle. While Childebert might well have acted on receipt of an appeal alone, it is clear that Clotild wanted to ensure his intervention and that is why she included the stained towel. This made certain that Childebert would be "moved" to undertake the dangers, the expense and the journey for a refusal would render him contemptible and threaten both his status and manhood before his peers.

Hildigunn's charge to Flosi indicates the nature of the sanctions which she could call on to force him to take revenge. She demands blood in the name of his "courage" and "manhood" or else, she pronounces, he will become a figure of scorn. Inherent in this charge is the accusation that a man who refuses the goad couched in these terms is less than a man; he is womanish. The aura of implied homosexuality hangs heavily in the background and colors the interaction.[17] Thus, in another example of goading in *Eyrbyggja saga*, when Thorarinn the Black is accused of stealing horses by Thorbjorn, his mother, Geirrid, who thought that he had reacted too mildly, came to the farmhouse door and said:

14 Sveinsson, *Laxdoela saga* ch. 60. Translation by Magnus Magnusson and Hermann Palsson, *Laxdoela Saga* (1972), p. 197.
15 Miller, "Choosing the Avenger" pp. 194–204.
16 Buchner, *Gregor von Tours* II: III, 10, p. 156. Translation by Lewis Thorpe, *Gregory of Tours. History of the Franks* (1979[2]), p. 170.
17 Folke Ström notes that "lack of courage, patent physical cowardice, implied such a flagrant deviation from what convention demanded that it could be branded as a symptom of perversion—of an abnormal, that is to say feminine, nature". Ström, *Nid, Ergi and Old Norse Moral Attitudes* (1973), pp. 3–20; Preben Sörensen, *The Unmanly Man: Concepts of Sexual Defamation in Early Norse Society*; Kari Gade, "Homosexuality and Rape of Males in Old Norse law and Literature" (1986), pp. 124–41.

What people say about you is all true, Thorarinn, that you have a woman's nature rather than a man's if you let Thorbjorn the Stout heap all kinds of insults on you; and I don't know why I have such a son.[18]

Unable to back down after the insult, Thorarinn replied: "Nor shall I stand here any longer" and rushed off to do battle. Later, after a second fight and a victory, Thorarinn returned to the farm and answered his mother's queries with a verse:

> Women's contemptuous taunts I
> turned from me—dun eagles
> fed there on the flesh of
> foemen—as I battled.
> Little spared I, strife-loving
> lady [Geirrid], to wield ruthlessly—
> loath though to boast—my bitter
> brand in mortal conflict.[19]

Geirrid demanded to know if this meant that Thorbjorn was slain and her son described in detail how his sword had "entered the warrior's gullet": " 'Then my egging you on did some good' exclaimed Geirrid. 'Now all go inside and bind your wounds'."

This episode, in turn, casts new light on other earlier materials. Consider, for example, a passage from the *Historia Francorum* in which one Sichar, after having killed Chramnesind's kinsmen, could still form a close friendship with him so that the two became devoted to each other and "often had meals together and even slept in the same bed". One day, however, when Sichar was drunk, he began saying that Chramnesind should be grateful to him for the killings since the compensation Sichar had paid him had made him rich:

> When he heard Sichar's remarks, Chramnesind was sick at heart. "If I don't avenge my relatives" he said to himself, "they will say that I am weak as a woman, for I no longer have the right to be called a man!" Thereupon he blew the lights out and hacked Sichar's skull in two. . . . Chramnesind stripped Sichar's corpse of its clothes and hung it from a post in his garden fence.[20]

Although Chramnesind was not here goaded by a woman, the significant fact is that he has internalized the terms of the expected insult so that he applies it himself—he worries about appearing like a woman. Nothing could more strongly show the dread of this idea in Frankish society. Chramnesind kills his friend because of a fear of what his relatives will say even though they have not yet said

18 Paul Schach and Lee M. Hollander, trans. *Eyrbyggja Saga* (1959), p. 29. See also Ursula Dronke, *The Role of Sexual Themes in Njals Saga* (1980).
19 Ibid. p. 30f.
20 Buchner, *Gregor von Tours* II: IX, 19, p. 256f. Translation by Thorpe, p. 501.

it. The passage does not identify the potential blamers among his relatives as women but we can well imagine that while he would consider it grim if men faulted him with being womanish, he would find it unendurable for women to do so.

A closer parallel to Thorarinn and his quarrelsome mother appears in a passage of the seventh century chronicle of Fredegar describing an episode from the life of Theodoric, king of the Goths:

> At one time, Theodoric and the Goths were making war against king Odoacer and the Heruli and, fleeing with his men, Theodoric entered Ravenna. His mother Lilia was there and came out to meet him, insulting him saying: "There is no place for you to flee to my son unless I raise my dress and you return to the womb from which you were born." [21]

In Mediterranean sources at least, [22] statements like this can be accompanied by an obscene gesture, a pointing at the genitalia or an actual raising of the dress. It is clear that it is not confined to the Germans alone, appearing among many peoples ancient and modern, but it is certain that its force is always greater in a simple society which exalts the warrior virtues. In all such cultures, the sex of the accuser is a critical datum. As Roberta Frank pointed out in a recent paper, some thirty-three named and four anonymous Icelandic scalds addressed poetry to women between 970 and 1210, and sometimes did so in unexpected circumstances. The reason for this female apostrophe, she concludes, is that "feud in Iceland was very much a woman's business" for women were constantly watching, judging and making comparisons of men. [23] Absent the bloody-shirt motif cited above, women could always appeal to the concept of manliness and it now appears that by doing so they became the most feared critics within these small population groups where reputation was a matter of life and death. As a corollary to this finding, it must also be postulated that many women would have felt a strong inducement to support this masculine ethos and to emphasize their function as arbiters of reputation. It was more than just gossip; the functioning of the heroic code, as the poets realized, was closely linked to their evaluations. Geirrid and Lilia certainly taught their sons the power of female criticism just as Hildigunn did to Flosi and many other examples could easily be adduced.

Let us now return to the elucidation of the plot itself. The episode of high-seat and table cloth can most conveniently be dealt with together. Both the context of

21 Bruno Krusch, ed. *Chronicarum quae dictuntur Fredegarii scholastici libri* (1888), IV, II, 57: Nam quadam vice apud Odoagrum rege et Aerolis Theudericus cum Gothis prilium concitasset, Theudericus fugiens cum suis, Ravennam ingressus est; ibique mater eius Liliam obviam veniens, increpans eum, dicens: "Non est, ubi fugias, fili, nisi ut levi vestimenta mea, ut ingredias utero, de quo natus est."
22 Carl Sittl, *Die Gebärdenden der Griechen und Römer* (1980), p. 104.
23 Roberta Frank, "Why Skalds Address Women" (1990), pp. 76, 78.

the scheme and Flosi's reaction to it point to an elaborately staged interdependent affront which stops just short of direct insult but is yet nicely calculated to give deep offense while remaining, to use a modern term, "deniable". Such a quality also makes it difficult to explain fully so that the scene must be approached in an oblique manner in order to reveal all implications. While the symbolism of the high-seat is obvious, that of the table and its accoutrements—and one must suppose that it was lavishly set—require considerable background exposition.

With its richness of costly vessels and ornaments, the lord's table was a cardinal symbol of status throughout the Early Middle Ages. As we have already seen, the seating order was a public visual statement of the hierarchy of the warband community while also expressing and renewing the bond which joined all who ate or drank from it. In the Sichar/Chramnesind passage cited above, it was said that both men became so close that they often had meals together and such behavior signified intimacy. Gregory of Tours provides plenty of examples showing that an invitation to a meal was an offer of friendship which obligated the guest to a political alliance; a refusal, on the other hand, signified enmity.[24] Consequently, tables were usually highly decorated and valued objects and those of royal halls were often kept in special storeroom with the treasure and other insignia of status.[25] One thinks of the so-called "table of Solomon" preserved by the Visigoths or the three beautiful silver tables possessed by Charlemagne, one of which was a favorite of Louis the Pious but was eventually chopped up and distributed as a reward to warriors.[26] Some courts might be noted for the display of these objects and become famous for the munificence surrounding them. It was said of prince Harald of the Danes in the ninth century that he wanted to visit Francia in order to see "the kingdom of the Franks, the piety of Caesar, his noble force and the service of his table . . . ".[27]

24 This point is widely noted in the literature. See, for example, Hauck, *Rituelle Speisegemeinschaft*, pp. 611–21; Weidemann, *Kulturgeschichte* II, p. 369f.; Dietrich Claude, "Untersuchungen zum frühfränkischen Comitat" (1964), p. 74f.; Brian Brennan, "Senators and Social Mobility in Sixth Century Gaul" (1985), p. 158.

25 Dietrich Claude, "Beiträge zur Geschichte der frühmittelalterlichen Königsschätze" (1973), pp. 5–24; Weidemann, *Kulturgeschichte* II, p. 360f.

26 Claude, "Königsschätze", pp. 9, 23; Thegan, "Vita Hlodovici", ch. 8 in Reinhold Rau, ed. *Quellen zur karolingischen Reichsgeschichte* I (1980), p. 223.; Reinhold Rau, ed. "Ann. Bertiniani" s.a. 842 in his *Quellen* II, p. 56.

27   Cernere namque placet Francorum regna fidemque
        Caesaris, arma, dapes, christicolumque decus,
        Culturamque Dei, cui servit cuncta potestas,
        Ut canis, atque fides firmiter alma tenet.

    Edmond Ferel, ed. *Ermold le Noir. Poème sur Louis le Pieux et épitres au roi Pépin* (1964), ll. 2036–2039, p. 154. The politico-theological background in Karl Hauck, "Der Missionsauftrag Christi und das Kaisertum Ludwigs des Frommen" (1990), p. 289f.; Idem, "Karolingische Taufpfalzen im Spiegel hofnaher Dichtung" (1985); Arnold Angenendt, *Kaiserherrschaft und Königstaufe: Kaiser, Könige und Päpste als geistliche Patrone in der abendlandischen Missionsgeschichte* (1984), p. 215f.

The silver dishes placed on these tables were equally loaded with symbolic freight and were themselves regarded as signs of high status. An indisputable connection exists between the munificence of the table setting and kingship. When king Childebert of the Franks wished to adopt a son who would succeed him, for example, he "gave him three pairs of everything which a king could need, arms, clothes and ornaments *with some silver dishes* and a team of horses."[28] Similarly, describing the treasure of the Vandals in a sixth century triumph, Procopius refers to the articles wont to be set aside for royal service. These included jewelry, "golden drinking cups" and "all the other things which are useful for a royal table".[29] Such beautiful objects were so rare and valuable that they might even be thought to symbolize the standing of an entire people. A community rich enough to possess them could not fail to be important. When Gregory of Tours was summoned to attend Chilperic at his manor in Nogent-sur-Marne, the king

> showed us a great salver which he had made of gold encrusted with gems and which weighed fifty pounds. "I have had this designed for the greater glory and renown of the Frankish people," he said. "If it is granted to me to live, I propose to have other objects made."[30]

The removal of these status symbols from an opponent signified great humiliation. Thus, king Guntram boasted of the table service he had confiscated from duke Mummolus. As one course was being served at a feast, the king said:

> All the plate which you see here belonged to the traitor Mummolus. By the grace of God, it has now passed into my possession. I have had fifteen other dishes out of the set broken up, all as large as the one you see. I have kept only this one plate, with a second one which weighs one hundred and seventy pounds.[31]

Naturally, then, such plates and cups were viewed as adjuncts to royalty and often presented as gifts to kings: "Queen Brunhild had a great salver of incredible size made out of gold and precious gems. This she dispatched to the king in Spain, together with a pair of wooden dishes, commonly called basins, which were also

---

28 Buchner, *Gregor von Tours* I: III, 24, p. 178. One should add that the small knives used for eating at table were also regarded as status symbols. As J. Werner notes, "übernahm aus dem spätrömischen Milieu zunächste die fränkische Oberschicht im Zeichen ständischer Repräsentation die Sitte, Einzelmesser oder Messerpaare mit Goldgriffen als Essbesteck mit sich zu führen und ins Grab zu nehmen." There is good evidence for later times as well. See Joachim Werner, "Das Messerpaar aus dem Basel-Kleinhüningen Grab 126" (1968), p. 647f.; Peter Paulsen, *Alamannische Adelsgraber von Niederstotzingen (Kreis Heidenheim)* (1967), p. 103; Percy Ernst Schramm, *Herrschaftszeichen und Staatssymbolik* II (1955), p. 542.
29 H.B. Dewing, ed. *Procopius* II (1924) "History of the Wars" IV, 9, 3f, p. 281.
30 Buchner, *Gregor von Tours* II: VI, 2, p. 6.
31 Ibid., VIII, 3, p. 164.

decorated with gold and jewels." [32] There are many such examples and a small mountain of archaeological evidence to accompany them. [33]

The table/treasure mentality was fully shared by the *Beowulf* poet. Consider, for example, the episode of the dragon's hoard which occurs while the old hero lies dying and just before he bequeaths kingship to his faithful retainer (ll. 2744–2800). He now orders Wiglaf to return to the creature's cave and bring out the "ancient wealth" for death will be easier, he says, if he surveys this prize. Wiglaf enters and finds jewels, standing cups, vessels, arm-rings and finely made old helmets. When he looks again, he sees "a standard all of gold, greatest of marvels made by hand, hanging high above the hoard." It was surrounded by a strange light which illuminated the treasure. Many objects were contained therein but the poet chooses to emphasize the dishes, jeweled drinking-cups and banner with which the retainer returns. On seeing them, Beowulf gives thanks to God that he has been allowed to win this treasure for his people before he dies and expresses satisfaction that his life has been well sold. His sentiment is hardly different from Chilperic's, who had a large dish made for the greater renown of the Franks and promised more such if he lived. Obviously, these utensils are not only valuable in themselves but also in what they represent. Indeed, scholars have remarked that the dragon's hoard with its golden banner "is an image for Beowulf's kingdom" which Wiglaf will inherit, just as he plunders the cave of its symbols of kingship. [34]

A reading of these passages can help us to appreciate Hildigunn's tactics but to fully comprehend her maneuverings we must recall that the wife of the lord, just as the wife of the free man, represents his status while at the same time being responsible for the utensils and ornaments of the home. [35] The wife holds the keys to the storerooms. [36] It is her right to prepare the table appropriately so as to honor the house and its guests and the way in which she does so can reflect her opinion of her husband's status and that of his friends. Such subtleties belong to a

32 Ibid., IX, 28, p. 278.
33 Weidemann, *Kulturgechischte* II, p. 360f.
34 Chaney, *Cult of Kingship*, p. 140f.
35 One scholar's analysis of Anglo-Saxon grave-goods of the sixth century led him to suggest that "it is tempting to conclude that the wealth bestowed on a woman may be a reflection of her husband's status as much as her own". C.J. Arnold, "Wealth and Social Structure: A Matter of Life and Death" (1977), p. 132. For women of the Swedish vikings (the Rus) the evidence is more direct: "each woman wears on either breast a box of iron, silver, copper, or gold; the value of the box indicates the wealth of the husband". H.M. Smyser, "Ibn Fadlan's Account of the Rus, with Some Commentary and Some Allusions to *Beowulf*" (1965), p. 96. He is referring, of course, to brooches. The association is otherwise indirectly made in *Njáls saga* where a husband does not defend his wife and so she loses her seat of honor. Or in *Laxdœla saga*: "Hrefna is to sit in the seat of honour". Kjartan insists, "and to be accorded the highest esteem as long as I am alive". Dronke, *Sexual Themes*, p. 20f.
36 Fell, *friwif locbore*, pp. 157–165; Dubner-Manthey, "Kleingeräte", p. 105f.; Vierck, "Tracht", pp. 271–83.

pre-industrial culture and are no longer easy for moderns to interpret but a glance at a plainer parallel from the *Historia Francorum* will show the nature of the by-play to be expected from the *Hetzerin* in this field. Amalaberg was the wife of Hermanfrid, the king of the Thuringians who ruled jointly with his brother Baderic after a third brother was killed. Amalaberg disapproved of the joint rule and so she "sowed the seeds of civil war" between the two remaining brothers:

> One day when her husband came in to have a meal, he found only half the table laid. When he asked what she meant by this, she answered: "A king who is deprived of half his kingdom deserves to find half his table bare." Hermanfrid was roused by this and by other similar things which Amalaberg did. He decided to attack his brother . . . .[37]

Would that we knew the nature of the "other similar things"! Nonetheless, this passage clarifies further the attitudinal atmosphere surrounding the symbolic order of the Germanic table—in the quotation above it represents the kingdom just as it represented the acme of kingliness for the Danish prince Harald—and the way in which women could exploit such associations for the sake of expressing their views and inciting conflict where they judged it necessary.

Equipped with this new understanding of the significance of the table and its ornaments we can more easily interpret Hildigunn's manipulation of power symbols. All her exaggerated formality and deference are calculated mockeries of Flosi's *chiefly* status and of his unworthy character exposed by a refusal to revenge her husband. In Hildigunn's opinion, revenge is the only manly response whereas Flosi holds honor to be satisfied by a court case. The high-seat and table, then, suggest an undeserved and unworthy lordship which is emphasized by the peasant-like towel full of holes so that the high status is contrasted with poverty of soul. When Flosi sits down he will do so with dirty hands and present a derisory tableau of a boor aping a lord in the home of a man who had truly possessed the quality of honor. Flosi shows himself to be keenly aware of the symbolism, however, and turns the tables, so to speak, when he knocks over the high-seat and uses the tablecloth to clean his hands. The first action demonstrates an utter contempt for Hildigunn's charade while the second returns the insult. At this

---

37 Buchner, *Gregor von Tours* I: III, 4, p. 146f. Translation by Thorpe, p. 164. The connection between the serving of meals and the goading woman has also been noted by Joaquin Martinez-Pizarro, "The Three Meals in *Heiðarviga saga*: Repetition and Functional Diversity" (1986), pp. 220–234. As he points out, the men's reaction to the food being served "is never so to speak gastronomic; they respond not to the food as food, but to the meaning they find in the victuals or attribute to them." It is all part of an elaborate domestic code. Clover connects Hildigunnr's actions with widowhood and ritual mourning. The associations do not seem unlikely and provide hints, to be discussed later in the present study, of a pattern of thought whereby women, prophecy and a cult of the dead form part of a single complex for the early Germans. See Carol J. Clover, "Hildigunnr's Lament" (1986), pp. 141–83.

point Flosi has bested Hildigunn at her own game. She, in turn, concedes the preliminary victory and must now, therefore, trot out the decisive weapons in her arsenal, the bloody cloak and the charge on Flosi's manhood. Against these potent talismans the angry leader cannot prevail and the magnitude of his defeat is reflected in his multi-hued visage. The best he can do is the weakly acquiescent riposte that "cold are the counsels of women". Thus, it is that Hildigunn gets what she wants from a chief who had been implacably determined not to give it.

No one who studies this elaborately knotted mobilization of status symbols can realistically conclude that the episode reflects anything other than a traditional mode of male-female conflict. The recognition of threat, speed of reaction, subtlety of manipulation and familiarity of employment betray a long-standing cultural comprehension which is little short of astounding and immediately suggests the existence of a practiced core of intensely held values of great antiquity. In fact, any lingering suspicion to the contrary must be set aside because citations from the *Historia Francorum* sustain the argument. Hildigunn's table manners are surely similar to those of Amalaberg and her bloody cloak is clearly comparable to Clotild's bloody towel. Even beyond these affinities, we must also recognize a noteworthy parallel in the fact that Amalaberg sought to influence a king and Hildigunn a chief. Evidently, high rank carries no immunity to the *Hetzerin*'s threat (actually it probably intensified it) for the association of women with service to table, and thus to authority in relation to control of home and hall, seems so thoroughly embedded in the collective psyche of all segments of Germanic society that alternatives are practically inconceivable. Power is exercised by men but many of the symbols of that power are maintained and arranged by women. Their manipulation forms a non-verbal language which can be either brutally direct or subtly provocative. It would also seem that the symbolic language must, *a fortiori*, be even more practiced and pointed in the exclusive and hierarchic society of a warrior sodality where the lord's wife must be present in the hall. That is not to say that female goading always works. Without her bloody relic, Hildigunn would have failed and Clotild might have remained in Spain. As Amalaberg was able to try "other similar things", however, one must also be willing to envision the employment of a variety of related feminine devices which will always have some effect because they rely on the fluid but perennial concepts of honor, status and shame which Germanic women frequently manipulated in attempts to influence men's design.

For these reasons, I think, one is justified in arguing that Wealhtheow's provocative behavior and ritual of status recognition are made more understandable when seen against the background of the *Hetzerin*'s durable tactics. As already established in several other areas, the queen's actions are not idiosyncratic. Just as the offering to husband and followers is traditional, so too is her incitement of the hero's dangerous promise. Her support of her children contrary to Hrothgar's wish, even though it threatens the security of the group, is a more personal undertaking but is unlikely to be anything novel or unusual in the behavior of Germanic wives whose outlook is much more thoroughly domestic and parochial than their more widely traveled and experienced menfolk.

It is possible to demonstrate that this type of behavior by Germanic women is much older than Gregory of Tours and the sixth century but, before doing so, it seems appropriate to take into account a recently advanced contrasting interpretation. The concept of the female goader has recently been severely criticized by Jenny Jochen who argues that it is largely the literary creation of the saga authors drawn from, she opines, the "mirage of male fantasies and fears".[38] She also suggests that at least some of the attributes of the *Hetzerin* should be associated with the "policies and attitudes of churchmen". Her thesis appeals to some modern sensibilities but is unconvincing for several reasons. In the first place, she overlooks the fact that the role of *Hetzerin* held many attractions but few dangers. It was an easy one for women to adopt since, in contrast to men, it was much less dangerous for them to act irresponsibly in serious cases.[39] Unlike their male counterparts, who had to reckon with the likelihood of woundings and deaths, women were not expected to take up arms in the causes they espoused and only very rarely, and in extreme circumstances, ventured to do so. The physical risks for them were far less for they might urge to battle but did not need to fight. The role of *Hetzerin* might also seem an attractive one since it could confer substantial power at a critical moment and was thus both a handy and appealing psychological tool. Moreover, because Icelandic women who were widows could not personally receive wergild anyway, they had little inducement to settle for compensation and might thus be expected to more lightly clamor for blood. But even in the rare cases that a woman personally participated in a bloodletting, it is unlikely that she would be held responsible or punished for it since any man affected might be judged cowardly for prosecuting her and this attitude, with few exceptions, must often have protected female goaders. It may have partaken of some of the qualities of an actual taboo. Also overlooked in Jochen's analysis is the very important social nexus in which both women and men functioned and which constantly created conditions encouraging *Hetzerei*. Although the passage of women created strategic political bonds between families, a wife often maintained close ties with her own kinsmen whose interests and loyalties could easily diverge considerably from those of her husband's family. In such cases it is only to be expected that a woman might sometimes urge her husband, perhaps against his own better judgement, to support her affines. The sagas provide many such instances and to deny what would appear to be a commonplace social reality in favor of an unproven theory of literary creation seems injudicious. Against this, Jochen's demonstration that the incidence of *Hetzerei* is higher in the "family sagas" than in other types of

---

38 Jochens, "Icelandic Heroine", p. 47f.; Idem, "Female Inciter", pp. 100–19.
39 See the studies by Miller cited in notes 8 and 11.

sources is useful but ultimately unconvincing since it relies on an assessment of the sources which is itself controversial.

Nor is it really fair to blame churchmen for the *Hetzerin* who, as we shall see below, existed in Germanic culture long before the introduction of Christianity. While the figure of Eve may sometimes have encouraged ambivalent feelings amongst clergymen, the same church was also responsible, as Jochen herself emphasizes,[40] for the most remarkable of all advances in the freedom and security of women in that the hierarchy insisted from the time of Gratian onwards on the mutual consent theory of marriage while also forbidding the widely prevalent practice of concubinage. Thus, there is no reason to believe that the clergy was any more intolerant than anyone else in the culture and a reasonable basis for holding the contrary view. Finally, to suggest as she does, that the authors of the Icelandic sagas were on the one hand "deeply imbued with pagan tradition" but on the other hand had also received a thorough clerical education and had perhaps thereby "absorbed" a two-track ecclesiastical attitude, is simply to set up a false dichotomy. The hidden assumption is that the pagan tradition was not ambivalent about females or female qualities. This is highly debatable but if one wishes to support it, one must hold strictly to one of two propositions each of which contains pitfalls: either pagans consistently thought highly of women or else consistently regarded them as inferior beings. Both the laws (which usually treat women as incompetent) and the *Hetzerin* motif suggest that the former is incorrect but if the latter be argued, then the grounds for blaming ecclesiastics disappear, for the bias is already present. Even if it could be shown that the clergy was marginally more prejudiced than the population at large, however, it might still be irrelevant since such demonstration would not necessarily affect the historicity of the motif in question but would merely suggest that churchmen might have tended to emphasize it more than some other authors. In view of these objections, one cannot accept the thesis as presented. Jochen's paper contains some acute observations of permanent worth but the existence of the female goader is difficult to dismiss as fictional.

So far I have discussed the darker side of the *Hetzerin* motif in order to demonstrate the palpable historicity of its roots in the common Germanic culture which probably affected the *Beowulf* poet's depiction of Wealhtheow. The task has been facilitated by the fact that explanations of causality in the sources naturally tend to cluster around cases of conflict rather than of settlement and thus the negative side of the female inciter is easier to document. That is not to say that the obverse of the coin is not also discernable. Previous discussion of Wealhtheow's behavior has established that women who can blame and provoke

---

40 Jochens, "Icelandic Heroine", p. 48; Idem, "The Church and Sexuality in Medieval Iceland" (1980), pp. 377–92; Idem, "Consent in Marriage: Old Norse Law, Life and Literature" (1986), pp. 142–76.

can also praise and mediate and thus reduce conflict among men. The Old English references to the offered cup followed by praise and advice clearly establish the positive role played by women of rank in the small but highly significant body of the *comitatus*. The combined witness of philology, literature and history all attest to this honored function. Citation of a few instances outside the warband, however, may prove useful in adding depth to the portrait of the cup-bearing woman within it.

A glance at the *Historia Francorum* shows that early medieval writers sometimes emphasized the prowess of a lord by showing that women praised him. A famous case, although its relevance to the explication of Germanic attitudes in this area has not hitherto been recognized, is that of king Childeric of the Franks, the father of Clovis. When Childeric was expelled from the kingdom for debauching the daughters of nobles, he fled to Thuringia where he took refuge with king Bisinus and his wife Basina. Some years later he was recalled to his throne and, thereafter, Basina deserted her husband and journeyed to Francia:

> He questioned her closely as to why she had come from far away to be with him, and she is said to have answered: "I know that you are a strong man and I recognize ability when I see it. I have therefore come to live with you. You can be sure that if I knew anyone else, even far across the sea, who was more capable than you, I should have sought him out and gone to live with him instead." This pleased Childeric very much and he married her. She became pregnant and bore a son whom she called Clovis. He was a great man and became a famous soldier.[41]

Si non è vero è ben trovato! Despite his career of furious debauchery, Gregory clearly admires Childeric and we can now recognize the significance of the fact that he has Basina, a woman, sing his praises. Nor does the bishop of Tours chastise Basina for breaking the marriage bond although that is what post-Tridentine moderns would expect of a bishop. Rather, he approves of Basina and applauds her judgement based on a rational assessment of the status and abilities of the two men. In the sentence introducing the quotation above, Gregory writes: "now that Bisinus and Childeric were both kings, Queen Basina . . . deserted her husband and joined Childeric". What primarily concerned Gregory, and also all those warlords, wives and warriors for centuries to come, was not an anachronistic concept of abstract morality but rather the living contemporary forces of status, honor and shame. For the chronicler of the Franks, the rightness of Basina's choice was amply demonstrated by Childeric's subsequent career and the fact that she bore a son who became a noted warrior.

A comparable incident is related of Clovis' grandson, Theudebert. Once again,

---

41 Buchner, *Gregor von Tours* I: II, 12, p. 94. Translation by Thorpe, p. 128f.

it concerns a woman who left her husband for a "better" man and who, thereby, highlights his superior qualities. The woman involved is named Deuteria and she came from a noble senatorial family. Her husband must have been noble as well but we know nothing about him. At the time of the incident Deuteria was living in or near the fortress of Cabrieres, then being threatened with a siege by Theudebert. She sent messengers to him to say:

> "No one can resist you, noble prince. We accept you as our ruler. Come to our town and do with it what you will." Theudebert marched to Cabrieres and entered the township. He saw that the inhabitants were offering no resistance. . . . Deuteria went to meet him. He found her attractive, fell in love with her, persuaded her to go to bed with him and had intercourse with her.[42]

Shortly afterwards, the two were married. This episode is particularly intriguing because a few paragraphs later Gregory tells us that Deuteria subsequently became jealous of her daughter by her first husband and drowned her because she was afraid Theudebert might desire her. Although it is a heinous crime, Gregory reports the murder without overt judgement, saying only that it happened in the city of Verdun. His only characterization of Deuteria is that she was "a married woman full of energy and resource". He takes the same relaxed attitude toward Theudebert. Despite exposing serious flaws in his character, he still describes him as being elegant, able, courageous; a man who "proved himself to be a great king, distinguished by every virtue. He ruled his kingdom justly, respected his bishops, was liberal to the churches. . . . "[43]

Quite obviously, neither of these episodes can be judged solely on the basis of clerical prejudice. Gregory has numerous biases but many are quite alien to moderns because his criteria for judgement are different. From his sixth century episcopal/senatorial viewpoint, the preponderant standards are those of nobility of lineage, the prowess of Christian warriors, generosity to the church and, most emphatically, the degree of respect accorded the office of bishop. Against these outstanding virtues, murder, rapine, brigandage, adultery and polygyny count for less. The correct choices of women do count, however, for the narratives indicate that the way in which women spoke of men was important for male reputations in both Romano–Frankish and Frankish contexts. While the *Hetzerin* motif predominates in many sources, then, that which we might term *Lobende*, the praise theme, is by no means absent. What the documents seem to be suggesting is this: the female provoker exists and there is prejudice against her in that guise. Once she turns to praise, however, her testimony becomes valuable but such is less commonly mentioned, perhaps because the more distracting negative tendencies come to be more often stressed and then routinized. Further research would be necessary to test this hypothesis but, for the present, would take us too

42 Ibid., p. 176.   43 Ibid., p. 178.

far afield since a number of more immediately relevant topics from ancient commentaries remain to be discussed. We may conclude, however, that the *Hetzerin* had another and brighter side which could sometimes be important.

Let us now examine the question of origins and *comitatus* association. Roman sources confirm that women acted as goaders and praisers, as exhorters in fact, from the very beginning of the tradition as we know it. In chapter seven of *Germania*, Tacitus lays great stress on the importance of individual reputation among the tribes of central Europe and indicates elsewhere that it is the reputation of warlords which often attract followers. If kings are chosen in this period on the basis of birth, military leaders are taken on the basis of ability. He says specifically that "if they are energetic, if they are conspicuous, if they fight in the front line, they lead because they are admired", *et duces exemplo potius quam imperio, si prompti, si conspicui, si ante aciem agant, admiratione praesunt.*[44] He then adds that two things "most stimulate their courage". The first is the fact that relatives fight together in formation and the second is that each warrior knows that *women* are the witnesses to his bravery:

> Close by them, too, are those dearest to them, so that they hear the shrieks of women, the cries of infants. *They* are to every man the most sacred witnesses of his bravery—*they* are his most generous applauders. *The soldier brings his wounds to mother and wife, who shrink not from counting or even demanding them and who administer both food and encouragement to the combatants.* Tradition says that armies already wavering and giving way have been rallied by women who, with earnest entreaties and bosoms laid bare, have vividly represented the horrors of captivity which the Germans fear with such extreme dread on behalf of their women, that the strongest tie by which a state can be bound is the being required to give, among the number of hostages, maidens of noble birth. They even believe that the sex has a certain sanctity and prescience, and they do not despise their counsels, or make light of their answers.

These lines certainly contain a hearty dose of exaggeration. We know that in times of dearth or emergency Germanic husbands sometimes sold their wives and children and we also know that maidens were not usually regarded as especially good sureties.[45] On the other hand, the general tenor of Tacitus' report

44 Hutton, *Tacitus. Germania* 7, p. 274. Translation by Church and Brodribb, p. 712.
45 Revolt among the Frisians, for example, followed only after they had first sold their cattle, their land and then their wives and children. See John Jackson, ed. *Tacitus. The Annals* III (1951²), IV, 72, p. 128. Commentary in Much, Jankuhn and Lange, *Germania*, p. 166f., and Reinhold Bruder, *Die Germanische Frau im Lichte der Runeninschriften und der antiken Historiographie* (1974), pp. 145–51. A useful discussion of Germanic society from a Marxist viewpoint will be found in Bruno Krüger, *Die Germanen: Geschichte und Kultur der germanischen Stämme in Mitteleurope* I (1988), pp. 121–91, 264–90. See also Rafael von Uslar, *Die Germanen vom 1. bis 4. Jahrhundert nach Christus* (1980); Eduard Norden, *Die germanische Urgeschichte in Tacitus Germania* (1959²); Malcolm Todd, *The Northern Barbarians. 100 BC–AD 300* (1987²); Nehlsen, *Sklavenrecht.*

on women as stimulators of courage, witnesses to bravery, demanders and counters of wounds, entreaters and counselors is confirmable from other sources and, despite some recent criticism, must be regarded as factual. An example of practice is contained in the *Historia* where Civilis surrounds himself with the standards of the defeated Roman cohorts to remind his men of their honor. He "directed his own mother and sisters, and the wives and children of all his men, to stand in the rear, where they might encourage to victory, or shame defeat. The warsong of the men, and the shrill cries of the women, rose from the whole line. . . ."[46] It must nevertheless be admitted that the mode of conflict described here is as much reminiscent of tribal folk-warfare as that of the *comitatus* where women and children are less likely to have been present. I do not regard that as a serious obstacle to the present interpretation, however, since a carryover of some such attitudes is a high probability.

These passages from Tacitus, as well as those from Frankish, Anglo-Saxon and Icelandic sources, provide strong support for the present hypothesis which emphasizes continuity in the *Hetzerin* motif and sees it as reflecting social reality. As in the sagas, it is mothers, sisters and wives who praise the brave and shame the cowards. The contrary view is more difficult to uphold. In recent times, however, the Tacitean references to women have been subjected to intense scrutiny by Reinhard Bruder who sought to depict them as primarily intentionally propagandistic and rhetorical but was forced to conclude that certain features probably rested on sound historical foundations.[47] Thus, he was driven to admit that women were sometimes present at battles—as exhorters but not as combatants as some scholars have argued—and that they did encourage the fighters through word and gesture. Although I do not discuss them, comparative materials from Celtic and Greek culture as well as anthropological data would all add weight to this conclusion.

Here, then, in the forests of *Germania,* is the archetype, the primordial *Hetzerin* whose descendant lives on in statelier guise in Hrothgar's hall. Although it was necessary to explore a number of byways before arriving at the site of her nativity, we have reached along the route a new understanding of the role of women as the formers of attitudes in simple societies. While the opinions of men were usually decisive, it may be regarded as established that women had a secure niche as judgers of reputation and it is, I suggest, the now demonstrated continuity of this function which partially explains Wealhtheow's speechmaking rights in the midst of a warrior band at Heorot. But this is only one link in a chain of associations each of which has a bearing on the other and can only be separated

---

46 Clifford Moore, ed. *Tacitus. The Histories* II (1951²), IV, 18, p. 34; Much, Jankuhn and Lange, *Germania,* p. 165f.; Bruder, *Germanische Frau,* pp. 128–42.

47 Bruder, *Germanische Frau,* p. 142.

for the purpose of analysis. The whole is greater than the sum of its parts as we shall see when discussing the relationship between liquor, women and initiation into lordship. Before examining that complex topic, however, a number of other Tacitean passages describing the odd *political* intimacy shared by warlords and prophetic women must be analyzed for these contain hitherto unnoticed clues which are essential to explaining the oracular-like pronouncements of Hrothgar's queen.

Although our study so far has resulted in some new insights into the character of the female exhorter, it is still too generalized a depiction for it does not yet bring her sufficiently into the ambit of the warlord nor endow her with the rather vague but nevertheless identifiable aura of sacrality which suffuses Wealhtheow's liquor ritual. The means of doing so are at hand, however, and lie in Tacitus' observation that the Germans believed their women to possess a certain sanctity and prophetic power which rendered their counsel worthy of hearing. He goes on to add that "in Vespasian's days we saw Veleda long regarded by many as a divinity. In former times, too, they venerated Aurinia, and many other women, but not with servile flatteries, or with sham deification." [48]

There are three broad ways of interpreting this Tacitean odor of sanctity said to surround at least some tribal females. The traditional approach, the one held by several generations of leading scholars, takes the cited passage largely at face value and associates Veleda and her "many other" companions with the oft-mentioned wise women, *matronae* and priestesses of the Germanic corpus. It views the passage as authentic in its essentials even while recognizing a certain amount of exaggeration in that the author's celebration of Germanic women in general is a tactic calculated to damn their increasingly immoral Roman sisters with faint praise. [49] The two other views seem more extreme. At one pole is the minimalist position held most strongly by Bruder who argues that such passages are primarily literary embellishments written not only to contrast Romans and Germans at the expense of the former but also to enliven a book by highlighting the exotic and picturesque. A dose of this skepticism is salutary for it is certain that not all Germanic women were virtuous, few were really venerated as prophetic wonders and Roman commentators on Germanic culture did have their own axes to grind and reputations to advance. Skepticism notwithstanding, however, we are still left with the undeniable facts, which Bruder must reluctantly but explicitly recognize, that certain Germanic women did wield influence because they were revered as sibyls, that they did function in the sacral area and did interact in a politically significant way with certain military leaders and rulers. The other interpretive extreme is represented by some modern feminists who ransack the literature on

48 Hutton, *Tacitus. Germania* 8, p. 276.
49 Among many works, see Much, Jankuhn and Lange, *Germania*.

Amazons, Norns, Valkyries and priestesses in an attempt to compile a heroic genealogy while at the same time proposing a wide degree of autonomy for the greatest possible number of early medieval women.[50] This approach draws inspiration less from the sources than from modern social movements and is best described as romantic and speculative. Much of it exhibits a yearning to identify an hypothesized long-lost golden age of "pre-patriarchal society" when a matriarch ruled the Noble Savage and the Indo-European sky god had not, it is argued, yet risen to prominence. Although a few insights have been achieved by some scholars influenced by this school, its assumptions are frequently characterized by wishful thinking.

In sum, while account must be taken of Bruder's criticism, the traditional interpretation remains soundest. That is not to say that it cannot be modified so as to achieve greater clarity and exactitude, particularity in the case of early *comitatus* politics which, of course, is a special interest here. The revised edition of Much's well-known *Germania* commentary speaks of the "political influence" of Veleda, the first century prophetess of the Batavian revolt, and Naumann, whose study of the *Seherin* is cited by Much, describes her as being "apparently the ally of the Batavian leader Civilis" who was "in a certain respect his equal".[51] Veleda's prophecies must, therefore, be seen in a political context and once this problem is squarely faced the key questions become these: who decided what Veleda was going to prophecy? Could she decide herself or was she controlled by someone else? Although the sources do not say a great deal about Veleda, they constantly associate her with Civilis and, when carefully analyzed, encourage the hypothesis that, like Wealhtheow, she was an instrument of the warlord employed to advance his cause. Let us now note the evidence which associates the two figures.

After a notable victory over the legions, after the warlord Civilis ceremonially cut the hair which he vowed never to trim until his triumph, the standing of the Romans reached a low ebb in the North. His intention of winning the supremacy over all Gaul and Germany seemed realizable to many and men from a variety of tribes flocked to his standard. He sent a captured Roman officer to Veleda, who had prophesied victory for the Germans.

> Munius Lupercus, legate of one of the legions, was sent along with other gifts to Veleda, a maiden of the tribe of the Bructeri, who possessed extensive dominion; for by ancient usage the Germans attributed to many of their

50 For example: Miriam R. Dexter, "Indo-European Reflections on Virginity and Autonomy" (1985), pp. 57-74; Fell, *Women*; Schrader, *Images*.
51 Much, Jankuhn and Lange, *Germania*, p. 169f.; Hans Naumann, "Der König und die Seherin" (1938), p. 347ff. A perceptive general discussion will be found in H.R. Ellis Davidson, *Myths and Symbols in Pagan Europe: Early Scandinavian and Celtic Religions* (1988), pp. 159–66.

women prophetic powers and, as superstition grew in strength even actual divinity. The authority of Veleda was then at its height, because she had foretold the success of the Germans and the destruction of the legions. Lupercus, however, was murdered on the road.[52]

In *Historia* 4, 65 Veleda is again mentioned. Civilis and his supporters were then deciding whether Colonia Agrippinensis (Köln) should be given over for plunder to the troops. The tribe of the Tencteri was especially bitter against the colony. When negotiations began, the colonists proclaimed:

"As arbiters between us we will have Civilis and Veleda; under their sanctions the treaty shall be ratified." The Tencteri were thus appeased, and ambassadors were sent with presents to Civilis and Veleda, who settled everything to the satisfaction of the inhabitants of the Colony. They were not, however, allowed to approach or address Veleda herself. In order to inspire them with more respect, they were prevented from seeing her. She dwelt in a lofty tower, and one of her relatives chosen for the purpose, conveyed, like the messenger of a divinity, the questions and the answers.[53]

There are two further brief references affecting our interpretation. One states that a captured Roman trireme was given as a gift to Veleda and another that the Roman commander Cerialis sent secret emissaries who

held out the prospect of peace to the Batavi, and of pardon to Civilis, while advising Veleda and her relatives to change by a well-timed service to the Roman people the fortunes of war, which so many disasters had shown to be adverse. He reminded them that the Treveri had been beaten, that the Ubii had submitted, that the Batavi had had their country taken from them, and that from the *friendship* of Civilis nothing else had been gained but wounds, defeat and mourning; an exile and a fugitive, he could only be a burden to those who entertained him . . . .[54]

This happened after the capitulation of Civilis.

Let us now examine these citations in an attempt to establish the nature of the relationship between Civilis and Veleda. Fragmentary as they are, some new insights may be attainable with regard to the elements of prophecy and the behavior of prophetesses. In a recent study, I argued that both Germans and Celts actually employed the apparently neutral device of casting lots to gain support for an intended action.[55] Prominently mentioned in *Germania*, lot-casting could be manipulated to achieve compromises between factions who could not otherwise honorably back down and to add supernatural force to secretly formulated

52 Moore, *Tacitus. Histories* II: IV, 61, p. 118.   53 Ibid., p. 126.
54 Ibid., pp. 212, 216.   55 Enright, *Iona, Tara and Soissons*, pp. 31–41 and n. 131.

plans. Thus, a ruler might cast lots, or cause lots to be cast for him, until they settled on the predetermined course which he wanted followed and which thereby seemed to have divine approval. It seems to me that warlords might well have made similar use of sibyls. We know that spaewomen and seeresses certainly existed among the early Germans and all indications are that tribesmen were deeply influenced by their opinions which, as in many other cultures, might often have marked political overtones. The fact that Veleda foretold victory for the revolt was obviously an important easily manipulable political datum since a positive prediction would inspire the tribes and attract followers to an anti-Roman resistance while a negative one would have the opposite effect. Civilis, of course, as a wily leader mindful of troop morale, was highly attuned to the value of signs and omens. Tacitus says that he "was naturally politic to a degree rarely found among barbarians" and then adds that he was given to representing himself as the long dead anti-Roman commanders Sertorius and Hannibal "on the strength of a similar disfigurement of his countenance".[56] For the sake of his followers' morale, then, Civilis had to take control of Veleda and shape her pronouncements but he also had to act as if her prognostications were the purest of divine enlightenments. That warleader and sibyl worked closely together is indicated by all the texts cited as well as by the specific reference to their "friendship". One must remember, however, that a truly egalitarian "friendship" in Germanic society only came into being when both individuals were of equal status and that otherwise an element of subordination existed. Whereas Civilis was a warleader of the Batavian royal family, Veleda is described simply as a "maiden of the Bructeri". The status-differential is vast. Moreover, Veleda was also kept isolated from others so that the colonists were not allowed to approach or address her themselves. Clearly, *someone controlled access to the oracle.* Messages were sent to her through a relative "chosen" for that purpose. Since her prophecies were favorable to Civilis, the question as to who ruled her and who chose the relative is hardly a difficult one to answer.

It might, however, still seem theoretically defensible to argue that Veleda was independent enough to support Civilis simply because she wished him well. This possible hypothesis founders on two objections. First, the texts suggest that both Romans and Germans thought Veleda's prophecies could be influenced by the right kind of timely intervention. Two passages mention the giving of gifts and Cerialis advised her that a change in her attitude would be a service to the Roman people. Simply stated: political allegiance determines prophetic utterance. Thus, even if we assume Veleda's good will, Civilis would still have needed to control her since prophecy is always a dangerous instrument and a willful prophetess is a loose cannon on any warlord's ship. To quote an appropriate proverb: "trust is good, control is better". Finally, Veleda's kinsmen are mentioned in two citations

56 Moore, *Tacitus. Histories* II: IV, 13, p. 22.

and in the second the legion's commander advises her "and her relatives" to serve the Roman people. He obviously assumes that her allegiance is negotiable! So whom had she served before? As an unmarried woman, Veleda would have been under the guardianship of her father or brothers who had no incentive to give her in marriage since she brought them both wealth and prestige. In this case, since Cerialis only talks to Veleda after the warlord's defeat, it seems probable that he is assuming his opponent's position as patron of the family. The conclusion that she was not a free agent is, despite generations of assumption to the contrary, inevitable.

Nor does it look as if Civilis and Veleda were doing anything really new. According to Tacitus, no people practiced augury and divination by lot more diligently than the Germans. Omens of all kinds were respected, among them the flight of birds and the neighing of certain horses. This latter means of gaining future knowledge was particularly venerated and it is explicitly stated that when the horses were taken out, they were accompanied by priest *and king* who "observe their neighing and snorting", *hinnitusque ac fremitus observant.*[57] In many cases, then, it would have been the sacral ruler who interpreted the omens for the tribe. Control of the omens, it seems, was nothing new to kings and it looks as if Civilis, who came from a royal family and wished to become king, was simply following tradition. In principle, at least, there appears to be little difference between the functions performed by Veleda and any other kind of oracle.

Although many types of oracles were respected, it is also clear that leaders often maintained women to interpret the supernatural. Cassius Dio mentions another warlord/prophetess pair when he says that Ganna, successor to Veleda, accompanied Masyos, king of the Semnones, to Rome where both were honored by Domitian before returning home, and Suetonius says that Vitellius kept a woman of the Chatti whom he trusted as an oracle.[58] Another piece of evidence for such pairing has been found in, of all places, the island of Elephantine near the southern border of Egypt. Written on an ostrakon in second century Greek occurs the name of Baloubourg (*recte* Waluburg), a sibyl of the Semnones, who is unlikely to have landed in those climes unless she accompanied a band of auxiliary troops of her people. This clue is particularly intriguing since it suggests that prophetesses like Veleda, Aurinia and Ganna may sometimes (often?) have traveled with the warlord's followers.

Another indication is provided by Caesar in his reference to Ariovistus, a

---

57 Hutton, *Tacitus. Germania* 10, p. 278. See also Davidson, *Myths and Symbols*, pp. 149–54; René Derolez, "La divination chez les germains" (1968), pp. 269–74.

58 For these and the following references see Cassius Dio, *Hist. Rom.* 67, 5; Suetonius, *Vita Vitellii* 14; Naumann, *Seherin*, pp. 347–58; Hans Volkmann, *Germanische Seherinnen in römischen Diensten* (1964); Edward Schröder, *Walburg, die Sibylle: Deutsche Namenkunde. Gesammelte Aufsätze zur Kunde deutscher Personen- und Ortsnamen* (1944), pp. 60–4; Jan de Vries, *Altgermanische Religionsgeschichte* I (1956), pp. 319–33.

warlord of the first century BC, although in this example several women are involved and not just one. The case is worth considering in greater detail, however, because it can provide us with a more specific instance of the manipulation of the readers of omens. In a passage from the *Gallic War* describing a long delay in an expected battle between the legions and the forces of Ariovistus, Caesar has this to say of the *matres familiae* of the opposing forces:

> It was a custom among the Germans that their matrons should declare by lots and divinations whether it was expedient or not to engage, and the matrons declared that heaven forbade the Germans to win a victory, if they fought an action before the new moon.[59]

On the face of it, this passage seems to emphasize the high degree of power accorded to certain wise women since, apparently, they were able to dictate when, or even if, battles were to be fought. Such impression is misleading. Caesar reports that he had great difficulty in bringing Ariovistus to engage. For "five days in succession" he ordered his troops to form for battle before the Roman camps and on each occasion Ariovistus would commit only his cavalry to minor encounters. On the sixth day, or perhaps somewhat later, Ariovistus still would not approach but instead ordered some of his men to a restricted and indecisive encounter from noon to sunset. It was on questioning some of the captured foemen as to the reason for these tactics that Caesar elicited the answer cited above. In fact, as is made likely by Ariovistus' reluctance to join battle, the divinations of the matrons were a delaying tactic, a device to gain time. As Delbrück and Walser suggested, the legions on this occasion probably outnumbered the Germans, although Caesar implies otherwise.[60] Thus, Ariovistus postponed battle as long as possible because he was waiting for reinforcements. It was only when Caesar advanced to his camp that "compelled by necessity", Ariovistus committed his full strength.

As in other comparable examples, then, the lot-casting and divinations served the warlord's wishes and interests. Although the device may seem a clumsy one, it is actually a highly sophisticated instrument of propaganda. Unlike the disciplined Roman legionnaire, the Germanic warrior's morale and steadiness of purpose often depended on the warlord's personal bravery and reputation for cleverness and success, qualities particularly necessary to a leader like Ariovistus whose troops were composed of men from six or seven different peoples and joined by no common bonds of tribal loyalty. Having led them to a face-to-face confrontation with the Romans, Ariovistus could not retreat even if the wives and children of his troops had not been present. To do so would have destroyed his

59 H.J. Edwards, ed. *Caesar. The Gallic War* (1980²), I, 50, p. 82.
60 Delbrück, *Kriegskunst* p. 445f.; Gerold Walser, *Caesar und die Germanen: Studien zur politischen Tendenz römischer Feldzugsberichte* (1956), p. 35f.; Siegfried Gutenbrunner, "Ariovist und Caesar" (1953), pp. 97–100.

reputation and his followers would have departed; the omens alone offered an honorable way out. When divination works, then, it redounds to the credit of the leader; when it fails the *matronae* can be blamed. That such may sometimes have happened is, perhaps, suggested by a passage in the *Getica* where Jordanes says that king Filimer of the Goths drove out the "witch women", *magas mulieres, Haliurunnas.*[61]

The foregoing analysis suggests that the warlord/sibyl/warband combination has ancient roots in Germanic culture which were still present in tradition at least in the age of the *Beowulf* poet who, however, only obliquely alludes to their existence through his references to incitement, the hint at the queen's oracular powers and through his general depiction of the woman who ritually presents the cup to the leader. The Hrothgar/Wealhtheow association as presented in the poem is an echo of an earlier more robust and vigorous politico-theological conception which requires considerable reconstruction to be understood. The poet's description is partial and some aspects may be deliberately shaded and elusive. Whatever the reason for his sensitivity—and it is difficult to know whether to ascribe it to the subtlety of his art or his Christian conviction—it seems quite probable that, on the whole, his portrait is reasonably realistic. He knows whereof he speaks but says less than he knows. Perhaps the most persuasive illustration of this is the now certain but never overtly emphasized delegatory role which is common to both Wealhtheow and Veleda who are further joined by ritual conduct, supernatural association and close ties to the warlord. While some differences in detail are present, and are only to be expected, one would need a high degree of faith in the lottery of circumstance to attribute the predominant congruity to an extra-institutional source. The political and religious needs of the *comitatus* warlord who rules a fictional family of warriors are undoubtedly the decisive variables. It is from a similar but even more ancient background in tribal warfare that the *Hetzerin* springs but here, too, certain modifications of her character have occurred; for, while the duality of her complementary qualities is noted by the Roman historian—she lauds courage and disdains cowardice, demands wounds but also heals them—the balance is already out of kilter in Gregory of Tours and the Icelandic sources may have gone further. But the church is probably not at fault here since Tacitus is overkind for his own reasons and the bias may be due to other variables or even be perennial. It may ultimately lie in the differing psychology of the sexes. The association of women with rank is certainly perennial, however, and we have noted the way in which they could

---

61 Mommsen, ed. *Jordanes. Getica* (MGH AA 5), XXIV, p. 121; Herwig Wolfram, *Geschichte der Goten. Von den Anfängen bis zur Mitte des sechsten Jahrhunderts: Entwurf einer historischen Ethnographie* (1980), p. 124. De Vries speaks here of a "pan-germanic concept" for the same word appears in OE as *hellerune* with the meaning "pythonissa, Zauberin" and in *Beowulf* is used to describe Grendel. See his *Altgermanische Religionsgeschichte* I, p. 231.

manipulate the same domestic status symbols and utter the same criticisms regardless of milieu and chronology. As members of this culture and participants in an organization where consciousness of relative status is ubiquitous, it would not be surprising if women like Wealhtheow, who were evidently expected to play that role, should combine the qualities of *Hetzerin* and sibyl in varying degrees at various times.

The association of women with magic will persist also. Magic is constantly associated with women in the Early Middle Ages and the *Libri pœnitentiales* show that there is actually a factual basis for this in the village rituals of archaic Europe.[62] Nor is it unusual to find the same beliefs in the halls of the mighty. One need only recall the repeated charges of witchcraft against Judith, the wife of Louis the Pious, or the death of Gerberga, sister of Bernard of Septimania, who was drowned in the river as a witch.[63] Such expresses the attitude of hostile witness. Within the Germanic *comitatus,* however, another pattern can be discerned – that of Ariovistus with his *matronae,* Civilis with Veleda, Masyos with Ganna, Waluburg with Germanic auxiliaries and Hrothgar with Wealhtheow. At this point, it might be objected that the chronological differential is so great as to reduce credibility in the association posited. There are at least two possible rejoinders. First, the evidence already presented strongly suggests otherwise. Second, and perhaps even more significant, so does the nature of the institution itself. One can reasonably posit continuity over many centuries because the *institutional* context, the warband itself, lasts for many centuries and *always* requires similar kinds of reinforcement. The supernatural will never lack for a welcome in the warband for those men who are *most* likely to provide it and seek to control it are leaders who cannot afford to neglect the morale of their troops. Even in modern armies, similar types of practitioners are still present, although they are now called chaplains, morale officers and political commissars.

Finally, one other observation may be added with regard to the offering of drink. It is instructive to note that Tacitus says that the *wives* and mothers of warriors gather at the sidelines during combat and minister to their menfolk by providing food and exhortation (*cibosque et hortamina pugnantibus gestant*) while checking wounds as proofs of valor.[64] Presumably, the offer of food to tired fighters would also include drink and, presumably also, the women would refuse to serve cowards or laggards. If so, then we have here the intriguing combination of drink-offering with incitement and the determination of status. The links in this

---

62 Monica Blocker, "Frauenzauber-Zauberfrauen" (1982), pp. 1–39; Pierre J. Payer, *Sex and the Penitentials: The Development of a Sexual Code 550–1150* (1984), pp. 19–55.

63 Reinhold Rau, ed. *Anonymi vita Hludowici imperatoris* 44, 53 in his *Quellen* I, pp. 334, 354. General discussion in Pierre Riché, "La magie à l'époque carolingienne" (1973), pp. 127–38.

64 Hutton, *Tacitus. Germania* 7, p. 274. Bruder is skeptical about this reference: *Germanische Frau,* p. 143f. On the whole, however, considering that women were sometimes present during tribal engagements to encourage the warriors, it hardly seems incredible.

case are less formal and secure; it would be speculative to place too much reliance on the passage. Nevertheless, when added to the dossier already compiled, the cultural associations do seem significant and encouraging since, once again, the constantly recurring pattern of warfare, women's service and warrior rank seem discernible. It is, therefore, utterly simplistic to label the heroic code a "male ideology" for women were crucial to its maintenance and propagation; that is one of the reasons for Wealhtheow's participation in the oaths of men and the giving of advice in the *comitatus*. Such a world view is not easy to appreciate in an era of industrial production and mass warfare but it is typical of the Early Middle Ages when neither were present to detract from the sheer joy of conflict and story. One concludes that Wealhtheow's role in the *comitatus*, exemplified by her acts of praise, warning, incitement and prophecy, is part of the warband institutional tradition itself. While such acts may well occur outside the *comitatus* framework, they lack the frequency, intensity and structural necessity that occurred within it. Consider the force of the fact that it is always the *same* woman who performs these acts for the same men. The pressure to respond appropriately must have been profound.

III

THE LIQUOR RITUAL AND THE BASIS OF THE

LORDLY POWER TO COMMAND FOLLOWERS

A partial review of major findings to this point may be helpful. Two mutually supportive, apparently independent, Old English sources, one of which is anecdotal and the other prescriptive, establish that aristocratic wives frequently executed a particular service ritual during which they named their husbands as heads of the household and confirmed their status by serving them liquor before others. Although the dating of these documents is controversial,[1] investigation has shown that the acts described are not; they are traditional and widely practiced and thus the early and long-term existence of the ritual seems assured.

While seeking to establish the actuality and presence of the pattern, an attempt has also been made to explain its broader significance and the reasons for the concentrated focus on the woman who conducted it. This approach has achieved some significant results. We have seen that the lord's wife is closely identified with his authority and, moreover, with the concept of authority itself in that she helps to affirm it in various ways among the group. The lady's symbolic status is both ancient and widely recognized. Hence, many different genres of sources as far back as the migration period refer to the capture of the queen as a technique for gaining legitimacy.[2] Even then it appears as traditional. Although Germanic candidates had other ways of expressing claims to the throne, those which appear to be most frequently present are cohabitation with the former ruler's wife and the capture of his *thesaurus*. The universality of these motifs in *historical* sources is a datum of such importance that it can hardly be overemphasized; it describes a fundamental and consistent mode of thought. Moreover, even after capture of woman and treasure, the relevance of the lord's wife does not sharply decline for legitimacy is the quality which is aimed at. We have seen that she is sometime regarded as the guardian of the royal insignia which make up an important part of the treasure and have great emblematic significance. True, from what little

---

1 See, for example, the variety of opinions offered by various contributors in Chase, *Dating of Beowulf.*
2 Schneider, *Königswahl*, p. 246f.; Köstler, "Raub-, Kauf- und Friedelehe", p. 92f.; Much, Jankuhn and Lange, *Germania*, pp. 282–94; Wenskus, *Stammesbildung*, pp. 17–32; Hans K. Schulze, *Grundstrukturen der Verfassung im Mittelalter* II (1986), p. 9; Weidemann, *Kulturgeschichte* I, p. 18f.

concrete evidence we have of actual behavior, the queen had to share her control with the *camerarius*,[3] and thus the exercise of her prerogative depends on her husband, but it is also the case that she is the one who often distributes gifts and in theory, it seems, was the one expected to do so under these conditions. All of this fits in well with her delegatory role in the *comitatus* described earlier.

Based, then, on the commonalty and significance of data—which alone might suggest antiquity for the liquor-service ritual—it now seems worthwhile to ask if it does not, in fact, go back even before the migration period and reveal something about the development of lordship among the early Germans. This is an extremely complex question about which certainty can hardly be achieved but it is also a fundamental one which must be posed. It may be that the introduction of the ceremonial elements outlined above can help us place the matter in a clearer light and to focus on relevant aspects hitherto overlooked.

We must first briefly review the early evidence for the sources of lordly power over companies. It is primarily but not exclusively philological. Leaving aside all other related but not (arguably) immediately relevant matters (although many of these are indeed important), the basic question is this: should one view the *comitatus* of the first three or four centuries as essentially a military institution based on voluntary entry, overall reciprocity and trust or, contrariwise, more as a domestic one based on command, hierarchy and obedience? If the former, which is in fact the majority opinion,[4] then one must perforce take up and defend certain positions regarding lordship, feudalism, the role of the church in influencing the Germans and so forth. If the latter, then contrasting interpretations must be expected.[5] The way in which one approaches this fundamental dilemma of constitutional scholarship will eventually affect every aspect of historiography (if held consistently) for it is, ultimately, a question about the nature of authority and the origins of the state in central and western Europe.[6]

A word on terminology is also important. The terms "military" and "domestic" here assume untoward significance which require some clarification for they point to two different spheres of lordly authority—on the one hand, that of the leader over followers who voluntarily join his warband and who grant obedience

3 Ewig, "Klosterpolitik", p. 577 and n. 89; Nelson, "Queens as Jezebels", p. 47.

4 Anne Kristensen, *Tacitus' germanische Gefolgschaft*; Green, *Carolingian Lord*; Walter Schlesinger, "Herrschaft und Gefolgschaft", pp. 9–52; Idem, "Über germanisches Heerkonigtum" (1963), pp. 53–87; Idem, "Randbemerkungen", pp. 296–316; Kroeschell, *Haus und Herrschaft*.

5 Kuhn, "Grenzen", pp. 1–83. Wenskus takes a position which draws on both Kuhn and Schlesinger in his *Stammesbildung*, p. 346f. A helpful summary discussion will be found in Schulze, *Grundstrukturen* I, pp. 39–53.

6 The warband attracts attention because it seems to be the crucial instrument of early political differentiation and hierarchy. In his article on *Gefolgschaft*, Kroeschell writes: "Gefolgschaft erscheint noch heute als der Prototyp aller politischen Herrschaft im Mittelalter, die mittelalterliche Verfassung als auf dem gefolgschaftlichen Prinzip, vor allem auf Treue, aufgebaut". clm. 1436.

because it is their unfettered will to do so and, on the other, that of the head of the household who exercises patriarchal authority over wife, minor sons, daughters, slaves and dependents whose desires need not be taken into account since they are not themselves free to make decisions but depend on him for protection and are, therefore, under his guardianship or *munt*.[7] The difference between these two forms may not always be clear and the opposition proposed is consciously somewhat exaggerated for the sake of lucidity. Nevertheless, one of these two alternative explanations is likely to be the more nearly correct one. The sources testify to both kinds of power from at least the time of Tacitus whose *Germania* is the origin and *locus classicus* for some of the formulations. I shall refer to crucial passages from this work below. But it will now be necessary to examine some linguistic evidence which is central to the problem and has assumed an important role in the debate.

The word *druht* (* *druhtiz*, OE *dryht*, ON *drótt*) is recognized as the most widespread and most important vernacular name for the *comitatus*.[8] As the root is also present in Gothic *driugan*, "to perform military service", it cannot be a new formation but must reflect primitive Germanic usage. The first extant example of *druht* appears in *Lex Salica* around 500 where, however, and this is most remarkable, it does not mean warband at all but "marriage procession" and appears in a chapter which describes the various forms of the kidnapping of women: "If anyone follows a betrothed girl in a wedding procession [*druete ducente*] who is on her way to be married and assaults her on the road and rapes her, what is called *gangichaldo* in the malberg, let him be held liable for 8000 denarii, which makes 200 solidi".[9] Kuhn has noted in an important critical monograph that this marital and festive meaning is supported by Lombard *troctingus*, OHG *truhting* and *truhti-gomo*, OS *druhting*, OE *dryht-guma*, *dryht-ealdor*, and *dryht-ealdorman*, all of which mean *Brautführer*, "bridesman", or in modern usage, "best man".[10] He argues that one of the very old meanings of *druht*

---

7 Werner Ogris, "Munt, Muntwalt" (1980), clm. 750–61; Schulze, *Grundstrukturen* II, p. 28f.

8 Ruth Schmidt-Wiegand, "Frankisch *Druht* und *Druhten*: Zur historischen Terminologie im Bereich der Sozialgeschichte" (1974), pp. 524–35; eadem, *Bezeichnungen*, p. 16f.; Green, *Carolingian Lord*, pp. 270–397; Von Olberg, *Gefolgsleute*, p. 208f.; Wenskus, *Stammesbildung*, p. 351f.; Kroeschell, *Haus und Herschaft*, p. 251; Schlesinger, "Heerkönigtum", p. 76f.; Alan Crozier, "The Germanic Root *dreug*- 'to follow, accompany' " (1986), pp. 127–48; idem, "Old West Norse *iprott* and Old English *indryhtu*" (1986), pp. 3–10; Lars G. Hallander, "Old English *dryht* and its Cognates" (1973), pp. 20–31; David Green, "Old English 'Dryht'—A New Suggestion" (1968), pp. 392–406; Kuhn, "Grenzen", p. 23f; Dick, *Ae. Dryht*; Lindow, *Comitatus*, p. 17f.

9 Karl August Eckhardt, *Pactus Legis Salicae: 65 Titel Text* (1955), p. 160: Si quis puella sponsata dructe ducente [ad maritum] et eam in via aliquis adsallierit et cum ipsa violenter moechatus fuerit, mallobergo gangichaldo, sunt denarii VIIIM qui faciunt solidos CC culpabilis iudicetur. The text is also available in MGH LL IV, 1, p. 63 and a new edition by Ruth Schmidt-Wiegand is forthcoming.

10 Kuhn, "Grenzen", p. 24.

must be "festive procession", or "wedding procession" and that at an early stage it must also have meant "festive gathering", "festival", "festival meal". This is demonstrated by several OHG and OE words all of which translate Latin *dapifer* and *discophorus*, he who carries the food and drink.[11] The conclusion is that all of these meanings could have evolved from a single (primitive) Germanic *druht*, "drink." One notes immediately how very closely this cluster of ideas—marriage procession, drink, festival meal—accords with the discussion above of the wife who gives drink to her husband and proclaims his leadership of the warband.

Between the meaning "armed band" and "marriage procession" one is compelled to seek a *tertium comparationis* which might lie in the fact that a marriage procession would include armed men even though many participants would be non-weapons-bearing women and children. Another lies in the observation, as Green pointed out, that there need be no real conflict between the meanings of festive group and warrior retinue since the *comitatus* which Tacitus describes also does double-duty; in time of war it serves the leader in the field and in time of peace it serves him in the hall where most effort is expended in getting drunk and in staying drunk for as long as possible: "if Tacitus, when describing the *comitatus*, so explicitly treats of it in its twofold aspect, then there is surely no reason why the one stem *druht*- should not have developed two specialized meanings (military and festive) from a common starting point."[12] To this one might add that in line 1231 of *Beowulf*, Wealhtheow casually refers to the followers as *druncne dryhtguman*, a fact which has unduly embarrassed some modern commentators who view the description as unfortunate or pejorative and who translate with "carousing" or "wine-glad".[13]

Evidence for another derivation has been offered by Ernst Dick. In his recent study of the word family of OE *dryht*, this scholar took up the idea of "marriage procession" and followed it through a variety of fascinating byways. In his view, there is no necessary original connection with the warband but a "far greater probability" of link with *indryhtu*, "*Wachstumsheil*", growth magic, and he would interpret *dryht* as primarily meaning "*Kultschar*" or cult-group.[14] His central concept is that of fertility. Ruth Schmidt-Weigand seems to have accepted at least

11 Ibid., p. 24f. See further Crozier, "*dreug*—'*to follow*' ", p. 137 who writes of OHG *truhtsazzo* that "it probably denoted originally the man responsible for seating the *druhtiz*, which in this compound can mean both 'bridal escort' and 'king's comitatus'."

12 Green, *Carolingian Lord*, p. 271. Schmidt-Wiegand, *Bezeichnungen*, p. 18 appears to favor this opinion also and writes that *druhtiz* "ist eine Gruppe, die unter gemeinsamen Anstrengungen etwas ausführt. Ihr Zusammenwirken kann sich - das zeigt die geschichte des Wortes—auf Kult und Brauch, auf Krieg und Waffendienst beziehen."

13 Magennis, "*druncne dryhtguman*", pp. 159–64. The phrase in question is not used pejoratively but "suggests powerfully through allusion to feasting her [Wealhtheow] belief in the harmony of the Danish court. In their carefree enjoyment of drinking together the Danes express their sense of loyalty and trust."

14 Dick, *Ae. Dryht*, pp. 396–464.

part of this analysis, for in her study of the *druht* references in early Frankish sources she concludes that they have "*agrarische Verhältnisse zur Voraussetzung*".[15] A recent commentary is that of Gabriele von Olberg who shares this view and refers to Dick's explanation.[16] Nonetheless, both Schmidt-Weigand and von Olberg hold that the primary common denominator is that of an armed band. Wenskus supports this also but is more skeptical of Dick's conclusions and also doubts that the "festive" meanings derive from the wedding procession.[17]

The mixture and variety of philological opinion on this topic is daunting. Viewed from the ritual perspective, however, it may be possible to develop other persuasive reasons for associating the *comitatus* with Germanic marriage custom and also for linking the bride in the procession—she is the only one normally left out of the discussion—with cultic practices within the warband. Some ways of doing so have been discussed in previous sections where we saw that the lord's wife must be accepted as part of the *comitatus* for many purposes and where she plays a crucial role in successions. It may be possible to build on these findings and add greater precision to the meaning of *druht* within the context of the overall problem of authority and subordination.

OE *dryht* means a "troop of retainers", a warband,[18] but it is fascinating to note that many compounds containing this element, which would naturally seem to be at home in the *comitatus*, are actually used of participants in marriage ceremonies. Words like *dryht-ealdor, dryht-ealdorman, dryht-guma, dryht-man, dryht-we-mend* and *dryht-wemere* can all be used in OE to gloss terms like *paranymphus*, "best man", who leads the marriage procession, and *architriclinus*, "master of the feast"—in this case the marriage feast.[19] As Roeder pointed out in an important study of 1909, such is also true of the important *comitatus* term *tacn-bora*.[20] This compound usually glosses the Latin *signifer, uexillifer* and refers to the man who walks ahead of the band and carries its banner or field-emblem. It is a highly honorable position. Bede provides an excellent example of usage in his early eighth-century *Historia ecclesiastica*: "So great was his majesty in his realm [king Edwin] that not only were the banners carried before him in battle, but even in time of peace, as he rode about among his cities, estates and kingdoms with his

15 Schmidt-Wiegand, *Bezeichnungen*, p. 18.
16 Von Olberg, *Gefolgsleute*, p. 209f.
17 Wenskus, "*Druht*" (1986), p. 202. See also Heike Grahn-Hoek, *Die fränkische Oberschicht im 6. Jahrhundert: Studien zu ihr rechtlichen und politichen Stellung* (1976), pp. 276–83.
18 See note 8. A particularly helpful summary discussion is provided by Crozier in the first article cited.
19 Dick, *Ae. Dryht*, pp. 229–44; idem, "The Bridesman in the Indo-European Tradition: Ritual and Myth in Marriage Ceremonies" (1966), pp. 338–47. The studies from note 8 onwards discuss this meaning also.
20 Fritz Roeder, *Zur Deutung der angelsächsischen glossierungen von "paranymphus" und "paranympha" ("pronuba"): Ein Beitrag zur Kenntnis des ags. Hochzeitsrituells: Nachrichten v. d. Köngl. Gesellschaft d. Wiss. zu Göttingen: Phil.—hist Kl.* (1907), p. 25f.

thegns, he always used to be proceeded by a standard-bearer. Further, when he walked anywhere along the roads, there used to be carried before him the type of standard which the Romans call a tufa and the English call a thuf." [21] This same word could also mean *paranymphus*. [22] In both types of groups, a specific man must have carried a banner. Thus, we conclude not only that *tacn-bora* designated a member of the *comitatus*, but also can conclude that it could mean "best man" in the marriage procession. In case of a lordly or royal marriage, then, the individual in each case would probably be the same. One thinks of all those widowed queens under the control of the warband and sought after by claimants to the throne.

Although this connection is a welcome hint that we are on the right track, it also serves to emphasize the point that something is missing from the equation and that the common denominator of arms-bearers (which Wenskus notes is "actually very broad") [23] may be somewhat superficial. There must be something else which explains the truly astonishing fact that the Germans applied the same word to both a warband and a marriage procession. The hitherto most widely accepted linkage may be questioned. In a society where many armed men would often have traveled together and where in any case all free men carried weapons, a single such linguistic usage could only have developed (it seems to the present author at least) if the community also perceived a single concept to have applied to both the married women and the retainer in the *comitatus*. The key concept, I suggest, one which can be shown to fit both criteria, is that of entry into an organization, a family; in the bride's case it is a true family, in that of the warrior it is fictive. [24] In each case there would be a festival and common meal and, although I have not searched the literature on this point, a procession is clearly a high probability as well. Recall Bede's description of the king and his retainers on the road. What we are pointing to, then, is a common contractual joining, in one case of man and wife and in the other of lord and man. Perhaps the word which comes closest to expressing both forms of union is "adoption" for such a concept seems to be present in each institution. At the same time, however, it is not adoption in the full technical sense. As Hans Kuhn has demonstrated, examples of "true adoption", are hard to find in Germanic sources and seem to be consistently linked with the Christian concept of a spiritual relationship (which does create strict mutual obligations) in the rites of baptism and confirmation. [25] As in *Beowulf* (ll. 946–949), however, where Hrothgar declares his wish to treat the hero like a son and bids the hero to hold to his *niwe sibbe*, "new family",

---

21 Colgrave and Mynor, *Bede*, II, 16, p. 192.
22 Roeder, *"paranymphus"*, pp. 14–41.
23 Wenskus, *"Druht"*, p. 202.
24 Among other studies, see Green, *Carolingian Lord*, p. 315f.; Roeder, *Die Familie bei den Angelsächsen: Eine kultur und literarhistorische Studie auf Grund gleichzeitiger Quellen* (1899), p. 83f.; Alfred Schultze, *Das Eherecht in den älteren angelsächsischen Königsgesetzen* (1941), p. 38f.
25 Hans Kuhn, "Philologisches zur Adoption bei den Germanen" (1971), p. 415.

the more general concept of drawing someone into the kin does exist and actually lies at the core of the warband ethos. It is in that sense that the term will be used here. Let us now examine the idea of adoption (drawing into the kin) in marriage and then to that of adoption in the *comitatus*.

In all Indo-European societies marriage was viewed as a hazardous undertaking, perilous for both the bride's family and the groom's.[26] The bride's family and her relatives were giving up a member for the sake of gifts, alliance and expected reciprocity.[27] All were valuable commodities which needed protection and guarantees. The groom's family, on the other hand, was accepting a stranger into its home and councils who had blood-ties to someone else and, therefore, could not be fully trusted. The bride was a serious potential threat to its well-being and security. Nonetheless, because she was necessary for the continuation of the family, she had to be accepted regardless of risk. The question was how to integrate this liminal individual into her new family. The solution was to immerse her departure from one home and arrival at another with powerful religious rites which would cauterize the loss for her natal family and safely and certainly graft her onto that of her husband.[28] Such activities, always regarded as sacred, are often thousands of years old so that, for example, the marriage-by-capture ritual (in which the bride seems to refuse the groom whom she had earlier ardently accepted and hides in her family home only to be removed by the groom's friends with much show of hostility) is an age-old practice not only common in Europe but to scores, if not hundreds, of different cultures elsewhere. This is a typical separation rite. The entire deliberately complicated process, like that of all *rites de passage*, is analogous to that of death and rebirth.[29] The bride "dies" to one group and is reborn, that is "adopted", into another. The religious rituals involved clearly establish this pattern. Typical adoption rites include a cutting of the hair, a sitting on the knee, an investment with weapons, a stepping into a new shoe, new ritual clothing, a ritual purification bath, a sprinkling with water or liquor, a common meal, and so on.[30] In one form or another, sometimes clearly, sometimes vaguely, all these rituals are found again in marriage. It could hardly be otherwise for the underlying concept is the same. The *domum deductio*, for example, the

---

26 Dick, *Ae. Dryht*, pp. 146–243.
27 Ibid.
28 Ibid. p. 150f.; Friedrich Kauffmann, "Braut und Gemahl" (1910), pp. 129, 153.
29 Dick, *Ae. Dryht*, pp. 146f., 191f.
30 Kauffmann, "Braut und Gemahl", pp. 143–51; Adalbert Erler, "Das Ritual der nordischen Geschlechtsleite" (1944), pp. 86–111; Max Pappenheim, "Über kunstliche Verwandtschaft im germanischen Rechte" (1908), pp. 304–33. For general and more modern discussions of Germanic marriage, see M. Rouche, "Des mariages païens au mariage chrétien" (1987), pp. 835–73; Peter Buchholz, "Die Ehe in germanischen, besonders altnordischen Literaturdenkmälern" (1977), pp. 887–900; Karl Schmid, "Heirat, Familienfolge, Geschlechterbewusstsein" (1977), pp. 103–37; Paul Mikat, *Dotierte Ehe—rechte Ehe. Zur Entwicklung des Eheschliessungsrechts in fränkischer Zeit* (1978); Ritzer, *Eheschliessung*.

taking home of the bride in the wedding procession, ends when the bride is symbolically reborn by being carried over the threshold into her new home. There, other rituals of integration await her but we need not examine these beyond remarking that their clear purpose is to bind her thoroughly to her new family, a process which may not be viewed as completed until she has borne a child and thereby repaid her in-laws for the gifts with which they bought her. In short, marriage for the Germans was a sacred drama of death and rebirth which ended for the bride in adoption into a new family. It should also be added that weapons often played a role in this process for they were undoubtedly part of the ritual hostilities between the bride's family and the groom's friends but they were also important for other reasons as can now be shown.

If the idea of adoption was necessary to the Germanic family who took in a "daughter", it is true to say that it was equally indispensable to the early *comitatus* which was extra-tribal in nature and hence accepted non-kinsmen as members. Already in the first century Tacitus reports the custom whereby "noble youths", tired of peace, seek out *nationes* waging war and attach themselves to other chiefs for the sake of renown (*Germania* 14). But how, given the universal conviction that only a relative could really be trusted and the only man one could truly call friend was a kinsman, could these other warrior bands have welcomed them, or the youths have expected a welcome? It seems unlikely that any leader would have done so unless he could make the stranger a "son"—a subordinate relative—and other members have made him a brother. Such must have been the case since the *comitatus* took its form and organizational concept from the institution of the family. As emphasized earlier, linguistics can only support this view. So, for example, the persons who collectively form the kin-group can be called *propinqui* or *parentes* but can also be referred to as *amici*, "friends." As in *Beowulf*, the members of the warband can be called *magas*, "kinsmen", *maguthegnas*, "young kin retainers", and the group as a whole can be called a *sibbegedryht*, "band of kinsmen".[31] How was this fictive kinship—this adoption—achieved? By the same means that Hrothgar made Beowulf his *sunu* at Heorot, by presenting him with weapons in the ritual of *Waffensohnschaft*.[32] Tacitus refers to this in *Germania* 13 although the passage is not always recognized as such:

> . . . in the presence of the council *one of the chiefs, or the young man's father, or some kinsman, equips him with a shield and a spear.* These arms are what the "toga" is with us, the first honour with which youth is invested. Up to this

31 Schlesinger, "Herrschaft und Gefolgschaft", p. 20; Donald Bullough, "Early Medieval Social Groupings: The Terminology of Kinship" (1969), p. 12; Karl Leyser, "Maternal Kin in Early Medieval Germany. A Reply" (1970), pp. 126–34. An important recent contribution is that of Murray, *Germanic Kinship Structure*.
32 Brunner, *Rechtsgeschichte* I, p. 103f. with further references in notes. Kuhn, "Adoption", pp. 410–19.

time he is regarded as a member of a household, afterwards as a member of the commonwealth. . . . Such lads attach themselves to men of mature strength and of long approved valor.

Once made a "son", the new member also becomes the brother of his companions and, as detailed above in chapter one, his status and condition is sealed with a ritual drink with his "family." He is doubly bound by the sacred symbols of his new life, by holy bonds of weapons and liquor. Such ties must be religiously and ritually sanctioned since the new member of the *comitatus* is just as potentially dangerous to that "family" as the new bride is to hers.

Weapons and liquor bind the follower in the *comitatus*; weapons and liquor, I suggest, also bind the new wife to the family. This hypothesis has not hitherto been fully argued in a comparative manner but it seems to follow ineluctably once one accepts adoption as the operative common denominator between the possible meanings of *druht*. It can be checked against the marriage pattern in *Germania* 18. Here we are told that the suitor brings gifts to his prospective bride whose parents and relatives are present to pass judgement on them. They are not, says Tacitus, meant to appeal to a woman's taste nor her desire for adornment but are composed of "oxen, caparisoned steed, a shield, a lance, and a sword. With these presents", he continues, "the wife is espoused, and she in her turn brings some piece of armor to her husband. This they count as their strongest bond of union, these their sacred mysteries, these their gods of marriage."

If the donation of arms is understandable for the follower—they are given by a leader in an act which obviously imitates a father's gift of weapons to a son on coming of age—what can be said of the astonishingly inapt gift of weapons to a bride who cannot wield them? Tacitus goes on to say that they demonstrate to a woman that she is not immune to the perils of war. The context is surely correct but the explanation is naive; one doubts that Germanic women needed any such reminder.[33] Scholars are united in this view but have not been able to offer any sustained specific explanation—a condition reflected in the confused discussion which appears in Much's otherwise excellent commentary.[34] Under present construction, however, the puzzle is solvable: the groom gave a present of weapons to his bride amidst parents and relatives because it was part of an adoption rite, a drawing into the kin which was common to both family and *comitatus*. The cultural consensus held that a fictive blood-relationship, at least, was necessary before gaining admission to the guarded inner workings, secrets, rites and machinations of the group. Ties to the natal family were regarded as so powerful that the one way they could be effectively countered was through a cultic

---

33 A good introduction to discussions of Germanic women by classical authors is contained in Bruder, *Germanische Frau*.
34 Much, Jankuhn and Lange, *Germania*, p. 285f.

duplication of the original affiliation. The nature of the bond is suggested by the kinds of gifts exchanged.

Nor do we need to rely on Tacitus alone for this conclusion, for it is certain that a gift of weapons also played a role in the establishment of legal marriage among the Visigoths. In his study *Über westgotisch-spanisches Eherecht*, Schultze fixed renewed attention on a formula dated to the fourth regnal year of king Sisebut (615—616) which prescribes the presents to be given to a noble Gothic bride as her *morgingeba* or "morning gift", that is, the things to be given by her husband after her wedding night.[35] These include ten boys, ten girls, ten stallions and, among others, a gift of weapons, *arma*. In the verse which describes it, this is called *Ordinis ut Getici est morgingeba vetusti*, "part of the ancient Gothic order", as Schultze translates.[36] The use of the folk-name *Getici* as well as the express reference to ancient custom clearly carries us back to a far earlier period, in fact back to the *Germania* with its horse and weapons which the warrior gives to his bride. The modern reader cannot but be struck by this surprising example of retention, evidence of a very specialized form of continuity.[37] Apparently the Visigoths thought it old-fashioned themselves for scarcely a generation later king Chindasvind issued a new decree in which the traditional *arma* was replaced by the word *ornamenta*, although the horse would continue to show up in later Spanish legislation.[38]

One can also point to supportive evidence from the Anglo-Saxon side where, if the weapons are no longer mentioned, the concept of the wife as follower of her husband is certainly present. In the OE poem called the *Wife's Lament*, for example, the abandoned woman laments the passing of *freondscipe* between her *hlaford* and herself.[39] The language is that of the warrior retinue and we may compare OE with OHG where *friunt* can mean "husband".[40] Witness also the *Husband's Message* which refers to an oath whereby the man will always keep the

---

35 Alfred Schultze, *Über westgotisch-spanisches Eherecht* (1944), p. 45f.; E.A. Thompson, *The Goths in Spain* (1969), p. 255f.

36 Ibid.

37 Walter Kienast, "Gefolgswesen und Patrocinium im spanischen Westgotenreich" (1984), p. 52f.

38 Schultze, *Westgotisch-spanisches Eherecht*, p. 47.

39 Roeder, *Familie bei den Angelsächsen*, p. 112f.

40 Wolfgang Fritze, "Die fränkische Schwurfreundschaft der Merowingerzeit. Ihr Wesen und ihre politische Funktion" (1954), p. 81f.; Reinhard Schneider, *Brüdergemeine und Schwurfreudschaft* (1964), pp. 8of, 115f. *Amicitia* between Alaric II and Clovis, according to Gregory of Tours, was created when they ate and drank together: coniunctique in insula Ligeris, quae erat iuxta vicum Ambaciensim terretorium urbis Toronicae, simul locuti, comedentes pariter et bibentes, promissa sibi amicitia, paxifici discesserunt. Buchner, *Gregor von Tours* I: II, 35, p. 128. See further Dietrich Claude, "Untersuchungen zum frühfränkischen Comitat" (1964), p. 74f, and Alfred Schultze, "Zur Rechtsgeschichte der germanischen Brüdergemeinschaft" (1936). The power of *Tischgemeinschaft* is well illustrated in Franz Irsigler, *Untersuchungen zur Geschichte des frühfränkischen Adels* (1981), p. 248f.

"covenant of companionship", *winetreowe*, with the wife.[41] Similarly, the much later (eleventh century) little tract *Be wifmannes beweddunge* refers to the presents which the groom must give the maiden in return for her acceptance of his will— *his willan geceose.*[42] As Roeder pointed out, this phrase is a *terminus technicus* to be used by a man who takes service with a lord—*ic . . . his willan geceas.*[43] Across the channel in ninth century Francia, the noblewoman Dhuoda would suggest something similar when she refers to her husband as her *dominus* and *senior.*[44] The terminology is that of vassalage.[45] Even the weaving of textiles, often described as *feminea opera*, can also be referred to by the typical vassalage term of *obsequium.*[46]

Such evidence casts new light on Walter Schlesinger's insight that the concept of lordship over a retinue helped to structure the Germanic law of marriage.[47] It seems to confirm the view that the wife stands in the same relation to her husband as the husband does to his lord; she is a follower just as he is. One must recognize, however, that the complete explanation is more complicated than this for marriage (as Schlesinger was certainly well aware) is by far the older institution just as it now seems clear that the *comitatus* lord is simply imitating the father of the family when he bestows weapons on his new *sunu*. What seems most probable, therefore, is that both types of weapon transfers have their home in the family. This is not to say that the *comitatus* did not exert influence but it is well to remember that the original "follower" is the biological son of his own sire. The warband imitates this relationship but is not the original model; rather, the overwhelming importance of the model is shown by its imitation and such copying then returns again to influence the marriage pattern. Consideration of the common denominator of adoption makes this conclusion more probable and so does the family organization of the leader's troop. Consequently, while the profound cultural significance of weapons as a binding element is conclusively demonstrated by these texts, one is under no compulsion to acknowledge that such weapon-rites are only to be associated with the warband. Every free head of household was armed and so was every non-minor son, as well as many dependents. So indeed, in a symbolic sense at least, was every free mother of a family. The examination of grave-goods by archaeologists has shown that many Germanic women carried very small knives

41 Roeder, *Familie bei den Angelsächsen*, pp. 112–18.
42 Ibid., pp. 25f., 83.
43 Ibid. Schlesinger ("Herrschaft und Gefolgschaft", p. 23) and Schultze reach the same conclusion. See the latter's, *Älteren angelsächsischen Königsgesetze*, p. 38: "In der gleichen Art, wie in der Gefolgschaft, der man den Willen seines Herren zu seinem eigenen macht, wird die Frau in der Ehe den Willen ihres Eheherrn zu ihrem eigenen machen, "erkiest sie" bei der Heirat "seinem Willen". See further Idem, *Westgotisch-spanisches Eherecht*, p. 50f.
44 Pierre Riché, ed. *Dhuoda. Manuel pour mon fils* (1975), pp. 84, 86.
45 Heinrich Fichtenau, *Lebensordnungen des 10. Jahrhunderts: Studien über Denkart and Existenz im einstigen Karolingerreich* (1984), p. 141 and n. 34.
46 Ibid., p. 149, n. 73 referring to *Gesta episcoporum Cameracensium* I, 117.

hanging from their girdles which seem to have been unusable for practical purposes. They probably served as tokens of free birth.[48] Again, there is no necessary
connection with the *comitatus* as such but there is an undisputable link with status.
Not the warband but the warlike worldview determined this symbolism.

I argued above that the integration rites in question included not just weapons
but weapons and liquor. This was partly based on the interpretation of historical
practices centering on the queen's service ritual and the role which liquor played
in *comitatus* life. It is all the more intriguing, therefore, that, on the basis of
philological evidence, Kuhn could reach the conclusion that *druht* originally
meant "drink". Although his findings have not found wide acceptance, Green
does allow that his derivation "may well be theoretically possible" in some cases[49]
and it is surely indicative of the force of his arguments that five philologically
competent scholars who have taken up the problem (Green, Dick, Schmidt-Weigand, von Olberg, Crozier) should each, in different ways, make room for the
association with festivity and marriage.[50] One may venture the opinion that the
under-investigated element in each case (family, marriage and *comitatus*) is the
power to command followers based on paternal authority. We have already seen
that the wife's condition approximated that of a follower too. Let us, therefore,
now seek for a more *specific* way—beyond the concept of festivity—in which the
offering of an intoxicating beverage could act to symbolize authority in both
marriage and warband.

Any scholar who seriously studies the drinking rites of the Germans will
quickly be impressed by the way in which women are frequently linked with
liquor in all of the sources. So common and internally consistent is this pattern
as to be practically impossible to overlook. Poets of the North Germans, for
example, very often refer to a woman by giving her the name of a goddess, Freya,
Gefion, Hlokk, etc., and then adding, of the cup, horn, beaker, or ale, mead, wine
and the like.[51] Although it is true to say that this is a poetic device, it is more
important to note that the incidence of usage (along with the many casual
mundane references) is so high as to indicate that it reflects a deep-seated attitude,
a pattern of thought which lies at the basic core of the culture. Simply stated, the
general concept "woman" is repeatedly associated with the general concepts of
liquor service and "contract service." That act which seems to most thoroughly
express and encapsulize the related notions of service and contract is the presentation of drink which also appears in literature as a powerful metaphor for the

47 Schlesinger, "Herrschaft und Gefolgschaft", p. 23.
48 A religious significance in some cases is not unlikely. Robert Koch, "Waffenförmige Anhänger
   aus merowingerzeitlichen Frauengräbern" (1970), pp. 285–93.
49 Green, *Carolingian Lord*, p. 271.
50 See the studies cited in note 8.
51 Rudolf Meissner, *Die Kenningar der Skalden: Ein Beitrag zur skaldischen Poetic* (1921), p. 401;
   Gudbrand Vigfusson and F. York Powell, ed. *Corpus Poeticum Boreale* (1883), p. 476.

ritual establishment of relative status in the Germanic world. Such emphasis will naturally show itself in a variety of ways. Einarsson (among others) has demonstrated that making oaths over liquor was a prevalent practice and that the act of drinking was considered a means to "add weight and authority to the spoken word".[52] Not surprisingly, examples are scattered throughout the sources. What is surprising, however, is the fact that not only do women commonly serve the drink but they are often the subject of the promise itself. Thus, in the saga of the Jomsvikings, when the men began to make vows over drink, Vagn swore to "kill Thorkel Leira and get into the bed of his daughter Ingeborg without the consent of her kinsfolk".[53] In the *Lay of Helgi Hjorvard's Son*, Hedin tells his brother that:

> on holy beaker
> in banquet hall
> thy bride I chose me,
> the child of kings.

In *Hervarar saga*:

> One Yule even in Bolm Angantyr swore at the Bragi cup, as then was customary, that he should get the daughter of Yngvi . . . king at Uppsalir, Ingibjorg by name, the fairest and wisest maiden within the Danish speaking world, or else fall [in battle].

In *Landnámabók*:

> At that feast Holmsteinn vowed that he should marry Helga, the daughter of Orn or else no other woman.

In *Svarfdoela saga*:

> Klaufi took for his [drinking] mate O—and vowed that he should go to bed with Yngvildr fogrkinn (faircheek) against the will of Ljótólfr godi.

These instances are culled from sources of varying date and reliability, of course, and it might fairly be asked if the practice described is really that frequent. The answer is found in the Snorra Edda poem *Málsháttakvaedi* where it is stated that the "maidens are chosen over the ale".[54] In other words, this is the method by which the vow to procure a woman is normally expressed. Such is only one example of the numerous ways in which the woman/liquor association affected the thinking of warriors. A woman, then, may be referred to by the beverage name, usually serves the drink, sometimes incites the oath, frequently is the subject of it and, as we shall see, is also bound to her mate by the same act of serving liquor.

52 Einarsson, "Old English *Beot*", p. 103.   53 Ibid. Citations are drawn from p. 108f.
54 Ibid., p. 114.

No marriage it seems was fully legal without a feast at which intoxicating drink was served, and there are many references to the "bridal ale" (but not the "groom's ale") in the sources.[55] More significant for present purposes is the fact that a specific ritual took place in which the woman presented her future husband with a drink. This was the formal symbolic statement by which she indicated that he was to be her husband. His acceptance of the cup signified his agreement as well as being a major part of the formal completion of the alliance. This ritual seems to be an extremely old one. The earliest non-Mediterranean example that I know of dates from the fourth century BC and describes a Celtic custom observed in the south of Gaul:

> Phocean traders from Ionia founded Marseilles. Now Euxenos the Phocean was guest-friend of the king, whose name was Nanos. When Nanos was preparing his daughter's wedding feast Euxenos happened to arrive by accident and Nanos invited him to the banquet. The marriage came about as follows. After the meal the girl had to come in and give a bowl which she had mixed to the one she chose among the suitors present. The suitor to whom she would give it was to be her bridegroom. When the girl, whose name was Petta, came in, she gave it to Euxenos, whether by chance or for some other reason. And then Euxenos took her, changing her name to Aristoxene; for even her father considered it right that he should have her on the grounds that the girl had been divinely prompted to give the cup to him.[56]

Euxenos was "guest-friend" to Nanos. This was an important institution and can be found amongst many Indo-European peoples. It was an alternative device to marriage for the creation of alliances and, as in marriage, was symbolically created by mutual drinking. On any other occasion, Petta might have served liquor to Euxenos in much the same way as she offered it in the citation but, in this case, because of the special purpose of the feast, the gesture was taken to symbolize a marriage contract between Petta and Euxenos rather than the friendship contract which she might otherwise have mediated between her father and his visitor. By offering the bowl to Euxenos, however, she chose him to be her husband i.e., expressed abstractly, she chose him to be her lord and to accept his lordship over her. Her father allowed this because she seemed to be divinely inspired.

Although the Greek anecdote about Petta and Euxenos describes the cup offering within a marriage context, it also demonstrates the antiquity of the association between such offering and authority in transalpine Europe. We have already seen that warband authority is to be linked with the domestic power of the husband and father. Celtic scholars tend to interpret the episode as an early

55 Cahén, *Libation*, p. 52f.; Roeder, *Familie bei den Angelsächsen*, p. 33f.
56 Ioannes Zwicker, *Fontes historiae religionis celticae* (1934), p. 2. Translation is by James Carney in his review in *Béaloideas* 1 (1937), p. 143.

and partial continental example of the traditional "king and goddess" theme whereby a supernatural woman bestows kingship on a candidate by offering him a drink of liquor in the *banais rigi*, "marriage feast of kingship", in which the ruler ritually marries the fertility goddess (or "sovereignty goddess") of his territory. The religious background of the Petta/Euxenos episode is suggested by Nanos' reference to divine prompting and the conceptual linking of the rite with authority is made manifest by the subsequent power of Euxenos to change his wife's name. A connection with Germanic culture is likely as well, although that will not become clear until later when much other material has been reviewed and when it will then be possible to outline the pattern of Germanic adaptation of Celtic status rituals and related practices. The present point to be emphasized is that the early Germans do not appear to have really distinguished very much between husbandly authority over wives and lordly authority over followers. That is why the husband can be refered to as the "lord" of his wife and the same term can be used for both warband and wedding procession. The Petta/Euxenos episode may be the earliest extant non-Mediterranean example of this archaic pattern.

The completed cup-offering among the Germans signifies the sealing of a contract between lord and man but it is ambiguous in that the same rite, when the presentation is by an unmarried woman, can also create marriage. Although we know comparatively little about the *specific* actions of the Germanic bride in the wedding ceremony, evidence from Paul's *Historia Langobardorum* suggests that a cup-offering was essential. In the story of Authari's marriage to Theude-linda cited above, it was related how the king disguised himself as an ambassador and asked to be allowed to take a cup of wine from her hand "as she will offer it to us hereafter". The girl's father interprets this to mean that the ambassador is a follower of Authari to whom his daughter will later attend and so he allows it. Authari, however, is actually surreptitiously alluding to the marriage rite in which the girl will serve him as bride and queen, as shown by his subsequent behavior.

> And when the king had assented to this that it should be done, she took the cup and gave it first to him who appeared to be the chief. Then, when she offered it to Authari, whom she did not know was her affianced bridegroom, he, after drinking and returning the cup, touched her hand with his fingers when no one noticed, drew his right hand from his forehead along his nose and face. Covered with blushes, she told this to her nurse, and her nurse said to her: Unless this man were the king himself and thy promised bridegroom, he would not dare by any means to touch thee. But meanwhile, lest this become known to thy father, let us be silent, for in truth the man is a worthy person who deserves to have a kingdom and be united with thee in wedlock.[57]

57 Waitz, *Historia Langobardorum* III, 30, p. 133f. Translation is by Foulke, p. 138f.

Anglo-Saxon sources convey the same message. That section of *Maxims I* which
states that a wife must always serve her lord first begins by declaring "a king shall
pay brideprice for a queen, with rings and goblets". The goblets in this citation
probably have symbolic significance since, as Roeder pointed out, a late Anglo-
Saxon manuscript painting of a marriage scene suggests that the bride has just
given a cup to her husband or future husband.[58] What Hugh Magennis has
recently noted of the significance of the cup in biblical imagery can also be applied
to these OE data: "the cup metonymically represents the wine which it contains,
and it shares the metaphoric associations of this wine."[59]

Another revealing example occurs in Saxo's *Historia Danorum*. He recounts
the tale of a certain high-spirited Erik who shamelessly cadges food and drink at
king Frothi's hall:

> "I've never met a more shameless request for food or drink," Frothi replied,
> to which Erik rejoined, "Few value or calculate the needs of a man who keeps
> quiet." The king's sister was then told to offer drink from a large bowl to Erik,
> who seized her right hand together with the extended vessel and said, "Didn't
> your generosity, noble sovereign, intend this as a present for me? Won't you
> agree to let me have what I'm holding as a permanent gift?" The king thought
> that by "gift" he meant only the bowl, and assented, but Erik then drew the
> girl to him as though she had been included in the donation.[60]

Although Frothi tried to escape from the consequences of his promise, he was
unable to do so and Erik kept his prize.

None of these actions are fully explainable unless one posits an essential
identity of purpose between the liquor offering within the *comitatus* and the liquor

---

58 Roeder, *Familie bei den Angelsächsen*, p. 31f. Schultze notes the association with cups as well
and points to Icelandic parallels: *Älteren angelsächsische Königsgesetzen*, p. 65f.

59 Magennis, "Cup", p. 518. Some other studies by this scholar are also relevant. See his *"druncne
dryhtguman"*, pp. 159–64; "The Exegesis of Inebriation: Treading Carefully in Old English"
(1986), pp. 3–6; "Water-Wine Miracles in Anglo-Saxon Saint's Lives" (1986), pp. 7–9; "The
Treatment of Feasting in the *Heliand*" (1985), pp. 126–33. See also Russom, "Drink of Death",
pp. 175–90; Stephen Glosecki, *"Beowulf* 769: Grendel's Ale-Share" (1987), pp. 1–9. On
brewing, utensils and linguistic usage, see Christine Fell, "Old English *Beor*" (1975), pp. 76–95;
eadem, "Some Domestic Problems" (1985), pp. 59–82; H.E. Kylstra, "Ale and Beer in
Germanic" (1974), pp. 7–14; Daniel Binchy, "Brewing in Eighth Century Ireland" (1981), pp.
6–9. On matters of cult and status, see Karl Kromer, "Das Situlenfest: Versuch einer Interpretation der Darstellungen auf figural verzierten Situlen" (1980), pp. 225–40; Georg Kossack,
"Trinkgeschirr als Kultgerät der Hallstattzeit" (1964), pp. 98–105; Ake V. Ström, "Die
Hauptriten des wikingerzeitlichen nordischen Opfers" (1966), p. 337f.; Grönvik, *'Funeral
Feast'*; Aaron J. Gurevich, "Edda and Law: Commentary upon Hyndlulióð" (1973), pp.
72–101; M. Rouche, "Les repas de fête à l'époque carolingienne: Manger et boire au moyen
âge" (1984), pp. 265–79. An excellent discussion of overall context is Otto Gerhard Oexle,
"Haus und Ökonomie im früheren Mittelalter" (1988), pp. 101–22.

60 H.R. Ellis Davidson and Peter Fisher, eds. *Saxo Grammaticus: The History of the Danes* I (1979),
p. 132.

offering at marriage. The only noteworthy difference seems to be the touching of the server's hand mentioned by both Paul the Deacon and Saxo Grammaticus for different societies four centuries apart. Even here, however, there are significant parallels for the "giving of the hand" and the formal kiss are common symbolic actions for both institutions. Formula I, 18 of Marculf in the first half of the seventh century refers to swearing fidelity "in our hand", *in manu nostra trustem et fidelitatem* and the Visigothic retainer, among others at later times, swore loyalty by kissing his lord's right hand. A vassal might then be termed a "man of mouth and hands".[61] The *osculum* over liquor was probably present in the early warband as well, although the sources (like Layamon's description of the continental Saxon wassail ceremony, ll. 7149–7157) are late and thus subject to question.[62] Nonetheless, such conjecture is rendered plausible by other evidence. Consider, for example, the very valuable "ring-swords" of certain early Germanic warriors recently studied by Heiko Steuer.[63] These weapons, fitted with a ring to the upper guard, are found in Northern Europe, Scandinavia and England with a chronological horizon from *c.*500 to *c.*700 and are widely understood to signify, as with the ring in marriage, the close bond between leader and most honored followers. Removal of the ring thereafter, attested archaeologically, seems to have signified the sundering of that bond. Once again, a parallel experience for wife and follower! Even the apparent exception of the touching of the girl's hand, therefore, is not a major departure from the conceptual framework and it now seems likely that a trace of the ancient Roman association between *manus* and *potestas* was also familiar to the Germanic tribes of the same period.

The presence of the woman in the *comitatus* is further clarified by this analysis as well. As we have seen, women were inseparably linked with notions of liquor and service and in both types of feasting, marital and martial, the outcome was the creation of a contract between principals mediated by a woman who was herself a binder and who carried the liquid which perfectly symbolized the pledge of unity because all drank from the same store and were served by the same hands. On formal occasions, as at Heorot, all seem to have drunk from the same actual cup[64] so that it is clear that the ritual linking lord to man is a close approximation

---

61 Zeumer, ed. *Form. Marc.* MGH Formulae Merowingici et karolini aevi I, 19, p. 55; Jacques Le Goff, "The Symbolic Ritual of Vassalage" (1980), pp. 237–87.

62 The connection between good fortune, mutual drinking and the kiss of peace is noted by Glosecki, "Grendel's Ale-Share", p. 4f.

63 Heiko Steuer, "Helm und Ringschwert: Prunkbewaffnung und Ringabzeichen germanischer Krieger. Eine Übersicht" (1987), pp. 189–236; Vera Evison deals more fully with the English evidence in: "The Dover Ring-sword and Other Sword-rings and Beads" (1967), pp. 63–118. On the burial of weapons in general, see now the very interesting study of Heinrich Härke, " 'Warrior Graves'? The Background of the Anglo-Saxon Weapon Burial Rite" (1990), pp. 22–43. The most important recent study in this field is Steuer, *Sozialstrukturen.*

64 Crépin, "Wealhtheow's Offering", p. 52. We also saw this in the case of Theudelinda and Agilulf. Bill Griffiths, "The Old English Alcoholic Vocabulary—a Re-examination" (1986), p. 236, cites

to the marriage rite (in which bride and groom share the same cup) which seems to have existed, among the Celts at least, already, in the fourth century BC. The importance of this latter point will later become clear for it can be shown that much Germanic thinking about marriage and warbands derived from the Celts of Gaul and southern Europe. It should be added, however, that the pattern described is normally a triangular one: it is usually the bride's father who "gives" or "sells" his daughter to the groom and thereby directs her offering just as it is the warlord who directs his wife to serve his sodality of "sons".

We now see that entry into marriage and entry into the *comitatus* are both initiations into a similar form of contract created by mutual drinking and female presentation. Once aware that the foundation of each is the idea of family unity, the occasional exploitation of the ritual by those who wished to fashion legal or social ambiguity is easily interpreted. Such also makes for a good story with plenty of dramatic appeal and writers, such as Paul and Saxo, could enjoy describing the equivocal by-play because they were perfectly aware of the underlying cultural assumptions and could expect their readers to understand too. Modern scholars usually mention the familial organization of the warband as well.[65] Nevertheless. while noting it as significant, they do not always recognize that it is truly the decisive socio-political fact which explains the warband's internal workings and hence have neglected to analyze the mentality evidenced in the passages cited above. A possible explanation, it seem to me, is this: the early Germans did not use *druht* for both warband and marriage procession because each consisted of a band of armed men but, rather, they perceived the armed men to be a band of adopted sons belonging to the family of the warlord just as they viewed the bride to be the adopted daughter of a new family lord. In each institution, the essential acts of entry and integration are the same but it is the family which provides the model for the *comitatus*. It is, then, from the dominating position of father of the ritually created fictive family that the warlord derives legitimacy for his power to command. It is the theoretical basis for his power over followers. Although a certain amount of reciprocity and affection is inherent in the giving of weapons and beer to sons, it is clearly far outweighed by the command authority wielded by the father over his household, the bestower over the receiver, for it is he who engenders sons and gives away daughters. It is around his table that the sons gather and their mother serves first her "lord"-husband and then her sons, both real and symbolic. A good example of the theory in practice actually occurs at Heorot where Hrothgar seats Beowulf with his children, publicly names him "son" and gives him gifts of horses and weapons. Drink is served thereafter. Wealhtheow thereby becomes a metaphoric "mother" to the hero although she

the late *Saga of Thorgils Skarthi*: "First they drank in companionship, passing the horn around; but then they began to drink individually, each draining his own horn; some of the men were by then quite drunk."

65 See note 30.

hardly wishes it and fears the consequences. Even if Beowulf's case be thought special, however, it is really only because of the extravagance of the gifts and the explicitness of statement. The other retainers are bound in essentially the same manner for all drink with Hrothgar from his table, live with him as a "band of kinsmen" and, as was normal upon entry into the *comitatus*, each had received a spear or sword from Hrothgar's hand.

While the aura of warfare hangs heavy in the background, the burden of the evidence also suggests that Kuhn was at least partly correct in arguing for a close connection between *druht* and "drink" even though the analysis he presented was not then sufficiently detailed to fully convince other scholars. Since both institutions established an hierarchical contractual relationship by weapon transfers and drink offering together, the underlying concept of relationship is likely to have been similar in each. The *munt* exercised by lord over follower approximated that exercised by husband over wife. While a variety of terms for "warband" may have existed, it can be suggested that the *druht*, both warband retainers and members of a wedding procession, were conceptually joined because of a common basis in festival and warband contract. They may occasionally have been called "the drinkers", a word which signified that they belonged to a *familia* and might, indeed should, sit together at table without fear of attack.

These findings add further nuance to the argument advanced on other grounds in chapter one, where it was suggested that a royal succession was regarded by the *comitatus* as analogous to the case of a family which had lost its father and which might, therefore, if the sons had reached majority, exercise their control over their mother by giving her in marriage to another husband who would then become king because, on the same theoretical basis, he would also become father. Such would seem to be the ultimate rationale behind Paul's story of the succession of Agilulf which will now repay further examination. Recall that upon Authari's death, the *prudentes* of the Lombards allowed Theudelinda to continue as queen because she pleased them. They also allowed her to "choose" a husband as long as he met the established criteria. Despite the element of exaggeration in the narrative, Theudelinda's subsequent ritual actions must be regarded as highly significant:

> And she, taking counsel with the prudent, chose Agilulf, duke of the people of Turin as her husband and king of the nation of the Langobards, for he was a man energetic and warlike and fitted as well in body as in mind for the government of the kingdom. The queen straightway sent word to him to come to her and she hastened to meet him at the town of Laumellum (Lumello). And when he had come to her, she, after some speech with him, caused wine to be brought, and when she had first quaffed it, she handed the rest to Agilulf to drink. And when he had taken the cup and had reverently kissed her hand, the queen said smiling, with a blush, that he should not kiss her hand who

ought to imprint a kiss upon her lips. And straightway raising him up to kiss her, she unfolded to him the subject of marriage and of the sovereign dignity. Why say more? The nuptials were celebrated with great rejoicing and Agilulf, who was a kinsman of king Authari on the mother's side, assumed the royal dignity at the beginning of the month of November. Later, however, in the month of May when the Langobards had met together in one place, he was raised to the sovereignty by all at Mediolanum.[66]

The taking of the cup is here accompanied with a kiss and the queen acts as mediatrix of authority. More graphically displayed in this text, one witnesses again the relationship between kingship, marriage and drink-offering (which is depicted in Anglo-Saxon ritual in *Beowulf* where it functions as a declaration of the lord's authority over his men). It is, ultimately, an assertion of his fatherly authority over his household and all of his *familia*, his band of "sons". The complex of ideas surrounding marriage, authority, fatherhood and lordship seem inextricably intertwined and royal succession, apparently, can thus be based on the concept of the remarriage of the widow in Germanic tradition. It is the "mother's" widowhood which explains her apparent "free" choice—but only in the medieval meaning of that term. We have already noted that Theudelinda does not act freely in the modern sense, although she may be free in the medieval sense of possessing the liberty to act appropriately under circumscribed conditions with the consent of her relatives. The inability of some commentators to appreciate this difference, despite Tellenbach's now classic exposition long since translated into English,[67] lies at the root of much incoherence in the literature, in that nineteenth century liberal ideas of personal freedom are often superimposed on sources to which they have no real relation since medieval thought is thoroughly grounded on the principles of status, counsel and assent. Barbarian law is even less amenable to such interpretation. But in nearly all cases, self-interest and political policy will be determinative and must often be given pride of place even where the word "freedom" is explicitly used. Schneider was in no way wrong to speak of *die Dominanz der Macht* amongst the Franks and Lombards in these situations[68] and when all is considered, it is the authority of the leader, which devolves on the *prudentes* during an interregnum, which counts most strongly. No family will allow a widow to remarry if it endangers the inheritance just as no group of powerful men with many hundreds of dependents will allow the king's

---

66 Waitz, *Historia Langobardorum*, III, 35, p. 141). The crucial lines are these: Quae cum prior bibisset, residuum Agilulfo ad bibundum tribuit. Is cum regina, accepto poculo, manum hororabiliter osculatus esset, regina cum robore subridens, non deberi sibi manum osculit, ait, quem osculum ad os iungere oporteret. Moxque eum ad suum basium erigens, ei de suis nuptiis deque regni dignitate aperuit.
67 Gerd Tellenbach, *The Investiture Contest* (1948), pp. 1–37.
68 Schneider, *Königswahl*, p. 240.

wife to choose a husband who might jeopardize its future. Theudelinda's apparent freedom of choice is necessary, however, because the theoretical basis for succession is marriage and adoption and the liquor ritual is an indispensable sign of both in all periods of the tradition until, at least, the ninth century when the influence of the Christian clergy becomes decisive in many regions. Note, however, that even in the citation above, the cup-offering and marriage are not enough and that Agilulf's status as king had to be confirmed in a second ritual at Milan.

The dual nature of Agilulf's initiation is itself significant and worthy of comment since it seems to ultimately derive from a concept which separates the sacral king from the military leader. Let us look at the ritual aspect of this more closely. One scholar has recently commented as follows:

> There is very little evidence concerning royal inauguration rituals among Germanic peoples before the church became involved here. It is possible that in many cases, regular ritual procedures did not exist, in the absence either of permanent political communities or of permanent kingships. The Merovingian dynasty, as Grierson has pointed out, was atypical in its relative stability, and yet, sacral features notwithstanding, it seems to have lacked a fixed ritual for the transmission of royal power. More relevant is the absence of any barbarian inauguration ritual exclusive to kingship: rather, the *rex* was a household-lord writ large, whose succession to his inheritance was thus aptly signified when he took his place on the high-seat in the paternal hall or beat the bounds of the paternal property. Similarly, the *dux* was set up through rituals of shield-raising and investiture with weapons which were common to all lords of military followings.[69]

The distinction between *rex* and *dux*, or sacral king and warleader, would seem to be a crucial one and, based on Schlesinger's analysis of 1954, has since been adopted by nearly all students of medieval kingship. But the evidence assembled here now seems to suggest that at least one "regular ritual procedure" for royal inaugurations did exist among the Germans prior to Christianity even if it were not exclusively royal. In fact, this latter aspect of non-exclusivity is a good argument in its favor. The wife's cup-offering symbolically expresses the ideas of both marital contract and lordship over the household and, because it also satisfies the requisite criteria of simplicity, antiquity and applicability to both house-lord and territorial ruler, also becomes a likely candidate for the earliest royal inauguration ritual within the *comitatus*. If the domestic ruler was recognized as such when his wife served him before others, then it seems to follow that in any formal gathering of such men the preeminence of the leader of the assembly would be established by the same action. In other words, the status of the *rex* would be

69 Janet Nelson, "Symbols in Context: Ruler's Inauguration Rituals in Byzantium and in the West in the Early Middle Ages" (1976), p. 264f.

shown to lie above that of the *dux* by the service itself. Although sacral elements may well have been present in both cases, they will have been more pronounced for the former. While the nature of the Germanic evidence is such that the distinction is difficult to draw for the continent, the likelihood of its existence will be shown below in chapter five where comparative Celtic material is examined. It will be seen that the cup-offering is made to both kinds of leaders but the mythic background is more clearly described and the difference between king of the tribe and "king" of the warriors is made clear. The claim to authority remained rooted in the domestic sphere and the contrasting qualities conferred at accession were manifest to participants through variances in speech—like the bestowal of the name of king in *Beowulf*—or by gesture or associated behaviors. Such an explanation would account for a great many inconsistencies which bedevil the study of barbarian succession rites. The warlord did not have to change the ritual upon becoming king; he simply claimed priority of service and the tribal rights and religious associations which went with it while at the same time maintaining the ceremonies which made him *dux*. The element of continuity clearly stands out in these acts. Shield-raising, taking the high-seat or investing with weapons are rituals which frequently appear over many centuries. For two reasons, however, because of its intimate familial basis and its association with marriage, the offering of drink based on precedence is likely to be older than any of them. It must have been an expected and perennial feature of every formal gathering. Hence, in the case of the cup-offering, it makes no crucial difference whether one refers to the first or ninth century warlord because the act and much of the conceptual background would have been familiar to both and the basic institutional context remained the same despite some shifts in its modality.[70]

As one approaches the material from this viewpoint, much else in the early sources takes on new meaning. Although the pre-migration evidence is scarce, we do know that inauguration to leadership was normally connected with a feast. While many scholars have referred to this in the past, it has hitherto proven impossible to explain why and in what way the feast was constitutive. One can now make that attempt. In *Historia* 4, 14 of Tacitus, Julius Civilis is described as one of the leaders of a rebellion. It is said that he collected the chiefs of the Batavians at a holy site where he had prepared a banquet. After they were "warmed with the festivities", i.e. after they had drunk a great deal, he began to encourage them with speeches to rebel against the Romans. When they had listened "with great approval", he "bound the whole assembly with barbarous rites [*barbaro ritu*] and the national forms of oath".[71] This feast is presented as the

71 On early oath-taking and associated matters, see Uwe Eckhardt, *Untersuchungen zu Form und Funktion der Treueidleistung im merowingischen Frankenreich* (1976), pp. 24–34; Schlesinger, "Herrschaft und Gefolgschaft", p. 24.

70 It is, of course, precisely because the family provided the model for warband authority that the cup-offering seems so appropriate a choice. For discussion of other rites, see Nelson, "Inauguration Rituals", pp. 259–307; Hauck, "Randkultur", pp. 1–91.

key starting point of the rebellion and also as the source of Civilis' dominance
during the course of the rebellion. Indeed, Schlesinger interprets the oath sworn
as a *comitatus* oath and goes on to stress that the entire procedure has strong sacral
overtones which Civilis himself emphasizes and exploits in order to legitimize
his leadership.[72] We may note in addition that Civilis is a member of a royal family,
the main speaker and convener of the feast and it looks as if he selects the "sacred
grove" where those who pledge support bind themselves with oaths. That the
nature of Civilis' lordship is different from that of others is made clear several
sentences later where a reference is made to Brinno, *dux* of the Canninefati, who
became such when he was raised on a shield by his followers.[73] He is a warlord,
but of a single tribal group, and clearly not one of the same type as Civilis who
may, however, also have been *dux* of the Batavians.

Exactly what form did these barbarous rites of pledging take? Unfortunately,
we have no direct evidence beyond the facts that they occurred during a feast
where liquor was drunk and in an atmosphere charged with the supernatural.
Based on this information, however, and on the results of the foregoing discussion, several deductions seem admissible: first, the liquor itself played a significant role in the deliberations (we note that Civilis did not begin speaking to the
chiefs until after they had been drinking for some time). Tacitus must personally
have believed this of the liquor for he wrote in *Germania* 22 that "it is at their
feasts" that the Germans decide on peace and war and "on the choice of chiefs"
since "they think that at no time is the mind more open to simplicity of purpose
or more warmed to noble aspirations. . . . They disclose their hidden thoughts in
the freedom of the festivity." Tacitus also seems to think that they do not make a
final decision until the following day but that is less likely since, as with Civilis,
the major choices were clearly taken at the feast itself. Tacitus seems to have been
right to emphasize the combined political and religious significance of such
gatherings.

Second, we may also deduce that where liquor is served there must be a server,
one who is not a member of the assembly since that might be beneath his dignity
or viewed as otherwise inappropriate. Third, the server in any formal instance is
likely to have been a woman, perhaps a woman held to be endowed with the power
of prophecy. Although one might argue that a priest would be the probable
celebrant at a ritual oath-taking in a sacred grove (and that would have been my
opinion prior to undertaking this study) we have already seen that, in later times
at least, oaths were usually made over liquor distributed by a woman. If Schlesinger (and others) are right in interpreting these Batavian oaths as belonging to the
sphere of the *comitatus*, then the hypothesis becomes even more likely. Even

---

72 Ibid.
73 Schlesinger, "Herrschaft und Gefolgschaft", p. 24: "Im Stamm werden *rex* und *dux* unter-
schieden, der Heerkönig dagegen ist *rex* und *dux* zugleich."

assuming for the sake of argument that this evidence is insufficient, however, other grounds urge the same conclusion. We saw in chapter two that Germanic warlords of the period were usually accompanied by prophetesses. Tacitus mentions several examples while noting that the Germans frequently turned to them for advice and pointing out by his emphasis that Civilis *in particular* valued this method of winning support. The fact that Ganna, "successor" to Veleda, accompanied king Masyos of the Semnones to Rome indicates that the warlord wished such women to be present on important occasions, especially since, as we have seen, ancient rulers often kept sibyls at their sides. For the Germans, we might suppose that the sibyl became the server who sanctified oaths when the warlord employed her in an institutional capacity. Consider also that a primary reason for the feast in the Batavian holy grove was a decision on the question of war or peace. In such a case the presence of a prophetess might well have been thought to be necessary, perhaps even normal in view of the setting. Ariovistus, for example, turned to the *matres familia* before making a decision while many tribes sought the visions of Veleda. Even as far away as Egypt there is evidence that Germanic troops required the presence of a sibyl. Who then was better placed to prophesy victory, serve the liquor and witness the oaths? All the evidence points to a woman under the control of Civilis. It was only some months later that Civilis and Veleda were together asked to decide another question of war and peace so that we know that their joint action was approved of in these contexts. Finally, we may also deduce that Civilis was elected as the foremost leader at this feast. In *Historia* 4, 13, Tacitus says that he and Julius Paulus were reckoned "very high above the rest of their nation" but in 4, 14 that it was "*he*", Civilis, who "bound the whole assembly with barbarous rites." Thereafter, it was Civilis also who seems to have taken the decision to send messengers to the Roman garrison at Mainz who would attempt to suborn the loyalties of the Celtic-British auxiliaries and Batavian cohorts serving with the legions. These directives affected the entire people and no other *princeps* seems to have exercised this level of power. It is a point explicitly recognized in *Historia* 4, 16 where Tacitus states that the true leader of the war was Civilis. Consequently, the feast where Civilis "bound them" must have been constitutive and it is not unlikely that the prophetess would have hailed Civilis in a special manner when, as the elected leader, he was served first. It would have been a key ritual or part of the ritual and would have been his warrant for headship of the rebellion, even if not for a right to exclusive rule or to rule beyond the time of the war, (although we also know that that is what he aimed for).

Further clues supporting this hypothesis will be discussed in chapters four and five. Until then, at least, a certain amount of skepticism seems appropriate for it cannot be denied that the distance between the Roman and early medieval sources is great and thus one cannot claim an identity of interpretation for each element discussed. A considerable amount of continuity has been demonstrated, however, and the accumulation of numerous clues makes it reasonable to argue that the Wealhtheow episode in *Beowulf* does reflect the force of early Germanic tradition. One aspect of this tradition emphasizes the creation of brotherhood in a rite which has decidedly sacramental overtones. Literally hundreds of scholars have referred to it in this manner without realizing that it is only part of the story, for the liquor ritual is perhaps even more significant as a device for the maintenance of lordship and authority and the allocation of status within a group. The "brothers" are also made subordinate "sons".

We must, however, be clear about the significance of the Batavian gathering in the groves. Although, for the reasons offered, one may argue that Veleda is likely to have been present, it can neither be securely demonstrated nor claimed as a fact. The association between the warlord and the woman who helps him govern the warband must have come into being at an early date, however, because it is a feature of that organization in the widely separated Lombard and Anglo-Saxon sources and also appears in texts concerning the Celts. Although it is not impossible that it existed for the Germans before the Batavian rebellion, the available evidence, such as it is, suggests that it was not created much before that time. When Ariovistus needed a prophecy about warfare in the preceding century, he had consulted the tribal matrons and not a single prophetess. On the other hand, we do know that Veleda had a "successor" named Ganna who traveled with king Masyos of the Semmones to Rome where both were honorably received by the emperor Domitian in 91 or 92 (Cassius Dio 67, 5). On important occasions, the prophetess travels with the warlord. In other words, her position was, or had become, an institutional one in which warlord and prophetess acted together. Considerably more subsequent analysis will be required to depict the full pattern. Even at this point in the discussion, however, it is striking, considering the overall paucity of the sources, that a tentative conclusion may be drawn. The line seems to run from Ariovistus with multiple prophetesses in the mid-first century BC to Civilis and Veleda in 69/70 AD and then to Masyos and Ganna in 91/92. All these leaders turned to prophecy at pivotal times which is, of course, another reason for thinking of Veleda at the oath-taking in the groves. A hint of continuity is also provided in *Germania* 8, although Tacitus is there speaking more of the prestige of the prophetess. He states that "even earlier", i.e. before Veleda, the Germans "showed a similar reverence for Aurinia and *a number of others*". Although this observation is insufficiently specific to cite as direct evidence, it does show that a fairly large number of prophetesses existed while also providing circumstantial support for the linkage posited. It seems reasonable to conclude, therefore, that in the century and a half or so from Ariovistus to Masyos, roughly the same period during which the Germanic *comitatus* came into existence as we shall see later, the warlord developed the technique of attaching a prophetess to his band in order to bolster his own status and further his military endeavors. The chronological convergence is not coincidental.

Given the great utility of the prophetess in the binding, morale building and governing of the *comitatus*, there is every reason to think that the warlord/prophetess pairing (which surely required a ritual affirmation) continued for as long as the pagan warband lasted. Under Christianity, belief in the supernatural powers of the prophetess must have declined but the fact is, as recent studies of early medieval magic and the process of Christianization have shown, religious change was not usually thoroughgoing and so it probably only slowly diminished or marginalized her standing without effacing her usefulness. Although unlikely to be provable, it would not be surprising if the newly Christianized warlord married his prophetess and thereby maintained a resource while reducing the chance of challenge or scandal. Various of her aspects and talents lingered, however, because the very makeup of the institution required them, even if, as I have suggested for *Beowulf*, they are only barely revealed in the mostly one-sided sources. The military chaplain eventually replaced the prophetess. Of that, there is no doubt. But it probably happened at widely different times in different regions, earlier at the core and later at the periphery of the Merovingian and early Carolingian era "states".

By way of conclusion, a few more general reasons may be offered for insisting on the great significance of the liquor ritual for the warband. Recall that the Anglo-Saxon lord is called *hlaford* and his followers *hlafoeta*. The former means "loaf-giver" and the latter "loaf-eater". This points to the supreme importance of food in archaic thinking and it has a long history. Speaking of a king of a first-century BC Gaulish tribe, Athenaeus says that "in an attempt to win popular favor", he made a large square enclosure "within which he filled vats with expensive liquor and prepared so great a quantity of food that for many days all who wished could enter and enjoy the feast prepared, being served without a break by the attendants."[74] Since Tacitus says that the Germans chose their kings during feasts, it might be appropriate to envision a similar lavishness for them. One might, on the other hand, suppose that it was the ordinary tribesman and not the noble who was influenced by this type of generosity with food. But such does not seem to be the case. In discussing the skeletal evidence for malnutrition in a large-scale survey of Anglo-Saxon cemeteries, Heinrich Härke recently pointed out that in spite of the wealth differential signaled by grave-dimensions and the presence or lack of weapons, "the risk of starvation seems to have been

74 J.J. Tierney, "The Celtic Ethnography of Posidonius" (1960), p. 248. Of course, many of the concepts expressed here would have been familiar to Romans as well. Suetonius notes (Dom. 5) that "Domitian himself was the first to eat" at a feast given for all orders during the festival of the Septimontium. D'Arms perceptively comments: "when the community sees that the *dominus* has begun to feast they may also join in the meal, thus transforming themselves from witnesses of, to participants in, a spectacular ceremony—a ceremony which symbolizes the orderly and harmonious functioning of society." See his "Control, Companionship and *Clientela*: Some Social Functions of the Roman Communal Meal" (1984), p. 344. The importance of the place of honor (*locus consularis*) at Roman *convivia* is stressed at length by Plutarch (*Moralia*, 619f.).

the same in both groups, indicating that no group in Anglo-Saxon society was shielded from the consequences of the inefficient system of food production and storage."[75] He goes on to note the following interesting correlation: "in the analyzed sample, fifty of 363 male adult weapons burials (13.8 percent) contained drinking vessels (including so-called "buckets" of various sizes) whereas only six of 337 male adult burials without weapons (1.8 percent) had drinking vessels."[76] The association of weapons with warrior graves seems clear but a link between drinking utensils and weapons is significant as well. Recall again the semantics of *druht* and the associations of marriage.

A glance at Old English poetry enables us to grasp something of the mentality behind the practice. In the thought world of the Early Middle Ages, ale, beer, wine and mead are constantly associated with love and companionship and, indeed, function as metaphors for delight and satisfaction. Their removal becomes a statement of poverty, alienation and reduced status.[77] As a whole, Germanic literature equates sharing out of drink with joy and prosperity while bitterness and loss are described as the distribution of a poisonous drink, the *poculum mortis*.[78] The motif is not uncommon. Even inspiration and the ability to speak well are associated with liquor while status is sometimes depicted in terms of types of liquor. Not surprisingly then, references to some kinds of drink signify profoundly felt emotions. As Christine Fell points out, the *Beowulf* poet's naming of Heorot as a *medoheal* seems partly functional but what are we to make of a pattern of thought which describes the path to Heorot as a *medostig* or which describes a victory as a winning of mead-seats in a hall (*medosetla ofteah* l. 5) or describes the wounds of warriors as payments for mead? As Fell suspects, "the strongly emotive terminology of *medu* is very closely linked with the loyalties and patterns of the heroic code".[79]

As far back as anyone can trace the tradition, Germanic concepts of contract, lordship, marriage, loyalty and community are all directly linked to the provision and distribution of liquor. Even if slight variations be suspected, the continuity of this conceptual structure, from the first through the ninth century at least, seems plausible. *Specifics* of ritual behavior are more difficult to discern. Nonetheless, when we find that Hrothgar is recognized as lord and king with a

---

75 Härke, "Weapon Burial Rite", p. 38.
76 Ibid., n. 31. In his dissertation, Härke points out that the weapon burial rite was itself a "symbolic action" which must be treated separately from the reality of warfare. It was, he argues, part of ritual behavior linked to warrior status. See Jankuhn's favorable discussion in "Neue Erkenntnisse zur Sozialstruktur germanischer Stämme im frühen Mittelalter auf Grund von Grabfunden" (1988), pp. 29–35.
77 Magennis, "*druncne dryhtguman*", pp. 159–64; Glosecki, "Grendel's Ale Share", p. 4f.; Fell, "Old English *Beor*", pp. 76–95.
78 Magennis, "Cup", p. 522f.; Carlton Brown, "*Poculum Mortis* in Old English" (1940), pp. 389–99; Russom, "Drink of Death", pp. 175–89.
79 Fell, "Old English *Beor*", p. 80.

cup-offering and when a husband is recognized as lord of a family in the same way, it seems difficult to believe that the people who originated the tradition, who chose their kings while drinking at feasts, did not follow the same ritual pattern. Although the sources are late, and hence I have not referred to them in detail, the North Germans seem to have preserved important aspects of this rite in matters of inheritance of property. At the heir's feast, the inheritor was not reckoned in full possession of an estate until he sat in the high-seat and drank a cup of liquor.[80] The Celts maintained a comparable ritual for king and king's "champion" at a much earlier period. A full discussion of this background will be delayed until the archaeological evidence for the mead cup motif has been examined.

80 See Grönvik, *'Funeral Feast'*, p. 9; Gurevich, "Edda and Law", pp. 72–84.

IV

THE ARCHAEOLOGY OF INTOXICATION AND
THE CONTINUITY OF TRANSALPINE HISTORY

The three previous chapters are based mostly on literary sources of varying quality and reliability. They are indispensable to any study of barbarian ritual from the early Roman imperial period to the Early Middle Ages of the *Beowulf* poem, that is, very roughly, from Augustus to about 800 AD. But every historian will immediately recognize the problems inherent in their usage. Classical sources like Caesar, Tacitus and Ammianus must be used for the early period but they are beset with technical problems of bias and the application of generalized *topoi* applied willy nilly to all barbarians who, viewed by the urban Mediterranean elite, were frequently seen as being all equally dim-witted and repulsive or else naive and childish in their appropriately primitive milieus. They were peoples without respectable histories whose customs and attitudes were mainly worthy of note for their entertainment value. An occasional noble exception merely demonstrated the rarity of the type. Five hundred years later, the nature of the biases had changed but the fact of extreme bias remained. Works like *Beowulf* were written, or recorded and modified, by Christian clerics out of sympathy with pagan ideas and customs which they often misrepresented, excluded or only briefly mentioned in order to condemn. The benighted barbarians had now become something even worse, the benighted non-Christians. And what of those who had lived outside of the empire in the vast regions of *Germania libera* or in the post-Roman Britain of the fifth and sixth centuries? For these areas, the literary sources are late and usually cursory at best. Although some reliable information is available and reasonable guesses can occasionally be made, the overall picture to be painted is unprepossessing and especially unimpressive to scholars accustomed to working in later periods with far richer literary remains.

Fortunately for the present study, one which seeks to explore the history and significance of the status-creating liquor ritual within the warband, a valuable control is available to be applied to the literary sources. They can be checked in a general way, and sometimes in very specific individual ways, by drawing upon archaeological data. The material is incredibly rich and varied and covers a much broader geographical area and chronological span than the one outlined above. Unlike other archaic rites which might be discussed, the liquor ritual is unique in that it has left bits and pieces of evidence throughout Europe. In parts of modern France, for example, peasants have been carting Roman amphorae away from their fields for over three centuries. These had originally been traded to the Gauls. Some fields are still difficult to plow because so many shards remain embedded in the soil.[1] A similar kind of trade occurred later with Britain and with some Germanic peoples and, outside of such zones of Roman occupation or strong influence, there is much related evidence for *Germania libera*. Consequently, although the interpretation of this material is not always easy—archaeological remains are "silent" by nature and thus require analysis—the evidence is undeniably present and available for the testing of hypotheses drawn from literary sources. It is accompanied by a huge, scattered and frequently highly specialized modern archaeological literature. I do not pretend to have surveyed more than a fraction of this expanse but I have constantly attempted to seek out the most relevant studies and to rely on the interpretations of respected specialists. I have occasionally questioned them. I am acutely conscious of the problems raised by doing so for I am not a trained archaeologist but rather an historian attempting to interpret material remains in the light of both text and artifact together. As Richard Warner has said, however, echoing remarks by Colin Renfrew on the relations between archaeologists and historians as "dialogues of the deaf",[2] I can only plead the best intentions and hope that archaeologists will forgive the amateur foray into their territory and the mistakes made while doing so.

Contrary to what might be expected, a reasonably reliable investigation of the early history of the drinking ritual is indeed possible and is, in fact, a major desideratum in the study of the Early Middle Ages. It is true that a number of works of various kinds dealing with drinking practices have appeared over the past few decades. Valuable as some of them are, many tend to be repetitive or derivative.[3] Grönbech's important work on the culture of the Teutons or Schücking's on Old English oath-making and drinking rituals have far too frequently been mined or paraphrased to produce pot-boiler essays of negligible value and less originality. Some other studies are very helpful but are often confined to individual personalities or groups during a restricted period. The literary sources are thus now in need of a somewhat more broad-based contextual discussion; they require placement in the *Gedächtniskultur*, that is, in the oral or memorial culture of early Europe which, with some exceptions, was largely disdained both by the

---

1 André Tchernia, "Italian Wine in Gaul at the end of the Republic" (1983), p. 90.
2 Richard B. Warner, "The Archaeology of Early Historic Irish Kingship" (1988), p. 47.
3 These remarks do not apply to a number of recent works which seek to go beyond traditional approaches. See, for some examples in this category, the insightful studies by D.A. Bullough, "Friends, Neighbors and Fellow-Drinkers: Aspects of Community and Conflict in the Early Medieval West" (1990); Gerd Althoff, *Verwandte, Freunde und Getreue: Zum politischen Stellenwert der Gruppenbindungen im früheren Mittelalter* (1990); Hayo Vierck, "Hallenfreunde: Archäologische Spuren Frühmittelalterliche Trinkgelage und mögliche Wege zu ihrer Deutung" (1990).

classical commentators and their ecclesiastical successors. Once this memorial context is understood, then it will also be possible to show why and how some peoples better preserved it than others. We will thereby have formed an approach towards demonstrating the important level of continuity which existed in European culture outside of, or aside from, the Christian literary tradition. Archaeology will provide a valuable perspective.

The section which follows presents a descriptive and analytic sketch of the famous Lübsow and Hasleben/Leuna graves together with some discussions of the row-graves of the Merovingian period and the continuity of some practices into the Viking Age. In the course of analysis, I will indicate some of the ways in which the surviving material suggests the existence of a carefully organized geographically extensive drinking ritual. Since the nature of the evidence will point to an originally strong Germanic dependence on things Celtic, I will repeat the process for Celtic culture in the next section beginning with the late Hallstatt period, continuing through La Tène and eventually providing some reference to the Celts of the islands. Section three will present a brief discussion of the nature of the oral culture highlighting some comparative Germanic and Celtic aspects. A broader purpose will also be evident. This chapter seeks, in addition, to elucidate the continuity of the material cultures of the peoples discussed over a long period; to illustrate some relevant aspects of the interplay between them; to demonstrate the way in which the archaeological evidence supports the literary sources and hence the age and durability of the mead cup motif in European history.

1. FROM LÜBSOW TO THE VIKINGS

Numerous cemeteries from the first century BC, the late pre-Roman Iron Age, have puzzled archaeologists by the fact that they contain either exclusively male or female burials. Stretching from Holstein to central Germany, these sex-segregated cemeteries include graves in which a sizable minority of men were buried with weapons and military equipment as well as bronze containers and Roman imports.[4] Many female graves contain ornaments such as items of jewelry. Puzzlement has arisen because no certain explanation for this novel segregation practice can be offered. Religious change, the coming of the *comitatus*, the creation of large-scale men's clubs (*Männerbunden*), have all been suggested as causative agents.[5] It is rather certain, however, that this burial custom points to

---

4 Malcolm Todd, "Germanic Burials in the Roman Iron Age" (1977), p. 40.
5 Steuer, *Sozialstrukturen*, pp. 157f., 190–8. See further Heiko Steuer, "Interpretationsmöglichkeiten archäologischer Quellen zum Gefolgschaftsproblem" (1992), p. 230f. The most recent anthropological analysis of the skeletal remains show that some women and children were indeed buried in these cemetaries. Actually, this might seem to strengthen the warband connection since women in some numbers, probably as slaves or concubines, can easily be

significant trans-regional social change. The importance of kinship, a primary organizational concept of tribal societies, must have declined in these areas for otherwise the more common practice of burial with family and relatives would not have been superseded. In the next century (outside of Holstein, the Altmark and some associated areas) this custom gives way to others but it remains an important and not fully explained indicator of widespread social ferment in Germania.

It is in the next century, however, beginning about the time of the birth of Christ and lasting into the mid-second century, that the clearest indication of strong class differentiation emerges. This is the period of the "princely graves" of the Lübsow type investigated by H.J. Eggers.[6] They are named after the Pomeranian cemetery of Lübsow where five such burials have been found. Their distribution stretches from Bohemia in a north-westerly direction up along the Baltic coast into Jutland and the Danish islands with an outlier in southern Norway. They are not numerous. Eggers identified thirty-two but recent research suggests that more could be added.[7]

These exceptionally rich graves are linked by a number of characteristics only the most important of which will be mentioned here. Most are inhumation burials and that alone makes them markedly different for cremation burial had been the rule among Germans for many centuries. Unusual care was also exercised in grave construction. Many of these "princes" were buried in coffins or in specially built chambers under barrows. An interest in the creation of political dynasties is also evident from the Lübsow site itself where three graves belong to the early imperial period and two to the later. Although Lübsow graves are normally weaponless, they do contain a broad range of imported Roman goods, especially very rich drinking vessels in bronze, silver and glass. One of the most impressive is the Hoby find from the Danish island of Lalland which can be dated to about the time of the birth of Christ.[8] It was the grave of a middle aged man who was buried with two joints of pork for his journey to the next world. His grave contained an astonishingly luxurious series of drinking vessels which included two silver cups on a bronze tray, a silver ladle, a bronze situla or bucket, a patera and a jug with two bronze-mounted drinking horns. There were also brooches of gold, silver and bronze, bronze belt-fittings and knife together with locally manufactured pottery.

One might compare this grave with that of a woman from Juellinge on the

---

envisioned as having been present and the appearance of children in these cemetaries would seem to follow.

6 H.J. Eggers, "Lübsow, ein germanischer Fürstensitz der älteren Kaiserzeit" (1950).

7 M. Gebühr, "Zur Definition älterkaiserzeitliches Fürstengräber vom Lübsow-Typ" (1974); Steuer, *Sozialstrukturen*, p. 52.

8 Mortimer Wheeler, *Rome Beyond the Imperial Frontiers* (1955), 36f.

same island towards the end of the Lübsow horizon.[9] She was in her thirties and had been buried with a joint of lamb for sustenance in the next life. Among her ornaments were two gold-headed silver hairpins and a gold pendant with two gold beads at her neck. Four silver brooches were found at her breasts and shoulders, beads of amber and glass under her right hand. Also in her right hand, she held a long-handled bronze wine-strainer. Among other grave goods were found glass beakers and drinking horns together with a ladle into which the strainer held by the dead woman fit. Both instruments were commonly used in ladling drink from a cauldron (also found in the grave) into beaker or horn since the various liquors of the time was thick, much like soup, often containing berries, seeds, nodules of spice or other kinds of additions. These might also be added to wine as well as to mead or beer. Analysis of the cauldron showed that it had contained a fermented liquor made from barley and fruit.

Here, surely, is an early example of our lady with a mead cup (holding a strainer for a barley/fruit liquor in this case) who was buried in such a way as to suggest both her respected functions as distributor of drink as well as her high social status. There is no doubt that the drinking assemblies buried in all the Lübsow type graves mirror the lifestyle of the contemporary Germanic upper class or nobility. A person's level of status was indicted by the very expensive and difficult to obtain imported goods while the fact that they were placed in the grave suggests not only a particular form of religious belief but also a necessity or desire on the part of the family for prestigious display at a time when many gathered together.[10] Luxury drinking vessels were not only appropriate objects to be associated with high rank, their very possession seems to have been a sign of elevated status throughout their broad range of distribution.

"Princely graves" similar to those of Lübsow also appear in the later Roman period with the designation "Hassleben-Leuna type" and are most common in the two or three decades on either side of AD 300.[11] Like Lübsow burials, they are widely distributed but now with concentrations in central Germany, the western Baltic shore and the Danish islands. They are mostly inhumations although that is no longer so unusual among Germans as it had been three

---

9 Ibid., p. 41f.
10 Excellent overviews, although often differing in matters of interpretation, will be found in the following works: Heiko Steuer, "Archaeology and History: Proposals on the Social Structure of the Merovingian Kingdom" (1991); Heinrich Härke, "'Warrior Graves'? The Background of the Anglo-Saxon Weapon Burial Rite" (1990); Herbert Jankuhn, "Neue Erkenntnisse zur Sozialstruktur germanischer Stämme im frühen Mittelalter auf Grund von Grabfunden" (1988); Bailey K. Young, "Exemple aristocratique et mode funéraire dans la Gaule mérovingienne" (1986); Edward James, "Burial and Status in the Early Medieval West" (1989), Donald Bullough, "Burial, Community and Belief in the Early Medieval West" (1983); Bergljot Solberg, "Social Status in the Merovingian and Viking Periods in Norway from Archaeological and Historical Sources" (1985).
11 Steuer, *Sozialstrukturen*, pp. 220–9.

centuries earlier. It seems clear that the inhumation custom, begun by the nobles or wealthy, had now become the model for the next lower social category who thereby distinguished themselves in death from the population as a whole who still retained the predominant practice of cremation.[12] Also copied was the lifestyle display. As in the Lübsow series, expensive imported bronze and silver drinking assemblies are prominent in graves of the Hassleben-Leuna type. The vessels are of the same kind as those used on the Rhine and Danube frontiers and it seems likely that many were taken in warband raids to the west and south. Although weapons are not normally present, silver arrowheads were placed in some graves, presumably as a sign of rank.

From the late fifth century onwards, in the wake of migration, Germanic service in Roman armies, conquest, Christianization and the establishment of barbarian successor states, the nature of burial customs change and fluctuate to such a degree in transalpine Europe that it would take a long disquisition to even partly describe them. I shall not attempt to do so here but will confine myself to a brief survey of a few selected themes.

The custom of inhumation, now aided by Roman, Gallo–Roman and Christian influence, begins a phase during which it will spread ever more widely to largely replace the older varieties of cremation types. Burial with weapons will become exceedingly important and widespread. Among the Germans, this practice had begun in a small way in the first century BC and was then taken up and abandoned numerous times in various cemeteries and in various regions. It was known to the Alemanni in the fourth century, for example, but not to the contemporary Franks in the homeland.[13] Both customs will come together in the eventually far-flung "row grave civilization" (*Reihengräberzivilization*) which begins in northeastern Gaul and reflects Gallo–Germanic origins.[14] Bodies are now buried in individual trenches without coffins and are disposed neatly in rows. Men are frequently buried with one or more weapons and women with ornaments and other items of dress. The number, types and quality of weapons frequently seem to reflect social differentiation but one cannot always confidently generalize since other features impinge and make it clear that weapon deposition alone does not determine social status.[15] Burials which must be described as "aristocratic" are not uncommon. Such graves are often earlier in date than others within the same cemetery which are oriented in various ways with regard to them and, as the collective evidence from many different cemeteries suggest, indicate the existence

12 Malcolm Todd, *The Northern Barbarians 100 BC–AD 300* (1987), p. 49f.
13 Edward James, "Cemeteries and the Problem of Frankish Settlement in Gaul" (1979), p. 71f.
14 Ibid. Bailey K. Young, "Le problème franc et l'apport des pratiques funéraires (III–Ve siècles)" (1980); Steuer, *Sozialstrukturen*, pp. 342–404.; G, Halsall, "The Origins of the *Reihen-gräberzivilisation*: Forty Years On" (1990).
15 Many of the works already cited refer to this point. See, for example, Steuer, "Archaeology and History", 106f.

of a lord/follower relationship in death as in life.[16] A good example of a rich aristocratic burial is grave 1782 of Krefeld-Gellep.[17] The warrior was buried with a full panoply of weapons including helmet, ring-handled long-sword (often taken to indicate a *comitatus* bond at the highest level),[18] lance, throwing axe and long knife. Other grave goods included a bronze jug, glassware, two small eating knives, a bronze hanging bowl and a wooden bucket with bronze fittings used for the distribution of liquor. This early sixth century grave is unusual for its richness but the overall pattern is typical of sixth and seventh century warrior burials which very frequently demonstrate links between weapons, social status and drinking utensils. The same is true of Anglo-Saxon England.[19]

Modifications occurred over time. Among seventh century Franks, for example, the burial of drinking vessels was gradually phased out, a development suggestive of Christian influence, and in the eighth century the deposition of grave goods ceases completely in much of western and central Europe.[20] There are exceptions. Saxony, northern German areas and the Scandinavian countries continue the older forms. Overall, however, it is reasonable to suppose that in the governing centers of the eighth century Frankish empire the lady with a mead cup had lost much of her original significance.[21] Greater complexity and bureaucracy would quickly have rendered her old-fashioned although certain of her aspects, titular control of the treasury, for example, or the yearly distribution of gifts to retainers, may have lasted longer.[22] Some retention of earlier practices is to be expected among contemporary local nobilities of the continent and England and the lady never really disappears among the Celts. The Vikings will maintain her for a long time too, just as they will continue the warband connection with drinking vessels and weapon burial. In Viking Age cemeteries, the combination of the bucket-container for distribution together with long-handled sieve and

16 Heiko Steuer, "Helm und Ringschwert. Prunkbewaffnung und Rangabzeichen germanischer Krieger, Eine Übersicht" (1987); Idem, "Interpretationsmöglichkeiten", pp. 225-240.
17 Renate Pirling, *Das römisch-fränkische Gräberfeld von Krefeld-Gellep 1960-63* (1974); James, "Cemetaries", pp. 79-83.
18 See the works cited in note 16.
19 Härke, " 'Warrior Graves' ", p. 37f.; Idem, "Early Saxon Weapon Burials: Frequencies, Distributions and Weapon Combinations" (1989).
20 Frauke Stein, *Adelsgräber des achten Jahrhunderts in Deutschland* (1967).
21 As D.A. Bullough pointed out, her presence seems to be "conspicuously lacking" in the Carolingian royal and imperial family. "Friends, Neighbors and Fellow-drinkers", p. 16f. Bureaucracy, the influence of churchmen with their own ideas of appropriate ritual, more complex notions of rank and the presence of many different leaders of varying status and relationships to the ruler, will all have played a role in her decline. The complexities of empire encourage other kinds of approaches to representations of authority and precedence although a concern for older types of ceremony may well linger for a long period.
22 For the yearly gift, see Timothy Reuter "Plunder and Tribute in the Carolingian Empire" (1985). One also wonders as to how long she was regarded as "nurse to the young men" in the *palatium*. Janet Nelson, "Queens as Jezebels", p. 47f.

drinking horn or cup remains very common as earlier on the continent.[23] Iconography makes this association especially clear. Beginning with the fourth or fifth century drinking horn from Gallehus and continuing to the end of the eleventh century, one of the most favored Scandinavian depictions is that of a female figure presenting a warrior (often on a horse) with a drinking horn.[24] One of her hands is usually shown raised in the offering gesture and in the other she sometimes carries a bucket. Woman, drinking horn and bucket containing a long-handled sieve all appear on the Halla Broa XVI picture stone, for example, a depiction which suggests that she had just passed a horn to a seated figure. The recent discovery of 2,300 stamped gold foils (*guldgubber*) from Sorte Muld (Bornholm) also offers significant new support for the present interpretation. Some of these small foils, roughly datable to circa 600, depict an aristocratic female in special costume bearing a drinking horn as attribute and a male figure sometimes holding a Frankish style drinking glass and sometimes a "long scepter". Although a complete archaeological analysis of this find has not yet been published, it has already attracted the attention of a number of scholars and a consensus is building which links the foils to "organized cult" and "ceremony" at royal and religious centers, sites whose politico-religious importance has only recently come to be recognized.[25]

In all of the regions of the Germanic world, from northern Scandinavia to Lombardy, a similar kind of rich or upper class lifestyle centered on the hall and its *Hallenfreude*, the "delight" of the hall, seems to have existed. This can be documented in various ways but the late Hayo Vierck did so through a survey of the costly glass remains found in and around some eight different halls of the late Iron Age and Viking periods.[26] A good example of such a site is that from the second to fifth century settlement of Westick, Kreis Unna. A large hall, forty-eight meters long and eight to twelve wide, was erected here, probably in the middle of the fifth century. At its front end, it also contained an installation for a ruler's high-seat. The remains of numerous expensive glasses were also found in the area, a pattern which remained consistent for the other halls. Not all of these buildings were (or were continually) warband halls. Some seem to have been used by merchants joined in a protective group in which cultic drinking rituals reinforced solidarity and vows of allegiance. It is clear, however, that the fortunate

23 Detlev Ellmers, "Zum Trinkgeschirr der Wikingerzeit" (1964/65).
24 Discussed in Birgit Arrhenius, "Zum symbolischen Sinn des Almandin im früheren Mittelalter" (1969).
25 Ellmers, "Trinkgeschirr", p. 26; Margarethe Watt, "Die Goldblechfiguren ("guldgubber") aus Sorte Muld" (1992); Idem, "Sorte Muld. Hövdingesaede og kultcentrum fra Bornholms yngre jernalder" (1991); Karl Hauck, "Frühmittelalterliche Bildüberlieferung und der organisierte Kult" (1992); Per O. Thomsen, "Die Goldblechfiguren ("guldgubber") der vierten Lundeborg-Grabung 1989" (1992); Karl Hauck, "Altuppsalas Polytheismus examplarisch erhellt mit Bildzengnissen des 5.–7. Jahrhunderts" (1994) esp. pp. 245–84.
26 Vierck, "Hallenfreunde".

lifestyle displayed by the material remains was very similar over many tribal areas and territories so that it may justifiably be described as trans-regional and, although somewhat anachronistically, international.

Even this very brief sketch of selected aspects of the archaeological evidence indicates the historical reliability of many of the central themes discussed in the first three chapters—even when the literary works themselves are later than the period described. The material evidence is critically important for it demonstrates the continuity of certain organizational and life modes over an entire millennium and in regions and at times for which there is no literary evidence whatsoever. The culture of the Viking period in the North is the tail end of a process which began for Germans in the late pre-Roman Iron Age.

Consider, for example, that something very much like *comitatus* organization probably existed in certain areas of Germania in the first century BC as Karl Peschel and others have argued.[27] The sex-segregated cemeteries of the period containing weapons demonstrate quite clearly that the concept of biological kinship as an organizational concept had been replaced for many with something else. Some have argued against warband influence because these cemeteries are very large and contain too many burials. But the contrasting possibility, that of men's clubs, does not seem completely convincing since such groups are usually closely connected with tribal concepts of kinship and not commonly with a deliberate and drastically separate type of association and burial which, in this case, would also seem to be intended as a means of separating kin in the afterlife. Nothing, on the other hand, forbids a combination of the two ideas or, probably more likely, a combination of more egalitarian warband burial with the burial of larger numbers of lower status clients heavily dependant on a particular patron who is also a *comitatus* leader. Both types of organization were well known and clearly defined in contemporary Gaul and other Celtic territories where powerful men might control a large warband but also be capable of assembling far larger numbers of clients. As a corollary, one would need to posit a high degree of control over such clients on the assumption that they would otherwise have chosen to be buried with relatives. As far as can be determined, both the warband principle and the appearance of sex-segregated cemeteries are contemporaneous developments and that supports the view of a connection between them. As we shall see in the following section, the warband form of organization is more flexible than many historians (and the archaeologists who have followed them) have supposed.

So far we have seen that the warrior lifestyle, connected with drinking displays, hierarchy, luxury containers and warband organization is a phenomena which

27 Karl Peschel, "Die Sueben in Ethographie und Archäologie" (1978); "Frühe Waffengräber im Gebiet der südlichen Elbgermanen" (1977); *Anfänge germanischer Besiedlung im Mittelgebirgsraum. Sueben-Hermunduren-Markomannen* (1978); Reinhard Wenskus, "Die neuere Diskussion um gefolgschaft und Herrschaft in Tacitus' *Germania*" (1992); Steuer, "Interpretationsmöglichkeiten"; Dieter Timpe, "Der Sueben-Begriff bei Tacitus" (1992).

lasts for more than a millennium among some cultures of the Germanic North—
although it loses ground much earlier at the continental core. But what about the
lady with her status ritual whom we have posited as belonging at the center of all
of this? It is, of course, very difficult to prove her kind of ceremonial behavior
from material remains alone. Nonetheless, some persuasive clues are available. In
a recent discussion of assemblies of objects appearing in women's graves, Max
Martin called attention to the way in which small objects, like keys of iron, bronze
and silver, usually attached to a ring at a woman's belt, served as status symbols.[28]
He pointed out that the same principle applied to spoon-sieves or spoon-strainers
carried on the same ring or chain. These instruments were well known in the
Mediterranean world where they might be carried by servers of either sex at feasts
or even brought by the guests themselves. In Germania, the situation was
different. The spoon-sieve there was an exclusively female object and is never
found in men's graves.[29] It also must have been an important status symbol for it
is only found in richer female graves. This radical difference in cultural mentality
is worth emphasizing. Whereas Romans did not assign the object to either sex,
the Germans did, and whereas the Romans thought of it as a simple table
instrument, the Germans, who associated liquor with rank and aristocratic
lifestyle, make it a status symbol for the upper class. The spoon-sieve appears in
burials from the late Roman period through the seventh century when the upper
class avidly took to the drinking of wine. The most beautifully decorated example
comes from Kent in southeastern England.[30] A different form of the object was
known earlier in the North, however. Attention has already been drawn to the
aristocratic woman's grave at Juellinge from the Lübsow horizon. As we now
recognize, the connection there between strainer and female rank was made
doubly manifest by those who buried her by placing it in the woman's right hand.
Similar long-handled sieves, sometimes made partly or completely of wood, also
appear in Viking Age graves and iconography.[31] The spoon-sieve, therefore, is a
peculiarly upper class female symbol of rank which has virtually no meaning
unless we accept a close link between women and the control and distribution of
drink. It is, in itself, a sign of prestige and another example of the continuity
between early Germania and the age of *Beowulf*.

28 Max Martin, "Bemerkungen zur Ausstattung der Frauengräber und zur Interpretation der
    Doppelgräber und Nachbestattungen im frühen Mittelalter" (1990); "Weinsiebchen und
    Toilettgerät" (1984); Birgit Dubner-Manthey, "Zum Amulettbrauchtum in frühmittelalter-
    lichen Frauen- und Kindergräbern (1990).
29 Martin, "Frauengräber", p. 94f.; "Weinsiebchen", p. 116. Larger examples of this symbolic
    instrument were well known in the Hallstatt and La Tène periods where they frequently appear
    with drinking vessels of various kinds. In the early medieval period, their distribution reaches
    from Britain through Northern Gaul, the Rhineland, southern Germany and Switzerland to
    Bohemia, Hungary and Italy. They appear to have been less common in middle and northern
    Germania where more perishable types were probably used.
30 Martin, "Weinsiebchen", p. 108.
31 Ellmers, "Trinkgeschirr", p. 26f.

A close link between women, the serving of liquor and the creation of fictive kinship is also demonstrable through the analysis of some peculiar drinking vessels called *Ringgefässe*.[32] These have a very long but obscure tradition in the Mediterranean world, especially the eastern Mediterranean, where they have been connected with fertility cults and the idea of a mystic marriage with a goddess.[33] Roman examples from the first century onwards have been found in the Rhineland and Britain.[34] They are rarer in the migration period but are found often enough in widely distributed graves of the Thuringians, Alemanni and Franks to demonstrate that they had a specific and well understood purpose.[35] Appropriately named, the *Ringgefässe* are characterized by a hollow ceramic ring which serves as both container and base. Upon this ring are mounted three (usually) cup-shaped containers with openings on the bottom so that liquor poured into any one cup will fill both the hollow ring and the cups on top of it as well. This type of vessel has a number of relatives worth mentioning. Among them are *Drillingsgefässe*, triple cup assemblies, in which the cups, steins or various kinds of containers are joined together and whose handles may occasionally intertwine.[36] Many have internal drilled holes to ensure that the same liquor mingles in each. Another type is the open circular vessel whose outer circumference extrudes three further containers at equidistant points.[37] A more distant cousin is the jug with three spouts for pouring instead of one.[38] All of these are known from the early medieval period or earlier. Some, like the *Drillingsgefässe*, are found among many different cultures throughout the world and were already being crafted in the late Neolithic. They continued to be produced in Central and Eastern Europe through the nineteenth century.

Neither *Ringgefässe* nor *Drillingsgefässe* were easy to manufacture and are far too unusual and complicated to have ever been suitable for ordinary usage. This explains their relative scarcity; they were preserved for special occasions and, one should note, many kinds were fragile and easily broken so that the small numbers that remain are only an indication of what once existed. In fact, they were ritual vessels used in the creation of fictive brotherhood and sisterhood. One sees this

32 A very useful, although now somewhat dated, discussion is that of Ernst Grohne, *Die Koppel-, Ring- und Tüllengefäse: Ein Beitrag zur Typologie und Zweckgeschichte keramischer Formen* (1932).

33 The eastern Mediterranean types were not meant for cultic drinking, however, whereas the northern examples were. See Elizabeth Ruttkay, "Ein urgeschichtliches Kultgefäss vom Jennyberg bei Mödling/Niederösterreich" (1974).

34 Waldemar Haberey, "Ein römisches Ringgefäss aus Kärlich, Landkreis Koblenz" (1952); P. Kupka, "Zwei germanische Tonlampen aus der Altmark" (1910).

35 Günter Behm-Blancke, "Trankgaben und Trinkzeremonien im Totenkult der Völkerwanderungszeit" (1979), p. 180f.; Pirling, *Krefeld-Gellep*, p. 99f.

36 Grohne, *Koppel-, Ring- und Tullengefässe*, p. 32f.

37 For a seventh century example, see Günter Behm-Blancke, "Das Priester- und Heiligengrab von Schlotheim. Zur Strategie und Mission der Franken in Nordthüringen" (1989), p. 217.

38 Or see the photo of the fourth century glass jug depicted in Renate Pirling, *Römer und Franken am Neiderrhein* (1986), p. 87.

most readily in the case of the *Drillingsgefässe* for they were not especially unusual during the late medieval and modern periods when they were used by some *Dutzbrüderschaften*, brotherhood groups in which arms were sometimes linked while drinking, a practice recalled by the intertwined handles of some of the modern triple-cup examples.[39] From the High Middle Ages, they were also linked to trinitarian symbolism and iconography in which Christ might be depicted as triple-headed or triple-faced.[40] The association was made possible by the vessel symbolism itself and also by the fact that God the Father was regarded as the patron of potters since he made man from clay.

Both kinds of associations are indicated for the *Ringgefässe* of the sixth and seventh centuries and earlier. The ritual brotherhood aspect is clearest in a Roman example from Britain where a human arm is shown rising from the foot of one of the ring-cups to grasp the center of the adjacent cup, a process which is repeated.[41] The trinitarian emphasis was also present in this period although it was not Christian. This is shown by the discovery of three *Ringgefässe* in the late Roman stratum of a small temple to the Celto-Germanic triple mothers near Mayen (Rheinland-Pfalz).[42] Only a fragment is preserved of one of these; the second is an especially elegant work (assignable to the third century) with an inscription pointing to a friendship between two women.[43] The third is unusual also since the hollow ring of the base is in the form of a four-spoked wheel, a Celtic symbol of godhood and sacrality, and it is surmounted by five cups, four at the circumference at the end of each spoke and a fifth in the center. It is difficult to understand the reason for the two extra cups in the last example but W. Haberey is probably right to regard it (along with the others) as an instrument belonging to some particular cult practice.[44] Such linkage with women which we find here in the mothers' cult (always linked to three figures) continues into the migration period. With perhaps one or two exceptions, all of the Germanic *Ringgefässe* come from women's graves.[45] This seems to confirm the interpretation frequently made in earlier chapters that women among the Germans were regarded as having a special responsibility for the public ritual creation of brotherhood. The religious significance of that act has already been pointed out. Similarly, all of the modern

39 Haberey, "Ringgefäss", p. 82.
40 Grohne, *Koppel-, Ring- und Tullengefässe*, p. 32f.
41 Haberey, "Ringgefäss", p. 81.
42 Ibid., p. 82.
43 Ibid.
44 Ibid.
45 Renate Pirling refers to an example from a man's grave near the end of the sixth century from Hugstetten, Kreis Freiburg/Br. but notes also that most come from women's graves. Their presence in female graves, she suggests, reduces the possibility of a relationship with the creation of brotherhood but she accepts the association with "magical" behavior. Actually, as I have argued here, the presence of these vessels in women's graves indicates that women were viewed as the proper *creators* of brotherhood. Pirling, *Krefeld-Gellep*, p. 100.

authors who have studied the *Ringgefässe* are agreed that they possess a pronounced religious or magical significance.[46] The ring, of course, is the most
perfect symbol of completion. By analogy, the drink which it contains, the
identical drink in each of the three cups, symbolizes the same perfection of unity
to be achieved by those who share it together. The ultimate justification for the
three cups is the same stress on unity again, only this time expressed through the
concept of the separate aspects of a triune deity or deities, an indication of the
way in which three might function as one.[47]

The *Drillingsgefässe* seem not to have had the same personal identification with
women but appears nonetheless to have possessed it at some times and places.
Perhaps the same can be said with regard to association with a triplicate or triune
deity. Such would seem to be a fair interpretation of the evidence from the grave
of an aristocratic woman of the Alemanni from Güttingen (Kreis Konstanz) from
the end of the sixth century.[48] The rich grave of this middle aged female occupied
a special place in the cemetery in that a number of other graves were oriented in
a half moon around it. The deceased wore a valuable necklace which included
three gold bracteates (coin-like amulets) each of which depicted the likeness of
an identical or near identical male head. According to Gerhard Fingerlin, from
whose complete catalogue the present partial description is drawn, each amulet
was created from the same model with slight differences ensuing because of later
touch-up.[49] From a chain attached to the woman's belt hung a small knife, a
number of other amulets and objects and an especially ornate spoon-sieve which
showed clear signs of long usage. At her pelvis were found two unusually large
disc broaches which seem to have originally been cut from late Roman silver
plates. One shows an imperial head in flat relief; the second depicts a rider
carrying a long cross on his right shoulder. Below the woman's feet lay a
Drillingsgefäss, three grouped cups joined by short pipes. Among other grave
goods were more conventional drinking implements and a ladle for serving. A
spindle whorl used in weaving was found on her chest and the remains of some
woven fabric (now completely decayed) was found over a bronze pan which also
lay at her feet.

The Güttingen grave is especially significant for several reasons. It draws
together a number of pertinent themes presented above but it also provides
valuable clues to an underlying mentality which is only found in bits and pieces,
the shards of a tradition, in a few later Christian literary sources. For one thing,

46 See the views expressed by Grohne, Haberey, Pirling and Behm-Blancke in the works cited
   above and, in addition: Tone Knez, "Neue Hallstattzeitliche Pseudokernoi aus Novo Mesto"
   (1974). Knez describes these as "emphatically cultic vessels" designed "very probably" for
   ritual drinking. He wonders if the buried woman should not be described as a "priestess".
47 This is essentially Haberey's formulation: "Ringgefäss", p. 82.
48 Gerhard Fingerlin, "Grab einer adligen Frau aus Güttingen" (1964).
49 Ibid., p. 38.

the lady's high status is unmistakable; it is shown by the conjunction of luxury grave goods with placement in the cemetery. That this status should also be associated with liquor service and fictive brotherhood is suggested by the spoon-sieve, ladle and *Drillingsgefäss*. In addition, however, the religious element, actu-ally the peculiarly female religious element, is very strong in the find so that it may be justifiable to go beyond Fingerlin's description of her as an "aristocratic woman" and suggest the possibility that she also fitted, although probably only in part, into a much older religious as well as social pattern. No single object from her grave leads ineluctably in this direction—except perhaps the *Drillingsgefäss* —but the presence of bracteate amulets, *Drillingsgefäss*, cross-bearing rider, spindle whorl, and woven material together do point to that possibility, for all seem to belong to a cultic context which has never been fully explained. This hypothesis will require a demonstration so that we may now turn to an examina-tion of the cultural connections of these Güttingen artifacts as a means toward more fully explaining their historical implications.

Although bracteates are also found in men's graves, they appear to have been worn far more often by women.[50] As amulets, they serve the religious purpose of warding evil or drawing supernatural support. The presence of the three "iden-tical" male head bracteates in conjunction with the three cups of the *Drillingsge-fäss* is difficult to accept as coincidence, however, for each seems to emphasize the same concept of triune unity.[51] The presence of the cut-out disc brooch depicting a rider bearing a long cross makes it possible to see this as evidence of Christian influence but that view requires nuance for the associational background and meaning of such objects in southern Germanic culture of the time is not what it was for the Mediterranean. Both bracteates and triple vessels antedate Christi-anity in northern Europe and neither plays much of a role in the only superficially understood mixed conversion-era mentality of sixth-century Germania. The trinitarian doctrine is especially troublesome here for it is the most esoteric of all Christian beliefs and its integration and effect on the Germanic cultures of different regions is a matter of guesswork. It is clear, on the other hand, that the remarkable concept of triune deities was well known in Iron Age Europe for triplicate heads and figures have been found scattered in many areas of La Tène culture on the continent and the British Isles.[52] We have already seen that this concept may be associated with the *Ringgefässe* of the late Roman period in the

50 Karl Hauck, *Die Goldbrakteaten der Völkerwanderungszeit I. Einleitung* (1985), p. 15f. Some further commentary in my review of this work in *Speculum* 63 (1988), p. 405f.
51 G. Behm-Blancke, "Heiligengrab von Schlotheim", p. 214f., prefers to regard the possible trinitarian conception as unproven even when the *Drillingsgefäss* is added to the evidence. Since both bracteates and vessel have undoubted religious significance, however, it seems to me that the triune concept in one form or another was meant to be understood.
52 See Anne Ross, *Pagan Celtic Britain: Studies in Iconography and Tradition* (1968²), pp. 61–127; Pierre Lambrechts, *L'Exaltation de la Tête dans la Pensée et dans l'art des Celtes* (1954).

Celto-Germanic cult of the triple mothers. From the Christian viewpoint, therefore, the most judicious deduction would seem to be that a conceptual evolution
may have taken place which maintained a connection with women, bracteates and
triple cup vessels while otherwise moving towards religious syncretism.

Consider, for example, the ways in which a "cross" can be depicted in
Alemannic culture and the way in which it can be associated with a prophetic
goddess who appears on bracteate amulets which, as in the Güttingen case, are
more commonly found in women's graves. One of these in the so-called category
of "Fürstenberg type"[53] bracteates derives from an unknown site in southwestern
Germany where it was originally found before 1855.[54] It depicts an enthroned,
large breasted female figure with skirt wearing a crown-like hairstyle and with an
Echoform of Byzantine diadem. In each hand she carries two very curious
cross-like objects which resemble the cross-staff and *globus cruciger* carried in
formal portraiture by the Byzantine emperor.[55] The ultimate model for these
amulets clearly lies in the East but the iconographic message has been adapted to
Germanic culture where the emperor has been replaced by a woman. This is also
shown by the fact that the long "cross" carried in the female figure's right hand
has crossbars on both top and bottom of the staff and such placement is
completely irreconcilable with orthodox thinking. The bracteate craftsman who
had originally seen the Byzantine depictions of the emperor's cross-staff did not
understand their significance but had reworked them to fit a familiar context with
a religious non-commercial meaning. It may be suggested that what the female
figure is actually carrying is not a long cross, however, but rather a weaving beam,
the shaft at the top of the warp weighted loom from which hangs the warp of
wool or flax to be woven into cloth.[56] Such looms were commonly used in Iron
Age and Early Medieval Europe and continued to be used in Scandinavian
countries into the twentieth century.[57] Larger weaving beams were sometimes
equipped with crossbars at one or both ends in order to facilitate the raising or
lowering of work frequently made quite heavy by scores of dangling loom weights.
As far as one can tell, peoples of Germanic culture always associated such looms
with the warp and woof of fate and the women who worked them were often
associated with magic.[58] Weaving implements like distaffs, spindles and whorls

53 Michael Enright, "The Goddess Who Weaves: Some Iconographic Aspects of Bractates of the
    Fürstenberg Type" (1990). Photos of these appear in the article but the fullest analysis will be
    found in the relevant volumes of Morten Axboe, Klaus Düwell, Karl Hauck, Lutz von Padberg
    et al., *Die Goldbrakteaten der Völkerwanderungszeit. Ikonographischer Katalog (= IK 1–3),
    Enleitungsband sowie je I Text und je I Tafelband* (1985ff.).
54 I refer to Enright, "Goddess who Weaves", p. 55f., for convenience but Hauck's catalogue, as
    noted above, must be consulted for finer details.
55 Ibid.
56 Ibid., p. 62f.
57 Full discussion in Marta Hoffmann, *The Warp-Weighted Loom. Studies in the History and
    Technology of an Ancient Instrument* (1964).
58 Enright, "Goddess who Weaves", p. 65f. with notes.

were thereby associated with prophecy and prophetesses in the Germanic tradition (and in the Celtic as well) and such women are often described as carrying them.[59] A weaving beam is therefore an appropriate symbol of divine prophetic talent although it does not always need to have crossbars. A variant of this bracteate type from Gudme, Fünen, shows the same figure carrying a long staff without bars.[60]

Here, then, in southern Germania, we find "crosses" associated with golden amulets, women, prophecy and magic so that it is clear that the religious context is quite different from what one might expect if one approached the question from the viewpoint of the Mediterranean tradition alone. The bracteate craftsman who saw portraits of the cross-bearing emperor on Byzantine coins transformed this depiction into that of a prophetic goddess carrying a weaving beam with cross-bars. At Güttingen, it may be suggested, we see another variation of the same process. Another craftsman has snipped the late Roman silver plate portraits of imperial head and cross-bearing rider to be made into brooches for a woman's clothing but that hardly means that she actually worshipped the emperor any more than the three bracteate heads, which may represent the Christian trinity, means that she was a convinced and knowing Christian. She was simply trying to ward evil and bring good luck by using symbols which are commonly interpreted within a purely Christian framework but which, since we know how other contemporary imperial portraits were interpreted in traditional Alemannic religion, may no longer be routinely explained in such a manner. The cross-bearing rider, as suggested by the imperial head for the other brooch, is close enough to the cross-bearing emperor to make sense. It seems clear, on the other hand, that the Güttingen female had been exposed to Christian ideas and knew something about them. More than anything else, she seems to have been a figure living in a syncretistic conversion period which easily gave rise to confused situations and surprising interpretive cross currents. She was certainly deeply interested in cultic paraphenalia.

A similar conceptual scheme is deducible from the "*globus cruciger*" in the Southwest Germany bracteate since it is not really a cross-surmounted globe at all but rather a flat-bottomed hemisphere which seems to resemble a swift, a common tool used by weavers for the winding of yarn.[61] One was buried with the "queen" of the famous Osberg ship.[62] This Fürstenberg type bracteate seems to be a sixth century product and comes from the same general region as the Güttingen burial. Another sixth century variant comes from the same Kreis

59 Ibid., p. 66f.
60 Morten Axboe, "Die Brakteaten von Gudme II" (1987), Tafel XIII, XIV.
61 On swifts, see Hoffmann, *Warp-Weighted Loom*, pp. 288–95. The late OE text *Gerefa* calls this tool *garnvinda*.
62 Thorleif Sjövold, *Der Oseberg-Fund und die anderen Wikingerschiffsfunde* (1958).

Konstanz in which Güttingen lies so that, considering the Gudme find, it now seems correct to speak of an actual widespread cult which emphasizes reverence for a staff-bearing prophetic goddess. All of the other hundreds of known bracteates feature divine and non-human figures, as Karl Hauck has shown, so that it is highly unlikely that these are exceptions.

The presence of spindle whorl and cloth in the Güttingen grave are further indications that it belongs to the context outlined above. Another Fürstenberg bracteate from the north-east, from Oberwerschen, Kreis Hohenmölsen, for example, shows the goddess standing with both hands raised.[63] The right is open in a gesture which can be identified as a signal for epiphany while the other holds a weaving sword, an implement used to manipulate threads on the loom.[64] Once again, it appears justifiable to connect this figure with prophecy, an act which is symbolized in Germanic culture by the carrying of weaving tools. In all of the cases cited, however, the "cross" is also present in some form or another and that is why one can make the connection with Güttingen. But it is not understood as a Christian symbol. In the Oberwerschen bracteate, for example, two "crosses" appear on the lower right perimeter but they seem unconnected with the goddess and look more like starfish than anything else. No convinced Christian would have depicted them in this way and it appears probable that the craftsman is working in an entirely different tradition. The fact that Fürstenberg type bracteates are only found in women's graves supports this view—for such would hardly be the case in Christianity—as also does, to a lesser extent, the *Drillingsgefäss*. One cannot maintain of course that this prophetic women's cult possessed the same attributes in all regions of Germania. Although the goddess seems much the same in the examples cited, she is sometimes depicted seated with staff and swift and sometimes shown standing with weaving sword or with upraised hands. The contours of the cult are unclear and subtleties escape us. A few literary sources help us to understand the mentality underlying the religious conceptions but they are completely silent on the cult itself and it is only through the analysis of the most diverse kinds of clues that any explanation becomes possible.

It may, on the other hand, be suggested that certain aspects of this cult may have had a long tradition in southern German regions although the evidence lies far back in early La Tène, that is, nine hundred to one thousand years earlier. The connection between women and various peculiar looking staffs and containers goes back at least that far in European prehistory, however, so that no matter how one interprets the evidence, the *pattern* of continuity between the southern

---

63 Enright, "Goddess who Weaves", p. 57. The woman's grave in which this bractate was found must also be connected with ritual and cult. See Berthold Schmidt, "Opferplatz und Gräberfeld des 6. Jahrhunderts bei Oberwerschen, Kreis Hohenmölsen" (1966).

64 Karl Gross, *Menschenhand und Gotteshand in Antike und Christentum* (1985), p. 19f. On weaving swords and their symbolism, see Max Martin, *Das fränkische Gräberfeld von Basel-Bernerring* (1976), p. 91f.; Wilfried Menghin, *Die Langobarden. Archaologie und Geschichte* (1985), p. 72.

German bracteate depictions and drinking vessels and the material of the earlier period is demonstrably present. As evidence, let us examine grave 118 of the Dürrnberg near Hallein, Austria.[65]

This rich female grave of the fifth century BC contained a large number of amulets, among them various kinds of animal teeth, stones and no less than a dozen snail shells.[66] In addition to brooches, rings and pots, it also contained a staff with hanging chains and a peculiar *Ringgefäss*. The wooden staff, 48.5 cm long and 0.7–1.1 cm in diameter, has small bronze knobs at top and bottom. A small loop is attached just beneath the upper knob and from it hang two 14.2 cm long chains. These are joined in turn to a flat half moon pendant from which hang three more chains (to about 21 cm long) tipped with three identical little club-like danglers. Two such staffs may once have existed at the cemetery of Hallstatt but it is difficult to be sure because of the disappearance of the wood. This staff type, however, together with a related type with ornamented top but without chains, derives from Italy and spread from there into southern Alpine regions and then eastward.[67] Others of these types, in whole or part, are known from such sites as Bologna, Este-Alfonsi, Padua, Montebelluna, Caversano, Albate (Como), Belmonte (Ascoli P.) while several others come from Slovenia and four from Hungary.[68] A staff of the second type was also found in grave 59 of the Dürrnberg and is comparable to one from Bargen, Kreis Konstanz—once again Konstanz—and Münsingen (Bern).[69]

Although von Duhn and Messerschmidt have called them "scepters", the connotation of political power seems unwarranted and Ludwig Pauli has rightly opted for "cult staff".[70] Apart from two children's graves (a four to five year old girl might also be buried with one of these staffs) and one of uncertain sex, such staffs "are always found in very rich female graves" and scholars appear to be agreed that "a cultic meaning must also be ascribed to them".[71] But the exact significance of the staff is unclear. It obviously serves no practical purpose but must nonetheless have had a symbolic association with leading women. Pauli thinks in terms of communal ritual and festival while E. Jerem has proposed links with a Venetic fertility goddess, an hypothesis which seems consonant with the

65 Ludwig Pauli, *Der Dürrnberg bei Hallein III. Auswertung der Grabfunde* (1978), pp. 530–2.
66 Ibid. There seems to be a correlation between women's graves, the occasional presence of snail shells and ideas of driving off hostile influences. See Ludwig Pauli, *Keltischer Volksglaube. Amulette und Sonderbestattungen am Dürrnberg bei Hallein und im eisenzeitlicher Mitteleuropa* (1975), p. 138f., 179f.
67 Ibid., pp. 531, 269–73.
68 Ibid., 270; Friedrich von Duhn, Franz Messerschmidt, *Italische Gräberkunde* (1939), p. 53f.
69 Pauli, *Dürrnberg*, p. 270.
70 von Duhn, Messerschmidt, *Gräberkunde*, p. 53f.; Pauli, *Dürrnberg*, p. 270.
71 See the works cited in note 70 and also E. Jerem, "Späteisenzeitliche Grabfunde von Beremend (Komitat Baranya)" (1973), p. 82; Idem, "The late Iron Age Cemetery of Szentlörinc" (1968), p. 187.

accumulated evidence even if one is doubtful about identification with any one particular divine figure.[72] Some type of religious or magical usage is indicated, particularly when one looks at the well-preserved Libna example (Slovenia) with its six hanging chains and diverse hanging amulets.[73]

Once again, the weaving context provides the most satisfactory interpretive scheme. The unique thing about these staffs, as with those on the bracteate depictions, is that they are nearly always found in female graves but also show up among various peoples at various times. Any answer must therefore fulfill the following criteria: it must find a common denominator linking women, staffs and magic over a very broad cross-cultural context lasting more than a thousand years. So stated, the only sufficient solution appears to be weaving. David Herlihy collected scores of supportive references from Middle Eastern cultures, from Greeks, Romans, Celts and Germans.[74] The earliest depictions north of the Alps seem to be the sixth-century BC pottery designs from Sopron in northwest Hungary.[75] One shows a woman working at an upright loom, while the other depicts a woman holding a long skein of wool from which dangles a spindle with whorl. The association with prophecy and the magical arts also seems constant. It might seem difficult to associate these phenomena with such perishable materials as wool, cloth and wooden weaving tools but the literature is actually quite rich in supportive clues. In his sixth-century *In Gloria Confessorum*, Gregory of Tours refers to a pagan sacred lake on Mons Helarius in the Gevaudan. The surrounding populace used to gather there for a three day festival which included animal sacrifice and offerings thrown into the lake. These offerings included tufts of unspun wool and woven cloth,[76] very probably a practice of considerable age. It also seems natural to associate weaving with "binding" and "loosing" spells, for example, and that principle might be applied to medicine: "For cheek disease, take the whorl, with which a woman spinneth, bind on the man's neck with a woolen thread";[77] or in other instances when "linen cloth" or "yarn thread" appear in the magical charms of Anglo-Saxon England.[78] Other studies support this view. In a recent paper, P. Scardigli observed that most of the runic inscriptions of the Suebic-Alemannic region derive from women's graves and appear on brooches, boxes or other feminine objects. One interesting example

72 Jerem, "Szentlörinc", p. 187 n. 103; Idem, "Beremend", p. 82 n. 78.

73 Pauli, *Dürrnberg*, p. 271.

74 David Herlihy, *Opera muliebria: Women and Work in Medieval Europe* (1990), pp. 25–48.

75 These are often reproduced. See, for instance, Stuart Piggot, *Ancient Europe* (1973²), p. 198.

76 Ad quem certo tempore multitudo rusticorum, quasi libamina lacui illi exhibens, lenteamina proieciebat ac pannos, qui ad usum vestimenti virile praebentur. . . . Gregory of Tours, *Liber in gloria confessorum*. MGH SS rer. Meror. 1(2)(1885), p. 299.

77 For examples and discussion, see Valerie I.J. Flint, *The Rise of Magic in Early Medieval Europe* (1991), p. 286f.; Audrey L. Meaney, *Anglo-Saxon Amulets and Curing Stones* (1981), p. 8f., 46f., 181–9.

78 Flint, *Magic*, p. 303.

comes from a loom fragment in a sixth century grave. Scardigli associates this with a widespread practice of consulting female diviners and so does S. Flowers in his recent book on runes.[79] One is also reminded of another weaving tool, a sley made of yew wood from Westeremden (Groningen) which probably dates to the late eight century. It bears two names in runic script and the context of yew wood, runes and weaving would seem to associate it with magic.[80] It all becomes more likely when one considers the many clerical condemnations recently discussed by David Herlihy and Valerie Flint. St. Eligius objected to women who sought supernatural power at the loom, in dying and in textile work, while Hincmar of Rheims associated weaving skills, colored threads and garments with the equipment of witches.[82] The penitential literature frequently forbids female "observances" while weaving, or making "consultations" of "woolen work" or the "vanities" and "incantations" of the "threads of the warp and of the woof".[83] As a small but indicative detail of the kind of continuity under discussion, one can also point to the fact that Hincmar of Rheims speaks of witches using snail shells in their work, a point which recalls the presence of a dozen snail shells in grave 118 of the Dürrnberg.

Considering the relatively small size of the Dürrnberg staffs, however, they do not represent the far larger weaving beam but rather the simple distaff. And the narrow chains, similar to hanging skeins of wool or flax in any case, are durable signs of hanging threads. Even those with ornamented ends and without the chains are a variant perfectly fitted to this milieu since distaffs were often provided with hooks, knobs, eyelets or projections to anchor the ball of wool from which hung the spindle with its whorl as flywheel and weight.[84] A further clue, mentioned by von Duhn and Messerschmidt but not followed up by them, is the fact that whorls and spindles may be found in conjunction with the staffs in Italian graves.[85] The two scholars interpreted this as an indication of the sex of the deceased without realizing that it also says something about the function of the

79 Piergiuseppe Scardigli, "Das Problem der suebischen Kontinuität und die Runeninschrift von Neudingen/Baar" (1986), p. 51; Stephen E. Flowers, *Runes and Magic: Magical Formulaic Elements in the Older Runic Tradition* (1986), p. 241f. Valerie Flint (*Magic*, p. 250) notes that the female magicians seem to appear "quite often" in Germanic areas.

80 R.W.V. Elliot, "Runes, Yews and Magic", (1991), p. 256. Elliot is cautious but I agree with Flint's opinion in *Magic*, p. 226 and n. 92.

81 Herlihy, *Opera muliebria*, p. 39f.; Flint, *Magic*, pp. 226–8.

82 Flint, *Magic*, pp. 226–8.

83 Ibid.

84 Many illustrations will be found in the photo section of Karl Schlabow, *Textilfunde der Eisenzeit in Norddeutschland* (1976). See especially *Abbildungen*, p. 22–8. In these early cultures in which distaffs and spindles were the most common tools possessed by women and known to all, the sight of a woman carrying a small staff would probably immediately bring both the weaving and magical contexts to mind.

85 von Duhn, Messerschmidt, *Gräberkunde*, p. 54f.

staff. But this proposed solution does not invalidate Jerem's fertility-goddess argument. Although it would take us too far afield to discuss the evidence here, and hence it will be investigated in the following chapter, late ancient Romans, Celts and Germans made very direct and graphic connections between weaving, sexuality and magic.

It is, on the other hand, now convenient to pause in our discussion of the genealogy of the Güttingen objects in order to note a significant relationship between weaving, prophecy and warfare in Germanic thinking. One does not need to repeat what has been said about tribal matrons choosing the time of battle or of Veleda's ceremonial predictions of victory although the improbability of Roman commentators understanding the background of these actions should be emphasized. Part of the background, at least, would seem to be described in the tenth century east Frankish magical formula known as the *First Merseburg Charm*:

> Once the women sat; sat here and there.
> Some made fetters; some restrained the hostile army;
> Some loosed the fetters.
> Free yourself from the fetters, escape the warriors![86]

This charm is much disputed for it may refer to actual physical battle but may also, alternatively, refer to a warding off of the hordes of disease invading the body. In either case, warfare is the central concept and women are involved because the binding and loosing of knots in the sunken weaving hut are interpreted as the magical equivalent of the binding and loosing of warriors on the battlefield. This religious notion of "fettering" must have been very important in Germanic culture for it already appears in Tacitus' laconic description of worship in the sacred groves (*Germania* 39). It appears again in Bede's story (HE IV, 22) of the captured thegn Imma whose fetters kept falling off, leading his captors to suspect that he possessed "loosing spells such as are described in stories". The "spells" turned out to be masses said for him by his brother, a priest. But the vocabulary of weaving has further connotations applied to both the physical and supernatural worlds of conflict. Old English *wigspeda gewiofu* occurs in *Beowulf* and means "web of battle luck" while a woman married off to create an alliance is called *freoðuwebbe*, "peace weaver".[87] The idea of women weaving fate is present in both contrasting metaphors. Old Norse, as in *sigrvefr*, "web of battle", extends the concept even further since the entire weaving loom can be compared to weapons and the act of weaving to the process of slaughter. The poem *Darraðarljóð* refers to the role of the "women's bower" and to weaving by valkyries in the Battle of Clontarf, fought between Scandinavians and Irish in 1014:

---

86 H.D. Schlosser, *Althochdeutsch Literatur* (1970), p. 252.
87 Enright, "Goddess Who Weaves", p. 66.

Blood rains
From the cloudy web
On the broad loom
Of slaughter
The web of man,
Grey as armour,
Is now being woven;
The Valkyries
Will cross it
With a crimson weft

The warp is made
Of human entrails;
Human heads
Are used as weights;
The heddle-rods
Are blood-wet spears;
The shafts are iron-bound,
And arrows are the shuttles.
With swords we will weave.
This web of battle.[88]

After the battle, the valkyrie women ripped their woven cloth from the loom "each keeping the shred she held in her hands". This reference to keeping a piece of the spelled cloth is, apparently, connected with the magic itself and helps to explain the appearance of bits of cloth in graves, as well as that of threads in amulet boxes and remarks about them in written charms. Although she does not cite *Darraðarljóð*, Audrey Meaney's research in the amulet usage of the Anglo-Saxons led her to a similar conclusion: "Scraps of textiles could have been preserved because of the magic powers within them".[89] That is why the church advocated a watch on weaving women; spells were being worked into the fabric. Actually, this category of magic appears to have been very nearly routine. It seems natural to assume that the woman of the house would seek to imbue the clothing made for her husband and children with whatever kinds of protection were available.

Even more significantly, the examples cited in the previous paragraph verify the archaic rationale for consulting women in the men's work of warfare and for the warrior sodality of the *comitatus* in maintaining a prophetess. The man's role was to fight; the woman's role was to protect him with the magic that was peculiarly hers and not accessible to him because it came from the *gynaeceum*. In addition, of course, Bede's story of Imma, long seen as a picturesque example of

88 The translation is by Magnusson, Palsson, *Njals Saga*, p. 349f.
89 Meaney, *Amulets*, p. 185.

Christian thaumaturgy, can now be seen in a new light, as a very precisely tailored substitution for *female* magic in warfare. Although the prophetess who would have been familiar to the thegn is not mentioned—deliberately not mentioned it would now seem and perhaps even slighted by the reference to *fabula*— it appears probable that the Christian priest is being presented as her proper substitute in the act of military binding and loosing in the same way as a new kind of Christian royal inauguration ritual will soon thereafter be substituted for her traditional liquor offering. I am emboldened to offer this interpretation because Bede's chapters surrounding the Imma story seem consciously designed to offer alternatives to the *pagan* warband system. Chapter 21 of book IV describes how archbishop Theodore brought peace to warring kings "by his wholesome advice". The new peaceweaver is the bishop. IV, 22 recounts the Imma incident; the priest replaces the prophetess. IV, 23 tells the story of Hild, a woman of high birth who might normally have offered the mead cup in secular life. Indeed, it seems quite probable that she did so for Bede says that "she spent her first thirty-three years very nobly in the secular habit". Thereafter, she abandoned the worldly life to become the revered abbess of Whitby. IV, 24 then recounts how Caedmon became a *Christian* poet through the intervention of abbess Hild; the new type of hall *scop* creates wonderfully pious songs but rejects all pagan ones and becomes a monk. The follower, the lady and the poet all appear in these artful chapters and it seems too curious a coincidence not to have been planned since the appearance of the three together indicates both an awareness of the *pagan* warband framework and the existence of a technique designed to modify its traditions. Except for the nuanced spells "described in stories" of the Imma chapter, however, no disquieting references to overt paganism mar the text so that the technique appears to be a variant of the subtle strategy of "exchanges" recommended by pope Gregory in his famous letter to Mellitus. Bede's approach, a damning by exclusion with a substitution remaining as the principle historical clue to the writer's purpose, is also comparable to the description of Wealhtheow in *Beowulf* where only hints of her full character and function are discernible. In this latter text, the magical background of the *comitatus* prophetess is largely submerged in Christian coloring to become part of the deodorized pagan memory of the monastic replacement program.

Grave 118 of the Dürrnberg also contained a *Ringgefäss*. The body of the vessel consists of a hollow ring about 17.2 cm in diameter and 22.7 cm in height. It clearly belongs to the same family of containers described earlier but it is a highly unusual variant (Ludwig Pauli called it "singular in all of La Tène culture") lacking cups or additional spouts.[90] The American reader can easily envision it by imagining a vertical doughnut on a stand surmounted by a conical spout resembling a funnel. Considering both context and form, its affinities also lie with the

90 Pauli, *Dürrnberg*, p. 296.

various kinds of "cult vessels" which, according to E. Ruttkay, are most frequently found in rich graves of the Celtic Hallstatt culture although they are known for long before that.[91] Some of these, like the three "pseudokernoi" found in a rich woman's grave from Novo Mesto are quite close to both the ring vessels and several of their relatives from early medieval Germanic graves.[92]

It may be concluded, therefore, that the manifold links between women, staffs and cultic drinking vessels are not at all peculiar to the *Völkerwanderungszeit* but go back a millennium earlier, sometimes even to the same region of Europe. The Güttingen lady with her spoon-sieve, spindle whorl, *Ringgefäss*, woven cloth and trinitarian bracteates may be considered as a point on a continuum. She seems to look backward to early La Tène and forward to the already vague perhaps fading tradition of Wealhtheow in the *Beowulf* poem. We must, however, further clarify this observation. It can be done by asking the following question: in view of the clearly mixed signals from the Güttingen grave, in view also of the only passing reference to binding spells in Bede and the late date of the *Beowulf* poem, are we still on solid ground in positing continuity in the area of magical weaving tools and textiles after several centuries of Christianization when, presumably, such pagan practices would have been constantly attacked? This may well be the crux of the matter.

A passage from the *Vita Leobae*, written or completed in 836 by Rudolf of Fulda, provides indisputable evidence. Leoba, an Anglo-Saxon woman and relative of St. Boniface, was abbess of Bischofsheim in the diocese of Mainz in the later eighth century. One night, after "she had succeeded in fixing her attention on heavenly things", she had a dream. She saw

> a purple thread issuing from her mouth. It seemed to her that when she took hold of it with her hand and tried to draw it out there was no end to it; and as if it were coming from her very bowels, it extended little by little until it was of enormous length. When her hand was full of thread and it still issued from her mouth she rolled it round and round and made a ball of it.[93]

Leoba knew that there was "some mystery" hidden in this dream and so she sent for explanation to one of her sisters in the convent, "an aged nun who was known to possess the spirit of prophecy, because other things which she had foretold had always been fulfilled". According to the monastic prophetess

---

91 Ruttkay, *Kultgefäss*, p. 47. Related vessels are known from as far back as the Neolithic so that it is clear that we are dealing with long established and widespread cultic conceptions. See further Z. Sochacki, "The Radical-decorated Pottery Culture", (1991), p. 325.

92 Knez, "Pseudokernoi", p. 53.

93 George Waitz, ed. *Vita Leoba* MGH SS 14 (1887), p. 129. The translation is that of C.H. Talbot, *The Anglo-Saxon Missionaries in Germany* (1954), p. 212f.

these things were revealed to the person whose holiness and wisdom made her a worthy recipient, because by her teaching and good example she will confer benefits on many people. The thread which came from her bowels and issued from her mouth signifies the wise counsels that she will speak from the heart. The fact that it filled her hand means that she will carry out in her actions whatever she expresses in her words. Furthermore, the ball which she made by rolling it round and round signifies the mystery of the divine teaching, which is set in motion by the words and deeds of those who give instruction and which turns earthwards through active works and heavenwards through contemplation, at one time swinging downwards through compassion for one's neighbor, again swinging upwards through the love of God. By these signs God shows that your mistress [Leoba] will profit many by her words and example, and the effect of them will be felt in other lands afar off whither she will go.

Here, against the background of the clerical prohibitions of the sixth and seventh centuries and of pagan sources like the *First Merseburg Charm* and *Darraðarljóð*, we find a clear *Christian* statement as to what threads and balls of threads (as well as whorls or spindles) signified in the ninth century. All are still directly linked to prophetic utterances by women. A Christian veneer has been placed over the pattern in that Leoba's thread is said to signify "wise counsels", "divine teaching" and "profit" to others but the fundamental assumptions are hardly modified at all. We thereby see how an apparently innocuous term like *freoðuwebbe*, when applied to women like Wealhtheow, really carries a heavy freight of magical thinking. Note too that the weaving context is extended. The writer is actually internally comparing the "swinging" ball to the thread hanging from the distaff and weighted by whorl and spindle. This passage seems to be unique in that it actually presents us with something of great value—a reliable non-hostile exegesis of an old and widespread European practice. It provides, so to speak, a pagan based (but still acceptably Christian) theological explanation for a traditional but largely hidden world view and the instruments associated with it. Recall again Gregory of Tours and the wool and woven cloth thrown into the sacred lake or the fact that Hincmar of Rheims associated colored thread with the equipment of witches. Because it was accompanied with the right switch in emphasis, ancient suspect usages had been made acceptable to pious monks and nuns. Is the monastic prophetess much different from the bracteate figure with her weaving implements?

If we now turn from the continent to England, from Güttingen and Bischofsheim to Bidford-on-Avon, we find that the trend of the evidence relating to women, liquor, weaving and prophecy remains much the same despite the shift in location. If the spoon-sieves from Kent and elsewhere serve as symbolic designators for the upper end of the aristocracy, there are other potent symbols equally revealing although, perhaps, they may in certain cases be more common somewhat lower down on the social hierarchy. One thinks of the evidence discovered in grave HB2 from the mixed Anglo-Saxon cemetery of Bidford-on-Avon. Some 200 burials were recovered from this site in the 1920s and some twenty more in recent years. 1971 saw the discovery of a young adult female buried at the extreme northern edge of the cemetery with grave goods which point to a date of deposition "probably within the first three-quarters of the sixth century".[94] This matches the Güttingen horizon fairly well as it also does that of the prophetic goddess of the Fürstenburg bracteates.

The Bidford woman was buried with two brooches, a small knife and a woolen garment under her neck. Several dozen glass and amber beads, perhaps originally ornamenting a cord or textile belt, were found in her grave. A damaged triangular "spangle" on a ring and four small alloy tubes were found at her neck area while a disc-shaped pendant and twelve small bucket pendants were found underneath the left shoulder blade. According to Tania Dickinson,[95] these bucket pendants seem to have been contained within a cloth-lined bag or to have been sewn to the cloth exterior of a leather bag. The decayed bag also appears to have originally contained two rings, one of heavy copper alloy and a second of iron, bearing remains of woven animal fiber. A deer antler cone and a stud were also present.

As Meaney and Dickinson point out, "such collections of objects hung from the girdle, with or without a bag, are an established feature of female graves throughout the Germanic world", in Bavaria, Austria, Francia, Thuringia, Iceland and elsewhere.[96] They point to a pan-Germanic set of ideas about females and their spheres of interest and competence. Such bags and similar collections of objects are also known from the Celtic world (as in the La Tène cemetery at Münsingen for example) so that here too there is congruity between Celts and Germans. The contents of such bags lack any clear utilitarian purpose and are normally associated by archaeologists with magic, prophecy and with the "cunning women" of Germanic societies. The twelve miniature bucket pendant amulets from HB2 share this magical character. They contained "remains of spun animal fiber thread" surrounded by a dark brown substance. At least twenty English finds containing bucket pendants can now be catalogued. Most are similar to the Bidford examples and are frequently found in clusters, sets of seven to twelve but occasionally considerably more. They appear to have most often hung from a women's necklace or from her girdle but in other cases might be placed within an attached bag or purse.

The English bucket amulets are always found in womens' (or in a few cases

94 Tania M. Dickinson, "An Anglo-Saxon 'Cunning Woman' from Bidford-on-Avon" in Martin Carver, ed. *In Search of Cult: Archaeological Investigations in Honour of Philip Rahtz* (1993), pp. 45–54 at p. 53.
95 Ibid., p. 51.
96 Dickinson, "Bidford-on-Avon", p. 51; Meaney, *Amulets*, p. 249f.

girls') graves and appear primarily in sixth century Anglian cultural contexts although a late seventh century example comes from Updown, Eastry, Kent. This amulet type is not English alone however; it is found in many regions of the continent and dates from the late Roman Iron Age. It was known in the Przeworsk culture and also to third and fourth century Goths of the Černjachov culture.[97] Schach-Dörges points out that bucket amulets appear among all three Germanic groupings, East, West, and North Germans.[98] They occur in no less than fifteen graves from the fourth century cemetery at Preetz, Kreis Plön, Schleswig-Holstein (where they seem to have been a more typical item of female costume than elsewhere) but other contemporary examples have been found in Niedersachsen and on the Danish islands of Fyn and Sjaelland.[99] They can thus be used to document not only an extensive kind of religious belief but also its persistence over a long span of centuries.

What did the bucket amulets signify in Germanic society? Meaney and Dickinson share a common view. In her discussion, Dickinson points out that "a simple iconographic explanation equates miniature buckets with full-sized ones, and in turn to drink; they might then symbolize the role of alcohol socially and perhaps ritually (as a means of prophetic communication) and women's role within this". She suggests that such interpretation could also be supported by the presence of the antler cone from the bag in HB2 which might symbolize a drinking horn. She notes, however, an objection to this view in the fact that the Bidford amulets contained textile fragments (at least three other examples of this textile in bucket pendant pattern are known) and finds it difficult to explain how they could be related to drink. Nonetheless, she concludes that the bag with miniature buckets and with cloth objects contained within them was a highly potent item which may have conferred or represented specific magical or symbolic functions and probably also have indicated by its emblematic appearance a special role or status for those women who wore them. Martin Carver agrees. He describes HB2 as providing "an exciting and credible confrontation with an Anglo-Saxon 'cunning woman' of the pagan period". He refers to her as a "local priestess".[100] Whatever terminology is used, the "ideology" which surrounded the bucket-with-textile pendants "was highly complex and unlikely to be easily explained".

Hopefully, the previous discussion of symbolic containers, weaving and weaving tools makes this "ideology" more intelligible even if more remains to be done before all aspects are explained. It seems to the present author that it reveals a

---

97 Ibid., p. 167.
98 Helga Schach-Dörges, *Die Bodenfunde des 3. bis 6. Jahrhunderts nach Chr. zwischen unterer Elbe und Oder* (1970), p. 84.
99 John Hines, *The Scandinavian Character of Anglian England in the Pre-Viking Period* (1984), p. 13.
100 In his introduction to *In Search of Cult*, p. vii.

hitherto half-submerged wealth of interpretative possibilities (for both paganism and Christianity) which only a few scholars have ventured to tackle. Both Meaney and Dickinson also make the potentially important observation that graves with large amulet bag collections often occur only once per cemetery.[101] This suggests the possibility that some sizable communities may have maintained their own spaewomen. If so, it provides further reason to believe that each warlord in the developing *comitatus* would have wanted his own. We might here recall that Leoba's monastery of Bischofsheim housed an aged woman "who was known to possess the spirit of prophecy". How often might this have been the case? The *vita* indicates that the nun's exercise of her prophetic talents was not a suspect occupation. On the contrary! It was clearly approved and frequently performed. The very pious Leoba consulted her about a dream "because other things that she had foretold had always been fulfilled". It begins to look as if an approach on this basis might have some consequence for an understanding of early medieval religiosity.

Further support for this view comes from Denmark where Lotte Hedeager has surveyed the archaeological materials from about 500 BC to AD 700/800 in order to form a comprehensive picture of socio-political development. As she points out, a new class of warriors and chieftains to be associated with the *comitatus* developed in Denmark during the later pre-Roman Iron Age. The prestige goods found in their graves are mainly Celtic and signify an evolving pre-eminence in relation to the community and the gods. Both society and religion were profoundly affected by the new institution. The process continued into the Roman Iron Age. Roman prestige goods now replace those of the Celts and the *comitatus* system becomes more dominant and complex over wide regions. A significant point is that warlords with their retinues "are geographically distributed at relatively even distances, so that each of them appears to have controlled an area the size of a *herred* [parish]".[102] In fact, a geographical and chronological survey of grave goods and settlements in several parts of the country can plausibly be interpreted as showing the development of a tiered ranking system from *herred* warlords to those of petty kingdoms. The pattern of change in votive finds are complementary so that it is clear that the new formations in both politics and cult go hand in hand. What now seems more likely is that the geographical pattern of warband distribution in Denmark (and in some parts of northern Germany) should be read in relation to Meaney and Dickinson's observations about the distribution of amulet bags and "cunning women" in Anglo-Saxon England. It all makes sense if one supposes that the warlord/warband/prophetess organization has replaced that of the sacral king, tribal troops

101 Meany, *Amulets*, p. 249; Dickinson, "Bidford-on-Avon", p. 53.

102 Lotte Hedeager, *Iron Age Societies: From Tribe to State in Northern Europe, 500 BC to AD 700* (1992), pp. 161, 243. Although, in my opinion, overly reliant on Marxist historical categories, this is a valuable work.

and tribal matrons of earlier communities. It also suggests that Christian writers like Bede did need to create some form of substitution policy for pagan aspects of the *comitatus* in transalpine Europe.

For the present investigation, these findings also add considerably more force to the picture presented of Wealhtheow in the *Beowulf* poem. Neither the antiquity, continuity, intensity nor popularity of the woman/liquor/prophecy complex can now be seriously doubted. The fact that it seldom clearly appears in the surviving literature says a great deal about the nature of the literature but says nothing useful about the prevalent acceptance of the paradigm among the population groups of the Early Middle Ages. Scrutiny of the archaeological remains suggests that we must be very careful in evaluating evidence from clerically influenced sources; the religious and social reality must often have been considerably different than that which they suggest. In the case of *Beowulf*, however, this judgement may be overly strong. Perhaps it is only to us, unaware of the clues and subtleties, that the author appears to be concealing more than revealing. Or perhaps he was trying to find a *via media* between the censorious opinion of committed ecclesiastics and the more mixed and varied opinions of the laity. It is difficult to reach a conclusion here; the only thing certain is that the image of the lady with a mead cup possessed an incomparably richer and more heterogeneous message for contemporaries than it does for us. It played a far more significant role in archaic Europe than has hitherto been known or suspected.

But why should this now demonstrated chain of associations with females have arisen in the first place? It would be possible here to draw on a large literature of "soft" evidence on the "mysteries of women", menstruation, phases of the moon, childbirth, notions of creation and so on. All of this deserves to be considered and undoubtedly played a certain role although it is often routinely used to explain everything from pimples to patriarchy. It is wanting as an explanation of specifics. The association of women with the technology of weaving and brewing, on the other hand, can clarify a great deal about early European attitudes and religiosity over millennia. The constants are these, that as far back as the evidence can take us, weaving was always considered women's work in transalpine Europe and analogies between the choosing of threads and the choosing of paths of life seem equally as old if not more so. The belief lasted as long as the technology and the division of labor and that was much the same in the age of *Beowulf* as it had been in the age of Civilis and Veleda. Although I have not checked the literature on this question, it would not be surprising to find, for example, that the triplicity of the triple mothers, one of whom is sometimes depicted with a distaff, might not only be related to purely religious concepts but that one should also think of the commonest operations of the almost superstitiously regarded *gynaeceum*,[103] the spinning, weaving and cutting of threads. This is not simple reductionism which

---

103 Herlihy, *Opera muliebria*, pp. 39f., 84f.

I do not favor as an explanatory tool; religious belief is a complex thing springing from too many sources to be easily isolated and pinned on the wall. At the same time, however, the pattern outlined here seems to me to be persuasive.

Consideration of the link between women and liquor leads to the same conclusions. It was a task normally performed away from men in separate buildings or environs. Although the evidence here is not as encompassing, the cultural attitudes already outlined in earlier chapters speak volumes, as do the hanging keys, spoon-sieves, ladles and containers of aristocratic women's graves. Doubtless also, one should think of the cottage gardens worked by women and of their role in agriculture which, observed Tacitus, men tended to avoid.[104] According to Herlihy, the brewing of ale was "the peculiar task of women"[105] in medieval Europe and, from the archaeological side, G. Behm-Blancke agrees that the preparation of mead and beer in the migration period lay in the hands of women.[106] Although neither discuss the reasoning behind the practice, it seems most probable that it was seen as analogous to cooking and the preparation of food—easy to understand since the liquor of archaic Europe was often thick and resembled soup. A previous chapter has outlined the way in which the preparation of the table constituted a symbolic speech for women over many centuries and the way in which the offer of liquor and containers might signify an offer of marriage. One late Norse saga refers to a quarrel between the two wives of a king as to which of them could brew the best mead for her husband. Odin himself, the god who gained mantic knowledge by stealing the beer brewed by Gunnlöð, was the judge of the contest.[107]

We now see that a survey of the archaeological evidence can provide striking and substantial support for the literary sources written down many centuries afterwards. One may confidently maintain that the concept of the aristocratic liquor-dispensing woman who confirms rank and creates brotherhood in the *comitatus*—what I have called the lady with a mead cup motif—derives from early La Tène and was already current among Germans during the Lübsow horizon from 0–150 AD at the latest. In other words, the evidence of the combined types of sources show that the concept was present during the first clearly demonstrable period of hierarchical differentiation among the Germans—roughly the time of the spread of the *comitatus*—and continued to influence political culture until its reshaping and realignment at the end of the Viking Age. The archaeological evidence also demonstrates that prophecy, although it is only weakly associated with the Wealhtheow figure, is indeed a crucial part of the mead- cup motif. Although a passage from *Beowulf* seems to imply that the queen might have prophetic ability, it is certainly subtle and one may decline to accept it until evidence like that from Bidford-on-Avon and the *Vita Leobae* demonstrates its

---

104 *Germania*, ch. 15.
106 Behm-Blancke, "Trankgaben", p. 209f.

105 Herlihy, *Opera muliebria*, p. 54.
107 Ibid., p. 189.

cogency. That is a central message of the conjunction of weaving tools and liquor containers in women's graves. Historians have overlooked the significant coupling because they are unaware of the archaeological pattern; archaeologists are aware but are insufficiently attuned to the full implications of the literary references and ecclesiastical prohibitions over the full span of the Early Middle Ages. The frequent allusions to weaving magic in the latter genre clearly indicate cultural continuity even when works like *Beowulf* only hint at its existence. As we shall see in part three of this chapter, such an approach by monastic scribes to unpleasant aspects of secular tradition is likely to have been part of an actual religious replacement policy. The finding that the mead cup motif is present in northern Germania during the Lübsow horizon, and in southern Germania for centuries before it, fits well with previous discussions of the relationships which existed between Civilis and Veleda in AD 69, almost the exact middle of Lübsow.

Against this background, the present state of the thesis can be further clarified. At the end of chapter three, it was possible to conclude that the warlord/prophetess link was an institutional one which probably developed between the time of Ariovistus and Masyos. We may now pose the question if, in the same institutional context of the Germanic warband, the prophetess also acted as a dispenser of liquor. Despite the nearly complete absence of relevant literary sources, the answer is sufficiently demonstrable in the positive because of the nature of the archaeological remains. The evidence on the La Tène Celtic side is perhaps plainer for here we have the conjunction of the weaving rod symbolism with the ritual vessel and magical paraphernalia in Dürrenberg grave 118 and there are ways to connect these with the partial literary hints from the Euxenos/Petta episode. The nature of the continuity in this case will become clearer in the following chapter in our discussion of the goddess Rosmerta and of several insular texts.

The evidence indicates that a very strong correlation existed between the concept of aristocratic femininity among the Germans and the ability to distribute liquor. In the Lübsow graves, the first series to provide indisputable evidence of hierarchic demarcation, we find a certainly high-status woman buried in a new type of way and with a wine strainer in her hand. These graves depict a dramatically changed conception of rank which many archaeologists now associate with foreign influence and the *comitatus*. Hence, it will not do to describe the strainer as simply a sign of generalized notions of open hospitality which might be connected with women. The strainer is not there to suggest commensality and an altruistic willingness to share good things. It is a notable cultural artifact which indicates an *ability* to provide the best for the best, a token of status but not hospitality. The secondary derivative notion must not be confused with the primary one. This is the clear message of the spoon strainers of the migration/Merovingian period of Central Europe and England. Serving the same function as the larger strainers, they hung on rich women's belts with keys. They were, at least, the female equivalent of the long swords in warriors' graves. Some of the Bornholm gold foils and later woman-with-horn depictions can be interpreted in much the same light and we have also seen that high status women are the ones who normally wear the Fürstenberg type bracteates indicating some type of allegiance or participation in the cult of a prophetic goddess.

Nor can the evidence be easily separated from the *comitatus* organization which formed the lifestyle that animated so many of the halls of barbarian Europe. Archaeologists frequently find large amounts of broken drinking vessels in and around these halls. As we saw earlier, the multi-tribal membership component of the warband made a formalized religiously sanctioned drinking ritual necessary in order to create the binding element of fictive kinship and such ritual would probably have been even more necessary in the earliest period of the *comitatus*. This correlates well with the fact that a woman who carries a spoon strainer might also be buried with a multiple cup vessel in the high status part of the cemetery. As many archaeologists have commented, such positioning is very frequently to be associated with warband organization in which the followers' graves are oriented with regard to the lord, his wife and their family. The multiple cup vessels may have had several meanings but the clearest one is the creation of a sense of unity among drinkers. As many are to be found in high status female graves of the migration/Merovingian period, the correlation with the *comitatus* and with the idea of female created unity among men would seem to be quite strong.

Such concept of female created brotherhood is clearly expressed for the *comitatus* in literary texts like *Beowulf* although we have to wait until then to actually see it in action and even then only see it infrequently. Consequently, it is only when one applies a number of widely scattered and sometimes disparate appearing clues that we can hope to reasonably depict the elusive earlier barbarian thoughtworld but that attempt must be made unless we wish to resign ourselves to a permanently partial picture of the Middle Ages. If the ability to provide food can be a decisive criterion of lordship, as attested by the term *hlaford*, then surely, from what we have seen, ladyship is to be linked with the provision of drink. As the OE text says, the noblewoman *must* serve her husband first but the clear implication is that she then serves his followers. It is difficult to imagine that rule being a new one. The burden of the archaeological and literary evidence thus indicates that liquor distribution was conceptually related both to aristocratic femininity and to the *comitatus* from the Lübsow period onwards. The prophetess, the companion of kings, warlords and warbands, must be located within the ambit of both constructs for her relations are most obviously tied to the military sphere. As will be seen in chapter five, a prophetess like Veleda can be linked to the very origins of warband religion and that discussion will further strengthen our conclusions here.

On the other hand, the clearly defined linkage of drink provision with the actual possession of political rank cannot have developed until the crystallization of a solidly rooted functionally hierarchic society in Germania. A great many archaeologists and historians see this as a feature of the Lübsow period with tendencies in that direction in the immediately preceding century. It is at this point, therefore, that attention must be turned to the Celts since they had many earlier centuries of experiences with religiously sanctioned hierarchical modes and the Germans would adopt a great deal of Celtic La Tène culture.

It must continually be emphasized that a strong religious element pervaded the lady's character from La Tène through Christianization. A concept of such importance could not have existed in the transalpine Europe of the period without the aura of divine approval and mundane patronage together. It should be easily possible to connect the lady with a goddess of the Germanic pantheon. Here nonetheless, one is confronted with the proverbial brick wall. As far as can be determined, no Germanic goddess fits the lady's precise bill of particulars until the Viking period and that is too late since no *confident* association on which we can build can be made with any of these female divinities *for the first century* AD. Only one contemporary goddess with suitable attributes is available and that is the goddess Rosmerta. Her cult is known from late La Tène and she was established in the central Rhineland by the mid first century. Her cult was then carried to Britain by Rhineland troops serving in the Roman army.[108] Although Rosmerta had achieved multiple citizenship by this time, her cult is Celtic in origin and not Germanic. Its spread in the Rhineland (a topic to be discussed later) is a perfect example of the religious and cultural fluidity so typical of that region in antiquity. More immediately relevant, however, it indicates that the cultural connections involved in the study of the mead cup theme must be quite complex. The evidence must also be examined from a Celtic perspective.

Although historians (and archaeologists) frequently refer to Celtic precedents, products and ideas when discussing early Germanic culture, the common tendency has been to look elsewhere when seeking explanation. Strongly influenced by classical thought, the knowledge of Roman conquest and subsequent Romanization has influenced many scholars to undervalue the vitality and staying power of Celtic culture. Classicists have often been interested in Gaul but mainly with the Romans in Gaul. Germanists know that little reliable *historical* material is known before Tacitus and generally work from Tacitus to the migration period when the ethnogenesis of the medieval Germanic peoples occur. Celticists have generally been preoccupied with linguistic problems—most who study the early period are linguists or archaeologists—and devote most of their time to the British Isles. All scholars, moreover, have been made somewhat gun shy by the great Celt vs. German debates of the early part of this century. Many students of the Middle Ages are therefore only vaguely aware that the Celts had been familiar with Mediterranean cultures for centuries and were especially knowledgeable in

---

108 Rosmerta will be discussed in detail in chapter five.

the two hundred years before Caesar's conquest. Moreover, because of the geographic range of early Celtic culture which separated North from South in a great swath from the Atlantic coast through southeastern Europe, Celts had been the recipients of a great deal of material of Mediterranean origin and had transmitted much else to the Germans. All of the objects—relatively new to the Germans—which we have discussed for the Lübsow and Hassleben/Leuna burials, had been used in much the same way by the Celts in previous centuries and their territories adjoined those of the Germans and were sometimes mixed among them. This is true even of lesser associations like those between women and keys as gravegoods, a topic usually related only to Germanic culture of the Early Middle Ages.[109] The question which archaeologists do not seem to ask about the luxury wares of the first century BC in Germania is this: is it clear that the Germans were imitating faraway Romans or is it not more likely, considering their previous history and the Celtic examples of importation, production and usage, that they were originally imitating Celts who were imitating Romans, or indeed, the practices of other Mediterranean elites who had long since influenced the Romans as well? Thus stated, the point may seem overly subtle; it is not. Despite the fact that both trans-Alpine peoples ultimately borrowed much from the South, the differences involved in chronology, as well as in modes and behaviors, may be very important for the interpretation of cultural history in northern Europe.

Consider, for example, the cultural pattern displayed in the customs of inhumation and weapons burial. Both practices were long familiar to Celts but were not known to Germans prior to the first century BC In his 1950 survey of the evidence for origins of the inhumation rite in the North, Ole Klindt-Jensen concluded that it was a borrowing from the Celts and had occurred in much the same way as the borrowing of certain types of pottery, weapon-turning techniques, some brooch types and, among women, a Celtic clothing fashion.[110] Berta Stjernquist argued against this interpretation in 1955.[111] Although conceding the possibility of Celtic influence, she maintained a case for the Sarmatians of Hungary as transmitters. Her evidence was scanty, however, and her views do not seem to have won acceptance. The material was re-examined in 1963 by Johannes Bröndsted who concluded, along with Klindt-Jensen, that the Germans took up this practice as a result of contact with the Celts of Silesia.[112] Diffusion seems to have proceeded in two waves, "the first in La Tène III from Celto-Germanic Middle Silesia with offshoots toward the north, then in early Roman times, from

---

109 Heinrich Jacobi, "Der keltische Schlüssel und der Schlüssel von Penelope, ein Beitrag zur Geschichte des antiken Verschlusses" (1930); Heiko Steuer, "Schlüsselpaare in früh-geschichtlichen Gräbern—Zur Deutung einer Amulett-Beigabe" (1982).
110 Ole Klindt-Jensen, *Foreign Influences in Denmark's Early Iron Age* (1950), pp. 176–9.
111 Berta Stjernquist, *Simris. On Cultural Connections of Scania in the Roman Iron Age* (1955), pp. 65–9.
112 Johannes Bröndsted, *Nordische Vorzeit III. Eisenzeit in Dänemark* (1963), pp. 63, 118, 156.

Celto-Germanic Bohemia via the Elbe, Oder and Vistula to Denmark and its neighboring countries".[113] Bröndsted went on to interpret the placing of food and drink in graves in the same way and concluded also that the custom of weapons burial is "doubtless" derived from Celtic influence.[114] More recently, Heiko Steuer has surveyed these questions against a broad chronological background and has agreed in essentials with Bröndsted.[115] The first phase of the Lübsow rite can be associated with Celtic practice and so too with weapon burial. Since both of these customs are critically important ones in terms of religion and warrior culture, the degree of Celtic influence must have been substantial. It is, finally, worth noting, considering the point made in the previous paragraph, that up until fairly recent times archaeologists typically regarded the Romans as the ultimate initiators of the inhumation rite in the North.[116]

The first century BC was an unusual time of social turmoil in Central Europe, one in which Germans were abandoning long-standing religious and social attitudes and adopting Celtic (not Roman) ones in their place. It is important to emphasize this because it is often assumed that Germans adopted Roman drinking styles as they imported luxury Roman wares. It was in this way, for example, that Joachim Werner interpreted in 1950 the paired appearance of silver cups and glass vessels in some of the Lübsow graves and that view is often repeated in the literature.[117] It is not clear that it is correct. The Celts had been importing huge amounts of Mediterranean luxury wares for centuries and had apparently followed the same pairing practice which Werner assumed to be Roman. Referring to the early La Tène princely grave from Kleinaspergle, Baden-Wurttemberg, for example, Franz Fischer commented: "What stands out is how things are paired, from the two drinking horns, usually found in Celtic tombs, to the two Attic *kylixes*".[118] In his recent study of Roman imports in *Germania libera*, Jurgen Kunow reached a similar conclusion. Close examination of materials indicated

113 Klindt-Jensen, *Foreign Influences*, p. 179.
114 See note 112.
115 Steuer, *Sozialstrukturen*, pp. 186, 199, 203. See further Peschel, "Frühe Waffengraber", pp. 261–81; Jan Lichardus, *Korpergräber der frühen Kaiserzeit im Gebiet der südlichen Elbgermanen* (1984), pp. 59–69. For further discussion of the variety of Celtic influences in these areas, see Kasimierz Godlowski, "Die Przeworsk-Kultur", (1992), pp. 10, 15, 19, 52–6. For evidence that it lasted up to and including Lübsow, i.e., that Celtic influence did not cease during the two generations after Caesar, see Otto-Hermann Frey, "Einige Überlegungen zu den Beziehungen zwischen Kelten und Germanen in der Spätlatenezeit", (1986), pp. 45–80.
116 Malcolm Todd, "Germanic Burials", p. 39; and see the convenient summary in Glenys Davies, "Burial in Italy up to Augustus" (1977).
117 Joachim Werner, "Römische Trinkgefässe in germanischen Gräbern der Kaiserzeit" (1950); Jürgen Oldenstein, "Die Zusammensetzung des römischen Imports in den sogennanten Lübsow Gräbern als möglicher Hinweis auf die soziale Stellung der Bestatteten" (1975).
118 Franz Fischer, "Kleinaspergle near Asperg, Kreis Ludwigsburg (Baden-Württemberg)" (1991), p. 178f.

that upper class Germans had little notion of actual Roman practice.[119] They sometimes used Roman cooking utensils as drinking ware and used drinking ware to cook in. Kunow commented that it is difficult to imagine them knowing or copying the carefully planned formal process of a Roman *comissatio*. The lifestyles of Germans and Romans was very different. So were their basic mentalities— even after hundreds of years of contact. One can more easily conceive of the difference by simply recalling the ways in which the two cultures made use of small spoon-strainers during the late empire. What was common table ware for one was an insignia of status for the other. The way of thinking about things in each case is a world apart—even in the fourth century. In the earlier Lübsow phase, a time of very superficial contact, the two peoples will have understood only the most basic things about each other. That was not the case between Germans and Celts who had a long history of relations. The differences between them were marked but were demonstrably bridgeable as we have already seen and shall see again in greater detail below.

As Steuer noted in his monumental study of early European social structure, changes in religious perceptions are critical to the introduction of new burial practices.[120] In such times, old cults are abandoned and new ones are developed to fit a changing scheme of things. In this case, it was the emerging upper class of Germania that sought to differentiate themselves from their ethnic fellows by adopting the religious and social modes of a more sophisticated neighboring people. At the same time, they introduced (imported, as I shall argue later) a new organization, the warband, and used it to undermine tribal bonds. Such kinds of transformations have happened many times in the past. It is a phenomenon which has its own rules. In his study of luxury graves, (Prunkgräber) G. Kosack commented:

> Contact with higher cultures and certain political constellations motivate an upper class to an identification with the partners viewed as culturally domi- nant. Through the borrowing of notably different customs or material culture

---

119 Jürgen Kunow, *Der römische Import in der Germania liberia bis zu den Markomannenkriegen. Studien zu Bronze- und Glasgefässen* (1983), pp. 77–80. Clara Redlich analyzes some of the same material in "Politische und wirtschaftliche Bedeutung der Bronzegefässe an Unterelbe und Saale zur Zeit der Römerkriege" (1980). One culture's misunderstanding and misuse of the peculiar containers of another's is now demonstrated for the Viking period as well. See Egon Wamers, "*Pyxides imaginatae*. Zur Ikonographie und Funktion karolingischer Silber- becher" (1991). Liturgical vessels in one area can become drinking cups in another. Similar usage and similar understanding of symbolism can only be reasonably assumed, it seems to me, after a long period of association between cultures when it can also be shown that one seeks to imitate the other in a variety of ways. That is demonstratable for the Celts and Germans in the last three centuries BC but the same level of interaction is not demonstrated for Romans and Germans until much later and even then, as the spoon-sieves show, the interpretative contrasts can be remarkable.

120 Steuer, *Sozialstrukturen*, p. 203.

and techniques, the new upper class seeks to demonstrate its own prestige, to create a sense of respect and greater social distance from tribal comrades. It seeks to show an aristocratic primacy both in this world and in the next. The means are constant ones: imposing ceremony on festive occasions. . . ; perennial feasting while adopting the highly regarded drinking customs of the foreigner; expensive clothing with stylishly artistic forms; ornaments with symbolic meaning; luxury products as indicators of an ability to gain and distribute riches.[121]

Let us now look to the people with whose leaders this new Germanic upper class sought to identify.

2. FROM HOCHDORF TO THE GAELS

Named after the site of Hallstatt in Austria, Hallstatt culture, from the eighth to the first quarter of the fifth century BC, is the earliest phase of the European Iron Age and the first phase of Celtic culture.[1] Hallstatt D, roughly its last century or so, is of special interest here for two reasons: one is the foundation of the Greek colony of Marseilles in southern France near the mouth of the Rhône for it established an important and highly influential trading network.[2] Second, and apparently directly related to the first in its later phase at least, is the more rapid evolution of a stratified hierarchical society characterized by massive tumulus graves for rulers, timber lined graves and wagon burial, centrally defended sites, large numbers of gold objects and bronze vessels sometimes accompanied by exotic objects like silk from faraway China.[3]

From about 600 onwards, the Hallstatt culture in certain regions, like eastern France and southern Germany, was heavily dependent on relations with the Mediterranean world and trade was largely in the hands of Greeks. By providing luxury goods to leaders, Mediterranean trade encouraged social differentiation since it provided added authority bolstered by the ability to maintain retinues of armed men eager to serve for the promise and fact of distribution.[4] Political and

---

121 Georg Kossack, "Prunkgräber. Bemerkungen zu Eigenschaften und Aussagewert" (1974), p. 31f.
  1 See, among many works, John Collis, *The European Iron Age* (1984), pp. 66–102.
  2 The best interpretive discussion that I know of is Barry Cunliffe, *Greeks, Romans and Barbarians: Spheres of Interaction* (1988), pp. 13–33. A more technical discussion in Peter S. Wells, *Culture Contact and Culture Change: Early Iron Age Central Europe and the Mediterranean World* (1980). Excellent overviews in K. Bittel, W. Kimmig, S. Schiek, eds., *Die Kelten in Baden-Württemberg* (1981); Jan Filip, *Celtic Civilization and its Heritage* (1977^2).
  3 See now the beautiful illustrated massive catalogue by Sabatino Moscati, Otto Hermann Frey, Vencesles Kruta, Barry Raftery and Miklós Szabó, eds. *The Celts* (1991), pp. 75–126.
  4 Ludwig Pauli, "Early Celtic Society: Two Centuries of Wealth and Turmoil in Central Europe" (1985); Peter S. Wells, "Mediterranean Trade and Culture Change in Early Iron Age Central Europe" (1985).

military leadership would come more easily to those able to provide access to Mediterranean wealth, prestige objects, diplomatic contacts and protection. In such a society, aristocratic rivalries would flourish, contractual bonds between leaders and followers could develop and armed bands of warriors would necessarily be maintained. A closely organized warrior society might thereby develop more quickly. It is important to add, however, that control of agricultural land, animals and clients remained fundamental throughout Hallstatt culture[5] and that Mediterranean trade and prestige goods may have simply encouraged or accelerated a process of social differentiation already present.

An idea of the wealth and lifestyle of those at the top of this tiered society— of those like the Lübsow "princes" of later times who sought more radical social separation—can be conveyed by glancing at some of the burials of the period. The most recently discovered is that of the wealthy "Celtic prince" of Hochdorf, a site located about ten km west of the famous oppidum of Hohenasperg in Baden-Wurttemberg.[6]

Found under a tumulus some sixty meters in diameter was the body of an impressively tall man of about forty.[7] He was buried in a timber lined chamber whose walls and floor were covered with multi-hued fabrics. A gold torc, the customary insignia of high rank, had been placed around his neck, two gold brooches on the right side of his chest, a golden armring on his right arm. He wore a dagger with a gold-wound grip hanging from a leather belt to which a strip of sheet gold had been fastened and his shoes had gold mounts. Toilet articles accompanied him in the grave. He must have been a fervent sportsman for so did fishing hooks and a quiver of arrows. He had been laid on an unusual 2.75 meter long (possibly Etruscan) bronze couch decorated with scenes of armed warriors fighting (or dancing) and riding in chariots. A disassembled four wheeled wagon with harness for two horses lay nearby.

His drinking service may be even more noteworthy. At the foot of the body lay a huge Greek bronze cauldron, 80 cm high, 104 cm in diameter and with a volume of 500 liters. Three large handles are attached to the top of the cauldron which is decorated with three small reclining lions. When placed in the grave, the cauldron had been three quarters full of thick honey mixture for making honey mead.

5 See the impressive analysis in Daphne Nash, "Celtic Territorial Expansions and the Mediterranean World" (1985). Françoise Audouze, Olivier Büchsenschütz, *Towns, Villages and Countryside of Celtic Europe: From the Beginning of the Second Millennium to the end of the First Century* BC (1992), pp. 177–8.

6 Jörg Biel, *Der Keltenfürst von Hochdorf* (1985). Helpful contextual discussions in S. Frankenstein, M.J. Rowlands, "The Internal Structure and Regional Context of Early Iron Age Society in South-Western Germany" (1978); J. Biel, "The Celtic Princes of Hohenasperg (Baden-Württemberg)" (1991); W. Kimmig, "The Heuneburg Hillfort and the Proto-Celtic Princely Tombs of Upper Rhineland" (1991); A. Hoffner, "The Princely Tombs of the Celts in the Middle Rhineland" (1991).

7 Biel, *Keltenfürst*, pp. 52, 61–91.

Chemical analysis showed that it had been mixed with at least 58 different herbs which could be identified and a number which could not. Jorg Biel reckoned that more than one hundred plants—some brought from distant places—had originally been used in creating the concentrated mixture.[8] From this analysis, we gain some idea of the enormous expenditure of time, effort and wealth needed to create such potently symbolic liquor. It must have been viewed with supernatural or quasi-magical veneration.[9] Such interpretation is further supported by the presence of a huge iron drinking horn in the grave which can only have belonged to the "prince" himself.[10] Made from nine different pipe-sections, this imposing artifact measures 97.5 cm long and tapers from a 14.5 cm diameter mouth to 3 cm at the foot. It could hold 5.5 liters of liquor. Originally attached to the base of the horn was a long complexly decorated finial so that the full length of the object was 123 cm. Various sections of the horn were wound with decorated strips of sheet gold.

All three of these artifacts, cauldron, mead-mixture and iron drinking horn must surely be identified as status symbols in themselves. The cauldron was worth a small fortune, the mead mixture took expeditions to create and the size of the iron horn means that it cannot have been designed for normal use. We get a partial idea as to what all of this might have meant by the fact that eight other (only partly preserved) normal sized drinking horns had originally been hung on the grave wall next to the one of iron.[11] The nine horns were matched by nine bronze platters, with two large knives for cutting meat and with a hemispherical bowl of beaten gold which had been placed in the cauldron and must have been used for serving the drink (note that handles on such vessels were rare in Hallstatt times so that servers were probably always present).[12] What is preserved here, in other words, is a banqueting service but it is one of a highly ceremonial type meant to portray the acme of aristocratic prestige and self-representation. Indeed, it may well have been even more than that for the outrageously complex liquor and the oversized iron horn would seem to indicate some kind of sacral gathering in which

8 Ibid., p. 130.
9 There is a long documented history of such attitudes among Celts and Germans and it will be discussed more fully in chapter five. See, for example, Hanscarl Leuner, "Über die historische Rolle magischer Pflanzen und ihre Wirkstoffe" (1970); Renate Doht, *Der Rauschtrank im germanischen Mythos* (1974).
10 Biel, *Keltenfürst*, p. 114f.
11 Ibid., p. 117. Karl Peschel argues strongly that the smaller drinking horns would have belonged to the closer members of the princely warband: "Zur kultischen Devotion innerhalb der keltischen Kriegergemeinschaft" (1989), p. 277f., and see further his "Kriegergrab, Gefolge und Landnahme bei den Latènekelten" (1984).
12 As is pointed out by Georg Kossack, "Trinkgeschirr als Kultgerät der Hallstattzeit" (1964), p. 99. For analysis of Hallstatt period feasts, see Karl Kromer, "Das Situlenfest: Versuch einer Interpretation der Darstellungen auf figural verzierten Situlen" (1980); Idem, "Gift Exchange and the Hallstatt Courts" (1982).

the prince (he may be the only one so far to actually merit the title), served with a golden bowl, conducted some special procedure with his eight advisors or favored followers. One will probably not be too far wrong in hazarding the guess that this festal apparatus is so unusual that it is likely to have had some link with ideas of government or kingship themselves and that the ceremonial banquet in which it was used was one with the utmost significance for the elite of this society. It was probably a sacral as well as communal gathering.

Although Hochdorf is unique because of the large iron horn and the chemically analyzed cauldron contents, all of the other forty or so rich graves from this period in west-central Europe display more or less similar characteristics.[13] They contain large quantities of impressive grave goods which frequently include gold torcs, luxury Mediterranean imports and many valuable cauldrons, vats, situla and drinking services. One thinks of the famous "princess" grave from Vix (Mt. Lassois, Côte d'Or). Along with the richly ornamented body of a woman about thirty five, it contained the largest Greek krater in existence, an astonishing work 1.64 m high, weighing 208.6 kg and surmounted by a strainer-lid decorated with the standing figure of a woman.[14] The neck of the krater has a large frieze of armed hoplites and charioteers. Two large gorgon-shaped handles are attached. As with the Hochdorf cauldron, this vessel must have been of marked social and cultic importance. It probably originated in Magna Graecia but is far too heavy to have been imported whole. The figures on the frieze around the neck have Greek letters scribed on them which correspond to letters on the body of the vessel but which were hidden when the figures were soldered on. The work must have been transported in parts along with at least one Greek craftsman to assemble them.[15] The strainer-lid also suggests that the krater was meant to contain specially prepared liquor since it would have been unnecessary for simple mixing. One scene from the situla art of the period shows a figure dropping nodules of some substance into such a container.[16] Both liquor and vessels must have had extraordinary significance. It seems, therefore, that the mentality of the elite of the widely separated sites of Hochdorf and Vix was quite similar and we may safely posit much the same pattern for this early Celtic culture as a whole.

Whence came the banqueting customs requiring these remarkably ceremonial and luxurious utensils? The possibility of Roman influence can be discounted here for the dates of the Hallstatt princely burials are too early and that suggests that we must look to the cultures of Magna Graecia and Marseilles, to Etruria or

13 Discussed by Wells, "Mediterranean Trade", p. 72f.
14 Jean-Pierre Mohen, "The Princely Tombs of Burgundy" (1991); Nadine Berthelier-Ajot, "The Vix Settlement and the Tomb of the Princess" (1991), p. 116f.
15 Collis, *Iron Age*, p. 95f.
16 Kromer, "Situlenfest", p. 237.

to Scythia.[17] The Greeks ultimately seem the most likely originators although some aspects may have been mediated by the Etruscans. As recent research indicates, the practice of drinking from costly gold-decorated drinking horns is first demonstratable for central Europe in the late Hallstatt period although it was a contemporary long-standing custom at the Greek and Etruscan *komos* symposium.[18] Dirk Krausse points out that drinking horns frequently appear on Greek black-figure vases of the sixth century BC where they are held by the symposiasts or depicted as hung on the walls as originally at Hochdorf.[19] The drinkers holding them sometimes recline on couches, a Greek custom taken up by the Etruscans.[20] In some areas of Greek or partly Greek culture, reclining at the feast was the privilege of the tested warriors. In Macedonia, for example, Athenaeus relates (*Diepnosophistae* I, 18) that no one could "recline at dinner unless he had speared a wild boar without using a hunting-net. Until then they must eat sitting." Such Greek notions surrounding the ideas of reclining, drinking and hunting (the Hochdorf ruler was also a huntsman) help explain the usages of Celtica.

Much of the rest of the festal pattern discussed for Celts and Germans also appears among the Greeks - the hierarchical seating arrangement, first service to the ruler and a formal cup-offering to a visiting dignitary for example. They are discussed at great length and with a multitude of historical and literary examples in the works of Athenaeus and Plutarch (*Quaestiones convivales* I, 2–3) among others. Similarly, Greek cauldrons and kraters like that of Vix were common diplomatic gifts and the *typical* reward for an outstanding warrior or athletic victor among the Greeks was an ornate cup or drinking vessel of precious metal.[21] Their reception was surrounded with elite formality and ritual as with the drinking of the *gerousios oinos*, the wine of honor, offered by the king of the city to the kings of the tribes.[22] As among the Celts, the Greeks honored the best warrior at a feast with a special cut of meat and a placement calling attention to his achievements.

It may be that the already mentioned pairing of vessels in some high-status burials of transalpine Europe (as at Kleinaspergle) also has Greek antecedents,

17 Bernard Bouloumié, "Le symposion gréco-étrusque et l'aristocratie celtique" (1988); Franz Fischer, "Thrakien als Vermittler iranischer Metallkunst an die frühen Kelten" (1983); Ludwig Pauli, "Zu Gast bei einem keltischer Fürsten" (1988/89).
18 Dirk Krausse, "Trinkhorn und Kline. Zur griechischen Vermittlung orientalischer Trinksitten an die frühen Kelten" (1993); On the symposium, see Klaus Vierneisel and Bert Kaeser, eds. *Kunst der Schale-Kultur des Trinkens* (1990), pp. 216–303.
19 Krausse, "Trinkhorn und Kline", p. 190f.
20 Burkhard Fehr, *Orientalische und griechische Gelage* (1971); Jean-Marie Dentzer, *Le motif du banquet couché dans le Proche-Orient et le monde grec du VIIe au IVe siècle avant J.-C.* (1982).
21 Vierneisel and Kaeser, *Kunst der Schale-Kultur des Trinkens*, pp. 130–3.
22 Dentzer, *Le motif du banquet couché*, p. 445.

possibly relating them to the worship of the gods or the honoring of high-status guests. The very beautiful Vaphio gold cups found at a site in Laconia not far from Sparta and dating to about 1500 BC are a famous example.[23] Athenaeus (*Diepnos.* XI, 482) refers to one individual who owned two drinking vessels: "the first was for the use of men, whereas he had acquired possession of the second in order to honor the gods." The vessels were apparently of dissimilar types, however, and so the answer may lie in another sphere. At some formal gatherings, ordinary guests were served only an allotted portion of wine. But heroes and rulers might be singled out, as in the *Iliad* (XII, 310) with the privilege of "seats" and "full cups." In *Iliad* IV, 257, Agamemnon proclaims that he wishes to honor Idomeneus "beyond all the Danaans" and so "even though the other long-haired Achaeans drink an allotted portion, thy cup standeth ever full, even as for mine own self, to drink whensoever thy heart biddeth thee." Could there be a hint here that the cups would be paired since the privilege was of the same kind as Agamemnon enjoyed? Something like this was done with food. Athenaeus (*Diepnos.* I, 14) says of the early Greeks that "they used also to present a part of their own portion to anyone they liked, just as Odysseus cuts off for Demodocus some of the chine which they had served to him". If this notion were applied to wine, might not a ruler be supplied with an extra cup in order to single out a friend? Herodotus says of the Spartan kings (VI, 57) that they "shall be first to sit down to the banquet, and shall be first served, each of them receiving a portion double of what is given to the rest of the company; theirs shall be the first libations, and theirs the hides of the sacrificed beasts". This was also their right when they "are bidden by private citizens to dinner". N.R.E. Fisher points out that after election to the *gerousia*, the victor is given king-like honors, a double set of rations at a feast, "the second of which he would give to the woman he honored most highly".[24] Although I am aware of no citation which can explicitly prove the point, it seems reasonable to suppose that the practices of "double portions" to kings and the giving of shares to friends provides a sound context for the Hallstatt pairing of festal vessels and might perhaps even have something to do with the prince's large drinking horn at Hochdorf. Since Herodotus says that the "hides and the chines of all sacrificed beasts" are taken by the kings, one might also speculate as to a connection with the butcher's tools discovered at Hochdorf, one specifically designed for the skinning of animals.[25]

It may be suggested that the numbers of Greek drinking utensils in aristocratic graves of the Hallstatt and La Tène periods indicate some knowledge and imitation of Greek custom. The evidence from Hochdorf is particularly persuasive. The impressive symmetry between Greeks and Celts in this regard will not

23 J.T. Hooker, *The Ancient Spartans* (1980), p. 34f.
24 N.R.E. Fischer, "Drink, *Hybris* and the Promotion of Harmony in Sparta" (1989), p. 40.
25 Pauli, "Zu Gast", p. 294f.

become clear until the next chapter, however, although Petta's cup-offering referred to earlier indicates a context and so of course do Caesar's remarks about the Gaulish knowledge of written Greek. The significant point here is the identification of a misapprehension among some historians and archaeologists who study the Germans of the Roman period and the Early Middle Ages and who frequently assume much Roman influence on both Germans and Celts with only a few generations difference in terms of initial impact. The evidence discussed here points to a different pattern: it indicates considerable Greco-Etruscan influence in the late Hallstatt and in the early La Tène although it declines thereafter. Roman influence among the Celts did not begin to make much headway until the later second century but Romans had by then borrowed consistently from the Greco-Etruscan pattern themselves. Since Roman export only begins after several centuries of Celto-Germanic interaction, the assumption that Germanic elites of the Lübsow period were imitating Roman manners in their use of costly Mediterranean ware is highly questionable.

Absent from all this is the lady with a mead cup who does not appear among either Greeks or Romans at a time when she might have entered the historical record. References to girls and women pouring wine do appear in early Greek literature but the increasing preoccupation with fashionable aristocratic pederasty in the later archaic period means that they are ousted by adolescents and boys.[26] The evidence from Latium may indicate a somewhat different emphasis for certain kinds of vessels used for the mixing of wine "have only been found in connection with women" and thus suggest a more significant role for them in the feasts of early Italy.[27]

The Etruscans are worthy of particular regard although, unfortunately, we know very little about them. It is certain that Etruscans exported massive amounts of material to the Celts during the seventh , sixth and fifth centuries BC until they gradually lost out in competition with the Greeks. They decisively influenced the development of Hallstatt art.[28] Apparently, the Celts of northern Italy—the most important tribes being the Boii, Senones, Cenomani and Insubres—reciprocated since the Etruscans later adopted the motif of the severed head and the wearing of torcs amongst them in the fourth century has been described as "ubiquitous".[29] Here too we find a marked cultural concern with omens and prophecy, what the Romans who adopted it called the "Etruscan discipline", and it is clear that Etruscans women, like the famous Tanaquil who predicted and promoted the rise of her husband, Tarquinius Priscus, to the kingship played a critical role. She did

26 Jan Bremmer, "Adolescents, *Symposion* and Pederasty" (1990), p. 140f.
27 Annette Rathje, "The Adoption of the Homeric Banquet in Central Italy in the Orientalizing Period" (1990), p. 283.
28 Otto-Hermann Frey, *Die Entstehung der Situlenkunst* (1969).
29 Larissa Bonfonte, "Daily Life and Afterlife" (1986), pp. 259, 262.

the same for her son-in-law, Servius Tullius, passing over her own sons in the process when she chose and presented him before an unwilling assembly. Tullia, the wife of Tarquinius Superbus, did much the same when she presented her husband before an indecisive crowd of men and was "the first to call him king," *regemque prima appellavit*, a phrase with a technical meaning (Livy, I, 34, 39, 48). These associations with prophecy and the giving of the royal name by women would seem to be significant. Roman historians like Livy condemned such past behavior (which seems much like euhemerized myth à la Dumezil) as they also did the morals of the Etruscans but that has a strangely familiar ring to anyone knowledgeable about reportage on the Celts and so it is not clear that modern scholars should accept it at face value. Although we cannot now be sure, the Etruscans may have contributed in important ways to Celtic political religiosity just as they did in the fields of art and aristocratic display.

The "feudal" Hallstatt world came to a turbulent finish not long after 500 BC.[30] The princely courts were plundered and from Burgundy to Bohemia the aristocratic practice of burial under a tumulus ceased. Hallstatt was now replaced by the vigorous and highly creative La Tène. It emerged first with two foci on the periphery of Hallstatt, one in the Marne region of northern France and the other in the Hünsruck-Eifel region of Germany. It spread thereafter in a broad band to include all of Gaul, northern Italy and much of central and eastern Europe. But the peoples of La Tène, especially those of the Hallstatt periphery, had developed along different lines and are best characterized as warrior societies in which leadership was based on military prestige and the ability to guarantee reward and plunder.[31] Such type of organization became characteristic of the entire Celtic world in the fourth and third centuries BC. One notes parenthetically that when La Tène culture succumbed in its turn to Roman conquest, that a similar process of transition occurred: it was the warlike peoples of the periphery, the Germans, strongly influenced by La Tène, who continued many of its traditions.

Expanding first into northern Italy in order to be near the source of luxury goods, the Celts now began a series of migrations, invasions and campaigns which would take them all over temperate Europe and beyond. In 387 BC, they took and occupied Rome, invaded Greece and sacked Delphi in 279 and established kingdoms in Thrace and Asia Minor thereafter. (Many centuries later, St. Jerome, who had lived in both Ancyra and Trier, would relate that the Galatians of Asia Minor and the Treveri of Gaul spoke the same language).[32] In these centuries the

---

30 Cunliffe, *Greeks, Romans and Barbarians*, pp. 32–5.
31 O.H. Frey, "The Formation of the La Tène Culture" (1991); V. Kruta, "The First Celtic Expansion" (1991); A. Duval, "Celtic Society" (1991); Wolfgang Dehn, "Einige Überlegungen zum Charakter keltischer Wanderungen" (1979).
32 Miklós Szabó, "The Celts and their Movements in the Third Century BC." (1991).

Celts also became the best regarded mercenaries of the Mediterranean world serving in large numbers with Philip of Macedon, Alexander, Hannibal and with the forces of most Hellenistic states and lordlings at one time or another.[33] The desire for conquest, travel, booty and payment all played a role. So characteristic was this long-lasting tradition of military service abroad that various groupings of Celts of the Alps and upper Rhine came to be called *gaesatae* by Greek and Roman writers who understood the term to mean "mercenary troops". It is actually a Celtic word meaning "spearman" which survived in early medieval Ireland as *gaiscedach*, a spear-bearing warrior.[34]

Although the fully developed *comitatus* with its accompanying religion emphasizing warlike gods and the warrior virtues may well have existed in Hallstatt culture, it can certainly be associated with La Tène in the fifth and fourth centuries when vast migrations, plundering expeditions and mercenary service combined to weaken the bonds of tribe and family. As K. Peschel and S. Deger-Jalkotzy point out, the former from the archaeological perspective and the latter from the historical and linguistic, the Celtic forces which attacked Italy, the Balkans and Asia Minor appear to have been organized according to the warband principle.[35] Brennus, for example, who led an army into Greece seems almost like a prototype warlord of the later Germanic type, an Ariovistus or Maroboduus,[36] with great numbers following him in the search for new land and plunder. The classical sources call him *regulus* or *basilius* but, like Julius Civilis of the Batavi, he seems to have actually been chosen as warlord at a public assembly by decision of the warriors present. Other contemporary leaders were chosen in the same way (Pausanius 10, XIX, 5–8). His power depended upon military reputation and achievement. After his forces were defeated and he himself wounded, although not mortally, he committed suicide. In the fighting, he had been surrounded by a special company of men, "the tallest and bravest of the Gauls", who killed all of the wounded unable to retreat with the disabled leader. Deger-Jalkotzy views their collective behavior as resembling that of a sworn brotherhood like the *soldurii* of Caesar's time.[37] These chosen followers would vow to share all benefits with their comrades "while if any violent fate befalls their fellows, they either endure the same misfortune along with them or take their own lives" (B.G. 3, 22). Caesar

33 Miklós Szabó, "Mercenary Activity" (1991); Daphne Nash, *Coinage in the Celtic World* (1987), pp. 13–18; G.T. Griffith, *The Mercenaries of the Hellenistic World* (1935), p. 78f.

34 Nash, *Coinage*, p. 14. Somewhat belied by the title, this work is actually an excellent guide to Celtic society and to politico-military activities as a whole in relation to the economy.

35 For Peschel's views, see the works cited in note 11 and Sigrid Deger-Jalkotzy, *E-QE-TA: Zur Rolle des Gefolgschaftswesens in der Sozialstruktur mykenischer Reiche* (1978), pp. 157–65. Again, this work is far wider-ranging than the title suggests.

36 The basic work is Walter Schlesinger, "Über germanisches Heerkönigtum" now in his *Beiträge*, pp. 53–87. On the Celtic side, see John T. Koch, "Brân, Brennos: An Instance of Early Gallo-Brittonic History and Mythology" (1990).

37 Deger-Jalkotzy, *E-QE-TA*, p. 158.

also related that Gaulish custom regards it as a crime for clients to desert their patrons "even in desperate case" (B.G. 7, 40). These remarks add depth to the observation of Polybius, writing about 140 BC, who noted the way in which the Celts of Italy formed *hetaeria*, the common Greek term for warband (*Histories* II, 17, 12): "They treated comradeship as of the greatest importance, those among them being the most feared and most powerful who were thought to have the largest number of attendants and associates". He too provides an example like that of Brennus (II, 31, 2). After the defeat of the paramount ruler of the Gaesatae, the subordinate king, Aneroestes, escaped with "a few followers to a certain place where he put an end to his life and to those of his friends". It must be emphasized that this kind of thinking, which vowed to loyalty and victory and to the collective death of the band upon defeat, continued to be typical of the Celtic elite long after the Roman conquest. In the year 21 AD, the nobles Julius Florus of the Treveri and Julius Sacrovir of the Aedui, led a revolt of some of the Treveri, Aedui and Turones. At this time, as Edith Wightman writes, "Gaul was still uneasily balanced between old and new traditions".[38] Certainly Sacrovir and his followers adhered to the former for, as Tacitus relates (*Annals* III, 47), after their defeat, he and his comrades committed suicide by mutually inflicted wounds.

The warband was probably a common aspect of Celtic culture from the fifth century onwards at the latest. Classical sources refer to all the typical behaviors and qualities of that form of organization: the extra-tribal grouping, the search for land and booty, the absolute bond to the leader, the sharing of his fate to death and beyond, the appearance of all together as a retinue, the hierarchy among followers, the communal drinking, the choosing of the best followers as counsellors. Strangely enough, however, the great similarity between the warbands of Celts and later Germans was not recognized until recently and is still very little known among medievalists. The essential barrier to understanding was that Caesar's linguistic usage had muddied the waters. As Gerhard Dobesch points out in his important study of the Celts of Austria (a book which deserves to be more widely known for its excellent analysis of Celtic society and politics in general), Caesar's ability to describe complex Gaulish conditions using mostly Roman terms is little short of astonishing.[39] With the exception of a few words like *soldurii* and *ambacti*, both terms for members of the *comitatus*, he constantly analyses Gaulish society using Latin concepts like *principatus, imperium, auctoritas, cliens, socius, fides, amicitia, equites, boni*, and so on.[40] He strives to explain the complex structures of a foreign society using language and categories familiar to his readers and unlikely to place any burden on their intellectual capacity. At

38 Edith Mary Wightman, *Gallia Belgica* (1985), p. 64.
39 Gerhard Dobesch, "Caesar als Quelle für keltische Verhältnisse" in his *Die Kelten in Österreich nach ältesten Berichten der Antike: Das norische Königreich und seine Bezeihungen zu Rom. im 2. Jahrhundert v. Chr.* (1980), pp. 406–7.
40 Ibid.

bottom, as Dobesch observes, he wishes his readers to know only as much about Gaulish life as will enable them to follow his story of conquest.[41]

Caesar constantly simplifies the variety and complexity of Gaulish politics, lifestyles and sociological relationships. His usage of the word *cliens*, "client", has been especially misleading. Although early Romans were quite familiar with warband organization, they had long since abandoned the *comitatus* for the patron-client relationship with its stress on obedience, subjection and lack of reciprocity.[42] Caesar's use of the word *cliens* for the *soldurii* suggests that they were of low status and had very few enforceable rights against the warlord. This is completely incorrect. As Dobesch's analysis shows, the *soldurii* belonged to the political and military elite and frequently came from powerful noble families. The degree of subjection present in the Roman *clintela* is impossible to envision for them. Actually, Tacitus uses both terms, *clientes* and *comites*, when describing the Germanic warband as well but some scholars have wished to deny the implied relational verticality for the Germans while affirming it for the Celts.[44] In part, this is due to the fact that earlier specialists like Camille Jullien and his followers identified the *ambacti* as the normal members of the Gaulish *comitatus* in Caesar's time.

The relationships between the warlord, *ambacti* and *soldurii* were complex and are unlikely to have been understood by most Roman commentators who, like Festus, commonly glossed Gaulish-Latin *ambactus* with *servus*, "slave".[45] The literal meaning of the word is "those who go around". To understand the true status of the *ambactus* and his cohorts—the point is an important one with ramifications for the Germanic warband as well—we need to look more closely at Gaulish political and economic structure over time. Daphne Nash, among others, has done important work in this area and some of her findings will be drawn upon below.

Celtic warrior societies of the fourth and third centuries BC seem to have been led by wealthy district chiefs who shared a tribal identity with others but recognized, or at least obeyed, no central ruler. As described by Polybius and Livy (referring to the time of Hannibal's invasion in 218 BC) these chiefs were called *principes castelli* or *reguli*, "lords of strongholds" or "kinglets" and Hannibal had to negotiate with each one separately.[46] Many would have been interested in mercenary leadership for their lifestyles were luxurious and their expenditures great. Take Dumnorix, for example, a noble among the Aedui, whom Caesar says was "unequaled in boldness" and "strong in the influence that his generosity gave

41 Dobesch, *Die Kelten*, p. 408.
42 Green, *Carolingian Lord*, pp. 64–79.
43 Dobesch, *Die Kelten*, p. 419f.
44 Ibid., 417f.; Green, *Carolingian Lord*, p. 71f.
45 The Roman glosses are analyzed in Alain Daubigney, "Reconnaissance des formes de la dépendance gauloise" (1979).
46 Nash, *Coinage*, p. 49.

him over the common folk".[47] Since he wished to become a king of his people, he distributed large bribes both at home and to neighboring states. He maintained a large body of cavalry "permanently at his own charges and kept them about his person". He had thus to feed, support and endow some hundreds of warriors of the upper class and this also required that he maintain craftsmen, druids, entertainers, guests and "men of art" of all kinds. But of what did his public generosity consist? We get some idea of what his status required and ambition encouraged by Posidonius' description of the great feast of Louerius, a Gaulish nobleman of about two generations earlier.[48] In an attempt to win popular favor, Louerius rode in a chariot over the plains distributing gold and silver to the thousands who followed him. Then he set up an enclave one and one half miles square filled with food and vats of expensive liquor so that "for many days" all who wished could enter and enjoy the feast while being served by his own attendants. A poet who came late, on the day that had been fixed for ending the feast, bemoaned his hard luck in verse. Louerius was so pleased at his song that he threw him a bag of gold from his chariot whereupon the poet proclaimed that the very tracks of his chariot provided largesse for mankind. Poets had to be maintained too! They traveled freely among the various states (along with druids but unlike others) and were indispensable tools for propaganda.

Caesar mentions many such leaders who thrive amidst their imposing retinues. Gaulish nobles, he states (B.G. 6, 15), are constantly engaged in military campaigns and "according to the importance of each of them in birth and resources, so is the number of liegemen and dependents that he has about him (*ita plurimos circum se ambactos clientesque habet*)". A powerful nobleman like Orgetorix has 10,000 *circum se*. Many of these would be of the common folk who are described as being "treated almost as slaves": The greater part of them "oppressed as they are either by debt, or by the heavy weight of tribute, or by the wrongdoing of the more powerful men, commit themselves in slavery to the nobles, who have, in fact, the same rights over them as masters over slaves".[49] From remarks like this, we would have to conclude that the great majority of Gaulish men, together with their families, were slaves—either that or, assuming honest reportage, that the word "slave" was being very loosely used. Compare from this perspective what Tacitus has to say about slavery among the Germans about a century and a half later. He is clearly puzzled about the whole question. German slaves, he says, "are not employed after our manner with distinct domestic duties assigned to them, but each one has the management of a house and home of his own. The master

---

47 BG I, 18.
48 J.J. Tierney, "The Celtic Ethnography of Posidonius" (1960), p. 248.
49 On various forms of dependance and slavery, see Karl Peschel, "Archäologisches zur Frage der Unfreiheit bei den Kelten während der vorrömischen Eisenzeit" (1990); Alain Daubigney, "Forme de l'asservissement et statut de la dépendance préromaine dans l'aire gallo-germanique" (1985).

requires from a slave a certain quality of grain, of cattle, and of clothing, as he would from a tenant, and this is the limit of subjection".[50] He goes on to say that slaves are rarely punished with bonds or hard labor, although they are often killed "on the impulse of passion".

In saying that "slaves" are like tenants, Tacitus is closer to the mark than Caesar who, nonetheless, also refers to debt and tribute. Both of them are actually groping towards the concept of the tenant farmer who also owes military service to the man who has given him land—a situation roughly analogous to that in a number of European regions up until recent times. Such explanations would account for the number of clients around Orgetorix. The full answer to the problem is to be found in early medieval Ireland which, comparable to Viking Age Scandinavia for the early Germans, preserved, only more faithfully, some of the customs and relationships of the early Celts.

Irish law texts of the seventh and eighth centuries show that society was thoroughly hierarchical with a variety of long-established forms of contractual clientships.[51] Broadly speaking, Irish jurists distinguished between two types of client or *céle*, the free client (*soerchéile*) and base client (*doerchéile*). These in turn are distinguished from the semi-freeman or tenant-at-will (*fuidir*), the hereditary serf (*sencléithe*) and the slave (*mug*, "male slave" and *cumal*, "female slave"). Clientship was established when the lord handed over a fief or "favor", frequently cattle, in return for which the client was bound to certain services and renders. These differed for each type of clientship. The free client was bound to return one third of the grant each year so that if he had received thirty cows, ten must be returned at the end of twelve months. If, after three years, the relationship was to be maintained for another three year period, the free client had to pay in milk and calves up to one third of their value and, upon continuance for a seventh year, no renders were required.[52] The contract also went beyond this. By accepting a man as his free client, the lord undertook to protect him against others and defend his rights while the client undertook personal and military service, as well as formal public demonstrations of respect. He must, for example always rise from his seat when his lord appears.[53] Free clientage was regarded as "the best of fiefs" because either party could terminate the contract at any time without penalty by returning the original grant or renders. That is unlikely to have been common practice since the immaterial benefits of the contract were often more valuable than the material because of the social and political bonds created. Hence, a man of equal rank to another might also wish to become his client. This was true of nobles and kings as well as free men so that clientship was spread throughout this

50 *Germania*, 25.
51 See now Fergus Kelly, *A Guide to Early Irish Law* (1988), pp. 29–35.
52 A useful analysis of socio-economic detail in Gearóid Mac Niocaill, *Ireland Before the Vikings* (1972), pp. 59–66; Donncha Ó Corráin, *Ireland Before the Normans* (1972), p. 42f.
53 Kelly, *Guide*, p. 32.

society from top to bottom with lesser kings the clients of more powerful ones. The debt involved in these multiple cases was permanently maintained and periodically reaffirmed because its real importance lay in the fact that it was an expression of ongoing affiliation and loyalty and *not* simply of economic dependence.[54]

The base client was also a free man but his obligations were more onerous. Although the actual renders were much smaller - less than one sixth those of the free client—the base client could not terminate his contract when he wished although his lord could. If the base client wished to withdraw, he must return twice the amount of the fief and, under certain conditions of ill will, also pay a fine of half of his lord's honor price or wergild.[55] In all such cases the lord was in a superior position for he was also the judge of any real or purported failures on his client's part whereas the client would probably have encountered great difficulty in legally attributing failure to his lord. Nonetheless, despite outlays and obligations, real benefits accrued to each party. The lord achieved increased status, military power and labor sources by the number of his clients. He also gained a guaranteed food supply because of various kinds of renders and might also guest with each of his clients for a night during part of the year.[56] The client gained a serviceable means of making or increasing his living, protection from depredation and a one time payment equal in value to his honor price. While remaining a free man, he was, however, bound to his lord's service for good or bad and for all practical purposes for the rest of his life.

The Irish warlord also possessed a special retinue or *dám* which would have been largely made up of specially sworn free men of ability and status.[57] It is difficult to envision anything else since the retinue was the primary instrument of prestigious display and public rank. His richer free clients will have been a part of this. In case of need, however, as with Orgetorix who faced criminal charges, the lord could create a powerful array by drawing his retinue and all of his clients together. Other kinds of warbands existed too although, most interestingly, they are associated from the seventh century onwards with pagan practices and are universally excoriated by the Christian clergy.[58] The evidence, such as it is, suggests that wherever the warband existed, it was the last holdout against Christianity. Undoubtedly, this was because of its collective sense of identity created by oaths, rituals and undertakings.[59] In sum, it seems probable that the

54 Robin C. Stacey, "Ties that Bind: Immunities in Irish and Welsh Law" (1990), p. 49. Further on background: Marilyn Gerriets, "Kingship and Exchange in pre-Viking Ireland" (1987).
55 Mac Niocaill, *Ireland Before the Vikings*, p. 62.
56 Ibid., p. 64f.
57 Deger-Jalkotzy, *E-QE-TA*, p. 165.
58 Richard Sharpe, "Hiberno-Latin *Laicus*, Irish *Láech* and the Devil's Men" (1979); Kim Mc Cone, "Werewolves, Cyclopes, *Díberga* and *Fianna*: Juvenile Delinquency in Early Ireland" (1986).
59 To this one must add the strong familial emphasis in the warband discussed in chapter one.

two types of Irish clients correspond to the devoted *soldurii* and *ambacti* of earlier Celtic society although an emphatic kind of bond is suggested for the *soldurii* by the very term "devoted".[60] A special kind of oath, a *sacramentum* such as Tacitus mentions in association with the Germanic warband, is likely. Also notable is the way in which Irish clients could be identified by the act of sitting or standing, a situation indicative of attitudes and socio-political arrangements very close to those outlined in chapter one for early medieval Germanic *comites*. The ranking arrangement of the Gaulish warband antedated both. As with *Beowulf*, it tells us much about lord/follower relationships and is worthy of remark.

Citing the lost work of Posidonius, written in the early first century BC, Athenaeus describes the Celtic feast as follows:

> When a large number dine together, they sit around in a circle with the most influential man in the centre, like the leader of the chorus . . . Beside him sits the host and next on either side the others in order of distinction. Their shieldsmen stand behind them while spearsmen are seated in a circle on the opposite side and feast in common like their lords.

Three distinct circles are described, two concentric and one separate from the others. The most significant inner circle has a specially honored place and (possibly aside from the host) rank proceeds from that point "in order of distinction". Not all may sit. The exterior circle is composed of men who stand and one may identify them as the *ambacti*. It is clear that they accompany the lords to war for they bear their shields but they are not regarded as troops of the first caliber and their lower status is indicated by the fact of permanent standing. The peculiar name of *ambactus* is thereby clarified as well for they are indeed those "who go around" or, in Caesar's reference to the warlord, those who are *circum se*.[62] The word does not refer to their general movements when the lord is underway but to their formal place at the feast. In contrast to the *ambacti*, the higher rank of the *soldurii* is indicated by the fact that they sit and eat separately and are described as the actual bearers of offensive weapons. They are the trusted fighters and comrades. It seems probable that they too must rise when their lord enters but, unlike the *ambacti*, they may sit and partake of the feast thereafter. We can conclude, therefore, that the festal hall of armed and sworn men was a microcosm of transalpine society for a thousand years before the *Beowulf* poem, a work which provides eloquent evidence for the continuity of an ancient warband pattern. The placement of warriors and the geography of the hall profoundly influenced language, social mores and attitudes. It was probably for feasts like these that the lord of Hochdorf brought forth his ceremonial mead-cauldron, iron horn and golden serving bowl.

60 See the discussion by Dobesch, *Die Kelten*, p. 251f. and p. 420 n. 7.
61 Tierney, "Celtic Ethnography", p. 247.
62 Daubigney, "Reconnaissance", p. 173f.

From what has been said above about Irish society, it can be suggested that the remarks about "slavery" by both Caesar and Tacitus are considerably wide of the mark. Caesar starts from the concept of Roman style clientage (which does not fit) and works from there to semi-slavery; Tacitus begins from Roman slavery (which does not fit either) and approaches the idea of tenant farming which is somewhat closer but lacks the military element. Both are applying Roman concepts to try and describe something which is foreign to Roman society and each seems to be describing something different when in fact they are probably describing the same thing—the institution of base clientage which, one may now suggest, would have been common to both Celts and Germans for some considerable time before Tacitus. Such clients would have belonged at the lower end of those several ranks which Tacitus said make up the Germanic *comitatus*, a point which draws the two institutions and the two societies even closer together and further clarifies their differences from the Mediterranean pattern. This conclusion would seem to support the earlier skepticism of G. Walser and R. Wenskus about Caesar's emphasis on extreme dependence within the Gaulish warband and is consistent with the more recent research of Dobesch and Deger-Jalkotzy which rejects that view completely.[63] The contractual grant of cattle, sometimes of land and cattle, indicated and reinforced status and was a crucial medium for the articulation of military and hierarchical relationships at every socio-political level.[64] None of this should be construed as a statement that slavery was uncommon, however. It was probably familiar all over Gaul and Germania but it is likely to have been more prevalent in areas closer to the Mediterranean.

All early Celtic class societies were alike in many respects and often evolved in similar ways over time. Political and military leadership were the exclusive preserve of an equestrian nobility among whom weaker nobles paid allegiance and tribute to stronger ones.[65] The same pattern followed all the way down the social pyramid. Both nobles and richer freemen were landowners and there was an unusually large pastoral component in the economy.[66] Each social grade sought clients among equals and inferiors. In such a society, aristocratic rivalries were constant and ordinary freemen must often have been threatened, in need of protection and in search of the means to grease social mobility. Entering the followings of powerful lords and/or mercenary service in distant lands would make a difference. Because the society was a dynamic one, some would flourish

---

63 Gerold Walser, *Caesar und die Germanen: Studien zur politischen Tendenz römischer Feldzugsberichte* (1956), p. 75; Reinhard Wenskus, *Stammesbildung und Verfassung*, p. 359; Deger-Jalkotzy, *E-QE-TA*, pp. 157–66; Dobesch, *Die Kelten*, pp. 417–32. There does, however, seem to have been a slow decline in the status of the *ambacti* in Gaul from the period of Celtic expansion to that of Caesar but the *soldurii* are a different case.

64 Nash, "Celtic Territorial Expansion", pp. 46–9.

65 Ibid.

66 For the interaction between the social and pastoral components of such a way of life, see A.T. Lucus, *Cattle in Ancient Ireland* (1989).

and others decline. It is possible, therefore, perhaps even likely in view of Mediterranean influence, that some devolution of status had occurred for the *ambacti* by Caesar's time as it certainly did for base clients in Ireland by the High Middle Ages.[67] Conditions during early and mid La Tène were different than those of the second and first centuries BC when the commercial economies of the South strongly affected Celtic institutions and values. Witness to this slow process is found in the beginnings and spread of Gaulish coinages in the various states and the creation of oppida, "the first towns north of the Alps",[68] in many regions of the Celtic world—a series of developments which heavily influenced some Germanic peoples of the periphery who drew on Celtic culture and products in the same way as the Celts drew on the Mediterranean.

Slavery brought changes, too. The demand for slaves in the Roman world "increased sharply in the mid-second century to reach unprecedented levels by the mid-first" so that Celtic warfare and slave-raiding to pay for Mediterranean imports was constantly stimulated from outside.[69] According to one estimate, some 30,000 of those who joined Spartacus in his Italian slave revolt were Celts.[70] Traditional kingship was another victim. It declined along with the status of the base clients. Among Celtic states closer to republican Rome, like those of the Arverni, Aedui and Helvetii, aristocratic oligarchies rose to overthrow kings and to rule in their own interests.[71] Again, as we shall see in the following chapter, these events would have reverberations in the Germanic world. The pattern is hard to overlook. Mediterranean influence wrought significant changes among the Celts of the second and first centuries BC. These were modified by Celtic interpretations, institutions and the stylistic approach of La Tène artists and craftsmen. Broadly speaking, it was in this Celtic guise that some aspects of the Mediterranean spirit eventually reached the pre-Lübsow Germans. Of course, some Romans and some Germans did have personal contact during the late Republic. These would become more significant in the first century AD but hardly before that. Something more must now be said about some of the cultural changes of late La Tène, the products that resulted and the influences that travelled beyond the Celtic world for that will make the mixed pattern of cultural transference clearer.

In keeping with our central theme, one way to begin is by examining some remarks of classical commentators on the then proverbial Gaulish love of wine. Drawing on Posidonius, both Athenaeus and Diodorus Siculus observe that the

---

67 Ó Corráin, *Ireland Before the Normans*, p. 44.
68 The phases of coinage introduction and the social context are discussed by Nash, *Coinage*, pp. 48–55. See also Hans-Jörg Kellner, "Coinage", pp. 451–9; John Collis, *Oppida: Earliest Towns North of the Alps* (1984).
69 Nash, *Coinage*, p. 20f.
70 Tchernia, "Italian Wine", p. 98.
71 Nash, *Coinage*, pp. 53f., 94–9.

Celtic nobility prefers wine to other drinks.[72] One is reminded of Kossack's analysis pointing out that the upper class of one culture will adopt the tastes of another in their search for self-glorification. "The drink of the wealthy upper classes", writes Athenaeus, "is wine imported from Italy or from the territory of Marseilles. This is unadulterated, but sometimes a little water is added. The lower classes drink wheaten beer prepared with honey, but most people drink it plain. They use a common cup, drinking a little at a time . . . ".[73] The wine trade seems to have become important to Roman merchants from the second half of the second century BC.[74] The Gauls of the time, according to Diodorus, were extremely fond of wine and would drink themselves into a stupor whenever they had it. Italian merchants capitalized on this fondness and looked on it as a treasure trove. They transported their cargo by boat and wagon and received incredible prices for it; "for one jar of wine they receive in return a slave, a servant in exchange for the drink".[75]

It is worth pausing to assess this observation for it is often cited but usually misinterpreted. While it may very well be true that Italian merchants sometimes received a slave in return for a jar of wine, the context is not, as Diodorus believed, that of economic exchange or, better stated perhaps, it is an economic transaction only from the viewpoint of the merchant. The Gaul involved probably saw it as something entirely different. It is now more difficult to think otherwise as we have seen that the Celts were well acquainted with Mediterranean values, particularly the value of money, since they had served for so long as mercenaries. We know from Livy (44, 26) that king Perseus of Macedonia (179–168 BC) offered Claodicus of the Danubian Bastarnae five gold staters apiece for infantry warriors, ten each for cavalrymen and one thousand for himself for a campaign. We also know that Greek coins were in use by communities close to the Mediterranean and that, inspired by Greek prototypes, some Celtic states began issuing their own coinages by about 300 BC.[76] Some two hundred years later, the Gaulish elite were operating mines, collecting state taxes and investing in the building of towns and factories for the mass production of goods. They were acutely aware of

---

72 Social and economic commentary in Tchernia, "Italian Wine", pp. 87–104; Christian Goudineau, "Marseilles, Rome and Gaul from the Third to the First Century BC", (1983), pp. 76–86; Michael G. Fulford, "Roman Material in Barbarian Society c.200 BC–c.AD 400", (1985), pp. 91–108. There is much relevant material in all of the essays in Sarah Macready and F.H. Thompson, eds., *Cross-Channel Trade Between Gaul and Britain in the Pre-Roman Iron Age* (1984).

73 Tierney, "Celtic Ethnography", p. 247.

74 Aside from the essays by Tchernia and Goudineau cited in note 72, see Franz Fischer, "Der Handel der Mittel- und Spät-Latène-Zeit in Mitteleuropa aufgrund archäologischer Zeugnisse" (1985); Dieter Timpe, "Der keltische Handel nach historischen Quellen" (1985).

75 Tierney, "Celtic Ethnography", p. 249.

76 Kellner, "Coinage", p. 451, states that "the first imitations date from the very beginning of the third century BC" Nash, *Coinage*, p. 48, refers to the mid-third century BC.

economics and finance and of the huge disparity between the value of a slave and that of a jar of wine; conservatively estimated, the former was worth sixty times the latter.[77] It was with this elite group that merchants dealt. Ordinary folk were unable to afford wine—may not even have had a taste for it—and so it can only have been a nobleman who could afford to give a merchant a slave.

The correct interpretation of the remark of Diodorus lies in the realm of culture, in the peculiar value placed on certain kinds of drink and ritual exchanges in the Celtic world. We have already noted the astonishing amount of labor and expense that early nobles might invest in specially prepared liquor and the great social and political value placed on cauldrons and vats. Such a mentality was not unfamiliar to the early Greeks who sealed personal friendships (also of a military nature) and diplomatic alliances by the gift of a drinking vessel, and to later Romans who gave gifts of silver vessels to German envoys and chiefs.[78] But the Gauls (quite apart from any propensity to drunkenness which upper class Romans exhibited to an even greater degree at their feasts) associated rare drink with honor, status and authority. It possessed for them a different kind of symbolism, a religious or quasi-religious significance which closely tied it to kinship, the warrior mentality and the heroic code. The transaction was not an economic one precisely *because* it concerned wine; the object to be exchanged transformed the nature of the exchange so that it became part of the gift-giving nexus wherein the concept of honor played the decisive role.[79] In order to maintain status and demonstrate appropriate regard, a "gift" of this kind had to be repaid with a greater counter-gift in keeping with the donor's rank and the receiver's desires—in some cases, apparently, with that of a slave, a human commodity known to be greatly in demand by Romans. This approach to certain kinds of exchanges is now difficult to fully appreciate but is aptly illustrated by some

77 Tchernia, "Italian Wine", p. 99.
78 As referred to by Tacitus, for example, in *Germania* 5. The full significance of these kinds of gifts is best explained by Franz Fischer, "*KEIMHIA*: Bemerkungen zur kulturgeschichtlichen Interpretation des sogenannten Südimports in der späten Hallstatt- und frühen Latène-Kultur des westlichen Mitteleuropa" (1973). See further David Braund, "Ideology, Subsidies and Trade: The King on the Northern Frontier Revisited" (1989); Paul Marie Duval, "Sources and Distribution of Chieftaincy Wealth in Ancient Gaul" (1986). The broader perspective in William J.H. Willems, "Rome and its Frontiers in the North: The Role of the Periphery" (1991); Michael Parker Pearson, "Beyond the Pale: Barbarian Social Dynamics in Western Europe" (1989).
79 Alain Daubigney, "Relations marchandes Méditerranéennes et procès des rapports de dépendance (*magu*—et ambactes) en Gaule protohistorique" (1983); C. Feuvrier-Prévotat, "Echanges et sociétés en Gaule indépendante: à propos d'un texte de Poseidonios d'Apamée" (1978). To better understand this kind of thinking, consider the fact that Celtic tribes (like the Tectosages) would sometimes maintain huge mounds of sacred temple treasure never used in trade or, for that matter, consider the great wealth buried in Germanic graves of the Early Middle Ages. Economic considerations played little role in such an approach to life.

Gaulish coins which depict ceremonial cauldrons and wine amphorae.[80] Such transactions cannot have continued for long. According to Andre Tchernia, the wine trade was just beginning to expand during the time of Posidonius, the writer upon whom Diodorus drew for his information about the Celts.[81] It is unlikely that Gaulish nobles would have continued to consistently react in this way with Italian merchants although that kind of behavior would have lasted longer outside of the nobility and in northern and eastern Gaul. It is a good example of the clash of two world-views, the status and prestige mentality of the warrior aristocrat and the commercial one of the merchant entrepreneur.

Urbanization, commerce and evolving production techniques and artistic styles are part of the structural mutations of late La Tène which not only affected Celtic societies but those around them. By the time of Caesar's conquest there were some 170 fortified oppida settlements scattered across Europe from the Germanic northeast through Gaul, Bohemia, Hungary, Austria, Switzerland, Britain and Bavaria.[82] The inhabitants of these towns were primarily engaged in trade and manufacturing which provided for their own needs and those of other regions. Oppida like Bibracte and Manching, Stradonice and Staré Hradisko maintained wide commercial relations with both North and South while continuing the Celtic foundation of the European iron-working tradition.[83] Such oppida produced over ninety different kinds of iron artifacts and high quality weapons, vast amounts of glass, vases and ornaments, amphorae, pots, locks, toiletry articles, gold, silver and bronze jewelry, frames for writing tablets and brooches of many types.[84] The *ferrum noricum* was praised by ancient writers while probably the largest number of brooches ever discovered in Europe, around 1300 examples, were discovered at Staré Hradisko.[85] Everything from luxury helmets to surgeon's tools, saddler's equipment and agricultural implements were made and traded while Italian products were also being imported and then exported elsewhere.[86] It is not surprising to find that it was during this period that the customs of inhumation and weapon burial were adopted by the Germans, that forms of organization like the *comitatus* came into being amongst them and that La Tène art styles became widely diffused. Although traces of cultural influences can be found at many sites in numerous areas of the continent and Britain, some areas, as Klindt-Jensen demonstrated for Denmark, were particularly affected (and the

---

80 Nash, *Coinage*, plate I.
81 Tchernia, "Italian Wine", p. 99.
82 Ferdinand Maier, "The *oppida* of the Second and First Centuries BC" (1991), p. 417; Collis, *Oppida*, pp. 8–14.
83 On iron working, see Collis, *Oppida*, pp. 87–92.
84 Susanne Sievers et al., "Handicrafts" (1991); Karl Horst Schmidt, "Handwerk und handwerker im Keltischen und Germanischen. Beiträge zu einem historischen Vergleich" (1983), pp. 265–85.
85 Jiri Meduna, "The Oppidum of Stare Hradisco" (1991), p. 546f.
86 For merchant activities, see Timpe, "Der keltische Handel", pp. 272–78.

same is very likely to be true of the Rhine-Weser Germans although the evidence is not always clear since they lacked the grave deposition practice). "Celtic taste", as F. Kaul comments, "become dominant far from the Celtic world".[87] One has only to think of the Brå cauldron, Dejbjerg carts or Gundestrup cauldron to realize the ways in which both products and ideas helped Celticize European culture in the century before Roman occupation.[88] Matters of religion were little different. M. Görman's recent study of the religiously related artifacts of southern Scandinavia during the first millennium BC concluded that belief in this region "had obvious Celtic traits".[89] Nor indeed may one conclude that Roman culture quickly or consistently changed all of this in the areas beyond southern Gaul. Assemblages from the Augustan period at the late Celtic horsemen's graves at Goeblingen-Nospelt "demonstrate that a long time after the conquest of Gaul, customs were still markedly Celtic in the territory of the Treveri".[90]

Beyond the continent, Britain and Ireland shared in the Celtic La Tène culture of the time but in varying degrees and with varying emphases. Fine metalwork is a prominent feature of the late centuries BC and the very impressive hillforts of Britain and the linear earthworks and promontory forts of Ireland testify to the presence of a military aristocracy, often fighting in chariots and carrying finely wrought weapons, who dominated a highly stratified society.[91] The evidence is particularly good for Britain which drew increasingly close to the continent during the first century BC when there was heavy immigration from Belgic regions as well as extensive cultic ties linking both parts of Celtica.[92] A very heavy maritime traffic also existed in the second and first centuries BC as is shown by the great quantities of the Dressel 1 A type of amphorae which can be traced from the ports of Quimper, Quiberon and St. Servin to those of central southern Britain and elsewhere.[93] The Roman occupation of the next century brought changes but not without rebellion and accommodation and it was never complete, even though Collingwood would mourn the situation of the Celtic artist in a vibrant tradition confronted by the "uniform and sordid ugliness of drab Romano-British daylight".[94] Nor, four hundred years later, was the Anglo-Saxon

87 Flemming Kaul, "The Dejbjerg Carts" (1991), p. 537.

88 As note 74, and see P. Mortensen, "The Brå Cauldron" (1991), p. 375; Flemming Kaul, "The Gundestrup Cauldron" (1991), p. 538f.

89 Marianne Görman, "Nordic and Celtic. Religion in Southern Scandinavia During the Late Bronze Age and Early Iron Age" (1990).

90 Jeannot Metzler, "Late Celtic Horsemen's Graves at Goeblingen-Nospelt" (1991), p. 521; Gustav Mahr, *Die Jüngere Latènekultur des trierer Landes* (1967).

91 Barry Raftery, "The Island Celts" (1991).

92 Barry Cunliffe, "Relations Between Britain and Gaul in the First Century BC and the Early First Century AD" (1984); Daphne Nash, "The Basis of Contacts between Britain and Gaul in the Late Pre-Roman Iron Age" (1984); I.M. Stead, "The Belgae in Britain" (1991).

93 Barry Cunliffe, "Maritime Traffic Between the Continent and Britain" (1991).

94 Cited from Piggott, *Ancient Europe*, p. 243.

conquest any more complete for the north and west of Britain remained independent and the Anglo-Saxons borrowed extensively from the more advanced cultures which they encountered.[95] Ireland, of course, was conquered by neither people although it had many and fruitful contacts with both which may have had important consequences for the vitality of its society.[96] Therein lies the uniqueness of Ireland; it was able to develop more naturally as a Celtic society free from outside threat and coercion. Unfortunately, the archaeological evidence for Iron Age Ireland is weak by continental or British standards and a great deal more remains to be done before a confident picture of prehistoric society can be created. Nonetheless, many beautiful artifacts of La Tène style are known so that it is clear that the continuity of La Tène art was unbroken and it remained to flourish, evolving and extending, throughout the first Christian millennium.

3. ASPECTS OF CONTINUITY AND ORAL CULTURE

How much continuity existed in the Celtic world from La Tène Gaul to early Christian Ireland and why did it exist? Up until very recently a strong consensus among scholars maintained that the answer to the first question was "a great deal", and to the second, "because of the teachings, conservative traditions and memories of the poets". In his well known survey of *Ancient Europe*, Stuart Piggott wrote that we should be cautious in comparing Manching with Emain Macha but also stated his view "that the picture of the structure and nature of Celtic society as given in early Irish literature is consonant with that contained in the classical writers, notably the Stoic philosopher and ethnographer Posidonius, writing in the first century BC, and upon whose account of Celtic customs Athenaeus, Diodorus, Strabo and Caesar all draw. It is also in accord with such inferences as we can make from the archaeological evidence".[1] He held that "the conservatism of barbarian Europe, as in other comparable groups of societies, led to retention and transmission of tradition, either orally, or by the handing on of skills by the direct precept of master to apprentice, or from priest to pupil".[2] His broad vantage point led him to conclude that, once certain not very ambitious demands had been adequately met, "innovation and radical change were exceptional" in Europe and accustomed modes could be "preserved and transmitted intact down the generations".[3] In arguing in this manner, Piggott drew extensively and eloquently on archaeological evidence but also on literary sources. He

---

95 Lloyd and Jennifer Laing, *Celtic Britain and Ireland, AD 200–800* (1990), pp. 67–70, 81–95; Patrick Wormald, "Celtic and Anglo-Saxon Kingship: Some Further Thoughts" (1986), pp. 151–83.

96 Harold Mytum, *The Origins of Early Christian Ireland* (1992), pp. 21–52.

1 Piggott, *Ancient Europe*, p. 226f.

2 Ibid., p. 259.

3 Piggott, *Ancient Europe*, p. 259.

frequently cited the Ulster cycle of tales, works preserved in eleventh and twelfth century manuscripts but containing references and very archaic linguistic passages widely regarded as reflecting a period four to six centuries earlier. He was particularly influenced by Kenneth Jackson's famous lecture on "a window on the Iron Age" in which Jackson argued that Irish texts, the earliest vernacular literature in Europe north of the Alps, preserved a reasonably accurate although fragmentary picture of earlier La Tène culture.[4]

Both Piggott and Jackson drew on a wide variety of evidence from material culture, linguistics, law, literature and religion. In recent years, an important modification of their perspective has been offered by J.P. Mallory and some discussion will help to clarify the state of scholarly opinion.[5] The most recent commentary by Mallory and McNeill, summarized below, appears in their book on the archaeology of Ulster published in 1991.[6]

In the early Irish annals, the events of the Ulster cycle are assigned to the first centuries BC and AD so that it is clear that chroniclers regarded the heroes and heroines of their stories (Cú Chulainn, Conchobur Mac Nessa, Fergus Mac Roig, Conall Cernach, Queen Medb) as living in the distant past, what to us is the Iron Age. "The behaviour and some of the descriptions of the Ulster warriors seem to accord well with that of the early Celts".[7] These include (although one may parenthetically note that the list is incomplete) fighting from chariots, a method of warfare that had disappeared on the continent by the first century AD and from Britain by the second century AD. Typical behaviors in Gaul and Ireland also include headhunting, worship of the severed head, feasting with "the champion's portion", pagan oaths by the gods of the tribe and the existence of druids and their primacy in prophecy and advice. Similarly, the Ulster cycle records the Ulaid capital of Emain Macha as having fallen in the fourth or fifth centuries AD. After this collapse, the kingdom of Ulster constricted to little more than the counties Antrim, Down and north Louth, "a small fraction of the area of Ulster regularly depicted in the Ulster tales",[8] so that the political geography of the texts recall an earlier period.

Placed against this evidence (of which more could be adduced) is the fact that the artifacts found do not closely fit the literary picture but seem to belong to the Early Middle Ages.[9] Cú Chulainn, for example, regularly applies a long sword to chop and decapitate his enemies. But Iron Age Irish swords were much shorter

---

4 Kenneth H. Jackson, *The Oldest Irish Tradition: A Window on the Iron Age* (1964).
5 J.P. Mallory, "Silver in the Ulster Cycle of Tales" (1986), pp. 31–78; "The Sword in the Ulster Cycle" (1981), pp. 99–114.
6 J.P. Mallory and T.E. Mc Neill, *The Archaeology of Ulster: From Colonization to Plantation* (1991).
7 Ibid., p. 168.
8 Mallory, Mc Neill, *Ulster*, p. 168.
9 Ibid.

and could hardly be used with the same élan. Similar discrepancies arise with spears and with silver ornaments which were not used as described in the tales until the early Christian period. Generally speaking, the archaeological artifacts of the Irish Iron Age rarely fit the descriptions of the tales but closely match those of the seventh to tenth centuries. The evidence for chariots is meager and the material on Emain Macha ambiguous.

Although all of this is important evidence that modifies the consensus, it leaves critical parts of the continuity argument intact. The authors do not comment, for example, on the *druidai*, *vates* and *bardoi* of the continent and their Irish equivalents of druid, poet and bard except to say that the large body of Irish material on the druids is untrustworthy.[10] That is true in some cases but false in others. The Irish monks who wrote down much of this material were not as ignorant of paganism as Mallory and Mc Neill suppose and, in cases where they were overtly hostile, their very antagonism is a useful sign of the druids' continuing influence. Actually, the two authors appear to be conscious of this and other approaches for they are by no means dogmatic and offer a nuanced conclusion which separates artifact and text: "We may imagine that the early Irish writers may have taken tales that were very ancient in structure but dressed them up in the clothes and weapons of their Early Christian contemporaries since they had no idea what Iron Age man looked like".[11] What the two authors seem to maintain is that the description of artifacts has been modernized to accord with current practice but authentic memories existed nonetheless "because both some of the practices and words used to describe them are not only found among the medieval Irish but also their Celtic neighbors and other related peoples of Eurasia".[12] Mallory and Mc Neill go on to note that both tradition and artifact "indicate that the Laigin, the people who gave their name to [the Irish province of] Leinster, were British and Gaulish in origin" and that "artistic inspiration directly from the continent, possibly northern France", would seem to have influenced the makeup of swords and scabbards in Ulster from about 300 BC.[13] They also suggest continuity with La Tène in political geography, kingship and royal ritual, in the sacred marriage of the king and the ritual drink presented to him by the goddess of the territory. In warfare, they are prepared to accept the antiquity and continuance of warbands who frequently adopt the names and behaviors of wolves and who sometimes fight virtually naked in battle, "the Irish equivalent of the Viking berserkers".[14]

The druids may have been responsible for the preservation of many of the techniques and traditions of La Tène culture in the Early Middle Ages. Their institutional importance as mobile repositories of native lore and sentiment is conspicuously demonstrated, as Piggott pointed out, by Roman legislation

10 Mallory, Mc Neill, *Ulster*, p. 170.   11 Ibid., p. 169.
12 Mallory, Mc Neill, *Ulster*, p. 170.   13 Ibid., p. 173.
14 Mallory, Mc Neill, *Ulster*, p. 170f.

against them in first century Gaul and, in the comparable case of the poets, by the savage English extermination policy in sixteenth and seventeenth century Ireland. The problem for organizers of conquest was not so much the fact that druids were priests but rather that they were teachers. There are explicit statements by Pomponius Mela and Caesar which there is no reason to doubt.[15] The former tells us that druids "teach many things to the nobles of Gaul in a course of instruction, lasting as long as twenty years, meeting in secret in a cave or in remote places". Caesar declares that "a large number of young men flock to them for training" and adds that their learning was orally transmitted (even though evidence suggests that some were literate): "It is said that they commit to memory large amounts of poetry". A similar system of aristocratic education seems to have existed in both Britain and Ireland where Cathbad, a druid often mentioned in the Ulster cycle, is depicted as teaching young noblemen, one hundred in one instance and eight in another.[16] In all three of these related cultures the druids possessed great authority and acted as judges of disputes. Their society was a pan-Celtic institution. It is worth noting that Cathbad is also associated with warbands in Irish tradition.[17]

We know more about the *filid* or poet-seers who found it easier to co-exist with Christianity. Possessed of sacral status and supernatural power, they regularly composed praise-poems, satires and elegies. They were also repositories of sacred knowledge, the *senchas*, i.e., history, genealogy, the meaning of names and place-names. According to one tenth and eleventh century tract containing materials of diverse origin and date, the poets were divided into a seven-grade system based on knowledge and training. "In its earliest form", according to P. Mac Cana, "the curriculum envisaged the student poet as passing through these grades in a period of seven years", an additional grade for each increase of knowledge. In theory at least, the course of study was lengthened to ten years at a later stage and in its final form the tract refers to a twelve year course of study. Aside from a broad palette of knowledge to be committed to memory, the *ollam filed* or "chief poet" must have learnt by heart at least eighty full tales although it is possible that more were demanded. Slips of memory were scorned and modifications of tales, although that did occur over time, were regarded as unworthy and illegitimate. "He is no poet", says the tract, "who does not preserve *coimgne* or all the stories". *coimgne*, according to Mac Cana, may have meant something like "knowledge held in common" or "comprehensive knowledge".[18] "At all events, it seems probable that initially it had general reference to learned knowledge of the past, as narrated by those persons whose proper function it was to preserve it intact by the power

15. Analyzed in Stuart Piggott, *The Druids* (1991[2]), p. 108f.
16 Ibid.
17 See Kim Mc Cone, *Pagan Past and Christian Present in Early Irish Literature* (1991), p. 223. All of his chapter on "Druids and Outlaws" is relevant here.
18 Proinsias Mac Cana, *The Learned Tales of Medieval Ireland* (1980), p. 112f.

of memory . . . ".[19] Such knowledge affected many aspects of life but was particu-larly relevant to kingship, status, property rights and law. "What has preserved the legal tradition of the men of Ireland?" asks the old introduction to the *Senchas Mór* [the great compilation of medieval Irish law] and goes on to answer "the common [i.e., concordant] memory of the elders, transmission from ear to ear, the chanting of the poets . . . ".[20] The collectors and compilers of the law codes were eminently literate men but their reverence for the oral tradition is worth emphasizing.

An exceedingly bitter controversy has recently erupted in the small world of Celtic scholarship concerning the manner in which the monastic scribes of the early medieval Irish were influenced by the pagan oral traditions of the *filid* and the degree to which they exercised literary creativity and personal interpretation. It is likely to be a topic of debate for years to come since both sides agree that the monks "were influenced by and drew upon an oral tradition with pagan roots", and it is the extent of monastic originality which is at issue. Much ink will be expended before the matter is settled, if at all, and I do not wish to become embroiled in the controversy here. Rather, I wish to look at the larger picture and to briefly sketch the undeniable pattern of accommodation reached by Irish Christians with pre-existing educational and legal institutions. It is this accom-modation which contributed to the preservation of earlier materials whereas it is the lack of it, and the lack of an institutional base, which affected the Germanic cultures of the continent outside of Scandinavia.

Unlike the continent, where learning in the crucial period of the seventh and eighth centuries was predominantly in the hands of the church, Irish society was unique in northern Europe in that it possessed separate learned groups, some of which had their own organized schools and arduous curricula of training. These were the elite of the *áes dáno*, the "learned men" or "men of art", of whom the most important were the poets (*filid*) and jurists (*brithemin*).[21] Each of these honored groups had a long tradition of native pagan learning. Many of their members had a status equal to that of a noble lord and the most learned amongst them had an honor-price equal to that of a petty king.[22] They belonged to the *nemed* class (cf. Gaulish *nemeton*), the meaning of which is "sacred" or "holy", and their standing was sustained by religious feelings as well as wealth.[23] It seems

---

19 Ibid., p. 125.
20 For the place of the poets in the legal tradition, see Kelly, *Guide*, pp. 43–49.
21 Discussion of both in Kelly, *Guide*, pp. 43–57. Among many studies, see J.E. Caerwyn Williams, "The Court Poet in Medieval Ireland" (1971); Richard Sharpe, "Dispute Settlement in Medieval Ireland: A Preliminary Inquiry" (1986).
22 On social classification and rank, see Thomas Charles-Edwards, "Críth Gablach and the Law of Status" (1986). *Críth Gablach* was edited by D.A. Binchy and translated by Eoin Mc Neill as "Ancient Irish Law. The Law of Status or Franchise" (1923). See further Kelly, *Guide*, p. 7f.
23 Kelly, *Guide*, p. 43f.

correct to call them a "mandarin class".[24] Such status was well recognized by the church in its legislation. Indeed, in the seventh and eighth centuries, it was the church which had to strive for equal recognition with the learned orders and not the other way around. Partly as a consequence, perhaps, the Irish church sought to accommodate, and succeeded in accommodating, a great deal of traditional vernacular learning and associated attitudes which, on the continent, would have seemed highly exotic and redolent of paganism.

Of all the learned orders, the Irish monks were most closely drawn to the *filid*, the poet-seers, and it is probably no accident that the great sixth century abbot, Columba of Iona, was closely connected with them in early medieval legend.[25] The association of churchmen and poets went further than is widely recognized. The grades of rank of the poetic hierarchy, for example, were synchronized with those of the church by 700 or so. Moreover, it is certain that many monks wrote poetry in both Latin and the vernacular. Large numbers of poets were actually attached to monasteries. One eighth century legal text declares that many of the learned professions could be practiced in both lay and monastic society without change of status.[26] Another makes clear that some churchmen were expected as a matter of course to be versed in both poetry and history.[27] According to one Middle Irish legal tract, each monastery was to have its own poet and jurist.[28] Evidence like this has caused more than one scholar to recently conclude that "the syllabus of the ideal or exemplary Irish monastic school comprised three interacting subjects—*léigenn* 'ecclesiastical learning', *filidecht* 'poetry or native lore' and *féinechas* 'native law'."[29] It is no surprise to find that the great and thoroughly pagan saga, *Táin Bó Cúailnge*, "The Cattle-Raid of Cooley", one or another version of which existed around 700, was either produced or written down in a monastery.[30]

To understand the way in which secular learning and tradition influenced Irish monks, one must know something more about the *filid*. As we have seen, the sources reveal the poet's order to have been organized in various grades depending upon skill.[31] They were greatly revered for they had the power to bless and to praise but were also feared since their contrasting ability to curse and satirize was

24 As does Donnchadh Ó Corráin who makes some perceptive observations in his "Nationality and Kingship in pre-Norman Ireland" (1978).
25 As in Whitley Stokes, "The Bodlein Amra Choluimb Cille" (1899). A recent discussion of this work is Maire Herbert, "Amra Coluim Cille" (1989).
26 Mc Cone, *Pagan Past* (1991), p. 22.
27 Ibid., p. 26.
28 Mc Cone, *Pagan Past*, p. 23.
29 Padraig O Riain, "Conservation in the Vocabulary of the Early Irish Church" (1989), p. 363.
30 The two main recensions have been edited and translated by Cecile O'Rahilly, *Táin Bó Cúailnge. Recension I* (1976); *Táin Bó Cúailnge From the Book of Leinster* (1967).
31 Liam Breatnach, *Uraicecht Na Ríar: The Poetic Grades in Early Irish Law* (1987).

universally acknowledged.[32] In fact, medieval Irish literature from the seventh century onwards is replete with examples of magical contests and flytings between poet/druid (the two are not easily distinguishable)[33] and saint, in which the saint only wins by trickery or great effort and does not always emerge unscathed. Like the saints, the poet/druids could successfully bless and curse, raise contrary winds, darken the sky and afflict with disease.[34] The cooperation between the two *nemed* groups, on the other hand, is again emphasized in the late seventh century *Vita Patricii* where it is the king's poet who rises as a mark of respect to the saint and becomes a witness to the new faith in Tara.[35] Also of special interest in the present context is the peripatetic or itinerant nature of the poets since they are depicted in the sources as constantly underway, moving from one lordly hall to another all over the island. Their status entitled them to expect and receive hospitality and reverence. Such travel was otherwise rare in Ireland for beyond one's own kingdom one became an endangered foreigner or exile, a *deoraid* of low status who was fair game without kin or protectors. In fact, the only two groups who normally traveled in this way were poets and religious *peregrini*, a point which again draws attention to the association and interaction of the church with the learned orders.[36]

Some aspects of the learning of the Irish monks also seem to have derived from the traditions of the *filid*. It is otherwise difficult to account for the pronounced love of exotic vocabulary, allusion and word play which is so impressively evident in Irish culture. It helps to explain why the *Etymologies* of Isidore received so welcome a reception in Ireland even before 650 and why it achieved such great prestige thereafter.[37] It also helps us to understand the development of the remarkable *Sondersprache* of the *Hisperica Famina* and other related literature. The *fili*'s love of subtle speech, hieratic language and public scholarly disputation to achieve rank is surely reflected there.[38] A similar *mélange* of pride and delight in language is displayed in *Auraicept na nÉces*, or the "Poet's Primer", a text much read in the

---

32 Tomas Ó Cathasaigh, "Curse and Satire" (1986), pp. 10–15.

33 Liam Mac Mathúna, *The Desingation, Functions and Knowledge of the Irish Poet: A Preliminary Semantic Study* (1982).

34 For some discussion with comparisons to continental hagiography, see Jean-Michel Picard, "The Marvellous in Irish and Continental Saints' Lives" (1981). Even in the Late Middle Ages the power of the poets was so feared that it might be incorporated among the formal sanctions of a treaty. See Charles Plummer, ed., *Vitae Sanctorum Hiberniae* (1968²), p. cii with notes.

35 Ludwig Bieler, ed. and trans., *The Patrician Texts in the Book of Armagh* (1979), p. 92. On the significance of this incident, see Kim Mc Cone, "Dubthach maccu Lugair and a Matter of Life and Death in the Pseudo-Historical Prologue to the *Senchas Már*" (1986); John Carey, "The Two Laws in Dubthach's Judgement" (1990).

36 T.M. Charles-Edwards, "The Social Background to Irish Peregrinatio" (1976), p. 52f.

37 Michael Herren, "On the Earliest Irish Acquaintance with Isidore of Seville" (1980), pp. 243–50.

38 Michael W. Herren, ed. and trans., *The Hisperica Famina I. The A-Text* (1974).

eighth century and later.[39] This has been described as "the first medieval grammar of a European vernacular".[40] What is most surprising about it, however, is the mentality of the scribe. He regards Irish as superior to all other forms of speech, including the three sacred ones of Hebrew, Greek and Latin. Anders Ahlqvist views this opinion as likely to have been a native idea for no other early medieval tradition dared to challenge the supremacy of the biblical and patristic languages.[41] Although the author was surely a monk, the manuscript tradition of the *Auraicept* demonstrates that it was the product of a school specializing in poetico-legal material.[42] Again, even allowing for the triumphalist tone of the prologue to *Lex Salica*,[43] it is difficult to imagine a Frankish monk maintaining that his language is superior to that of the bible. As we shall see below, it is a concept that would have shocked him to the core.

Perhaps the most revealing of all citations about learned Christian attitudes towards the materials of the *filid* is contained in the *Book of Leinster* recension of *Táin Bó Cúailnge*. The twelfth century monastic scribe who recorded the text was perfectly aware that it glorified the pagan past. Writing in Latin, he criticized the work he had just performed by stating that he gave no credence to the fable:

> For some things in it are the deceptions of demons, others poetic figments; some are probable, others improbable; while still others are intended for the delectation of foolish men.

Writing in Irish, however, in a wonderful example of linguistic and cultural diglossia, a more intense and warmly emotional feeling comes to the fore:

> A blessing on everyone who shall faithfully memorize the *Táin* as it is written here and shall not add any other form to it.[44]

This is an extraordinary statement! Here is a man who believed so strongly in the universal religion of Christianity that he had dedicated himself to a severely ascetic life of pious devotion. Once he elected to think in Irish categories, however, a switch indicated by language, he felt so committed to his demon deceived text that he regarded it as a semi-holy work which should be memorized in the same way that his colleagues might memorize the psalms or books of the bible. Like these works, the words of the *Táin* might not be altered. Such an attitude is

---

39 Anders Ahlquist, ed. and trans., *The Early Irish Linguist: An Edition of the Canonical Part of the Auraicept Na nÉces* (1983).
40 Jack Fellmann, "The First Medieval Grammar of a European Vernacular" (1978), p. 55f.
41 Ahlquist, *Auraicept*, p. 12f., 19f.
42 Ibid., p. 13.
43 Ruth Schmidt-Wiegand, "*gens francorum inclita*: Zu Gestalt und Inhalt des langeren Prologs der *Lex Salica*" (1955), pp. 233–70.
44. His attitude is discussed in Proinsias Mac Cana, "Early Irish Ideology and the Concept of Unity" (1985), p. 56f.

consistent and understandable against the background of the Irish tradition as I have sketched it here but who can imagine a continental monk bestowing a blessing on everyone who would memorize the *Völuspá* or the *Merseburger Zauberspruch*? Even the act of recommending memorization is itself worthy of note when it is done by a monk literate in two languages. It suggests that the oral and written cultures co-existed in an atmosphere of respectful interaction as late as the twelfth century. The *Táin* is also a long work, about one hundred and fifty pages or so in a modern translation, and the fact that a scribe might think of a (fairly large?) number of readers prepared to memorize it says much about the status and appeal of oral learning among the Irish literati.

Of course, many of the *filid* may have themselves become literate as time went on but that hardly means that they abandoned their familiar repertoire. Ireland is that place in early medieval Europe where heathen myth and ritual is recorded more fully than anywhere else and where the links with Indo-European material are strongly attested. Christian monks would make many efforts to domesticate the most egregious aspects of all this but it looks very much like an effort to partially contain that which they could not control. As we shall see below, a high percentage of the continental clergy enjoyed the diverse lore of the past as well but they were mostly brought to heel by official policy by about 900 or so. But the multitude of kings, lay abbots and tribal particularism made any attempts at such an approach more difficult in Ireland. In addition, the influence and patronage power of the institutional learned orders, each of which wished to preserve a full account of their own experience, meant that the church could not develop an encompassing interpretative monopoly on the history of the past or the *senchas* of the bards and *filid*. The imposition of any official scheme or policy in early medieval Ireland would be hindered by the same conditions which frustrated later invaders seeking to conquer the country—too much dispersal of power and influence, too few resources available to enforce uniformity, too strong a veneration for the person and knowledge of the *filid*.

The Germanic peoples of the continent also possessed a powerful oral tradition documentable from scattered remarks by classical authors and by early medieval writers like Gregory of Tours, Bede, Paul the Lombard and Alcuin. In the migration period the songs and recitation of professional poets were closely associated with the aristocratic lifestyle, as were the instruments which they played in accompaniment. In Köln, in Alemannia, in north Francia, harps and lyres have been found in aristocratic graves along with weapons, ornaments and drinking vessels so that it is clear that all were part of a flourishing upper class culture.[45] One is reminded of ancient Greece when Achilles strummed his lyre and sang of the glorious deeds of warriors. As in the *Beowulf* poem, where the hero was called upon several times to speak publicly in the hall, the skills taught by poets

45 Joachim Werner, "Leier und Harfe im germanischen Frühmittelalter" (1954), pp. 9–15.

were valued by young aristocrats, the future advisors of kings, who might gain in reputation by a knowledge of the past and a skill in repartee and rhetoric. Initially, at least, the clergy did not oppose these aspects of the inherited conventions.

In the eighth century, the professional performers of the tradition were still well regarded by the literate clergy who distinguished between high-status *poetae* and lowly *scurri*, the *scop* and the joker or mime. It is probably the former who is mentioned in a mid-ninth century *vita* (describing a scene from *c.*790) by bishop Altfrid of Hildesheim. He was a blind singer named Bernlef who lived on the estate of a noble Frisian woman and was greatly favored by the inhabitants of the area for he knew how to accompany "the deeds of the ancients and the battles of kings" with the music of his lyre.[46] Bernlef was a pagan, converted by St. Luidger of Münster, who cured him and thereafter taught him the psalms. There is no mention here of any antagonism between bishops and poets, indeed it looks more like an alliance existed between the two carriers of different traditions. It was the kind of association that could give rise to literary records. Among the schoolbooks of a Reichenau book catalogue of 821/22 appears the title *De carminibus theodiscae* vol[umen] I, "Of Songs in the German Language, One Volume", and in the next generation *XII carmina Theodiscae lingua formata*, "Twelve Songs Composed in the German Language", and *carmina diversa ad docendam Theodiscam linguam*, "Diverse Songs for Teaching the German Language".[47] We do not know the genre of these songs which may well have been a mixture of various types.

All of this is sad to recall since a fragment of the *Hildebrandslied* is the only sizable surviving piece of Germanic heroic poetry south of Scandinavia. The answer to the apparent contradiction – a flourishing oral tradition but few written remains—appears to lie in the increasing hostility of the Christian clergy. Over the course of the ninth century, the poets and wandering minstrels of the Carolingian Age are constantly criticized for their crudity and morals. Before 900, as W. Haubrichs notes, the word *scop* was frequently glossed with *vates, psalta, psalmista*.[48] Thereafter, it is usually glossed with *ioculator, mimus, tragicus, satyricus* and so on, occupational terms for individuals considerably lower down on the social scale. The *idiota et illerati*, the unlettered multitude, are now more rigidly distinguished from the *docti et cauti*, the Christian clergy, who had abandoned the *simplex natura* of the rustics and possessed *eruditio*, Latin learning. Even the

---

46 Wolfgang Haubrichs, *Geschichte der deutschen Literatur von den Anfängen bis zum Beginn der Neuzeit I: Von den Aufängen zum hohen Mittelalter* (1988), p. 84. See further Egon Werlich, "Der westgermanische Skop: Der Ursprung des Sängerstandes in semasiologischer und etymologischer Sicht" (1967).

47 Ibid., p. 103f.

48 Haubrichs, *Anfang*, p. 89. Michael Richter is currently preparing several new works in the area and I wish to thank him for allowing me to see in advance of publication a draft of his *The Oral Tradition in the Early Medieval West* to appear soon in the series *Typologie des sources du môyen-age occidental*. See now his *The Formation of the Medieval West. Studies in the Oral Culture of the Barbarians* (1994).

vernacular itself is criticized as an unworthy tool for learned expression. Writing in the first half of the ninth century, Walahfrid Strabo speaks in the most contemptuous tones, likening Germanic speech to that of monkeys in comparison with that of the Latin speaking children of Augustus. Terms like *inculta*, "un-kempt", *indisciplinabilis*, "untamable" and *agrestis lingua*, "peasant speech", are frequent in the literature.[49]

This is not to say that continental clergy were immune to the charms of native learning. In 802, repeating a prohibition of 789, Charlemagne admonished abbots and abbesses against maintaining entertainers, and the renewed warnings of succeeding generations show that churchmen found it difficult to live up to the ordinance.[50] A deep cleft existed between public and private attitudes. Nonethe-less, the drumbeat of official condemnation did succeed in attaching the taint of crudity, sinfulness and paganism to the carriers of Germanic *carmina*—not so much in driving their material underground for it remained popular outside official purview—but in degrading the status of the poets and in excluding their works from the affirming literary record. Largely deprived of monastic support and increasingly of the patronage of secular lords, vernacular learning which did not serve a religious purpose came to reside largely in the *Volk* rather than the hierarchy.

Even though we know of the continuity of oral tradition on the continent, ecclesiastical reluctance to dignify it by recording it deprives scholars of the most central evidence. One way to attempt recovery is through a combination of archaeological and art-historical research of the type that Karl Hauck has con-ducted over the past generation. This has proven to be immensely fruitful. In the case of the motifs and scenes of migration period gold bracteates, for example, it has been possible to show in minute and specific detail a close relationship with the picture stones of Scandinavia and with the content of scaldic and eddic poetry.[51] These studies, apparently, are little known to literary scholars and many archaeologists are insufficiently aware as well since so much of the work deals with the art-historical field of iconography. It must be stressed, however, that cultural continuity for the Germanic periphery has *already* been demonstrated in many areas and much of this is directly relevant to conditions at the core for it illuminates in a completely novel way the conditions and clues that do exist there. Most importantly, it demonstrates the power of the oral or *Gedächtniskultur* in all of Europe to the High Middle Ages and clarifies the role of the periphery as a repository of tradition. Although the scalds of the North lacked the established educational base of the *filid*, their persons and their craft were held in high honor

---

49 Haubrichs, *Anfang*, pp. 43f., 61f.
50 See Richter's discussion in *Formation*, pp. 125–80.
51 Amidst a flourishing literature, see now the conference papers in Karl Hauck, ed., *Der historische Horizant der Gotterbild-Amulette aus der Übergangsepoche von der Spätantike zum Frühmittelalter* (1992).

by the leaders of society who might also be trained in poetry themselves. Indeed, it is highly probable that the two cultures, Irish and Scandinavian, mutually reinforced and affected each other. The Vikings maintained strongholds and then petty kingdoms in Ireland for over two centuries so that there was frequent intermarriage, bilingualism, mixed lordships and cultural exchange. One famous scald, Kormakr Ogmundarson, bears an Irish name and plenty of others have Irish, Welsh or Scottish contacts and associations.[52] The literature of all these peoples demonstrate a history of diverse interaction. Purists of all groups dislike the implications but the interaction is there nonetheless.

Similarly, the compilers of North Germanic oral tradition might demonstrate attitudes much like that of the copyist of *Táin Bó Cúailnge*. At the end of the second poem of Helgi Hundingsbani, the thirteenth century scribe reveals his divided allegiance:

> It was a belief in heathen times that men could be reborn, but that is now called old women's foolishness. Helgi and Sigrun are said to have been reborn. He was named Helgi, Prince of the Haddings, and she was Kara, the daughter of Halfdan, as is told in the poem *Karuljod*, and she was a Valkyrie.[53]

As R. Kellogg remarks, the scribe wants to tell the story but also to dissociate himself from it.[54] His references to "heathen times" and "old women's foolishness" sound like condescension but are more probably a tactical device which allows him to go on writing about that which he clearly loves without incurring censure: it is part of an uneasy cultural synthesis which tolerates a certain amount of contradiction in dealing sympathetically with explicit paganism. The scribe cannot bless anyone who memorizes his pagan poems but it does seem likely that he has memorized them himself.

The surviving literature of Anglo-Saxon England is unique in one instance in that it provides us with a relatively detailed description of the creation of an early medieval poet. It is the story of Caedmon found in Bede's *Historia Ecclesiastica* (IV, 24) completed in 731. Caedmon bears an anglicized Celtic name indicating a bi-cultural background. His career may be placed between 660 and 680. As Bede describes him, he lived a secular life as a simple worker near abbess Hild's monastery of Whitby and "had never learned any songs". Even at a feast, when

52 E.O.G. Turville-Petre, *Scaldic Poetry* (1976), pp. xxiv, 45f.
53 Cited in Robert Kellogg, "Literacy and Orality in the Poetic Edda" (1991), p. 94f.
54 Ibid. Many questions can be raised here. For background discussions, see D.H. Green, "Orality and Reading: The State of Research in Medieval Studies" (1990); Michael Richter, "Kommunikationsprobleme im lateinischen Mittelalter" (1976); Lars Lönnroth, "Hjálmar's Death-Song and the Delivery of Eddic Poetry" (1971); Joseph Harris, "Eddic Poetry as Oral Poetry: The Evidence of Parallel Passages in the Helgi Poems for Questions of Composition and Performance" (1983); Jurgen von Ungern-Sternberg and Hansjorg Reinau, eds., *Vergangenheit in mundlicher Überlieferung* (1988); Morton W. Bloomfield and Charles W. Dunn, *The Role of the Poet in Early Societies* (1989).

"it had been decided that they should all sing in turn, when he saw the harp approaching him, he would rise up in the middle of the feasting, go out, and return home". After one such occasion, he fell asleep in a cattle byre and had a dream in which God appeared to him and told him to sing. Caedmon suddenly found it possible to do so marvelously well and "when he awoke, he remembered all that he had sung while asleep". After describing his experience to the reeve, Caedmon was passed on to the abbess and then to a panel of *doctores* who "read to him a passage of sacred history of doctrine, bidding him make a song out of it, if he could, in metrical form". He returned next morning when he had turned the passage "into excellent verse". Recognizing that he was inspired by the grace of God, abbess Hild

> instructed him to renounce his secular habit and to take monastic vows. She and all her people received him into the community of the brothers and ordered that he should be instructed in the whole course of sacred history. He learned all he could by listening to them and then, memorizing it and ruminating over it, like some clean animal chewing the cud, he turned it into the most melodious verse . . . He sang about the creation of the world, the origin of the human race, and the whole history of Genesis . . . and of many other of the stories taken from the sacred Scriptures.

A number of biblical epics have been ascribed to Caedmon and the short vernacular lyric known as *Caedmon's Song* was exceptionally popular for centuries. There are also many analogues, Celtic and Germanic, to his story—the dream inspiration, the night of rumination and memorization, the recital thereafter. Jeff Opland is reminded of Egil Skallagrimsson laboring through the night to compose a *drapa* for Erik[55] but the story sounds suspiciously like a description of a poetic test of the type one might expect for a novice *fili* in an established curriculum before examiners, perhaps then, another example of substitution. Caedmon's Celtic name may be a significant clue. In any case, we note again a phenomenon referred to earlier: Caedmon is illiterate and seems to have remained so throughout his life; he composes, memorizes what he has composed and literate monks write down his verses. They are then memorized by others so that an almost natural commingling and symbiosis of the oral and literate modes comes into being.

The attitudes surrounding Old English literature seem comparable to those of the continent in that considerable hostility existed to the usage of non-Christian themes of the pagan past and the partially Christianized early medieval present. Bede says that none could compare with Caedmon because "he received the gift of song freely by the grace of God. Hence he could never compose any

55 Jeff Opland, *Anglo-Saxon Oral Poetry: A Study of the Traditions* (1980) p. 114; Margaret C. Ross, "The Art of Poetry and Figure of the Poet in *Egil's saga*" (1989).

foolish or trivial poem but only those which were concerned with devotion . . . ". His songs inspired others to "despise the world and to long for the heavenly life". In all of his works "he sought to turn his hearers away from delight in sin" and, submitting himself to monastic discipline, "he opposed all those who wished to act otherwise with a flaming and fervent zeal". It looks again as if "a deliberate replacement programme" is underway.

In comparing English and Irish modes of literary expression, Hildegard Tristram writes: "The Christianizing policy in England seems to have been a wholesale replacement of pagan mythology by Christian doctrine, whereas the Irish strategy was to harmonize the two. By rendering it inoffensive and legiti-mizing it by synchronisms with Old Testament history à la Eusebius, they [the Irish] were able to preserve large parts of their pre-Christian heritage".[56] As J.D. Niles has argued, however, some kinds of integration with the past did take place in Anglo-Saxon England—in the remaking of Wodan into a descendant of Noah, in the reinterpretation of runic letters, in the reworking of tradition so that the *Beowulf* poem recognizes some aspects of paganism while at the same time overlaying the work as a whole with a Christian consciousness and a strong "Christian coloring".[57] The result is a less offensive and bowdlerized (one might almost say "politically correct") form of understanding which, nonetheless, mediates between the Germanic heritage and Christianity—but only in a few works deemed worthy of placement on expensive monastic vellum. Even then, *Beowulf* survived in only one manuscript. The oral tradition continued to flourish outside of the monastery, it simply wasn't written down. As for the "harmoniz-ing" strategy of the Irish, it seems unclear as yet that it operated in that way, or worked consistently in that way, although Kim Mc Cone has convincingly demonstrated the existence of many carefully developed techniques to make it do so.[58] Some of these will have worked. But what are we to make of the *Táin* scribe who directly links part of the opus to the deception of demons while blessing those who memorize it, or of the druids who might be sympathetically described even while battling Christian saints? There is so much of this that it seems difficult to speak of a real symmetrical "fit" between approaches. Another possibility is equally valid: it is that, in the case of both Ireland and Iceland, of conservative cultures drawing on a millennium of experience and willing to harbor incompatible concepts as long as ultimate allegiance goes to Christianity. The perspective is not unlike that of a twice married man who retains an affection for his first wife and her children. The second wife may well tolerate visits in order to prevent strife and disaffection. Anything more than a surface harmony

---

56 Hildegard L.C. Tristram, "Early Modes of Insular Expression" (1989) p. 431.
57 John D. Niles, "Pagan Survivals and Popular Belief" (1991). See further Craig R. Davis, "Cultural Assimilation in the Anglo-Saxon Royal Geneologies" (1992).
58 That is a central theme of his *Pagan Past*.

between the women is unlikely but that is perfectly acceptable under the circumstances and is really all that is necessary. Anthropologists tell us that cultures often
behave like individuals and can be just as ambivalent. It is because of these
qualities of ambivalence and tenacity that the *Randkulturen* preserved much of
the thought-world that was largely omitted from the written records of the
continent and England.

Armed with this knowledge—the continuity of material remains, the archaeological evidence for the mead cup motif, the long continental history of La Tène
cultural interaction, the conserving traditions of the insular Celts and northern
Germans—we may now return to the lady and the warlord in the *comitatus*
tradition.

V

WARBAND RELIGION AND THE CELTIC WORLD

Analysis in previous chapters suggests that the warlord/consort behavior pattern described by the *Beowulf* poet originates in the Germanic past and is parallelled in surprising ways by Tacitus' descriptions of similar duos contained in the *Germania* and *Historia*. A comparison of Wealhtheow with Veleda has proven to be particularly instructive in that both women have been found to be delegates of a warlord who help him to control his followers and achieve his goal of greater hierarchically based solidarity. While the fact that one is a wife and the other a virgin prophetess might seem to be a noteworthy difference at first glance, the delegatory status of each in relation to the warlord is surely a weightier datum especially when joined to the finding that Wealhtheow exhibits hints of vacinatory power as well. Moreover, the association of each woman with the ritual-political sphere is quite clear. Wealhtheow's proclamation of kingship during her cup-of-fering is a momentous ritual act for the warband and something similar may also have occurred with the early Germanic sibyls for we have seen that they could be the companions of kings during embassies, that is, on formal occasions, and links with regard to promises of victory and oaths seem probable. Despite the intervening centuries and scarcity of detailed references—a gap which now looms less formidably because of the demonstrated continuity of the archaeological evidence —the warlord's need to bolster his position and influence the morale of his troops through control of the supernatural provides a convincing logical connection for the activities of both women since this need is a perennial one which operates regardless of chronology and geography. It may not, however, be separate from the sphere of *comitatus* warfare and may well be tied to it since frequent reassurance will naturally be more important for those groups often in harm's way and less so for those who are not commonly raiders and who are more or less peaceful or sedentary. The kind of binding performed by the prophetess/consort may also be less necessary outside of the warband where the fictive kinship element declines in importance.

Building on previous discussion, the present chapter seeks to deepen our understanding of the relationship between women like Veleda and Wealhtheow and the warleader by shifting focus to the evidence of personal names, by drawing on comparative material relating to the Celts and by a discussion of the origin of the *comitatus* and *comitatus* religion. In studies of the present type in which results are inevitably based on scattered clues, all avenues must be explored before reaching conclusions. As we shall see, one type of evidence, that of names, leads ineluctably to the other, that of comparative institutions, and both can profitably be interpreted against the background of evolution in military organization from about the third century BC to the time of Tacitus. The rise of the warlord/prophetess team in northern Europe, it will be argued, is closely related to changes in technology, warfare and kingship which, in turn, are due to a long period of intense interaction between Celts and Germans in the Rhineland and elsewhere.

1. DRUIDS, FEMALE MAGIC AND WEAVING BEAMS

We may begin by stating that Veleda, the first female companion of a warlord of whom we know, is a remarkable name to be borne by a woman of the Germanic tribe of the Bructeri, living east of the Rhine in the area of the Lippe.[1] It is remarkable because it is not readily explainable on the basis of Germanic culture and is probably not a personal name at all but rather a "cult-name" or the name for a particular occupation or office. A long list of scholars, Holder, Vendryes, Dottin to name a few, interpret the name as Celtic while others like Müllenhoff, Krahe and Meid, treat it as more likely to be Germanic.[2] Krahe, for example, holds it to be a Germanic "inherited word", as "a common form (isogloss) with Celtic, but not a borrowing from it". He, nevertheless, concludes with the observation that "it is impossible to escape from the fact that 'Veleda' is isolated in Germanic". and notes a similar isogloss in *nimidas*, "*sacra silvarum*", in the *Indiculus Superstitionum* which corresponds to Gaulish *nemeton* and Old Irish *nemed*.[3] The problem recognized by most scholars of the latter group is that only faint signs of the relevant root word are present in Germanic but, as Much-Jankuhn notes, the name Veleda corresponds "exactly to Irish *fili* derived from *velet*—'poet,' actually 'prophet,' which belongs to Middle Welsh *gwelet*, now *gweled*".[4] Krahe and Meid share this view as well. The conclusion follows that "Veleda therefore now means 'prophetess' and is thus an epithet (Beiname)".[5] Guyonvarc'h also maintains this opinion and so does Helmut Birkhan, the most recent commentator, who agrees that Veleda is not the actual name of the

---

1 A good discussion of the first century Bructeri with full bibliography is contained in Wolfgang Will, "Römisch 'Klientel-Randstaaten' am Rhein? Eine Bestandsaufnahme" (1987), pp. 38–44. See further Ludwig Schmidt, *Geschichte der Deutschen Stämme bis zum Ausgang der Völkerwanderung. Die Westgermanen* II (1940²), p. 200ff.; Much, Jankuhn and Lange, *Germania*, p. 397f.

2 A summary of views will be found in Gerold Walser, "Veleda" (1955), clm. 617–21. See further: Hermann Reichert, *Thesaurus Paleogermanicus: Lexikon der altgermanischen Namen* I (1987), p. 770; Helmut Birkhan, *Germanen und Kelten* (1970) pp. 553–7; Moritz Schonfeld, *Wörterbuch der altgermanischen Personen- und Völkernamen* (1911), p. 102f.

3 Hans Krahe, "Altgermanische Kleinigkeiten" (1961), p. 43; Wolfgang Meid, "Der germanische Personenname *Veleda*" (1964), p. 256f.

4 Much, Jankuhn and Lange, *Germania*, p. 169.

5 Ibid.

prophetess but is instead a "sacred name" or "cultic epithet".[6] He associates it with the very close relations between Celts and Germans in the Rhineland where, as he points out, ancient authors have often referred to the existence of druidesses and *dryadae*.[7] The OI evidence shows that female druids, called *banfilid*, *banfathi*, *bandrui*, did have an established place in society. The Gaulish name for such a woman may have been **uelētā* or **ueletā*.[8]

This interpretation which emphasizes that Veleda was not actually the personal name of the prophetess and which explains its existence by reference to cognate Irish and Welsh terms for poet, seer and prophet is almost certainly correct. One may point out, however, that these linguists seem to have reached their conclusions in default of a key piece of evidence which clinches the Celtic link but which has not to my knowledge hitherto been adduced. In order to understand its significance, we must first pause to clarify the relationship between Celtic druid and poet-seer, the *fili* whose designation best explains the name Veleda. This is necessary not only because it strengthens the overall trend of the modern *communis opinio* but also because it modifies it slightly and offers a further clue regarding the relationship obtaining between prophetess, warlord and warfare. Thereafter, we shall see that it also contains some implications for the study of Wealhtheow.

Posidonius (*c*.135—*c*.50 BC), who had himself traveled in southern Gaul, was the great authority on the Celts for the ancient world.[9] Book 23 of his *History* was dedicated to them. Although the work is no longer extant, much of his material survives in summary form (with some changes and additions) in three later Greek authors, Diodorus Siculus, Strabo and Athenaus. As is well known, Posidonius divided the learned classes in Gaulish society into three groups: "druids", *druidai*, "seers", *ouateis* and "poets", *bardoi*. Words cognate with each of these exist in OI and MI: *drui*, "druid", *faith*, later *faidh*, "seer, prophet", and *bard*, "poet". [10]The term *fili* might seem to interrupt this symmetry but it is actually to be equated with *faith* and, as Mac Mathúna points out in his illuminating semantic study of

---

6 Christian J. Guyonvarc'h, "A propos de la VELLEDA des Bructeres et du mot irlandais FILE "poète, prophète voyant" (1969), pp. 321–5; Christian J. Guyonvarc'h and Françoise Le Roux, *Les Druides* (1986), p. 438f.; Birkhan, *Germanen und Kelten*, p. 557.
7 Ibid. Further discussion below.
8 Birkhan, *Germanen und Kelten*, p. 557.
9 Tierney, "Celtic Ethnography", pp. 189–275. Cf. Daphne Nash, "Reconstructing Posidonius' Celtic Ethnography: Some Considerations" (1976), pp. 111–26; T.C. Champion, "Written Sources and the Study of the European Iron Age" (1985), pp. 9–22; Norden, *Urgeschichte*, pp. 59f., 105f., 116f., 142f. et passim; H.D. Rankin, *Celts and the Classical World* (1987), pp. 259–94.
10 There are many studies to draw upon. Most helpful in the present context are Liam Mac Mathúna, *The Designation, Functions and Knowledge of the Irish Poet: A Preliminary Study* (1982), pp. 225–38; J.E.C. Williams, "Celtic Literature: Origins" (1986), pp. 123–44; Idem, "The Court Poet in Medieval Ireland" (1971); Proinsias Mac Cana, "Conservation and Innovation in Early Celtic Literature" (1972), p. 89f.

the Irish wordfield dealing with poetry and knowledge, its emergence before the
fifth century in Ireland reflects a realignment of the dynamic intellectual classes
whose functions were not as sharply divided as has often been supposed.[11]

Female seers existed among the Gauls on the continent and are also known
from early Irish texts, although in both areas they do not appear to have been very
common. The best known example is Feidelm, mentioned in both Recension I
and II of the preface to *Táin Bó Cúailnge*.[12] She is characterized by the inter-
changeable terms *banfaith* and *banfili*, "seeress".[13] The passage in question describes the gathering of queen Medb's army for a great cattle raid on Ulster. The
army was forced to delay its departure, however, because "their prophets and
druids did not permit them to go thence, but kept them for a fortnight awaiting
an auspicious omen".[14] On the day on which Medb finally decided to depart, she
was still worried about the outcome of the expedition (which was indeed destined
to be ill-fated) and her charioteer suggested that they turn right-handwise in order
to strengthen their luck. It was on doing so that they saw before them a grown
"maiden" who proclaimed that she was Feidelm, the *banfili* of Connacht, Medb's
own kingdom. She was dressed in rich garments with a golden brooch and a tunic
with red embroidery. Her shoes had golden fastenings; "in her hand she carried
a weaver's beam of white bronze, with golden inlay".[15] Medb questioned her and
was told that she possessed the art of divination or *filidecht* (the corresponding
abstract noun of *fili*) part of which was *imbas forosnai*, "the great knowledge which
illuminates".[16]

Recension II of the *Táin* belongs to the twelfth century and is thus about two
to three centuries younger than Recension I. It preserves, or adds, a few other
details to this passage while modifying in a number of places. In Recension II, for
example, Medb turns to a druid for a prophecy of the outcome and receives an
unsatisfactory answer. It is then that the charioteer performs the turn and Feidelm
approaches. She is now described as "weaving a fringe, holding a weaver's beam
of white bronze in her right hand with seven stripes of red gold on its points".[17]
She tells Medb that she is "promoting your interest and prosperity" and, when
asked why, replies: "I have good reason to do so. I am a bondmaid [*banchumal*] of
your people".[18] While the weaving rod is mentioned in both texts, the second
recension thus adds the interesting information that Feidelm serves Medb's

11 Mac Mathúna, *Irish Poet*, p. 237f.
12 Cecile O'Rahilly, ed., *Táin Bó Cúailnge. Recension I* (1976), pp. 2, 126; Idem, *Táin Bó Cúailnge From the Book of Leinster* (1970), pp. 5, 143.
13 For these terms, see Mac Mathúna, *Irish Poet*, p. 227f.; Guyonvarc'h and Le Roux, *Druides*, p. 438f.
14 O'Rahilly, *Táin. Recension I*, p. 125.
15 Ibid., p. 126.
16 Ibid., pp. 2, 126.
17 O'Rahilly, *Táin From the Book of Leinster*, p. 143.
18 Ibid.

interests because she is expected to do so; she is a slave of her people who is also a prophetess.

Several aspects of this portrait are relevant to the present analysis and will be discussed below. Most immediately instructive is the occasion of the meeting in Recension II for Medb only encounters the *banfili* after first consulting a druid. Although an apparently insignificant detail, this seems to underline the fact that in both Gaulish and Irish traditions the prophets serve as the mouthpieces of the druids since the latter are mostly occupied with religious knowledge, the judgement of quarrels and legal cases and the teaching of the young. Whereas the druids are more like professors in that they study "the science of nature" and "moral philosophy", the vates are more like "interpreters" of sacrifice and we know that the great sacrifices were performed by druids.[19] The distinction may not always be a clear one but it did exist. In the Irish tradition the distinction is easier to draw because the prophets are also poets. Mac Mathúna cites and translates several MI texts which illustrate the point: "the seven druids to bewitch (?) them through spells, the seven poets [*filid*] to lampoon them and to proclaim them". Or: "and their druids chanted a charm and their poets [*filidh*] extempore incantations for them".[20] Feidelm does the same in Recension I of the *Táin* in that her prophecy is given in verse and in Recension II she "began to prophesy and foretell Cú Chulainn to the men of Ireland, and she chanted a lay".[21] The druids, apparently, "are thought of as wielding supernatural power by means of stereotyped spells; the poets would verbalize the process using newly composed satires and formal proclamations".[22]

This relationship between druid and *fili*, in which the former searches for knowledge and the latter proclaims it in a special manner, seems to illuminate a small but significant detail in Tacitus' discussion of Veleda's *modus operandi*. The occasion of his report was a quarrel between the Tencteri and the people of Köln in which the latter, most of whom were Ubii who had allowed Roman veterans to settle amongst them, were called upon to kill the foreign settlers. The Ubii protested that they could not do so because the veterans had intermarried with them and became their parents, brothers and children. They proposed instead a compromise solution by asking that Civilis and Veleda act as arbiters "before whom all our agreements shall be ratified": *arbitrum habebimus Civilem et Veledam, apud quos pacta sancientur.*[23] With this proposal the Tencteri were "calmed" and a delegation was sent with gifts to Civilis and Veleda who "settled everything". But the embassy was "not allowed to approach" Veleda directly:

19 Tierney, "Celtic Ethnography", pp. 251, 269; Guyonvarc'h and Le Roux, *Druides*, pp. 14–44, 425–44.
20 Mac Mathúna, *Irish Poet*, p. 227.
21 O'Rahilly, *Táin From the Book of Leinster*, p. 144.
22 Mac Mathúna, *Irish Poet*, p. 227.
23 Moore, *Tacitus. Histories*, IV, 65, p. 126f.

In order to inspire them with more respect, they were prevented from seeing her. She dwelt in a lofty tower, and one of her relatives chosen for the purpose, conveyed, like a messenger of a divinity, the questions and answers.[24]

Scholars have not hitherto devoted much attention to the peculiar connection between Veleda and her relative who conveys her answers "like the messenger of a divinity". He has been neglected, perhaps, because his function seems to be little more than that of an errand-boy, a simple carrier of the sibyl's oracles. But examination of the Gaulish, and especially the Irish, evidence suggests otherwise for the Veleda/messenger link reproduces that of druid/*fili*. Introduction of this material—an explanatory foray perfectly justified by the name of the prophetess herself—suggests that the Bructeri messenger's position may have been an established institutional one which also existed at other times for other prophetesses. Although Tacitus does not say so (for him the allusion was casual) the "messenger" was probably expected to deliver the oracles in a particular way, no doubt expounding and interpreting them in formal verse as did the Irish *fili*, who was also a poet. The conclusion is justified for other reasons too. If Veleda was at all like other prophets, then her answers were seldom clear and she may also have used exotic devices, gestures or phraseology to express her meaning.[25] A grunt, a glance, a movement, a word, might all have had special import and have required an interpreter to translate them into understandable language which, because of its source in divine revelation, would naturally require an appropriately eloquent style of delivery and locution. If correct, this may be a significant clue to the nature of early Germanic religious practice. The question is too involved to enter into here. For present purposes it is enough to note that the analysis offered would seem to confirm the view that Veleda is not a personal name. Instead, it would seem to be a Germanic borrowing of a Celtic appelative for a special type of religious practitioner. This confirmation of the linguistic evidence by a separate route is doubly important because it shows that some Germanic peoples at least had adopted a Celtic word to describe the general category of office of the "prophetess". Regardless of personal name, each would be called "*veleda*".

A problem arises with this interpretation. In Irish tradition it is the messenger

24 Ibid: sed coram adire adloquique Veledam negatum: arcebantur aspectu quo venerationis plus inesset. Ipsa edita in turre; delectus e propinquis consulta responsaque ut internuntius numinis portabat.

25 Plutarch speaks, for example, of the Pythia's *mania* which he compares to a turbulent sea: "incapable of remaining passive and offering herself, still and tranquil, to him who moves her, she roils inwardly like a stormy sea, for within her, movements and passions rage. Think of bodies that rotate as they fall: they do not move in a regular or certain manner, but rather, owing to the circular impetus they receive and because of their tendency to fall, exhibit an irregular and disorderly turbulence". A recent extended discussion in Giulia Sissa, *Greek Virginity* (1990), pp. 15–32. Two useful essays on mantic techniques are Françoise Le Roux, "La divination chez les Celtes" (1968), pp. 233–56, and Derolez, "Divination chez les Germains", pp. 257–302.

who would have been called *fili*, not Veleda, and this discrepancy might seem to suggest that the comparative evidence is misleading. But such is probably not the case for there are at least two likely appropriate explanations at hand. In its migration from one culture to another such an occupational title might well have been mistakenly applied to the druidess rather than to the druidical interpreter and then have become institutionally established as the designation for a holder of a particular office. Another possibility is that the functions of druid and *fili* were simply not always clearly differentiated. Mac Mathúna's discussion of the medieval evidence demonstrates a certain fluidity of usage and, in his opinion, the two types of practitioner may not always have been easy to distinguish in any period.[26]

Recourse to Celtic evidence can also help us to better understand the Tacitean passage as a whole. We recall that the Veleda reference occurs within the context of conflict and threatened warfare between Tencteri and Ubii and that it is purely to arbitrate the quarrel that Veleda and Civilis are called upon. Both sides are satisfied with the notion and each accepts the subsequent decision. Although such might seem to be a reasonable bargain to moderns, and doubtless that is the reason for the lack of scholarly commentary, it is not at all a common Germanic way of settling disputes among peoples. While vaguely related instances probably could be found somewhere in the corpus, I know of no clear early medieval parallel. The *matres familiae*, for example, certainly advised on omens but did not normally operate as arbiters. On the other hand, the Gaulish druids constantly did so.

Posidonius relates that "the Celts have in their company even in war (as well as in peace) companions whom they call parasites. These men pronounce their praises before the whole assembly and before each of the chieftains in turn as they listen". They are, however, separate from the bards ("poets who deliver eulogies in song") and seem to have had an association with oratory and wisdom. As Caerwyn Williams has shown, the Greek word *parasitos* did not simply mean a hanger-on or sponger but also designated an honored "companion at a sacred feast" who had sacrificial and religious duties.[27] In the Celtic context, they resemble druids. It is especially noteworthy that these druids accompanied warriors on campaigns. Drawing on Posidonius, Diodorus Siculus wrote of the Celts:

> Their custom is that no one should offer sacrifice without a philosopher; for they say that thanks should be offered to the gods by those skilled in the divine nature, as though they were people who can speak their language, and through them also they hold that benefits should be asked. And it is not only in the needs of peace but in war also that they carefully obey these men and their

26 Mac Mathúna, *Irish Poet*, p. 237f.
27 J.E. Williams, "Posidonius's Celtic Parasites" (1980), p. 314f.

song-loving poets, and this is true not only of their friends but also of their enemies. For oftentimes as armies approach each other in line of battle with their swords drawn and their spears raised for the charge these men come forth between them and stop the conflict, as though they had spellbound some kind of wild animals.[28]

Similarly, in a famous phrase, Strabo calls the druids "the most just of men" who often "arbitrated in war".[29] Citations like these of course cannot prove that Germanic prophetesses might not have sometimes have performed the same type of acts but it is still true to say that Germanic tradition does not demand it of them, whereas the Celtic one does require it of their equivalents. The Celtic tradition also sanctioned a certain amount of female participation. Writing in the early second century AD, Plutarch (*De virtute mulierum* 6) recalled an earlier incident of women negotiating between armies which resonated down to his own time:

> . . . a dire and persistent factional discord broke out among them which went on and on to the point of civil war. The [Celtic] women, however, put themselves between the armed forces, and, taking up the controversies, arbitrated and decided them with such irreproachable fairness that a wondrous friendship . . . was brought about between both states and families. As a result of this, they continued to consult with the women in regard to war and peace, and to decide through them any disputed matters in their relations with their allies . . . in their treaties with Hannibal they [the Celts] wrote the provision that, if the Celts complained against the Carthaginians, the governors and generals of the Carthaginians in Spain should be the judges; and if the Carthaginians complained against the Celts, the judges should be the Celtic women.

Plutarch notes that the Celts "continued" to act in this way. But he is vague when he speaks of "women" since, just as it was only the "governors and generals" of the Carthaginians who might settle disputes, it must also have been only a certain small number of women of recognized honor and experience who might intervene for the Celts. Any large body is unlikely. Considering what we now know, it appears probable that the females in question were druidesses or associated with druids. In other words, they were veledas. It is therefore, not simply Veleda *and* the "messenger" who recall the Celtic world but also the peculiar manner of arbitration itself. Finally, it is interesting to note that Veleda communed with the divine in a tower. On the basis of what we now know, can this easily be separated from the fact that the Gothic word for tower, *kelikn*, is derived from Gaulish *celicnon*, "tower"? The borrowing cannot be classed as a late one simply because it appears

28 Tierney, "Celtic Ethnography", p. 251f.
29 Ibid., p. 269.

in the bible of Ulfilas. As Wenskus commented, "the borrowing must lie further back since the ending has been dropped from Gothic as in true Germanic words".[30]

Nor does the evidence for an institutional link between the sibyl and her interpreter conflict in any way with what has been said earlier about Civilis' influence on the same individual. Indeed, it may thereby be corroborated. Whatever may have been the relationship between druids and kings in Gaul, and the texts certainly deserve further study, Irish druids and *filid* often took orders from the warlord. They were not necessarily subservient but the pivotal facts are that a ruler could keep one or dismiss one, raise a rival if he wished or follow a different prophecy if he chose. One sees this quite clearly in a number of texts concerning the coming of Christianity to Ireland in which the ruler of Tara *judges* a contest of magic between St. Patrick and the druids of the court.[31] On the other hand, the early high status of the druid is reflected in the not infrequent naming of a Christian saint as *drui* or in the similar description of Christ: *is e mo drui Crist mac De*, "Christ the son of God is my druid".[32] A number of texts also suggest the existence of rivalry and/or resentment between the learned orders and this may be a hint that we might expect the same between veledas and "messengers". *Bethu Phatraic*, for example, contrasts the spiteful sustained opposition of the druids to the saint with the surprisingly speedy support given by Dubthach moccu Lugair, *rigfile ind rig*, "the kingly *fili* of the king", who was "the first man who believed in God in Tara".[33] Mac Mathúna's comments are apropos:

> Whatever the likelihood of an important *fili* of the mid-fifth century actually embracing the new religion with such alacrity, one is justified in assuming that by about AD 900, the date of composition of this text, the *filid* wished that such had been the case and knew that such a claim would not be dismissed out of hand by their public. In other words, whereas the druids had resolutely

---

30 Wenskus, *Stammesbildung*, p. 408. The origins of this word continues to be debated, however. See Winfred P. Lehmann, "Linguistic and Archaeological Data for Handbooks of Proto-languages" (1987), pp. 72–87; Edgar C. Polomé, "Who are the Germanic People?" (1987), pp. 216–44. Lehmann is convincing when he argues that the debate is sterile in view of the way in which archaeological finds, and the history of technology and linguistics combine to indicate that the Celts were "givers" in this and other areas. As he points out (pp. 80, 82): "It is scarcely a large intellectual leap to conclude that the Germanic borrowers, as of Gothic *reiks*, had a less highly developed political organization than the Celts. When we compare the archaeological evidence for the late Hallstatt and La Tène cultures with that of areas inhabited by the Germanic speakers, it seems almost willful to deny for the Celts political superiority in much of the millenium before our era, espically since this is a period of documented expansion by Celtic speakers, as into the Balkan, Anatolian, Iberian and Italian peninsulas. . . . Archaeology provides the evidence to give solid support for hypotheses drawn from linguistics".

31 The late seventh century *Vita S. Patricii* of Muirchú devotes several chapters to such contests. See Ludwig Bieler, ed. *Patrician Texts in the Book of Armagh* (1979), pp. 84–99.

32 Cited in Mac Mathúna, *Irish Poet*, p. 233.

33 Ibid., p. 228. Muirchú makes a similar statement. Bieler, *Patrician Texts*, p. 92.

opposed Christianity and subsequently been deprived of their power and status by its success, the *filid* had adjusted to the new order, and perhaps actually collaborated with it.[34]

Especially worthy of note is the fact that the trio of warband, druid and *fili* frequently appear together in early Irish sources. From the seventh, eighth and ninth century texts, most recently examined by Richard Sharpe and Kim Mc Cone,[35] it is apparent that such association represents the continuation of an established pre-Christian (i.e. pre-fifth century) social institution which ecclesiastical writers sought to denigrate and eliminate whenever possible; it was too much a stronghold of paganism. The term for warband was *fían* but the wild young bachelors who belonged to it were often called *díberga*, "brigands", *maic báis*, "sons of death" or, more reflective of the aristocratic component, *maic ríg*, "sons of kings". A number of passages and glosses refer to their practice of wearing "diabolical marks" and to a "vow of evil" while their banquet is referred to as a *fled demundae*, "devilish feast", attended by beggar-poets, "bandits, pagans and whores". Similarly, the *cáinte*, the poet who typically accompanies the band, is described as a base "satirist", an "intolerable" insulter of virtue. His barbs must often have been aimed at the clergy. One text derives *cáinte* from *canis*, "hound", "on account of the head of a hound on a *cáinte* as he bays (satirizes?)".[36]

Of great interest to Celticists, the value of this material for the present analysis is twofold: it confirms the institutional context of the dispersed Tacitean reportage by showing that the trio was conceived as a unit. Although classical reference to a "successor" to Veleda who is the companion of a king on an embassy is a strong hint of this, the clearest corroboration of the nature of the link comes from Irish sources which, as will be seen below, can themselves be supplemented by recently discovered first century Gaulish texts. At least as significant is the indication that it is not simply warlord and druidess who belong to the early Germanic warband but warlord, druidess and poet whom we can now plausibly identify with the apparently minor figure described by Tacitus as Veleda's "messenger", the transmitter of her prophecies. Once again we see that while the Roman historian provides the essential information for an interpretation, his own understanding of discrete events and personages is vitiated by an incomplete knowledge of the institutional milieu from which they spring. The essential context is the warband with its leader and his delegates, the magico-religious practitioner and the publicist-poet. Each exercises a function essential to group survival and continuity and it seems likely that we can perceive them again in the

---

34 Mac Mathúna, *Irish Poet*, p. 228.
35 Sharpe, "Hiberno-Latin *Laicus*", pp. 75–92. Citations in this paragraph are drawn from Kim Mc Cone, "Poet and Satirist", pp. 122–43 at p. 125f. See further his "Juvenile Delinquency", pp. 1–22; "*Aided Cheltchair Maic Uthechair*: Hounds, Heroes and Hospitallers in Early Irish Myth and Story" (1984), pp. 1–30.
36 Mc Cone, "Poet and Satirist", p. 128.

figures of Hrothgar, Wealhtheow and Unferth, the *þyle*, the *cáinte* as he may be called, who insults Beowulf in the service of his master. This latter individual is less important than the prophetess but is worthy of some remark in our discussion because of his place in the organizational pattern.

In Old English, *þyle* is glossed as both *orator* and *scurra*[37] and Unferth the *þyle*, the follower who occupies a special seat before the king, who questions and insults Beowulf but who yet has Hrothgar's approval, is a figure who has aroused even more controversy that Wealhtheow. It would be fruitless to review all of the literature concerning his actions in the hall since no agreement has ever been reached. In German scholarship he is often called a *Kultredner*,[38] Eliason has suggested that he is the person called *Hroðgares scop*,[39] Opland excluded him from his discussion of poet-words in OE for he believes the *þyle* to have been an orator alone,[40] and Hollowell has argued that he is a pagan religious practitioner with a special connection to the utterance of gnomic wisdom, a man like the Norse *þulr* who also holds a particular hall-seat and is often involved in Odinic sacrifice.[41] Others suggest he is more like a jester or mime.

There is something to be said for all of these interpretations but each seems incomplete in one way or another and none adequately deals with the require-ments of the historical warlord concerned to maintain organization and morale. Another lacuna, of course, is that the comparative evidence from Irish texts on warbands and poets has never been discussed at all. These two contexts, however, provide the essential key to understanding. It is significant that the *cáinte* is often described in Early Medieval Ireland as the lowest of the seven or more grades of poets and is frequently excluded from the poetic company altogether.[42] Mc Cone has recently pointed out that there is considerable variation and inconsistency in the terminology applied to humbler bards and low-status poets and that much of this should be related to clerical hostility.[43] An important contrast is between those who operated within the respectable confines of the more Christianized tribal kingdoms and those associated with warbands within which pagan traditions seem to have been assiduously maintained; the former were often praised and their high status recognized but the latter were uniformly disparaged. This situation seems relevant to the *þyle* in *Beowulf* in light of Brodeur's observation that there is a "complete cleavage between Beowulf's attitude toward Unferth, and that of the poet".[44] Whereas Beowulf accepts Unferth's friendship and gift,

37 For discussion, see Baird, "Unferth the *þyle*", p. 4f.; Hollowell, "Unferth", p. 252f.
38 De Vries, *Altgermanische Religionsgeschichte* I, p. 403.
39 Eliason, "The *þyle* and Scop", pp. 267–84.
40 Jeff Opland, *Anglo-Saxon Oral Poetry: A Study of the Traditions* (1980), p. 232.
41 Hollowell, "Unferth", p. 243f.
42 Liam Breatnach, *Uraicecht na ríar: The Poetic Grades in Early Irish Law* (1987); Mc Cone, "Poet and Satirist", p. 127f.
43 Mc Cone, "Poet and Satirist", p. 128f.
44 Arthur G. Brodeur, *The Art of Beowulf* (1959), p. 150f.

the poet's attitude is antagonistic and calculated. Although the hostility is artfully depicted in *Beowulf*, it is certainly there.

Similarly, Opland's exclusion of *þyle* from his list of poet-words like *scop*, *gleoman*, *woþbora* and *leopwyrhta* seems challengeable on the same grounds, but is more worrisome because of the very large number of Irish words for poet, for types of poetry and for the fine distinctions that are often made between them. Granted a divergence in cultural approaches, the widespread acceptance of an association between poetry and "gnomic wisdom", a form of discourse frequently poetic, would seem to indicate some such background for the *þyle*. The connection of *þyle* with *þulr* points in the same direction. So, perhaps, does his seat before the king for a poet, or at least a harpist, is described as having the same place in *The Fortunes of Men*. It is also hard to imagine a more apt description of Unferth, a name which means either "Mar-peace" or "Hun-spirited",[45] than that applied to the *cáinte*, a figure who belongs to an extra-tribal band of predators, attends "devilish feasts" and is notable on account of the "virulence and the fieriness of the words from him".[46] Irish texts tell us that the *cáinte* is destined for Hell "unless God himself curtail it", a view which is hardly different from that of the *Beowulf* poet who depicts the *þyle* as a traitorous fratricide who will suffer damnation. All of these insular Christian references are alike in that they seem to denigrate the status and character of pagan-connected officials. The two figures need not, of course, be alike in all ways; that is not the purpose of a cultural comparison. Their similarity is, nonetheless, remarkable. Finally, it should be noted that the same kinds of strictures are applied by clerics to druids who are frequently linked with both warband and *cáinte*. Applying these findings, *mutatis mutandis*, to the Germanic context, it is immediately clear that they may well have a bearing on the strange name given to Hrothgar's queen, Wealhtheow. The *-theow* element, signifying baseness and servility, has always been a great puzzle to scholars and, like "Unferth", has generated much dispute in itself. We shall examine it more closely later. Progress towards understanding the two names can be made, however, provided that one assigns each holder a role in an earlier more overtly pagan warband and accepts that the *Beowulf* poet is both as cognizant and disapproving as his Irish colleagues.

Historians seem to have consistently misread the evidence on those figures whom I have called the warlord's delegates.[47] Hence, Veleda is normally examined as a member in the category *Seherin* or the *þyle* in the hall as a member in the

---

45 John D. Niles, *Beowulf: The Poem and its Tradition* (1983), p. 82 with further references in notes.
46 Mc Cone, "Poet and Satirist", p. 128.
47 As do Niles and Damico. The most obvious problem is that scholars have failed to interpret them as delegates at all even though neither are actual fighters (such, at least, does not seem to be Unferth's main role) and both minister to the warband under Hrothgar's direction. Their places and actions are ultimately dependant on his patronage. Under such circumstances, what they could do and say was limited.

category *scop*, *orator*, or *scurra* while the other associations are treated as more or less incidental, episodic or temporary. In some cases, or for some individuals, that approach may be justified, but it is not one which aids much in comprehending the nature of the *comitatus* in which the roles of each are interlocking. Indeed, one important part of such traditional association is demonstrated by the course of the *Beowulf* poem itself for Wealhtheow does not come forth to distribute liquor until immediately after Unferth's attack on Beowulf and the hero's response. It is then that she begins to serve drink and provokes Beowulf's vow. The hero has obviously been "double-teamed" and the poet depicts it in a wonderfully subtle fashion—so well in fact that it has gone unrecognized. Whereas the poet and his audience intimately understood the operation of the warband, most modern literary critics have been more interested in other topics and have failed to see that Wealhtheow and Unferth are working in shifts to forward Hrothgar's policy of finding someone to defeat Grendel. That is one of the ways in which they pay for their mead.

The prominence of the *aspect théâtral* in the Unferth/Wealhtheow episodes in the poem is unmistakable once it is recognized. A delightful symmetry emerges upon analysis. In one sense, the behavior of the characters before the high-seat is a piece of pure entertainment, a way to enliven the tedium of life in the camp between bouts of brawling and drunkenness. Like the seating arrangements discussed in chapter one, however, it also nicely epitomizes a critical social function which goes far beyond the practiced duet between blamer and praiser. The concept of group survival is the foundation of the scene. The challenge, provocation, seating and service of the visitor are all ways of drawing him out and thereby assessing and appraising an intrusive influence. His performance can be enjoyed by all while simultaneously providing time and a tool of judgement to the leader and *seniores* of the retinue who may then develop some preliminary lines of policy based on the level of the visitor's skills and connections. These episodes of the poem are not mere literary embellishments but are unique testimony to an actual contemporary survival strategy. We are here privileged to witness the operation of a customary extended greeting ritual to an eminent stranger to the *comitatus*.

But no single tool is sufficiently formable to delve through every strata and expose all of the qualities and intentions requiring assessment. Hence every warlord *must* have other instruments at his disposal and the male/female duo is the combination which is most flexible. The *þyle*, who otherwise serves as the mouthpiece of the prophetess, also acts as the speaker of the warlord. In both cases, his office requires that he possess a full repertoire of linguistic skills including the important one of composing poetry, a skill greatly valued in his society for it indicates a divinely endowed creative capacity. His sacral status enables him to legitimately give voice to the reservoir of doubt, envy or hostility which may well flow beneath the surface of hospitality to a stranger but cannot easily be publicly vented by others. If handled properly, the *þyle*'s interrogation provides useful information for decision-making. The obligation to avenge insult does not apply to him and neither guest nor kin-group member in the hall or elsewhere can rightly take umbrage. His badinage is a palpable service to the band although it probably often included scurrilous commentary at least partly as a means of unmasking and exposing character. Even if the *þyle* be severely insulting, however, he is protected by other considerations of importance in his milieu: first, everyone in the warband must sometime or another undergo his public questioning and it is a matter of pride and reputation to do well but a sure loss of face to resort to weapons. Second, the entire affair is a ritual which everyone wishes to preserve. It partakes of all of the emotional and protective qualities which ritual entails and is thereby robbed of much of its apparently malignant intent. Third, the ritual also possesses a safety valve in the subsequent soothing ministrations of the woman of the hall. Like the *þyle*, she too is protected in a variety of ways which are necessary because she will often need to manipulate the guest in another manner and provoke in other fashions. The ways in which she acts will be determined by her sense of the *þyle*'s encounter and the warlord's wishes. Because she is a woman, it is unmanly to insult her and discourteous to defy her. She can cajole, antagonize or placate in ways which the *þyle* cannot and she is probably also the lord's wife or chief wife. Finally, and most significantly, she is the prophetess of the warband who has persuaded the followers that she has direct access to the supernatural and is thus peculiarly qualified to proclaim kingship and provoke oaths, to witness them and in some way to "bear" them. Thereby, she becomes a part of every warrior's destiny, a key to his future. It is worth remembering that if she can prophesy, then it is also likely that she can curse and bless. She is part of a socially indispensable pattern.

Between the necessarily coordinated attentions of *þyle* and prophetess, the visitor is clearly at a disadvantage. If he is boxed-in, however, he is not completely without resources. If he is anything like Beowulf, he has been raised in the *comitatus* and knows perfectly well what to expect. Part of his education has been directed at achieving excellence in exactly these kinds of confrontations. Better than anyone else, he knows his own strengths and weaknesses and has developed flexible strategies to exploit them. He too can manipulate the tableau if he is capable of doing so. Indeed, he is now presented with a wonderful chance to take center stage and apply the kinds of pressures allowed him by status, reputation and experience. A talented man can do much with this opportunity; an inferior one can do less. But that is exactly what the greeting ritual is meant to elicit, an understanding of the talents, temper and intentions of the stranger. The coordinated ballet of the warlord's delegates is a superb unmasking mechanism. It cannot be omitted if the band is to be long successful.

If the association between Civilis/Veleda and Hrothgar/Wealhtheow might previously have seemed somewhat daring, the fact that a third member can now be assigned in each case drastically affects the hypothesis. We may more properly describe the linkages as Civilis/Veleda/"messenger" and Hrothgar/Weal-htheow/*þyle*. In each case, the latter two members of the trio are employed in a politico-religious manner to carry out the policies of the former. Civilis wishes to defeat the Romans; Hrothgar wishes to defeat Grendel. The high probability of continuity because of *institutional form* has now been demonstrated in a way which helps to explain the durability of the Germanic *comitatus* in the first millennium. To govern the warband, the warlord must control and direct the prophetess and her interpreter. The differences in this regard in *Beowulf* are not minor but they are explainable on the basis of institutional evolution and poetic hostility to overt paganism. It is the citation of comparative evidence which makes the pattern clear and enables us to glimpse the reality of relationships upon which the poem is founded.

One fascinating point, of course, despite certain observable discrepancies, is that the essential constellation of these relationships has been found among each of the groups discussed, Celts and Germans in the Roman period and Anglo-Saxons and Irish in the Early Middle Ages. Additional witness was provided by the Lombards in earlier chapters and the Scandinavian evidence, although much has remained uncited because of its late date, provides many other parallels. Of course these peoples *are* different in significant ways. No one denies it. During the Early Middle Ages, however, they are all joined by the common denominators of the figure of the weaving prophetess, the warband organizational form and participation in the memorial culture discussed earlier. In each area, the sources which survive describe only part of the whole which I am here attempting to elucidate. It derives from the Iron Age of La Tène.

That aspects of Celtic culture affected both Civilis and Veleda can also be demonstrated by several other means. Before 69 AD, that is before Civilis took over leadership of the Batavian revolt, it is likely that he spent some undetermined period of time in Britain. Tacitus says that Batavian cohorts gained renown by their service in that land. They were, he adds, "commanded according to ancient tradition by the noblest men in the nation". A few sentences later he initiates a summary of Civilis' early career by describing him and his brother as "ranking very high above the rest of their nation".[48] Chances are very good, therefore, that the warlord and some of his followers served in the northern island campaigns. We know that he was commander of a cohort and that no less than eight cohorts of Batavians, who were attached to legio XIV gemina, were withdrawn from there in 67.[49] Indeed, other members of his family may have served as well for his sister's son, Julius Briganticus, bears a cognomen which might well recall the northern

48 Moore, *Tacitus. Histories*, IV, 13, p. 22f.
49 Geza Alföldy, *Die Hilfstruppen der römischen Provinz Germania inferior* (1968), p. 36f.

British tribe of the Brigantes.[50] M.W.C. Hassel has argued that the Batavians probably served in Britain from AD 43 and that Civilis, who claimed to have been a friend of Vespasian before he became emperor, would have met him then.[51] The same author regards it as "very likely" that Batavian cavalry served under Suetonius Paulinus in 60 when they attacked the island of Anglesey which contained a sacred site and was a refuge for druids.[52] If so, then, they would also have encountered "a troop of frenzied women", priestesses who accompanied the druids and who encouraged the Celtic forces during a battle. Tacitus declares that the Roman soldiers were so shocked by the curses of the druids and the wild dashing-about of the women that they had to be rallied by their general's appeals before regaining courage and attacking.[53] The Batavians, if involved, might well have learned something useful from all this. In any case, whether or not Civilis was present, it would be surprising if he did not hear of an account of this famous battle from his friends. We also know that Civilis was intimately aware of Gaulish custom, little different in broad terms from that of the British. A full discussion of this topic will be reserved for subsequent analysis but it may be mentioned in advance that Civilis may have traveled in Gaul, at least in 68, and that this was also the year in which a contingent of Batavians served in Arvernian territory against the Gaulish leader Julius Vindex, then in revolt against Nero. The *same* contingent would follow Civilis into rebellion.[54] During the revolt, of course, the Gaulish tribes of the Treveri and Lingones were crucial allies of Civilis.

It is important to emphasize that druidic activity was on the upsurge in the late 60's and played a significant, perhaps even a pivotal role, in the rebellion.[55] Recent archaeological finds indicate the possibility that some women might have been involved, as they also were on Anglesey. In the course of excavation at Sources des Roches near the village of Chamaliéres between 1968 and 1971, a ritual site was discovered containing literally thousands of wooden *ex votos*.[56] The village of Chamaliéres is in the arrondisement of Clermont-Ferrand in the Auvergne, that is, the same general area in which a detachment of Civilis' Batavian troops served in 68. The chronology seems to fit also for the deposition of *ex votos*

50 M.W.C. Hassall, "Batavians and the Roman Conquest of Britain" (1970), p. 134.
51 Ibid., p. 133.
52 Hassall, "Batavians", p. 132. See, however, Will, " 'Klientel—Randstaaten' ", p. 19 and n. 132. On Roman recruitment of auxiliaries, see Alföldy, *Hilfstruppen*, pp. 81–136. For site and provincial background, see Christoph B. Rüger, *Germania Inferior* (1968), especially pp. 32–92; and for Rhineland relations, Harald von Petrikovits, *Rheinische Geschichte: Altertum* I (1978), pp. 57–76. For Anglesey and the British background, see Graham Webster, *Rome Against Caractacus. The Roman Campaigns in Britain AD 48–58* (1981); idem, *Boudica and the British Revolt Against Rome AD 60* (1978), pp. 83, 86f.; Ross, *Pagan Celtic Britain*, p. 56f.
53 Jackson, *Tacitus. Annals* : XIV, 30, p. 154f.
54 Alföldy, *Hilfstruppen*, p. 14.
55 Tacitus is quite certain of this. See *The Histories* IV, 54.
56 Claude Vatin, "Wooden Sculpture From Gallo-Roman Auvergne" (1972), pp. 39–42; idem, "Ex-voto de bois gallo-romains à Chamalièrs" (1969), pp. 103–14.

ceased roughly about the time of the reign of Nero.[57] The abandonment of the sanctuary during this period has seemed suspicious to several scholars for it may be associated with the Gaulish revolt in 68 and would thus have suffered from reprisals against the druids.[58]

One especially important find at the site was a small inscribed leaden tablet containing 336 characters in Roman cursive but in the Gaulish language.[59] The object of the inscription seems to be the attestation of a group oath by the god of the fountain. One of these oath-takers, a man called Asiatic(os), bears a rare name and may be, according to Leon Fleuriot, identical with a Gaulish leader mentioned by Tacitus (Hist. 2, 94) who fought with Vindex.[60] The tablet makes clear that these men were engaged in a major endeavor from which they expected an important result. The oath may have been a military one for the events of the time would have called for it and only men are mentioned. We cannot be sure of any of this, however, since the inscription presents numerous linguistic problems and the interpretation of formulas is a matter of controversy.[61] Nonetheless, it should be noted that the most recent translation of the tablet takes the second sentence to be an attempt to draw on the magical power of women: "through the incantations of women expedite us . . .". According to P.L. Henry, the formula in question, BRIXTIA ANDERON, is the Gaulish equivalent of OI *brichta ban*, "the enchantments of women", which can be directly related to the druidesses and seeresses of early medieval tradition.[62] If correct, then, we have again a peculiar coincidence of events in which warfare, rebellion and female magic are combined. This rebellion of 68, of course, is the one which helped to inspire Civilis in 69.

In any case, particular attention should probably be focused on the magical role of women in fortifying groups of warriors since female magicians are again referred to in a newly discovered lengthier tablet from the village of Larzac (Aveyron, canton de Nant).[63] It was found in a grave dating to about 100 AD and

---

57 Vatin, "Wooden Sculpture", p. 40.
58 Leon Fleuriot, "Note additionnelle sur l'inscription de Chamalières" (1979), p. 139; idem, "La Tablette de Chamalières: Nouveaux commentaires" (1980), p. 158; idem, Deux inscriptions Gauloises, p. 107; Pierre-Yves Lambert, "La tablette gauloise de Chamalières" (1979), p. 164.
59 Aside from works cited in note 56, see Patrick L. Henry, "Interpreting the Gaulish Inscription of Chamalières" (1984), pp. 141–50; Pierre-Yves Lambert, "A Restatement on the Gaulish Tablet From Chamalières" (1987), pp. 10–17; Karl Schmidt, "The Gaulish Inscription of Chamalières" (1980), pp. 256–68; Michel Lejeune and Robert Marichal, "Textes gaulois et gallo-romaine en cursive latine" (1976), p. 156f.; Leon Fleuriot, "Le vocabulaire de l'Inscription Gauloise de Chamalières" (1976), pp. 173–90.
60 Fleuriot, "Vocabulaire", p. 183.
61 Lambert, for example, now believes that "there is no political background behind the Chamalières tablet" ("Restatement", p. 17). He alludes to a variety of opinions among experts regarding translations.
62 Henry, "Gaulish Inscription", p. 145f.
63 Michel Lejeune et al., "Textes gaulois et gallo-romaine en cursive latine: Le plomb du Larzac" (1985), pp. 95–177.

seems to be an example of hostile magic or counter magic. The names of a "troop of female magicians" are mentioned.[64] Both of these inscriptions are currently undergoing intensive study but it is already clear that the Irish references to female druids and seeresses can now be *certainly* regarded as related evidence. For present purposes, the most significant points are these: we now know that some rather unclear connection existed between druids and female practitioners of magic in the Celtic world and that the sphere of warfare and/or hostility was involved. It also seems probable that Civilis and some Batavians were aware of this. An enlarged contemporary context for a Bructeri prophetess bearing a Celtic title is thereby provided. Taken individually, none of the clues from the sources appears to explain very much. Examined as a whole, they seem to fit a pattern which consistently recalls the Celtic world even when the practitioners are Germanic. This closely fits the archaeological evidence which shows Rhineland Germans to have adopted the entire panoply of La Tène material culture by the first century BC.[65]

A brief analysis of one further characteristic of the prophetess will help confirm the validity of the present methodology. We have already alluded to several Tacitean passages concerning the presence of prophetesses amongst the Germans and the veneration accorded them. We know the names of several as well as the significant datum that Ganna, a woman who accompanied king Masyos to Rome, was Veleda's "successor".[66] As with Veleda, a glance at these names can be revealing. Ganna, for example, is widely recognized as deriving from Germanic *Gand-no* to be compared with ON *gandr*, "magical staff". The name would thus mean something like "she who carries the magical staff" or, according to Krahe, "she who controls the magical staff or something similar".[67] So too with Balouburg, rectified to Walburg or Waluburg, the prophetess of the Semnones who accompanied troops to Egypt in the second century. Her name also contains the word for "staff": Gothic *walus*, ON *vǫlr*.[68] It has been suggested that Gambara, the name of the famous wise woman of the Lombards described by Paul the Deacon as "most prudent in counsel among her people", should be interpreted

64 Ibid., pp. 96, 133f. 152f. The six women mentioned in the text seem to belong to an organized group and can be compared to several in insular Celtic literature or, for that matter, to the Furies at Anglesey mentioned by Tacitus.
65 Karl Peschel, "Die Kelten als Nachbarn der Germanen" (1970), pp. 1–36; Idem, "Kelten und Germanen während der jüngeren vorrömischen Eisenzeit (2.–1. Jh. v. u. Z)" (1988), pp. 241–63; Ernst Wahle, *Zur ethnischen Deutung frühgeschichtlicher Kulturprovinzen* (1941); Hermann Ament, "Der Rhein und die Ethnogenese der Germanen" (1984), pp. 37–47; Waldtraut Schrickel, "Die Nordgrenze der Kelten im rechtsreinischen Gebiet zur Spätlatenèzeit" (1964), pp. 138–53. There are, of course, many statements of this point. The linguistic evidence will be discussed below along with aspects of technology.
66 "Masyos, king of the Semnones, and Ganna, a virgin who was priestess in Germany, having succeeded Veleda, came to Domitian and after being honoured by him returned home". Cary, ed. *Cassius Dio. Roman History* (1955), LXVII, 12, p. 347.
67 Krahe, "Kleinigkeiten", p. 41.
68 Ibid.

as *Gand-bara*, "carrier of the magical staff".[69] The same term is found in ON *vǫlva*, "prophetess". and, as von Amira pointed out early in this century, a staff was possessed by the Icelandic *spakona* of the sagas.[70] All of these women, therefore, including Veleda, must have carried a staff as a sign of their abilities or as a symbol of office.

But what kind of staff are we to imagine them carrying? The answer has already been provided by the discussion of weaving beams, distaffs and weaving magic in chapter four. It seems to be confirmed by Irish sources in which a prophetess bearing a weaving beam appears in a military context and advises on warfare. We may thus conclude that the evidence linking Celts and Germans in the field of magical and prophetic practice is quite strong: Both peoples possessed sibyls who advised rulers on warfare, who carried weaving beams as attributes and who even bore the same occupational titles. Similarly, Veleda and her "messenger" seem to reproduce the druid/*fili* association of the warbands of Ireland and Gaul while her act of arbitration appears to be one of the traditional Gaulish priestly functions. Finally, the way in which women of the Celts and Germans played a role in judging conflicts among men provides another broader context for interpreting, as was discussed in chapter two, the provoking and peacemaking functions of females in archaic cultures.

It begins to look as if some Germanic peoples borrowed a variety of Celtic practices at the same time as they were adopting the material culture of La Tène. Such pattern may have continued to exercise an influence in the mid first century. Although it is in no way necessary to the present thesis, one may also consider the possibility that previous episodes of anti-Roman activity might have affected the plans and techniques of control exercised by Civilis and Veleda. Like revolutions, revolts often follow noticeable patterns. In two recent papers, S.L. Dyson has argued that the Batavian War, which he compares to those of Vercingetorix, Arminius and Boudicca, was a typical "nativist" revolt against colonial domination by an overbearing foreign power.[71] In the nineteenth and twentieth centuries, such episodes typically involved charismatic leaders (significantly, these are often members of upper class society regarded as acculturated to the conqueror's ideals) and are further marked by a re-emphasis on traditional religion and prophecy. The prevailing mood amongst Gauls and Germans in the sixties of the first century seems conducive to such an interpretation. One thinks, for example, of the case of Mariccus whom Tacitus describes (Hist. II, 61) as a low-born member of the Boii, a tribe settled on the middle Loire. Sometime in 69, Mariccus

---

69 Ibid., p. 41f.
70 Von Amira, *Stab*, p. 8f. In general, see Hans Volkmann, *Germanische Seherinnen in römischen Diensten* (1964), pp. 5–18; Hans Naumann, "Der König und die Seherin" (1938), pp. 347–58; De Vries, *Altgermanische Religionsgeschichte* I, pp. 319–33; Schröder, *Walburg*, pp. 60–4.
71 Stephen L. Dyson, "Native Revolts in the Roman Empire" (1971), pp. 239–74; idem, "Native Revolt Patterns in the Roman Empire" (1975), pp. 138–75.

began "pretending to divine inspiration" and "ventured to thrust himself into fortune's game and to challenge the arms of Rome". Calling himself "the champion of Gaul and a god (for he had assumed this title)", he raised the considerable force of 8000 men and took possession of villages of the Aedui. The Aedui counterattacked with the help of Roman cohorts sent by Vitellius but for a time, at least, Mariccus was believed "by the senseless multitude to be invulnerable".

In comparison with the Batavian rebellion, this local uprising is of little consequence and may have had an entirely different set of goals.[72] Given the terse stylistic report of Tacitus, the only writer to mention it, one can hardly draw grand conclusions. The Boian's charismatic leadership and claim of divine inspiration, on the other hand, are eminently comparable to those of Civilis for whom, as we shall see in more detail later, the evidence is considerably clearer. Two views are possible. The similar techniques may be coincidental, no more than a chance array of like methods to achieve related ends. Casting the net wider, one can also interpret the evidence otherwise: of the three rebellions against Roman rule between AD 60 and 69 which Tacitus finds noteworthy and which were certainly known to the Batavians (Boudicca and the Iceni, Vindex and the Arverni, Mariccus and the Boii), all three were by Celtic peoples while the fourth, that of the Batavians, was joined by the Treveri and Lingones. The Celts may well have influenced Germanic upper class concepts of, for lack of a better term, the decorum of revolt. Religious belief probably played a lesser role in the case of Vindex than in the others but even here scholars concede it some relevance.[73] Religious belief was crucially important, according to Tacitus, in the other three. In two of the cases, moreover, the first and fourth, the Roman-prohibited but otherwise revered druidic priesthood (leading families three centuries later would still claim druids as ancestors) played a central propagandistic role.

The Batavian revolt was no simple affair. The lengthy comparative analysis above demonstrates the presence of non-Roman and non-Germanic influence; so too a discussion of other contemporary revolts. Hence, any discussion of Civilis and Veleda in terms of Romano-Germanic conflict alone can only result in a partial understanding of what was, in reality, a very complex weaving of cultural, religious and political interactions involving the Gauls as a third major force.

72 G.E.F. Chilver, *A Historical Commentary on Tacitus' Histories I and II* (1979), p. 223, declares that Mariccus "was of the people, hostile to the aristocracy, and of a different stamp from either Vindex or Classicus". This seems speculative. It is not, for example, impossible that Mariccus was a druid. We simply do not know.

73 P.A. Brunt, "The Revolt of Vindex and the Fall of Nero" (1959), p. 549; J.F. Drinkwater, *Roman Gaul. The Three Provinces, 58 BC–AD 260* (1983), p. 43; Ronald Syme, *Tacitus* I (1958), p. 458f. Syme's remarks, p. 462, seem apropos: "What impelled Julius Vindex will never be known . . . . The protest against the tyranny of Nero at once and inevitably took the form of a native insurrection against the Roman power, recalling Julius Florus and Julius Sacrovir, chieftains of the Treveri and Aedui, who raised war in Gaul in the days of Tiberius Caesar. Julius Vindex was not only a Roman senator—he was the descendant of kings in Aquitania".

2. WEALHTHEOW

We may now turn to the vexed question of Hrothgar's queen. Having already traced aspects of Wealhtheow's behavior back to a similar institutional model in Tacitean Germania, it may not be surprising to find that the operation can also work in reverse in another area, that of name studies. To students familiar with this complex field, however, (the present author claims only amateur status) this statement requires justification and some brief reference to previous opinion is necessary in order to highlight the current state of research and the need for an innovative approach "where angels fear to tread".

Scholars have not always been inclined to accept personal appellations as important since we live in an age in which they have largely lost their meaning and in which etymology is a rarefied field for specialists. An antidote for this view can be found in Robinson's impressive study on the significance of names in Old English literature in which, following Curtius in part, he demonstrates that literary onomastics was "a dominate mode of thought" for the Anglo-Saxons.[1] Quite simply, the giving of a name was an act of profound import because the givers understood it to provide a key to character, to the inner workings of the receiver's soul, so that even in literary works where the selection of a name might be dictated by tradition, the poet can, as in *Beowulf*, focus on the latent etymological sense through the setting or the words or the actions of the person named. As Heusler remarked many years ago, names had a "hypnotic power" for the Germans[2] and for an eighth-century example one need only think of that passage, much loved by contemporaries, in which Bede recalls Gregory the Great's prophecy concerning the conversion of the Anglo-Saxons achieved by a series of "onomastic inspirations" involving the names Angle, Aella and Deira.[3]

Wealhtheow, more correctly Wealhþeow, is by all accounts the most puzzling and surprising, not to say shocking, name in Old English literature. Among the host of scholars who have referred to it are Müllenhoff who regarded it as a purely Anglo-Saxon invention because the name is emphatically *"nicht altnordisch"*,[4] Klaeber who described it as "strange",[5] Bjorkmann who called it "extraordinary",[6] and Damico, the latest commentator, who views it as "perplexing" and

---

1 Robinson, "Names", pp. 14–58; Curtius, "Etymology as a Category", pp. 495–500.
2 Heusler, "Gelehrte Urgeschichte", p. 39f.
3 Colgrave and Mynors, *Bede*, II, 1, p. 133f. A variant form will be found in the Whitby *vita* of St. Gregory.
4 Mullenhoff, "Beovulf", p. 26: "Die Gemahlin ist sicherlich nur eine angelsächsische Erfindung, denn der Name, der 'welsches Weib' bedeutet, ist gar nicht altnordisch".
5 Klaeber, *Beowulf*, p. xxxiii: "the strange name of Hroðgar's queen, Wealhþeow (i.e. 'Celtic servant') indicates that she was considered of foreign descent".
6 Erik Björkman, "Zu einigen Namen in Beowulf: Breca, Brondingas, Wealhtheow" (1919), p. 177f. "Man könnte sich deshalb denken, dass er vom Dichter erfunden war, obgleich es nicht recht ersichtlich ist, wie dieser zu dem ganz sonderbaren Namen gekommen wäre. Bei der Beurteilung von Wealhpeow müssen wir von der Tatsache ausgehen, dass der Name weder mit

argues that it is a nickname associated with someone else.[7] The primary source of confusion is that one or perhaps even both elements of the name signify servitude and such condition is exceedingly difficult to reconcile with the idealized archetypical *ides Helminga*, the stately noble queen of the poem. The OE noun *wealh* (pl. *wealas*) has the primary meaning of Celt or Briton but carries the secondary meaning of "slave", "servant" and then "foreigner" in general.[8] Although the laws of king Ine of the late seventh century show that upper class *wealas* did exist within the area of Saxon domination and also served the ruler in socially estimable ways, their reduced wergild demonstrates that they occupied a generally inferior position analogous to that of the Roman *homo possessor* of *Lex Salica* who was also allotted a half wergild.[9] The significance of *wealh* could vary according to time and place, however. In the seventh century, for example, it is found in the names of four members of the royal house of Mercia and of one member each of the West Saxon and Sussex royal houses.[10] As Faull points out in her superb study of the semantics of *wealh*, "it is scarcely conceivable that six royal children would have been given names implying servility, particularly as the royal houses showed great care in the selection of the names given to their members".[11] Intermarriage must have been common during this period of English history and communication easy in many areas. The secondary meanings of *wealh* on the other hand follow more or less predictably from the facts of conquest, conflict and of serfdom for many of those of British descent in English areas. Tribal prejudice is also indicated (especially in later texts) in that *wealas* are often associated with darkness and deviousness.[12]

The second name element, *theow*, always means "slave" or "servant" and is commonly applied to those of very low status.[13] There are exceptions. It is not infrequently used in the abstract sense of "one who serves" so that people in religious orders may honorably be referred to as *Godes theowas*.[14] When combined

englischen noch mit nordischen Namenbildungsgepflogenheiten im Einklang steht und dass er nur als ein ursprüngliches Appellativum erklärt werden kann".

7 Damico, *Wealhtheow*, p. 58f. She adds that the name is "troublesome". It is an example "of the strong tendency of Anglo-Saxon writers to engage in name-play . . . . [Such] enables authors to convey information directly about their *dramatis personae* outside the strictures of plot. It thus affords them the opportunity to keep in continuous focus certain aspects of the character or theme which either decorum or the exigencies of the narrative would otherwise prohibit them from presenting . . . . Each etymology served as a departure point for investigating diverse characteristics that might comprise the bearer's spiritual essence".

8 Margaret L. Faull, "The Semantic Development of Old English *wealh*" (1975), pp. 20–44.

9 Attenborough, *Laws*, p. 42. *The Laws of Ine* (ch. xxiii, 3) states: Wealh gafolgelda cxx scill . . . . See Faull, "Old English *wealh*", pp. 21, 26.

10 Faull, "Old English *wealh*", p. 32.

11 Ibid.

12 Ibid., p. 30f.

13 J. Bosworth and T.N. Toller, *An Anglo-Saxon Dictionary* (1882) s.v. *Wealh*, p. 1173. The name appears to have originally derived from the Celtic tribe of the Volcae mentioned by Caesar. See Leo Weisgerber, "Walhisk. Die geschichtliche Leistung des Wortes Welsch" (1954), pp. 155–232.

14 E.V. Gordon, "Wealheow and Related Names" (1935), p. 171.

with *wealh*, however, the most immediate meaning of Wealhtheow would seem to be "British slave" or "British servant". The only solution for those who find the status anomaly intolerable is to discover another etymology. Gordon tried this in 1935 when he constructed an etymology based on the ON masculine name of *Valþjofr*.[15] When combined with other hypotheses, this would permit the reading of "chosen servant" for Wealhtheow with the sense that the chosen was the servant of the ideal or of a god. Even to one unversed in philology, however, such translation presents serious obstacles. The most obvious one is that while *theow* names with this meaning are not uncommon for Germanic *warriors*, neither a scouring of OE or ON turns up a single instance of that element in a woman's name with the elevated sense that Gordon wishes it to convey (Otto Höfler rejected this interpretation partly for that reason and Helmut Birkhan is also skeptical).[16] Gordon was thus driven to postulate a female *theow* name with a religious sense which once existed in proto-Norse, (although nothing like it is mentioned in even the earliest sources) which then disappeared for centuries only to be resurrected by the Anglo-Saxons.

In short, neither of the two main contenders, "British slave" or "chosen servant", provides an easily acceptable explanation for Wealhtheow. The first would seem to be incompatible with royal status and behavior and, even if one supposes that Wealhtheow may have been captured in war and then released, not in itself inherently unlikely (Höfler), it is not credible that her husband's warriors would abandon her birth name and still continue many years later to call her "slave". She is identified in the poem as *freolic wif*, "freeborn woman", and *freolicu folccwen*, "freeborn queen of the people". The second derivation is also unsatisfactory because neither OE or ON offers a comparable name containing the requisite sense of religious devotion by a female and it thus seems more like a despairing hypothesis than anything else. What is clearly needed is a solution in which status and name can be more easily reconciled.

Even if Gordon's elucidation is rejected and even if the *theow* names in the honorable sense are exclusively masculine in Germanic, his search does further the investigation for it emphasizes again the curious religious aura which dogs Wealhtheow's steps. Moreover, Gordon raises a significant point when he notes that although the name element *Val-*, as in ON *Valþjofr*, "is not equivalent to OE *wealh* but goes back to Germanic **wala-*, 'chosen', 'beloved'", the two could easily become "confused" in later Germanic.[17] He cites an example of such misunderstanding and concludes that on that basis an OE rendering in *wealh* "is not surprising" and presents no etymological difficulty.[18] In his recent study of

15 Ibid.
16 Hofler, *Geheimbunde*, pp. 266, n. 354, 269, n. 369; Birkhan, *Germanen und Kelten*, p. 571f. and
     n. 1795. Björkman makes the same point: "Namen im *Beowulf*", p. 177.
17 Gordon, "Wealhþeow", p. 170.
18 Ibid., p. 170f.

devotional names of this type, Birkhan agrees that such could have occurred and is "formally possible" but unlikely because of the doubtfulness of *uala* as a name-element.[19] One might then ask the linguist this: if it is possible to accept *Val-*, as in Val þjofr, becoming *Wealh-*, is it not easier to envision *Vel-*, as in Veleda, becoming *Wealh-* or even (on the same basis of "confusion" over a long period of time) *-eda* or *-eta* becoming *-theow*? In this case, Birkhan's skepticism because of a lack of a comparable personal name element does not arise for we have already seen that *veleda* is a purely occupational designation applied to all prophetesses and have seen too that these sibyls had an institutional existence among the Germans for a long period of time. Like Veleda, then, Wealhtheow might not be a personal name at all but rather the old occupational designation present in new guise due to linguistic and geographical change. It seems to me that this is a possibility worth mentioning since it provides some basis for comparison while also providing a clarification as to what it is that Wealhtheow is devoted to or serves.

If the problem of the *theow* element still seems to be insufficiently resolved, however, we might point to some other clues which might mitigate the tension. We have already noted that the presence of *wealh* as a name element in several royal Saxon families points to frequent intermarriage and social and cultural exchange at the very highest levels. Might not this cultural exchange also have exerted influence on masculine *theow*? The idea, at least, is worth voicing and Gordon seems to have been thinking along these lines as well for he notes that "in so far as these 'servant' names arose from dedication to gods, they form a curiously close heathen parallel to the Gaelic Christian names in *Mael-* and *Gil-*, as in *Maelmuire* '(tonsured) servant of Mary', *Gilchrist* 'servant of Christ'."[20] In drawing the "curiously close" parallel, Gordon seems to have been unaware that such names merely continue a very old pre-Christian practice familiar to all Celts —Gauls, Britons and Irish alike. Names of similar import in *Mug* and *Cú* are best known but there are others as well. In their studies of such names, both Schramm and Birkhan note that signs indicating *Gottesknechtschaft*, slavery to a god, are particularly prominent in two IE languages, Celtic and Germanic. In each, moreover, the name-types in question are often associated with the *comitatus*.[21] It is this coincidence of cultic service and warband which seems to fit Wealhtheow so closely and again indicates that the warband connection is critical.

The most instructive parallel, however, is probably still that of the *fili*

---

19 Birkhan, *Germanen und Kelten*, p. 571f. and n. 1795.
20 Gordon, "Wealhþeow", p. 173.
21 Gottfried Schramm, *Namenschatz und Dichtersprache: Studien zu den zweigliedrigen Personen-namen der Germanen* (1957), p. 70f.; Birkhan, *Germanen und Kelten*, p. 576f.; Höfler, *Geheim-bünde*, p. 266f.; T.F. O'Rahilly, *Early Irish History and Mythology* (1946), p. 217.

Feidelm.[22] As with the prophetesses of the Germanic tradition, she too carries a staff, a weaving beam, and despite her beauty, noble bearing and rich dress symbolic of high status, she describes herself as promoting Medb's interests because she is a "bondmaid", a *theow* in other words, of the queen's people. Significantly, her service is also associated with the military sphere for Feidelm is engaged in "gathering and mustering" the men of Ireland for Medb's raid into Ulster. Is this much different from Veleda's service to Civilis or that of Walburg to the troops with whom she travels? And does not Wealhtheow perform similar service to the warlord by helping to maintain his *comitatus*, encouraging vows and retaining recruits? Among the Celts, at least, this type of religious military service has very ancient roots. In describing the attack of the Roman governor Paulinus on Anglesey, holy center of druidic worship in 61 AD, Tacitus says that between the ranks of armed Celtic warriors "dashed women, in black attire like the Furies, with hair dishevelled, waving brands. All around, the druids lifted up their hands to heaven, and pouring forth dreadful imprecations, scared our soldiers by the unfamiliar sight, so that, as if their limbs were paralyzed, they stood motionless, and exposed to wounds".[23] These black-dressed "Furies" at a cult-site encouraging the warriors and seemingly aiding the druids may well lie at the core of the tradition.

This hypothesis of cultural influence and continuity might well strike some as daring. It is, however, consonant with the archaeological evidence. The most recent large-scale investigation of early Anglo-Saxon cemeteries by Heinrich Härke indicates that a high percentage of the contemporaries buried in these graves are Celts.[24] Such is also consonant with the most recent maritime research which shows that the nature of the boats of the period, together with the preparations and dangers of the voyage from the continent to Britain, mean that the very large numbers of Germanic settlers once assumed by scholars is unlikely.[25] The Anglo-Saxon warbands of the sixth, seventh and eighth centuries were not Anglo-Saxon alone but must have included Britons and many men of mixed ancestry. At least one scholar now regards the ratio of Anglo-Saxons to Britons during the "Dark Ages" as lying somewhere between 1:20 and 1:50.[26]

The *theow* element in Wealhtheow's name indicates that she was thought to be a slave to somebody or something. Such a name, assuming its use in an honorable

---

22 See part one of the present chapter. The fact to be noted, of course, is that features, dress and ornament all mark her as belonging to the highest class of society. So does her freedom of speech with Medb. Nonetheless, she is a *theow*! The Anglo-Saxons might describe her aptly as Wealtheow.

23 Jackson, *Tacitus. Annals*, XIV, 30, p. 154f.

24 Härke, "Weapon Burial Rite", p. 40. For discussion of Härke's overall findings, see Jankuhn, "Neue Erkenntnisse", pp. 29–35.

25 Michael E. Jones, "The Logistics of the Anglo-Saxon Invasions" (1987), pp. 62–9.

26 Lloyd Laing, *Celtic Britain and Ireland, AD 200–800* (1990).

sense, might partially reflect her delegatory status in the *comitatus* where masculine names of this kind had a revered traditional place. Feminine names in *theow*
did not, however, and so, for an explanation in a positive sense, one must draw on
the surprising parallels with Feidelm of the *Táin* (prophecy, warfare, slavery
despite appearance of nobility) which suggests the influence of British culture.
Another possibility is that Wealhtheow is a "confused" derivation of the occupational term *veleda*, "prophetess". Actually, both of these aspects may have
interacted over time so that it is difficult to choose between them. A third
possibility arises from earlier discussion of Wealhtheow's predecessors and the
relationship between *þyle* and *cáinte*. We saw there that the poet's hostile description of the *þyle* reflects the wider insular practice of stigmatizing the holders of
pagan-associated offices within the *comitatus*. Since prophetess and *þyle* work
together, as Wealhtheow and Unferth seem to do in the poem, then it might no
longer seem unusual that the poet slights each by his choice of names, the kind
of movement exemplified by the transition from *orator* to *scurra*. Reaction to the
disparagement of the queen (which seems implicit in the Anglo-Saxon name) is
stronger because she is a more sympathetic figure and it is harder for us to
appreciate that the *þyle*'s duty might have required him to blame in the same
measure that her's required that she praise. The poet cannot conceal the fact that
the *þyle* was a significant and honored court practitioner; Beowulf publicly treats
him in that fashion. The poet's attitude toward Wealhtheow, on the other hand,
is less censorious and more subtle and her prophetic competence is underplayed.
Her true role *is* easier to conceal. Nonetheless, it cannot be coincidental that the
two most controversial names in *Beowulf*, those which have caused more puzzlement than all others combined, belong to figures whom we have identified as
having *interlocking* pagan associations. In effect, the poet concedes their original
standing in the warband but diminishes their characters in different subtle ways
in accord with a religious viewpoint which requires that they somehow be
criticized.

The interplay of possibilities is too varied to make a reliable choice between
them. One may submit, however, that previous approaches to Wealhtheow are
unsatisfactory because of a lack of understanding of her institutional functions
within the warband. Comparison with Veleda and Feidelm bring this out. A
comparative procedure is again supported by the fact that the name of each
woman, Veleda and Wealhtheow, is completely isolated in Germanic, a point
which underlines the necessity of looking elsewhere. Whatever the difficulty of
establishing confident specificities, therefore, the probability that Veleda and
Wealhtheow occupy the same niche and fulfill similar roles in the warband is high.
As in the case of Unferth, the name Wealhtheow may well indicate the poet's
oblique (to us) criticism of a suspicious, even obnoxious, institutional ancestry. If
the *Beowulf* poem is not of the eighth but of the ninth or tenth centuries, as many
scholars now argue, then the presumption becomes even stronger, for later OE

texts link both parts of her name to deceit and deviousness and the poet cannot but have been aware of this. In such case, the parallels between the semantic history of *þyle* and *wealh* become even more striking.

3. THE CELTO-GERMANIC WARBAND AND THE RISE OF THE WARLORD

In the course of the preceding discussion solutions have been proposed for several etymological and historical puzzles but it is true to say that the same solutions raise problems of their own. If we can now be more confident of the possibility that a form of institutionally driven continuity existed from the *veleda*s to Wealhtheow, the Celtic element, which may be present to some degree in the case of the latter as well, requires further exploration for it suggests that the war-lord/prophetess/*comitatus* dynamic is not yet fully explained. A more through examination of the origins of the *comitatus* would seem to be necessary. This need to mine so deeply into the ancient sources was not apparent when the study began. At that time it seemed that a sufficient explanation for the pattern described would be achieved once it had been demonstrated that it was discernable in the remote age of Tacitus where the supportive delegatory function of the prophetess vis à vis the warlord seem to offer a sound if distant parallel to the perplexing rituals of the Danish hall. It seemed unwarranted for the historian, as opposed to the archaeologist or philologist, to seek to go beyond that because so little is known of the politico-religious currents within pre-Roman Germanic society and hence any conclusions reached in this area, at least, would have to be tentative.

At the same time, however, it was clear that the largely independent warlord of the type so prominent in these pages had not always existed among the Germans. Rather, that institution seems to have arisen during the course of the first century BC and only gradually over the course of several centuries to have become a permanent fixture.[1] Until then, tribal kingships and/or tribal councils of oligarchs predominated. So too with *comitatus* warfare which had originally been a type of *ad hoc* arrangement without permanent seat or permanent leader conducted in part, at least, to simply bloody the men. It was a tribal affair in which recruitment to the select band from outside the recognized community was uncommon if not forbidden. While it is not always easy to distinguish *comitatus* warfare from tribal warfare in the historical sources, it is obvious that the latter was much more exclusive with loose knit armies being gathered and organized according to family and clan and with little or no room, either political or economical, for the leader with an extra-tribal group of followers supported at his expense and living more or less constantly in his hall. This is the distinction based on the classical opposition between *rex* and *dux* and between the concept

---

1 Wenskus, *Stammesbildung*, p. 356f.; Kuhn, "Grenzen", p. 77f.; Rafael von Uslar, *Die Germanen vom 1. bis 4. Jahrhundert nach Christus* (1980), p. 49f.; Steuer, *Sozialstrukturen*, p. 57.

of *comitatus* warfare and tribal warfare originally devised by Schlesinger and now part of the arsenal of all scholars of early European institutions.[2]

But if this be true, and it is the current *communis opinio*,[3] then the warlord/prophetess relationship, which we now know to have been both politically intimate and militarily enterprising, must also have originated roughly during the same period as the institutionalized warband. As far as I can determine, scholars have constantly assumed that the warlord and the prophetess were unrelated figures wielding power in separate spheres and joined only occasionally when mutual interest dictated common action or, somewhat naively perhaps, in cases where the former might earnestly wish to consult the latter as to the future success of an endeavor.[4] The political dimensions of this tableau—and such must have existed because of the status and function of the warleader—were never worked out; in fact, they were ignored. An erroneous impression was thereby created and embedded in the literature. As a further consequence, scholars also seem to have assumed that the genealogy of the prophetess could not realistically be investigated; it probably reached back somewhere to the primordial past and must be taken for granted as if perhaps she were an expected echo of early Mediterranean oracles like those of Delphi or even Dodona and not a product of the far northern forests which knew neither one. But in view of the fact that *veleda* is an occupational designation borrowed from the Celts, that interpretation does not appear likely. It seems best, therefore, to seek for the origin of the warlord/prophetess/*comitatus* connection within the context of Celto-Germanic contact in the

2 Schlesinger, "Herrschaft und Gefolgschaft", pp. 9–52; Idem, "Heerkönigtum", pp. 53–87; Idem, "Randbemerkungen", pp. 286–334. For criticism of Schlesinger's views see Kroeschell, *Haus und Herrschaft*, pp. 11–47.

3 There are, of course, many questions remaining about the origins of lordly power and the nature of the lord/follower relationship. See the studies of Kuhn and Kroeschell cited in notes 1 and 2 and also Anne K.G. Kristensen, *Tacitus' germanische Gefolgschaft* (1983); Green, *Carolingian Lord*, pp. 59–80.

4 The problem with this interpretation was discussed in chapter two. In the cases of men like Ariovistus and Civilis, for example, canny and capable leaders who laid plans on the basis of logistics, recruitment and overall military strategy, it is difficult to imagine them not taking account of the need to maintain morale by controlling, and not just soliciting, soothsayers and sibyls. Exposure to other cultures, Celtic and Roman, will only have encouraged this necessary concern of all commanders. The possibility of their own faith in prophecy is a perhaps related but not necessarily significant datum since the propagandistic emphasis must be maintained for the sake of unity and efficiency in guiding large forces of warriors from different social and tribal strata. A certain level of independence may be allowed in the case of mantic practitioners who belong to a traditional and venerated organization such as the druidic priesthood. That was not the case with the Germans who, as H. Roe points out, ("Rome and the Early Germans: Some Sociolinguistic Observations" [1980], p. 104) possessed "no common Germanic word for 'priest' ". Even in the Celtic case, best illustrated by early medieval Irish evidence, a druid, *fili* or bard was always *ceile* or "vassal" of some kind to his lord and the best known seeress of the tradition was a slave, albeit one of special status. See Williams, "Celtic Literature", p. 143.

late La Tène (first century BC) which is in fact that period that establishes the true foundation for the subsequent political development of Germanic culture.

Classical historians had great difficulty distinguishing Celts from Germans; modern historians are little better off and archaeologists find it a struggle to do so by the late La Tène period. With Strabo, we may say that "these people are similar and akin to one another both in their nature and in their citizen life . . . they are wont to change their abode on slight provocation, migrating in bands with all their battle-array, or rather setting out with all their household when displaced by a stronger enemy".[5] In keeping with a recent modern interpreter, however, one must also add that "it is established that the northern tribes of the pre-Roman Iron Age stand largely within the shadow of Celtic culture".[6]

From about 500 BC, roughly the beginning of the La Tène culture, until the time of Caesar and beyond, groups of Celts and Germans were frequently in fairly close contact. Contrary to later Roman commentators who wished to simplify a complex situation, the Rhine was in no way a boundary between them, although it is true to say that in the immediate centuries BC and AD, the Rhineland was the area of most intense cultural exchange.[7] The contact zone also extended beyond that. As late as the last pre-Roman half-century, as Gerhard Mildenberger has recently stated, Celtic-speaking groups still "certainly" existed east of the Rhine and even the question as to whether the highly Celticized Germanic groupings west of the river (*Germani cisrhenani*) continued to speak a Germanic language is "completely open".[8] "Intense cultural contact", therefore, is precisely the appropriate descriptive phrase and it is the one frequently used by linguists who point to the remarkable store of social, legal and, above all, institutional words common to both peoples.[9] In the case of the Rhineland, it is possible to speak of "linguistic

---

5 Tierney, "Celtic Ethnography", p. 267f. All of this material comes originally from Posidonius writing near the beginning of the first century BC.
6 Peschel, "Kelten", p. 29f.; idem, "Kelten und Germanen", pp. 167–200; idem, *Anfänge germanischer Besiedlung im Mittelgebirgsraum. Sueben—Hermunduren—Markomannen* (1978), p. 37f.; idem, "Kriegergrab, Gefolge und Landnahme bei den Latènekelten" (1984), pp. 445–69; idem, "Die Sueben in ethnographie und Archaologie" (1978), pp. 259–309; Birkhan, *Germanen und Kelten*, p. 44; Wenskus, *Stammesbildung*, pp. 346f., 409f.; Harald von Petrikovits, "Germani Cisrhenani" (1986), pp. 91, 97, 102; Rolf Hachmann, "Germanen und Kelten am Rhein in der Zeit um Christi Geburt" (1962), pp. 61, 64; Ament, "Ethnogenese", p. 39f.
7 See the studies by Ament, von Petrikovits and Hachmann cited in note 6 and von Petrikovits, *Rheinische Geschichte* I, pp. 39–44, 57–62.
8 G. Mildenburger, "Germanen in der archäologischen Forschung nach Kossinna" (1986), p. 320; von Petrikovits, "Germani Cisrhenani", pp. 88–106; Günter Neumann, "Germani cisrhenani—die Aussage der Namen" (1986), pp. 107–29; Birkhan, *Germanen und Kelten*, pp. 181–250.
9 See, for example, Karl H. Schmidt, "Keltisch-germanische Isoglossen und ihre sprachgeschichtlichen Implikationen" (1986), pp. 231–47.

and cultural fusion, as well as outright diglossia"[10] but even for tribes like the Batavians and Usipetes (whose name appears to mean "good riders" and is "presumably Celtic") there are enough clues available to show that we must reckon with considerable influence in the northern Rhine region as well.[11] Indeed, it would be surprising if otherwise, for centers of Celtic activity were present not only in the West and South where one would expect them but also within Germania, in the Jutland peninsula where astonishing amounts of late La Tène goods have been found, and also on the East where, as Filip and Peschel have shown, the cultural province of the Volcae and Boii must be considered.[12]

Linguistic evidence does not contradict this portrait. The many Celto-Germanic isoglosses have often been studied by philologists and are well known.[13] Although it is true to say that only two important legal/institutional words can be conclusively demonstrated to have been borrowed from the Celts (Gaul. *rik-s, Got. reiks, "ruler"; Gaul. ambaktos, OHG ambaht, "servant"),[14] seven other words can be described as "probable" borrowings on the basis of their semantics:

10 T.L. Markey, "Social Spheres and National Groups in Germania" (1986), p. 256. The author goes on to speak of reciprocal influence, cross-fertilization and acculturation in the areas of art and religion as well as language. Speaking of territories outside of the core areas of Celtic culture, von Petrikovits ("Germani Cisrhenani", p. 91) notes: "Dass man hier eine andere Sprache benutzte als die Gallier, wird vielen nicht aufgefallen sein, weil sie sich eines Dolmetschers bedienten und die Germanen dieses Gebietes vielleicht auch mit Handlern oder den seltenen Reisenden ein 'basic'-Gallisch (-Keltisch) radebrechen konnte, das wohl auch hier eine 'lingua Franca' war."; Karl H. Schmidt, "Celtic Languages in Their European Context" (1986), p. 208: "During the earlier period, in which the Celts enjoyed technical and military superiority in middle Europe the continental Celtic languages acted as models for other languages. This process is reflected e.g. by Celtic words in Germanic . . . ". Rudolf Much, *Deutsche Stammeskunde* (1900), p. 50: "Doch kann es als sicher gelten, dass die Sprache des mehr verfeinerten gallischen Nachbarvolkes auch in hoheren germanischen Gesellschaftskreisen der Grenzbezirke gepflegt wurde". He goes on to emphatically demonstrate "ein besonders enges Verhältnis". See further, Hans Krahe, *Sprache und Vorzeit. Europäische Vorgeschichte nach dem Zeugnis der Sprache* (1954), pp. 122–43; Günter Neumann, "Die Sprachverhältnisse in den germanischen Provinzen des römischen Reiches" (1983), pp. 1061– 88; Edgar C. Polomé, "The Linguistic Situation in the Western Provinces of the Roman Empire" (1983), p. 527f.; Hermann Reichert, "Zum problem der rechtsrheinischen Germanen vor und um Christi Geburt: Wie kann die Namenkunde helfen, die Sprachzugehörigkeit der Namenträger zu bestimmen?" (1976), pp. 557–76.
11 See, for example, Markey, "National Groups in Germania", p. 256f.; Neumann, "Sprachverhältnisse", p. 1067f.
12 Filip, *Celtic Civilization*, p. 127f.; Peschel, "Kelten", p. 23f. and the works cited in note 6; Natalie Venclova, "Das Grenzgebiet der Latènekultur in Nordwestböhmen" (1988), pp. 121–128. The Volcae are discussed by Weisgerber, "Walhisk", pp. 155–232.
13 Schmidt, "Keltisch-germanische Isoglossen", pp. 231–47; Idem, "Celtic Languages", pp. 199–221; Idem, "Die keltischen Matronennamen" (1987), pp. 133–53; Krahe, *Sprache und Vorzeit*, pp. 122–43; D. Ellis Evans, "Celts and Germans" (1981), pp. 230–55; Birkhan, *Germanen und Kelten*, p. 120f. *et passim*.
14 These words are discussed in all of the works cited in note 13 to which may be added Tristano Bolelli and Enrico Campanile, "Sur la préhistoire des noms gaulois en -rix" (1972), pp. 123–40.

Celto-Germ. **oitos*, OI *oeth*, Got. *aiþs*, "oath".
Celto-Germ. **orbhio-*, OI *comarbe*, Got. *arbja*, "heir".
Celto-Germ. **priios*, Welsh *rhydd*, Got. *freis*, OHG *frî*, "free".
OI *giall*, Welsh *gwystl*, OHG *gisal*, "hostage".
OI *fine*, "kin, tribe, family", Gaul. personal name Veni-carus, ON *vinr*, "friend", OHG and AS *wini*, "friend".
OI *cath*, Welsh *cad*, Gaul. *catu-*, OHG *hadu-*, "battle".
OI *búaid*, "victory", Welsh *budd*, "profit", OHG goddess name Baudihillia.[15]

It seems very likely, especially when one introduces historical and archaeological evidence, that a high proportion of these latter words are borrowings as well. Speaking of Celto-Germanic contact and of the marked separation between Germanic nobles and commoners which evolved over the course of the last five centuries BC, Reinhard Wenskus has this to say:

> This aristocratic culture, originating on the borderlands of the Mediterranean area and the eastern Alps, spread quickly to the west into the core territory of the Celts and became rooted in the most fruitful period of Celtic culture (La Tène). In this area, a social model for less cultivated neighboring groups developed. It is for that reason that Celtic influence on many of the similar Germanic words relating to law, politics, social life and the conduct of war can be accepted although linguistic means alone cannot prove borrowing in the majority of these words.[16]

One should note that the same seems to be true in the field of personal name studies. Much, Krahe and Birkhan, among others, have all called attention to the "extraordinarily high number" of similar two-element personal names shared by Celts and Germans to the point where "hardly any other pair of Indo-Germanic languages can offer a parallel".[17] Birkhan's partial selective list of such names contains over eighty items. Examples are: Gaul. Ver-corius, Burgundian Gundi-charius; Gaul. Vandelos, ON Vandill; Ir. Ali-therus, OHG Eli-land; Brit. Cuno-morus, OHG Hun-mar; Welsh Drut-guas, OHG Trut-man; Cornish Jud-hent, Lombard Teude-sindus; Breton Uuiu-ho-march, Vandal Visu-mar(h).[18]

Such evidence has often been used in the past to argue the thesis of early Celtic rule over a large number of Germanic tribes.[19] Considering the great Celtic advantage in weaponry, this is likely to have been true in the early and mid La

It may, perhaps, be noted in passing that the views of Jan de Vries, *Kelten und Germanen* (1960), pp. 62–79 seem to have been superseded in this area as in some others dealing with similar topics.
15 Convenient discussions of this list will be found in the studies by Schmidt cited in note 13.
16 Wenskus, *Stammesbildung*, p. 356f.
17 Much, *Deutsche Stammeskunde*, p. 51f.; Krahe, *Sprache und Vorzeit*, p. 138f.; Birkhan, *Germanen und Kelten*, p. 40f.
18 Birkhan, *Germanen und Kelten*, p. 40f.
19 For example: H. D'Arbois de Jubainville, *Les premiers habitants de l'Europe* (1894), p. 328f.

Tène just as the position was often reversed in the late La Tène. Caesar says (B.G. 6, 24): "There was a time in the past when the Gauls were superior in valor to the Germans and made aggressive war upon them". Tacitus cites him to the same effect in chapter 29 of *Germania*. Neither Krahe or Birkhan fully accept this view, however, although both are clearly impressed by the phalanx of clues which they themselves have assembled. Krahe declares that the evidence leaves a "weighty impression" and admits it can be interpreted "in the sense of the theory of an earlier Celtic hegemony" but seeks himself to explain it as proof of an "extremely close culture-community" of the two groups.[20] Birkhan, for his part, suggests that Celtic names may simply have been fashionable in the same way that, for example, Patriz is favored in the modern Steiermark, Leopold in Lower Austria or Eugen in Vorarlberg. On the other hand, since Germanic kings and nobles show a remarkable desire to copy the Celts, he argues that there must have existed a "*snobistische*" tendency towards Celtic pronunciation and name-borrowing *even* in cases where Germanic possessed an exact semantic or phonetic parallel.[21] To Birkhan's first hypothesis one must reply, despite the exceptional range of that scholar's knowledge and his magisterial control of the subject, that it seems to be inadequate to explain such a widespread phenomenon, especially in view of the convincing remarks on the importance of name giving in archaic societies made in the essay by Robinson cited earlier.[22] The second is open to the same criticism but here one may simply observe that if the "tendency" towards adopting Celtic pronunciation and name-style had indeed gone as far as Birkhan allows, then Gaulish cultural ascendancy must have been of heroic proportions and it seems unnecessary to argue beyond that.

We may now turn to the *comitatus* itself. The most recent reference to the origins of Germanic warband organization that I know of is that by Schulze in his very useful book on basic elements of the medieval constitution. As he states: "The Germanic and Celtic warband forms possess closely similar basic elements without it being possible with certainty to determine an influence on

---

20 Krahe, *Sprache und Vorzeit*, p. 138f.

21 Birkhan, *Germanen und Kelten*, p. 76. One would not wish, as some have done, to go so far as to argue that those who bore Celtic names were necessarily Celtic in culture and language. On the other hand, the notion that these names have "Mode-Ursachen" alone must be emphatically rejected for Germanic dependence on some Celtic vocabulary, politics and technology is too clear to allow one to follow the minimalist interpretation. De Vries' attempt in this direction (*Kelten und Germanen*, p. 69f.) is inadequate. "Prunksucht" is simply too weak to bear the evidence and is, in itself, speculative. It is the desire and fact of emulation that is significant.

22 Robinson, "Names", pp. 14–58. In many cases, intermarriage will provide the most cogent interpretation. A probably high frequency has been noted by von Petrikovits and Markey (see note 10) for the Rhineland zone, by Faull, "Old English *wealh*", pp. 20–44, and the presence of large numbers of Britons in the Anglo-Saxon *comitatus* is a further significant indication. Northumbria, the probable home of the *Beowulf* poem, is a clearly analogous area to the Rhineland.

the Germanic warband by the Celts".[23] His conclusion is based largely on the frequently contrasting research findings of Schlesinger, Kuhn, Kroeschell and von Olberg, although in this matter, as he does in others, it might have been appropriate to cite the well-known study of Wenskus on *Stammesbildung* which seems, at least to me, to offer the most useful synthesis of argumentation on the question.[24] In any case, the pivotal phrase in the citation is the cautious "with certainty" which is less justifiable in this instance than in many others. To demonstrate, let us first approach the topic by way of analogy. Consider, for example, that the only early extensive statement that we possess about the nature of the Germanic *comitatus* for the entire ancient period is that which appears in chapters 13 and 14 of *Germania* and that this is the foundation upon which practically all major judgements of that institution are based. Those brief observations by other classical commentators like Caesar, Strabo, Cassius Dio or Ammianus Marcellinus, who frequently confuse Celts and Germans and almost routinely transmit the confusion of others, are difficult to interpret without reference to Tacitus whose spirit pervades most modern analyses as well.

It is, therefore, surprising to find that most students of warband organization do not even cite the findings of Norden reached as long ago as 1923 in which he demonstrated that several critical Tacitean expressions derive ultimately from a reference of Polybius (*Hist.* II, 12, 17), quoted in chapter three of the present study, to the power of Celtic leaders and the nature of the comradeship they enjoy with their followers.[25] These may have reached Tacitus by way of some second-stage reworking of the lost book of Posidonius, who was writing specifically on Celtic tribes and customs.[26] One can, of course, simply retort that Tacitus' reliance on the language of Polybius does not necessarily mean that the ideas expressed do not also apply to Germanic institutions. That is undeniably true. But it is equally undeniable that the remarks of Tacitus are thereby rendered ambiguous. Historians must be particularly skeptical at two specific points in the logical chain: first, when arguing on the basis of Tacitus' choice of words or vocabulary that the warbands are different at all (since his usage of Polybius or Posidonius inherently suggests that he personally may have believed otherwise) and second, in arguing for specific but subtle types of distinctions between organizations on the basis of his remarks. Clearly one cannot do so "with certainty". The point may be otherwise formulated as follows: given the universally acknowledged close similarity between the Celtic and Germanic *comitatus* and the fact that the former predates the latter by several centuries at least, any methodology will seem inconsistent and challengeable if it treats Tacitus' borrowing of language originally applied to the Celtic warband as inconsequential but at the same time argues

23　Schulze, *Grundstrukturen der Verfassung* II, p. 39.
24　See notes 1–3. von Olberg, *Gefolgsleute*, 202–15; Wenskus, *Stammesbildung*, p. 346f.
25　Norden, *Urgeschichte*, p. 124f.
26　Ibid. and p. 142f.

that Celtic influence is uncertain even though a durable pattern of cultural borrowing from Celts in a variety of fields has long been established.

If we narrow our focus somewhat from the broader pattern of cultural interplay to those sectors most likely to have been of interest to warlords and followers, then we find considerable evidence, linguistic, archaeological and historical, to suggest that the uncertainty of some modern scholars is unjustified. We have already seen that the Gaulish word for "king", which often appears in the names of warlords, cannot easily be explained as due to fashion. The Gaulish word *ambaktos* (OHG *ambaht*) "servant", may be even more significant for it was commonly applied to followers. If no one doubts its place in the Gaulish *comitatus*, however, the reason for its possible adoption by Germanic troops has not hitherto been completely elucidated.

Arguing that the Germanic warband was not based on a vertical relationship between lord and man but that the Gaulish one was, some scholars have viewed the servile connotations of *ambaktos* as a key piece of evidence demonstrating that the two organizations were dissimilar.[27] As we saw in chapter three, this conclusion is now doubtful but it is doubtful for additional reasons as well. In chapter 13 of *Germania*, Tacitus states that graduations of honor exist within the *comitatus* and these ranks are determined by the will of the chief. Given this hierarchical structure, considerable social distance must have separated the trusted, experienced, mature warrior from the untried newcomer who would normally have been considerably younger and who, as in practically every closely knit military organization that ever existed, would have been assigned the most menial tasks and often ordered to serve the seniors until he rose in rank. This ordinary technique of introduction has been applied over many millennia because it is the most effective means of integrating recruits and creating a functioning unit. Neither noble nor commoner can escape this stage (except under unusual circumstances) and thus it says nothing about the extra-organizational status of the man being tested. All beginners are called "plebes", "fags" or "slaves". We know this to have been the case among the first century Chatti, for example. Tacitus says that the youths of this people were not accounted men and not allowed to shave or cut their hair until they had killed an enemy. Until that day they also had to wear an iron ring in token of chains (clearly reminiscent of slavery). It even became popular for older men to continue to wear the "chain", perhaps as a sign of a willingness to be constantly tested.[28] Procopius confirms the general concept in the sixth century for he states that the young men of the Heruli were called *douloi*, literally "slaves" until they demonstrated their bravery by fighting without a shield,[29] and

---

27 For example, Green, *Carolingian Lord*, pp. 59–79.
28 Hutton, *Tacitus. Germania* 31, p. 308.
29 Dewing, *Procopius* "De bello Persico" II, XXV, 27, p. 486f.; Herwig Wolfram, *Geschichte der Goten. Von den Anfängen bis zur Mitte des sechsten Jahrhunderts: Entwurf einer historischen Ethnographie* (1980), p. 125 and n. 104.

Ammianus Marcellinus, writing in the fourth century, says that young men of the Taifali, a tribe closely associated with the Goths and Vandals, were shamefully used by adult warriors until they gained their freedom by killing a boar or capturing a bear.[30]

All of these passages seem to reflect a widespread Germanic practice whereby young men of the warband, whom Anglo-Saxon sources call the *geoguð*, "youths", as opposed to the *duguð*, "veterans", were ill-treated (as was Beowulf) until they had proved their worth.[31] Purely tribal societies make use of this technique as well but it need not be so pronounced among them because of the natural glue of blood ties. The *comitatus*, on the other hand, recruiting from outside the kin and tribe and often enduring lengthy journeys in hostile territory, must constantly stress a long period of harsh initiation in order to create that pervading sense of *esprit de corps* which will make it possible for members to support one another despite a desire for flight as well as, in some cases, to attack people of their own tribe if it be judged necessary by the leader. The system is not arbitrary; it is essential— but only at the stage where the *comitatus* has emerged since a harsh lengthy initiation is less necessary within the tribe. Something like this may have also

---

30 John C. Rolfe, ed. *Ammianus Marcellinus* (1964), p. 444f. Hist. XXXI, 9, 5.

31 Klaeber, *Beowulf*, ll. 2183–9; Green, *Carolingian Lord*, p. 268, n. 2, notes that "whereas the 'Männerbund' may indeed be a particular form of the *comitatus*, we certainly cannot argue conversely that every *comitatus* is therefore also a 'Männerbund.' The two institutions may well have a lot in common but they cannot be called identical". It is unlikely, however, that societies which favor the "Männerbund" system would have abandoned that approach with the *comitatus* which accepted boys at a very early age. As pointed out above, the very nature of the *comitatus* would require harsh initiation and training in order to instill a thorough-going group identification. Kristensen, *Germanische Gefolgschaft*, p. 67f. and n. 189 seems to agree: "trotzdem eröffnet die Schilderung [*Germania* 13] die Möglichkeit, indirekt einen eventuellen Zusammenhang zwischen der Entwicklung der unfreien Begriffe und der Mitgliedschaft im Gefolge zu schliessen, da in der eigentlichen Männerbund-Institution, in den Vorstellungen verschiedener Art, die an die Jünglingsperiode geknüpft sind, Voraussetzungen dafür bestan- den zu haben scheinen". One stone inscription from Valsfjord, dated to *c.*400, refers to a *comitatus* member as a slave (Schramm, *Namenschatz*, p. 72). Gothic sources, such as the *Passio S. Sabae* also support the view that followers could indeed be described as "slaves" of a leader. Thompson notes, *Visigoths*, p. 52f., that "when the tribal chief Atharid was helping to enforce the persecution of the Christians of Gothia he came to a village with 'a company of lawless brigands' who referred to Atharid as their 'master' (*despotes*) and who included one of his sons among their number. It is difficult to see what can have been the relationship of those men with their 'master' if it was not that of a retinue with its leader; for the men were not slaves, and who else had a master in Gothia?" If one assumes this company was a retinue, as Thompson adds, then "it is of the utmost interest to observe that it was used not in a plundering raid against other people but so as to enforce 'order' at home and to coerce a refractory tribesman". This example illuminates many of the themes already discussed—the conflict between tribal and warband organization, the necessity of the lord's power to command and, of special note, the way in which paternal power becomes involved since the warlord's son is a member of the band. Recall that the same is true at Heorot where Beowulf sits between Hrothgar's sons who are members of the *geoguð*. Kinship and the power of the warlord are concepts which must be related.

existed among the Gauls who possessed two names for followers, *soldurii*, "the devoted ones", and *ambacti*, "the servants", literally "those who move around" the lord.[32] In some cases, there may have been an age-differential between the two or perhaps—it is now difficult to tell—between certain members of each group. It has, of course, been pointed out earlier that many Germanic warriors known to have been respected were given *theow*- names which signify cultic "slavery".

Contrary to the traditional assertion, therefore, *ambaktos*—assuming for the sake of argument an original servile taint—does not demonstrate that the two warbands were dissimilar; quite the reverse, they may be most alike at precisely that point where they have hitherto been called most different. At the same time, however, the foregoing interpretation should not be construed to mean that slaves or lower class bondsmen of various types did not also have a place in the warbands of both peoples. Already in 1956, Hans Kuhn demonstrated that the Germanic warbands of various periods contained both free and unfree members and Reinhard Wenskus, one of the few scholars to draw the necessary consequences from the studies of Norden and Kuhn, associated the *ambacti* with the latter although the idea of base clientship is probably closer the mark.[33] While I have emphasized the initiatory metaphoric significance of the word "slave" in this context, such would naturally only be true with regard to free men. A recent lengthy discussion of the Celtic *comitatus* is that by Dobesch who demonstrates the untenability of the older view, showing it to derive from an indiscriminate usage of the word "client" by classical Latin writers and the only partial description by Caesar.

Military organization has always been affected by technology and the types of weapons that technology can provide. Thus, for example, when the huge army of the Cimbri and Teutones faced the new model Roman forces of Marius near the end of the second century BC, their cavalry was already armed on the Celtic model. Unlike the German horse soldiers bearing a lance,[34] these troops wore helmets, were equipped with iron breastplates, carried shields, two lances, and at close quarters used large, heavy swords.[35] This obviously encouraged new types of strategy and tactics and makes it easier to understand why one word for "cavalry", OE *eored*, is a borrowing from Celtic, or why the wearing of spurs was adopted by the Germans from the Celts.[36] There are many other clues. The

---

32 Edwards, *Caesar. Gallic War*, III, 22; VI, 15, pp. 168, 338f.; Wenskus, *Stammesbildung*, p. 358f.
33 Wenskus, *Stammesbildung*, p. 360.
34 A good discussion of weapons and tactics, which notes the shortage of iron available to Germanic communities in Tacitean Germania, will be found in E.A. Thompson, *The Early Germans* (1965), pp. 111–30. See also Hans Delbrück, *History of the Art of War II. The Germans* (1980), p. 47f.
35 Bernadotte Perrin, ed. *Plutarch's Lives* "Caius Marius" XXV, 7, p. 532.
36 Wenskus, *Stammesbildung*, p. 357, n. 556; Bruno Krüger, *Die Germanen: Geschichte und Kultur der germanischen Stämme in Mitteleuropa* I (1988), p. 341.

Germanic for "iron", **isarna-*, is borrowed from the Celts and so also are the words for "oven", **ufna-*, and "lead", **lauða* (although this latter occurred in the second century AD) as well as **brunio* (Got. *brunjo*) "mail coat", **uira-*, "metal wire" and "perhaps", **uepna*, "weapon".[37]

Since both metal working techniques and significant *termini* of the *Handwerk-ersprache* were owed to the Celts, it should not be surprising that the Germans also drew on the weapons of their neighbors. Thus it is that Raddatz, in his study of Germanic weaponry of the pre-Roman period, could speak of "intense" Celtic influence during the mid La Tène and of late La Tène Germanic weapons as being "decisively influenced by those of the Celts".[38] An extraordinary example is that of the mid La Tène Danish find at Hjortspring containing 20 to 24 mail coats, "whose presence in the framework of the primitive appearing armament is surprising".[39] Similar conclusions can be drawn regarding methods of fighting and of the coordination between cavalryman and footsoldier. The nobility, of course,—those who carried Celtic names, borrowed the Celtic word for "king", wore Celtic mail coats in order to distinguish themselves from other warriors and recruited the *ambacti* in the first place—were especially impressed for they were the only ones who could afford Celtic type swords, shields and mail coats whereas the other warriors, particularly in the northeast, often had to make do with small-bladed iron spears, stag-horns or clubs made from bone.[40] The word **uira*, "metal wire", is also intriguing in the present context since twisted wire was often used for arm-rings and perhaps bestowed by the "ring-giver". Birkhan wonders if this term might not belong to the same period as the borrowing of the "king" word and comments: "objectively speaking, this borrowing would fit well in the area of the warband".[41] Even the oldest native word for the *comitatus* may be related to the Celts. As Kuhn points out, the warband *termini* *Gesind* and *Gesinde*,

---

37 These and other examples are discussed in Birkhan, *Germanen und Kelten*, pp. 140–66. Many others might be cited—in the area of building techniques, fortifications and the spread of oppida, for example. A strong eastern influence on some Germanic weapon forms is clear and explainable on the basis that the Cotini functioned "als Eisenlieferanten der Quaden". For the spread of oppida, see J.R. Collis, *Oppida: Earliest Towns North of the Alps* (1984), pp. 8–15.

38 Klaus Raddatz, *Die germanische Bewaffnung der vorrömischen Eisenzeit* (1966), pp. 429–46; idem, *Die Bewaffnung der Germanen in der jungeren römischen Kaiserzeit* (1967), pp. 3–17. See also Kurt W. Zeller, *Kriegswesen und Bewaffnung der Kelten* (1980), pp. 111–32; F. Fischer, "Bewaffnung" (1976), pp. 409–16.

39 Raddatz, *Germanische Bewaffnung*, p. 436.

40 Ibid., p. 440: "Einen sehr primitiven Zug in der Bewaffnung lassen die knöchernen Speer-spitzen erkennen, die in beträchtlicher Menge sowohl in Hjortspring als auch in Krogsbolle belegt sind". p. 446: "Während in Mitteleuropa in der Latènezeit die keltische schwere Bewaffnung entwickelt wurde, bedingte der Eisenmangel im Norden ein Festhalten am Späthallstattischen Kampfmesser und erzwang die rationelle Ausnutzung des verfügbaren Metalls und den Rückgriff auf Hirschgeweih und Knochen".

41 Birkhan, *Germanen und Kelten*, p. 154.

"traveling companions", derive from Germanic *sinþ-*, "path", whose closest linguistic relative is Celtic *sent-*, "path".[42]

Despite a documentable multiplicity of contacts, the poverty of detailed testimony does not allow us to point with confidence to any specific date when it can be categorically stated that certain Germanic groupings had adopted the Celtic warband form of organization.[43] As a reasonable guess, one would probably not be too far off the mark in supposing that the Cimbri/Teutones invasions of the last decades of the second century BC provide an attractive context for some initial contacts. Neither Greek nor Roman commentators, who had difficulty distinguishing the two peoples and who exaggerated or diminished differences to suit propagandistic purposes, can be expected to know or care much about this. In the case of an historian like Tacitus, one finds that much that he wrote is dubious because it is saturated with ancient rhetorical *topoi*.[44] It is possible, however, to provide a relatively reliable picture of the way in which such a transition might have occurred if we take a brief look at the career of Ariovistus, the earliest known warlord of whom we possess any information going beyond the most basic type of casual classical reference. Schlesinger, Wenskus, Walser and Peschel, among others, have all commented on his biography in some detail and all that is necessary here is a review of the high points with a few analytic remarks.

Called *rex* by Caesar and *rex Sueborum* by Pliny, Ariovistus crossed the Rhine during the seventies of the first century BC. Whether this should be classified as a tribal migration or a warband raid is difficult to say although it must be noted that Peschel has advanced strong arguments for holding that the Suebi were already under Celtic influence and that their name is less a *Sammelbezeichnung* or group designation for different tribes than it is for raiding warbands.[45] According to Caesar (B.G. 1, 31), Ariovistus had 15,000 followers when he was called in as a mercenary by the Sequani to aid in their war with the Aedui. With his support they were successful and won the major battle of Magetobriga in 61 BC. Thereafter, according to Caesar, he settled or seized one third of the territory of the Sequani and three years later demanded another third. But these references to land taking are grossly exaggerated for Caesar is seeking to justify his own campaigns by picturing the Germans as a great danger to Roman security who

---

42 Kuhn, "Grenzen", p. 78.
43 Peschel makes a strong case for the first-century BC Suebi. See his "Sueben", pp. 259–309. He argues that the military organization of the Suebi, especially cavalry and warband, were based on the Celtic model.
44 A.A. Lund, "Zum Germanenbegriff bei Tacitus" (1986), pp. 53–87; Dieter Timpe, "Ethnologische Begriffsbildung in der Antike" (1986), pp. 22–39.
45 Peschel, "Sueben", pp. 259–309.

cannot be repulsed by the Gauls alone.[46] This too is his reason for constant harping on the rapacity and ferocity of Ariovistus as well as for the inflated numbers of his supporters—15,000 initially, then control of 120,000 and a further 24,000 said to be coming to aid him. None of this is fully credible. On the other hand, it is clear that Ariovistus was a powerful warband leader, though not one of a tribe. He is said to have stated that his men were highly trained in the use of arms and, although this is obviously exaggerated, that they had not "lived beneath a roof for fourteen years".[47] He personally led his troops into battle, collected hostages, demanded tribute and based his legitimacy on the right of conquest. In his final battle with Caesar in 50 BC his army was made up of men from at least seven different tribes: Harudes, Marcomanni, Triboces, Vangiones, Nemetes, Sedusi, and Suebi.[48]

If Ariovistus certainly exercised a new type of non-tribal lordship, it is difficult to think of him in terms of purely Germanic culture. To begin with, his name is probably not Germanic. Disagreement persists about its precise components but the most likely derivation is Celtic or "Celto-Germanic".[49] The first element *ario-/areo-*, apparently "a nobleman, a master, a chief"(?), is cognate with Irish *aire*, "a noble, a chief, a freeman, a free peasant".[50] The name is otherwise attested as that of the leader of the Gaulish Insubres and of a physician in Britain but no Germanic bearers are known.[51] Ariovistus was also a "fluent" speaker of Gaulish. When Caesar wished to parlay with him, he sent a young man versed in that tongue.[52] Moreover, of the two known wives of Ariovistus, one was Suebian and the other Celtic. She was not from Gaul, however, but was the sister of king Voccio

---

46 Norden, *Germanische Urgeschichte*, p. 94f.; Wenskus, *Stammesbildung*, p. 220f.; W.M. Zeitler, "Zum Germanenbegriff Caesars: Der Germanenexkurs im sechsten Buch von Caesars Bellum Gallicum" (1986), pp. 41–52. A useful (although sometimes exaggerated) overview in Walser, *Caesar und die Germanen*. See also the studies by von Petrikovits, Hachmann and Ament cited in note 6.

47 Edwards, *Caesar. Gallic War*, I, 36, p. 56.

48 Ibid., p. 78.

49 Rolf Kodderitzsch, "Keltoide Namen mit germanischen Namenträgern" (1986), p. 202f.; Anton Scherer, "Die keltisch-germanischen Namengleichungen" (1955), p. 203f.; D. Ellis Evans, *Gaulish Personal Names: A Study of Some Continental Celtic Formations* (1967), pp. 54f., 141f. Interestingly, among all the recorded personal names of the Ubii, most are Roman. Of the remainder, however, only 4% are German and 7% are Celtic. See J.H. Weisgerber, *Die Namen der Ubier* (1968), pp. 172–97; Neumann, "Sprachverhältnisse", p. 1072f. Among older scholars, Much thought the name Ariovistus to be Celtic but Moritz Schonfeld, *Wörterbuch der altgermanischen Personen-und Völkernamen* (1911), p. 28, thought it to be Germanic. Reichert, "Problem der rechtrheinischen Germanen", p. 560, states that the name Ariovistus "zweifelsfrei als keltisch angesehen werden muss . . . . Also muss Ariovist einem Kulturkreis entstammen, in dem zumindest der Adel Keltisch lernte . . . ".

50 Evans, *Gaulish Personal Names*, p. 141f.

51 Ibid., p. 54 and see the studies by Kodderitzsch and Scherer cited in note 49.

52 Edwards, *Caesar. Gallic War*, I, 47, p. 78.

of Noricum.[53] This suggests a wider dimension to the warlord's diplomacy and also a close connection with another Celtic people. The same paradigm should also be assumed for his followers who would certainly have copied their king and so a pattern of intermarriage and cultural adaption is to be expected. As Reinhard Wenskus and Harold von Petrikovits have argued, such cases are found all over the world under similar circumstances and they often occurred elsewhere in the Iron Age, among the *Germani cisrhenani* for example.[54] Taken together, then, these clues are sufficient to indicate that we are not dealing with a man of purely Germanic culture at all. He appears to be, like the tribe he is in the process of creating, a Celto-Germanic hybrid at home on either bank of the Rhine or Danube. His name suggests that the Celtic influence is of long standing while his languages and marriages show that he has adopted a consistent policy of accommodation with the Celts and not simply, as Caesar depicts it, one of ferocious hostility and exploitation. While tribal rivalries certainly existed, the conditions of life in the Celto-Germanic contact zones over several centuries created exactly the right kind of climate for cultural interchange and not just for tribal conflict. An important reason for Germanic success in the first century is that the military organizations of both peoples were becoming more alike.

If it is true to say with Krahe that linguistics provides proof of an "extremely close culture-community", the cumulative effect of the further evidence, personal names, institutional and artisan terminology, weaponry, cavalry. etc., is so powerful as to admit of only one conclusion: Germanic *duces* consciously and deliberately set out to form their dependents into a military organization on the model of the Celtic warband. Separately, each item on any list of parallels and borrowings can be challenged or reduced by a minimalist interpretation which asserts that even close similarity does not prove influence of one on the other. But the pattern here goes far beyond that for we are dealing with peoples who were sometimes neighbors, traders and fighters for half a millennium and among whom, as numerous scholars have pointed out, the cultural influence most frequently operated from South to North and West to East. It is not simply the remarkable profusion of the evidence which convinces but rather the way in which the archaeological, linguistic and historical material combines to form an interrelated pattern (which is, probably, in itself the most significant datum of all). The Celtic invasions of Greece and Rome in the fourth and third centuries BC probably had a profound impact on Germanic warrior attitudes and early Celtic hegemony over some Germanic tribes will also have played a significant role. It will have endowed them with the kind of prestige which encourages emulation. I also agree, however, with Wenskus' remarks in *Stammesbildung und*

---

53 Ibid., p. 84; Geza Alföldy, *Noricum* (1974), p. 40f. The probability is that Voccio and Ariovistus formed an alliance against the Boii and Helvetii.

54 Wenskus, *Stammesbildung*, pp. 220f., 384; Von Petrikovits, "Germani Cisrhenani", p. 102.

Verfassung where he points out that "certain beginning approaches and pre-forms" must have existed amongst the Germans, for otherwise they would not have taken so readily to the Celtic model.[55] Elsewhere, he associates these with a Gaulish *clientela* and a patron-client relationship which may be helpful in interpreting a complex pattern.[56]

These findings are an important aid to understanding the general milieu. They indicate that warlords or proto-warlords were the true carriers of innovation in Germanic society for they were willing to adapt, adopt and manipulate in order to develop and solidify their revolutionary power. The cultural situation is not very different from early medieval England where one finds a similar mixture of religious and military elements. Whereas many early missionaries and *wealhsto-das*, "interpreters", are from Celtic areas, it is especially intriguing to note that it was a retired military man like Guthlac, a former *comitatus* leader, who had learned how to speak British.[57] Like Guthlac and like Ariovistus, Julius Civilis of the Batavi would have known Celtic as well. Long before his time, as linguists are agreed, Gaulish had become a kind of lingua franca of the North.[58] Civilis was acquainted with both Gauls and Britons, both served in his armies and he aimed to become king of a multicultural state. It is difficult to imagine him not knowing the Celtic language so closely associated with Germanic aristocratic culture. Except for the matter of scale his policies cannot have been much different from Ariovistus. Although it is true to say that he was a far more widely travelled and experienced man than Ariovistus, it is also now clear that both were familiar with Celtic culture and that each knew how to make use of it.

How did the prophetess come to fit in with the schemes of such ambitious would-be kings and conquerors? The question of origins in this case may not be as difficult as it looks. Although the available evidence is sparse, it remains possible to develop an hypothesis which fits it. The first point to note is that Germanic warriors did not normally turn to women for advice on the future. In chapter 10 of *Germania*, we are told that the Germans are immensely interested in augury and divination. The casting of lots is particularly popular and the method of doing so is uniform. If the occasion be an official one concerning the public the "priests of the state" presides; if it be private the *pater familias* invokes the gods and takes up the rune-chipped sticks. Aside from lots, the Germans will often consult the flight of birds and are especially drawn to the omens furnished by horses. But again these rituals are carried out by the "priest or king or leader of the state". and it is stated that "no species of augury is more trusted". Otherwise, in times when they "seek to learn the result of an important war" they set up a duel with a prisoner from an opposing tribe with each fighting with the weapons of his own

55 Wenskus, *Stammesbildung*, p. 360.
56 Reinhard Wenskus and Dieter Timpe, "Clientes" (1984), pp. 20f., 23–30.
57 Bertram Colgrave, ed. *Felix's Life of Saint Guthlac* (1956), XXXIV, p. 110f.
58 See the studies cited in note 10.

country. The victory of one over the other will determine the omen. This list of oracular methods is a broad one for Tacitus seems to be interested in the topic and it looks like he wants to be inclusive. Notice that there is no role for women. Divination belongs to priests, kings, chiefs and family fathers. The same is true with regard to councils and assemblies where priests and rulers exercise marked authority and only armed men are admitted.[59]

How does one reconcile the apparent contradiction—the fact that some women were held in high regard and consulted as prophetesses with the contrasting fact that the most respected and popular auguries, public, private and military, were all performed by men. In chapter 8 of *Germania*, Tacitus says that the Germans did *not* scorn to consult women whom they credited with possessing an uncanny and prophetic sense. In this group he places Veleda, Albruna "and many others" among whom we may include Ganna and Walburg. But it seems curiously inapt for we have already seen that these women exist in an institutional context and not simply as some talented women among others. That is why Ganna can accompany king Masyos of the Semnones to Rome and is described as "successor" to Veleda. Tacitus may have been aware of this but it is in any case simply one of those details which he considered unworthy of commentary. He was more interested in Germanic women as a species than in contextual accuracy or differentiation for all of that was unrelated to his theme of their un-Roman-like morality and virtue. Lund has recently taken him to task for precisely this type of selective idealism and exaggeration.[60]

59 Kristensen, *Germanische Gefolgschaft*, has recently re-emphasized the role of the *concilium*.
60 Lund, "Germanenbegriff bei Tacitus", pp. 53–87. The frequent credulity of classical writers is paralled by some modern scholars with far less justification. In her recent book, for example, Miranda Green seeks to more strongly emphasize the socio-religious role of goddesses in Celtic art and assumes for her model an historical equality between the sexes (*Symbol and Image in Celtic Religious Art* [1989], p. 67): ". . . we know from Greco-Roman sources that Gaulish women were nearly as large and powerful as their men and just as formidable in warfare. We know also from early Irish tradition that the mother-goddess had a warrior role as well". As evidence she cites Ammianus Marcellinus, XV, 12 who, speaking of the tall stature of the Gauls, says that "a whole band of foreigners" will be unable to defeat "one" Gaul "if he calls in his wife, stronger than he by far and with flashing eyes; least of all when she swells her neck and gnashes her teeth, and poising her huge arms, proceeds to rain punches mingled with kicks, like shots discharged by the twisted cords of a catapult". One would expect that the notion of one Gaul and his wife defeating a whole band of foreigners in this humorous fashion would be treated as the joke that it clearly is. Such is not the case. Patrick Ford makes the same kind of assumptions in "Celtic Women: The Opposing Sex" (1988), pp. 417–33 where he speaks of their "belligerant", "aggressive" and "bellicose" nature and, along with Ammianus, cites Posidonius: "the Gallic women are not only equal to their husbands in stature, but they rival them in strength as well" (Diodorus Siculus, V, 32). Diodorus goes on to say that their children are mostly born with grey hair and the most savage of the Gaulish tribes to the north are cannibals just like the Britons. Once again, we are clearly dealing with exaggerated classical *topoi* reflecting Greek views about the barbaric customs of non-Greeks as well as the sense of strangeness and shock with which smaller Mediterranean peoples viewed the "pale savages" of the North. The same is true of reports of lack of sexual restraint referred to by some authors or, in the case of Tacitus and the Germans, their praiseworthy sexual morality.

We can reduce the level of confusion and present what I suggest may be a more accurate picture if we assume that Tacitus has here confused two separate often mutually hostile institutions, the tribe and the warband. Chapter 10 of *Germania* is best explainable from this angle for he specifically refers to the priest of the state (*civitas*) who acts in an official capacity for all (*si publice consultetur*) in contrast to the father of the family who performs religious acts for the household. The consultation of the horses is said to be even more important and its public significance is emphasized by the participation of both priest and king. Finally, the word "tribe" or "people" (*gens*) is used with reference to the decision concerning warfare and virtually proves the context in itself. In contrast, chapter 8 is devoted to the role of women in warfare and thus to a special situation. It begins by noting (although it may be more correct to view chapter 8 as an extension of 7) that women typically encourage their menfolk to bravery by incessant prayer and by baring their breasts in order to graphically depict the consequences for them of defeat. After relating that men greatly fear slavery for their women and that this makes females more valuable hostages, he then makes reference to Veleda and Albruna. If the context still seems to be that of tribal warfare, however, it is now less believable. Not only is there no reference to the tribal prognostication mentioned in chapter 10 but the *matres familiae* are not even mentioned. Since they would be the ones most likely to accompany their men to the battlefield the clear impression is one of confusion.

The modern assumptions cited here are historically naive. We know, for example, that women died two to four years earlier than men in early medieval and ancient societies north of the Alps. Since the mortality rate for children generally exceeded 50%, most women were pregnant during most of their adult years. Not much time for warfare here! Similarly, knowledge of sexual dimorphism, which is characteristic of practically all human population groups and many primates, is hardly a help. There is a large body of literature on skeletal and cemetary studies which demonstrate that the classical authors were wrong but none of this is cited by Green or Ford. Nor do they consider that the pelvic structure of females is designed more for child-bearing than speed or that the average upper-body strength of modern women is 55% that of men. It is unlikely that this was different in earlier societies where poor nutrition and iron deficiency anemia, particularly prevalent among women who had borne one or two children, caused frequent suffering and much early death.

As for the well documented significant role of goddesses, there is considerable evidence to show that mythological concepts about female deities are no reliable guide to actual social practice. The relationship may well be an inverse one. See Ruth Katz Arabagian, "Cattle Raiding and Bride Stealing: The Goddess in Indo-European Heroic Literature" (1984), pp. 107–42. See further Lund, "Germanenbriff bei Tacitus", p. 85f.; J.C. Russell, *Late Ancient and Medieval Population* (1958); Bernd Herrmann and Rolf Sprandel, *Determinanten der Bevölkerungsentwicklung im Mittelalter* (1987), which contains copious bibliographies. Bruder, *Germanische Frau*, pp. 128–51, provides a useful analysis of classical reports about women in and near battles which *mutatis mutandis* is also helpful for the Celts. Much ancient reportage, of course, is extremely valuable but aspects like those mentioned here require careful treatment so that what was once Greco-Roman prejudice does not now masquerade as fact simply because it appeals to certain sensibilities.

In the *Germania*, where Tacitus generalizes, he sometimes gets things wrong; in the *Historia*, on the other hand, where he reports actual events, he correctly places Veleda in the company of the man who would be king and there is no reference to the *sacerdos* or *rex*. Under battlefield conditions, then, a certain group of respected women of the tribe may be consulted in addition to the priests but Veleda and Albruna probably do not belong to that group but to the warband. It should be added, however, that in the case of men like Civilis a certain lack of clarity is probably inevitable for, despite his being the leader of a *comitatus*, there may also have been marked tribal elements in this war against Rome. In such transitional circumstances various kinds of shifts in personnel and institutions are easy to envision even if the lineaments of change be also discernable.

This interpretation would seem to offer some clues worthy of expansion. As Schlesinger has rightly emphasized, the early warlord constantly suffered from a lack of that sacral power which helped maintain the authority and status of the tribal king who was bolstered by the traditional priesthood and an ethos of reverence. It is only to be expected that the warlord, who was seeking to create an extra-tribal lordship based on reputation and the distribution of booty and land, would also seek a supernatural mantle with which to wrap himself and would look for it outside the tribe since the sources within the tribe were tied to its original institutions. In the case of Ariovistus, Schlesinger sees such "sacral indications" in his consultation of the lots cast by the *matres familiae* even though he finally decides to ignore them. Schlesinger is surely correct in his interpretation insofar as it explains the warlord's attempt to draw on the glamour of tribal magic but he underestimates the crucial nuance, namely, that Ariovistus does so for a politico-military purpose which in this case, as described earlier, enabled him to delay an engagement. Referring to Civilis, Schlesinger notes that the evidence for sacral legitimation is stronger here and he makes some acute observations:

> Civilis' undertaking was thus structurally a *comitatus* war, not a tribal war. But it is highly characteristic that in these cases sacral elements played a significant role. One needs only to mention the name Veleda to make this clear. How much different her position was from that of the *matres familiae* with Ariovistus! To her were presented prisoners and war booty, surely for sacrifice. A three-step war dance is also reported before a battle. Civilis, moreover, on the basis of his barbarian oath, as it is called, had dyed his hair red to let it grow from the beginning of taking of arms against Rome and allowed it to be cut only after victory. The sacral meaning of such hair-wearing is known. The oath-taking of the warband followers took place in a holy grove to which Civilis had invited them for a feast (*epulae*) which may have had a sacred character. One may suppose that this ambitious offspring of a royal family, one not unacquainted with Roman culture, had purposely brought those apparently traditional

sacred elements to bear in order to strengthen his position, particularly in regard to the sought-after kingship. *Comitatus* warfare was married to the form of tribal warfare and this process must also have brought with it a change in the position of the leader.[61]

Again, Schlesinger rightly notes the marked difference in the positions of the *matres familiae* and Veleda, who now gets gifts and captives to sacrifice. His illuminating interpretation of this contrast as an indication of the narrowing gap between tribal and *comitatus* war to the advantage of the warleader makes perfect sense. Because of his concentration on the warlord, however, he does not fully appreciate that the linkage between warlord and prophetess is a crucial one. The *matres* are a select group of trusted magical counselors who belong wholly to the tribe. Their place is with those women who stand behind the battle lines, urge on the family warriors and tend to their wounds. They are part of the war of the folk whereas Veleda and her successors belong to the warlord. He is the dynamic force changing forever the nature of this society and she is his instrument for controlling the supernatural.

It is in this fluid transitional environment that the Celtic words for "follower", "oath" and "prophetess" have their true home. The words were used earlier but it is likely that they were popular among the nobility or *Oberschicht* and not the people as a whole. The warlord appears to be consciously applying partially known terminology to create a new type of military and religious organization tied to him and opposed to the tribal leaders and the tribal past. Therein we see the real significance of the fact (recalling the material cited earlier on language, weapons, names and tactics) that the early warlords cited by Schlesinger (Ariovistus, Maroboduus, Arminius and Civilis)[62] can all be shown in one way or another, directly or indirectly, to have been familiar with some aspects of Celtic culture. The conclusion may be stated as follows: because ambitious Germanic leaders could not utilize the institutions of the tribe to gain power, they turned instead to the institutions of outsiders, the Celts, and applied them to do what native forces would not allow. Similar calculation explains the choice of a woman to predict future success. Among the Germans, prophets and not prophetesses performed the most important divinations but the predictions of one group of women, the *matres*, were closely linked with hope of victory. The warlord needed to draw on the association but could not because it was too much a part of tribal thinking based on concepts of kinship and traditional forms. Hence, he turned to the Celts among whom individual women, despite a status differential,[63] were occasionally recognized to possess similar powers to those of the druids or vates.

61 Schlesinger, "Heerkönigtum", p. 69.
62 Ibid., p. 64f.
63 Around AD 300, for example, one of these *dryadae* is working as a waitress. Birkhan, *Germanen und Kelten*, p. 557, suggests that this may be "eine sekundäre Verfallserscheinung" but one can

A single woman, of course, was also more amenable to control than a group. That is why Veleda was chosen and also why she bears a Celtic title. Much that was hitherto obscure is explainable on this construction or, at least, is more difficult to explain without it.

If the coming of the Romans helped solidify the vectors of change north of the Alps, it is nonetheless accurate to say that long before that the Celtic world had provided a model, a terminology and a plenitude of historical example for their neighbors. In early medieval scholarship much is made of the fact that Romans and Germans had dealings with each other for five hundred years; scholars sometimes overlook the fact that the same was true of Celts and Germans in the preceding half millennium and that was why the Romans had so much difficulty telling them apart by the first century BC.

4. GOVERNMENTAL FORMS

Celtic inspiration in the evolution of the Germanic *comitatus* would seem to presuppose an effect on the development of governmental forms as well since it is by virtue of control of a warband that the new type of non-tribal ruler achieves dominance. Previous discussion of linguistic, organizational and historical evidence makes this deduction unsurprising inasmuch as the institutional tendencies are joined at the root. But one cannot simply proceed on that basis alone without discussing the broader constitutional pattern and noting the relevant connections. Fortunately, other scholars have also been interested in this question. For England, for example, it has most recently been discussed by Francis Wormald, who showed that Anglo-Saxon kingship of the sixth through eighth centuries is much more like that of the Celts than is often assumed.[1] The earlier pattern of dispositions on the continent, on the other hand, is best delineated by Wenskus in his magisterial analysis of the Gaulish-West Germanic "revolution" in which he exposes the rationale for the similarities of governmental forms among the Celts and Germans.[2] In the following several paragraphs I can do no

---

hardly be sure about the original nature of the druid-*dryada* association. Was it official or unofficial? Was she of high or low status? In Ireland, where the evidence is better, there are only a few mentioned in the earlier literature and in the most famous example, the woman concerned is described as a slave. The safest presumption would seem to be that *banfilid* were warily respected, and this gained them a certain influence, but that their social status was somewhat anomalous, akin perhaps to that of early medieval nuns.

1 Patrick Wormald, "Celtic and Anglo-Saxon Kingship: Some Further Thoughts" (1986), pp. 151–83; T.M. Charles-Edwards, "Kinship, Status and the Origins of the Hide" (1972), pp. 3–33; Rosemary Cramp, "Northumbria and Ireland" (1986), pp. 185–201; Hermann Moisl, "The Bernician Royal Dynasty and the Irish in the Seventh Century" (1983), pp. 99–124.

2 Wenskus, *Stammesbildung*, pp. 409–29.

better than simply summarize his results which demonstrate the existence of a close political relationship between the two people over broad regions of central Europe.

As Wenskus points out, the migration of tribes and the settling of warbands presented leaders with a multitude of novel tasks and functions which help to explain the growth of a new type of kingship among the Germans of the late Iron Age and the early Roman period. But this is far from being a complete explanation, for the greatest tribal movements had occurred earlier and had not produced a classical warband society or, at least, one which lasted. On the other hand:

> If one transcribes on a map the names of the Celtic and Germanic tribes for whom Caesar and Tacitus name kings, along with those for whom only *principes* are recorded, the result is a surprising picture which shows that the frontiers of the two constitutional forms cut through the ethnic bounds and that the territory of the Germanic *civitates* with chieftainly form [*Prinzipatsverfassung*] is bound together with an associated corresponding Celtic complex. Eastern Germans on the contrary, like eastern Celts (Noricum for example) remain under kings. The same holds for the northern sphere of both linguistic areas. That cannot be coincidence.[3]

One can only agree. A geographical distribution of such extensive type in which Germanic tribes with kings are territorially associated with like-ruled Celtic tribes and in which the same is true of tribes rules by *principes* can only be explained on the basis of far-reaching cultural interaction. The political map thus provides significant confirmation of the arguments already presented, for it reflects a pattern whereby Germanic political custom in one area is gradually aligned with that of the Celts in an adjacent area so that, from the Germanic cultural perspective, ethnic boundaries become less important than the socio-political imitation of high prestige neighbors whose basic language is the lingua franca of diplomacy.

Although a precise chronology is impossible to work out in most cases, an approximate one is not. Like a number of other Indo-European peoples, Celtic history begins with kings and kings still ruled the tribes of southern Gaul when Rome began her conquest of Provincia Narbonensis. By Caesar's time, however, the picture had changed considerably so that only comparatively few peoples still maintained kings although a *stirps regia* or royal family would continue to be recognized by many and a multitude of *principes* could still point to a father or grandfather who had been rulers. This is what Grenier called the Gaulish "revolution"—the abandonment of kingship in favor of a variety of non-royal leaders.[4] Drawing on the work of Grenier and Powell,[5] Wenskus notes several

3 Ibid., p. 413.
4 A. Grenier, *Les Gaulois* (1945), p. 183f.
5 Ibid.; T.G.E. Powell, *The Celts* (1958), p. 79f.

reasons for this metamorphosis. First is the influence of republican Rome which, although it cannot explain the event, should not be discounted. The second factor is the creation of the oppida culture near the end of the second century BC which reflects the concepts of a Mediterranean urban culture and which would be further encouraged by the invasions of the Cimbri-Teutones.[6] Such developments in urbanization and fortification must have had negative consequences for the old type of governments and have led to the weakening of tribal and cultic ties.[7] This widely held view finds strong support from the Germanic sphere where an "almost legal like connection" can be established between the distribution areas of kingless groups and that of the fortified hill settlements.[8] At the same time, however, one is still looking at something which is more a symptom than a cause. More important than any other contributing element seems to have been the expansion and misuse of the various kinds of retinues and the warbands of the aristocracy who built so solidly on this basis that no traditional tribal ruler could stand before them. When, as Caesar reports, a *princeps* like Orgetorix could appear before a tribal court with 10,000 followers, the days of tribal government were numbered and it is not surprising to find *principes* attempting to subject several *civitates* to their authority.[9]

The same decay of kingship also occurred among the Germans but it will not do to associate it simply with sedentary settlement and Roman advance (as Schlesinger did) since the transition to princely rule had already been completed before this among a number of tribes like the Ubii, Usipetes and Tencteri who, one should add, lived near the Rhine close to similarly governed Celts.[10] One inscription, now generally regarded as dating to the first century, shows the Batavians possessing a (probably) Celtic type *summus magistratus*[11] so that once again we see how warlords like Civilis might be affected.

A full explanation of this process of governmental transformation does seem to demand an assumption of close contact with the Celts for even the negative evidence of the Gothic east suggests the strength of the outside influence in the west. Among the Goths the "old" designation for king, *thiudans*, survived alongside of Celtic **reiks* and eventually overcame it whereas in the west **reiks* dominated.[12] Wenskus goes on to discuss further evidence with regard to the Cherusci and Chatti where the clash between tribal and warband values often

6 Jan de Vries, "Kimbern und Teutonen (Ein Kapitel aus der Beziehungen zwischen Kelten und Germanen)" (1951), pp. 7–24; Norden, *Germanische Urgeschichte*, pp. 207–65.
7 Wenskus, *Stammesbildung*, pp. 409–29; Collis, *Oppida*, pp. 39–50, 65–86, 177–89.
8 Wenskus, *Stammesbildung*, p. 415.
9 Edwards, *Caesar. Gallic War*, I, 4, p. 6f.; Wenskus, *Stammesbildung*, p. 416.
10 Wenskus, *Stammesbildung*, p. 418.
11 J.E. Bogaers, Civitas en stad, p. 5ff.; Rüger, *Germania Inferior*, p. 94; Will, "'Klientel-Randstaaten'", p. 11f. For a general overview, see William J.H. Willems, "Romans and Batavians: Regional Developments at the Imperial Frontier" (1984), pp. 105–27.
12 Wenskus, *Stammesbildung*, p. 419.

provoke conflict. We need not repeat that here except to note that it is compatible with the overall conclusion: "it should now be clear that we cannot understand early Germanic constitutional history without considering that of the Celts, just as the later period cannot be understood without knowledge of the Roman inheritance".[13] It seems to me that this demonstration is of capital importance in assessing the nature of the forces at work in *Germania* in the century before and after Christ.

5. MERCURY, WODAN AND THE ONE-EYED WARLORD

Like Schlesinger, Wenskus also suggests that a major socio-political transformation like that which produced the warband and warband kingship is unlikely to have occurred without affecting religious views and practices. It might perhaps be correct to state this even more forcefully since it would be astonishing were the warlord to refrain from seeking a new form of legitimization centered on the warband when he could no longer turn to the tribe (except, of course, insofar as he made use of the concepts of family and kin). If one inquires as to what the recognizable religious differences were, however—the political logic of the case almost demands their existence—then the only clues that I can discern in the contemporary sources are those which relate the warlord to the prophetess and those which connect the warband to a new type of god, Wodan probably, or at least to a god very much like him. In what follows I will discuss the basis for these religious changes and attempt to explain how they were related to Civilis and Veleda who, as the burden of the evidence suggests, were the prototype for the warlord/prophetesses pattern still discernable in *Beowulf*.

Most scholars of comparative religion now accept that the primitive **uoðanaz*, should be identified with Roman and Gallo-Roman Mercury of whom Caesar and Tacitus say: *Deorum maxime Mercurium colunt.*[1] His characteristic qualities— wanderer, inventor, companion of the dead—were a further common denominator among the Gauls and Germans near the Rhine. This Mercury was also associated with war and wisdom. The *Mercurius Vassocaletis* of the Celtic Treveri was the "companion of heroes" and is identical with *Mercurius Visucius*, also of the Treveri, the "Mercury with the raven".[2] It was from the west bank of the

---

13 Ibid., p. 427.
1 Many works might be cited. See, for example, Karl Helm, *Altgermanische Religionsgeschichte* I (1913), p. 361; Siegfried Gutenbrunner, *Die germanischen Götternamen der antiken Inschriften* (1936), p. 58; Gerhard Bauchhenss, "Mercurius in Bornheim" (1981), pp. 223–38; Norbert Wagner, "Ein neugefundener Wodansname" (1988), p. 238f.; Phyllis F. Bober, "Mercurius Arvernus" (1945), pp. 19–46; Jan de Vries, *Keltische Religion* (1961), pp. 40–54; Much, Jankuhn and Lange, *Germania*, p. 171f.
2 Wolfgang Jungandreas, *Sprachliche Studien zur germanischen Altertumskunde* (1981), p. 33.

Rhine apparently that his cult passed to the Germanic tribes.[3] Celtic associations are also suggested by the fact that *uoðanaz is cognate with Latin *vates*, a word borrowed from the Gauls or cisalpine tribes, and OI *faith*, "poet, seer".[4] In a brief reference to Wodan, Birkhan also makes the interesting point (not hitherto noted elsewhere as far as I know), that the root of Celtic *uatis* and Germanic *uoðanaz also had an aggressive accent in Irish despite its connection with poetry and wisdom: *con-fad*, "rabies", *confadach*, "rabid".[5] The basis always seems to be that of *furor* or warlike ecstasy. Dumézilians, of course, routinely associated this wisdom/warfare complex with the first function of sovereignty, just as they associate Celtic Lug and Germanic Wodan with Indic Varuna.[6] In a certain ultimate sense they may well be correct. What the present clues suggest, however, is that the original passage of aspects of the Wodan cult, or at least of a cult with very similar characteristics, occurred at much the same time and from the same source as the inspiration for the *comitatus*.

The spread of the Wodan cult (though not necessarily its origin) may well owe something to the interest of one particular warlord. Just as the later idea of the ravens Huginn and Muninn whispering wisdom into Odin's ear may be a simple extrapolation from "Mercury with the raven", so it is not implausible to propose that Odin's known one-eyedness, among other characteristics, derives from the same early period when the warlord was searching for a supernatural patron. This hypothesis is suggested by an intriguing remark which Tacitus casually drops in *Historia* 4, 13 in which he links Hannibal, Sertorius and Civilis. An investigation of the rationale for this association can help us to gain a much better understanding of the strategy of the latter named individual whose techniques may well have had a more catalytic effect than hitherto supposed.

Throughout his narrative of the Batavian rebellion of AD 69 the Roman historian paints a convincing portrait of Civilis as a man of the most acute sensitivity to image and symbol and to the value of propaganda. Coming from a royal family, he lacked neither the attitudes nor the training to exploit the credulity of the tribesmen by "speaking of the renown and glory of their race",[7] by letting his dyed hair grow until victory in traditional warrior fashion,[8] by employing Veleda to prophesy future success,[9] by utilizing feasts and "barbarous rites" to strengthen devotion and by calling meetings and oath-takings in a "sacred grove".[10] His

---

3 Ibid. Aside from the works cited in note 1, see also Karl Helm, *Wodan. Ausbreitung und Wanderung seines Kultes* (1946), p. 5f.
4 Birkhan, *Germanen und Kelten*, p. 471; Heinrich Wagner, *Studies in the Origins of the Celts and of Early Celtic Civilization* (1971), pp. 47–57.
5 Birkhan, *Germanen und Kelten*, p. 471.
6 See, for example, Georges Dumézil, "Magic, War and Justice: Odin and Tyr" (1973), pp. 26–48.
7 Moore, *Tacitus. Histories*, IV, 14, p. 24f.
8 Ibid., IV, 61, p. 116f.
9 Ibid.
10 Ibid., IV, 14, p. 24f.

ultimate aim, says Tacitus, was kingship over large regions of Gallia and Germania.[11] Thus, we are not surprised to hear the historian note that "he was naturally politic to a degree rarely found among barbarians. He was wont to represent himself as Sertorius or Hannibal, on the strength of a similar disfigurement of his countenance".[12] The common disfigurement, it seems, was the loss of an eye.

Although little noticed by scholars, it will be maintained here that this brief sentence from the *Historia* offers the best guide we are likely to find to the psychology and actual contemporary popular propaganda of the Germanic warlord. It may well be the single most important piece of information about Civilis' approach to leadership over Germans and Gauls.[13] From it alone we can deduce several significant facts: first, that Civilis viewed his one-eyedness as a powerful asset which he could exploit to influence his followers; second, that stories of Hannibal and Sertorius were circulating amongst peoples north of the Alps and particularly in the milieu about Civilis; third, that the warlord perceived these legends as so important that he wished contemporaries to believe that a mystical connection existed between these two famous generals and himself. We should now seek to determine why these links were maintained by Civilis and by what means they could have been manipulated to influence those to whom "he was wont to represent himself".

Quintus Sertorius and Hannibal had a number of things in common. Both were very famous generals who fought long and frequently successfully against Rome. Each led large numbers of Celtic tribesmen during their wars. Aside from one-eyedness, a characteristic related to wizardry and mantic wisdom among all three peoples we are concerned with, Romans, Celts and Germans,[14] both leaders were also masters of disguise. Polybius (3, 78), Livy (22, 1) and Zonaras (8, 24) all mention this curious stratagem when referring to Hannibal. The former notes that Hannibal was worried about assassination attempts by Celtic chiefs since his friendship with them was recent. Hence, says Polybius, "he had a number of wigs made, dyed to suit the appearance of persons differing widely in age, and kept constantly changing them, at the same time also dressing in a style that suited the wig, so that not only those who had seen him but for a moment, but even his familiars found difficulty in recognizing him".[15] Sertorius, later the revered leader of Celtic warbands in Spain, was well known to have employed the same kind of artifice in the Cimbrian war when he disguised himself as a Celt and mingled with the enemy to learn their plans.[16] He afterwards (97 BC) practised the same

---

11 Ibid., IV, 18, p. 34f.: sic in Gallias Germaniasque intentus, si destinata provenissent, validissimarum ditissimarumque nationum regno imminebat.

12 Ibid., IV, 13, p. 22f.: sed Civilis ultra quam barbaris solitum ingenio sollers et Sertorius se aut Annibalem ferens simili oris dehonestamento . . . .

13 Such a view is not shared or even discussed by most authors cited in the present study.

14 Georges Dumézil, "'Le Borgne' and 'Le Manchot': The State of the Problem" (1974), pp. 17–28.

15 W.R. Paton, ed. *Polybius. The Histories* II (1967²), III, 78, p. 190f.

16 Perrin, *Plutarch* VIII "Sertorius" III, 2, p. 6f.

tactic against the Celtiberians.[17] These, of course, are exactly the kind of subter-
fuges which create admiring legends among soldiers and could easily give rise to
stories of disguised old one-eyed warriors, even of shamanic shape-shifters, all of
which are repetitive components of the later Wodan cult.[18] We know from Tacitus
that such tales were circulating two centuries after the events in the northern
world so that it is *certain* that they give rise to tribal legend.

Plutarch also provides a fascinating hint of something deeper in the personality
of Sertorius which might have connected him with a cult of the dead. At a low
point in his career, Sertorius became acquainted with a "firm belief" among the
barbarians that the "Elysian Fields and the abode of the blessed" were to be found
among the Atlantic islands. He was "seized with an amazing desire" to go and
dwell in these "Isles of the Blest" and was only dissuaded when pirates who spoke
of them refused to sail there.[19] Although we hear nothing more of this episode,
the fact that Plutarch knew of it again suggests that stories connecting Sertorius
with the Elysian Fields, that is, with a paradisiacal kind of supernatural existence
frequently associated with an afterlife, were not uncommon.

The traits of one-eyedness, disguise, war leadership and a possible connection
with a cult of the dead are simply too specific and arresting to easily be dismissed
as coincidental. Inspired by these, Thomas Africa argued in 1970 that such themes
were absorbed into the Wodan cult and Walter Moeller argued several years later
that the historical figures were actually reflexes of the mythologem rather than
the reverse.[20] Africa, it seems to the present author, is more nearly right but, in
any case, both scholars were seriously misled by the belief that the Wodan cult
was already "flourishing long before Hannibal".[21] Neither explored all aspects of
the material or thoroughly investigated the institutional and religious contexts
which are the only ones allowing us to make sense of the panoply of evidence.

17 Ibid., III, 5, p. 8f. Two modern biographies are available: Philip O. Spann, *Quintus Sertorius and
    the Legacy of Sulla* (1987); Adolf Schulten, *Sertorius* (1926).
18 See, for example, Peter Buchholz, "Odin: Celtic and Siberian Affinities of a Germanic Diety"
    (1983), pp. 428–36; E.O.G. Turville-Petre, *Myth and Religion of the North. The Religion of
    Ancient Scandinavia* (1975²), pp. 6of., [65.] Buchholz also emphasizes the "Celtic affinities" of
    the god.
19 Perrin, *Plutarch* VIII "Sertorius" VII, 3–9, I, p. 2of. Spann, *Sertorius*, p. 5of. It has been pointed
    out that Horace's *Epod.* 16 was inspired by the story of this yearning of Sertorius, another
    indication of how his life captured the imagination of later Romans. Schulten, *Sertorius*, p. 48ff.
    Some possible implications are discussed by Hendrick Wagenvoort, "The Journey of the Souls
    of the Dead to the Isles of the Blessed" (1971), pp. 113–61; Idem, "Nehalennia and the Souls
    of the Dead" (1971), pp. 239–92. There are many Celtic mythic connections. To the Celts, these
    Isles were Tír nan Og, 'Land of the Ever Young' and Magh Mell, 'Field of Happiness.'
20 Thomas Africa, "The One-Eyed Man Against Rome: An Exercise in Euhemerism" (1970), pp.
    528–38; Walter Moeller, "Once More the One-Eyed Man Against Rome" (1975), pp. 403–10.
21 Africa, "One-Eyed Man Against Rome", p. 538; Moeller, "Once More the One-Eyed Man",
    p. 402. All arguments that the Wodan cult existed before Gaulish Mercury are purely specula-
    tive. See, for example, Helm, *Wodan*, pp. 5–20, who demonstrates this point in a thoroughly
    convincing fashion.

One may, therefore, seek to discover the other links between Wodan, Civilis and Sertorius (it is the latter who is the key figure and not Hannibal). These will include the motifs of prophecy, spear-bearing, human sacrifice, relation to a *comitatus*, kingship and presence of a consort. In all of these the Iberian-Gaulish connection is critical.

Sertorius, who died in 72 BC and who was thus a contemporary of Ariovistus, looms large in the present context because his career would have particularly appealed to Civilis. Like him, Sertorius was a personally courageous ex-Roman army officer who turned against Rome or, if one prefers, was eventually forced into an anti-Roman stance. Actually, he was both a "new man" and a Sabine and thus, to the upper class Romans of the time, was not a completely proper Roman at all.[22] The element of alienation is definitely present in his biography and would surely have impressed a Roman citizen who was also a Batavian and thus subject to a similar kind of patronization.[23] Much of Sertorius' career was spent among those "lesser breeds without the law". He was very knowledgeable about the Cimbri-Teutones, had worn their clothes and ornaments, learned Celtic,[24] and formed a famous band of devoted Celtiberians who took an oath to fight to the death for him.[25] Moreover, one of the chief means by which he won the loyalty of his followers was by exploiting their religious sentiments. Here, too, he was much like Civilis whose similar methodology was outlined above. But Sertorius did not have a prophetess. Instead, he made use of a closely analogous device given him by a goddess—a prophetic animal, an unusually colored pure white doe, whom he tamed and who "obeyed his call and accompanied his walks" even through the crowds of the camps. Plutarch wrote of him that he gradually

> tried to give the doe a religious importance by declaring that she was a gift of Diana, and solemnly alleged that she revealed many hidden things to him, knowing that the Barbarians were naturally an easy prey to superstition. He also added such devices as these. Whenever he had secret intelligence that the

22 Schulten, *Sertorius*, pp. 17–25; Spann, *Sertorius*, p. 1f.
23 The Roman attitude to peoples of the North ran all the way from mild patronization to the views of Velleius Paterculus, *praefectus alae* on the Rhine under Augustus, that the Germans were animals who had nothing in common with humans except limbs and voices. Ammianus Marcellinus tended more in this direction but Tacitus, of course, is an exception in some regards although he too had a low opinion of the German's trustworthiness and thought them ignorant. In this respect, Civilis was unique because of his cleverness. See, among many studies, Saddington, *Race Relations*, pp. 112–37. Roman exploitation could have severe consequences. A recent paper about the Low Countries is entitled by W. Groenman-Van Watering, "The Disastrous Effect of the Roman Occupation" (1984), pp. 147–58. For the frontier regions of Germania and Britain, see the many contributions in John Barrett, Andrew Fitzpatrick and Lesley Macinnes, *Barbarians and Romans in North-West Europe From the Later Republic to Late Antiquity* (1989).
24 Perrin, *Plutarch* VIII "Sertorius" III, 1, p. 6f.
25 Ibid., XIV, 4, p. 38f.

enemy had made an incursion into the territory he commanded, or were trying to bring a city to revolt from him, he would pretend that the doe had conversed with him in his dreams, bidding him hold his forces in readiness [cf. the explanation of the *matres* with Ariovistus]. Again, when he got tidings of some victory won by his generals, he would hide the messenger, and bring forth the doe wearing garlands for the receipt of glad tidings, exhorting his men to be of good cheer and to sacrifice to the gods, assured that they were to learn of some good fortune. By these devices he made the people tractable, and so found them more serviceable for all his plans; they believed that they were led, not by the mortal wisdom of a foreigner but by a god.[26]

Appian, a contemporary of Plutarch, adds other important information for he makes it clear that Sertorius took the deer with him when he went on campaign. He states that when she was not in sight, Sertorius "abstained from fighting". On the other hand, "when she made her appearance running through the woods Sertorius would run to meet her, and, as though he were consecrating the first fruits of a sacrifice to her, he would at once direct a hail of javelins at the enemy".[27]

Plutarch goes on to say that Sertorius was also "admired and loved" because he taught the Celtiberians how to fight against Roman armies. He introduced "Roman arms and formations and signals"; he eliminated "their frenzied and furious displays of courage and converted their forces into an army, instead of a huge band of robbers".[28] Catering to their love of beautiful array, he also "used gold and silver without stint for the decoration of their helmets and the ornamentation of their shields".[29] The children of the most powerful of his followers became especially devoted (and their fathers "wonderfully pleased") for Sertorius set up a special school for them "with the assurance that when they became men he would give them a share in administration and authority". Constant examinations were held and Sertorius would distribute prizes to the deserving, "golden necklaces which the Romans call '*bullae*' ".[30] Indeed, the Celtiberians respected him so much that they "gave him the name of Hannibal, whom they considered the boldest and most crafty general ever known in their country".[31] The Sertorius/Hannibal identification borrowed by Civilis was apparently first made by the Celtiberians.

It is certain that much of this information was known in Gaul where Sertorius had won fame earlier because of his exploits against the Cimbri-Teutones (who had in fact invaded Spain and been repulsed by the Celtiberians). Caesar makes it rather explicit for his own time for he relates that during the campaign of

26 Ibid., XI, 2–XII, 2, p. 28f.
27 Horace White, ed. *Appian's Roman History* I (1933²), XIII, 110, p. 204f.
28 Perrin, *Plutarch* VIII "Sertorius" XIV, 1, p. 36f.
29 Ibid., XIV, 2, p. 36f.
30 Ibid., XIV, 2–3, p. 36f.

Publius Crassus in Aquitania, the Vocates and Tarusates sent representatives to Spain "inviting succors and leaders from thence". The men with whom they returned to fight against the Romans had "great prestige" and were selected as leaders for they "had served for the whole period with Quintus Sertorius and were believed to be past masters of war". Caesar notes that they proceeded against the Romans "in Roman fashion".[32] For much the same reasons, as Tacitus indicates, we must also assume that Civilis paid close attention to the stories of Sertorius - not only because they were widespread among the Gauls (many of whom played an important role in his plans as will be shown below) but also because Sertorius was a legendary figure in the Roman army, in which Civilis had served for twenty-five years,[33] and Romans would be just as impressed by the model as the barbarians. Sertorius possessed a charismatic glamour for all three *ethnica*. We have noted Tacitus' explicit statement that Civilis exploited an accidental likeness to the extent, apparently, that he wanted to be viewed as Sertorius reborn. All of this material is worth pondering for it seems to provide grounds for a new approach towards the solving of several significant problems.

It is surprising that students of the Germanic *comitatus* (Schlesinger, Wenskus, Green, Much-Jankuhn, for example) have not more thoroughly explored these rather substantial clues. Aside from the *Germania* there are few texts available which illustrate the early history of that institution and Plutarch's *Life of Sertorius* clearly offers many important parallels. He provides, for example, relatively detailed references to the transition to a more disciplined form of organization, to ritual gift-giving and ornamentation, to the use of a prophetess by a warlord (in this case, a doe who carried messages from a goddess), and also to a school for the children of aristocrats that (although Plutarch interprets it as a canny form of hostage-taking), in principle at least, is not unlike the Gaulish and Germanic practice of beginning the process of induction for some members of the warband at a very early age. A close study and nuanced analysis of this work would surely repay the effort.

Most immediately relevant is the phenomenon of the one-eyed warleader. Although we cannot conclusively prove that this well-known characteristic of the war god in the Viking period reaches back to the first century AD, a connection with Celtic Lug with whom Mercury is often associated in the *interpretatio Romana* does seem likely.[34] But one should note that Lug's one-eyedness is

31 White, *Appian. Roman History* I: XIII, 112, p. 208f.
32 Edwards, *Caesar. Gallic War*, III, 24, p. 170f.
33 Moore, *Tacitus. Histories*, IV, 32, p. 60f.
34 De Vries, *Keltische Religion*, pp. 51–5. The similarities are so impressive that de Vries concluded that Lug should be placed "in die unmittelbare Nähe des germanischen Odhin und des indischen Varuna". As Karl Helm showed, however, Wodan does not belong to the Indo-European past and the Dumézilian hypothesis is unnecessary here. Davidson, *Myths and Symbols*, pp. 89–101 argues for a close association between the two gods as well and speaks of "striking resemblances". See also H.R. Ellis Davidson, *The Battle God of the Vikings* (1972), pp. 1–33.

achieved by simply closing one eye in a magical ritual.[35] The overall similarity has long been recognized by scholars and we shall refer to it again below. Nevertheless, a truly one-eyed god of the warband only occurs among the Germans and the crucial figure would seem to be Civilis who had more to gain by propagating that link than anyone else. But this interpretation needlessly assumes that a one-eyed Wodan already existed. Perhaps even more likely is the notion that the god subsequently acquired that disfigurement because of the impression made on the popular mind by the stories of *three* great one-eyed generals, each of whom had led armies with large numbers of barbarian troops who had personally pledged to him against Rome. Can the god of warfare and the *comitatus* really be separated from the first great leaders of a *comitatus* who bear his attribute?

Other evidence supports this hypothesis while also adding something new. In Scandinavian poetry and saga Odin is called "lord of the spear", *geirs dróttinn*, and his spear Gungnir, is closely associated with kings and human sacrifice, above all with the killing of kings.[36] Those to be sacrificed are "marked for Odin" with this weapon. In one verse ascribed to Bragi (*c*.850), Odin is called "Gungnir's shaker", *Gungnirs váfaðr*.[37] It is instructive to note, however, that similar kinds of ideas appear to have flourished among Celts and Celtiberians. Annaeus Florus (*c*.75–140 AD), who traveled in Spain and who wrote a rhetorical history of the Roman wars, had this to say of one campaign in the second half of the second century BC:

> There would have been trouble also with all the Celtiberians had not the leader of their rising, Olyndicus—a man of great craft and daring, if only fortune had favored him—been put out of the way early in the war. This man, *brandishing*

35 De Vries, *Keltische Religion*, p. 52.
36 Turville-Petre, *Myth and Religion*, p. 43f. Bracteate iconography now provides the best evidence for Wodan's linkage to spears and sacrifice in some late ancient and early medieval Germanic areas. The key studies are by Karl Hauck: *Die Wiedergabe von Göttersymbolen* (1986), pp. 477f., 487f., 494f.; idem, *Varianten des göttlichen Erscheinungsbildes* (1984), pp. 266–313; idem, "Text und Bild in einer oralen Kultur. Antworten auf die zeugniskritische Frage nach der Erreichbarkeit mündlicher Überlieferung" (1983), pp. 510–99. This latter study is particulary useful for its discussion of the relationship between the god and the prophetess (his bestowal of her staff of office) and for the way in which the god intervened to aid warriors in casting a spear. See also Dietrich Hofmann, " Die Bezeichnung Odins in *Húsdrápa* 9" (1984), pp. 314–20; Michael Müller-Wille, "Opferplätze der Wikingerzeit", (1984), pp. 187–221; Herbert Jankuhn, "Archäologische Beobachtungen zu Tier und Menschenopfer bei den Germanen in der römischen Kaiserzeit" (1967); Heinrich Beck, "Germanische Menschenopfer in der literarischen uberlieferung" (1970), pp. 240–58; Paulson, *Adelsgräber*, pp. 104–21; idem, "Flügellanzen: Zum archäologischen horizont der Wiener 'sancta lancea' " (1969), pp. 289–312; Schramm, *Herrschaftszeichen und Staatssymbolik* I (1954), p. 492f. Useful studies of Celtic spears, weapons and warrior groups in William Sayers, "Warrior Initiation and Some Short Celtic Spears in the Irish and Learned Later Tradition" (1989), pp. 89–108; idem, "Martial Feats in the Old Irish Ulster Cycle" (1983), pp. 45–80; Helmut Bauersfeld, "Die Kriegsältertumer im Lebor na h-Uidre" (1933), pp. 294–345; O'Rahilly, *Early Irish History*, pp. 58–74.
37 Turville-Petre, *Myth and Religion*, p. 43f.

a silver spear which he claimed had been sent from heaven, and behaving like a prophet, had attracted general attention; but having, with corresponding temerity, approached the consul's camp under the cover of night, he ended his career *by the javelin of a sentry* close to the very tent of the consul.[38]

This "silver spear" sent from heaven must have been an important religious and political symbol for the Celtiberians. The portrait of their prophetic warleader, who might also be called "Gungnir's shaker", being killed by a spear certainly gives food for thought since Wodan/Odin also died mystically in the same way.[39] The spear seems to have been a royal symbol among British Celts as well. Not only do we hear of it being carried in a symbolic way by rulers[40] but it is also associated with Mercury who, in Roman religion of course, carries a caduceus as attribute.[41] At his temple at Uley (Gloucestershire), for example, Mercury appears wearing a silver neck torc, symbol of authority and kingship. Offerings of model caducei and bronze figurines at this site demonstrate that the classical concept of deity prevailed but, adds Martin Henig, "the presence of miniature iron spears and of little metal rings (presumably stylized torques) reminds us that a local, British element survived as a subsidiary element in temple ritual".[42] Nor do these examples exhaust the list of coincidences for Sertorius was said to have lost his eye through a spear-cast. Although the wound actually occurred during the Social War, one Roman writer, Nepotianus, has it occurring during a battle with the Cimbri-Teutones. He has Sertorius swimming across the river Rhône, weighed down with arms and breastplate and with a spear hanging from his

---

38 The Celtiberians, of course, worshipped Lug whose weapon was the spear. Just as the doe was sent to Sertorius by Diana (in the *interpretatio Romana*) so, the implication seems to be, was the spear a sign of Lug's approval and support. In general, see Antonio Tovar, "The God *Lugus* in Spain" (1982), pp. 591–99; J. Loth, "Le dieu Lug, la Terre Mère et les Lugoves" (1914), pp. 205–30; Thévénot, "Genie de Lyon", pp. 94–107: E.S. Forster, ed. *Annaeus Florus. Epitome of Roman History* I (1947²), XXXIII, 14, p. 148f.: Fuisset et cum omnibus Celtiberis, nisi dux illius motus initio belli vi oppressus esset, summi vir astus et audaciae, si processisset, Olyndicus, qui hastam argentam quatiens quasi caelo missam vaticininti similis omnium in se mentes converterat. Sed cum pari temeritate sub nocte castra consulis adisset, iuxta tentorium ipsum pilo vigilis exceptus est.

39 The Gaulish god Esus would seem to have played a role here as well. See Ross, *Pagan Celtic Britain*, pp. 248–64.

40 In describing queen Boudica of the Iceni, Cassius Dio, (LXII, 6) remarks on her necklace, tunic, mantle and brooch and adds that she "grasped a spear to aid her in terrifying all beholders". As Dyson cogently notes, however, "the sight of a women grasping a spear does not seem sufficient to stupify a group of tough, blood-thirsty Britons. In fact, if the description is at all accurate, it would sound as if she were using all her dress and attributes to create an impression of inspired awe in her followers". ("Native Revolts", p. 262) He compares the spear as a "sacred talisman" to the one mentioned above as being brandished by Olyndicus.

41 Much, Jankuhn and Lange, *Germania*, p. 171.

42 Martin Henig, *Religion in Roman Britain* (1984), p. 59.

eye-socket.[43] This episode was famous. The most recent biographer of Sertorius has pointed out that his escape from the Roman debacle at Arausio "became a minor legend in antiquity".[44] It was, incidentally, after this battle that the Cimbri-Teutones hung their Roman captives from trees, a form of human sacrifice which was later commonly associated with the Wodan cult.[45] We now have cause to further extend our catalogue.

A common method of dedicating a victim to Odin was to hurl a spear over his head while saying "you all belong to Odin". In *Eyrbyggja saga*, for instance, a chief hurled a spear over the opposing force "following an ancient custom", *at fornum sið*, in order to claim it for the battle-god, and Odin himself in his capacity

---

43 Spann, *Sertorius*, p. 13. There is another interesting coincidence here as well. When Marius achieved power in Rome, he formed a group of ex-slaves and thugs into a bodyguard known as the *Bardyaei* or "Spiked-Boots". Sertorius was so disgusted with their terrorism that he had them surrounded by a Gaulish unit and shot down, to a man, *with javelins*. Plutarch refers to this incident in both his lives of Sertorius and Marius and it is clear that it was much talked about in antiquity. The involvement of a Gaulish troop is suggestive. It is one more item to add to the list which associates spears, one-eyed men, Celts, war-leadership and, perhaps, sacrifice. The Celtiberians, in particular stressed the connection for they gave Sertorius the name of Hannibal. He, in turn, was quite proud of the wound and the effect it created. Concerning the wound, writes Plutarch, IV, 2: "he actually prided himself at all times. Others, he said, could not always carry about with them the evidences of their brave deeds, but must lay aside their necklaces, spears and wreaths; in his own case, on the contrary, the marks of his bravery remained with him, and when men saw what he had lost, they saw at the same time a proof of his valor. The people also paid him fitting honours. For, when he came into the theatre, they received him with clapping of hands and shouts of welcome, testimonials which even those who were far advanced in years and honours could not easily obtain". It seems clear that Sertorius actively sought the name of "Hannibal" and exploited it in the same way that Civilis did with that of the Roman. There is little that is haphazard in all of this for by the time of Civilis a tradition had already been established which emphasized the one-eyed warleader's enmity to the empire.

44 Spann, *Sertorius*, p. 13.

45 Again, therefore, indirectly but intriguingly in view of all of the connections noted above, Sertorius is brought into the ambit of Wodanistic acts. As with his disguises and the Isles of the Blessed episode, such were elements which soldiers would typically exalt and memorialize so that in later sagas all would be linked to the one-eyed god. On the practice itself, see de Vries, *Altgermanische Religionsgeschichte* II, p. 28f. One further possibly significant association may be mentioned. We have seen that Sertorius made use of a prophetic doe, sent by Diana, in order to strengthen morale and loyalty among troops. Civilis did essentially the same by manipulating the prophecies of Veleda. Sertorius may, however, have been associated with an actual prophetess in another way since, during his service with Marius against the Cimbri-Teutones, that leader had been sent a Syrian seeress by his wife. She successfully predicted victory during a gladiatorial duel and Marius admired her: "As a general thing, she was carried along with the army in a litter, but she attended the sacrifices clothed in a double purple robe that was fastened with a clasp, and carrying a spear that was wreathed with fillets and chaplets. Such a performance as this caused many to doubt whether Marius, in exhibiting the woman, really believed in her, or was pretending to do so and merely acted a part with her" (Caius Marius, XVII, 2).

as warleader observed the ritual in his war against the Vanir.[46] Although the custom is generally thought to be purely Germanic, or even Scandinavian alone, one can now recognize that such is not the case for it also appears among the Celtiberians of the first century BC. As Appian wrote, Sertorius had directed that javelins be hurled at the enemy when he saw the deer of the goddess "as though he were consecrating the first fruits of a sacrifice to her".[47] The implication is that he followed this ritual consistently, just as he also carried the deer with him on every campaign. One might, of course, object that the parallel is not complete for Sertorius ordered javelins to be thrown *at* the enemy and not over them. But even assuming that Appian is correct in this, I do not think that it substantially alters the overall picture for it is not alone the comparison of a spear-cast as a means of dedication to a deity which is so remarkable but rather the additional facts that it is ordered by a one-eyed warleader of a band of *soldurii* who, as Tacitus states, was imitated in the Rhineland by another one-eyed warlord of a *comitatus*. All this at a time when that institution was still in its infancy and when the cult of Wodan was hardly much further advanced! The worship of a spear-bearing prophetic wargod, accompanied perhaps by a consort with a fawn (Lug with Diana in the *interpretatio Romana*), would seem to have existed among the Celtiberians from an early period. Sertorius exploited that belief in order to attach it to himself as a "god" as Plutarch wrote. Such exploitation and fame paved the way for a northward spread.[48] Considering the very unusual clustering of characters, motifs and chronologies, therefore, an hypothesis might well be developed which argues that the original of the disguised, one-eyed Germanic god of wisdom, prophecy and *comitatus* warfare was Sertorius, the manipulator of Celtic belief in the early first century BC.

One should emphasize that certain aspects of the Mercury/Wodan connection, sans Sertorius, have been discussed in the past and that some scholars, probably the majority, favor the view of Wodan's derivation from Mercury. One of the clearest statements came from A. Closs writing in 1934: "There can be no doubt that the actual true root area of this god lies in the Istavaonic West and that the Wodan belief first spread from there with a warrior culture movement over Germany".[49] For this view, he was taken sternly to task by Jan de Vries whose own

46 Turville-Petre, *Myth and Religion*, p. 47. For the various types of spears used by Celts and Germans, see Dagmar Hüpper-Dröge, *Schild und Speer: Waffen und ihre Bezeichnungen im frühen Mittelalter* (1982).

47 White, *Appian. Roman History* I: XIII, 110, p. 204f.

48 It is highly likely that the god was Lug (whose characteristics are remarkably similar to those of Wodan/Odin), who was worshipped not only by Celtiberians but also by the Cis- and Transalpine tribes. On the widely spread deer cult in Spain, see José Maria Blázquez, *Religiones primitivas de Hispania* I (1962), p. 17f.; idem, "Einheimische Religionen Hispaniens in der römischen Kaiserzeit" (1986), p. 189f. Blázquez notes that the deer cult possessed divinatory characteristics and was sometimes associated with a cult of the dead. Sertorius and the Isles of the Blessed episode again come to mind.

49 A. Closs, "Neue Problemstellungen in der germanischen Religionsgeschichte" (1934), p. 482.

opinion that Wodan was already worshiped by the Cimbri-Teutones before their travels in the late second century BC was itself rejected by Much-Jankuhn.[50] More recently, Thomas Africa developed some of the evidence for a relationship between Hannibal, Sertorius, Civilis and Wodan but his perceptive paper does not seem to have aroused much interest among Germanists or students of comparative religion.[51] Hans Kuhn has also contributed to the debate in a typically original fashion. Although he appears to think (wrongly in my view) that the Roman act of throwing a spear over a boundary in order to declare war is a significant parallel to the Germanic practice of dedicating an opposing group to Wodan, he also argues that some critical aspects of the Scandinavian tradition in this field derive from the northern English Danelaw where, he emphasizes, Celtic tradition played a crucial role.[52] In his opinion, Bragi's "Gungnir's shaker" reference comes from this area and so too does the famous episode of Odin's self-sacrifice: "we must unfortunately leave open the question whether the Death Spear, and what is connected with it, already before the Viking period and outside the North, was connected with this god [Odin]".[53] We may now conclude, however, that Wodan was identified with the spear at an early date. Although Kuhn was not wrong in his tendency to look to the British Isles, present evidence suggests that the British/Viking connection is secondary to the Celtiberian/ Gaulish/South Germanic context wherein Mercury/Wodan worship evolves within the sphere of the developing extra-tribal *comitatus*.

Appian also wrote of Sertorius that "wherever he went he surrounded himself with a bodyguard of Celtiberian spearmen [!] instead of Romans and gave the care of his person to the former instead of the latter".[54] Plutarch goes into greater detail about the nature of the relationship:

It was the custom among the Iberians for those who were stationed about their leader to die with him if he fell, and the barbarians in those parts call this a 'consecration.' Now, the other commanders had few such shield-bearers and companions, but Sertorius was attended by many thousands of men who had thus consecrated themselves to death. And we are told that when his army had been defeated at a certain city and the enemy were pressing upon them, the Iberians, careless of themselves, rescued Sertorius, and taking him on their shoulders one after another, carried him to the walls, and only when their leader was in safety, did they betake themselves to flight, each man for himself.[55]

50 Much, Jankuhn and Lange, *Germania*, p. 172.
51 Africa, "One-Eyed Man Against Rome", pp. 528–38.
52 Hans Kuhn, "Der Todesspeer. Odin als Totengott" (1971), pp. 247–58.
53 Ibid., p. 257.
54 White, *Appian. Roman History* I: XIII, 112, p. 208f.
55 Perrin, *Plutarch* VIII "Sertorius" XIV, 4, p. 38f.

These citations are important for the history of the warband in that they are a statement of the institutional ideal that the follower should fight to the death for the leader and should not survive him if he falls in battle. Although Tacitus also ascribes this conception to the Germanic *comitatus* it has long been known that it is more emphasized in sources relating to the Celts than in the later texts on the Germans.[56] This has led some scholars, most notably Kuhn, to view the idea as a cultural borrowing contemporary with the adoption of the warband itself.[57] The debate is an old one and can, of course, be endlessly continued because of the scarcity of relevant sources. The only way in which the balance would be substantially altered is if it could be shown that such personal devotion was tied to a *network* of characteristics in which one largely depended on the other and in which several of these others, at least, originated elsewhere. This condition is fulfilled by the evidence of the preceding citations, providing one accepts that Civilis set out to follow the example of Sertorius. His one eye would have helped, of course, but it would not have made a really substantial difference unless he also sought to foster the impression in other ways. One can, I think, draw this inference from relevant remarks in the *Historia*.

Nor should one neglect to note that the followers of Sertorius were known to the Gauls for the Roman-like discipline which he had inculcated, a fact which Caesar indirectly corroborates. Since Civilis was surely aiming for the same goals of strict training and control—Tacitus mentions a number of examples—the assumption that he applied the model of Sertorius for several purposes beyond the more obvious one of drawing attention to a common disfigurement would seem to be fully warranted. It is, therefore, in the perfunctory and adventitious sentence of Tacitus that one finds the most remarkable clue to the politico-theological postulates of the rebellious warlord. Both his person and his arguments seem to have contributed significantly to the rise of a new type of warrior religion.

Along with manipulation of prophecy and relentless exploitation of local religious belief, one other crucial factor joins Sertorius and Civilis: each aimed to become the ruler of a multi-cultural kingdom. By the time of his assassination in 72 BC, Sertorius was de facto king of much of Spain and had been a feared figure in an alliance with Mithridates. He had led mixed Roman, Celtiberian and (Celtic or part Celtic) Lusitanian forces in victorious battle against commanders as capable as Pompey.[58] In all of this he constantly took pains to appear as a Roman general and governor of Spain, which capacity he had originally filled. Mommsen,

---

56 For example, Edwards, *Caesar. Gallic War* II, 22, p. 168f.: "the rule of these men [*soldurii*] is that in life they enjoy all benefits with the comrades to whose friendship they have committed themselves, while if any violent fate befalls their fellows, they either endure the same misfortune along with them or take their own lives; and no one yet in the memory of man has been found to refuse death after the slaughter of the comrade to whose friendship he devoted himself".

57 Kuhn, "Grenzen", p. 7; Wenskus; *Stammesbildung*, p. 357f.

58 Spann, *Sertorius*, p. 108ff.; Schulten, *Sertorius*, pp. 87–125.

who considered him to be perhaps the greatest of the Romans, shrewdly noted that "his successes were bound up with the peculiarities of the country and the people".[59] In the case of Civilis, the dimensions of his proposed rule are less clear but we know that Tacitus thought his aim to include "kingship over the strongest and richest nations" in both the Gauls and the Germanies (*Hist.* 4, 18). He too, for the first part of the rebellion at least, acted as a Roman officer, prefect of a cohort, caught between the conflicting claims of Vespasian and Vitellius just as Sertorius had been between those of the followers of Marius and Sulla.

Civilis also looked for allies and found them among the Gauls, particularly the Treveri and Lingones whose leaders were disquieted by the revolt of Julius Vindex, a descendent of the princes of Aquitania, who had received much support (although Treveran auxiliary troops had fought against him) but had been defeated in the previous year, AD 68.[60] While not joining at the outset, many thousands of the Gauls did go over to the Batavian rebellion by the beginning of 70. They were led by Julius Classicus of the royal line of the Treveri and commander of an *ala Treverorum*, Julius Tutor of the same people, *praefectus ripae Rheni*, and Julius Sabinus of the Lingones.[61] These, along with some members of the Ubii and Tungri, took oaths to establish an *imperium Galliarum*.[62] Tacitus says that Gauls and Germans worked in alliance for this purpose and, for those west

59 Mommsen, *Römische Geschichte* III, p. 19f.
60 On the region in general, see the excellent studies by Edith Mary Wightman, *Gallia Belgica* (1985); Von Petrikovits, *Rheinische Geschichte* I. On the Treveri: Wightman, *Roman Trier and the Treveri* (1970); Jungandreas, *Sprachliche Studien*; Heinz Heinen, *Trier und das Trevererland in römischer Zeit* (1985); Ralf Urban, "Die Treverer in Caesars *Bellum Gallicum*" pp. 244–56. On the Lingones; Edith Mary Wightman, "The Lingones: Lugdunensis, Belgica or Germania Superior" (1977), pp. 207–17; Georges Drioux, *Cultes indigènes des Lingons* (1934). On Vindex: Camille Jullian, *Histoire de la Gaule* IV (1913), p. 179f.; Brunt, "Revolt of Vindex", pp. 531–59. For tribal groupings and politics, see Nico Roymans, "The North Belgic Tribes in the 1st Century BC: A Historical-Anthropoligical Perspective" (1984), pp. 43–69; M.E. Marien, "Tribes and Archaeological Groupings of the La Tène Period in Belgium: Some Observations" (1980), pp. 213–41; J.H.F. Bloemers, "Acculturation in the Rhine/Meuse Basin in the Roman period: A Preliminary Study" (1984), pp. 159–210; Michael Parker Pearson, "Beyond the Pale: Barbarian Social Dynamics in Western Europe" (1989), pp. 198–226; David Braund, "Ideology, Subsidies and Trade: The King on the Northern Frontier Revisited" (1989), pp. 14–25. Also useful are C.M. Wells, *The German Policy of Augustus: An Examination of the Archaeological Evidence* (1972); Wells, *Culture Contact and Culture Change*; Jean-Jaques Hatt, *Celts and Gallo-Romans* (1970); Paul-Marie Duval, *Les dieux de la Gaule* (1976); Andrée Thénot, *La civilization celtique dans l'est de la France* (1982); Drinkwater, *Roman Gaul*.
61 Alföldy, *Hilfstruppen*, pp. 37f., 82f., 111f.; Urban, *Der 'Bataveraufstand' und die Erhebung des Iulius Classicus* (1985), p. 48ff.; Heinen, *Trier und das Trevererland*, 71ff.; Von Petrikovits, *Rheinische Geschichte* I, p. 70f.
62 Moore, *Tacitus. Histories*, IV, 54–IV, 60, p. 102f. See further Urban, *'Bataveraufstand'*, p. 58f.; Heinen, *Trier und das Trevererland*, p. 73f. These scholars view Tacitus' reportage on this point as sheer propaganda. Some of their skepticism, at least, seems exaggerated. Hence, I have tended to rely more on P.A. Brunt, "Tacitus on the Batavian Revolt" (1960), pp. 484–517; P.G. van Soesbergen, "The Phases of the Batavian Revolt" (1971), pp. 238–56. Von Petrikovits,

of the Rhine, it was also a purpose hallowed by priests and prophecy. What chiefly inspired the Gauls was the recent news of the burning of the Roman Capitol (4, 54): "Once, long ago, Rome was captured by the Gauls but since Jove's home was unharmed, the Roman power stood firm . . . ". Now, however, the druids were spreading "vain and superstitious prophecies" of the passage of sovereignty to the peoples beyond the Alps. While Civilis may have had plans beyond the *imperium Galliarum*, or even in conflict with it (4, 61), each of the anti-Roman confederacies tried to work closely together and coordinate strategies even if they were only occasionally successful. Finally, when the Treveri and Germans were defeated at Trier by Petilius Cerialis, Classicus took the remainder of his forces and joined Civilis across the Rhine where they made a last stand on one of the Batavian islands.[63]

Knowing the cast of mind of the Treveri, Batavians and their mutual allies, and knowing also the explosive role which prophecy played in this revolt, we can be sure that the alliance was propped and maintained by priests and religious rites on both sides. Whereas the druids would have represented the Treveri, the Germans would have been represented by Veleda. One recalls how the Ubii had requested Civilis and Veleda as mediators and the fact that the suggestion and solution were accepted by the Tencteri, *as well as* the Treveri who were also involved (4, 63). One is justified in assuming a number of such cosmopolitan meetings for they are necessary for both leaders and followers in an alliance and are deducible from many remarks in the *Historia* of Tacitus. Language would not have presented much of a problem at these gatherings. Already in 1920 Much pointed out that it may "be taken as certain that the language of the more refined Gaulish neighboring folk was cultivated in the higher Germanic social circles of the frontier areas".[64] A common religious focus would also have been easy to achieve since both groups worshiped the same god, Mercury. Although this significant fact is often alluded to by specialists in the period, it is less widely known to those of the Early Middle Ages who naturally tend to emphasize the

Rheinische Geschichte I, p. 73 speaks of Civilis joining with "gallischen Utopisten". This may only be true in retrospect. Only about one third of the Belgic tribes and a few of the Gaulish (at most) took part in the revolt but an extra victory or two might well have changed the wary and ambiguous stance of others (since we know that pro-revolt sentiment did exist). Wider support would surely have made a substantial difference and the leaders of the revolt were probably counting on this. Some scholars seem to underestimate the degree of resentment felt by conquered and colonialized peoples and speak as if the process of "Romanization" changed these views radically. Actually, as many studies show, that resentment is often felt most strongly by the upper classes, outwardly the *most* Romanized. See Dyson, "Native Revolts", pp. 239–74; idem, "Native Revolt Patterns", pp. 138–75. For the second and third centuries, however, one can argue otherwise but even then a strong sense of Gaulish separatism persisted.

63 Moore, *Tacitus. Histories*, V, 19–20, p. 206f.
64 Much, *Deutsche Stammeskunde*, p. 50.

religious developments of the core areas of western and central Europe and who thus often neglect the Rhineland.

In recent years, however, both Celticists and Germanists have more fully come to the recognition that the tribes closest to the Rhine are a special case.[65] Centuries of warfare, intermarriage and accommodation had made them thoroughly familiar with each other's languages and customs and the presence of the Romans, as in the Batavian revolt, caused many to think in terms of mutual aid and alliance against the overbearing newcomers who exacted taxes and tribute and conscripted their young men. While it certainly took considerable time for resentment to reach the level of action, nothing tends more quickly to cement differences between two parties than the arrival of a third who threatens both. Of course this is not to say that each people emphasized the same aspects of cult or characteristics of deity—important contrasts existed as well but, especially when one thinks of Mercury and the *matronae* who were largely responsible for the pivotal areas of war and fertility,[66] one is compelled to recognize wide areas of significant accord. When a Roman historian like Tacitus who may not have known the basic languages of the Rhineland yet could relate so much about the beliefs of its inhabitants, one can be certain that many of those who lived there were better informed. The Gauls respected Veleda just as the Germans respected the druids and both peoples revered the memory of Sertorius. Although the period of combined action came too late, the Batavian revolt demonstrates the realization among the Rhineland tribes that if they did not hang together they would all hang separately. We may now look more closely at some aspects of this phenomenon of Rhineland acculturation in order to expand our hypothesis of the Celtiberian/ Gaulish/Germanic connection. Particular attention will be focused on those aspects which turn on warband religion and kingship ritual.

The weight of the evidence examined so far in this chapter suggests that the Celts, particularly those living just east and west of the Rhine, played a significant role in the development of both warband organization and warband cult among the Germans. Although other contemporary nodes of significant interaction further to the east and south can also be identified, it seems legitimate to concentrate attention on this area. As soon as one does so the tribe of the Treveri begins to stand out from the others since, apart from the Britons of the Early Middle Ages, few other peoples have had so close an association with the Germans over so long a period of time.[67] This sense of identification went so far, according to Tacitus in *Germania* 28, that the Treveri claimed a Germanic origin for

---

65 See, for example, Ament, "Ethnogenese", pp. 247–56; Hachmann, "Germanen und Kelten am Rhein", pp. 9–68; Markey, "National Groups in Germania", pp. 248–65.
66 See now Gerhard Bauchheness and Günter Neumann, eds. *Matronen und verwandte Göttheiten* (1987); Christoph B. Rüger, "Gallisch-Germanische Kurien" (1972), pp. 251–60; Green, *Symbol and Image*, pp. 189–205.
67 See studies cited in note 60.

themselves. From what source this datum derives is unknown but as a point of information it is certainly false; history, linguistics, religion, place names and personal names conclusively demonstrate that the Treveri were Celts. On the other hand, allowing the Roman historian a certain latitude, the spirit of the remark is not entirely misleading especially since the tribal name itself seems to mean "river crossers".[68] As the numerous Treveri occupied a highly strategic territory in the southern part of the Ardennes, the Eifel and the Hunsrück, the rationale for the name might apply to the Mosel as well as the Rhine or even to both rivers. If one accepts the evidence of Caesar, however, who has a great deal to say in the matter, then the Rhine is indicated for he frequently refers to the way in which the Treveri and the Germans worked together against the Romans.

It is worth noting some of these instances from *De bello Gallico* for the light they cast on the Treveri's German connection. In B.G. 5, 2, for example, we are told that Caesar sent an expedition against the Treveri because they would not come to his councils but were instead "stirring up the Germans beyond the Rhine". In 5, 55 the Treveri under Indutiomarus sent "deputies across the Rhine" promising money to the reluctant Germans if they would take up arms. In 6, 2, after the death of Indutiomarus when the "chief command" had passed to his kindred, the Treveri try again and in 6, 5 the Treveri mediated a formal friendship between the Menapii, neighbors of the Batavians, Ambiorix of the Eburones and the tribes beyond the Rhine. This episode is particularly revealing because it suggests that the Treveri were so well known and trusted by the transrhenane peoples that they could act as middlemen in a highly significant diplomatic rapprochement—a view which is confirmed in 6, 8 where the relatives of Indutiomarus, who had encouraged the failed anti-Roman policy, are reported to have departed across the Rhine with their German allies. Ambiorix had wished to accompany them. Thousands of people must have been involved on this occasion for all of these nobles had their own clients and followers. Such back and forth movements of large numbers must have been frequent. In 8, 45, for example, we are informed that Labienus fought a cavalry engagement in the territory of the Treveri killing both Treveran *and* German tribesmen. A generation later, in 30 or 29 BC, Nonius Gallus defeated the Treveri who again "brought in the Germans to help them". In the next two Gaulish rebellions under Julius Florus of the Treveri and Julius Sacrovir of the Aedui in 21 AD and of Julius Vindex in 68, we hear nothing of German involvement but can nonetheless be sure that relations continued for in late 69 or January of 70 the Treveri are once more in the field in alliance with Civilis and other German leaders and have carried the Lingones along with them.

In discussing such multi-tribal coalitions one need hardly point out that they were prey to all of the regrettably normal episodes of conspiracy, connivance and

68 Wightman, *Trier and the Treveri*, p. 20.

betrayal which a loose command and organizational structure encourages. Factions quickly developed and at various times bands of Treveri would fight for and against Rome, for and against the Germans. The same was true of Batavi, Ubii and others. Roman rule did not alter the pattern decisively in the first century. Just prior to the development of a common front in December of 69 or January of 70, for example, the Batavians raided Treveran territory because each supported rival imperial claimants, Vitellius and Vespasian.[69] It was not until after the death of Vitellius, accompanied by simmering Treveran resentment at nearly two years of Roman high-handedness,[70] that the alliance actually took shape. While Civilis could then have stopped the revolt, were it only an aspect of Roman civil war, the Treveri had to reckon with far worse treatment since, in choosing Vitellius, they had backed the wrong horse. The design for an *imperium Galliarum* was the result. It now seems to have been a poorly developed strategy, one which was nearly predestined to failure due to a lack of support from other Gauls (many of whom resented the tribes of the Rhineland zone). Proponents of an *imperium Galliarum*, therefore, may have been willing to settle for something less if it could be obtained. We simply cannot say much about specific aims since a broad palette of mixed motives is likely and since we have no certain idea of the political strategies involved.

At least as arresting, however, despite the unusual circumstances which persisted through much of 69, is the documentation of a long-term readiness among the Rhineland ethnica to form alliances and the inclination to cooperate for the sake of mutual interest. The political and cultural attitudes of the Rhineland are clearly very similar. This is precisely the opposite of the picture which Caesar (and sometimes Tacitus) presents and, if it be true to say that politics sometimes makes strange bedfellows, it is also true that hundreds of years of recorded cohabitation is likely to induce familiarity and smooth rough edges. One may remark again how unlikely is Caesar's depiction of the brutal oppressor Ariovistus who, however, bears a Celtic name and maintains a handy alliance through his Celtic wife.

Although Caesar does not refer to the ethnic affiliation of the transrhenane Germanic allies of the Treveri, we do know that a number of different groupings were involved. Among them, perhaps, were the Suebi who were definitely present in 30/29 BC.[71] More interesting is the relationship with the Bructeri, Tencteri and Usipetes. As Jungandreas has recently emphasized, the evidence of linguistics and place names suggests that the Treveri once lived much closer to these tribes than they did in Caesar's day.[72] Moreover, just as the suffix -avi in Batavi, Chamavi

---

69 Moore, *Tacitus. Histories*, IV, 28, p. 52f.
70 Wightman, *Trier and the Treveri*, p. 44f.; Heinen, *Trier und das Trevererland*, p. 72f.; Urban, '*Bataveraufstand*', pp. 46–61.
71 Peschel, "Sueben", p. 285f.
72 Jungandreas, *Sprachliche Studien*, pp. 11–30.

and Frisiavi shows an original close association between three coastal peoples, so does the -eri suffix, in Bructeri, Treveri and Tencteri, indicate some kind of affinity if not actual affiliation.[73] The Tencteri and Usipetes, at least, are mentioned as moving south and crossing the Rhine to Treveran territory in support of Indutiomarus in the 50s BC[74] and we find them—Bructeri and Tencteri generally acted together[75]—also allied with the Treveri in AD 70. For the intervening period we can only say that "Germans" were involved as the sources do not identify them further. Nonetheless, Jungandreas' view that the three -eri tribes were united in traditional *Waffenbrüderschaft* is persuasive and suggests that Bructeri and Tencteri were indeed among the "Germans" mentioned.[76] Even without the evidence presented, the assumption itself is not unreasonable. The Treveri may also have had additional reason to think kindly of the Batavi and Usipetes (whose Celtic tribal name means "good riders"). All three were famous for horse-raising and for their cavalry units and while such hardly creates alliances it does provide grounds for mutual respect and makes understanding easier.[77] Both Civilis' nephew and Julius Classicus were cavalry commanders. Caesar regarded the Treveri as the best cavalrymen of Gaul and Hirtius noted that they differed little from the Germans "in habits of barbarity".[78] We also know that troops of Batavian and Treveran horse were serving together in 69 AD under Munius Lupercus in the Rhineland and Tacitus says the Batavians were then disaffected.[79] Civilis later sent the same Munius Lupercus as a sacrificial gift to Veleda.

This evidence helps deepen our understanding of inter-tribal relations in the Rhineland; it also adds a further dimension to our knowledge of the politics of Civilis. We have argued above that the Tacitean passages relating to Veleda indicate the presence of Celtic influence among the Germans. This is now considerably bolstered because of the revelation of traditional Celto-Germanic alliances and a probably traditional tie of loyalty between Tencteri, Bructeri and Treveri, those tribes which, next to the Batavians themselves, were highly visible in the rebellion. As that revolt did not begin until May or June of 69, however, and since the Treveri did not join until six or seven months later, it appears that one must envision a period during which Civilis and his supporters earnestly tried to gain their support. A conspiracy certainly existed before the actual Treveran entry since

---

73 Ibid., p. 14f.
74 Edwards, *Caesar. Gallic War*, VI, 36, p. 364f.
75 Schmidt, *Westgermanen*, pp. 189–205; Jungandreas, *Sprachliche Studien*, p. 14.
76 Jungandreas, *Sprachliche Studien*, 14f.; Wightman, *Trier and the Treveri*, p. 16f.
77 Alföldy, *Hilfstruppen*, p. 13f. 37f. The author points out also that troops from Belgica and the two German provinces shared a number of characteristics in their army service in general (p. 86f.).
78 Edwards, *Caesar. Gallic War*, II, 24; V, 2; VIII, 26, pp. 120f., 236f., 552f.
79 Moore, *Tacitus. Histories*, IV, 18, p. 34f.

Tacitus notes that "messengers passed to and fro between Civilis and Classicus" and we also know that Classicus and Tutor were in communication with "German chiefs", not just Civilis, and concluded at least one agreement with them (*Hist.* 4, 57): *cum ducibus Germanorum pacta firmavere.* Under such conditions the choice of a "maiden of the Bructeri" as prophetess might perhaps be interpreted as, among other things, a calculated appeal to the Treveri. Her rise to influence would seem to have taken place within the relevant time-frame. If we now know that Veleda was a creature of Civilis it is yet true that she also came from a tribe that the Treveri were, perhaps, more likely to trust than many others. Because of her Celtic title and behavior, she may also have been more acceptable to the druids and poets of the Treveri whose status and mode of worship had been under attack since the age of Augustus.[80]

In AD 69 these druids seem to have been busy spreading the already mentioned prophecy of Rome's imminent demise. Indeed, there is good reason to believe that it may have originated with the Treveri. According to Tacitus, the burning of Jove's home reminded the Gauls of their capture of Rome in the fourth century BC and presaged for them "the passage of the sovereignty of the world to the peoples beyond the Alps", *possessionem rerum humanarum Transalpinis gentibus portendi . . . .*[81] The only claim to a new sovereignty among the Gauls, however, was that made by Julius Classicus who donned imperial insignia and required oaths to a new *imperium Galliarum* under his rule.[82] Since a conspiracy or at least rumors of a conspiracy had already existed for some time (*Hist.* 4, 54–55) and since the most tangible benefits flowed to Classicus, the ancient maxim of *cui bono* clearly shifts the evidence in favor of Treveran instigation of the prophecies or, at minimum, in favor of speedy cooption by Treveran propagandists.

The evidence indicates more combined Gaulish-Germanic preparation to the second phase of the rebellion than has sometimes been thought. While Civilis may have felt increasing dissatisfaction with the idea of second place, he may have behaved differently at the inception of the plot. In any case, the apparently coordinated appearance of prophets under both leaders, druids for Classicus and a veleda for Civilis, also suggests solid, transrhenane support amongst those of traditional religious attitudes. One further important reason for this was Roman prohibition of the widely practiced Celtic and Germanic rite of human sacrifice. This ritual death-dealing, reverently regarded by all Rhineland tribes as the great mysterium of religion, horrified the Romans who much preferred the joys of the

---

80 Rankin, *Celts and the Classical World*, p. 285f. The ostensible ground for prohibition of the druids was human sacrifice. As Ronald Syme, *Tacitus* (1958), p. 457f. notes, however, "whether ritual murder among the Gauls was the true reason or only the inevitable pretext is another question". Cf. Guyonvarc'h and Le Roux, *Druides*, pp. 66–76.

81 Moore, *Tacitus. Histories*, IV, 26; IV, 54, pp. 50f., 102f.

82 Ibid., IV, 58–60, p. 110f.

gladiatorial arena where the infinitely more frequent flow of blood served the higher secular purpose of pure entertainment. Such attitudes will have affected all the riverine peoples drawing them together in a somewhat more intense type of Mercury cult than that known in the west and south (where Mercury was less popular) and molding their institutions in similar ways.[83] In fact, even without the evidence of coordinated prophecy in support of an allied undertaking in AD 70, joint political and religious ventures usually accompany each other among tribal peoples and a good deal more can be learned by examining things from this perspective.

As Edith Wightman points out in her superlative study of the pagan cults of the province of Belgica, the picture which results from an analysis of Gaulish Mercury is not quite that of Caesar's "discoverer of the arts and supervisor of commercial transactions, but a more mysterious creature linked with fertility, seasonal change and the underworld".[84] As Helm and Much-Jankuhn note, it is the Gaulish Mercury whose characteristics are associated with Wodan.[85] The inscriptional evidence for this is quite strong. All seven inscriptions to Mercurius Arvernus, for example, are found on German soil.[86] Another, to Mercurius Arvernorix, was found on the Greinberg near Miltenberg[87] in the company of two dedications to Mercurius Cimbrianus while two others to the Cimbrian deity were found on the Heiligenberg near Heidelberg and one in the region of Mainz.[88] One group clearly points to connections with the Gaulish tribe of the Arverni while the others indicate, as many scholars agree, the settlement of remnants of the Cimbri in Rhineland areas.[89] The Cimbri (and Teutones) are particularly interesting in view of the fact that they were among the most heavily Celticized Germanic peoples whose sacrificial ritual, in which captives had their throats cut over a cauldron in order to prophesy from the flow of blood, is certainly Celtic.[90] This is admitted even by de Vries whose view that Wodan might already have been

---

83 One thinks of triple-headed Mercury and the rider-god columns. See Edith Mary Wightman, "Pagan Cults in the Province of Belgica" (1986), p. 563.

84 Ibid., p. 553. See also Émile Thévénot, *Divinités et sanctuaries de la Gaule* (1968), pp. 73–96; Duval, *Dieux de la gaule*, pp. 27f., 29f.; De Vries, *Keltische Religion* pp. 41–55; Ferdinand Benoit, *Mars et Mercure. Nouvelles Recherches sur l'interprétation gauloise des divinités romaines* (1959); Mac Cana, *Celtic Mythology* (1970), p. 24f.

85 Helm, *Altgermanische Religionsgeschichte*, p. 361; Much, Jankuhn and Lange, *Germania*, p. 171f.

86 The classic study is Gutenbrunner, *Germanischen Götternamen*, pp. 52–8; Bober, "Mercurius Arvernus", pp. 19–46.

87 Rudolf Simek, *Lexikon der germanischen Mythologie* (1984), p. 260; De Vries, *Altgermanische Religionsgeschichte* II, p. 30.

88 Simek, *Lexikon*, p. 261; De Vries, *Altgermanische Religionsgeschichte* II, p. 29f.

89 Bober, "Mercurius Arvernus", pp. 22f., 28f.; Norden, *Urgeschichte*, p. 225, n. 3; Simek, *Lexikon*, p. 261; De Vries, *Altgermanische Religionsgeschichte* II, p. 29f.

90 de Vries, "Kimbern und Teutonen", p. 12f.

worshipped by the Cimbri in their homeland is generally regarded as "*wohl zu gewägt*".[91] The name Mercurius Gabrinius which appears on ten inscriptions from Bonn is also Celtic.[92] The further spread of the cult among the Germans, on the other hand, is shown by dedications like those to Mercurius Channin(i)us from Blankenheim, Erausius (?) from Ubberbergen near Nijmegen, Leudisius (?) from Weisweiler (Kr. Düren) or Mercurius Rex from Nijmegen.[93] Both Mercurius Rex and Mercurius Arvernorix (king of the Arverni) indicate a link to kingship which fits well with the view presented here. All of these inscriptions, moreover, are decisive evidence of a Gaulish-Germanic religious connection.

One Gaulish god much worshipped in the east under the name of Mercury may have been Esus whose woodchopper figure, standing by a tree, appears on a first century relief in Trier, the city of the Treveri, where it is "associated or identified with Mercury".[94] Esus was a god who loved human sacrifice. The Berne Scoliast on Lucan recorded that he demanded a type of sacrifice whereby men were hung on trees and then chopped or stabbed so that omens could be told from the direction of their blood flow.[95] Anne Ross has rightly noted that the

91 Much, Jankuhn and Lange, *Germania*, p. 172; Helm, *Wodan*, p. 5f.; De Vries, *Altergermanische Religionsgeschichte* II, p. 30. Although Helm did not wish to argue that the characteristics of Gaulish Mercury and Wodan were identical, he did recognize a close association and his work conclusively demonstrated the inadequacy of all claims for the existence of Wodan before the first century AD. de Vries continued to maintain his earlier position, however, but was unable to provide evidence until he converted to the Dumézilian approach. This enabled him to claim that Mercury/Lug and Wodan all derived from an Indo-European background and he was then able to accept, even emphasize, the similarites as he did in his book on Celtic religion. The origins of Wodan in Celto-Germanic contact along the Rhine are now becoming difficult to dispute. See, most recently, Bauchhenss, "Mercurius in Bornheim", pp. 224–38; Wagner, "Wodansname", p. 238f. The evidence will be discussed more fully below.

92 Along with the works cited above, see Christoph B. Rüger, "A Husband for the Mother Goddess —Some Observations on the Matronae Aufaniae" (1983), pp. 210–19.

93 Gutenbrunner, *Germanischen Götternamen*, p. 54f.; Simek, *Lexikon*, p. 261f.

94 On Esus, see de Vries, *Keltische Religion*, p. 100: "[the evidence shows] dass Esus ein Name für eine der Hauptgottheiten der Gallier war und wohl am ehesten mit Mercurius und dem nordgermanischen Odhin zu vergleichen ist".; Paul-Marie Duval, "Teutates, Esus, Taranis" (1958), p. 42f.; idem, *Dieux de la Gaule*, p. 34f.; Thévénot, *Divinités et sanctuaires*, p. 142f.; Mac Cana, *Celtic Mythology*, p. 25f. According to the Lucan commentary, Esus was sometimes equated with Mercury and sometimes with Mars. Mercury, Rosmerta and Esus all appear on one stone from Trier and, given the nature of Esus' sacrifices, this is a significant piece of evidence when considering the characteristics of Wodan and the possible transmitters of the cult.

95 Zwicker, *Fontes* I, p. 50: Hesus mars sic placatur: homo in arbore suspenditur, usque donec per cruorem membres digeserit. Victims dedicated to Teutates were drowned by being plunged head first into a vat while those for Taranis were burned. One thinks of the death of the Norse king Fjolnir which may be compared to those of the Irish Diarmait mac Cerbaill and Murchertach mac Ercæ. See Mac Cana, *Celtic Mythology*, p. 27. Links with Wodan/Odin, however one chooses to interpret them, seem obvious. Kuhn, "Todesspeer", p. 256, argued that Odin's tree-hanging self-sacrifice derived from Celtic-Viking contact in Britain but that now seems too late.

peculiar nature of sacrifice to Odin may well owe something to Esus and cites the lines of *Hávamál*: "I know that I hung full nine nights on the gallows tree, wounded by the javelin and given to Odin, myself to myself". The tendency of the evidence to lead to the Treveri is really quite extraordinary. Not only do we note a probable tie between that people and the Bructeri but also with sacrificial hanging, with the raven attribute of Wodan, and then find them in alliance with a one-eyed general, much given to warrior tradition and the sacred groves. Taken together with the epigraphic material and the other evidence offered in this chapter, we now have a strong case for the Celtic origins of many of the identifying characteristics of the cult of Wodan and warband religion as it began to develop under Civilis.

One must ask, however, if it could all be legitimately regarded as a series of unusual coincidences? Although a certain skepticism is appropriate in this area, that conclusion would lead to an even greater series of puzzles. For what then would one do with the surely related Celtiberian figure of the spear-bearing prophet who was stabbed with a spear, or with the practice of dedicating an enemy as a sacrifice with a spear-throw? The argument for coincidence can hardly be pushed to such extremes especially since, as we have already shown, all evidence centers on the institution of the warband which is itself a cultural borrowing from the Celts. Suppose nonetheless, that one were to take a critical stance on the basis of the facts that not all Celtiberians were Celts (although they seem to have been[96]) and that Hispania is no short distance from the Rhineland. Perhaps the evidence from the two regions should be separated. That inference would also be unwarranted since we can deduce from Caesar that travel between Spain and Gaul was not uncommon, that knowledge of Sertorius was widespread and appreciated by both Civilis and many Gauls (Caesar and Tacitus) and since, in any case, the striking consistency of cult practice is completely understandable on the grounds of shared Celtic culture alone but is difficult to explain outside of it. The conclusion thus seems to be compelling: many of the attributes of Wodan and the practices associated with his worship were first borrowed from the Celts among whom the Treveri appear to have played a significant role as transmitters. The Wodan cult, however, although it may be overly daring to seek a true chronology, probably postdates Caesar's conquest since the Germans, it appears, mostly sacrificed to him under the guise of Mercury and are unlikely to have done so until, at the earliest, the first consistent stage of Romanization perhaps two generations thereafter. One can, of course, envision a somewhat earlier date of origin but such assumption seems to lack a secure evidentiary basis. The Batavian revolt, on the other hand, provides an attractive context for early development of the cult. Assuming that Civilis was about forty-three years old in 70 AD after

96 Antonio Tovar, "The Celts in the Iberian Peninsula: Archaeology, History and Language" (1986), pp. 68–101.

twenty-five years of Roman service, one might think of the early foundation as being laid, if it did not come after him, not long before his birth. In either case, it would appear to be correct to hold, as suggested above, that this one-eyed warlord was a crucial propagator of the cult and the cruel/deceptive character of the god was fixed during a period of conspiracy and rebellion, victory and defeat, hope and despair. Wodan's friendship was rarely offered without cost and frequently difficult to hold; his friends suffered as much as his enemies. The associations surrounding Veleda would seem to favor this view as well and we may now explore them further in order to compare them with the trend of the evolving interpretation.

6. ROSMERTA AND VELEDA

Throughout this study, attention has focused on the relationship between the warlord and his female delegate, aspects of which, it has been argued, derive from the earlier institution of warband prophetess (Veleda, Ganna, Walburg etc.) and, finally, from the peculiar and unique mixture of the Celto-Germanic civilization of the Rhineland. From all that we have seen, the warlord/prophetess association, which centered on the warband, must have had a cultic basis just as was the case with the earlier *rex* and matrons of the tribe. It is thus a matter of special interest to note that the Rhineland Mercury also had a consort whose place in the cult is not yet fully worked out but whose presence and attributes, it may be suggested, could almost be predicted from the findings already outlined. As Wightman remarks in her already cited work on Belgic cults, "the chain of associations visible in the monuments links Mercury with . . . a female principle denoting fertility, fate or both . . . ".[1] This is no peripheral aspect of the cult for it is documented not only for the Rhineland but also for the other areas of Gaul, Britain and Spain where the connection is clearly conventional and significant.[2] The same association had previously existed in the cult of the mothers.[3] Stressing the necessity of a husband for the mother goddesses, Rüger notes that the sacred precincts of the *matronae Aufaniae* also contained a temple of Mercurius Gebrinius whose building inscription, along with eight other dedications to that god, was found among

---

1 Wightman, "Pagan Cults", p. 553.
2 A good overview in Green, *Symbol and Image*, pp. 54–61, 107f.; Idem, *Gods of the Celts*, 98f.; Graham Webster, *Celtic Religion in Roman Britian* (1986), pp. 57–61; De Vries, *Keltische Religion*, p. 118f. Green states (*Symbol and Image*, p. 61) that of the two deities, "it is Rosmerta who provided the cult's profundity". The people originally concerned might be surprised at this interpretation. Although Rosmerta was an important figure, the cult of Mercury was immensely more popular and widespread and she was only one of many consorts possessing more or less similar characteristics.
3 See now the variety of important contributions in Bauchhenss and Neumann, *Matronen*; Green, *Symbol and Image*, 189–205.

the inscriptions to the Aufaniae under Bonn Minster.[4] Similarly, Harald von Petrikovits writes that Mercury appears to have been a *parhedros* or cult companion of the *matronae*.[5] Other scholars (Horn, Schmidt) have recently noted the thoroughly hybrid Celto-Germanic features of this Rhineland cult as well as the frequently "military context" of the epigraphic dedications.[6] In Britain, for example, most are found near Hadrian's wall.

Rüger also refers to the *Matres Castrorum*—"motherly guards and protectors of the military camp"—and states that the connection of soldiers to mother worship belongs to the field of psychology.[7] That does not make it difficult to interpret. Throughout history, most soldiers have been farmers and, as Birkhan rightly concludes, there is no doubt that the dangers of the military life could result in the unconscious yearning for security as represented in the religious area by the fictional personal relations of the inscriptions.[8] From the present perspective it seems to make sense to regard the cult of the *matronae* as most closely tied to the tribe and not to the warband, although in the religious field, so full of crossover phenomena, it is surely less a case of opposition as such and more that of a different place on the same spectrum. Nonetheless, cultic innovation in the Rhineland does seem to have accompanied the process of institutional transition.

The goddess described by Wightman as linked to fertility and fate is Rosmerta whose dual name-elements may translate to the "great provider".[9] It is, perhaps, at least as correct to call her the "great prophetess", however, since Vendryes' argument that the root *smer* in her name means "fate" or "prophecy" has never been refuted.[10] Both concepts are connected as we shall see. She is often named on the monuments, especially after the first century, and appears as consort somewhat more often in rural areas of Belgica than in urban.[11] She is the female figure who appears with Mercury on the already mentioned first century relief from Trier and her inscriptions and reliefs are concentrated in the Rhineland: Mannheim, Trier, Metz, Wiesbaden and Heidelberg, although they are found in

4 Rüger, "Husband for the Mother Goddesses", pp. 210–19.

5 Von Petrikovits, *Rheinische Geschichte* I, p. 156.

6 Heinz Günter Horn, "Bilddenkmäler des Matronenkultes im Ubiergebiet" (1987), pp. 31–53; Karl H. Schmidt, "Die Keltischen Matronenbeinamen" (1987), pp. 133–53; Christoph B. Rüger, "Beobachtungen zu den epigraphischen Belegen der Muttergottheiten in den lateinischen Provinzen des Imperium Romanum" (1987), pp. 1–30, esp. p. 8.

7 Rüger, "Beobachtungen", p. 3. Rüger's discussion of the association between men's sodalities and Matronengruppen seems to me to contain some important insights. This linkage appears to have been especially strong in the Rhineland. See pp. 18f., 26f.

8 Birkhan, *Germanen und Kelten*, p. 537.

9 Wightman, "Pagan Cults", p. 553f.; Green, *Symbol and Image*, p. 54f.

10 J. Vendryes, "La racine *smer*- en celtique" (1937), pp. 133–6; A.L.F. Rivet, Colin Smith, *The Place Names of Roman Britain* (1979), p. 460f.

11 Wightman, "Pagan Cults", p. 574.

other areas as well.[12] Graham Webster notes that "all the inscriptions and many of the sculptured reliefs link Rosmerta with Mercury" and there "seems little doubt" that it was from the Rhineland that the goddess was brought to Britain.[13] In view of what we now know about the Rhineland origins of many of Wodan's characteristics and also of his special patronage of the warband, the figure of Rosmerta is of peculiar interest for it is conceivable that if the attributes of Wodan derive from the Gaulish Mercury, then some of those of the veledas might well derive from or otherwise be associated with those of his companion.

A study of the Rosmerta sculptures clearly links her to those characteristics which would seem to have been typical of the prophetess in the *comitatus*: distributions of drink and gifts (especially in their cultic aspects), connections with fate and prophecy and the carrying of a rod or staff as attribute. One relief from Wiesbaden, for example, shows Mercury pouring from his purse into a patera held by Rosmerta while an Eros at her right hand holds a cornucopia as symbol of her ability to provide.[14] Other reliefs show the goddess carrying her own purse in imitation of Mercury. Her ties to fate and the future are shown by her "close affinity" to Fortuna in the *interpretatio Romana*,[15] an approach made easier, apparently, by an earlier tradition in which certain gods and goddesses were associated with wheels, perceived as appropriate symbols of the turning of fortune.[16] On the Gundestrup cauldron, for example, found in the old territory of the Cimbri and now often regarded as a Gaulish or Celtic product of the first century BC,[17] a goddess is shown flanked by two stylized wheel symbols and this concept carried over to Rosmerta and Fortuna's wheel. In this guise, she is sometimes shown holding a rudder, wheel or sphere of the world, all objects which could be turned for or against the supplicant to indicate his rise or fall.[18]

Depictions from Britain seem to be less Romanized and are especially instructive. According to Webster, a good example of Rosmerta's special attribute there appears on a relief from Gloucester where the goddess, partnered with Mercury, holds a staff in her right hand with a pelta-shaped terminal, "presumably a symbol of authority".[19] In her left hand she holds a patera from which she is pouring something into a small wooden tub. At Bath, Mercury and a female deity are again

---

12 A catalogue and discussion will be found in Colette Bémont, "Rosmerta" (1960), pp. 29–43; eadem, "A propos d'un nouveau monument de Rosmerta" (1969), pp. 23–44; De Vries, *Keltische Religion*, p. 118f.

13 Webster, *Celtic Religion*, p. 57f.

14 Ibid., p. 58.

15 Ibid.; Green, *Symbol and Image*, p. 59.

16 Green, *Gods of the Celts*, p. 46f.

17 Garrett Olmsted, *The Gundestrup Cauldron* (1979); Richard Pittioni, *Wer hat wann und wo den Silberkessel von Gundestrup angefertigt* (1984). See, however, Ruth Megaw and Vincent Megaw, *Celtic Art From Its Beginnings to the Book of Kells* (1989), p. 176.

18 Webster, *Celtic Religon*, p. 58.

19 Ibid., p. 59.

shown and she "appears to be carrying a short staff" in her left hand and in her right, over a small wooden tub, an object which "could have been intended as a large stirring spoon".[20] A figure interpreted as Mercury also appears to the right of two female figures on a relief from Wellow in Somerset. The central one holds what appears to be "a bunch of rods" in her left hand while the other figure holds a "thin scepter" in her left hand and in the right a "large spoon with a long handle".[21] At her side is a tall bucket or tub. The four bands around the top, notes Webster, represent the bronze bindings on a "typical Celtic mixing bucket".[22] The mixing bucket and stirrer "confirms the identification of the figure as Rosmerta" and other reliefs show the same attributes again. The containers seem to have primarily functioned as "wine buckets" or, alternatively, as water buckets "used to dilute the wine". Such buckets were definitely associated with a cult of the dead as well as the living since, with only three possible exceptions, all of the many British examples were found in graves and in four cases actually contained ashes of the deceased.[23] These depictions clearly indicate the existence of a well-established conception of Rosmerta's sphere of authority, one which, as the sculptures themselves suggest, must be connected to a widespread set of contemporary ritual behaviors (see V, 8).

Rosmerta, then, the companion of Mercury with her attributes of staff, purse and wine bucket, fulfills, as no other contemporary figure does, all of the qualifications for an identification with the veledas of the warlords and may well recall the feast in the sacred grove presided over by Civilis. The association is supported not only by her holding of a staff which is the symbol of office of the Germanic sibyl but also by her connection with a cult of the dead (Mercury the *Seelenbegleiter*) which is later reflected in the association of Wodan with the *völva* who calls up the dead. Karl Hauck has shown the *völva* of Eddic poetry to be a continuation of the bracteate prophetess of the migration period.[24] One recalls also the frequent presence of buckets and spoon-shaped strainers with handles in northern graves of the Early Middle Ages.[25] Indeed, it may be suggested that the object held by Rosmerta is more likely to be a spoon-shaped strainer rather than a simple spoon stirrer as that would better fulfill the demands on the goddess for distribution. The liquor brewed by both ancients and early medievals often

20 Ibid.
21 Ibid.
22 Ibid. For extended discussion, see I.M. Stead, "A La Tène III Burial at Welwyn Garden City" (1967), pp. 1–62.
23 Webster, *Celtic Religion*, p. 61. An association of Rosmerta's attributes with cauldrons of renewal and regeneration is a widely held view. See Green, *Symbol and Image*, p. 58; eadem, *Gods of the Celts*, p. 97; Mac Cana, *Celtic Mythology*, p. 25.
24 Karl Hauck, "Motivanalyse eines Doppelbreakteaten. Die Trager der Goldenen Götterbilda-mulette und die Traditionsinstanz der fünischen Brakteaten produktion" (1985), pp. 153f., 181f.; Idem, "Text und Bild in einer oralen Kultur", p. 569f.
25 Ellmers, "Zum Trinkgeschirr der Wikingerzeit", pp. 21–43.

required straining and one can easily envision the liquor being drawn through the strainer and then poured into the cup or horn. Very long-handled *Löffelseiher* of this type were already quite common in the eastern Alpine and Venetic cultural area from the Hallstatt period onwards.[26] This was true further north as well. The Viking Age picture stone Halla Broa XVI, for example, shows a drinking scene within a house in which a standing figure passes a drinking horn to a sitting one. On the ground between the two stands a bucket from which one can discern the protruding handle of a strainer.[27] In a British context, this scene might well be identified as one depicting Mercury and Rosmerta. Thus, all indications point to the conclusion that the reliefs and inscriptions to these two figures can provide answers to many of the questions which bedevil the study of early Germanic religion. In *Germania* 9, Tacitus states that during the reign of Vespasian Veleda was regarded by many *as a deity*. As Civilis represented himself as Sertorius redivivus (who had a special cultic relationship with the goddess Diana, who presented him with a prophetic doe) so did he also wish Veleda to be linked with Rosmerta. The later literary texts are explained by the iconography of the monuments of Britain and the Rhineland.

A problem concerning the staff must be discussed before preceding to a discussion of other evidence and implications. In his very useful summary discussion of Rosmerta, Webster notes that the appearance of the staff in the goddess' hand is a "special attribute" of the British reliefs and he does not mention it for Gaul.[28] At one point this seemed to me to be a severe enough deficiency to cast doubt on the identification made above. Could one rightly speak of Rosmerta as the supernatural archetype legitimizing the Germanic sibyl if the Gaulish-type monuments, presumably those most likely to be known to the Rhinelanders, did not endow her with this attribute? A number of explanations are possible. Speaking of the Batavians before the rebellion, Tacitus says that their cohort gained renown by service in Britain where they had been transferred and where they were "commanded according to ancient tradition, by the noblest men in the nation". We have already seen that Civilis and many of his Batavian followers probably served there. One might even note an intriguing and very unusual relief from Easton Grey near Malmesbury, Wilts., which shows a goddess accompanied by three male figures. The inscription reads *Civilis fecit*.[29] Who can say whether or not a connection might exist? Even so, would this Batavian presence in Britain, where they would have continued to worship Mercury, do as a substitute for the loss of the staff in Gaul? Another possible solution is provided by the identification of Rosmerta with Fortuna (and occasionally with Victoria as well).[30] It might

---

26 Kossack, "Trinkgeschirr", pp. 97–105; Ellmers, "Trinkgeschirr", p. 26..
27 Ellmers, "Trinkgeschirr", p. 22f.
28 Webster, *Celtic Religion*, p. 59.
29 Ross, Pagan Celtic Britain, p. 211.
30 Ibid., p. 217f.; Green, *Symbol and Image*, pp. 59, 198.

be suggested that the vagaries of the *interpretatio Romana* gave her rudder, wheel and sphere instead of a staff since, apparently, all could signify knowledge or control of the future. When combined, the two hypotheses might seem to offer a way out of the problem even if it be a bit belabored and not entirely satisfactory. But a more attractive explanation eventually evolved. It starts from the fact of occasional possession by both deities of a caduceus.

In their discussion of the reasons for the identification of Wodan with Gaulish Mercury, Much-Jankuhn noted that Mercury's cap and herald's staff—that is what caduceus means—can be compared to the hat and spear of Wodan.[31] It may be, then, that both Wodan's spear and sibyl's staff have the same origin and the difference is accounted for by the fact that each denotes authority in different areas. In Wodan's hand the staff becomes a spear because that is an ancient symbol of warrior rule; Veleda's emblem remains a staff-like weaving beam or distaff, however, because it still suggests some type of authority and is also easy to associate with weaving sticks, spindles and weaving-swords, all of which remind one of the widespread concept of the weaving of fate. Complicated as it may seem, that is very likely what occurred. The monuments themselves bear witness to a transfer and reversal of functions. The purse-bearing attribute of Mercury, for example, is also acquired by Rosmerta and we have already seen Mercury pouring the contents of his purse into Rosmerta's patera.[32] Sometimes Mercury will be depicted holding a patera as well.[33] In an entirely different context, Emile Thévenot makes this matter of transmission of function rather clear. When stating that Rosmerta is *"très rarement invoquée ou représentée de façon isolée"* but usually appears to the right of Mercury and often carries a cornucopia, he adds that she sometimes carries a caduceus suggestive of an affinity of functions.[34] In Mediterranean religion, of course, Mercury might also act as a prophet so that it is likely that we are dealing with a mixture of religious concepts which also draw on the long transalpine tradition of linking female prophecy with distaffs and weaving. It may be noted parenthetically that scholars of religion have not drawn on the archaeological evidence linking "cult staffs" and liquor service discussed here in chapter four. Examples of Rosmerta with caduceus have been found at, among other places, the temple of Mercury at Donon in Treveran territory as well as Langensulzbach, Schorndorf, Stetten, Neustadt a. Haardt, Bierstadt near Wiesbaden, Devant-les-Ponts near Metz.[35]

31 Much, Jankuhn and Lange, *Germania*, p. 171f. The way in which spear and caduceus might be intermingled has been noted for Mercury's temple at Uley. Similarly, Celtic spear shafts often carried knobs at the end and Ross has noted (*Pagan Celtic Britian*, p. 231) that Mercury may appear with "a caduceus with a knobbed end like the spears of some of the northern warriors". For other forms of the caduceus, see H. Vertet, "Remarques sur l'aspect et les attributs du Mercure gallo-romaine populaire dans le centre de la Gaule" (1962), pp. 1605–16.

32 Webster, *Celtic Religion*, p. 58; Green, *Symbol and Image*, p. 56f.

33 Webster, *Celtic Religion*, p. 60.

34 Thévenot, *Divinites et sanctuaires*, p. 30.

35 Bémont, "Rosmerta", p. 40f.

The combined staff-bearing of Mercury and Rosmerta was a common motif in the Rhineland from where her worship also spread as far afield as Britain. Although her monuments cannot certainly be identified north of the middle Rhine on the continent, it is not unlikely that this is a matter of archaeological accident for conditions in Germania Inferior certainly encouraged a wide mixture of cults. B.H. Stolte made the following remarks:

> The population of Germania Inferior was not homogeneous; aside from Celtic and Germanic elements one must also reckon with a pre-Celto-Germanic stratum. Moreover, Germania Inferior was a frontier province with a sizable occupation force of legions and auxiliaries. People from a variety of countries accompanied the army into the province and brought their gods with them. We may thus expect a colorful variety of every kind of religion.[36]

He goes on to note the popularity of Mercury in the Rhineland and Netherlands where inscriptions and bronze statues (32 from the Netherlands) demonstrate a notable pattern of veneration along with native influence.[37]

Nor, in the specific case of the Batavians, does one need to assume that they had to travel very far to become acquainted with Mercury and Rosmerta. We know that at least some Batavians bore Celtic names (e.g. *Vassio, Suandacca*) and it has been suggested that they intermarried with the neighboring Celtic tribe of the Menapii who, according to a disputed passage in Caesar's *Gallic Wars*, "possessed lands, buildings, and villages on both banks of the river".[38] Although the dating is uncertain, the cult of Mercurius Rex also played some role in Batavian territory and a first century inscription from Ruimel suggests that a Celtic style leader exercised some authority amongst them (*summus magistratus civitatis Batavorum*).[39] Moreover, the very sizeable number of eight cohorts of Batavians were serving in Britain in the 60s AD.[40] The proposed solution answers all outstanding questions, therefore, and actually supports the overall argument in other ways. Here, for example, is a further reason why a staff-bearing Germanic sibyl would bear a Celtic title meaning "prophetess" and here too is a vindication of the identification made between the staff of the Germanic prophetess and the "weaving rod" carried by the druidess in *Táin Bó Cúailnge*. Both symbols are to be associated with the "staff", "scepter" or "rod" of Rosmerta, the goddess of fertility and fate whose name and whose affinity with Fortuna (and occasionally with Victoria) in the *interpretatio Romana* demonstrates that knowledge of the future was her traditional stock in trade.

36 B.H. Stolte, "Die Religiose Verhältnisse in Niedergermanien" (1986), p. 591f.
37 Ibid., p. 632f.
38 Neumann, "Sprachverhältnisse", p. 1067; Ernst Schwarz, *Germanische Stammeskunde* (1956), p. 146. The name Noviomagus, Nijmegen, for example, is Celtic in origin.
39 Rüger, *Germania Inferior*, p. 94; Will, "'Klientel-Randstaaten'", p. 11f.
40 Alföldy, *Hilfstruppen*, p. 13f., 136f.

Further confirmation comes from Spain. In his study of native Spanish religion, J.M. Blazquez calls attention to a third century altar from Salvatierra de Santiago (Prov. Cacares) dedicated to Mercurius Colualis.[41] Colu- is also found as a prefix in the Spanish personal name Coulupata. He compares it to IE *kuel-*, "to turn", and especially to Latin *colus*, "spindle". Perhaps, he comments, "Mercury may thereby be identified as the protector of housework".[42] This latter tentative suggestion is not very convincing but in view of what we now know of the Celtiberian/Gaulish/Germanic connection, it adds a further significant piece of evidence to that assembled above. The Celtic linkage between prophecy and weaving tools must also have been made in the case of Hispanic Mercury. One recalls again the spear-bearing prophet and the Celtiberian reverence for one-eyed generals.

Mercury's association with weaving tools is also significant in another way for it provides a hint which helps to explain the transition from tribal dependence on the *matres* to warband reliance on the prophetess. In the Rhineland and elsewhere the mothers usually appear in triplicate. One stone from Trier, for example, depicts one of the mothers with swathing band and the other two with distaffs as if, writes Miranda Green, they "take on the role of the Fates, spinning out men's lives".[43] She adds that they are frequently connected with Fortune or

41 Blázquez, "Einheimische Religion", p. 215. Hispanic Mercury must also be identified with Lug who, in Spain as well as in Gaul, is associated with the raven (p. 216).
42 Ibid.
43 Green, *Gods of the Celts*, p. 81. One of the mothers carries a spindle. At Metz, notes Green (*Symbol and Image*, p. 194) the mothers stand with breasts exposed and wearing diadems: "one bears a palm-leaf (a victory symbol) and a patera; another has distaff and spindle; the third a goblet". At the temple of Nettersheim near Bonn, one of the Aufaniae carries a distaff. Victories may also appear with the mother goddesses. So can the Celtic Mercurius Arvernus, as at a temple at Gripswald. Such symbolism is echoed in Britain where Rosmerta and another goddess resembling Fortuna appear on a stone from the Bon Marché site at Gloucester where each "wear elaborate headresses reminiscent of the 'coiffure' of the Germanic mothers" (p. 59). Isabella Horn has noted the possibility that "die Matronenheiligtümer als Orakelstätten eine Rolle gespielt haben". She states: "Die AUDRINEHAE (auch in den Varianten AUTHRINE-HAE und AUTRIAHENAE) lassen sich mit an. *auðinn*, ags. *eaden*, as. *odan* 'vom Schicksal bestimmt' und an. *auðna* 'Schicksal, Glück' zusammenstellen. Wenn das verwandte an. *auðr* 'Schicksal, Tod' ursprünglich wirklich 'Gewebe' bedeutete (idg. Wurzel *AUDH), so besitzen wir in den AUDRINEHAE einen Hinweis auf die Möglichkeit des Wirkens der Matronen als Schicksalweberinnen". See Isabella Horn, "Diskussionsbemerkung zu Ikongraphie und Na-men der Matronen" (1987), p. 155f. Christoph Rüger has argued that a men's group called a *curia* was directly associated with each of the many mother-groups in the Rhineland and that their temples were the assembly houses. He points out that Indo-European peoples have constantly linked agriculture and the agonal principle and that such would explain the constant presence of Mercury in such locales. A "männerbundischer Initiationsritus" would be the logical consequence. The trend of his explanation is quite persuasive. If he is correct, then it would mean that the mothers were not just connected with the tribe as a whole but had a special relationship, sanctified by myth and cult, with men's clubs within the tribe. The transition to a warband prophetess might thus be even easier. See Rüger, "Gallisch-Germanische Kurien", pp. 251–60; idem, "Beobachtungen", pp. 18f., 26f.

Good Luck. At Trier, Mercury also appears as a three-headed god in company with the mothers and, on one bronze statuette from Tongres, he is triple phallused.[44] Rosmerta and the mothers appear together as well, a fact which is not surprising since all are fertility goddesses who may carry a staff and predict the future. At Bath, in Britain, the subtle but definite linkage is palpably manifested. Here, Mercury and Rosmerta share a relief with three *genii cucullati* and ram—"both fertility symbols and the former at least linking them directly with the mothers".[45]

In other words, looked at from the perspective of the warlord, the religious basis for an institutional transition is fairly easy and fluid for it does not involve a totally new creation but rather a new emphasis. Mercury was the husband of both the *matres* and Rosmerta and all were linked to Fortuna.[46] But, whereas the mothers were generally tied to a specific locale or group (hence the dedications to *matronis assingenehis*, *matronis mahlinehis*, *aufanibus* and many others), Rosmerta was trans-regional with an international following and was thus best suited to the warlord's purpose. A new means of political legitimation could thus slowly emerge. Mercury and the mothers continue to be worshipped for tribal roots remain important but Mercury and Rosmerta, in one guise or another, could become the supernatural patrons for the extra-tribal warband. Similarly, the matrons of the tribe might continue to predict for their menfolk but a single woman would do so for the warrior sodality.

When the people of the Rhineland called their sibyls "veledas" they were not simply bestowing a Celtic title on a traditional native figure for if the institution of the single prophetess tied to warfare had really originated on the east bank of the Rhine then the likelihood is high that she would also have borne a Germanic

---

Without necessarily sharing the views expressed here, Rüger refers to Mercurius as a combination of Esus/Mercury/Mars/Odin. It is surely significant that the distaff-bearing mothers appear at Trier where, as noted earlier, Mercury, Rosmerta and Esus also come together on another stone. One is again encouraged to think of the Treveri as the transmitters of the more darkly sacrificial and prophetic aspects of the cult later to be linked to Wodan/Odin.

44 Green, *Gods of the Celts*, p. 85; Idem, *Symbol and Image*, p. 194. The tricephalos is certainly to be associated with Mercury. Green notes that at Trier the mothers appear to trample the triple-headed god underfoot and that such action symbolizes his subordination among the Treveri. Whatever the symbolism actually suggests, this view is improbable. The number and nature of Mercury's reliefs and inscriptions in Belgica clearly indicate his dominant status among a wide variety of worshippers. Some dedicants or groups might have wished it to be otherwise, however, in the same way that some might have favored certain aspects of the god over others or have preferred Lenus Mars, Cernunnos or the mothers. Although Mars was popular among the Treveri, for example, Mercury has more representations (12% to 1.5%) and inscriptions (18% to 12.5%). See Wightman, "Pagan Cults", p. 563. Factors such as tribal enmities, politics, progaganda, even personal idiocyncracies, can all play a role in artistic conceptions.

45 Green, *Gods of the Celts*, p. 97.

46 Rüger, "Husband for the Mother Goddesses", pp. 210–19.

title. It is important to remember that the *comitatus* to which she was attached was not an originally Germanic institution whereas that of the tribal sibyls whom she replaced, was. Additional support for this view comes from the evidence regarding Veleda's staff, her "messenger", her act of mediation of conflict in the Celtic fashion and now her proposed association with Rosmerta and Mercury. Outside of the Rhineland, the closest contemporary parallels to Veleda are the Gaulish druids and druidesses while non-contemporary parallels do not lie only in Iceland, as hitherto believed, but rather also in Ireland. Nor may one argue that Veleda represents a unique outlier of Gaulish influence since, aside from Rosmerta and the prophetic ritual of the priestesses of the Cimbri, a wide variety of Celtic goddesses were venerated along the lower Rhine.[47] Viradecdis, worshipped both by soldiers and civilians, is a good example. Five inscriptions to her have been found from Vechten, Birrens, Mainz, Trebur, and Stree-lez Huy. Parts of her altars have been found in De Woerd near Valkenburg and Kestern in the Betuwe.[48] Gutenbrunner identified her as a war goddess since her name corresponds to the Irish *feardhacht*, "manliness", but Stolte conjectures that she may have been responsible for fertility.[49] In recent years, inscriptions to three other Celtic goddess have been found, in Köln and near Alem, Noord-Brabant. The larger implications of this summary are now obvious: in the case of Veleda, it has become awkward to maintain the view that a Celtic title does not suggest the presence of Celtic practice and, in addition, a search for the locus of practice consistently leads to the *comitatus*.

7. MERCURY, ROSMERTA AND A CONCEPT OF RHINELAND KINGSHIP

As soon as one begins to examine the literature on the origins of Wodan one finds that, despite the universal recognition of a close connection with Gaulish Mercury, it is frequently assumed or argued on dubious grounds that he predates Mercury and must have been some kind of *"uralt"* storm demon or leader of the dead.[1] None of these conclusions seem satisfactory or demonstrable. As Karl Helm showed, Wodan was not a common Germanic god and had in fact taken the place of the war god Tiu who continued to be worshipped into the Early Middle Ages.[2] Whereas the name Tiu (*Tiwaz, ON Tyr) is Indo-European, Uoðanaz is, depending upon whose etymology one accepts, either Celtic or Germanic, and while Odin appears in Scandinavian literature as the discoverer of the runes, his name does not appear in the runic alphabet whereas Tiu's does.[3]

47 Stolte, "Religiose Verhältnisse", p. 652f.

48 Ibid., p. 653f. and n. 279.

49 Gutenbrunner, *Germanische Götternamen*, p. 104f.; Stolte, "Religiose Verhältnisse", p. 655.

1 Helm, *Wodan*, pp. 6, 15f.

2 Helm, *Wodan*, p. 7f.; Much, Jankuhn and Lange, *Germania*, pp. 54, 176.

3 de Vries, *Altgermanische Religionsgeschichte* II, p. 21; Turville-Petre, *Myth and Religion*, p. 180f.; Helm, *Wodan*, p. 7f.; Wagner, *Early Celtic Civilization*, pp. 49f., 54f.

Efforts to argue that his name was too holy to mention are utterly unconvincing.[4] A survey of the Roman evidence—brief references to Mercury in Caesar and Tacitus—cannot modify this conclusion. Since Tiu was widely known and his cult long established, it is most likely Tiu to whom Caesar refers in the *Gallic Wars*. The *interpretatio Romana* is notoriously encompassing.

It is only with Tacitus, writing some 150 years later that one begins to find a few tentative indications but even here Helm confidently asserts otherwise for the Rhineland.[5] Nonetheless, that scholars did think that Wodan was worshipped among the Hermunduri (who inhabited the middle Elbe-Saale region) in the first century for Tacitus says in *Annals* 13, 57 that during a war with the Chatti each side vowed to destroy all opponents in the name of Mars and Mercury. Because two gods are called on, he reasons, Mars must be Tiu and Mercury must be Wodan.[6] Although an attractive hypothesis on the surface, this too fails for several reasons. First, because the Germanic peoples worshipped a multitude of gods, we cannot confidently discern the native name for the gods mentioned. Why should we not think of Ing of the Ingaevones, Irmin of the Herminones, the comparable god of the Istaevones or many scores of others now forgotten? Second, while it may not be unlikely that Tiu is one of these gods, we cannot know if two separate gods are actually being referred to. This is the horribly tangled problem of the *interpretatio Romana* which often produces strange hybrids. In Gaul, for example, it is clear that Taranis = Jupiter, but Esus = Mars or Mercury and Teutates = Mercury or Mars.[7] This confusion appears in both monumental and literary sources and directly implicates the same two gods mentioned by Tacitus. No conclusion is possible on this basis. Third, even if one sets aside these objections, the battle in question was fought in the year 58 AD, that is, probably, a minimum of two generations after the establishment of Gaulish Mercury and we cannot tell how far his name or cult-concepts had spread in *Germania libera*. Fourth, since Tacitus published his *Annals* in 116 AD, one can hardly place much credence in his ability to accurately relate the names of the gods called on by the Hermunduri in an obscure battle in a distant place some fifty years earlier. All that can reasonably be deduced from this passage is that Germanic warriors might often vow to completely destroy an opposing group in the name of their god or gods.

The basis for the contrary view—that the Wodan cult derives from Celtic practice centering on Gaulish Mercury—is stronger. Avoiding needless repetition of detail, we may simply note that most of Wodan's major attributes, or motifs associated with him in later sources, are first documented for figures linked with

---

4 Dumézil, "Odin and Tyr", p. 33f. On Odin's rise in the pantheon, see further Stephen P. Schwartz, *Poetry and Law in Germanic Myth* (1973), p. 27f.
5 Helm, *Wodan*, p. 16f.
6 Ibid., p. 18f.
7 Hatt, *Celts and Gallo-Romans*, p. 271.

Gauls, Celtiberians or both. These include: one-eyedness, raven as cult animal, spear-bearing prophet stabbed by spear, sacrifice by hanging and stabbing, disguised appearance, dedication of a hostile force by spear-throw, leadership of a band of warriors sworn to die for him, association with a prophetess with ties to a cult of the dead. These are not minor similarities; they are essential to the character of the deity described and form an immediately recognizable pattern. The mode of transmission has also been indicated and the above-named characteristics can all be directly, or else indirectly but plausibly, related to a Rhineland milieu between Caesar and Tacitus. Even the distinctly Roman attributes of Mercury, petasos and caduceus, reach the Germans by way of the Gaulish monuments.[8]

The inscriptions provide further testimony whose value in this regard does not seem to have been fully utilized. Consider, for example, the dedications to Mercurius Arvernus, Mercurius Arvernorix and Mercurius Rex. All seven of those to the first named and the singlet to the second were found together with two inscriptions to Mercurius Cimbrianus on the Greinberg near Miltenberg (Kr. Würzburg).[9] The presence of so many inscriptions in one place "on Germanic territory" to a god of a Gaulish tribe has caused no little discomfort to those arguing for a purely Germanic Wodan. They have been driven to suggest, as Rudolf Simek does (following after de Vries rather than Gutenbrunner) in the most recent reference I have noted, that "it is not out of the question that with him [Arvernian Mercury] we are dealing with a Germanic deity although the byname then remains unexplained".[10] Stolte is willing to entertain a similar idea.[11] What they all appear to have overlooked is the most obvious reason for the great fame of the god. In book 34, 18 of his *Natural History*, Pliny the Elder, who died in 79 AD, devoted a section to famous colossal statues of his world. He refers, among others, to the Apollo of the Capitol at 45 ft. high and to the huge and greatly admired statue of the sun at Rhodes at 105 ft. high:

> But all the gigantic statues of this class have been beaten in our period by Zenodorus with the Mercury which he made in the community of the Arverni in Gaul; it took him ten years and the sum paid for its making was 40,000,000 sesterces. Having given sufficient proof of his artistic skill in Gaul he was summoned to Rome by Nero, and there made the colossal statue, 106 1/2 ft.

8 Much, Jankuhn and Lange, *Germania*, p. 171f. They add (p. 54) that, as "highest god", Wodan may first have been worshipped in areas bordering on those of the Celts.
9 Gutenbrunner, *Germanische Götternamen*, pp. 52–8. In general, see Bober, "Mercurius Arvernus", pp. 19–46.
10 Simek, *Lexikon*, p. 260. By now, however, the pattern is much clearer for we not only see the Mercury of the Arverni being honored but also note the appearance of Mercurius Hranno with Rosmerta. See below.
11 Stolte, "Religiose Verhältnisee", p. 650.

high, intended to represent that emperor but now, dedicated to the sun after the condemnation of that emperor's crimes, it is an object of awe.[12]

Pliny then goes on to discuss the great skill of Zenodorus.

The Mercury of the Arverni, was depicted as seated on a throne and the actual height of the statue is unknown.[13] Even allowing for a measure of exaggeration in Pliny, however, little doubt exists that it was the greatest work of its type in Europe north of the Alps. Unfortunately, we do not know exactly where the statue was located or what became of it although there is reason to believe that it may have been placed on the summit of Puy-de-Dôme overlooking Clermont.[14] As Thévenot has pointed out, an important reason for building such a gigantic statue would have been to impress the multitudes who would travel to view it. Those who came or told of it would also have passed on news of the cult and customs associated with Gaulish Mercury. One should, doubtless, also imagine the statues which once accompanied the inscriptions on the Greinberg as being smaller copies of that greater model.[15] We can be fairly confident that the Rhinelanders

---

12 H. Rackham, ed. *Pliny. Natural History* (1952), XXXIV, xviii, 45, p. 160f.: verum omnem amplitudinem statuarum eius generis [large bronzes] vicit aetate nostra Zenodorus Mercurio facto in civitate Galliae Arvernis per annos decem HS CCCC manipretii, postquam satis artem, ibi adprobaverat, Romam accitus a Nerone, ubi destinatum illius principis simulacro colossum fecit CVIS pedum in longitudinem qui dicatus Soli venerationi est damnatis sceleribus illius principis. Aside from the fame of their great statue, the Arverni, as Bober notes ("Mercurius Arvernus", p. 28), seem to have been well known in Belgica and Germania inferior. Some seem to have migrated and, apart from possible recruits to the legions stationed there, "it appears that many craftsmen from Aquitania, among the Arverni in particular, shifted their activity to Germania inferior. It is apparant that workers in metal and terra sigillata transferred their ateliers to the flourishing cities of the Lower Rhine, just as the center of the provincial glass industry moved from Lyon to Cologne in the second century. Domestic utensils and sigillata vessels from the region in question—Vechten, Xanten, Cologne, Nijmegen, etc. —are often stamped with the inscriptions, ARVERNI, ARVERNICI or ARVERNICUS". She notes, too, that Auvergne and the Lower Rhineland shared ties "rooted in certain ramifications of Emperor worship". This point is demonstrated more thoroughly by Annalis Leibundgut, "Der 'Traian' von Ottenhusen. Eine neronische Privatapotheose und ihre Beziehungen zum Mercur des Zenodorus" (1984), p. 282f.

13 The most recent study is by Leibundgut, "'Traian' von Ottenhusen", pp. 257–89, who provides an excellent discussion of the statue based on a variety of enthroned Mercury monuments. See also Bober, "Mercurius Arvernus", pp. 19–46.

14 Thévenot, *Divinités et sanctuaires*, p. 93f.; Leibundgut, "'Traian' von Ottenhusen", p. 276f.; Bober, "Mercurius Arvernus", p. 21. de Vries does not discuss Bober's study in his *Altgermanische Religionsgeschichte*. In discussing Mercurius Cimbrianus and Mercurius Arvernorix, both of whom were worshipped on the Greinberg, he states that it is not possible to determine their original affiliation. He wishes, however, to identify Mercurius Cimbrianus with Wodan: "die Verehrung auf einem Berge steht vielleicht mit einem germanischen Wodankult in Einklang, da wir ja mehr Belege dafür haben". He is certainly correct here but it does not help his thesis since this hill-placement is also in imitation of the Arvernian deity (Puy-de-Dôme overlooks much of Clermont) whom Thévenot describes as "dieu des sommets". He provides several examples, including Montmartre of Paris or, among the Lingones, that of Aigu (Côte-d'Or). See *Divinités et sanctuaires*, p. 90f.

15 Leibundgut, "'Traian' von Ottenhusen", p. 278f.; Bober, "Mercurius Arvernus", p. 24f.

knew of Mercury before the sixth decade AD, just as they knew of Mercury and Rosmerta before they appeared on the Mainz column of 66 AD, but the fame of this Arvernian deity probably helped to establish his cult among the Germans as a whole during the first century. Such explanation makes considerably more sense than the vague guesses about a Germanic god named Arvernus for whom there is no shred of evidence. Mercurius Arvernorix and Mercurius Rex are probably best explained on the same basis. Just as a great temple will enhance the status of the god who dwells there, so will a huge statue, larger than any other, suggest that the god depicted is the most king-like of all. Nero certainly felt that way when he ordered a higher statue created for himself, and the Germans must have been even more amazed to hear of the great statue.

While Mercury was never a king in Roman religion he did assume that rank among some tribes of the Gauls and Iberians. Thus, we find a Mercurius Arvernus from the Pays Bas seated on a throne as king of the gods, another enthroned Mercury at Köln and a third from Dampierre in the territory of the Lingones, a people who were noted Mercury cultists and also allies of Civilis.[16] The Mercurius Rex from Nijmegen in the land of the Batavi, on the other hand, documents the borrowing and extension of this conception among Germans of the lower Rhine.[17]

One final inscription, only recently discovered, would seem to confirm the argument. In 1984, in Bornheim-Hemmerich, a small town between Bonn and Köln, a badly fragmented dedication to Mercurius-Hranno was found. It raises to six or seven the number of reliefs and inscriptions discovered in the general area and seems to confirm A. Oxé's suggestion from the turn of the century that a temple to Mercury must have existed somewhere in the locale.[18] The most recent discussion by Gerhard Bauchhenss dates the beginning of this cult to "at least" the second half of the first century.[19] On one relief Mercury appears in company

16 Ibid., pp. 279f., 24f.
17 Simek, *Lexikon*, p. 262f. He states that the title "Mercury the king" "bezieht sich wie die meisten anderen niederrhein. Nennungen des Merkur auf den german . . . was hier durch den Beinamen Rex nur bestätigt wird, denn der röm. Merkur nahm keine so hervorragende Stellung im röm. Pantheon ein, während Wodan/Odin dieser Titel im Rahmen der german. Götterwelt sehr wohl zukommen konnte". Unfortunately, Simek has confused Roman and Gallo-Roman Mercury for it is only the latter who is called king. The pattern is the same as that for Mercurius Arvernorix. Wodan, whose cult did not become widespread until after the Roman period, was not originally a king of the gods. It is not a Roman concept which is here being amplified but a Gallo-Roman concept which is being confirmed. Despite the assertions of Simek and de Vries, there is no evidence whatsoever for the contrary view. With regard to the Batavians, one might wonder if the *summus magistratus* inscription from Ruimel, apparently roughly contemporary with Civilis, might be of some relevance.
18 A. Oxé, "Ein Merkurheiligtum in Sechtem" (1902), pp. 246–51.
19 Bauchhenss, "Mercurius in Bornheim", p. 236. The author notes that the dedications suggest that the Mercury shrine from Bornheim-Sechtem appears "zumindest im 2. und 3. Jahrhundert n. Chr.- vorzugsweise von Frauen besucht worden zu sein". The hypothesis which he offers as explanation—that in the neighboring Celtic areas of Treveri and Mediomatrici, Mercurius Iovanticarus is responsible for the well-being of the young—seems quite reasonable. There may

with a female figure, most likely the goddess Rosmerta. Each originally carried a caduceus. The inscription in question appears on the base of a largely destroyed statue: *Mercurio / Hrannoni / Nigrinia / Titula ex / visu monita / l(ibens) m(erito)*.

As Norbert Wagner points out, the nominative of Mercurio Hrannoni is Mercurius Hranno, a certainly Germanic name.[20] He notes that it appears in an expected mutated form in *Hrolfs saga Kraka* (ch. 23, 30) from about 1400, a reworked version of an earlier account.[21] Here, Odin is mentioned as appearing in the guise of a farmer named Hrani. This appellation is also a modern Icelandic substantive meaning "brutal man", "brawler", or "trouble-maker", all attributes typically ascribed to Odin.[22] The name appears again as that of an apparently North Germanic tribe in the OE poem *Widsith*, a fact which demonstrates that it is many centuries earlier than the saga.[23] In fact, it must ultimately derive from the partially Romanized Celto-Germanic area of the Rhineland. Referring to the brutality component of the divine name Hrani, Wagner concludes as follows:

> This means then that a very remarkable characteristic of the god Odin, hitherto known only from relatively late sources and only for the North, is now confirmed by the existing inscription for a far earlier period for the middle-western part of continental Germania and for the god Wodan/Mercurius. [24]

To this one might only add a slight modification: it is not Roman but Gallo-Roman Mercury who is documented and the evidence already presented for Veleda provides a very close geographic, historical and religious parallel. After all, Mercurius Hranno, Wodan, here appears as the consort of Rosmerta, the Gaulish goddess of prophecy and fertility. It is thereby clear that Germanic speakers, already tied to the Celts by many aspects of material, political and military culture, had certainly borrowed in the religious sphere as well. A Celtic goddess of prophecy is the consort of the god of the *comitatus*. As will be shown in the following section, Rosmerta was also a goddess who distributed drink to rulers as a sign of their right to rule, and who, while doing so, made prophecies about their future.

The warband context of Mercury/Wodan is also fortified by the new find. Despite the huge interval of nearly 1400 years, the saga demonstrates that the institutional background remains the same in essentials. When the Danish king Hrolf first encounters Hrani, he is leading a warband to Uppsala, a famous

---

not, however, as he seems to think, be any conflict between this concept and Wagner's translation of Mercurius Hranno as "Polterer, rauher Mensch, Prahler", to be discussed below. As Rüger has pointed out ("Beobachtungen", p. 27) the concept of fertility (and one might add its associated qualities of health and prosperity) is constantly associated, on the male side, with aggression and conflict. For present purposes, one notes again the probability that it is a Celtic concept of deity which is here displayed.

20 Wagner, "Wodansname", p. 238f.
21 Ibid.   22 Ibid.   23 Ibid.   24 Ibid.

sacrificial site. The god sets three tasks for the followers which only a few can accomplish. The two protagonists meet again on the return journey when Hrani offers weapons to Hrolf. The latter does not accept them, however, and this refusal leads to his downfall. Both these episodes belong to the sphere of the *comitatus*. The first recalls an initiation rite that determines who is the most fit to enter Odin's company. The second, of course, centers on the traditional and binding gift of weapons by which the lord of a warband accepts a new retainer and rewards him. Refusal of these sometimes constituted an insult and so it was interpreted in Hrolf's case. Beowulf was luckier when he accepted the same type of gift from Hrothgar but was not then compelled to join his following. Incidentally, Hrolf recognized that Hrani was Odin since the glowering farmer had only one eye.[25]

One might now recommend that specialists re-examine the evidence which seems to associate Mercury with certain British and Gaulish men's clubs called *curiae*. For various reasons, these groups cannot be identified with the familiar Roman or Romanized municipal organizations of the same name although the coincidence of terminology makes differentiation difficult. In 1934, C.E. Steven explained a British *curia* inscription, the Curia Textoverdorum, by reference to the Irish word *cuire*, "army", and the **cori-* root with tribal and place names such as Coriovallum, Petrucorii, Coriosolites etc.[26] In Kenneth Jackson's view, however, this is a misconception since the -o- to -u- vowel change happened only in Irish from the fifth century and not at all in British or Gaulish.[27] On the other hand, C.B. Rüger's recent investigation of some Gaulish, British and Rhineland inscriptions suggests that some *curiae* may well have been separate men's and women's groups worshipping a god and his female companions, the *matronae*. In his view they would have had both a cultic and social character and, in eastern Gaul and the Rhineland, the god most closely associated with this pattern is Mercury.[28] The inscriptional evidence in this area is especially complex, however, and there is no *necessary* connection between cult-group and warband. Nonetheless, the trend of the evidence now indicates that this direction is a promising one to explore.

Not only was Mercury worshipped as king by the Arverni but Rosmerta was also worshipped as queen. In 1970, a ritually broken vase, dating from the reign of Tiberius, was discovered in a rectangular trench from the necropole of Lezoux

---

25 Gwyn Jones, ed. *King Hrolf and His Companions: Eirik the Red and Other Icelandic Sagas* (1961), pp. 289–306.

26 C.E. Steven, "A Roman Inscription from Beltingham" (1934), pp. 138–45

27 Kenneth Jackson, "On Some Romano-British Place-Names" (1948), pp. 54–8.

28 Rüger, "Gallisch-Germanische Kurien", pp. 251–60; idem, "Beobachtungen", pp. 18f., 26f. Rüger speaks of Mercurius as being actually Esus/Merkur/Mars/Odin. I would prefer to say Lug/Esus/Gallo-Roman Mercury/Wodan but it might not be incorrect to include some influence from a Mars cult. Although I have approached the matter from a different angle, these two studies strike me as being particularly valuable.

(Puy-de-Dôme).[29] When reassembled, it was found to bear a Gaulish dedication in Latin cursive to the *rigani* Rosmerta and has been translated by M. Lejeune as *hoc dicavi Reginae atque Rosmertae*.[30] This is important new evidence of Rosmerta's status since, until recently, it was not at all certain that the Gauls worshipped any goddess as "queen". Rosmerta now seems much more like the liquor-dispensing "sovereignty" goddesses of the insular Celts (especially Medb whom we have already seen seeking prophesies from the seeress Feidelm and of whom more later). The context also confirms again the close connection of Rosmerta with a cult of the dead—a fact which was already emphasized when dealing with the British evidence where Rosmerta's wine-buckets are found in graves. Celtic religious concepts, Gaulish and British, appear to provide the clearest indication of the origins of Wodan's special attributes and associations.

The monumental and inscriptional evidence persuasively corroborates much of the overall argument. The concepts of Mercury as king and Rosmerta as queen had evolved among the Arverni no later than the reign of Augustus (see below). Both the great statue and the *rigani* vase are products of the same belief system in the Puy-de-Dôme region. Although a great many scholars have maintained otherwise, it seems to follow, particularly in light of Mercurius Hranno's connection with "queen" Rosmerta, that the kingship of Mercury theme, found in Batavia as well as the Rhineland, is most probably Gaulish in origin and not Germanic. Among Germanic speakers, on the other hand, even postulating the beginnings of a specific Wodan cult in this period, Wodan as a distinctly Germanic divine figure, cannot yet have been perceived as king for if anyone deserved that honor it would have been the older and better known Tiu. No matter what his status, however, Tiu is unlikely to have played much of a role for the characteristics of one-eyedness (perhaps also reminiscent of magic making) would become attached to Wodan's cult and not that of his rival. Moreover, as far as we know, Tiu was never associated with a goddess of prophecy and fertility. Hence, all evidence tends to indicate that the only extra-tribal king-god available to the warlord and possessed of the requisite qualities was the enthroned Mercurius Arvernus of the Gauls. That is what the Rhineland inscriptions to Mercury have always most clearly suggested. But it was never Mercury alone who should have been considered but rather Mercury and Rosmerta as the supernatural patrons of Civilis and Veleda. As we have seen, a similar type of debate has continually surrounded the figure of Veleda as well but that too has only muddied the waters for it is the conjunction of the figures in the historical Rhenish context of the first century which provides the best aid to understanding. Religion along the Rhine was at least as fluid as the other aspects of culture already examined.

29 A good photo in J.M. Demarolle, "Céramique et religion en Gaule romanie" (1986), plate IV.
30 Lejeune and Marichal, *Textes gaulois*, p. 151f.; Michel Lejeune, "En marge d'une *rígani* gauloise" (1981), p. 29f. See further Jean-Jaques Hatt, "La divinité féminine souveraine chez les Celtes continentaux d'après l'épigraphie gallo-romaine et l'art celtique" (1981), pp. 12–28.

Consider also that the concept of the kingship of Wodan is often thought to be a late one and efforts to relate this attribute to passages in Tacitus have been controversial because of Tiu's common Germanic worship and his patronage of war and warriors. After all, if, as is often asserted, Wodan were originally a storm demon or leader of the dead, how are we to imagine him ending up as king of the gods and usurper of Tiu? The early runic script can be traced to the second or, perhaps, the first century, and still shows Tiu as the god most venerated.[31] What is required, therefore, is a well-founded *specific* explanation for without it we are left only with vague hypotheses and an act of faith. Dumézil tried to provide this by relativising the evidence for Tiu and maximizing that for Wodan but, despite immense learning, his arguments are not persuasive.[32] Whatever may ultimately be said for the Sanskrit evidence, it hardly seems necessary to journey to India when the Rhineland is right next door and the god mentioned in all of the texts is Mercury. By accepting the obvious implications of the inscriptions, on the other hand, we arrive at a completely satisfactory demonstration of the origins of Wodan's kingship—a matter of no small gain for it also validates the arguments for continuity with the Scandinavian texts. Our catalogue on the Celtic side is thereby enriched with another item as well—kingship—and that really places the thesis of direct relationship and assimilation on an even more secure footing.

Nor should it go unremarked that the politico-theological context of the rebellion of 69/70 thereby emerges in clearer focus. Knowing that Civilis and Classicus both wanted to be kings of Gallo-Germans makes it more likely that the concept of Mercurius Rex played a significant role in the revolt. A success on the Batavian side would have produced a one-eyed king with a *comitatus* ruling over regions of Gallia and Germania. Here, I suggest again, is the best piece of evidence for the origin of a Wodan cult: first, because the combination of kingship, one-eyedness and control of a prophetess becomes especially striking when one can securely connect the two to a Germanic leader aware of Mercury and Rosmerta and open to Celtic influence; second, because these conditions create precisely that kind of specificity needed to convincingly close the ethnic gap between Mercury and Wodan and the chronological gap between the classical and early medieval sources; third, because it exactly pinpoints the *origins* of famous Wodanistic attributes in the only area where all the evidence makes sense, the Rhineland.

We may now seek for a higher degree of exactitude by asking if Civilis can be certainly shown to have know of Mercurius Arvernus. Were one to ignore Pliny's

---

31 Klaus Düwel, *Runenkunde* (1983²), p. 19f.; idem, "Runes, Weapons and Jewelry: A Survey of Some of the Oldest Runic Inscriptions" (1981), pp. 69–91; Flowers, "Runes and Magic", pp. 71f., 92f., p. 116, n. 54. Flowers follows de Vries and Dumézil rather than Helm and thus, in my opinion, is misled.

32 Dumézil, "Odin and Tyr", pp. 26–48.

remarks (as does de Vries, for example)[33] one would still be able to make a good case for his knowledge. The evidence of the statue, however, makes it virtually indubitable. We know that Zenodorus was working on Nero's colossus in Rome during the first few years of the sixties. Mercurius Arvernus, on which he had labored for ten years, was completed before that time.[34] News of his great work would have traveled very speedily around Gaul and a Romanized Batavian aristocrat could hardly have avoided hearing of it. He may well have seen it personally. Civilis was a Roman citizen of noble birth with the right to travel in the provinces and it is difficult to believe that he would not have done so. He was in Rome at least once when he was sent in chains to Nero but freed by Galba on Nero's death in 68. This was the year of Julius Vindex's rebellion in which he was joined by the Arverni and we know that Batavian troops helped put it down. Soon after returning home, Civilis went into rebellion himself and began (or continued) looking for support among Gaulish tribes. His grievances were his own but it is not too much to suggest that he was animated by the Gaulish examples and, perhaps, specifically by the Arvernian. Aside from Vindex, might he not have thought as well of Vercingetorix, a prince of the Arverni, Caesar's greatest opponent? As Tacitus makes clear (*Hist.* 4, 54–56) many different Gaulish tribes were considering joining Civilis and so one must accept the idea of at least some degree of carryover from one crisis to the other, even while noting that Civilis had a number of strictly personal reasons for his animosity against the Romans. What better way of gaining support and cementing it once he had it than by a costless emphasis on a common cult for a mixed group of peoples?

As a token of the superiority of this Mercury worship, Civilis could unhesitatingly point to the colossus of the Arverni made famous during the previous decade. One must also emphasize that Civilis and many of his Batavians, who had served for years with the legions, would quite naturally have tended to think in this extra-tribal fashion. They would have been thoroughly aware that it was official Roman policy to directly equate Gaulish Mercury with Jupiter and both with the cult of the emperor.[35] One of the means by which art historians have

33 de Vries does discuss the inscriptions in some detail in *Altgermanische Religionsgeschichte* II, pp. 28–32. Simek, *Lexikon*, p. 260f. does not mention the statue although the connection with the Rheinland inscriptions had already figured prominently in the works of Bober and Thévenot, for example.

34 Pliny states: statuam Arvernorum cum faceret provinciae Dubio Avito praesidente. L. Dubius Avitus was *legatus pro praetore* in Aquitania circa 54 AD. The building of the statue is more fully discussed in Leibundgut, "'Traian' von Ottenhusen", p. 276f.

35 The topic is a large one. See, for example, D. Fishwick, "The Development of Provincial Ruler Worship in the Western Roman Empire" (1978), pp. 1201–1253. A bibliography to 1977 is contained in ANRW 16, 2. Bober notes ("Mercurius Arvernus", p. 31) that the Mercury temple on the Puy-de-Dôme "seems to have been erected during the period of Augustus, at a time when great stress was placed upon uniting the 'barbarians' of the Celtic and Germanic provinces by their participation in the reverence of Rome and the emperor". Lug was closely indentified with Mercury and the first day of August (!) was his great feast. Leibundgut

been able to reconstruct the great Mercurius Arvernus statue, for example, is by reference to several enthroned Rhineland depictions, most notably that from the Mercury-Augustus temple in Köln, first consecrated in the period of the colony's foundation under Claudius.[36] The rationale for this official artistic propaganda—which endowed Augustus with the attributes of Mercury, including the caduceus[37]—was the unification of the provincial peoples through a common participation in the cult of the emperor. Such identification went so far that Rosmerta, Mercury's companion, was also associated with the living emperor in inscriptions.[38] Although only two examples have been found and their dating is uncertain (one dates to around 200), the idea itself is not uncommon in either Roman or Celtic history. Julius Caesar often exploited links with the goddess Venus and initiation to royal rule among the Celts, included marriage to the territorial goddess.[39] In other words, it is not only important to be aware that Civilis knew of the kingship of Mercury theme, it is also highly significant that Rosmerta the "queen" was included in the pattern. Recall that Veleda was a prophetess and Rosmerta a goddess of prophecy. One is thus consistently confronted with supernatural pairings: Mercury/Rosmerta, Augustus/Rosmerta, Wodan/Rosmerta. The first duo appears to be the prototype for the others and, one may also suggest, for legitimation of the warband combination of Civilis/Veleda.

As the present hypothesis seems to become more compelling, the contrary one seems tenable only with difficulty. One would then need to postulate an experienced and educated leader needing allies and described by Tacitus as "naturally politic to a degree rarely found among barbarians", who would yet decline to utilize the most obvious of all tools of statecraft, the closely aligned religious perceptions of all anti-Roman forces. One must remember that Civilis was brought up with both the *interpretatio Gallica* and *Romana* constantly before his eyes. It was the policy of the conquerors to identify the gods of the transalpine peoples with their own in order to weld them into a common loyalty to the *imperium Romanum*. Could the leaders of the proposed *imperium Galliarum* afford to do any less?

("'Traian' von Ottenhusen", pp. 257–89) follows Bober and more thoroughly demonstrates the connection between statue, Jupiter cult and provincial Augustus worship.

36 Leibundgut, "'Traian' von Ottenhusen", p. 279f.

37 Apparently, Augustus was worshipped at Lyon, the town of Lug, under the guise of Mercury. Many of the coins depicting the Ara Lugdunensis show, on the obverse, Augustus carrying Mercury's caduceus. Bober, "Mercurius Arvernus", p. 31. For other links, see Kenneth Scott, "Merkur-Augustus und Horaz C.12". (1928), pp. 15–33; Ludwig Voit München, "Horaz-Merkur-Augustus (zu Hor. C. II. 17. I 10. 12)" (1982), pp. 479–96.

38 Bémont, "Nouveau monument de Rosmerta", pp. 23–44. L. Dubius Avitus was closely allied with the imperial house and his patronage of Zenodorus is likely. In conjunction, now, with the find of the *rigani* vase from the time of Tiberius in the Puy-de-Dôme area, an early connection between Augustus and Rosmerta seems probable.

39 Detailed discussion in the following section.

8. THE INAUGURATION OF THE WARLORD

Aiming for kingship, we may expect that Civilis took an interest in the rituals of kingship and, both on the basis of Rhineland origin and the Mercury/Rosmerta model, it seems reasonable to hold that the rituals would have been familiar to Celts and Germans alike. It might be objected that Civilis did not become king (although we do not know what happened after 70 when he and Classicus fought their last battle against Rome) and hence any question of inauguration rites would not have been raised. This cannot be persuasive, however, since, as will be shown, the liquor ritual had roots among both peoples and since, in the Early Middle Ages at least, it was common to both lords and rulers. Moreover, because Julius Classicus was certainly claiming the prerogatives of kings—donning imperial insignia and demanding oaths to the *imperium Galliarum*—the rituals and protocols of authority probably assumed great significance for both leaders. Indeed, Tacitus makes it clear *inter alia* that the question of who would rule the new empire became a bone of contention between them. In such an atmosphere, we can be quite sure of the topic's pertinence. Let us, therefore, first look at what can be said of the Gaulish rite and then turn to the evidence for that of the Germans, keeping in mind in all cases that while the leaders were more aware of Roman ways their followers had to be courted on the basis of tradition.

As previously discussed, there are very few clues available to the scholar who seeks to establish the nature of the earliest king-making rituals in the Germanic *comitatus* even though it appears obvious that such rites must have existed. From the Anglo-Saxon and Lombard references examined in chapter one, it seems likely that a drinking ritual including a royal naming by the lord's consort or former ruler's wife was central to the *comitatus* in the Early Middle Ages and other documents from a variety of Germanic peoples at different times and places frequently indicate that a feast played a notable and probably a constitutive role in inauguration rituals.[1] The original significance of the female element has been shown by our analysis of the bride's offering of the cup to her future husband in marriage for the gestures of offering, accepting and drinking seem to have been the archetypical method of acknowledging lordship and accepting subordination which easily carried over into the hierarchical family of the warband. This liquor ritual is of considerable antiquity, reaching back to mid La Tène as shown in chapter three. I have further suggested that something like this demonstration of status through first service probably occurred when Civilis was recognized as leader of a rebellion *during a feast* in the sacred groves when he bound those present with "barbarous rites" and oaths and when he, arguably, may have been served by the prophetess.

---

1 Janet Nelson, "Ritual and Reality in the Early Medieval Ordines" (1975), p. 330f.; eadem, "Inauguration Rituals", p. 287. Early Celtic and Germanic references to be discussed below.

Findings in the present chapter have furthered this interpretation. The evidence indicates that Celtic governmental forms and military institutions and techniques had been adopted by neighboring Germanic tribes, that the Wodanistic concept of kingship traditionally associated with the *comitatus* derived from ideas surrounding Gallo-Roman Mercury and that the earliest known monument which can convincingly be associated with Wodan shows him as the Gallo-Roman husband of a Gaulish goddess of prophecy, a queen depicted as the distributor of liquor with attributes of spoon-strainer, mixing bucket, staff and patera. Since Civilis and Veleda can plausibly be linked to this divine pair—for the same reasons that Augustus claimed Mercury's caduceus and Rosmerta—all of the discrete parts of the pattern appear to be present. The question now to be posed is this: can Rosmerta's attributes as prophetess and provider of liquor be persuasively joined to a kingship ritual similar to that later used by Anglo-Saxons and Lombards? Having already seen that a long series of the major traits exhibited by Mercury/Wodan in the Viking Age are traceable to a Rhineland milieu of approximately the first century AD, the prognosis does not seem unfavorable.

Once again, it is convenient to clear the underbrush, so to speak, by making preliminary decisions on several issues. First, would a positive finding for Gaulish kingship ritual have any necessary import for the Germans? A large part of the answer is already known. Wodan, the patron of warband rule, is not yet Germanic! He is Mercurius Hranno of the Rhineland, a composite figure made up of aspects of Lug, Esus and Mercury, and his wife is not Scandinavian Frigg but Rosmerta of the Rhineland and Britain. The process of settling Mercurius Hranno's citizenship had only just begun during the time of Civilis and the kingship he represents is not yet Germanic either but rather Gallo-Roman and Rhenish. Its origins lie in the Auvergne, the same region, as the *rigani* vase attests, where Rosmerta was known as queen and prophetess. Hence, because it is from the hybrid cultural region of the Rhineland that this cult expands, it is reasonable to hold that what the Gauls did in making kings is likely to have had a marked influence on Germanic practice. The god's Germanic name, Hranno, meaning essentially "the brawler", seems especially appropriate to the warband and indicates again that the rise of his cult accompanied the spread of that institution.

Second, the Gaulish king-making rites to be discussed involve a ritual drinking at a feast. May one justifiably regard Civilis as being aware of this? Again, cultural geography suggests that he was. So, too, does his familiarity with Gauls, especially Treveri and Lingones, his own noble descent and his (probable) years of service with Batavian cohorts in Britain. The rituals in question are Celtic with no Roman admixture and hence are likely to have been familiar in the riverine territories for many generations. They are exactly the kind of thing that druids and veledas know about. At this point, however, one might object that Civilis' desire to rule both Gauls and Germans (as Tacitus states) presumes the influence of the Roman idea of *imperium* and thus of a departure from native tradition in favor of Roman-style ceremony.[2] We have seen, for example, that Classicus, the Treveran leader, took up Roman imperial insignia. Some Roman influence was certainly present, therefore, but its extent should not be exaggerated. A certain shock value is inherent in Tacitus' references to the usurpation of Roman symbols and oaths and this would have been absent in any description of comparable native acts. After all, Tacitus wrote for a Mediterranean audience and his references to Germans emphasize their barbarian simplicity. As for the idea of *imperium*, that hardly requires Roman precedent since the Celts had no need to look elsewhere for a concept of multi-tribal authority. That had existed amongst them long before the time of Vercingetorix.[3] Some manipulation of Roman ideas is only to be expected but if we wish to know how a contemporary leader actually appealed to his followers in this milieu, we may simply point to the behavior of Civilis who, despite twenty-five years of Roman service, acted thoroughly according to tradition by letting his hair grow long, conducting meetings in sacred tribal groves under religious auspices, bringing out the war emblems of the tribes and calling to service a prophetess of the Bructeri. At the same time he is ready to apply Roman concepts where they can advance his anti-Roman cause—as when he tries to teach his men the use of Roman siege engines.[4] One sees again, perhaps, why his model was Sertorius, the general who had taught his Celtic followers to fight against the Romans "in Roman fashion" but who had also manipulated native prophetic beliefs and institutions to strengthen his position.

Let us now examine the rituals in question. There are, actually, two which seem appropriate. One involves the recognition of the ruler's chief warrior or champion while the others centers on much the same type of ceremonial actions but creates the king himself. The earliest material which can establish a general pattern derives from Athenaeus and Diodorus Siculus who depend on the lost history of Posidonius.[5] Writing about the feasts of the Gauls, the former has this to say:

2 Such assumptions seem to be implied in, for example, Heinen, *Trier und das Trevererland*, p. 72f.; Von Petrikovits, *Rheinische Geschichte* I, p. 73.
3 Wenskus, *Stammesbildung*, p. 417, Celtillus, father of Vercingetorix, exercised *principatum totius Galliae*. Diviciacus was *totius Galliae potentissimus*. In Britain, one might point to Cassivellaunus. Development of the oppida and high levels of technology (the Romans would borrow some weapons-making techniques from the Gauls) help to provide an economic background.
4 It seems to me that this deduction follows from Moore, *Tacitus. Histories*, IV, 23, 28, 30, pp. 44, 54, 56. Aside from teaching Roman formations and discipline to the tribes of Spain, Plutarch notes that Sertorius undertook "the construction of all sorts of engines of war and the building of triremes" (Perrin, *Plutarch* VIII "Sertorius" VI, 5, p. 18f.). Such abilities greatly impressed the barbarians who had turned to Sertorius because they "were lacking in a commander of great reputation and experience as they faced the terror of Roman arms". In later sources, both Lug and Wodan are described as "master of all arts". Again, a strong likelihood of linkage would seem to exist. Of course, this is not to maintain that peoples might not endow their gods with such qualities aside from any mundane exemplar. In the case of Wodan, however, there is so much contrary evidence that is closely related to the *comitatus* and anti-Roman warfare that it is impossible to interpret as coincidence.
5 See Tierney, "Celtic Ethnography", pp. 189–275.

When a large number dine together they sit around in a circle with the most influential man in the centre, like the leader of the chorus, whether he surpasses the others in warlike skill, or nobility of family, or wealth. Beside him sits the host and next on either side the others in order of distinction. Their shieldsmen stand behind them while spearsmen are seated in a circle on the opposite side and feast in common like their lords. The servers bear around the drink in terra cotta or silver jars like spouted cups . . . . The drink of the wealthy classes is wine imported from Italy or from the territory of Marseilles. This is unadulterated but sometimes a little water is added. The lower classes drink wheaten beer prepared with honey, but most people drink it plain. It is called *corma*. They use a common cup, drinking a little at a time, not more than a mouthful, but they do it rather frequently. The slave serves the cup towards the right, (not) towards the left. That is the method of service. In the same way they do reverence to the gods, turning towards the right.

Athenaeus then refers to the conflicts which often occur at these festal assemblies:

Posidonius, in the twenty-third book of his *Histories*, says: 'The Celts some-times engage in single combat at dinner. Assembling in arms they engage in a mock battle-drill, and mutual thrust-and-parry, but sometimes wounds are inflicted, and the irritation caused by this may lead even to the slaying of the opponent' unless the bystanders hold them back.' 'And in former times,' he says, 'when the hindquarters were served up the bravest hero took the thigh piece, and if another man claimed it they stood up and fought in single combat to the death.'[6]

Diodorus adds a few variant details:

At their meals they are served by their youngest grown-up children, both boys and girls. Beside them are hearths blazing with fire, with cauldrons and spits containing large pieces of meat. Brave warriors they honour with the finest portions of the meat, just as Homer introduces Ajax, honoured by the chief-tains, when he conquered Hector in single combat: 'He honoured Ajax with the full-length chine'. . . . At dinner they are wont to be moved by chance remarks to wordy disputes, and, after a challenge, to fight in single combat, regarding their lives as naught. . . .[7]

A problem immediately arises. It is noticeable that these passages do not refer specifically or uniquely to a woman as cup-bearer at the feast. Athenaeus refers to "servers" in general, which might seem to suggest both sexes and Diodorus

6 Ibid., p. 247.
7 Ibid., p. 250.

refers to "boys and girls" which seems to confirm the point. Nevertheless, these generalized descriptions are difficult to accept as accurate for all occasions. The analysis of pre-Roman Gaulish utensil design and the associated artistic motifs clearly indicate that a profoundly ritualistic religious significance attached to festal vessels and to the gatherings at which they appeared.[8] Such is not easy to reconcile with the idea of miscellaneous servers for that tends to reduce the ceremonial component which we know to have otherwise been so pronounced. Other kinds of iconographic evidence, like the Rosmerta monuments with patera and vat, for example, indicate that the act of serving liquor was an activity predominantly connected with females. To go further back, the transalpine situla of the late Hallstatt period often depict musical and drinking scenes where women appear as the bearer of cups and bowls.[9]

If we then move forward into the Early Middle Ages, we find the same equation to be true since Celtic and Germanic societies consistently linked women and liquor service.[10] The name of the Irish fertility goddess Medb, for example, means either "the intoxicated one" or "the one who intoxicates".[11] The latter is more likely for Medb is one of the goddesses who offers drink and sexual favors to candidates for kingship. The connection between kingship and liquor service is so constant and ubiquitous that literary puns could be made in the sources on the words *laith*, "drink" and *flaith*, "sovereignty".[12] An essential parallel with Germanic tradition lies in the fact that Medb's liquor is a preliminary to marriage which is itself an inauguration to kingship. Thus, in citing the fourth century BC

8 Venceslas Kruta, "Le corail, le vin et l'arbre de vie: Observations sur l'art et la religion des Celts du Ve au Ier siècle avant J.-C" (1986), p. 18f.

9 The Hallstatt culture, of course, is the direct ancestor of La Tène. See Filip, *Celtic Civilization*, pp. 28–59. Speaking of these warrior/women drinking scenes and their material remains, Kossack notes ("Trinkgeschirr", p. 103) that "hier eine soziale Sonderung, ihren Niederschlag gefunden habe und dass es sich bei diesen Kriegern um eine Gruppe handeln müsse, die nicht nur durch übereinstimmende Vorstellungen vom Werte 'ritterlichen' Daseins zusammengehalten wurde, sondern der darüber hinaus noch über weite Entfernungen hinweg eine spezielle Trinksitte gemeinsam war". Such practices seem to have passed to the Celts and thence to the Germans. The latter, during the Hallstatt period, lacked the wealth and rich vessels for emulation. Many depictions contained in Otto-Herman Frey, *Die Situla in Providence (Rhode Island). Ein Beitrag zur Situlenkunst des Osthallstattkreises* (1962).

10 Meissner, *Kenningar*, p. 401; Einarsson, "Old English *Beot*", p. 108ff. In *Tochmarc Étaíne*, "The Wooing of Etain", for example, a daughter who resembles her mother is substituted for her but recognized because she did not pour out drink in the same way. See Francis John Byrne, *Irish Kings and High-Kings* (1973), p. 61.; T.F. O'Rahilly, "On the Origin of the Names Érainn and Ériu" (1943), pp. 7–28.

11 T. O Maille, "Medb Cruachna" (1927/28), pp. 129–46; Rudolf Thurneyson, "Göttin Medb?" (1929), pp. 108–10; Georges Dumézil, *The Destiny of a King* (1973), pp. 81–99; Josef Weisweiler, *Heimat und Herrschaft: Wirkung und Ursprung eines irischen Mythos* (1943), p. 112f. Medb is from **medhua*, feminine of the adjective **medhuo-* from whence Welsh *meddw*, "drunk".

12 Myles Dillon, *The Cycles of the Kings* (1946), p. 13 and n. 1.

text on Petta's cup-giving to Euxenos in southern Gaul,[13] it was possible to point to an identical marriage custom among Lombards, Anglo-Saxons and Danes of a far later period when that rite was also intimately related to kingship. Recall also the by-play to which it gave rise—the cup and hand-touching or kissing between Authari and Theudelinda, Theudelinda and Agilulf, or between Erik and the king's sister at Frothi's court. Compare this with a Middle Irish account of Cú Chulainn's combat with the champion Fer Díad in which Medb's daughter, Findabair, "used to lay her hand on every goblet and every cup for Fer Díad" as a sign that he was "her beloved and chosen wooer".[14] Remove the names from these episodes and it would be impossible to say which culture, Celtic or Germanic, was being discussed. In each important case, however, a woman acts as server.

A recent paper by Wolfgang Meid on "popular" Gallo-Latin inscriptions sheds further light on the woman-drink association.[15] These brief messages are found on *pesons de fuseau*, spindle whorls from northeastern Gaul of the third or fourth century AD and are of great interest to linguists because they document the existence of a certain kind of mixed Gaulish-Latin jargon.[16] They are always directed to girls or women and grammatically are in the form of an imperative. Thus, Latin examples often begin with *salve, ave vale* or *accede*, "come here". The speaker sometimes hints at his intentions:

ave domina sitiio[17]

If he "thirsts", however, it is not for drink or just for drink alone. As Meid remarks, all of these many inscriptions are part of the ritual of amorous games between the sexes.[18] They frequently refer to liquor:

nata vimpi	*curmi da*
"Pretty girl,	give beer".
nata vimpi	*pota vi(nu)m*
"Pretty girl,	drink wine".

---

13 The Irish ritual of king making was known, significantly, as *banais rigi*, "wedding feast of kinship". A wedding ceremony, in which the bride handed the bridegroom a cup of liquor, was called *banais* or *banfhess*, literally "wife-feast". Petta's cup-giving is discussed by Murphy in his review of Zwicker's *Fontes* (1937), p. 143f.; O'Rahilly, "Érainn and Ériu", p. 14f.
14 Murphy, "Review", p. 144.
15 Wolfgang Meid, "Gallisch oder Lateinisch? Soziolinguistische und andere Bemerkungen zu populären gallo-lateinischen Inschriften" (1983), pp. 1019–1044.
16 Karl Schmidt, "Keltisch-lateinische Sprachkontakte im römischen Gallien der Kaiserzeit" (1983), p. 1009; Polomé, "Linguistic Situation", p. 529f.
17 Meid, "Gallisch oder Lateinisch", p. 1030.
18 Ibid., pp. 1035, 1043.

Others are more outspokenly erotic:

> geneta   vis cara
> "Pretty girl,   do you want to?"

Some can be obscene.

These inscriptions show that, at a popular level of expression, the Gauls also associated women and liquor service. They point to a geographic area of special interest. While *vimp-* appears widely in personal names of the frontier provinces of Gallia Belgica, Germania Inferior and Superior, it is infrequent or non-existent in the core areas of Gaul.[19] Finally, in view of the Celtic/Germanic linkage between the giving of drink and sexual favor or marriage, the erotic aspect of the inscriptions is worth emphasizing. It is quite explicit, even in those apparently neutral messages which might be though susceptible to other interpretations. The reasons lies in the objects themselves. The whorl or weight is in the form of a ring which is fitted over the pencil-like weaving spindle. The metaphorical association, documented also by the etymology of a number of words in IE languages which refer to spinning and twisting, is simply this: spindle = *membrum virile.*[20]

Here too, perhaps, one finds the answer to other questions. Attention was earlier drawn to a series of sixth century bracteates depicting a large breasted goddess carrying what appears to be a weaving beam.[21] The attribute indicates that she is a prophetess but the lush figure, as well as a probable connection with Odin's wife, Frigg, suggests fertility. How does one get from one to the other, from weaving to fertility?

According to the evidence now assembled, we must not only posit a link between weaving tools and prophecy but also between the same tools and sexuality. This opens a fascinating perspective on the thought-world of archaic societies and helps to explain some hitherto confusing conjunctions. One thinks of the cult of the mothers, for example, where members of a triad might carry spindle, distaff, goblet or napkin, as well as fruit.[22] They are generally associated

19 Ibid., p. 1033, n. 38.
20 Ibid., p. 1043 and n. 68. As Meid notes, these spindle whorls belong in the area of the weaving hut. He suspects "das mit diesen Objekten gewisse Spielchen getrieben wurden, etwa amouröse Pfänderspiele oder Liebesorakel". The pattern in archaic thinking is always weaving/prophecy, sexuality, liquor. Recall, again, the roughly contemporary Spanish altar to Mercurius Colualis in which the identifying by-name is to be compared to IE *kuel-*, "to turn", and Latin *colus*, "spindle".
21 See section one of the present chapter.
22 See part six, n. 43. At the beginning of the present section, attention was called to the great popularity of the cult of the mothers among soldiers in the Rhineland and Britain. The psychological explanation of *Mutterbindung* is surely partly right but it may be suggested that notions of prophecy (especially important for soldiers concerned with survival and victory), sexuality and drunkenness (recall *Beowulf*'s *druncne dryhtguman*) were even more emphatically involved. This combination is practically irresistable for any company of men, especially one removed from the restraints of kin-group relationships and serving in foreign areas. Occasional

with fertility and child-care but, on the basis of the considerations offered here, one can now understand why the association was made in the first place. We may therefore reiterate an argument made constantly in this study—that prophecy, sexuality and the offering of liquor were all part of the same mental construct for Celts and, perhaps somewhat later, for Germans. As is well known, Celtic goddesses could always be depicted in triplicate and such necessarily applies to Rosmerta.[23] It also follows that the cult of the mothers encouraged the same kind of association between drink-offering and prophecy that is established for Rosmerta alone. The significance of the ritual act, therefore, must have been widely understood among peoples living in the Rhine-Weser region during the time of Civilis. As corollary, the present interpretation of Veleda and Wealhtheow must also be involved. Prophetic ability is established for the former and a royal liquor offering along with prophetic-like utterances for the latter. We must now recognize that both types of behavior were originally inseparably related. That is why we find distaffs and peculiar kinds of cultic drinking vessels in women's graves from Hallstatt through the Early Middle Ages. The decline of an explicit linkage among Anglo-Saxons seems apparent by the time of the composition of *Beowulf* but one might need to allow for some Christian-influenced understatement since the clues are still fairly easily recognizable once the basic conceptual pattern is exposed. Unfortunately, the Germanic side of the whole evidence is less clear. Nonetheless, Meid can refer to an OHG analogue copied into a St. Gallen manuscript:

> *ue ueru taz ist spiz*
> *taz santa tir tin fredel ce minnon*
> *ue ueru* that is spear-like
> it was sent by your companion as an offering.

As he observes, "this statement may also originally have appeared on a pointed object that functioned as a declaration of love".[24]

Evidence like this suggests that Mediterranean writers did not always explain, or did not always understand, the archaic thought-world associated with drink and festal assemblies. Both Athenaeus and Diodorus are citing a third work and their remarks are slightly divergent. They may simply have compressed the material that they drew on or else have chosen to speak in a general way about what, to classical commentators, might have seemed an unimportant detail irrelevant to the picturesque scenario. On the other hand, it may be that some distinction should be made as to the type of feast in the Posidonius citations since not all will be equally formal or ceremonial in nature. More likely, perhaps, one

---

attempts to associate such cults with long discredited concepts of matriarchy are simply naive and are usually in inverse proportion to the evidence.

23 The best discussion in Ross, *Pagan Celtic Britain*, pp. 205–33. See also Green, *Symbol and Image*, pp. 169–205; Horn, "Bilddenkmaler des Matronenkultes", 44f.

24 Meid, "Gallisch oder Lateinisch", p. 1044.

should think of certain periods during gatherings when greater formality was expected or enforced. This was the case in *Beowulf*, for example, where ll. 1160–1162 refer to "cup-bearers" or "stewards" pouring wine from wondrous vessels until Wealhtheow appeared wearing her golden diadem. At that point, all scurrying-about stopped while the queen presented the cup to her husband and named him as lord and ruler.[25] The analogy with the classical citations seems rather close here for, were it not for the Wealhtheow passages and *Maxims I*, we would constantly think of cup-bearers in general and never know about the queen's ritual at all. Hence, the great burden of evidence indicates that certain high-status women did indeed play a crucial ritual role as bearers of liquor. The Petta/Euxenos episode demonstrates that a key aspect of the tradition—the bridal offering of cup to husband—was already established in Gaul by the fourth century BC and, given what we now know, it is possible to recognize that such ritual illustrates the underlying patterns by which concepts of precedence and authority were articulated in royal halls. That is one reason why the Irish kingship rite is called the "marriage-feast of kingship". The descriptions drawn from Posidonius are accurate as far as they go but it is clear that the reportage is impressionistic; some parts of the pattern are mentioned, others are not. Further discussion below will corroborate this view.

One might now pause for a moment, however, to parenthetically note the accumulation of what is really a formidable list of Celto-Germanic cultural identifications in the areas discussed. These include, but are not confined to, a series of ideas surrounding women, liquor and cups, sexuality, fertility, weaving tools and staffs, contentions at feasts, hierarchy of seating and first serving of a ruler. Some of these conventions, as in the case of cups, are so intimate as to reach the profound level of innuendo. But the unpersuaded skeptic might still justifiably ask if some of these are not more or less unsurprising conjunctions in view of the similar lifestyle of the peoples concerned. In other words, would it not be equally valid to interpret the cultural similarities as more or less generic responses to comparable challenges rather than as legacies of one group to the other? The answer is that the lifestyles of the two cultures did not really become strictly comparable until late La Tène. Before then, the tribes of Germania lived a very simple existence indeed, as many archaeologists have noted. Moreover, the generic approach cannot explain the striking extent of the documentable borrowing pattern. Consider the cases of inhumation burial, weapons burial, the adoption of the *comitatus* (governmental forms) or the pattern of imitation in weaponry, religion, technology, naming practices and linguistic terms. As soon as one begins to compile such a list, the woeful inadequacy of any "generic" argument becomes clear. Hence, the similar lifestyle is not something that developed out of parallel evolution. It is the

25 This was the case also at the feast described in ll. 607–41. Cf. l. 2014f. where queen, cup-bearers and daughter are mentioned and a special emotional bond implied between the queen's young daughter and the veteran warriors.

result of a historical process which took place in several different regions of central Europe in the mid and late La Tène where two cultures, at least, met, married and evolved in similar ways since one borrowed the forms and institutions of the other. In the case of the Germani Cisrhenani, for example, they not only crossed and settled west of the river, they also adopted Gaulish political forms and probably the Gaulish language.[26] There is nothing accidental here! The origins of some of these cultural concepts can be associated with Mediterranean trade reaching north of the Alps in the late Hallstatt period and continuing thereafter. Subsequent social and political transformations last for centuries among the Celts but do not affect Germanic peoples until relatively late in prehistory as the archaeological evidence shows.

We may now return to the central argument. In the passages cited from Posidonius, one notes many of the elements and motifs earlier described for Germanic culture—most notably the jockeying for warband status mentioned by Tacitus and the *Beowulf* poet which frequently led to woundings and killings. We know that this was intimately related to the hierarchical pattern of the liquor service, one rationale for which is probably revealed by the remark that the circular passage of the cup follows the same pattern as in the worship of the gods. This passion for public status finds an especially noteworthy outlet in the combats to determine the "bravest hero" who will receive the honored portion of the meat, a custom which, as Diodorus acutely noted, was also typical of early Greek warrior society (where, incidentally, it can also be associated with warbands). One expects, naturally, the provision of liquor for the best warrior to follow a similar precedence pattern and one would wish to know more about it. Although the classical sources convey little further about the "champion's portion", those of the insular Celts do so frequently. It is a common motif of the early medieval Irish sagas which, Jackson maintains for *Táin Bó Cúailnge*, often faithfully reflect the tradition of the continent and offer an invaluable "window on the Iron Age".[27] As

26 A serious problem in the study of Germanic religion is the apparent unwillingness of specialists to seriously come to grips with the implications of large-scale cultural borrowing for much of the La Tène period. Polomé's suggestion ("Germanentum und religiöse Vorstellungen" [1986], p. 295) should be examined in depth: "Weiter sollte man bei der Besprechung der ältesten Formen der germanischen Religion auch an mögliche Verbindungen mit der keltischen Welt denken. Wenn die Archäologen, die behaupten, dass das Germanentum unter dem Einfluss der keltischen Eisenzeitkultur als Katalysator in der Jastrow-Kultur als selbständige Kultur zur Reife gekommen ist, recht haben, dann lohnt es sich vielleicht, gewisse Thesen Birkhans neu zu untersuchen". Over the past generations, archaeologists have demonstrated many more connections than have been discussed here. See further the remarks of Reichert, "Problem der rechtrheinischen Germanen", p. 572.

27 The phrase was made popular by Jackson in his famous lecture: *The Oldest Irish Tradition: A Window on the Iron Age* (1964), p. 155. The "champion's portion" is discussed on pp. 21f., 38. Jackson argued that the "account of the life and civilization depicted in the Ulster tales is demonstrably older than the fifth century and extraordinarily similar to that of the Gauls and Britons in the couple of centuries before they were absorbed by Rome; and that the reason for

Wolfgang Meid has expressed it: "The relationships (in early medieval) Ireland
. . . may be regarded as typical of older Celts and, in the broader sphere, of
Indo-European earlier cultures".[28] Although recent criticism makes these views
seem overly strong in some cases, they continue to be sustainable in the area of
kingship, always a repository for an early culture's mythic impulse.

In reviewing this insular literature one learns several important details unknown or omitted in the impressionistic classical travelogues. Most important are
the facts that the best warrior occupied the "champion's seat", *fochla feindida*,[29]
by virtue of his right to the *curadmir*, the "champion's portion" of the meat,[30] and
also that the symbol of his status was a special cup from which he drank the liquor
of the feast. Most likely, the presenter of the cup was always a woman. That was
certainly the case amongst the Irish and Welsh.

The most famous tale which centers on the *curadmir* motif is the ninth century
Fled Bricrend, "Bricriu's Feast", in which several warriors claim the same honor
and queen Medb uses much the same language in presenting the champion's cup
to each of them as a ruse in order to prevent violence. I cite only the first instance:

> "Welcome! You deserve the champion's portion, and so we make you king over
> the warriors of Eriu from this time forth, and we give you the champion's
> portion and this bronze cup, with a bird of white gold at the bottom, to bear
> before all as a token of our judgement. Let no one see it until you appear in
> Conchobar's Craebruad [Red Branch hall] at the end of the day, and then,
> when the champion's portion is set out, display your cup to the chiefs of Ulaid.
> The champion's portion will be yours, and no Ulaid warrior will challenge you
> for it, for your cup will be a token of recognition to the Ulaid". Then the cup,
> filled with undiluted wine, was given to Loégaire, and there, in the center of
> the royal house, he drained it at a swallow. 'Now yours is the feast of a
> champion,' said Medb. . . .[31]

this is that Gauls, Britons and Irish were all living in cultures which were local expressions of a
Celtic Early Iron Age whose common roots lay in Gaul in the third century BC". Modification
of some of Jackson's views may be necessary in some areas. See J.P. Mallory, "Silver in the Ulster
Cycle of Tales". N.B Aitchison's remark ("The Ulster Cycle: Heroic Image and Historical
Reality" [1987], p. 91) that the champion's portion does not indicate Gaulish-Irish similiarity
but "is what might be expected among the members of a warrior aristocracy within almost any
barbarian society" is simply incorrect. He does not state what other barbarian societies he has
in mind. The champion's portion is not a common motif in Germanic literature, for instance,
and the citation of the Greek example alone is insufficient proof of universality.

28 This view is discussed more fully in Christian J. Guyonvarc'h and Françoise Le Roux-Guyon-
    varc'h, "Remarques sur la Religion Gallo-Romaine" (1986), pp. 423–55.
29 O'Leary, "Contention at Feasts", p. 116f. and n. 8. The author also draws attention to the
    remarks of Posidonius.
30 Ibid. See further William Sayers, "Conall's Welcome to Cet in the Old Irish *Scela Mucce Meic
    Datho*" (1982), pp. 100–8; Anne O'Sullivan, "Verses on Honorific Portions" (1968), pp. 118–23;
    Mac Cana, "Conservation and Innovation", p. 89f.
31 Henderson, ed. *Fled Bricrend*, p. 58f. I cite from the translation of Jeffrey Gantz, *Early Irish
    Myths and Sagas* (1984), p. 239.

It is the presentation of the cup, then, and the drinking of the "undiluted wine" in the "royal house" which is an important part of the champion's accession ritual and, just as in *Beowulf*, the giving of the name of (in this case metaphorical) "king" accompanies the drink.[32] One might note, incidentally, that in the same saga the king strikes his "silver scepter" against a pillar as a signal for the warriors to sit and that the champion's wife gains precedence when her husband does as she is then allowed to be the first of the women who "enter the drinking house".

Within the present context the most significant aspect of the passage cited is the further demonstration of a relationship between the offering of a cup of liquor by a queen and the bestowal of the royal title of "king". Since this is definitely a warrior's ritual, however, and since the warlord is perceived as the best of warriors, as the "champion" in fact, then it would seem to be a peculiarly appropriate ritual for a *comitatus* in which the leader establishes himself because of ability and not birth and in which his reputation is the crucial spur to recruitment.

At this point, one must be careful to distinguish between institutions. Early medieval Celtic society differed from that of the Germans in one crucial way: whereas a more tightly organized form of hierarchical organization developed out of warband kingship on the continent, Irish kingship continued to center on the tribe and the *dux* never *consistently* emerged to replace the sacral *rex*.[33] On the other hand, although to my knowledge Celticists have not commented on the relationship, the tales focussing on the champion's portion do indicate that a kind of warband leader called a "king" did develop. While remaining subordinate to the tribal king, he must nonetheless have exercised considerable influence over the warriors of the tribe for his inauguration parallels that of the ruler and is conducted by the same goddess. Warbands were probably more important in early Irish society than has often been thought and more research on this topic, of the kind conducted by Sharpe and Mc Cone, is urgently needed.

The champion was inaugurated by Medb who poured the liquor into the cup which served as a "token of recognition" for the warriors of the Ulaid. In the sagas she is often described as a queen but it is abundantly clear that she is a

---

32 Aside from cup-offering and contention about precedence, there is a further interesting analogue to *Beowulf* in that the hero who wins the contest, Cu Chulaind, must guard the hall during the night against monsters impervious to sword strokes. The beheading sequence from this tale appears again in *Sir Gawain and the Green Knight*. See David Dumville, "*Beowulf* and the Celtic World: The Use of Evidence" (1981), pp. 109–60.

33 For the Germanic pattern, see Alexander Demandt, "Die Anfänge der Staatenbildung bei den Germanen" (1980), pp. 265–91 with bibliography. Much work remains to be done for the Celts. See, however, Byrne, Tribes and Tribalism pp. 128–71; Sharpe, "Hiberno-Latin *Laicus*", pp. 75–92; Enright, *Iona, Tara and Soissons*, p. 49f.

goddess *and a prophetess* who possesses the power to grant kingship.[34] She normally appears in tales that involve conflict over tribal rule. A prominent motif in many of these is a hunt for a doe or deer. The deer is the goddesses' animal and its capture by one of the candidates demonstrates her favor and thus the candidate's right to govern.[35] This motif of possession of the prophetic goddesses' deer already appears in the career of Sertorius although neither Plutarch nor Appian fully understand the rationale and cannot, therefore, connect it with kingship except in an indirect manner (although they do relate it to prophecy). Nonetheless that is why the white deer is held in such awe and why it inspires such devotion among the Celtiberian tribesmen. The key fact here is the followers' belief that it was sent by a goddess—remember that Sertorius claimed it as a gift of Diana —who must therefore have imparted to Sertorius the right to command along with knowledge of the future. This was a chief reason why Sertorius "tried to give the doe a religious importance". For the Celts, a claim to command, a relationship with a goddess and possession of her animal *always* meant kingship.

This finding is significant for a number of reasons: first, it demonstrates that it is both correct and necessary to draw on prominent aspects of early medieval insular material to illuminate Celtic traditions on the continent.[36] Second, the religious basis for Sertorius' leadership of Celtiberian followers, misunderstood by Plutarch and Appian, is thereby explained. Whatever Romans believed, the rationale noted above was the Celtiberian view—one which Sertorius was fully capable of manipulating. Again we see why he was so appropriate a model for Civilis. Whereas Celtiberians proclaimed that Sertorius was Hannibal returned to them (Plutarch was surely right to see the canny general's own hand involved), the third one-eyed warlord did the same once removed for he needed the mythic model at least as much. Not only was he fighting the Romans but he was seeking to create a multi-tribal kingship which included both Gauls and Germans of the Rhineland zone. On the politico-religious front, the weapons which he brought to bear—Mercurius Rex, Veleda and Sertorius—were all exceptionally well chosen for each had roots, or had achieved popular veneration, amongst at least two of the peoples concerned. Tacitus' statements of his political acuteness, his

34 See the works cited in note 11. The most thorough discussion is by Proinsias Mac Cana, "Aspects of the Theme of King and Goddess in Irish Literature" (1955/6), pp. 76–114, 356–413 and, in a subsequent volume, pp. 59–65. For early Britain, see T.M. Charles-Edwards, "Native Political Organization in Roman Britain and the Origin of MW *brenhin*" (1974), p. 35–45; John T. Koch, "A Welsh Window on the Iron Age: Manawydan, Mandubracios" (1987), p. 34f.

35 E. Gwynn, *The Metrical Dindschenchas* (1935), pp. 134–43; R. Bromwich, "Celtic Dynastic Themes and the Breton Lays" (1961), p. 445f.; Enright, *Iona, Tara and Soissons*, p. 36f.; idem, "The Sutton Hoo Whetstone Sceptre: A Study in Iconography and Cultural Milieu" (1983), p. 130f.

36 See, for example, Guyonvarc'h and Le Roux-Guyonvarc'h, "Remarques sur la Religion Gallo-Romaine", pp. 423–55; Mac Cana, *Celtic Mythology*, pp. 20–53.

knowledge and his goals seem perfectly fitting. Finally, it now seems even more likely that the Batavian's use of a prophetess is properly comparable to Sertorius' device of a prophetic deer. Both serve the same purpose. Of course this is not to claim that Civilis invented the stratagem of making a soothsayer work for him. Such is too common among ancient rulers to require comment. In view of the evidence adduced, however, we should now regard his special *elevation* and dispute-settling use of a prophetess as a device which had roots both in Gaulish practice and in the legend of Sertorius. Remember that Civilis wished to be regarded as Sertorius reborn and it is, therefore, undeniable that the one-eyed Sabine general with his devoted Celtic warband played a crucially important role in his religious propaganda and military efforts. Civilis probably knew of the white doe; he probably also knew, as both Plutarch and Appian remarked, that the animal was difficult to control. He solved the problem by picking, amongst the occasional veledas of the countryside with reputations for second sight, a maiden of the Bructeri who was best for his purpose. In doing so, he appears, as far as the sources can inform us, to have established the warlord/prophetess model of the *comitatus* that would be copied in subsequent centuries.

Although Medb is the most famous of the "sovereignty" goddesses in Celtic literature, she is only one of many very closely related figures who populate the female pantheon in Irish, Welsh and British sources.[37] Broad common denominators generally include dispensation of drink, promotion of fertility and bestowal of kingship, often in conjunction with capture of a sacred animal, usually a deer. Similarly, many are connected with springs, rivers or lakes.[38] The Gaulish goddesses, insofar as one can determine original associations through art, archaeology and literature, do not differ very much from this pattern. The nature and characteristics of the goddess Epona, for example, are universally recognized as having their clearest reflection and explanation in insular texts.[39] Most important for the present argument, however, is the goddess Rosmerta who has no place in a Mediterranean milieu. In classical religion, Mercury is not a king-god and has no divine consort. In eastern Gaul and the Rhineland, on the other hand, he is an enthroned god of kingship who frequently appears in company with a goddess of prophecy, fortune and fertility, who carries a patera, or, in Britain, is depicted with bucket or vat. In both Gaul and Britain, this goddess also has links with a cult of the dead. Such a pattern is hardly explainable from a classical background but perfectly fits the pan-Celtic kingship theme. A further noteworthy example of that fit may now be offered.

The concept of the drink-giving prophetess of kingship is well illustrated in two related Irish texts of great interest. The first is of the late ninth century and

---

37 See Mac Cana as in note 34; Hatt, "Divinité féminine souveraine", pp. 12–28.
38 Green, *Symbol and Image*, pp. 155–64.
39 See, most recently, Laura Oaks, "The Goddess Epona: Concepts of Sovereignty in a Changing Landscape" (1986), pp. 77–83.

the second of the late seventh. *Baile in Scáil*, the "Phantom's Ecstasy", purports to be a prophecy uttered by the god Lug before king Conn of Tara. Having been transported to an otherworld dwelling, Conn and his druids and poets encounter a *scál*, a "phantom", and a woman called the "sovereignty of Ireland". It is Lug who directs the goddess to distribute drink to kings:

> They then went into the house, and they saw a young woman in the house with a diadem of gold upon her head; a silver kieve (vat) with hoops of gold by her, and it full of red ale; a golden can [*escra*] on its edge; a golden cup at its mouth. They saw the *Scál* himself in the house before them, in his king's seat . . . . "Lug, son of Edlenn, son of Tighernmas, is my name. What I have come for is, to reveal to thee the life of thine own sovereignty, and of every sovereign who shall be in Tara." And the maiden who was in the house before them was the sovereignty of Erinn forever.
>
> It was this maiden who gave the two articles to Conn, namely, an ox-rib and a hog-rib . . . . When the maiden came to distribute the drink, she said to them: 'Who shall this bowl be given to?' The *Scál* answered, that every sovereign from Conn down forever should be named. They went from out of the shadow of the *Scál* . . . . The kieve was left with Conn, and the golden *escra* and the bowl.[40]

The remainder of the text is a recitation of a dialogue between the woman of sovereignty and the phantom. She repeatedly asks "who shall this bowl with the red ale [*dergflaith*] be distributed to?" The phantom replies in each case with a prophetic naming of a king and more than fifty kings are mentioned although many are not historical. We note that the symbols of kingship are left with Conn and these are clearly intended to be used again.

Appended to this text is another from the last quarter of the seventh century called *Baile Chuind*, "Cond's Ecstacy".[41] It contains a list of kings from Art, son of Conn, to Finnachta who reigned from 675 to 695. The coming to kingship and deeds of these rulers are alluded to in terms of the liquor which they receive or demand from "her", the goddess of sovereignty of the kingdom.[42] The language is archaic and difficult but Gerard Murphy has ventured a translation which I reproduce in part in order to give some of the flavor of the thinking:

> Art shall drink it after forty nights, a mighty hero . . . . Corbmac shall drink it up; an ancient drink; a pleasant warrior; he shall die at Scoilicc (?); he shall be a glorious man over her; he shall wash her; Coirpre shall drink it, a fitting

40 Edition and translation in Eugene O'Curry, *Lectures on the Manuscript Materials of Ancient Irish History* (1873), p. 618f.; Dillon, *Cycles of the Kings*, p. 11f.
41 O'Curry, *Manuscript Materials*, p. 621; Dillon, *Cycles of the Kings*, p. 13.
42 Gerard Murphy, "On the Dates of Two Sources Used in Thurneysen's *Heldensage*" (1952), p. 145f.

contestant with righteousness of rule. Fiachri shall demand it . . . till Broad-faced Daire shall distribute it for a plenteous month . . . . Finnachta who shall pour shall drink it . . . .[43]

Whether or not the early Germans laid quite so much emphasis on the royal drink is difficult to say since we simply do not have comparable texts of similar age from the continent where a learned order of poets in partial opposition to the Christian clergy did not exist and where the clergy took a far more hostile attitude toward pagan learning. Having noted the caveat, however, a number of exceptionally strong reasons exist for holding that the essential concept underlying the Celtic ritual appears again in the Germanic *comitatus*. Most persuasive, it seems to me, is the remarkable parallel between Lug and the maiden of sovereignty and Mercury and Rosmerta. Celticists have not hitherto emphasized (nor, in most cases, noted) this relationship because of a failure to recognize that the goddess-prophecies in the king-tales are to be associated with one of Rosmerta's attributes, of which the caduceus in Gaul and the scepter and rod in Britain are tokens.[44] Once that foundation has been established, however, it can be maintained that the Irish texts give every sign of being very much like a literary exposition of the monumental iconography of Britain and the Rhineland. The archetype of the maiden of sovereignty, the fertility goddess with her vat of red ale, is Rosmerta standing over her wine-bucket with its strainer or, in the more Romanized versions, with her patera and cornucopia. Lug in his "king's seat" is none other than the enthroned Mercurius Rex. The constant insular references to the distribution of royal liquor accompanied by prophecy are thereby explainable on the basis of Rosmerta's attributes on the monuments. Vendryes' argument that her name derives from a word meaning "prophecy" or "fate" is vindicated not only by the evidence for the significance of her staff—we have already related it to weaving and prophecy—but also by *Baile in Scáil* which shows her to be the recipient of Lug's vaticinations. She then becomes the keeper of these and their transmitter just as on the continental monuments Mercury's herald's staff is passed to Rosmerta signifying the same transmission of function. This is a striking example of cultural retention. The Mediterranean divine herald is equated with Lug, the spear-bearing magician with a raven who then becomes Mercurius Hranno, another spear-bearing magician with a raven.

Once again, however, one must emphasize that the present interpretation does not apply to the Celts alone, who simply preserve the tradition better than the Germans, but rather to the entire Rhineland milieu where the monuments and

---

43 Ibid., p. 147f.
44 With a large body of literature it is hard to be certain. The exception, however, is Mac Cana who describes *Baile in Scáil* (*Celtic Mythology*, p. 25) and states that the descriptions of Lug and the goddess of sovereignty "can scarcely be dissociated from the Gaulish monuments to Mercury and Rosmerta". Idem, "Women in Irish Mythology" (1980), p. 8: "In the ninth century *Baile in Scáil* 'The Phantom's Frenzy' the setting is almost iconographic".

inscriptions to Mercury and Rosmerta are most thickly clustered. Additional proof of this contention lies in the often demonstrated ease with which Mercury/Lug and Mercury/Wodan can be compared. The reasons for this lie in the plasticity and magnetism of the *interpretatio Romana* which, particularly in the case of male gods, mixed and mingled a variety of originally separate divine attributes so that those of figures like Esus and Lug (god of kingship, poetry, inspiration, master of all arts) were quickly assimilated to Gaulish Mercury and then passed to Mercurius Hranno who eventually became Wodan. A long exposition with copious references to Rhineland iconography would certainly prove this Lug/Wodan identification but, fortunately, much of that may be omitted here since several scholars, most notably de Vries, have already discussed the evidence. With regard to Esus, for example, de Vries concludes that he is a leading Gaulish god who shows a particular affinity for Mercury and who may best be compared with North Germanic Odin.[45] The homology of Lug and Wodan is even clearer for the qualities of the former "place him very close to Germanic Odin and Indic Varuna".[46] de Vries advances a long list of reasons:

1. Lug is chief god of the Gauls, so is Wodan of the Germans.
2. Lug is a warleader, so is Odin.
3. Lug plays a critical role in the war between the gods at Mag Tured, as Odin does in that between the Aesir and Vanir.
4. Lug fights with a spear, Odin also. (One should note here that de Vries is apparently unaware of the Celtiberian prophet with the spear and does not refer to the spear dedications of Sertorius).
5. Lug uses magic in battle, so does Odin in marked degree.
6. Lug closes one eye when he performs magic, Odin has only one eye (de Vries does not remark the Hannibal/Sertorius/Civilis material).
7. Lug is the patron of poetry, as Odin is patron of the *skald*s.
8. Lug is in some way connected with the raven; this bird is also the cult-animal of Odin.
9. Lug is the father of heroes, especially of Cú Chulainn; so is Wodan.

So far de Vries with some noted omissions. To this list we may now add a few further points of schematic commentary and a conclusion. First, not only are both gods identified with Mercury, but Mercury's companion, Rosmerta, appears as a divine prophetess. We know from Tacitus that many Germans thought of Veleda as a deity and that Civilis claimed a supernatural nature. Such claims have a cultic basis. Second, Lug closes one eye to perform magic and is linked with a prophetess in *Baile in Scáil*. This clearly recalls Hranno's relationship with

45 de Vries, *Keltische Religion*, p. 100.
46 Ibid. p. 53.

Rosmerta, Odin's with the *völva* and Veleda's with Civilis. Third, Odin's prophetess is closely connected with a cult of the dead and so is Rosmerta whose buckets and vessels are found in Gaulish and British graves. The same practice is followed in Scandinavia. Fourth, both Lug and Wodan are connected to kingship through Mercurius Rex and, because this link is confirmed by Rhenish, Irish and Scandinavian texts, it *must* have been a distinctive and critical feature of the cult of the Gaulish and Rhineland god. One may conclude that the figures of Mercury and Rosmerta served as the Rhineland paradigm of royalty in the second half of the first century. Hence, since the Mercury and Rosmerta monuments were familiar to both Celts and Germans; since Rhineland iconography deliberately accentuates contemporary concepts of kingship and the serving of liquor by a goddess of prophecy; since Gaulish, Irish and Germanic rituals of hierarchy consistently feature status declaration by cup-offering at assemblies; since aristocratic women's graves suggest the existence of this concept during the Lübsow period in northern Germania; since the offering can be associated with governmental forms and warband leadership borrowed from Celts; since Civilis sought kingship, emphasized the supernatural nature of his monocularity, employed a prophetess with a Celtic title and was made leader at a feast in which drink was served; it is difficult to avoid concluding that the kingship ritual in use among first century Rhineland warlords was, at the least, very similar to that used by the Celts of eastern Gaul. To maintain otherwise, it seems to the writer, is ultimately to defy the repeatedly demonstrated pattern of the evidence which has been shown to be remarkably consistent in the matter of cultural borrowing and in those areas which touch on Wodan, Veleda, Civilis and the *comitatus*. No single point convinces, for each can be minimized or relativized at will, it is the *pattern* which demonstrates the thesis.

The evidence indicates that Mercury/Lug, Mercury/Hranno and Mercury/Wodan may no longer be regarded as gods with surprisingly parallel attributes; they appear to be too closely related for simple parallelism. But one should note two significant differences or additions; namely, that Wodan's cult shows signs of influence by that of Esus as well as Lug and that his one-eyedness is only partially paralleled by Lug whereas the fixing of this characteristic on the Germanic Mercury occurs through Civilis in his imitation of Sertorius. These variations hint again at transmission by the Treveri although other tribes may easily have been involved. In addition, one must also stress that de Vries' hypothesis of a connection with Indic Varuna as an explanatory device for parallel development is totally unnecessary. While Dumézil's tripartite system of analysis is often helpful, its application to the Rhineland gods in the face of the evidence accumulated is no longer persuasive since every aspect of the cult can be justified by reference to the same fairly small region of Europe. A different interpretation might be required if it could be shown that Wodan's name is of Indo-European origin but no scholar has convincingly argued that this is the case while most recognize that Tiu was the original god of war and kingship among the Germans.

If the early Wodanistic concepts of kingship may now be viewed as deriving from Lug and Esus via Mercurius Rex and Rosmerta, the directly related inauguration ritual itself requires some additional commentary for here one needs to take account of probabilities which are not historically demonstrable but which seem justifiable in themselves. One should point out, for example, that the method of establishing precedence through an ordered drinking ritual is a common device peculiar to no single people; it is a custom based on the intrinsic concept of hierarchy itself and is at home in many formal gatherings from the ancient Near East to modern times.[47] So too with the motif of the woman who serves drink at feasts for that is already a feature of the transalpine situla of the late Hallstatt period.[48] Moreover, the links between drink, feasting and kingship are established for the Germans by Tacitus when he states that the Germans consult on the choice of chiefs when they are drunk at feasts[49] and the evidence he provides for Civilis in somewhat more detail indicates that the feast itself was probably the constitutive act. Against the trend of this argument, however, lie the facts that Tacitus was writing at the end of the first century, i.e. after several centuries of Celto-Germanic contact, and that all indications point to a very close cultic association between Civilis and Veleda, Mercury and Rosmerta. These cannot realistically be separated from Gaulish practice. Hence, spreading the net of clues as widely as possible, the most judicious conclusion seems to be this: insofar as the sequential offering of drink implies precedence alone, the hierarchical service pattern is just as likely to be Germanic as Celtic; insofar as it became an actual formalized ritual involving prophecy which established kingship over the warband, however, all of the available evidence indicates Celtic priority and/or pronounced Celtic influence.

One might, finally, wish to know if the Germanic tradition preserves any clear traces of the Rhineland kingship myth aside from those in the Anglo-Saxon and Lombard sources. At this point we can hardly avoid the concept of the *hieros gamos* which appears to lie at the root of a great deal of early thinking about kingship whether it be Indic, Hittite, Greek, Celtic or Germanic. Although there are only a few scraps of South Germanic evidence, the North Germanic corpus, while admittedly much later in date, does help to bridge the gap. In Hallfredr Ottarsson's *Hákonardrápa*, for example, one finds Odin's wife Jord being equated with the land of Norway and now being made available to the virile lover Hakon of Hladir,[50] while other similar concepts are applied elsewhere to the goddess Thorgerðr Holgabruðr and the family of the same earl who were zealous defenders of

---

47 Wagner, *Early Celtic Traditions*, p. 11ff.
48 Kromer, "Situlenfest", pp. 231, 237f.
49 Hutton, *Tacitus. Germania* 22, p. 296.
50 See Folke Ström, "Hieros gamos-motivet i Hallfredr Ottarrssons Hákonardrápa och den nordnorska jarlavärdigheten" (1983), pp. 67–79; Margaret Clunies Ross, "Style and Authorial Presence in Scaldic Mythological Poetry" (1981), p. 284f.

the old faith.[51] Here too, in Scandinavia, one finds a ritual of succession centering on the drinking of liquor in that an heir to an estate was not formally recognized as such until he prepared a funeral feast.[52] He had to remain sitting on the lower step of the high-seat until the *bragafull*, "holy beaker", was brought out. He then blessed the liquor, drank of it, and after that ascended to his father's place. We do not know who presented the drink nor can we be sure that changes had not taken place in the ritual by the twelfth or thirteenth centuries. Nevertheless, since the concept of the *hieros gamos* certainly existed in Scandinavia and since it is also clear that the early Germanic marriage rite included a liquor offering to the husband, it seems highly probable that the mead would not have been omitted from the "mystic marriage" in the pagan period at least.

Recent research also suggests that a "knowledge criterion" played a role in such successions especially in the case of a ruler. According to Jeri Fleck and Einar Haugen such is discernable in a number of sources where mantic wisdom and genealogical awareness are required for eligibility.[53] In the *Lay of Hyndla*, for example, Ottar can only succeed to his father's throne by demonstrating the possession of numinous knowledge which includes a full recitation of the genealogy and deeds of his forbears. He is able to do so because the goddess Freya, his "lover", procures for him the "beer of memory" from the wise woman who guards it.[54] As in the *Lay of Grim*, where Odin grants Agnar his father's kingship because he gave him a beaker of liquor (and also added a long lecture on the mystic and cosmological verities), the core concept seems to be that the holy drink opens the mind to divine inspiration and thus prepares the ruler to receive that perpetually valid sagacity which describes all that is true of the art of governance. Such a drink is always charged with supernatural significance. In the *Lay of Sigrdrífa*, where the valkyrie bride gives a horn full of mead to Sigurd in order to teach him wisdom, there is a clear statement as to how it was perceived in a numinous context. It is called the "holy mead" and Sigrdrifa says:

> First I will bring beer to the warrior—might brewed it, mingled with fame—
> full of spells and potent songs, rich in charms and runes of joy.[55]

As in the *Hyndlulióð* and *Grímnismal*, there follows a long series of verses describing essential truths of thought and behavior, wisdom as seen through the eyes of the poet. One is reminded that Odin only gained this wisdom when a

51 Nora Chadwick, "Þorgeror Hölgabrúðr and the Trolla þing" (1950), pp. 397–417.
52 Grönvik, '*Funeral Feast*', pp. 5–25; Einarsson, "Old English *Beot*", p. 109f. Ström, "Hauptriten", p. 337f.
53 Jere Fleck, "*Konr-Otarr-Geirrodr*: A Knowledge Criterion for Succession to the Germanic Sacred kingship" (1970), pp. 39–49; Einar Haugen, "The Edda as Ritual: Odin and His Masks" (1983), pp. 3–24.
54 Gurevich, "Edda and Law", pp. 72–101.
55 Translation by Patricia Terry, *Poems of the Vikings. The Elder Edda* (1980), p. 167.

woman, Gunnlöð, in whose keeping it was, promised him a drink of the holy liquor after sleeping with him for three nights.[56] This myth, and the concept which underlies it, is fundamental to all scaldic poetry where the act of poetic inspiration is repeatedly compared to the drinking of liquor whereas the poet's declamation is linked to the spewing of liquor into the ears of the hearers.[57] Theoretically speaking, that is really the point of it all—the causal association between liquor and inspiration, the divinely granted ability to reach through and grasp the otherwise veiled understanding which enables one to create a structure of poetic truths.

But is not this very similar to what Tacitus says about the state of mind which the Germans believe they must reach through drinking before deciding on questions of peace and war and the choosing of kings? It is a state of mind mediated by women, which, under Celtic influence, came to be associated with kingship itself just as its presentation became a ritual of kingship. From all that we have seen, the Germans did not separate this concept of intuitive comprehension from their attitudes toward the women of the household who, it must be noted, were the ones who always brewed the liquor.[58] It is this simple domestic linkage which, in my view, provides the final key to understanding the entire process of myth-building surrounding the sacral kingship. Because women brew the liquor and serve it, they are directly tied to the inspiration that it produces which enables the men to rightly choose and the king to rightly know. In the mythological realm, which we cannot fully appreciate because we lack so many of the early texts, this homely process finds its archetypical paradigm in the sexual encounter of the candidate who is given a drink of the "beer of memory" by the goddess and thereby learns that which is essential to gain his inheritance. Even in the case of Odin and Agnar where the supernatural woman does not appear, we are probably only viewing the myth at one step further from its source. Recall that the name Wodan/Odin means frenzy and this divine madness, really the result of truly seeing the universe whole, probably came about because of Gunnlöð's mead. The god's name is cognate with Latin *vates*, "prophet", borrowed from the Celts, and OI *faith*, "poet".[59] Poetry and prophecy both spring from the identical-source. Since that source is typically carried by a woman, we can now finally understand all of the ramifications of the prophecy/sexuality/liquor-offering paradigm. The association between OI *faith* and the name Veleda seems entirely natural.

If the written texts are late, many of the archaeological documents are not. In

---

56 A full discussion in Doht, *Rauschtrank*, who also notes the Celtic sovereignty associations.
57 Carol J. Clover, "Skaldic Sensibility" (1978), pp. 63–81.
58 The process of brewing and related activities are discussed in Fell, "Old English *Beor*", p. 76–95; eadem, "Some Domestic Problems", pp. 59–82; Kylstra, "Ale and Beer", pp. 7–16.
59 Wagner, *Early Celtic Civilization*, pp. 46–57.

Scandinavian iconography, a female figure is frequently depicted as offering a drinking horn to a rider on a horse. The oldest such scene is depicted on the fourth or fifth-century horn from Gallehus and thereafter on picture stones of the Viking period.[60] A female figure with horn in upraised hand, and sometimes with ladle or bucket in the other, is also a common amulet-type from the beginning of the eighth century to the end of the eleventh.[61] The theme represented is usually thought to be that of the "woman who welcomes a house-guest with a drink" and that is surely correct in most instances but may not be so in all for drinking horns of certain types have often been associated with high status[62] and the warrior on the horse need not necessarily be a guest or a guest alone. But such a gesture, of course, is always a way of *honoring* a guest and, thus, the welcoming concept must be closely joined to recognition of a certain status. The fact that the womanly cup-offering can be traced back to the migration period is itself an important datum. So, too, is the knowledge that this iconographic scene, despite its clearly Germanic modifications, derives in part from the Roman *adventus* ceremonial where the goddess Victoria presents the victor with a wreath.[63] Add Celtic concepts of cup, kingship and warband and we have a fuller picture. The notions of triumph, victory and high rank were often commingled by the Romans and the same is surely true of the Germans as well, although it is clear that for them the drink-offering itself played the most important ritual role and that it had other roots. That is not to say that scenes from the picture stones do not more directly support the present hypothesis. On Halla Broa XVI from Gotland we have already noted that a figure sitting on what appears to be a high-seat holds a drinking horn which he seems to have received from another figure beside whom stands a bucket or a vat. One is inevitably reminded of Wealhtheow and Hrothgar and of the noblewoman who must always present the first drink to the prince before she serves his followers.

The North Germans appear to have best preserved the Rhineland tradition. This is not surprising since they were the peoples farthest removed from Christian influence. They are much like the Irish who, for other reasons, hardly deviated from the ancient practice at all. That is not to say that every aspect was identical but many were quite similar. Like Germanic rulers, for example, Irish kings were inaugurated at feasts. The most famous was the *Feish Temro*, "Feast of Tara", but each territorial ruler also had his own feast in which the motifs of

60 Detlev Ellmers, "Zum Trinkgeschirr der Wikingerzeit" (1965), p. 24f.
61 Birgit Arrhenius, "Zum symbolischem Sinn des Almandin im früheren Mittelalter" (1969), pp. 47–59.
62 Steuer, *Sozialstrukturen*, p. 243f.; Clara Redlich, "Zur Trinkhornsitte bei den Germanen der älteren Kaiserzeit" (1977), pp. 61–120.
63 For Victoria in the North, see now Hauck, *Goldbrakteaten der Völkerwanderungszeit* I, 1, p. 139f.; idem, "Ein neues Drei-Götten-Amulett von der Insel Funen" (1974), pp. 92–159.

marriage, liquor service and kingship were intermingled.[64] In their understanding of what the drink of liquor accomplished, however, there may have existed a subtle difference between the two cultures. In Germanic thinking as we have seen, a drink of the goddess's liquor enabled the king to recall or to discover the knowledge appropriate to his new status and that entailed an understanding of custom, behavior and individual motivation. The Irish texts, on the other hand, focus more thoroughly on what is called the "truth of lordship", the ability to discern the right answer to a problem and to make a "true judgement" in legal cases.[65] A king who is unable to do this will be rejected by the natural elements themselves—the earth will move or the waters will drown him—and his successor must then meet the goddess. Nonetheless, a fundamental similarity is present in both traditions, since the end result is always the imparting of transcendental knowledge to the ruler even if its content may reveal some difference in emphasis. One also finds this type of thinking being applied by monks writing hagiography. In the Irish *Life of Berach*, for example, king Aedan must decide which of two men, a saint or a poet-druid, is the stronger.[66] Since both are powerful miracle workers, the decision is a difficult one. The *vita* says that the king ordered his druids to find the answer and that in order to do so "the druids went on to their hurdles of rowan, and *new beer was brought to them*".[67] Thereafter, each devised a poem giving victory to the saint. In the same way, says Tacitus, the Germans would consult about kings when they were drunk.

---

64 O'Rahilly, "Érainn and Ériu", pp. 7–28; Daniel A. Binchy, "The Fair of Tailtiu and the Feast of Tara" (1958), pp. 113–38.
65 Myles Dillon, "The Hindu Act of Truth in Celtic Tradition" (1947), pp. 137–40; David Greene, "The Act of Truth in a Middle Irish Tale" (1976), pp. 30–7; Calvert Watkins, "Is Tre Fir Flathemon: Marginalia to Audacht Morainn" (1979), pp. 181–98.
66 Plummer, ed. *Life of Berach* in his *Bethada* II (1968), xxiii, p. 32f.
67 Ibid., p. 33.

VI

CONCLUSION

Criticized by some and praised by others, the Germanic *comitatus* played a crucial role in the creation of the early medieval state or proto-state. Continental scholars have devoted much attention to its legal and constitutional significance but have tended to neglect its social and religious dimensions. Anglophone scholars, with some notable exceptions, have often simply adopted the views of their continental brethren. No one, to my knowledge, has sought to directly associate the *comitatus* with the Germanic prophetess or to propose for her an institutional and instrumental part in its maintenance and continuity. That such was the case has been a central argument of the present work which has traced her drinking ritual, a distinctive organizational binding ceremony most clearly described in *Beowulf*, to three often related sources—to the hierarchic pattern of the Germanic household, to Gaulish custom and to the cult of the goddess Rosmerta (who should probably now be regarded as the earliest known consort of Wodan). This work was written in the belief that the many studies referring to the sociology of Germanic drinking practices - scores have done so over the past generation alone —have become banal and diagnostically sterile. The brilliant insights achieved by Wilhelm Grönbech and Levin Schücking are now constantly reiterated with only superficial modification or nuance and hence the time seemed ripe, not so much to go beyond these fundamental interpretations, but to reexamine some central aspects and to expand them in a way which might cast new light on the ethos and religious beliefs of the Germanic warband and on the continuity of northern European culture.

As an occasional gathering of predators, members of a non-tribal warband required little beyond capable leadership, a willingness to fight together and a motive in the shape of lavish booty. Success, together with the comradeship, fostered by mutual effort and the survival of hardship, encouraged more frequent forays and the leader, whose power grew through accomplishment and the creation of a planning and command structure, constantly sought to encourage stability. Since institutional permanence was the warlord's goal, he required techniques for the establishment of cohesion, order and peaceful interaction for those not related by blood. Oath-swearing with structured communal drinking was indispensable since it imitated the intimate household pattern; it created a fictive family. And so a mother of the family was also needed—a woman at the core of the group who might hearten, reward and calm the young men, many of whom, as the institution took root and flourished, were no more than boys seeking training and status. According to Tacitus, these men were accustomed to accepting food and encouragement from women gathered at the sideline during tribal engagements and to accord them a degree of sanctity and prescience. Certain tribal matrons who traditionally prophesied for warriors were especially revered.

Early warlords adapted, tightened and streamlined tribal practices while also reaching beyond them. Based on a tribal approach to kinship, they expanded the concept of adoption into a family to include that of adoption into a familially organized group and replaced the prescient matrons with a single prophetess who, most probably, became over time one of the leader's wives. In order to control this rambunctious military gathering, greater emphasis than ever before had to be placed on ideas of hierarchy, service, reward and lordship. Such qualities could be magnified and manipulated through a communal drinking ritual which, however, required a special emphasis, sacralization and ritual practitioner. A simple concept of precedence alone was insufficiently weighty to properly lionize the ascending dignity of the warlord claiming kingship and an ordinary woman who could not claim prophetic powers lacked the influence needed to convincingly reassure and embolden men who constantly faced mortal danger. Actually, the whole concept of kingship itself needed an expanded definition to include extra-tribal and territorial components as well as innovative religious propaganda. In rivalry with traditional oligarchs and tribal kings, the warlords needed contrasting systems of governance and legitimation. Whence came the new arsenal?

Although Mediterranean peoples might have provided advanced examples of various socio-political structures, they were, originally at least, too sophisticated, bureaucratized, distant and strange to be of much use or meaning to the tribes of Germania. Archaeologists and historians are agreed that Germanic society of the mid La Tène was generally dispersed, tribally organized, exceptionally simple and lacking in technology as well as the resources to advance it. The earlier Celts had been in much the same condition until extended contact with Greeks and Etruscans had brought about significant changes in lifestyle. Such changes, suitably adapted to simpler transalpine needs, were now passed on to others so that by late La Tène many Germanic groupings had borrowed numerous aspects of kingship, politico-military organization, technology and religion from the geographically intermediate Celts. A "*sehr enge Kulturgemeinschaft*" of Celts and Germans came into existence. This was a decisive moment in northern European history although it has been much neglected by modern historians. It was probably during this period that the terms and concepts later associated with Veleda and Wodan began to be disseminated among Germans of the Rhine-Weser archaeological group, among others to the east.

The coming of the Romans under Caesar around mid-firstcentury BC added a third force to this traditional pattern but may only have hastened or intensified some aspects of change since many Germans had already shifted to a more complex way of life. Developments in the first century AD became more complicated. By this time, the warlord/prophetess partnership, hitherto misunderstood and only superficially sketched by scholars, had come into being. Its ultimate source was Celtic, as we have seen, but new circumstances and contemporary needs encouraged further modulations along with additional borrowings. A single Batavian warlord, providentially one-eyed, now began to emphasize a novel kind of warrior religion based on an acquired facial resemblance to famous military leaders of the past, Hannibal and Sertorius. In the circumstances of the time, as can be gleaned from Tacitus, he clearly wished to recall and exploit memories of their successful anti-Roman campaigns, their multi-tribal alliances and the storied efficiency and devotion of their troops. Sertorius was a particularly attractive model for a disaffected Batavian, an outsider who had served in the Roman army for many years but who also wished to make use of some of its techniques. Two other roots of the new warband religion can also be traced. One derives from the Gallo-Roman concept of the kingship of Mercury/Lug and the other from the tribal king's mystic marriage to Rosmerta, a deity prominent in eastern Gaul and the Rhineland.

These findings are significant for several reasons. First, they are an aid to understanding the native side of the multifaceted Batavian rebellion, a matter usually regarded as only partially explainable through Tacitus and otherwise lost in the mists of the unchronicled past. Second, the nature of warband religion in the Early Middle Ages has attracted increased attention over the past two decades. Its sources, however, are usually seen to derive from a combined Romano-Germanic interaction which, from the present perspective, is not a sufficient answer in itself. Analysis of *comitatus* organization, especially the warlord/prophetess association with its Gallo-Roman dimension, adds a second investigatory framework while providing valuable new information upon which to form a judgement. Warband organization, together with many of its associated practices, seems to be a borrowing from the Celts of late La Tène. Third, the god Wodan/Odin was, by all accounts, the most important as well as puzzling and contradictory god of the pagan Germans of the Early Middle Ages. His origins, characteristics and cult have long been topics of pronounced scholarly interest and controversy. Practically all of his intriguing qualities may now be explainable on the basis of the context provided. The earliest identifiable Wodanistic monument places him in a Gallo-Roman Rhineland milieu and shows him as the consort of a liquor-dispensing Gaulish sovereignty goddess. This is singularly important new information which makes examination of the mixed Rhineland culture of the time obligatory. It is fully consonant with findings which show both the Germanic *comitatus* and inhumation rite to be adaptations of Gaulish and eastern Celtic practices. Similarly, Wodan's monocularity cannot now be separated from the magic-making of Mercury/Lug, Rosmerta's former husband, or from the one-eyedness of three renowned anti-Roman warleaders. His kingship and kingship ritual must, in the present author's view, be regarded as closely related phenomena pointing to the same contextual sphere. They are part of the religious changes accompanying the new organization and burial customs in Germania during the first century BC and the following several generations.

Our understanding of the Germanic *comitatus* and its warrior religion would thereby seem to be usefully advanced. The archaeological, epigraphical and historical literary evidence can now be more convincingly interpreted as part of an interrelated whole. It casts new light on the creative ferment of the late pre-Roman Iron Age and enables us to discern the roots of a pattern that lasted for another millennium in the Germanic North. The foundations for tighter organization, stronger kingship and at least a partially common transalpine religiosity were laid long before the *Völkerwanderungszeit* and were largely a product of Celto-Germanic interaction and the somewhat later stress of Roman occupation, training and example. In addition, knowledge of the roots of organization and cult, particularly in the case of Wodan/Odin and the prophetess, provide a new means of interpreting the cultural monuments of the Viking period and the High Middle Ages, while also contributing to the evidence for a central European origin of the one-eyed god and the distribution and dispersal of his worship thereafter.

We have also arrived at a new way of looking at several apparently unrelated concepts in early Germanic culture. Prophecy, sexuality and the distribution of liquor are not infrequently affiliated themes in the literature of the Middle Ages. Nonetheless, with some exception for the latter two, scholars have commonly discussed them separately. They have failed to recognize the complete rationale for Tacitus' attribution of the power of prophecy to women and the cogency of his remarks on the state of inebriation and the choosing of chiefs. These are now explainable. Both weaving and the brewing of beer or mead were women's work. The weaving of cloth was universally regarded as closely analogous to the weaving of fate and weaving tools like the spindle and whorl were also imbued with strong sexual connotations. The goddess on sixth century bracteates is depicted with large breasts and carrying a weaving beam and weaving sword as attributes. The brewing of liquor was similarly mystical. In effect, it produced pleasure while encouraging inspiration and furthering community. So too did the woman herself but then she also served the drink and, because of the method of service on significant occasions, formalized status. Any other result would be surprising since the adoption of the thoroughly hierarchic *comitatus* guaranteed that the liquor offerings would become a more officially symbolic statement of ranking than ever before even though fictive kinship was also created. For the mythopoeic mentality of the time, each of these associations led ineluctably to the other. Hence, the warlord, the husband and the follower all received their cup and commonly made oaths and heard wishes for the future when they drank from it.

Notions of kingship, the inspirational effects of alcohol and the expressive significance of its distribution were thereby intimately and inextricably linked in Germanic culture—not only in the time of Beowulf when the evidence is plainer but also in the distant age of Civilis. An organizational and cultural bridge formed by *comitatus*, warlord, prophetess and poet joins the two periods. The complex of ideas which I have called the "lady with a mead-cup motif" existed for well over a millennium and profoundly shaped the thinking and attitudes of Transalpine peoples.

In seeking the origins of the liquor ritual, therefore, something else has also been discovered, the origins of Germanic warband religion on the continent. One now perceives that the search could lead in no other direction for the rite belongs to the band and acts on the warrior group itself by focusing its energies, maintaining its integrity and exalting its leadership. The ritual may be described as a perdurable, religiously sanctioned, primary organizational technique of Germanic military society. The beginnings of this warband religion lie in the first century BC; its crucial formative impulse occurs during the Batavian revolt and its spread is ensured by the warband's greater efficiency, its expanded role for social mobility through competence, and by the wandering of peoples in the fourth, fifth and sixth centuries. More needs to be said but that would require a book on the history and sociology of the warband, not on its ritual and religion, even though certain aspects of both have been discussed in passing.

Finally, the matter of the continuity of transalpine culture has taken on a different coloring in the present interpretation. Probably from the late Hallstatt period but certainly by mid La Tène, the warband organizational form operated to determine the future of Celtic society. It was borrowed by enterprising Germanic leaders in the two or three generations before Caesar's conquest arrested independent Gaulish political development. It continued thereafter to influence the Germans, just as it lasted in the British Isles, to become the politically dominant mode of the late ancient and Merovingian periods. The heroic ethos and warlike religiosity pervaded Germanic culture for a near millennium from Civilis to Beowulf and would continue to do so after Carolingian disintegration. Feudalism is no more than a mutation of the *comitatus* principle. Looked at from this wider perspective, the four centuries of Roman culture in the North are not the wholly encompassing phenomenon that they are often made out to be. The rhythm of time returned the old institution (long lodged in the barbarian periphery) to the core where it also influenced the new religion of Christianity which sought to preserve some aspects of Mediterranean Roman ideals. A great many scholars are accustomed to think of transalpine history in terms of Roman decline and the transition to the Early Middle Ages. That is only a partial picture half a world removed from the full panorama. Stated somewhat paradoxically but no less meaningfully, early medieval culture begins with La Tène.

BIBLIOGRAPHY

Actes du Colloque de Nice (15–17 Octobre 1982), Vol I. Nice, 1984.

Affeldt, Werner, ed. *Frauen in Spätantike und Frühmittelalter. Lebensbedingun-Lebensnor-men-Lebensformen*. Sigmaringen, 1990.

——, and Annette Kuhn, eds. *Frauen in der Geschichte*, Vol VII. Dusseldorf, 1986.

Africa, Thomas W. "The One-Eyed Man Against Rome: An Exercise in Euhemerism". *Historia* 19 (1970): 528–38.

Ahlbäck, Tore, ed. *Old Norse and Finnish Religions and Cultic Place-Names*. Åbo, 1990.

Ahlqvist, Anders, ed. and trans. *The Early Irish Linguist: An Edition of the Canonical Part of the Auraicept Na nÉces*. Helsinki, 1983.

Ahrens, C., ed. *Sachsen und Angelsächsen. Ausstellung des Helms-Museums 18 November 1979 bis 28 Februar 1980. Hamburgisches Museum für Vor und Frühgeschichte*. Hamburg, 1980.

Aitchison, N.B. "The Ulster Cycle: Heroic Image and Historical Reality". JMH 13 (1987): 87–116.

Alcock, Leslie. *Economy, Society and Warfare Among the Britons and Saxons*. Cardiff, 1987.

Alföldy, Geza. "Epigraphisches aus dem Rheinland II". ES 4 (1967): 1–43.

——, *Die Hilfstruppen der römischen Provinz Germania inferior*. Düsseldorf, 1968.

——, *Noricum*. London, 1974.

Althoff, Gerd, *Verwandte, Freunde und Getreue: Zum politischen Stellenwert der Gruppen-bindungen in früheren Mittelalter*. Darmstadt, 1990.

——, Dieter Geuenich, Otto Gerhard Oexle and Joachim Wollasch, eds. *Person und Gemeinschaft in Mittelalter: Karl Schmid zum fünfundsechzigsten Geburtstag*. Sigmaringen, 1988.

Ament, Hermann. "Der Rhein und die Ethnogenese der Germanen". PZ 59 (1984): 37–47.

von Amira, Karl. "Der Stab in der germanischen Rechtssymbolik", in *Abhandlungen der Könglich.-Bayerischen Akad. d. Wiss. Phil.-Hist. Klasse* 25 (1909). No. 1.

Angenendt, Arnold. *Kaiserherrschaft und Königstaufe: Kaiser, Könige und Päpste als geistliche Patrone in der abendländischen Missionsgeschichte*. Berlin and New York, 1984.

Angles and Britons: The O'Donnell Lectures. Cardiff, 1963.

Anton, Hans Hubert. *Fürstenspiegel und Herrscherethos in der Karolingerzeit*. Bonn, 1968.

Antonsen, Elmer. "On the Mythological Interpretation of the Oldest Runic Inscriptions". In *Languages and Cultures: Studies in Honor of Edgar C. Polomé*, eds. Mohammed Ali Jazayery and Werner Winter, pp. 43–54. Berlin, 1988.

——, "Die ältesten Runenschriften in heutiger Sicht". In *Germanenprobleme in heutiger Sicht*, ed. Heinrich Beck, pp. 321–43. Berlin, 1986.

Arabagian, Ruth Katz. "Cattle Raiding and Bride Stealing: The Goddess in Indo-European Heroic Literature". *Religion* 14 (1984): 107–42.

Arnold, C.J. "Wealth and Social Structure: A Matter of Life and Death". In *Anglo-Saxon Cemetaries 1979*, eds. P. Rahtz, T. Dickinson and L. Watts, pp. 81–142. Oxford, 1980.

——, "Social Evolution in Post-Roman Western Europe". In *European Social Evolution*, ed. J. Bintliff, pp. 277–94. Bradford, 1984.

——, *Roman Britain to Saxon England*. London, 1984.

——, *An Archaeology of the Early Anglo-Saxon Kingdoms*. London, 1988.

Arrhenius, Birgit. "Zum symbolischen Sinn des Almandin im früheren Mittelalter". FM St. 3 (1969): 47–59.

Attenborough, F.L., ed. *The Laws of the Earliest English Kings*. Cambridge, 1922.

Audouze, Françoise and Olivier Büchsenschütz, *Towns, Villages and Countryside of Celtic Europe: From the Beginning of the Second Millennium to the End of the First Century B.C.*. Bloomington, 1992.

Aus Verfässungs—und Landesgeschichte, Vol I. Lindau-Konstanz, 1954.

Axboe, Morten "Die Brakteaten von Gudme II". FM St. 21 (1987): 76–81.

——, Klaus Düwel, Karl Hauck and Lutz von Padberg, eds. *Die Goldbrakteaten der Völkerwanderungszeit. Ikonographischer Katalog (=IK 1–3), Einleitungsband sowie je 1 Text-und je 1 Tafelband*. München, 1985f.

Bäck, Hilding. *The Synonyms for 'Child', 'Boy', 'Girl' in Old English*. Lund, 1934.

Baird, Joseph. "Unferth the þyle". MA 39 (1970): 1–12.

Baker, Derek, ed. *Medieval Women*. Oxford, 1978.

Barrett, John, Andrew Fitzpatrick and Lesley Macinnes, eds. *Barbarians and Romans in North-West Europe From the Later Republic to Late Antiquity*. Oxford, 1989.

Bassett, Stephen. "In Search of the Origins of Anglo-Saxon Kingdoms". In his *The Origins of the Anglo-Saxon Kingdoms*, pp. 3–27.

——, *The Origins of the Anglo-Saxon Kingdoms*. London, 1989.

Bauchhenss, Gerhard. *Die Jupitersäulen in den germanischen Provinzen*. Köln and Bonn, 1981.

——, and Günter Neumann, eds. *Matronen und verwandte Gottheiten*. Köln, 1987.

——, "Mercurius in Bornheim". BJ 188 (1988): 223–39.

Baudy, Gerard. "Hierarchie oder: Die Verteilung des Fleisches. Eine ethnologische Studie über die Tischordnung als Wurzel sozialer Organization". In *Neue Ansätze in der Religionswissenschaft*, eds. Burkhard Gladigow and Hans Kippenberg, pp. 131–74. München, 1983.

Bauersfeld, Helmut. "Die Kriegsältertumer im Lebor na h-Uidre". ZCP 19 (1933): 294–345.

Bauschatz, Paul. "The Germanic Ritual Feast". In *The Nordic Languages and Modern Linguistics 3. Proceedings of the Third Internatioal Conference of Nordic and General Linguistics*, ed. John Weinstock, pp. 289–95. Austin, 1978.

Becher, Matthias, "Drogo und die Königserhebung Pippins". FM St. 23 (1989): 131–53.

Beck, Heinrich. "Germanischen Menschenopfer in der literarisch Uberlieferung". In *Vorgeschichtlicher Heiligtumer und Opferplatze in Mittel-und Nordeuropa*, ed. Herbert Jankuhn, pp. 240–58. Göttingen, 1970.

——, ed. *Germanenprobleme in heutiger Sicht*. Berlin, 1986.

——, Detlev Ellmers and Kurt Schier, eds. *Germanische Religionsgeschichte: Quellen und Quellenprobleme*. Berlin—New York, 1992.

Behm-Blancke, Günter. "Trankgaben und Trinkzermonien im Totenkult der Völkerwan-
derungszeit". *Alt-Thüringen* 16 (1979): 171–227.
—, "Das Priester- und Heiligengrab von Schlotheim. Zur Strategie und Mission
der Franken in Nordthüringen". *Alt-Thüringen* 24 (1989): 199–219.
Bellows, Henry Adams, ed. *The Poetic Edda*. New York, 1923.
Bémont, Colette. "Rosmerta". EC 9 (1960): 29–43.
—, "A propos d'un nouveau monument de Rosmerta". *Gallia* 27 (1969): 23–44.
Benoit, Ferdinand. *Mars et Mercure. Nouvelles Recherches sur l'interprétation gauloise des
divinités romaines*. Aix-en-Provence, 1959.
Benveniste, Emile. *Indo-European Language and Society*, trans. Elizabeth Palmer. Coral-
Gables, 1973.
Berger, L. "Posidonios Fragment 18: Ein Beitrag zur Deutung der spätkeltischen Viereck-
schanzen". *Ur-Schweiz* 27 (1963): 26–8.
Berthelier-Ajot, Nadine. "The Vix Settlement and the Tomb of the Princess". In *The
Celts*, eds. Sabatino Moscati, Otto Hermann Frey, Venceslas Kruta, Barry Raftery
and Miklós Szabó, pp. 116–17. New York, 1991.
Bessinger, J.B. and S.J. Kahrl, eds. *Essential Articles for the Study of Old English Poetry*.
Hamden, 1968.
Beyerle, Franz, ed. *Die Gesetze der Langobardenreiche*, Vol I. Wietzenhausen, 1962.
Beumann, Helmut. "Nomen imperatoris. Studien zur Kaiseridee Karls des Grossen". In
Zum Kaisertum Karls des Grossen, ed. Günther Wolf, pp. 174–216. Darmstadt, 1972.
—., ed. *Historische Forschungen für Walter Schlesinger*. Köln, 1974.
Biel, Jörg. *Der Keltenfürst von Hochdorf*. Stuttgart, 1985.
—. "The Celtic Princes of Hohenasperg (Baden-Württemberg)". In *The Celts*, eds.
Sabatino Moscati, Otto Hermann Frey, Venceslas Kruta, Barry Raftery and Miklós
Szabó, pp. 108–13. New York, 1991.
Bieler, Ludwig, ed. *Patrician Texts in the Book of Armagh*. Dublin, 1979.
Binchy, Daniel A., ed. *Studies in Early Irish Law*. Dublin, 1936.
—., ed. *Crith Gablach*. Dublin, 1941.
—. "The Fair of Tailtiu and the Feast of Tara". *Eriu* 18 (1958): 113–38.
—. *Celtic and Anglo-Saxon Kingship*. Oxford, 1970.
—. "Brewing in Eighth Century Ireland". In B.G Scott, *Studies on Early Ireland:
Essays in Honour of M.V. Duignan*, pp. 68–73. Galway, 1981.
Bintliff, J., ed. *European Social Evolution*. Bradford, 1984.
Birley, Eric. "The Deities of Roman Britain". ANRW II, 18, 1 (1986): 3–112.
Bittel, Kurt, Wolfgang Kimmig and Siegwalt Schiek, eds. *Die Kelten in Baden-Württem-
berg*. Stuttgart, 1981.
Birkhan, Helmut. "Gapt und Gaut". ZdA 94 (1965): 1–17.
—. "Das gallische Namenselement *Cassi- und die germanisch-keltische Kontak-
tzone". In *Beiträge zur Indogermanistik und Keltologie: Julius Pokorny zum 80.
Geburtstag gewidmet*, ed. Wolfgang Meid, pp. 115–44. Innsbruck, 1967.
—. *Germanen und Kelten bis zum Ausgang der Romerzeit. Der Aussagewert von
Wörtern und Sachen für die frühesten Keltisch-Germanischen Kulturbezeichnungen*.
Wien, 1970.
—. and Otto Gschwantler, eds. *Festschrift für Otto Höfler*. II vols. Wien, 1968.
—., ed. *Festgabe für Otto Höfler zum 75. Geburtstag*. Wien, 1976.

Björkman, Erik. "Zu einigen Namen im *Beowulf*: Breca, Brondingas, Wealhtheow". *Anglia, Beiblatt* 30 (1919): 170–80.

Blagg, T.F.C. and A.C. King, eds. *Military and Civilian in Roman Britain: Cultural Relationships in a Frontier Province*. Oxford, 1984.

Blázquez, José Maria. *Religiones primitivas de Hispania*, Vol I. Roma, 1962.

——. *Primitivas Religionas Ibericas. Religiones Preromanes*. Madrid, 1983.

——. "Einheimische Religionen Hispaniens in der römischen Kaiserzeit". ANRW II, 18, 1 (1986): 164–275.

Bleiber, Waltraut. *Das Frankenreich der Merowinger*. Berlin, 1988.

Blockley, R.C. "Roman-Barbarian Marriages in the Late Empire". *Florilegium* 4 (1982): 63–79.

Bloemers, J.H.F. "Acculturation in the Rhein/Meuse Basin in the Roman Period: A Preliminary Survey". In *Roman and Native in the Low Countries: Spheres of Interaction*, eds. Roel Brandt and Jan Slofstra, pp. 59–210. Oxford, 1984.

Blocker, Monica. "Frauenzauber—Zauberfrauen". *Zeitschrift für schweizerische Kirchengeschichte* 76 (1982): 1–39.

Bloomfield, Morton. "Understanding Old English Poetry". AM 9 (1969): 5–25.

——. and Charles W. Dunn, *The Role of the Poet in Early Societies*. New Haven, 1989.

Boardman, John, M.A. Brown and T.G.E. Powell, eds. *The European Community in Later Prehistory: Studies in Honour of C.F.C. Hawkes*. London, 1980.

Bober, Phyllis F. "Mercurius Arvernus". *Marsyas* 4 (1945): 19–46.

Boehmer, R.M. and H. Hauptmann, eds. *Beiträge zur Altertumskunde Kleinasiens. Festschrift für Kurt Bittel*. Mainz, 1983.

Bogaers, J.E. "Civitas en Stad". In *Germania Romana III: Römisches Leben auf germanischem Boden*, ed. Herman Heinz, pp. 20–42. Heidelberg, 1970.

——. *Noviomagus. Auf den Spuren der Römer in Nijmegen*. Nijmegen, 1980.

Bolelli, Tristano and Enrico Campanile. "Sur la préhistoire des noms gaulois en -rix". EC 13 (1972): 123–40.

Bonfonte, Larissa, ed. *Etruscan Life and Afterlife*. Detroit, 1986.

Borst, Arno. "Kaisertum und Nomentheorie im Jahre 800". In *Zum Kaisertum Karls des Grossen*, ed. Gunther Wolf, pp. 216–40. Darmstadt, 1972.

Bossy, John, ed. *Disputes and Settlements: Law and Human Relations in the West*. Cambridge, 1983.

Bosworth, J. and T.N. Toller. *An Anglo-Saxon Dictionary*. Oxford, 1882.

Bouloumié, Bernard. "Le symposion gréco-étrusque et l'aristocratie celtique". In *Les princes celtes et la Méditerranée*, pp. 343–83. Paris, 1988.

Braat, Wouter C. "Die Besiedlung des römischen Reichsgebietes in den heutigen nördlichen Niederlanden". In *Germania Romana III: Römisches Leben auf germanischem Boden*, ed. Herman Heinz, pp. 43–61. Heidelberg, 1970.

Brady, Caroline, " 'Warriors' in *Beowulf*: An Analysis of the Nominal Compounds and an Evaluation of the Poet's Use of Them". ASE 11 (1983): 199–246.

Brandt, Roel and Jan Slofstra, eds. *Roman and Native in the Low Countries: Spheres of Interaction*. Oxford, 1984.

Braund, David, *Rome and the Friendly King: The Character of Client Kingship*. London, 1984.

——. "Ideology, Subsidies and Trade: The King on the Northern Frontier Revisited".

In *Barbarians and Romans in North-West Europe From the Later Republic to Late Antiquity*, eds. John Barrett, Andrew Fitzpatrick and Lesley Macinnes, pp. 14–25. Oxford, 1989.

Braunfels, Wolfgang and Percy Ernst Schramm, eds. *Karl der Grosse*. Lebenswerk und Nachleben 4. Düsseldorf, 1967.

Breatnach, Liam, ed., *Uraicecht na ríar: The Poetic Grades in Early Irish Law*. Dublin, 1987.

Breatnach, Padraig A. "The Chief's Poet". PRIA, C 83 (1983): 37–79.

Bremmer, Jan. "Adolescents, *Symposion* and Pederasty". In *Sympotica: A Symposium on the Symposion*, ed. Oswyn Murray, pp. 279–88. Oxford, 1990.

Brennan, Brian. "Senators and Social Mobility in Sixth Century Gaul". JMH 11 (1985): 145–61.

Brennan, Malcolm M. "Hrothgar's Government". JEGP 84 (1985): 3–15.

Bringmann, Klaus. "Topoi in der taciteischen Germania". In *Beiträge zum Verstandnis der Germania des Tacitus* I, eds. Herbert Jankuhn and Dieter Timpe, pp. 59–78. Göttingen, 1989.

Brodeur, Arthur. *The Art of Beowulf*. Berkeley, 1960.

Bröndsted, Johannes. *Nordische Vorzeit III. Eisenzeit in Dänemark*. Neumünster, 1963.

Bromwich, R. "Celtic Dynastic Themes and the Breton Lays". EC 9 (1961): 445–59.

Brown, Carleton, *"Poculum Mortis* in Old English". *Speculum* 15 (1940): 389–99.

Bruder, Reinhold. *Die Germanische Frau im Lichte der Runeninschriften und der antiken Historiographie*. Berlin, 1974.

Brunner, Heinrich. *Deutsche Rechtsgeschichte*. II vols. Berlin, 1961².

Brunt, P.A. "The Revolt of Vindex and the Fall of Nero". *Latomus* 18 (1959): 531–59.

—. "Tacitus on the Batavian Revolt". *Latomus* 19 (1960): 494–517.

Buchholz, Peter, "Die Ehe in germanischen, besonders altnordischen Literaturdenkmälern". SSCI 24 (1977): 887–900.

—. "Odin: Celtic and Siberian Affinities of a Germanic Deity". MQ 24 (1983): 427–36.

Buchner, Rudolf, ed. *Gregor von Tours: Zehn Bücher Geschichten*. II vols. Darmstadt, 1974.

Buisson, Ludwig. *Der Bildstein Ardre VIII auf Gotland: Göttermythen, Heldensagen und Jenseitsglauben der Germanen im 8. Jahrhundert n. Chr.*. Göttingen, 1976.

Bullough, Donald A. "Early Medieval Social Groupings: The Terminology of Kinship". PP 45 (1969): 3–18.

—. "Burial, Community and Belief in the Early Medieval West". In *Ideal and Reality in Frankish and Anglo-Saxon Society*, eds. Patrick Wormald and Donald Bullough, pp. 177–201. Oxford, 1983

—. *"Aula Renovata*: The Carolingian Court Before the Aachen Palace". PBA 71 (1985): 267–301.

—. *Friends, Neighbors and Fellow-Drinkers: Aspects of Community and Conflict in the Early Medieval West*. Cambridge, 1990.

Bullough, Vern L. and James Brundage, eds. *Sexual Practices and the Medieval Church*. Buffalo, 1982.

Burkert, Walter. "Opfertypen und antike Gesellschaftsstruktur". In *Der Religionswandel unserer Zeit im Spiegel der Religionswissenschaft*, ed. Günther Stephenson, pp. 168–187. Darmstadt, 1976.

Burnham, Barry and Helen Johnson, eds. *Invasion and Response: The Case of Roman Britain*. Oxford, 1979.

Burrow, J.A. *The Ages of Man: A Study in Medieval Writing and Thought.* Oxford, 1986.

Byock, Jesse L. "Governmental Order in Early Medieval Iceland". *Viator* 17 (1986): 19–34.

Byrne, Francis John. "Tribes and Tribalism in Early Ireland". *Ériu* 22 (1971): 128–171.

——. *Irish Kings and High-Kings.* New York, 1973.

Cahén, Maurice. *Études sur le vocabulaire religieux du Vieux-Scandinave: La libation.* Paris, 1921.

Calder, Daniel and Craig Christy, eds. *Germania. Comparative Studies in the Old Germanic Languages and Literatures.* Wolfeboro, 1988.

Callies, H. "Ariovistus". *Reallexikon* 1 (1973): 407–8.

——. "Arminius". *Reallexikon* 1 (1973): 417–20.

Campbell, James. *Bede's Reges and Principes.* Newcastle upon Tyne, 1979.

——. "Early Anglo-Saxon Society According to Written Sources". In his *Essays in Anglo-Saxon History*, pp. 131–38.

——. *Essays in Anglo-Saxon History.* London, 1986.

Campbell, Miles. "Queen Emma and Aelfgifu of Northampton: Canute the Great's Women". *Medieval Scandinavia* 4 (1971): 66–79.

Caquot, André and Marcel Leibovici, eds. *La divination.* Paris, 1968.

Carey, John. "The Two Laws in Dubthach's Judgement". CMCS (1990): 1–18.

Carney, James. "Review of Zwicker's *Fontes*". *Béaloideas* 1 (1937): 143–45.

——. "Society and the Bardic Poet". *Studies* 62 (1973): 233–50.

——. and D. Greene, eds. *Celtic Studies: Essays in Memory of Angus Matheson.* London, 1968.

Carver, Martin, ed. *In Search of Cult: Archaeological Investigations in Honour of Philip Rahtz.* Bury St. Edmunds, 1993.

Cary, Ernest, ed. *Dio's Roman History.* IX vols. Cambridge, 1955².

Chadwick, Hector Munro. *Studies on Anglo-Saxon Institutions.* Cambridge, 1905.

Chadwick, Nora. "Þorgerðr Hölgabrúðr and the trolla þing". In *The Early Cultures of North-West Europe*, eds. C.Fox and B. Dickens, pp. 397–417. New York, 1950.

Champion, T.C. "Mass Migration in Later Prehistoric Europe". In *Transport Technology and Social Change*, ed. P. Sörbom, pp. 33–42. Stockholm, 1980.

——. "Written Sources and the Study of the European Iron Age". In *Settlement and Society: Aspects of Western European Prehistory in the First Millenium BC*, eds. T.C. Champion and J.V.S. Megaw, pp. 9–22. New York, 1985.

——. and J.V.S. Megaw, eds. *Settlement and Society: Aspects of Western European Prehistory in the First Millenium BC.* New York, 1985.

Chaney, William. *The Cult of Kingship in Anglo-Saxon England: The Transition from Paganism to Christianity.* Berkeley, 1970.

Charles-Edwards, T.M. "Kinship, Status and the Origins of the Hide". PP 56 (1972): 3–33.

——. "Native Political Organization in Roman Britain and the Origin of MW *brenhin*". In *Antiquitates Indogermanica: Gedenkschrift für Hermann Guntert*, eds. M. Mayrhofer, W. Meid, B. Schlerath and R. Schmitt, pp. 35–45. Innsbruck, 1974.

——. "The Distinction between Land and Movable Wealth in Anglo-Saxon England". In *Medieval Settlement: Continunity and Change*, ed. Peter Sawyer, pp. 180–87. London, 1976.

—. "The Social Background to Irish Peregrinatio". *Celtica* 11 (1976): 43–59.

—. "Críth Gablach and the Law of Status". *Peritia* 5 (1986): 53–73.

—. "Early Medieval Kingships in the British Isles". In *The Origins of Anglo-Saxon Kingdoms*, ed. Stephen Bassett, pp. 28–39. London, 1989.

Chase, Colin, ed. *The Dating of Beowulf.* Toronto, 1981.

Chilver, G.E.F. *A Historical Commentary on Tacitus' Histories I and II.* Oxford, 1979.

—. and G.B Townend. *A Historical Commentary on Tacitus' Histories IV and V.* Oxford, 1985.

Christlein, Reiner. *Die Alamannen: Archäologie eines lebendigen Volkes.* Stuttgart, 1978.

Chropovsky, Bohuslav, ed. *Symposium. Ausklang der Latène-Zivilization und Anfänge der germanischen Besiedlung im mittleren Donaugebiet.* Bratislava, 1977.

Church, Alfred J. and W.J. Brodribb, trans. *Complete Works of Tacitus.* New York, 1942.

Claude, Dietrich. "Untersuchungen zum frühfränkischen Comitat". ZSSR (GA) 81 (1964): 1–79.

—. "Beiträge zur Geschichte der frühmittelalterlichen Königsschätze". HA 54 (1973): 5–24.

—. "Königs-und Untertaneneid im Westgotenreich". In *Historische Forschungen für Walter Schlesinger*, ed. Helmut Beumann, pp. 358–78. Köln, 1974.

—. "Die ostgotischen Konigserhebungen". In *Die Völker an der mittleren und unteren Donau im fünften und sechsten Jahrhundert*, eds. H. Wolfram and F. Daim, pp. 149–86. Wien, 1980.

—. "Zur Begründung familiärer Beziehungen zwischen dem Kaiser und barbarischen Herrschern". In *Das Reich und die Barbaren*, eds. Evangelos Chrysos and Andreas Schwarcz, pp. 25–56. Wien, 1989.

Closs, A. "Neue Problemstellungen in der Germanischen Religionsgeschichte". *Anthropos* 29 (1934): 477–96.

Clover, Carol J. "Skaldic Sensibility". ANF 93 (1978): 63–81.

—. "The Germanic Context of the Unferth Episode". *Speculum* 55 (1980): 444–68.

—. "Hildigunnr's Lament". In *Structure and Meaning in Old Norse Literature: New Approaches to Textual Analysis and Literary Criticism*, eds. John Lindow, Lars Lonnroth and Gerd Wolfgang Weber, pp. 141–83. Odense, 1986.

Coles, Bryony and John Coles. *People of the Wetlands: Bogs, Bodies and Lake-Dwellers.* New York, 1989.

Colgrave, Bertram, ed. *Felix's Life of Saint Guthlac.* Cambridge, 1956.

—. and R.A.B. Mynors, eds. *Bede's Ecclesiastical History of the English People.* Oxford, 1969.

Collis, John R. "Pre-Roman Burial Sites in North-Western Europe". In *Burial in the Roman World*, ed. Richard Reese, pp. 1–13. London, 1977.

—. *The European Iron Age.* New York, 1984.

—. *Oppida: Earliest Towns North of the Alps.* Sheffield, 1984.

Colpe, Carsten. "Muttergottinnen und keltisch-germanischen Matronen: Ein historisch-psychologisches Problem". In *Matronen und verwandte Gottheiten*, eds. Gerhard Bauchhenss and Günter Neumann, pp. 229–40. Köln, 1987.

Contamine, Philippe. *War in the Middle Ages.* London, 1984.

Corolla Linguistica: Festschrift Ferdinand Sommer. Wiesbaden, 1955.

Craik, Elizabeth M., ed. *Marriage and Property.* Aberdeen, 1984.

Cramp, Rosemary. "Northumbria and Ireland". In *Sources of Anglo-Saxon Culture*, ed. P.E. Szarnach, pp. 185–201. Kalamazoo, 1986.

Crawford, Barbara E. "Marriage and the Status of Women in Norse Society". In *Marriage and Property*, ed. Elizabeth Craik, pp. 71–88. Aberdeen, 1984.

Creed, Robert P. "Beowulf and the Language of Hoarding". In *Medieval Archaeology. Papers of the Seventh Annual Conference of the Center for Medieval and Early Renaissance Studies*, ed. Charles L. Redman, pp. 155–167. Binghamton, 1989.

Crépin, André, "Wealhtheow's Offering of the Cup: A Study in Literary Structure". In *Saints, Scholars and Heroes: Studies in Medieval Culture* I, eds. Margot King and Wesley Stevens, pp. 45–58. Collegeville, 1979.

Chrysos, Evangelos and Andreas Schwarcz, eds. *Das Reich und die Barbaren*. Wien, 1989.

Crozier, Alan. "The Germanic Root *dreug- 'to follow, accompany' ". ANF 101 (1986): 127–48.

——. "Old West Norse *iþrott* and Old English *indryhtu*". SN 53 (1986): 3–10.

——. "*Orlygis draugr* and *orlog drygja*". ANF 102 (1987): 1–12.

Cunliffe, Barry. "Relations Between Britain and Gaul in the First Century BC and Early First Century AD". In *Cross-Channel Trade Between Gaul and Britain in the Pre-Roman Iron Age*, eds. Sarah Macready and F.H. Thompson, pp. 3–23. London, 1984.

——. *Greeks, Romans and Barbarians: Spheres of Interaction*. New York, 1988.

——. "Maritime Traffic Between the Continent and Britain". In *The Celts*, eds. Sabatino Moscati, Otto Hermann Frey, Vencesles Kruta, Barry Raftery and Miklós Szabó, pp. 573–80. New York, 1991.

Curtius, Robert. "Etymology as a Category". In his *European Literature and the Latin Middle Ages*, pp. 495–500. New York, 1953.

——. *European Literature and the Latin Middle Ages*. New York, 1953.

Damico, Helen. *Beowulf's Wealhtheow and the Valkyrie Tradition*. Madison, 1984.

Dannell, G.B. "Eating and Drinking in Pre-Conquest Britain: The Evidence of Amphora and Samian Trading Ware and the Effect of the Invasion of Cladius". In *Invasion and Response: The Case of Roman Britain*, eds. Barry Burnham and Helen Johnson, pp. 177–86. Oxford, 1979.

Dannheimer, Hermann and Heinz Dopsch, eds. *Die Bajuwaren von Severin bis Tassilo 488–788*. Salzburg, 1988.

D'Arbois de Jubainville, H. *Les premiers habitants de l'Europe*. Paris, 1894.

——. *La famille celtique*. Paris, 1905.

D'Arms, John H. "Control, Companionship, and *clientela*: Some Social Functions of the Roman Communal Meal". *Échos du Monde Classique* 3 (1984): 327–48.

Daubigney, Alain. "Reconnaissance des formes de la dépendance gauloise". *Dialogues d'histoire ancienne* 5 (1979): 145–89.

——. "Relations marchandes Méditerranéennes et procès des rapports de dépendance (*magu*—et ambactes) en Gaule protohistorique". In *Modes de contacts et processus de transformation dans les sociétés anciennes*, ed. Giuseppe Nenci, pp. 659–83. Pise-Rome, 1983.

——. "Forme de l'asservissement et statut de la dépendance préromaine dans l'aire gallo-germanigne". In *Antike Abhängigkeitsformen in den griechischen Gebieten ohne Polisstruktur und den römischen provinzen*, eds. Heinz Kreissing and Friedmar Kühnert, pp. 108–30. Berlin, 1985.

Davidson, H.R. Ellis. *Gods and Myths of Northern Europe*. Harmondsworth, 1964.

—. *The Battle God of the Vikings.* York, 1972.

—. and Peter Fischer. *Saxo Grammaticus: The History of the Danes.* II vols. Cambridge, 1979.

—. *Myths and Symbols in Pagan Europe: Early Scandinavian and Celtic Religions.* Syracuse, 1988.

—. ed. *The Seer in Celtic and Other Traditions.* Edinburgh, 1989.

—. "The Training of Warriors". In *Weapons and Warfare in Anglo-Saxon England,* ed. Sonia C. Hawkes, pp. 11–24. Oxford, 1989.

Davies, Glenys. "Burial in Italy up to Augustus". In *Burial in the Roman World,* ed. Richard Reese, pp. 13-19. London, 1977.

Davies, Wendy. *Wales in the Early Middle Ages.* Leicester, 1982.

—. "Celtic Women in the Early Middle Ages". In *Images of Women in Antiquity,* eds. A. Kuhrt and A. Cameron, pp. 145–66. London, 1983.

—. and H. Vierck. "The Contexts of the Tribal Hidage: Social Aggregates and Settlement Patterns". FM St. 8 (1982): 223–93.

—. and Paul Fouracre, eds. *The Settlement of Disputes in Early Medieval Europe.* Cambridge, 1986.

Davis, Craig R. "Cultural Assimilation in the Anglo-Saxon Royal Geneologies". ASE 21 (1992): 23–36.

Deger-Jalkotzy, Sigrid. *E-QE-TA: Zur Rolle des Gefolgschaftswesens in der Sozialstruktur mykenischer Reiche.* Wien, 1978.

Dehn, Wolfgang. "Einige Überlegungen zum Charakter keltischer Wanderungen". In *Les Mouvements Celtiques du Ve au Ier siècle avant notre ère,* eds. Paul-Marie Duval and Venceslas Kruta, pp. 15–21. Paris, 1979.

Delbrück, Hans. *History of the Art of War II. The Germans.* trans. Walter J. Renfroe. Westport, 1980.

Demandt, Alexander. "Die Anfänge der Staatenbildung bei den Germanen". HZ 230 (1980): 265–91.

—. "The Osmosis of Late Roman and Germanic Aristocracies". In *Das Reich und die Barbaren,* eds. Evangelos Chrysos and Andreas Schwarcz, pp. 75–86. Wien, 1989.

Demarolle, J.M. "Céramique et religion en Gaule romaine". ANRW II, 18, 1 (1986): 519–41.

Dentzer, Jean-Marie. *Le motif du banquet couché dans le Proche-Orient et le monde grec du VIIe au IVe siècle avant J.-C.* Rome, 1982.

Derolez, René. "La divination chez les germains". In *La Divination,* eds. Andre Caquot and Marcel Leibovici, pp. 257–302. Paris, 1968.

de Vries, Jan. "Kimbern und Teutonen (Ein Kapitel aus der Beziehungen zwischen Kelten und Germanen)". In *Erbe der Vergangenheit,* pp. 7–24. Tübingen, 1951.

—. "Das Königtum bei den Germanen". *Saeculum* 7 (1956): 289–309.

—. *Altgermanische Religionsgeschichte.* II vols. Berlin, 1956.

—. *Kelten und Germanen.* Bern, 1960.

—. *Keltische Religion.* Stuttgart, 1961.

Dewing, H.B., ed. *Procopius.* VII vols. London, 1924.

Dexter, Miriam R., "Indo-European Reflections on Virginity and Autonomy". MQ 26 (1985): 57–74.

Dick, Ernst S. *Ae. dryht und seine Sippe. Eine wortkundliche, kultur- und religionsgeschicht-*

liche Betrachtung zur altgermanischen Glaubensvorstellung vom wachstumlichen Heil. Münster, 1965.

—. "The Bridesman in the Indo-European Tradition: Ritual and Myth in Marriage Ceremonies". JAF 79 (1966): 338–47.

Dickinson, Tania. "An Anglo-Saxon 'Cunning Woman' from Bidford-on Avon" in *In Search of Cult: Archaeological Investigations in Honour of Philip Rahtz*, ed. Martin Carver, pp. 45-54. Bury St Edmunds, 1993.

Die Kelten in Mitteleuropa. Kultur-Kunst-Wirtschaft. Salzburger Landesausstellung Hallein. Salzburg, 1980.

Diesner, Hans-Joachim. *Westgotische und Langobardische Gefolgschaften und Untertanenverbände.* Berlin, 1978.

Dillmann, Francois-Xavier. "Katla and her Distaff: An Episode of Tri-Functional Magic in the *Eyrbyggja Saga*". In *Hommage to Georges Dumézil*, ed. Edgar C. Polomé, pp. 113–24. Washington, 1982.

Dillon, Myles. *The Cycles of the Kings.* London, 1946.

—. *The Archaism of Irish Tradition.* Oxford, 1947.

—. "The Hindu Act of Truth in Celtic Tradition". MP 44 (1947): 137–40.

—. and Nora Chadwick. *The Celtic Realms.* New York, 1967.

Doane, A.N. and Carol B. Pasternack, eds. *Vox intexta. Orality and Textuality in the Middle Ages.* Madison, 1991.

Dobesch, G. *Die Kelten in Österreich nach den ältesten Berichten der Antike.* Wien, 1980.

Doherty, Charles. "Exchange and Trade in Early Medieval Ireland". JRSAI 110 (1980): 67–89.

Doht, Renate. *Der Rauschtrank im germanischen Mythos.* Wien, 1974.

Donahue, Charles. "Potlatch and Charity: Notes on the Heroic in *Beowulf*". In *Anglo-Saxon Poetry: Essays in Appreciation for John C. McGalliard*, eds. Lewis E. Nicholson and Dolores Warwick Frese, pp. 23–40. Notre Dame, 1975.

Donaldson, E. Talbot. *Beowulf: A New Prose Translation.* New York, 1966.

Dottin, Georges. *Manuel pour servir à l'étude de l'antiquité celtique.* Paris, 1915.

—. *La langue gauloise.* Paris, 1920.

Drescher, Hans and Karl Hauck. "Götterthrone des heidnischen Nordens". FM St. 16 (1982): 237–301.

Drew, Katherine Fischer. "The Law of the Family in the Germanic Barbarian Kingdoms: A Synthesis". SMC 11 (1976): 17–26.

Drinkwater, J.F. "The Rise and Fall of the Gallic Iulii: Aspects of the Development of the Aristocracy of the Three Gauls Under the Early Empire". *Latomus* 37 (1978): 817–50.

—. *Roman Gaul. The Three Provinces, 58 BC–AD 260.* Ithaca, 1983.

—. and Hugh Elton, eds. *Fifth Century Gaul: A Crisis of Identity.* Cambridge, 1992.

Drioux, Georges. *Cultes indigènes des Lingons.* Paris, 1934.

Driscoll, Stephen T. and Margaret R. Nieke, eds. *Power and Politics in Early Medieval Britain and Ireland.* Edinburgh, 1988.

Dronke, Ursula. *The Role of Sexual Themes in Njals Saga.* London, 1980.

von Duhn, Friedrich and Franz Messerschmidt, *Italische Gräberkunde.* Heidelberg, 1939.

Dumézil, Georges. *The Destiny of a King.* Chicago, 1973.

—. *Gods of the Ancient Northmen.* Berkeley, 1973.

—. "Magic, War and Justice: Odin and Tyr". In his *Gods of the Ancient Northmen*, pp. 26–48.

—. *From Myth to Fiction: The Saga of Hadingus*, trans. Derek Coltman. Chicago, 1973.

—. " 'Le Borgne' and 'Le Manchot': The State of the Problem". In *Myth in Indo-European Antiquity*. eds. Gerald James Larson, Scott Littleton and Jan Puhvel, pp. 17–28. Berkeley, 1974.

Dumville, David N. "Beowulf and the Celtic World: The Use of Evidence". *Traditio* 37 (1981): 109–60.

—. "The Origins of Northumbria: Some Aspects of the British Background". In *The Origins of Anglo-Saxon Kingdoms*, ed. Stephen Bassett, pp. 213–24. London, 1989.

Dubner-Manthey, Birgit. "Kleingeräte am Gürtelgehänge als Bestandteil eines charakteristischen Elements der weiblichen Tracht: Archäologische Untersuchungen zu einigen Lebensbereichen und Mentalitäten der Frauen in Spätantike und Frühmittelalter". In *Frauen in der Geschichte* VII, eds. Werner Affeldt and Annette Kuhn, pp. 88–125. Düsseldorf, 1986.

—. "Zum Amulettbrauchtum in frühmittelalterlichen Frauen-und Kindergräbern". In *Frauen in Spätantike und Frühmittelalter*, ed. Werner Affeldt, pp. 65–88. Sigmaringen, 1990.

Düwel, Klaus. "Runes, Weapons and Jewelry: A Survey of Some of the Oldest Runic Inscriptions". MQ 22 (1981): 69–91.

—. "Runeninschriften auf Waffen". In *Wörter und Sachen im Lichte der Bezeichnungsforschung*, ed. Ruth Schmidt-Wiegand, pp. 128–67. Berlin, 1981.

—. *Runenkunde*. Stuttgart, 1983².

—., Herbert Jankuhn, Harold Siems, Dieter Timpe, eds. Untersuchungen zu Handel und Verkehr in vor-und Frühgeschichtlichen Zeit im Mittel-und Nord Europa. IV vols. Göttingen, 1985.

Duval, Alain. "Regional Groups in Western France". In *Cross-Channel Trade Between Gaul and Britain in the Pre-Roman Iron Age*, eds. Sarah Macready and F.H. Thompson, pp. 78–91. London, 1984.

—. "Celtic Society". In *The Celts*, eds. Sabatino Moscati, Otto Hermann Frey, Venceslas Kruta, Barry Raftery and Miklós Szabó, pp. 485–90. New York, 1991.

Duval, Paul-Marie. "Le dieu SMERTRIOS et ses avatars gallo-romaine". EC 6 (1953): 219–38.

—. "Teutates, Esus, Taranis". EC 8 (1958): 41–58.

—. *Les dieux de la Gaule*. Paris, 1976.

—. "Sources and Distribution of Chieftaincy Wealth in Ancient Gaul". In *Proceddings of the Seventh International Congress of Celtic Studies*, eds. D. Ellis Evans, John G. Griffith and E.M. Jope, pp. 19–24. Oxford, 1986.

—. and Venceslas Kruta, eds. *Les Mouvements Celtiques du Ve au Ier siècle avant notre ère*. Paris, 1979.

Dyson, Stephen L. "Native Revolts in the Roman Empire". *Historia* 20 (1971): 239–274

—. "Native Revolt Patterns in the Roman Empire". ANRW II, 3 (1975): 138–175.

Earle, John and Charles Plummer, eds. *Two of the Saxon Chronicles Parallel*, Vol I. Oxford, 1892.

Ebel, C. *Transalpine Gaul: The Emergence of a Roman Province*. Leiden, 1976.

Eckhardt, Karl August, ed. *Pactus Legis Salicae: 65 Titel-Text*. Göttingen, 1955.

Eckhardt, Uwe. *Untersuchungen zu Form und Funktion der Treueidleistung im merowingischen Frankenreich*. Marburg, 1976.

Edwards, H.J., ed. *Caesar. The Gallic War*. Cambridge, 1980².

Eggers, H.J. "Lübsow, ein germanischer Fürstensitz der älteren Kaiserzeit". PZ 34/35 (1950): 58–112.

Eichmann, Edward. "Die Adoption des deutschen Königs durch den Papst". ZSSR (GA) 37 (1916): 291–312.

Einarsson, Stefan. "Old English *Beot* and Old Icelandic *Heitstrenging*". In *Essential Articles for the Study of Old English Poetry*, eds. J.B. Bessinger and S.J. Kahrl, pp. 99–123. Hamden, 1968.

Eliason, Norman. "The þyle and Scop in *Beowulf*". *Speculum* 38 (1963): 268–273.

Elliot, R.W.V. "Runes, Yews and Magic". *Speculum* 32 (1975): 250–260.

Ellmers, Detlev. "Zum Trinkgeschirr der Wikingerzeit". *Offa* 21/22 (1965/6): 21–43.

Engelhardt, George. "On the Sequence of *Beowulf's Geogoð*". MLN 68 (1953): 91–95.

Enright, Michael J. "King James and his Island: An Archaic Kingship Belief?" SHR 55 (1976): 29–40.

——. "Charles the Bald and Aethelwulf of Wessex: The Alliance of 856 and Strategies of Royal Succession". JMH 5 (1979): 291–302.

——. "Disease, Royal Unction and Propaganda: An Interpretation of Alfred's Journeys to Rome". *Continuity* 3 (1982): 1–16.

——. "The Sutton Hoo Whetstone Sceptre: A Study in Iconography and Cultural Milieu". ASE 11 (1983): 119–34.

——. "Royal Succession and Abbatial Prerogative in Adómnan's *Vita Columbae*". *Peritia* 4 (1985): 83–103.

——. *Iona, Tara and Soissons: The Origin of the Royal Anointing Ritual*. Berlin, 1985.

——. "Lady With a Mead-Cup: Ritual, Group Cohesion and Hierarchy in the Germanic Warband". FM St. 22 (1988): 170–203.

——. "The Goddess Who Weaves: Some Iconographic Aspects of Bracteates of the Fürstenberg Type". FM St. 24 (1990): 54–70.

——. "*Iromanie—Irophobie* Revisited: A Suggested Frame of Reference for Considering Continental Reactions to Irish *peregrini* in the Seventh and Eighth Centuries". In Jörg Jarnut, Ulrich Nonn and Michael Richter, eds. *Karl Martell in seiner Zeit*. Sigmaringen, (1994): 367–380.

Erbe der Vergangenheit. Germanistische Beiträge. Festgabe für Karl Helm zum 80. Geburtstag 19. Mai. 1951. Tübingen, 1951.

Erler, Adalbert. "Das Ritual der nordischen Geschlechtsleite". ZSSR (GA) 64 (1944): 86–111.

Espérandieu, E. *Recueil général des bas-reliefs, statues et bustes de la Gaule romaine*. X vols. Paris, 1907ff.

Evans, D. Ellis, *Gaulish Personal Names: A Study of Some Continental Celtic Formations*. Oxford, 1967.

——. "Celts and Germans". BBCS 29 (1981): 230–255.

——. "The Celts in Britain (up to the Formation of the Brittanic Languages): History, Culture, Linguistic Remains, Substrata". In *Geschichte und Kultur der Kelten:*

Vorbereitungskonferenz 25–28 Oktober 1982 in Bonn, eds. Karl H. Schmidt and Rolf Kodderitzsch, pp. 102–15. Heidelburg, 1986.

—., John G. Griffith and E.M. Jope, eds. *Proceedings of the Seventh International Congress of Celtic Studies*. Oxford, 1986.

Evelyn-White, Hugh, ed. and trans. *The Homeric Hymns and Homerica*. Cambridge, 1959.

Evison, Vera I. "The Dover Ring-sword and Other Sword-rings and Beads". *Archaeologia* 101 (1967): 63–118.

Evolution, Zeit, Geschichte, Philosophie: Universitätsvorträge. Münster, 1982.

Ewig, Eugen. "Studien zur merowingischen Dynastie". FM St. 8 (1974): 15–59.

—. *Spätantikes und fränkisches Gallien. Gesammelte Schriften (1952–1973)*. II vols. München, 1976.

—. "Das Privileg des Bischop Bethefried von Amiens für Corbie von 664 und die Klösterpolitik Königin Balthilds". In his *Spätantikes und fränkischen Gallien. Gesammelte Schriften (1952–1973)*, pp. 538–84.

Faral, Edmond, ed. *Ermold le Noir. Poème sur Louis le Pieux et épitres au roi Pépin*. Paris, 1964.

Farrell, R.T. "Beowulf, Swedes and Geats". SBVS 18 (1972): 226–86.

—, ed. *Bede and Anglo-Saxon England*. Oxford, 1978.

Faull, Margaret L. "The Semantic Development of Old English *wealh*". LSE 8 (1975): 20–44.

Feist, Sigmund. *Indogermanen und Germanen: Ein Beitrag zur europäischen Urgeschichtsforschung*. Halle, 1919.

—. *Germanen und Kelten in der antiken Überlieferung*. Halle, 1927.

Fell, Christine E. "Old English *Beor*". LSE 8 (1975): 76–95.

—. "A *friwif locbore* Revisited". ASE 13 (1984): 157–65.

—. *Women in Anglo-Saxon England*. Bloomington, 1984.

—. "Some Domestic Problems". LSE 16 (1985): 59–82.

Fellmann, Jack. "The First Medieval Grammar of a European Vernacular". *Linguistics* 206 (1978): 55–56.

Fehr, Burkhard. *Orientalische und griechische Gelage*. Bonn, 1971.

Fenske, Lutz, Werner Rösener and Thomas Zotz, eds. *Institutionen, Kultur und Gesellschaft im Mittelalter: Festschrift für Josef Fleckenstein zu seinem 65. Geburtstag*. Sigmaringen, 1984.

Feste und Feiern im Mittelalter: Paderborner Symposion des Mediävistenverbandes. Sigmaringen, 1991.

Feuvrier-Prévotat, C. "Echanges et sociétés en Gaule indépendante: à propos d'un texte de Poseidonios d'Apamée". *Ktema* 3 (1978): 243–259.

Fichtenau, Heinrich. *Lebensordnungen des 10. Jahrhunderts:Studien über Denkart and Existenz im einstigen Karolingerreich*. II vols. Stuttgart, 1984.

Filip, Jan. *Celtic Civilization and its Heritage*. 1977².

Finberg, H.P.R. *Agricultural History of England and Wales 432–1042*. Cambridge, 1972.

Fingerlin, Gerhard. *Grab einer adligen Frau aus Güttingen*. München, 1964.

Fischer, Andreas. *Engagement, Wedding and Marriage in Old English*. Heidelberg, 1986.

Fischer, Franz. "*KEIMHL IA*: Bemerkungen zur kulturgeschichtlichen Interpretation des sogenannten Südimports in der späten Hallstatt—und frühen Latène—Kultur des westlichen Mitteleuropa". *Germania* 51 (1973): 436–459.

—. "Bewaffnung". *Reallexikon* 2 (1976): 409–416.

—. "Thrakien als Vermittler iranischer Metallkunst an die frühen Kelten". In *Beiträge zur Altertumskunde Kleinasiens. Festschrift für Kurt Bittel*, eds. R.M. Boehmer and H. Hauptmann, pp. 191–202. Mainz, 1983.

—. "Der Handel der Mittel- und Spät-Latène-Zeit in Mitteleuropa aufgrund archäologischer Zeugnisse". In Untersuchungen zu Handel und Verkehr vor-und Frühgeschichtlichen Zeit im Mittel-und Nord Europa I, eds. Klaus Düwel, Herbert Jankuhn, Harold Siems, Dieter Timpe, pp. 285–98. Göttingen, 1985.

—. "Kleinaspergle near Asperg Kreis Ludwigsburg (Baden-Württemberg)". In *The Celts*, eds. Sabatino Moscati, Otto Hermann Frey, Vencesles Kruta, Barry Raftery and Miklós Szabó, pp. 485–90. New York, 1991.

Fisher, N.R.E. "Drink, *Hybris* and the Promotion of Harmony in Sparta". In *Classical Sparta. Techniques Behind her Success*, ed. Anton Powell, pp. 126–50. Normon, 1989.

Fishwick, D. "The Development of Provincial Ruler Worship in the Western Roman Empire". ANRW II, 16, 2 (1978): 1201–1253.

Fitzpatrick, A.P. "The Uses of Roman Imperialism by the Celtic Barbarians in the Later Republic". In *Barbarians and Romans in North-West Europe From the Later Republic to Late Antiquity*, eds. John Barrett, Andrew Fitzpatrick and Lesley Macinnes, pp. 27–54. Oxford, 1989.

Flach, Dieter. "Die Germania des Tacitus in ihrem literaturgeschichtlichen Zusammenhang". In *Beiträge zum Verstandnis der Germania des Tacitus* I, eds. Herbert Jankuhn and Dieter Timpe, pp. 27–58. Göttingen, 1989.

Fleck, Jere. "*Konr-Otarr-Geirrodr*: A Knowledge Criterion for Succession to the Germanic Sacred Kingship". SS 42 (1970): 39–49.

—. "Odin's Self-Sacrifice: A New Interpretation". SS 43 (1971): 119–42; 385–413.

—. "The Knowledge Criterion in the *Grimnesmál*: The Case Against 'Shamanism'". ANF 86 (1971): 49–65.

Fleckenstein, Josef. *Grundlagen und Beginn der deutschen Geschichte*. Göttingen, 1974.

—. "Von den Wurzeln Alteuropes: Die 144. Veranstaltung des Mittelalterkreises anlasslich des 70. Geburtstages von Karl Hauck". FM St. 22 (1988): 6–15.

Fleuriot, Leon. "Le vocabulaire de l'Inscription Gauloise de Chamalières". EC 15 (1976): 173–190.

—. "Note additionelle sur l'Inscription de Chamalières". EC 16 (1979): 135–39.

—. "La Tablette de Chamalières: Nouveaux commentaires". EC 17 (1980): 145–159.

Fleury, J. *Recherches historiques sur les empêchements de parenté dans le mariage canonique des origines aux fausses décrétales*. Paris, 1933.

Flint, Valerie I.J. *The Rise of Magic in Early Medieval Europe*. Princeton, 1991.

Flowers, Stephen E. *Runes and Magic: Magical Formulaic Elements in the Older Runic Tradition*. New York-Frankfort, 1986.

Ford, Patrick K. "Celtic Women: The Opposing Sex". *Viator* 19 (1988): 417–33.

Forster, E.S., ed. and trans. *Lucius Annaeus Florus. Epitome of Roman History*. Cambridge, 1947².

Foster, B.O., ed. and trans. *Livy*. XIII vols. London, 1925.

Foulke, William Dudley, trans. *Paul the Deacon. History of the Lombards*. Philadelphia, 1974².

Frank, Roberta. "Why Skalds Address Women". In *Poetry in The Scandinavian Middle Ages: The 7th International Saga Conference*, pp. 67-83. Spoleto, 1990.

Frankenstein, S. and M.J. Rowlands. "The Internal Structure and Regional Context of Early Iron Age Society in South-Western Germany". *Bulletin of the Institute of Archaeology. University of London* 15 (1978): 73–112.

Frere, Sheppard. *Britannia: A History of Roman Britain*. London, 1987³.

Frey, Otto-Herman, *Die Situla in Providence (Rhode Island). Ein Beitrag zur Situlenkunst des Osthallstattkreises*. Berlin, 1962.

——. *Die Entstehung der Situlenkunst*. Berlin, 1969.

——. "Einige Überlegungen zu den Beziehungen zwischen Kelten und Germanen in der Spätlatenezeit". In *Marburger Studien zu Vor-und Frühgeschichte. Gedenkschrift für G. von Merhart*, pp. 45–79. Marburg, 1986.

——. "The Formation of the La Tène Culture". In *The Celts*, eds. Sabatino Moscati, Otto Hermann Frey, Vencesles Kruta, Barry Raftery and Miklós Szabó, pp. 127–46. New York, 1991.

Fritze, Wolfgang. "Die fränkische Schwurfreundschaft der Merowingerzeit. Ihr Wesen und ihre politische Funktion". ZSSR (GA) 71 (1954): 74–125.

Fröhlich, Hermann. *Studien zur langobardischen Thronfolge von den Anfängen bis zur Eroberung des italienische Reiches durch Karl den Grossen (774)*. II vols. Tubingen, 1980.

Fulford, Michael G. "Roman Material in Barbarian Society *c.*200 BC–*c.*AD 400". In *Settlement and Society: Aspects of Western European Prehistory in the First Millenium BC*, eds. T.C. Champion and J.V.S. Megaw, pp. 91–108. New York, 1985.

Gade, Kari Ellen. "Hanging in Northern Law and Literature". *Maal og Minne* (1985): 159–83.

——. "Homosexuality and Rape of Males in Old Norse Law and Literature". SS 58 (1986): 124–41.

——. "The Naked and the Dead in Old Norse Society". SS 60 (1988): 219–45.

Galliou, Patrick. "Days of Wine and Roses? Early Armorica and the Atlantic Wine Trade". In *Cross-Channel Trade Between Gaul and Britian in the Pre-Roman Iron Age*, eds. Sarah Macready and F.H. Thompson, pp. 24–36. London, 1984.

Ganshof, Ferdinand. "Le statut de la femme dans la monarchie franque". RSJB 12 (1962): 5–58.

Gantz, Jeffrey, trans. *Early Irish Myths and Sagas*. Harmondsworth, 1984.

Garnsey, Peter, Keith Hopkins, C.R. Whittaker, eds. *Trade in the Ancient Economy*. Berkeley, 1983.

Geary, Patrick J. *Aristocracy in Provence: The Rhône Basin at the Dawn of the Carolingian Age*. Philadelphia, 1985.

——. *Before France and Germany: The Creation and Transformation of the Merovingian World*. Oxford, 1988.

Gebühr, M. "Zur Definition älterkaiserzeitliches Fürstengräber vom Lübsow-Typ". PZ 49 (1974): 82–128.

Gerriets, Marilyn. "Kingship and Exchange in pre-Viking Ireland". CMCS 13 (1987): 39–72.

——. "The King as Judge in Early Ireland". *Celtica* 20 (1989): 29–52.

Gibson, Margaret and Janet Nelson, eds. *Charles the Bald: Court and Kingdom*. Oxford, 1981.

Giot, P.-R. "Stabilité ou instabilité des populations dans le Nord-Ouest de la Gaule celtique". In *Les Mouvements Celtiques du Ve au Ier siècle avant notre ère*, eds. Paul-Marie Duval and Venceslas Kruta, pp. 21–9. Paris, 1979.

Gladigow, Burkhard and Hans Kippenberg, eds. *Neue Ansätze in der Religionswissenschaft.* München, 1983.

Glasser, Marc. "Marriage in Medieval Hagiography". SMRH 4 (1981): 3–36.

Glendenning, Robert J. and Haraldur Bessason, eds. *Edda: A Collection of Essays.* Manitoba, 1983.

Glosecki, Stephen. "*Beowulf* 769: Grendel's Ale Share". ELN 25 (1987): 1–9.

Gneuss, Helmut. "Die Battle of Maldon als historisches und literarisches Zeugnis". *Bayerische Akad. d. Wiss. Phil.- Hist. Kl.* 5 (1946): 15–40.

Godden, Malcolm and Michael Lapidage, eds. *The Cambridge Companion to Old English Literature.* Cambridge, 1991.

Godley, A.D., ed and trans. *Herodotus.* IV vols. Cambridge, 1950.

Godlowski, Kasimierz. "Die Przeworsk-Kultur". In *Beiträge zum Verstandnis der Germania des Tacitus*, eds, Günter Neumann and Henning Seemann, pp. 9–90. Göttingen, 1992.

Godman, Peter and Roger Collins, eds. *Charlemagne's Heir: New Perspectives on the Reign of Louis the Pious (814–840).* Oxford, 1990.

Goody, Jack. *Cooking, Cuisine and Class: A Study in Comparative Sociology.* Cambridge, 1982.

——. *The Development of the Family and Marriage in Europe.* Cambridge, 1983.

Gordon, E.V. "Wealhþeow and Related Names". MA 4 (1935): 169–75.

Görman, Marianne. "Nordic and Celtic. Religion in Southern Scandinavia During the Late Bronze Age and Early Iron Age". In *Old Norse and Finnish Religions and Cultic Place-Names*, ed. Tore Ahlbäck, pp. 329–43. Åbo, 1990.

Goudineau, Christian. "Marseilles, Rome and Gaul from the Third to the First Century BC". In *Trade in the Ancient Economy*, eds. Peter Garnsey, Keith Hopkins, C.R. Whittaker, pp. 76–86. Berkeley, 1983.

Grahn-Hoek, Heike. *Die fränkische Oberschicht im 6. Jahrhundert: Studien zu ihrer rechtlichen und politischen Stellung.* Sigmaringen, 1976.

Grat, F., J. Vielliard and S. Clemencet, eds. *Annales de Saint-Bertin.* Paris, 1964.

Graus, Frantizek. "Über die sogenannte germanische Treue". *Historica* 1 (1959): 71–121.

——. *Volk, Herrscher und Heiliger im Reich der Merowinger.* Prague, 1965.

Green, David H. *The Carolingian Lord: Semantic Studies on Four Old High German Words: Balder, Fro, Truhtin, Herro.* Cambridge, 1965.

——. "Old English 'dryht'—A New Suggestion". MLR 63 (1968): 392–406.

——. "Orality and Reading: The State of Research in Medieval Studies". *Speculum* 65 (1990): 267–80.

Green, D.R., C.C. Haselgrove, and M. Spriggs, eds. *Social Organization and Settlement.* Oxford, 1978.

Green, Miranda J. "The Iconography and Archaeology of Romano-British Religion". ANRW II, 18, 1 (1986): 113–62.

——. *The Gods of the Celts.* Totowa, 1986.

——. *Symbol and Image in Celtic Religious Art.* London, 1989.

Greene, David. "The Act of Truth in a Middle Irish Tale". Saga och Sed (1976): 30–7.

Grenier, A. *Les Gaulois.* Paris, 1945.

Grierson, Philip. "Election and Inheritance in Early Germanic Kingship". CHJ 7 (1941): 1–22.

Griffith, G.T. *The Mercenaries of the Hellenistic World*.Cambridge, 1935.

Griffiths, Bill. "The Old English Alcoholic Vocabulary—a Re-examination". *Durham University Journal* 47 (1986): 231–7.

Groenmann-Van Waateringe, W. "The Disasterous Effect of the Roman Occupation". In *Roman and Native in the Low Countries: Spheres of Interaction*, eds. Roel Brandt and Jan Slofstra, pp. 147–58. Oxford, 1984.

—. "Food for Soldiers, Food for Thought". In *Barbarians and Romans in North-West Europe From the Later Republic to Late Antiquity*, eds. John Barrett, Andrew Fitzpatrick and Lesley Macinnes, pp. 96–107. Oxford, 1989.

Grohne, Ernst. *Die Koppel-, Ring- und Tüllengefäse: Ein Beitrag zur Typologie und Zweckgeschichte keramischer Formen*. Bremen, 1932.

Grönbech, Wilhelm. *The Culture of the Teutons*. II vols. Copenhagen, 1932.

Grönvik, Ottar. *The Words for 'Heir', 'Inheritance' and 'Funeral Feast' in Early Germanic*. Oslo, 1982.

Gross, Karl. *Menschenhand und Gotteshand in Antike und Christentum*. Stuttgart, 1985.

Gross, Thomas and Rudolf Schieffer, eds. *Hincmarus de ordine palatii*. MGH Fontes III. Hannoverae, 1980.

Grunert, Heinz. "Zur Bedeutung und zur Bild der Frau in den keltischen und germanischen Stammesgesellschaften". In *Frühe Volker in Mitteleuropa*, eds. Fritz Horst and Friedrich Schlette, pp. 247–74. Berlin, 1988.

Gulick, C.B., ed. and trans. *Athenaeus. The Deipnosophists*. VII vols. Cambridge, 1951.

Gurevich, Aaron J. "Wealth and Gift-Bestowal Among the Ancient Scandinavians". *Scandinavica* 7 (1968): 126–38.

—. "Edda and Law: Commentary upon *Hyndlulióð*". ANF 88 (1973): 72–84.

Gussone, Nickolaus and Heiko Steuer. "Diadem". *Reallexikon* 5 (1984): 350–75.

Gutenbrunner, Siegfried. *Die germanischen Götternamen der antiken Inschriften*. Halle/Saale, 1936.

—. "Ariovist und Caesar". RH 96 (1953): 97–100.

Guyonvarc'h, Christian-J. "A propos de la VELLEDA des Bructeres et du mot irlandais FILE 'poète, prophète, voyant' ". *Ogam* 21 (1969): 321–25.

—. and Françoise Le Roux. *Les druides*. Paris, 1986.

—. and Françoise Le Roux. "Remarques sur la Religion Gallo-Romaine". ANRW II, 18, 1 (1986): 423–55.

Gwynn, E. ed. and trans. *The Metrical Dindshenchas*, Parts 1–5. Dublin, 1900–1935.

Haberey, Waldeman. "Ein römisches Ringgefäss aus Kärlich, Landkreis Koblenz". *Festschrift* RGZM III (1952): 79–82.

Hachmann, Rolf. "Zur Gesellschaftsordnung der Germanen in der Zeit um Christi Geburt". AG 5/6 (1957): 7–24.

—. *Die Germanen*. München, 1971.

—. "Germanen und Kelten am Rhein". In *Völker Zwischen Germanen und Kelten*, eds. Rolf Hachman, Georg Kossack and Hans Kuhn, pp. 9–68.

—. "Gundestrup-Studien. Untersuchungen zu den spätkeltischen Grundlagen der frühgermanischen Kunst". *Bericht der Römisch-Germanischen Kommission* 71 (1990): 565–904.

—., Georg Kossack and Hans Kuhn, eds. *Völker Zwischen Germanen und Kelten*. Neumünster, 1962.

Haefele, Hans, ed. *Notker Balbulus, Gesta Karoli Magni Imperatoris.* MGH SS. rer. Germ. 12. Berlin, 1962².

Hallander, Lars-G. "Old English *dryht* and its Cognates". SN 45 (1973): 20–31.

Halsall, G. "The Origins of the *Reihengraberzivilisation*: Forty Years On". In *Fifth Century Gaul*, eds. J. Drinkwater and H. Elton, pp. 196–207. Cambridge, 1992.

Hamp, Eric P. "The Indo-European Terms for Marriage". In *Languages and Cultures: Studies in Honor of Edgar C. Polomé*, eds. Mohammed Ali Jazayery and Werner Winter, pp. 179–82. Berlin, 1988.

Hannig, Jürgen. *Consensus Fidelium: Frühfeudale Interpretationen des Verhältnisse von Königtum und Adel am Beispiel des Frankenreiches.* Stuttgart, 1982.

Hansen, Elaine Tuttle. "*Precepts*: An Old English Instruction". *Speculum* 56 (1981): 1–9.

—. "Hrothgar's 'Sermon' in *Beowulf* as Parental Wisdom". ASE 10 (1982): 53–67.

Hanson, W.S. "The Nature and Function of Roman Frontiers". In *Barbarians and Romans in North-West Europe From the Later Republic to Late Antiquity*, eds. John Barrett, Andrew Fitzpatrick and Lesley Macinnes, pp. 55–63. Oxford, 1989.

Härke, Heinrich. "Early Saxon Weapon Burials: Frequencies, Distributions and Weapon Combinations". In *Weapons and Warfare in Anglo-Saxon England*, ed. Sonia C. Hawkes, 49–62. Oxford, 1989.

—. "'Warrior Graves'? The Background of the Anglo-Saxon Weapon Burial Rite". PP 126 (1990): 22–43.

Hartley, Brian and John Wacher, eds. *Rome and Her Northern Provinces.* London, 1983.

Harbison, Peter. *Pre-Christian Ireland. From the First Settlers to the Early Celts.* London, 1988.

Harman, M., T.I. Molleson and J.L. Price. "Burials, Bodies and Beheadings in Romano-British and Anglo-Saxon Cemetaries". *Bulletin of the British Museum of Natural History (Geol.)* 35 (1981): 145–88.

Harris, Joseph. "Eddic Poetry as Oral Poetry: The Evidence of Parallel Passages is the Helgi Poems for Questions of Composition and Performance". In *Edda: A Collection of Essays.* eds. Robert J. Glendenning and Haraldur Bessason, pp. 210–42. Manitoba, 1983.

Haselgrove, Colin. "'Romanization' Before the Conquest: Gaulish Precedents and British Consequences". In *Military and Civilian in Roman Britain: Cultural Relationships in a Frontier Province*, eds. T.F.C. Blagg and A.C. King, pp. 5–64. Oxford, 1984.

Hassall, M.W.C. "Batavians and the Roman Conquest of Britian". *Britannia* I (1970): 131–36.

Hatt, Jean-Jaques. *Celts and Gallo-Romans.* London, 1970.

—. "La divinité féminine souveraine chez les Celtes continentaux d'après l'épigraphie gallo-romaine et l'art celtique". AIBL (1981): 12–28.

—. "Les deux sources de la religion gauloise et la politique religieuse des empereurs romains en Gaule". ANRW II, 18, 1 (1986): 410–21.

Hauck, Karl. "Rituelle Speisegemeinschaft im 10. und 11. Jahrhundert". SG 3 (1950): 611-621.

—. "Lebensnormen und Kultmythen in germanischen Stammes—und Herrscher-genealogien". *Saeculum* 6 (1955): 186–223.

—. "Die geschichtliche Bedeutung der germanischen Auffassung von Königtum und Adel". *Congrès international des sciences historiques* 11 (1960): 96–120.

——. "Carmina antiqua. Abstammungsglaube und Stammesbewussein". ZBL 27 (1964): 1–33.

——. "Von einer spätantiken Randkultur zum karolingischen Europa". FM St. 1 (1967): 3–93.

——. "Ein neues Drei-Götten-Amulett von der Insel Funen". In *Festschrift Karl Bosl*, pp. 93–159. Stuttgart, 1974.

——. "Zur Ikonologie der Goldbrakteaten XV: Die Arztfunktion des seegermanischen Götterkönigs, erhellt mit der Rolle der Vögel auf den goldenen Amulettbildern". In *Festschrift für Helmut Beumann zum 65. Geburtstag*, eds. Kurt-Ulrich Jaschke and Reinhard Wenskus, pp. 98–116. Sigmaringen, 1977.

——. "Brakteatenikonologie". *Reallexikon* 3 (1978): 361–401.

——. "Die Veränderung der Missionsgeschichte durch die Entdeckung der Ikonologie der germanischen Bilddenkmäler, erhellt am Beispiel der Propagierung der Kampfhilfen des Mars-Wodan in Altuppsala im 7. Jahrhundert". *Westfalen* 58 (1980): 227–307.

——. "Gemeinschaftsstiftende Kulte der Seegermanen". FM St. 14 (1980): 463–609.

——. "Die bildliche Wiedergabe von Götter-und Heldenwaffen im Norder seit der Völkerwanderungszeit". In *Wörter und Sachen im Lichte der Bezeichnungsforschung*, ed. Ruth Schmidt-Wiegand, pp. 168–270. Berlin, 1981.

——. "Fünfzig Jahre Historische Sachforschung—das Vordringen in das ethnologische Europa". In *Evolution, Zeit, Geschichte, Philosophie: Universitatsvorträge*, pp. 65–87. Münster, 1982.

——. "Dioskuren in Bildzeugnissen des Nordens vom 5. bis zum 7. Jahrhundert: Zur Ikonologie des Goldbrakteaten, XXVIII". JRGZM 30 (1983): 435–64.

——. "Text und Bild in einer oralen Kultur. Antworten auf die zeugniskritische Frage nach der Erreichbarkeit mündlicher Überlieferung". FM St. 17 (1983): 510–99.

——. "Formenkunde der Götterthrone des heidnischen Nordens (Zur Ikonologie der Goldbrakteaten XXIX)". *Offa. Berichte und Mitteilungen zur Urgeschichte, Frühgeschichte und Mittelalterarchaologie* 41 (1984): 29–39.

——. "Missionsgeschichte in veränderter Sicht: Sakrale Zentren als methodischer Zugang zu den heidnischen und christlichen Amulettbildern der Übergangsepoche von der Antike zum Mittelalter (Zur Ikonologie der Goldbrakteaten XXVII)". In *Institutionen, Kultur und Gesellschaft im Mittelalter: Festschrift für Josef Fleckenstein zu seinem 65. Geburtstag*, eds. Lutz Fenske, Werner Rösener and Thomas Zotz, pp. 1–34. Sigmaringen, 1984.

——. Variante des göttlichen Erschenungsbildes im kultischen Vollzug erhellt mit einer ikonographischen Formenkunde des heidnischen Altars". FM St. 18 (1984): 266–313.

——. *Die Goldbrakteaten der Völkerwanderungszeit I. Einleitung*. München, 1985.

——. "Karolingische Taufpfalzen im Spiegel hofnaher Dichtung". *Nachrichten d. Akad. d. Wiss. in Göttingen. Phil-Hist Klasse*, 1985.

——. "Motivanalyse eines Doppelbreakteaten. Die Trager der Goldenen Götterbildamulette und die Traditionsinstanz der fünischen Brakteaten Produktion". FM St. 19 (1985): 139-194.

——. "Die Wiedgabe von Göttersymbolen und Sinnzeichen der A-, B-, und C-brakteaten auf D- und F- Brakteaten". FM St. 20 (1986): 474–512.

——. "Macht und Meer im völkerwanderungszeitlichen Ostseeraum, erhellt mit

Schiffsresten, Goldhorten und Bildzeugnissen (Zur Ikonologie der Goldbrakteaten, XLIII)". In *Gesellschaftsgeschichte: Festschrift für Karl Bosl zum 80. Geburtstag* I, ed. Ferdinand Siebt, pp. 139–56. Munchen, 1988.

——. "Zum Problem der Götter im Horizont der völkerwanderungszeitlichen Brakteaten (Zur Ikonologie der Goldbrakteaten, XLII)". In *Person und Gemeinschaft in Mittelalter: Karl Schmid zum fünfundsechzigsten Geburtstag*, eds. Gerd Althoff, Dieter Geuenich, Otto Gerhard Oexle and Joachim Wollasch, pp. 73–98. Sigmaringen, 1988.

——. "Zwanzig Jahre Brakteatenforschung in Münster/Westfalen (Zur Ikonologie der Goldbrakteaten, XL)". FM St. 22 (1988): 17–52.

——. "Ein Königsname in einer Brakteateninschrift". In *Historiographia Medievalis: Festschrift für Franz-Josef Schmale zum 65 Geburtstag*, pp. 38–59. Darmstadt, 1989.

——. "Der Missionsauftrag Christi und das Kaisertum Ludwigs des Frommen". In *Charlemange's Heir: New Perspectives on the Reign of Louis the Pious (814–840)*, eds. Peter Godman and Roger Collins, pp. 275–308. Oxford, 1990.

——. "Frühmittelalterliche Bildüberlieferung und der organisierte Kult". In his *Der historische Horizont der Götterbild-Amulette*, pp. 433–574.

——., ed. *Der historische Horizant der Gotterbild-Amulette aus der Übergangsepoche von der Spätantike zum Frühmittelalter*. Göttingen, 1992.

——. "Altuppsalas Polytheismus exemplarisch erhellt mit Bildzengnissen des 5.–7. Jahrhunderts". In *Studien zum Altgermanischen. Festschrift für Heinrich Beck*, ed. Heiko Uecker, pp. 197–302. Berlin, New York, 1994.

Haugen, Einar. "The Edda as Ritual: Odin and His Masks". In *Edda: A Collection of Essays*, eds. Robert J. Glendenning and Haraldur Bessason, pp. 3–24. Manitoba, 1983.

Haubrichs, Wolfgang. *Geschichte der deutschen Literatur von den Anfängen bis zum Beginn der Neuzeit I: Von den Aufängen zum hohen Mittelalter*. Frankfurt, 1988.

Hawkes, Sonia C., ed. *Weapons and Warfare in Anglo-Saxon England*. Oxford, 1989.

Hedeager, Lotte. "A Quantitative Analysis of Roman Imports in Europe North of the Limes (0–400 AD) and the Question of Roman-Germanic Exchange". In *New Directions in Scandinavian Archaeology*, eds. Kristian Kristiansen and Carsten Paludan-Muller, pp. 191–216. Odense, 1984.

——. Iron Age Societies: From Tribe to State in Northern Europe, 500 BC to AD 700. Cambridge, 1992.

Heinen, Heinz. *Trier und das Trevererland in römischer Zeit*. Trier, 1985.

Heller, Rolf. *Die literarische Darstellung der Frau in den Islandersagas*. Halle, 1958.

Hellmuth, Leopold. *Gastfreundschaft und Gastrecht bei den Germanen*. Wien, 1984.

Helm, Karl. *Altgermanische Religionsgeschichte*, Vol I. Heidelberg, 1913.

——. *Wodan. Ausbreitung und Wanderung seines Kultes*. Giessen, 1946.

Henderson, G., ed. *Fled Bricrend: The Feast of Bricriu*. London, 1899.

Henig, Martin. *Religion in Roman Britain*. New York, 1984.

——. and Anthony King, eds. *Pagan Gods and Shrines of the Roman Empire*. Oxford, 1986.

Henry, Patrick L. "Interpreting the Gaulish Inscription of Chamalières". EC 21 (1984): 144–50.

Herbert, Maire. "Amra Coluim Cille". In *Sages, Saints and Storytellers: Celtic Studies in Honour of Professor James Carney*, eds. Donnchadh Ó Córrain, Liam Breatnach and Kim Mc Cone, pp. 67–76. Naas, 1989.

Herlihy, David. *Opera muliebria: Women and Work in Medieval Europe*. New York, 1990.

Herren, Michael. "On the Earliest Irish Acquaintance with Isidore of Seville". In *Visigothic Spain: New Approaches*, ed. Edward James, pp. 243–50. Oxford, 1980.

—., ed. and trans. *The Hisperica Famina I. The A-Text.* Toronto, 1974.

Herrmann, Bernd and Rolf Sprandel. *Determinanten der Bevölkerungsentwicklung im Mittelalter.* Weinheim, 1987.

Herzig, Heinz E. and Regula Frei-Stolba. *Labor omnibus unius. Gerold Walser zum 70. Geburtstag dargebracht von Freunden, Kollegen und Schülern.* Stuttgart, 1989.

Hess, Henner. "Die Entstehung zentraler Herrschaftsinstanzen durch die Bildung klientelärer Gefolgschaften". KZS 29 (1977): 762-778.

Hill, John M. "Beowulf and the Danish Succession. Gift-Giving as an Occasion for Complex Gesture". *Medievalia et Humanistica* 11 (1982): 177-197.

Hill, Rosalind. "Marriage in Seventh Century England". In *Saints, Scholars and Heroes: Studies in Medieval Culture* I, eds. Margot King and Wesley Stevens, pp. 67–75. Collegeville, 1979.

Hillgarth, J.N. "Ireland and Spain in the Seventh Century". *Peritia* 3 (1984): 1-16.

Hillmann, Michael. "'Geschlecht' als Masstab der Rechtsordnung. Überlegungen zur Geschlechterpolarität in den altenglischen Gesetzen". In *Frauen in der Geschichte* VII, eds. Werner Affeldt and Annette Kuhn, pp. 171–91. Dusseldorf, 1986.

Hines, John. *The Scandinavian Character of Anglian England in the Pre-Viking Period.* Oxford, 1984.

Hinz, Hermann. *Germania Romana III: Römisches Leben auf germanischen Boden.* Heidelberg, 1970.

Historiographia Medievalis: Festschrift für Franz-Josef Schmale zum 65 Geburtstag. Darmstadt, 1989.

Hoekstra, T.J., H.L. Janssen and I.W.L. Moermann, eds. *Liber Castellorum: 40 variaties op het thema kasteel.* Zutphen, 1981.

Hoffmann, Erich. "Die Einladung des Königs bei den skandinavischen Völkern im Mittelalter". MS 8 (1975): 100–39.

—. *Königserhebung und Thronfolgeordnung in Danemark bis zum Ausgang des Mittelalters.* Berlin, 1976.

Hoffmann, Marta. *The Warp-Weighted Loom. Studies in the History and Technology of an Ancient Instrument.* Oslo, 1964.

Hoffner, A. "The Princely Tombs of the Celts in the Middle Rhineland". In *The Celts,* eds. Sabatino Moscati, Otto Hermann Frey, Venceslas Kruta, Barry Raftery and Miklós Szabó, pp. 155–62. New York, 1991.

Höfler, Otto. *Kultische Geheimbunde der Germanen.* Vol. I. Frankfort, 1934.

Hofmann, Dietrich. "Die Bezeichnung Odins in Húsdrápa 9". FM St. 18 (1984): 314-20.

Holder, A. *Altceltischer Sprachschatz.* III vols. Lepzig, 1896–1913.

Hollander, Lee M., ed and trans. *Heimskringla: History of the Kings of Norway.* Austin, 1964.

Hollowell, Ida Masters. "Unferth and the þyle in *Beowulf*". SP 73 (1976): 239-65.

Hommages à Albert Grenier, Vol II. Bruxelles, 1962.

Hooker, J.T. *The Ancient Spartans.* London, 1980.

Horn, Heinz Günter. "Bilddenkmäler des Matronenkultes im Ubiergebiet". In *Matronen und verwandte Gottheiten*, eds. Gerhard Bauchhenss and Günter Neumann, pp. 31–54. Köln, 1987.

Horn, Isabella. "Diskussionsbemerkung zu Ikonographie und Namen der Matronen". In *Matronen und verwandte Gottheiten*, eds. Gerhard Bauchhenss and Günter Neumann, pp. 155–56. Köln, 1987.

Horst, Fritz and Friedrich Schlette, eds. *Frühe Völker in Mitteleuropa*. Berlin, 1988.

Hubert, Henri. *The Greatness and Decline of the Celts*. London, 1934.

Hughes, Diane Owen. "From Brideprice to Dowry in Mediterranean Europe". JFH 3 (1978): 262–296.

Hume, Kathryn. "The Concept of the Hall in Old English Poetry". ASE 3 (1974): 63–74.

Hüpper-Dröge, Dagmar. "Schutz-und Angriffswaffen nach den Leges und verwandten fränkischen Rechtsquellen". In *Wörter und Sachen im Lichte der Bezeichnungsforschung*, ed. Ruth Schmidt-Wiegand, pp. 107–27. Berlin, 1981.

——. *Schild und Speer: Waffen und ihre Bezeichnungen im frühen Mittelalter*. Frankfurt a/M, 1982.

Hutton, Maurice, ed. *Tacitus. Agricola and Germania*. Cambridge, 1963[2].

Hyam, Jane. "Ermentrude and Richildis". In *Charles the Bald: Court and Kingdom*, eds. Margaret Gibson and Janet Nelson, pp. 133–56. Oxford, 1981.

Irsigler, Franz, *Untersuchungen zur Geschichte des frühfränkischen Adels*. Bonn, 1981.

Irving, Edward B. *A Reading of Beowulf*. New Haven, 1968.

Jackson, John, ed. *Tacitus. The Annals*. IV vols. Cambridge, 1951[2].

Jackson, Kenneth. "On Some Romano-British Place-Names". JRS 38 (1948): 54–8.

——. *Language and History in Early Britain*. Edinburgh, 1953.

——. *The Oldest Irish Tradition: A Window on the Iron Age*. Cambridge, 1964.

Jacobi, Heinrich. "Der keltische Schüssel und der Schüssel der Penelope, ein Beitrag zur Geschichte des antiken Verschlusses". In *Schumacher—Festschrift*, pp. 213–32. Mainz, 1930.

James, Edward. "Cemetaries and the Problem of Frankish Settlement in Gaul". In *Names, Words and Graves*, ed. P.H. Sawyer, pp. 55–89. Leeds, 1979.

——. "Merovingian Cemetary Studies, and Some Implications for Anglo-Saxon England". In *Anglo-Saxon Cemetaries 1979*, eds. P. Rahtz, T. Dickinson and L. Watts, pp. 35–58. Oxford, 1980.

——., ed. *Visigothic Spain: New Approaches*. Oxford, 1980.

——. "Burial and Status in the Early Medieval West". TRHS 39 (1989): 23–40.

——. "The Origins of Barbarian Kingdoms: The Continental Evidence". In *The Origins of Anglo-Saxon Kingdoms*, ed. Stephen Bassett, pp. 40–54. London, 1989.

Jankuhn, Herbert. *Archäologische Bemerkungen zur Glaubwurdigkeit des Tacitus in der Germania*. Göttingen, 1966.

——. "Archäologische Beochtungen zu Tier- und Menschenopfer bei der Germanen in der römischen Kaiserzeit". *Nachr. d. Akad. d. Wiss. Göttingen. Phil.-Hist- Klasse* 6 1967.

——., ed. *Vorgeschichtliche Heiligtümer und Opferplätze in Mittel-und Nordeuropa*. Göttingen, 1970.

——. "Siedlung, Wirtschaft und Gesellschaftsordnung der germanischen Stämme in der Zeit der römischen Angriffskriege". ANRW II, 5, 2 (1976): 65–126, 1262–1265.

——. "Das Germanenproblem in der älteren archäologischen Forschung (Von der Mitte des 19. Jh.s bis zum Tode Kossinnas)". In *Germanenprobleme in heutiger Sicht*, ed. Heinrich Beck, pp. 298–309. Berlin, 1986.

——. "Neue Erkenntnisse zur Sozialstruktur germanischer Stämme im frühen Mittelalter auf Grund von Grabfunden". In *Gesellschaftsgeschichte: Festschrift für Karl Bosl zum 80. Geburtstag* I, ed. Ferdinand Siebt, pp. 29–35. München, 1988.

—. and Dieter Timpe, eds. *Beiträge zum Verstandnis der Germania des Tacitus*, Vol I. Göttingen, 1989.

Janssen, Walter. "Essen und Trinken im frühen und hohen Mittelalter aus archäologischer Sicht". In *Liber Castellorum: 40 variaties op het thema kasteel*, eds.T.J. Hoekstra, H.L. Janssen and I.W.L. Moermann, pp. 324–37. Zutphen, 1981.

Jarnut, Jorg. *Geschichte der Langobarden*. Stuttgart, 1982.

—. Ulrich Nonn und Michael Richter, eds. *Karl Martell in seiner Zeit*. Sigmaringen, 1994.

Jaschkc, Kurt-Ulrich und Reinhard Wenskus, eds. *Festschrift für Helmut Beumann zum 65. Geburtstag*. Sigmaringen, 1977.

Jazayery, Mohammed Ali and Werner Winter, eds. *Languages and Cultures: Studies in Honor of Edgar C. Polomé*. Berlin, 1988.

Jenkins, Dafydd and Morfydd Owen, eds. *The Welsh Law of Women: Studies Presented to Professor Daniel A. Binchy on his Eightieth Birthday*. Cardiff, 1980.

Jennings, Lee and G. Schultz-Behrend, eds. *Vistas and Vectors: Essays Honoring the Memory of Helmut Rehder*. Austin, 1979.

Jerem, E. "The Late Iron Age Cemetery of Szentlörinc". AAH 20 (1968): 166–90.

—. "Späteisenzeitliche Grabfunde von Beremend (Komitat Baranya)". AAH 25 (1973): 65–86.

Jochens, Jenny M. "The Church and Sexuality in Medieval Iceland". JMH 6 (1980): 377–92.

—. "Consent in Marriage: Old Norse Law, Life, and Literature". SS 58 (1986): 142–76.

—. "The Medieval Icelandic Heroine: Fact or Fiction?". *Viator* 17 (1986): 35–50.

—. "The Female Inciter in the King's Sagas". ANF 102 (1987): 100–19.

—. "The Politics of Reproduction: Medieval Norwegian Kingship". AHR 92 (1987): 327–49.

John, Eric. *Land Tenure in Early England: A Discussion of Some Problems*. Leicester, 1964.

—. "Beowulf and the Margins of Literacy". *Bulletin of the John Rylands Library* 56 (1973–74): 388–422.

Jones, Gwyn, ed. and trans. *King Hrolf and his Champions: Eirik the Red and Other Icelandic Sagas*. London, 1961.

Jones, Michael E. "The Logistics of the Anglo-Saxon Invasions". In *Naval History: The Sixth Symposium of the United States Naval Academy*, ed. Daniel M. Masterton, pp. 62–9. Wilmington, 1987.

Jope, E.M. "Celtic Art: Expressiveness and Communication Through 2500 Years". PBA 73 (1987): 99–123.

Jullian, Camille. *Histoire de la Gaule*, Vol IV. Paris, 1913.

Jungandreas, Wolfgang. *Sprachliche Studien zur germanischen Altertumskunde*. Wiesbaden, 1981.

Kabell, Aage. "Unferð und die dänischen Biersitten". ANF 94 (1979): 31–41.

Kajanto, I. "Epigraphical Evidence of the Cult of Fortuna in Germania Romana". *Latomus* 47 (1988): 554–83.

Kalifa, Simon. "Singularités matrimoniales chez les anciens germains: le rapt et le droit de la femme à disposer d'elle-même". RHDFE 48 (1970): 199–225.

Kanner, B., ed. *The Women of England From Anglo-Saxon Times to the Present*. London, 1980.

Karras, Ruth M. *Slavery and Society in Medieval Scandinavia*. New Haven, 1988.

Kantorowicz, Ernst. *The King's Two Bodies: A Study in Medieval Political Theology*. Princeton, 1970².

Kaufmann, Ekkehard. "Formstrenge". HdR I, clm. 1163–8.

Kauffmann, Friedrich. "Braut und Gemahl". ZdP 42 (1910): 129–53.

Kaul, Flemming. "The Dejbjerg Carts". In *The Celts*, eds. Sabatino Moscati, Otto Hermann Frey, Vencesles Kruta, Barry Raftery and Miklós Szabó, pp. 536–37. New York, 1991.

——. "The Gundestrup Cauldron". In *The Celts*, eds. Sabatino Moscati, Otto Hermann Frey, Vencesles Kruta, Barry Raftery and Miklós Szabó, pp. 538–39. New York, 1991.

Kearney, Richard, ed. *The Irish Mind: Exploring Intellectual Traditions*. Dublin, 1985.

Keay, S.J. *Roman Spain*. London, 1990.

Keller, Hagen. "Alemannen und Sueben nach den Schriftquellen des 3. bis 7. Jahrhunderts". FM St. 23 (1989): 89–111.

Kellogg, Robert. "Literacy and Orality in the Poetic Edda". In *Vox intexta. Orality and Textuality in the Middle Ages*, eds. A.N. Doane and Carol B. Pasternack, pp. 89–101. Madison, 1991.

Kelly, Fergus. *A Guide to Early Irish Law*. Dublin, 1988.

Kennedy, Charles W., trans. *Beowulf: The Oldest English Epic*. New York, 1940.

Kienast, Walter. "Germanische Treue und Königsheil". HZ 227 (1978): 265–324.

——. "Gefolgswesen und Patrocinium im spanischen Westgotenreich". HZ 239 (1984): 23–75.

King, Margot and Wesley Stevens, eds. *Saints, Scholars and Heroes: Studies in Medieval Culture*. II vols. Collegeville, 1979.

Kirchner, Horst, ed. *Ur und Frühgeschichte als historische Wissenschaft. Festschrift Ernst Wahle*. Hiedelberg, 1950.

Klaeber, Fr., ed. *Beowulf and the Fight at Finnsburg*. Lexington, 1950².

Kliman, Bernice. "Women in Early English Literature, *Beowulf* to the *Ancrene Wisse*". NMS 21 (1977): 32–49.

Kimmig, W. "The Heuneburg Hillfort and the Proto-Celtic Princely Tombs of Upper Rhineland". In *The Celts*, eds. Sabatino Moscati, Otto Hermann Frey, Vencesles Kruta, Barry Raftery and Miklós Szabó, pp. 114–15. New York, 1991.

Klinck, Anne. "Anglo-Saxon Women and the Law". JMH 8 (1982): 107–21.

Klindt-Jensen, Ole. *Foreign Influences in Denmark's Early Iron Age*. Copenhagen, 1950.

Klingenberg, H. "Dichter". *Reallexikon* 5 (1984): 376–92.

Kneissl, Peter. "Entstehung und Bedeutung der Augustalität. (Zur Inschrift der ara Narbonensis [CIL XII 4333])". Chiron 10 (1980): 291–326.

Knez, Tone. "Neue Hallstattzeitliche Pseudokernoi aus Novo Mesto". *Antike Welt* 5 (1974): 53–54.

Koch, John T. "A Welsh Window on the Iron Age: Manawydan, Mandubracios". CMCS 14 (1987): 17–52.

——. "Brân, Brennos: An Instance of Early Gallo-Brittonic History and Mythology". CMCS 20 (1990): 1–20.

Koch, Robert. "Waffenförmige Anhänger aus merowingerzeitlichen Frauengräbern". JRGZ 17 (1970): 285–93.

Kodderitzsch, Rolf. "Keltoide Namen mit germanischen Namenträgern". ZCP 41 (1986): 188–213.

Konecny, Silvia. *Die Frauen des karolingische Königshauses: Die politische Bedeutung der Ehe und die Stellung der Frau in den fränkischen Herrscherfamilien vom 7. bis zum 10. Jahrhundert.* Wien, 1976.

Kossack, Georg. "Prunkgräber. Bemerkungen zu Eigenschaften und Aussagewert". In *Studien zur Vor- und Frühgeschichtichen Archäologie. Festschrift Joachim. Werner* I, eds. Georg Kossack and Günter Ulbert, pp. 3–33. München, 1974.

——. "Trinkgeschirr als Kultgerät der Hallstattzeit". In *Varia Archaeologica*, pp. 97–105. Berlin, 1964.

——. and Günter Ulbert, eds. *Studien zur Vor- und Frühgeschichtichen Archäologie. Festschrift Joachim Werner*, Vol I. München, 1974.

Köstler, Rudolf. *Die väterliche Ehebewilligung: Eine kirchenrechtliche Untersuchung auf rechtsvergleichender Grundlage.* Stuttgart, 1908.

——. "Raub-, Kauf- und Friedelehe bei den Germanen". ZSSR (GA) 63 (1943): 92–136.

Krahe, Hans. *Sprache und Vorzeit. Europäische Vorgeschichte nach dem Zeugnis der Sprache.* Heidelberg, 1954.

——. "Altgermanische Kleinigkeiten". IF 66 (1961): 35–43.

Krapp, George Philip and Elliot van Kirk Dobbie, eds. *The Exeter Book.* New York, 1936.

Kratz, Dennis, ed. *Waltharius and Ruodlieb.* New York, 1984.

Krausse, Dirk. "Trinkhorn und Kline. Zur griechischen Vermittlung orientalischer Trinksitten an die frühen Kelten". *Germania* 71 (1993): 188–97.

Kreissig, Heinz and Friedmar Kühnert, eds. *Antike Abhangigkeitsformen in der griechischen Gebieten ohne polisstruktur und den romischen Provinzen.* Berlin, 1985.

Kreutzer, Gert. *Die Dichtungslehre der Skalden: Poetologische Terminologie und Autorenkommentäre als Grundlagen einer Gattungspoetik.* Meisenheim am Glan, 1977.

Kristensen, Anne K.G. *Tacitus' germanische Gefolgschaft.* Köbenhavn, 1983.

Kristiansen, Kristian and Carsten Paludan-Muller, eds. *New Directions in Scandinavian Archaeology.* Odense, 1984.

Kroeschell, Karl. *Haus und Herrschaft im frühen deutschen Recht.* Göttingen, 1968.

——. "Söhne und Tochter im germanischen Erbrecht". In *Studien zu den germanischen Volksrechten: Gedächtnisschrift für Wilhelm Ebel*, ed. Gotz Landwehr, pp. 87–115. Frankfurt, 1982.

Kromer, Karl. "Das Situlenfest: Versuch einer Interpretation der Darstellungen auf figural verzierten Situlen". *Situla* 20/21 (1980): 225–40.

——. "Gift Exchange and the Hallstatt Courts". BIA 19 (1982): 21–30.

Krüger, Bruno. "Stamm und Stammesverband bei den Germanen in Mitteleuropa". Zf.A. 20 (1986): 27–37.

——. *Die Germanen: Geschichte und Kultur der germanischen Stamme in Mitteleuropa.* II vols. Berlin, 1988.

Krumbein, A. "Civilis". *Reallexikon* 5 (1984): 7–10.

Krusch, Bruno, ed. *Vita S. Balthildis.* MGH SS. rer. Merov. 2. Hannoverae, 1888.

——. *Liber in gloria confessorum.* MGH SS. rer. Merov. 1(2). Hannoverae, 1885.

——., ed. *Ionas Vita Columbani abbatis.* MGH SS. rer. Merov. 4. Hannoverae, 1902.

——., ed. *Ionas Vita Vedastis episcopi.* MGH SS. rer. Germ. Hannoverae, 1905.

Kruta, Venceslas. "Les Celtes des Gaules d'après l'archéologie". In *Geschichte und Kultur der Kelten: Vorbereitungskonferenz 25–28 Oktober 1982 in Bonn*, eds. Karl H. Schmidt and Rolf Kodderitzsch, pp. 33–51. Heidelburg, 1986.

——. "Le corail, le vin et l'arbre de vie: Observations sur l'art et la religion des Celts du Vᵉ au Iᵉʳ siecle avant J.-C". EC 23 (1986): 7–32.

——. "The First Celtic Expansion". In *The Celts*, eds. Sabatino Moscati, Otto Hermann Frey, Vencesles Kruta, Barry Raftery and Miklós Szabó, pp. 195–214. New York, 1991.

Kuhn, Hans. "Die Grenzen der germanischen Gefolgschaft". ZSSR (GA) 17 (1956): 1–83.

——. "König und Volk in der germanischen Bekehrungsgeschichte". *Kleine Schriften* II (1971): 277–86.

——. "Philologisches zur Adoption bei den Germanen". *Kleine Schriften* II (1971): 410–19.

——. "Der Todesspear. Odin als Totengott". *Kleine Schriften* IV (1971): 247–58.

Kuhrt, A. and A. Cameron, eds. *Images of Women in Antiquity*. London, 1983.

Kunow, Jürgen. *Der römische Import in der Germania libera bis zu den Markomannenkriegen. Studien zu Bronze- und Glasgefässen*. Neumünster, 1983.

Kupka, P. "Zwei germanische Tonlampen aus der Altmark". PZ (1910): 81–3.

Kylstra, H.E. "Ale and Beer in Germanic". In *Iceland and the Medieval World: Studies in Honour of Ian Maxwell*, eds. E.O.G. Turville-Petre and J.S. Martin, pp. 7–14. Victoria, 1974.

Laing, Lloyd. *The Archaeology of Late Celtic Britain and Ireland*. London, 1975.

——. "The Romanization of Ireland in the Fifth Century". *Peritia* 4 (1985): 261-278.

——. *Celtic Britian and Ireland, AD 200–800*. New York, 1990.

Lambert, Pierre-Yves. "La tablette gauloise de Chamalières". EC 16 (1979): 141-169.

——. "A Restatement on the Gaulish Tablet From Chamalières". BBCS 34 (1987): 10-17.

Lambrechts, Pierre. *L'Exaltation de la tête dans la pensée et dans l'art des Celtes*. Bruges, 1954.

Landwehr, Gotz, ed. *Studien zu den germanischen Volksrechten: Gedächtnisschrift für Wilhelm Ebel*. Frankfurt, 1982.

Lancaster, Lorraine. "Kinship in Anglo-Saxon Society". BJS 9 (1958): 230–50, 359–77.

Larson, Gerald James, Scott Littleton and Jan Puhvel, eds. *Myth in Indo-European Antiquity*. Berkeley, 1974.

Larson, Laurence, trans. *The Earliest Norwegian Laws: Being the Gulathing Law and the Frostathing Law*. New York, 1935.

Laske, Walter. *Das Problem der Mönchung in der Völkerwanderungszeit*. Zürich, 1973.

Lee, Alvin. *The Guest Hall of Eden*. New Haven, 1972.

Le Goff, Jacques. *Time, Work and Culture in the Middle Ages*. trans. A. Goldhammer. Chicago, 1980.

——. "The Symbolic Ritual of Vassalage". In his *Time, Work and Culture in the Middle Ages*, trans. A. Goldhammer, pp. 237–88. Chicago, 1980.

Lehmann, Winfred P. "Linguistic and Archaeological Data for Handbooks of Proto-Languages". In *Proto-Indo-European: The Archaeology of a Linguistic Problem. Studies in Honor of Marija Gimbutas*, eds. Susan Nacer Skomal and Edgar C. Polomé, pp. 72–87. Washington, 1987.

Leibundgut, Annalis. "Der 'Traian' von Ottenhusen. Eine neronische Privatapotheose und ihre Beziehungen zum Mercur des Zenodorus". JDAI 99 (1984): 257–89.

Lejeune, Michel and Robert Marichal. "Textes gaulois et gallo-romaine en cursive latine". EC 15 (1976): 151–90.

—. "En marge d'une *rigani* gauloise". AIBL (1981): 29–30.

—. "Rencontres de l'alphabet grec avec les langues barbares au cours du Ier millenaire avant J.-C". In *Modes de contacts et processus de transformation dans les sociétés anciennes*, ed. Giuseppe Nenci, pp. 731–53. Pise-Rome, 1983.

—., et al. "Textes gaulois et gallo-romaine en cursive latine: Le plomb du Larzac". EC 22 (1985): 95–177.

Les princes celtes et la Mediterranée. Rome, 1988.

Leuner, Hanscarl. "Über die historische Rolle magischer Pflanzen und ihre Wirkstoffe". In *Vorgeschichtliche Heiligtümer und Opferplätze in Mittel-und Nordeuropa*, ed. Herbert Jankuhn, pp. 279–96. Göttingen, 1970.

Le Roux, Françoise. "La divination chez les Celtes". In *La Divination*, eds. Andre Caquot and Marcel Leibovici, pp. 233–56. Paris, 1968.

Leyser, Karl. "The German Aristocracy from the Ninth to the Early Twelfth Century: A Historical and Cultural Sketch". PP 40 (1968): 25–53.

—. "Maternal Kin in Early Medieval Germany. A Reply". PP 49 (1970): 126–34.

Liberman, Anatoly. "Germanic *sendan* 'to make a sacrifice' ". JEGP 77 (1978): 473–88.

Lichardus, Jan. *Korpergräber der frühen Kaiserzeit im Gebiet der südlichen Elbgermanen*. Bonn, 1984.

Liebermann, Felix, ed. *Die Gesetze der Angelsachsen*. III vols. Halle, 1903–16.

Lincoln, Bruce. "The Druids and Human Sacrifice". In *Languages and Cultures: Studies in Honor of Edgar C. Polomé*, eds. Mohammed Ali Jazayery and Werner Winter, pp. 381–96. Berlin, 1988.

Lindow, John. *Comitatus, Individual and Honor: Studies in North Germanic Institutional Vocabulary*. Berkeley, 1976.

—., Lars Lönnroth and Gerd Wolfgang Weber, eds. *Structure and Meaning in Old Norse Literature: New Approaches to Textual Analysis and Literary Criticism*. Odense, 1986.

Lönnroth, Lars. "Hjálmar's Death-Song and the Delivery of Eddic Poetry". *Speculum* 46 (1971): 1–20.

Loth, J. "Le dieu Lug, la Terre Mère et les Lugoves". RA 23 (1914): 205–30.

Loyn, H.R. "Kinship in Anglo-Saxon England". ASE 3 (1974): 197–209.

Lucas, A.T. *Cattle in Ancient Ireland*. Kilkenny, 1989.

Lund, A.A. "Zum Germanenbegriff bei Tacitus". In *Germanenprobleme in heutiger Sicht*, ed. Heinrich Beck, pp. 53–87. Berlin, 1986.

Mac Cana, Proinsias. "Aspects of the Theme of King and Goddess in Irish Literature". EC 7 (1955/56): 76–114; 8 (1958): 59–68.

—. *Celtic Mythology*. London, 1970.

—. "Conservation and Innovation in Early Celtic Literature". EC 13 (1972): 61–119.

—. "*Regnum* and *Sacerdotium*: Notes on Irish Tradition". PBA 65 (1979): 443–79.

—. *The Learned Tales of Medieval Ireland*. Dublin, 1980.

—. "Women in Irish Mythology". *The Crane Bag* 4 (1980): 7–11.

—. "Early Irish Ideology and the Concept of Unity". In *The Irish Mind. Exploring Intellectual Traditions*, ed. Richard Kearney, pp. 56–78. Dublin, 1985.

Mac Curtain, Margaret and Donnchadh Ó Córrain, eds. *Women in Irish Society*. Westport, 1979.

Mac Mathúna, Liam. *The Designation, Functions and Knowledge of the Irish Poet: A Preliminary Semantic Study*. Wien, 1982.

Mac Neill, Máire. *The Festival of Lughnasa*. Oxford, 1962.

Mac Niocaill, Gearoid. *Ireland Before the Vikings*. Dublin, 1972.

Macready, Sarah and F.H. Thompson, eds. *Cross-Channel Trade Between Gaul and Britain in the Pre-Roman Iron Age*. London, 1984.

Magennis, Hugh. "The Cup as Symbol and Metaphor in Old English Literature". *Speculum* 60 (1985): 517–36.

—. "The *Beowulf* Poet and His *druncne dryhtguman*". NM 86 (1985): 159–64.

—. "The Treatment of Feasting in the *Heliand*". *Neophilologus* 69 (1985): 126–33.

—. "The Exegesis of Inebriation: Treading Carefully in Old English". ELN 23 (1986): 3–6.

—. "Water-Wine Miracles in Anglo-Saxon Saint's Lives". ELN 23 (1986): 7–9.

Magnusson, Magnus and Hermann Palsson, trans. *Laxdaela Saga*. Harmondsworth, 1972.

—, trans. *Njals Saga*. Harmondsworth, 1960.

Mahr, Gustav. *Die Jüngere Latènekultur des trierer Landes*. Berlin, 1967.

Maier, Ferdinand. "The *Oppida* of the Second and First Centuries BC". In *The Celts*, eds. Sabatino Moscati, Otto Hermann Frey, Vencesles Kruta, Barry Raftery and Miklós Szabó, pp. 411–25. New York, 1991.

Mallory, J.P. "The Sword in the Ulster Cycle". In *Studies in Early Ireland: Essays in Honour of M.V. Duignan*, ed. B.G. Scott, pp. 99–114. Galway, 1981.

—. "Silver in the Ulster Cycle of Tales". In *Proceedings of the Seventh International Congress of Celtic Studies*, eds. D. Ellis Evans, John G. Griffith and E.M. Jope, pp. 31–78. Oxford, 1986.

—. and T.E. Mc Neill. *The Archaeology of Ulster: From Colonization to Plantation*. Antrim, 1991.

Marburger Studien zu Vor- und Frühgeschichte. Gedenkschrift für G. von Merhart. Marburg, 1986.

Mariën, M.E. "Tribes and Archaeological Groupings of the La Tène Period in Belgium: Some Observations". In *The European Community in Later Prehistory: Studies in Honour of C. F.C. Hawkes*, eds. John Boardman, M.A. Brown and T.G.E. Powell, pp. 213–41. London, 1980.

Markey, T.L. "Social Spheres and National Groups in Germania". In *Germanenprobleme in heutiger Sicht*, ed. Heinrich Beck, pp. 248–66. Berlin, 1986.

Martin, Max. *Das fränkische Gräberfeld von Basel-Bernerring*. Basel, 1976.

—. "Weinsiebchen und Toilettgerät". In *Der spätromische Silberschatz von Kaiseraugst* I, eds. Herbert Cahn and Annemarie Kaufmann-Heinimann, pp. 97–122. Derendingen, 1984.

—. "Bemerkungen zur Ausstattung der Frauengräber und zur Interpretation der Doppelgräber und Nachbestattungen im frühen Mittelalter". In *Frauen in Spätantike und Frühmittelalter*, ed. Werner Affeldt, pp. 89–104. Sigmaringen, 1990.

Martindale, Jane. "The French Aristocracy in the Early Middle Ages: A Reappraisal". PP 75 (1977): 5–45.

Martinez-Pizarro, Joaquin. "The Three Meals in *Heiðarviga saga*: Repetition and Functional Diversity". In *Structure and Meaning in Old Norse Literature: New Approaches to Textual Analysis and Literary Criticism*, eds. John Lindow, Lars Lönnroth and Gerd Wolfgang Weber, pp. 220–34. Odense, 1986.

Matthews, John. *The Roman Empire of Ammianus*. Baltimore, 1989.

Mattingly, H. and S.A. Handford, trans. *Tacitus. The Agricola and the Germania*. Harmondsworth, 1975.

Mauss, Marcel. *Essai sur le don: Forme et raison de l'échange dans les sociétés archaiques*. Paris, 1950.

Mayer-Maly, Theo. "Das Notverkaufsrecht des Hausvaters". ZSSR (RA) 75 (1958): 116–55.

Mayrhofer, M., W. Meid, B. Schlerath and R. Schmitt. *Antiquitates Indogermanicae: Gedenkschrift für Hermann Guntert*. Innsbruck, 1974.

Mc Cone, Kim. "*Aided Cheltchair Maic Uthechair*: Hounds, Heroes and Hospitallers in Early Irish Myth and Story". *Ériu* 35 (1984): 1–30.

—. "Dubthach maccu Lugair and a Matter of Life and Death in the Pseudo-Historical Prologue to the *Senchas Már*". *Peritia* 5 (1986): pp. 1–35.

—. "Werewolves, Cyclopes, *Díberga* and *Fíanna*: Juvenile Delinquency in Early Ireland". CMCS 12 (1986): 1–22.

—. "A Tale of Two Ditties: Poet and Satirist in *Cath Maige Tuired*". In *Sages, Saints and Storytellers: Celtic Studies in Honour of Professor James Carney*, eds. Donnchadh Ó Córrain, Liam Breatnach and Kim Mc Cone, pp. 122–43. Maynooth, 1989.

—. *Pagan Past and Christian Present in Early Irish Literature*. Maynooth, 1991.

Mc Neill, Eoin. "Ancient Irish Law. The Law of Status or Franchise". PRIA, C 26 (1923): 265–316.

Meaney, Audrey L. *Anglo-Saxon Amulets and Curing Stones*. Oxford, 1981.

—. "The Ides of the Cotton Gnomic Poem". MA 48 (1979): 23–39.

Meduna, Jiri. "The Oppidum of Stare Hradisco". In *The Celts*, eds. Sabatino Moscati, Otto Hermann Frey, Vencesles Kruta, Barry Raftery and Miklós Szabó, pp. 546–47. New York, 1991.

Megaw, Ruth and Vincent Megaw. *Celtic Art from its Beginnings to the Book of Kells*. London, 1989.

Meid, Wolfgang. "Der germanische Personenname *Veleda*". IF 69 (1964): 256–58.

—. *Beiträge zur Indogermanistik und Keltologie: Julius Pokorny zum 80. Geburtstag gewidmet*. Innsbruck, 1967.

—. "Gallisch oder Lateinisch? Sociolinguistische und andere Bemerkungen zu populären gallo-lateinischen Inschriften". ANRW II, 29, 2 (1983): 1019–44.

Meissner, Rudolf. *Die Kenningar der Skalden: Ein Beitrag zur skaldischen Poetic*. Bonn, 1921.

Melicher, Theophil. *Der Kampf zwischen Gesetzes—und Gewohnheitsrecht im Westgotenreiche*. Weimar, 1930.

—. *Die germanischen Formen der Eheschliessung im westgotisch-spanischen Recht*. Wien, 1940.

Menghin, Wilfried. *Die Langobarden. Archäologie und Geschichte*. Stuttgart, 1985.

Merschberger, Gerda. *Die Rechtsstellung der germanische Frau*. Leipzig, 1937.

Merten, Hiltrud. "Der Kult des Mars im Trevererraum". TZ 48 (1985): 7–113.

Metzler, Jeannot. "Late Celtic Horsemen's Graves at Goeblingen-Nospelt". In *The Celts*, eds. Sabatino Moscati, Otto Hermann Frey, Vencesles Kruta, Barry Raftery and Miklós Szabó, pp. 520–21. New York, 1991.

Meyer, Marc. "Land Charters and the Legal Position of Anglo-Saxon Women". In *The Women of England From Anglo-Saxon Times to the Present*, ed. B. Kanner, pp. 57–82. London, 1980.

Meyer, Willy. "Wealhtheow". *Anglia, Beiblatt* 33 (1922): 94–101.

Middleton, P.S. "Army Supply in Roman Gaul: An Hypothesis for Roman Britain". In *Invasion and Response: The Case of Roman Britian*, eds. Barry Burnham and Helen Johnson, pp. 81–98. Oxford, 1979.

Mikat, Paul. *Dotierte Ehe—rechte Ehe. Zur Entwicklung des Eheschliessungsrechts in fränkischer Zeit*. Opladen, 1978.

Mildenberger, Gerhard. *Sozial-und Kulturgeschichte der Germanen*. Stuttgart, 1972.

—. "Die Germanen in der archäologischen Forschung nach Kossinna". In *Germanenprobleme in heutiger Sicht*, ed. Heinrich Beck, pp. 310–20. Berlin, 1986.

Miller, William Ian. "Choosing the Avenger: Some Aspects of the Bloodfeud in Medieval Iceland and England". *Law and History Review* 1 (1983): 159–204.

—. "Justifying Skarpheðinn: Of Pretext and Politics in the Icelandic Bloodfeud". SS 55 (1983): 314-344.

—. "Dreams, Prophecy and Socery: Blaming the Secret Offender in Medieval Iceland". SS 58 (1986): 101–23.

Mills, Stella M., trans. *The Saga of Hrolf Kraki*. Oxford, 1933.

Moeller, Walter O. "Once More the One-Eyed Man Against Rome". *Historia* 24 (1975): 402–10.

Mohen, Jean-Pierre. "The Princely Tombs of Burgundy". In *The Celts*, eds. Sabatino Moscati, Otto Hermann Frey, Venceslas Kruta, Barry Raftery and Miklós Szabó, pp. 103–7. New York, 1991.

Moisl, Hermann. "Anglo-Saxon Royal Genealogies and Germanic Oral Tradition". JMH 7 (1981): 215–48.

—. "The Bernician Royal Dynasty and the Irish in the Seventh Century". *Peritia* 2 (1983): 103–26.

—. "Kingship and Orally Transmitted Stammestradition Among the Lombards and Franks". In Herwig Wolfram and Andreas Schwarcz, *Die Bayern und ihre Nachbarn* I, pp. 111–19. Wien, 1985.

Mommsen, Theodor. *Römische Geschichte*. III vols. Leipzig-Berlin, 1854–6.

—., ed. *Jordanes. Getica*. MGH AA 5. Hannoverae, 1882.

Moody, T.W., ed. *Nationality and the Pursuit of National Independence*. Belfast, 1978.

Moore, Clifford H., ed. *Tacitus. The Histories*. III vols. Cambridge, 1951[2].

Moorhead, John. "Culture and Power Among the Ostrogoths". *Klio* 68 (1986): 112–22

Moosleitner, Fritz. "Handwerk und Handel". In *Die Bajuwaren. Von Severin bis Tassilo 488–788*, eds. H. Dannheimer and H. Dopsch, pp. 208–19. Salzburg, 1988.

Mortensen, P. "The Brå Cauldron". In *The Celts*, eds. Sabatino Moscati, Otto Hermann Frey, Vencesles Kruta, Barry Raftery and Miklós Szabó, p. 375. New York, 1991.

Moscati, Sabatino, Otto Hermann Frey, Venceslas Kruta, Barry Raftery and Miklós Szabó. *The Celts*. New York, 1991.

Motz, Lotte. "The Sacred Marriage—a Study in Norse Mythology". In *Languages and Cultures: Studies in Honor of Edgar C. Polomé*, eds. Mohammed Ali Jazayery and Werner Winter, pp. 449–60. Berlin, 1988.

Much, Rudolf. *Deutsche Stammeskunde*. Leipzig, 1900.

—., Herbert Jankuhn and Wolfgang Lange. *Die Germania des Tacitus*. Heidelberg, 1967.

München, Ludwig Voit. "Horaz—Merkur—Augustus (zu Hor. C. II 17. I 10. 12)". *Gymnasium* 89 (1982): 479–96.

Müllenhoff, Karl, *Beovulf: Untersuchungen über das angelsächsische Epos und die älteste Geschichte der germanischen Seevölker*. Berlin, 1889.

Müller-Wille, Michael. "Opferplatze der Wikingerzeit". FM St. 18 (1984): 187–221.

Murray, Alexander Callender. *Germanic Kingship Structure: Studies in Law and Society in Antiquity and the Early Middle Ages*. Toronto, 1983.

Murphy, Gerard. "Review of Zwicker's *Fontes*". *Béaloideas* 1 (1937): 143–45.

—. "On the Dates of Two Sources Used in Thurneysen's *Heldensage*". *Ériu* 16 (1952): 145–51.

Murphy, Michael. "Vows, Boasts and Taunts and the Role of Women in Some Medieval Literature". ES 66 (1985): 105–12.

Murray, A.T., ed. and trans. *Homer. The Iliad*. II vols. Cambridge, 1946.

Murray, Oswyn, ed. *Sympotica: A Symposium on the Symposion*. Oxford, 1990.

Myres, J.N.L. *The English Settlements*. Oxford, 1988.

Nash, Daphne. "Reconstructing Posidonius' Celtic Ethnography: Some Considerations". *Britannia* 7 (1976): 111–26.

—. "Territory and State Formation in Central Gaul". In *Social Organization and Settlement*, eds. D.R. Green, C.C. Haselgrove and M. Spriggs, pp. 455–75. Oxford, 1978.

—. "The Basis of Contact Between Britain and Gaul in the Late pre-Roman Iron Age". In *Cross-Channel Trade Between Gaul and Britain in the Pre-Roman Iron Age*, eds. Sarah Macready and F.H. Thompson, pp. 92–107. London, 1984.

—. "Celtic Territorial Expansion and the Mediterranean World". In *Settlement and Society: Aspects of Western European Prehistory in the First Millenium BC*, eds. T.C. Champion and J.V.S. Megaw, pp. 45–68. New York, 1985.

—. *Coinage in the Celtic World*. London, 1987.

Naumann, Hans. "Der König und die Seherin". ZdP 63 (1938): 347–58.

Naumann, H.-P., R. Wenskus and D. Claude. "Dux". *Reallexikon* 6 (1986): 296–306.

Neckel, Gustav. *Liebe und Ehe bei den vorchristlichen Germanen*. Leipzig, 1932.

Nehlsen, Hermann. *Sklavenrecht zwischen Antike und Mittelalter*. Vol. I. Göttingen, 1972.

Nelson, Janet. "National Synods, Kingship as Office and Royal Anointing: An Early Medieval Syndrome". SCH 7 (1971): 41–59.

—. "Royal Saints and Early Medieval Kingship". SCH 10 (1973): 39–44.

—. "Ritual and Reality in the Early Medieval *Ordines*". SCH 11 (1975): 41–51.

—. "Symbols in Context: Rulers' Inauguration Rituals in Byzantium and the West in the Early Middle Ages". SCH 13 (1976): 97–119.

—. "Queens as Jezebels: The Careers of Brunhild and Balthild in Merovingian History". In *Medieval Women*, ed. Derek Baker, pp. 31–77. Oxford, 1978.

—. "Inauguration Rituals". In *Early Medieval Kingship*, eds. Peter Sawyer and Ian Wood, pp. 50–71. Leeds, 1979.

—. "The Church's Military Service in the Ninth Century: A Contemporary Comparitive View?" SCH 20 (1983): 15–30.

—. *Politics and Ritual in Early Medieval Europe*. London, 1986.

Nenci, Giuseppe, ed. *Modes de contacts et processus de transformation dans les sociétés anciennes*. Pise-Rome, 1983.

Neumann, Eduard. *Das Schicksal in der Edda I: Der Schicksalbegriff in der Edda*. Giessen, 1955.

Neumann, Günter. "Die Sprachverhältnisse in den germanischen Provinzen des römischen Reiches". ANRW II, 29, 2 (1983): 1061–88.

——. "Germani cisrhenani—die Aussage der Namen". In *Germanenprobleme in heutiger Sicht*, ed. Heinrich Beck, pp. 107-129. Berlin, 1986.

——. "Die germanischen Matronenbeinamen". In *Matronen und verwandte Gottheiten*, eds. Gerhard Bauchhenss and Günter Neumann, pp. 103–32. Köln, 1987.

——. and Henning Seemann, eds. *Beiträge zum Verständnis der Germania von Tacitus*, Vol. II. Göttingen, 1992.

Ní Brolcháin, Muireann. "Women in Early Irish Myths and Sagas". *The Crane Bag* 4 (1980): 12–19.

Nickels, André. "Les Grecs en Gaule: L'example du Languedoc". In *Modes de contacts et processus de transformation dans les sociétés anciennes*, ed. Giuseppe Nenci, pp. 409–28. Pise-Rome, 1983.

Nicholson, Lewis E. and Dolores Warwick Frese, eds. *Anglo-Saxon Poetry: Essays in Appreciation for John C. McGalliard*. Notre Dame, 1975.

Niles, John D. *Beowulf: The Poem and its Tradition*. Cambridge, 1983.

——. "Pagan Survivals and Popular Belief". In *The Cambridge Companion to Old English Literature*, eds. M. Godden and M. Lapidge, pp. 126–41. Cambridge, 1991.

Nolan, Barbara and Morton Bloomfield. "*Beotword, Gilpcwides* and the *Gilphlaeden* Scop of *Beowulf*: JEGP 79 (1980): 499–516.

Norden, Eduard. *Die germanische Urgeschichte in Tacitus Germania*. Stuttgart, 1959².

Oaks, Laura S. "The Goddess Epona: Concepts of Sovereignty in a Changing Landscape". In *Pagan Gods and Shrines of the Roman Empire*, eds. Martin Henig and Anthony King, pp. 77–84. Oxford, 1986.

Ó Cathasaigh, Tomás. "Curse and Satire". *Eigse* 21 (1986): 10–15.

Ó Córrain, Donnchadh. *Ireland Before the Normans*. Dublin, 1972.

——. "Nationality and Kingship in pre-Norman Ireland". In *Nationality and the Pursuit of national independence*, ed. T.W. Moody, pp. 1–35. Belfast, 1978.

——. "Women in Early Irish Society". In *Women in Irish Society*, eds. Margaret Mac Curtain and Donnchadh Ó Córrain, pp. 1–13. Westport, 1979.

——., Liam Breatnach and Kim Mc Cone, eds. *Sages, Saints and Storytellers: Celtic Studies in Honour of Professor James Carney*. Naas, 1989.

O'Curry, Eugene. *Lectures on the Manuscript Materials of Ancient Irish History*. Dublin. 1873.

Ó Cuív, Brian. "A Poem Composed for Cathal Croibhdhearg O'Conchubhair". *Ériu* 34 (1983): 157–74.

Oexle, Otto Gerhard. "Mahl und Spende im mittelalterlichen Totenkult". FM St. 18 (1984): 401–20.

——. "Haus und Ökonomie im früheren Mittelalter". In *Person und Gemeinschaft in Mittelalter: Karl Schmid zum fünfundsechzigsten Geburtstag*, eds. Gerd Althoff, Dieter Geuenich, Otto Gerhard Oexle and Joachim Wollasch, pp. 101–22. Sigmaringen, 1988.

Ogris, Werner. "Munt, Muntwalt". HRG 19 (1980): clm. 750–61.

von Olberg, Gabriele. *Freie, Nachbarn und Gefolgsleute: Volkssprachige Bezeichnungen aus dem sozialen Bereich in den frühmittelalterlichen Leges*. Frankfurt a/M., 1983.

——. *"Leod* 'Mann'. Soziale Schichtung im Spiegel volkssprachiger Wörter der Leges". In *Wörter und Sachen im Lichte der Bezeichnungsforschung*, ed. Ruth Schmidt-Wiegand, pp. 91–106. Berlin, 1981.

Oldenstein, Jürgen. "Die Zusammensetzung des römischen Imports in den sogennanten Lübsow gräbern als möglicher Hinweis auf die soziale Stellung der Bestatteten". AK 5 (1975): 299–305.

O'Leary, Philip. "Contention at Feasts in Early Irish Literature". *Eigse* 20 (1984): 115–27.

——. "The Honour of Women in Early Irish Literature". *Ériu* 38 (1987): 27–44.

Olivecrona, Karl. *Das Werden eines Königs nach schwedischem Recht*. Lund, 1947.

Olmsted, Garrett. *The Gundestrup Cauldron*. Brussels, 1979.

——. "Gaulish and Celtiberian Poetic Inscriptions". MQ 28 (1988): 339–87.

——. "The Meter of the Gaulish Inscription from Larzac". JIES 17 (1989): 155–63.

Ó Máille, T. "Medb Cruachna". ZcP 17 (1927/28): 129–46.

Opitz, Stephen. "Runeninschriftliche Neufunde: Das Schwert von Eichstetten/Kaiserstuhl und der Webstuhl von Neudingen/Baar". ANB 27 (1981): 26–31.

Opland, Jeff. *Anglo-Saxon Oral Poetry: A Study of the Traditions*. New Haven, 1980.

O'Rahilly, Cecile, ed and trans. *Táin Bó Cuailnge From the Book of Leinster*. Dublin, 1970.

——., ed and trans. *Táin Bó Cuailnge. Recension I*. Dublin, 1976.

——., ed and trans. *The Stowe Version of Táin Bó Cuailnge*. Dublin, 1978.

O'Rahilly, T. F. "On the Origin of the Names Érainn and Ériu". *Ériu* 14 (1943): 7–28.

——. *Early Irish History and Mythology*. Dublin, 1946.

Ó Riain, Pádraig. "Conservation in the Vocabulary of the Early Irish Church". In *Sages, Saints and Storytellers: Celtic Studies in Honour of Professor James Carney*, eds. Donnchadh Ó Córrain, Liam Breatnach and Kim Mc Cone, pp. 358–66. Naas, 1989.

O'Sullivan, Anne. "Verses on Honorific Portions". In *Celtic Studies: Essays in Memory of Angus Matheson*, eds. James Carney and D. Greene, pp. 118–23. London, 1968.

Owen-Crocker, Gale R. *Dress in Anglo-Saxon England*. Manchester, 1986.

Oxé, A. "Ein Merkurheiligtum in Sechtem". BJ 108/109 (1902): 246–51.

Palmer, Robert E. *Roman Religion and Roman Empire: Five Essays*. Philadelphia, 1974.

Palsson, Hermann and Paul Edwards, eds. *The Book of Settlements*. Manitoba, 1972.

Pappenheim, Max, "Über kunstliche Verwandtschaft im germanischen Rechte". ZSSR (GA) 29 (1908): 304–33.

Paton, W.R., ed. *Polybius. The Histories*. VI vols. Cambridge 1967².

Patterson, Nerys T. "Material and Symbolic Exchange in Early Irish Clientship". *Proceedings of the Harvard Celtic Colloquium* I (1981): 53–61.

Patzelt, Erna, ed. *Alfons Dopsch. Gesammelte Aufsätze I. Verfassungs-und Wirtshaftsgeschichte des Mittelalters*. Aalem, 1968².

Pauli, Ludwig. *Keltischer Volksglaube: Amulette und Sonderbestattungen am Durrnberg bei Hallein und in eisenzeitlichen Mitteleuropa*. München, 1975.

——. *Der Dürrnberg bei Hallein III. Auswertung der Grabfunde*. München, 1978.

——. "Early Celtic Society: Two Centuries of Wealth and Turmoil in Central Europe". In *Settlement and Society: Aspects of Western European Prehistory in the First Millenium BC*, eds. T.C. Champion and J.V.S. Megaw, pp. 23–44. New York, 1985.

——. "Zu Gast bei einem keltischen Fursten". MAGW 118/119 (1988/89): 291–303.

Paulsen, Peter. *Alamannische Adelsgräber von Niederstotzingen (Kreis Heidenheim)*. Stuttgart, 1967.
—. "Flügellanzen: Zum archäologischen Horizont der Wiener 'sancta lancea'".
FM St. 3 (1969): 289–312.
Payer, Pierre J. *Sex and the Penitentials: The Development of a Sexual Code 550–1150*.
Toronto, 1984.
Pearson, Michael Parker. "Beyond the Pale: Barbarian Social Dynamics in Western
Europe". In *Barbarians and Romans in North-West Europe From the Later Republic
to Late Antiquity*, eds. John Barrett, Andrew Fitzpatrick and Lesley Macinnes, pp.
198–226. Oxford, 1989.
Pelling, C.B.R. "Caesar's Battle Descriptions and the Defeat of Ariovistus". *Latomus* 40
(1981): 741–66.
Pelteret, David. "Slave Raiding and Slave Trading in Early England". ASE 9 (1981) 99–144.
Perrin, Bernadotte, ed. *Plutarch's Lives*. XI vols. Cambridge, 1949².
Peschel, Karl."Die Kelten als Nachbarn der Germanen". Zf.A 4 (1970): 1–36.
—. "Frühe Waffengräber im Gebiet der südlichen Elbgermanen". In *Symposium.
Ausklang der Latène -Zivilization und Anfänge der germanischen Besiedlung im mit-
tleren Donaugebiet*. ed. Bohuslav Chropovsky, pp. 261–81. Bratislava, 1977.
—. *Anfänge germanischen Besiedlung im Mittelgebirgsraum. Sueben—Hermunduren—
Markomannen*. Berlin, 1978.
—. "Die Sueben in Ethnographie und Archäologie". *Klio* 69 (1978): 259–309.
—. "Kriegergrab, Gefolge und Landnahme bei den Latènekelten". *Ethnogr.—Ar-
chaol. Zeitschrift* 25 (1984): 445–69.
—. "Kelten und Germanen während der jüngeren vorrömischen Eisenzeit (2.–1.
Jh. v. u. Z)". In *Frühe Volker in Mitteleuropa*, eds. Fritz Horst and Friedrich Schlette,
pp. 167–200. Berlin, 1988.
—. "Zur kultischen Devotion innerhalb der keltischen Kriegergemeinschaft". In
Religion und Kult in ur-und frühgeschichtlichen Zeit, eds. Friedrich Schlette and Dieter
Kaufmann, pp. 273–82. Berlin, 1989.
—. "Archäologisches zur Frage den Unfreiheit bei den Kelten während der vor-
römischen Eisenzeit". *Ethnogr.-Archäol. Zeitschrift* 31 (1990): 370–417.
Peters, Edward. *The Shadow King: Rex Inutilis in Medieval Law and Literature 751–1327*.
New Haven, 1970.
von Petrikovits, Harald. "Ein Mädchenkopf und andere Plastiken aus dem Heiligen
Bezirk in Zingsheim". BJ 165 (1965): 192–227.
—. *Rheinische Geschichte: Altertum*. Düsseldorf, 1978.
—. "Lixae". *Roman Frontier Studies* 12 (1980): 1027–34.
—. "Sacramentum". In *Rome and Her Northern Provinces*, eds. Brian Hartley and
John Wacher, pp. 179–201. London, 1983.
—. "Germani Cisrhenani". In *Germanenprobleme in heutiger Sicht*, ed. Heinrich
Beck, pp. 88–106. Berlin, 1986.
—. "Matronen und verwandte Gottheiten. Zusammenfassende Bemerkungen". In
Gerhard Bauchhenss and Günter Neumann, *Matronen und verwandte Gottheiten*,
pp. 241–60. Köln, 1987.
Picard, Jean-Michel. "The Marvellous in Irish and Continental Saints' Lives". In
Columbanus and Merovingian Monasticism, eds. H.B. Clark and Mary Brennan, pp.
91–103. Oxford, 1981.

Piggott, Stuart. *Barbarian Europe*. Edinburgh, 1965.

—. *Ancient Europe*. Chicago, 1973².

—. *The Druids*. London, 1991².

Pirling, Renate. *Das römisch-fränkische Gräberfeld von Krefeld-Gellep 1960–63*. Berlin, 1974.

—. *Römer und Franken am Niederrhein*. Mainz, 1986.

Pittioni, Richard. *Wer hat wann und wo den Silberkessel von Gundestrup angefertigt?* Wien, 1984.

Plummer, Charles, ed., *Vitae Sanctorum Hiberniae*. II vols. Dublin, 1968².

—., ed. and trans. *Bethada Náem nÉrenn: Lives of Irish Saints*. II vols. Oxford, 1968².

Polomé, Edgar C. "Some Aspects of the Cult of the Mother Goddess in Western Europe". In *Vistas and Vectors: Essays Honoring the Memory of Helmut Rehder*, eds. Lee Jennings and G. Schultz-Behrend, pp. 193–208. Austin, 1979.

—., ed. *Hommage to Georges Dumézil*. Washington, 1982.

—. "Celto-germanic Isoglosses (revisited)". JIES (1983): 281–98.

—. "The Linguistic Situation in the Western Provinces of the Roman Empire". ANRW II, 29, 2 (1983): 509–53.

—. "Germanentum und religiöse Vorstellungen". In *Germanenprobleme in heutiger Sicht*, ed. Heinrich Beck, pp. 267–97. Berlin, 1986.

—. "Muttergottheiten im alten Westeuropa". In *Matronen und verwandte Gottheiten*, eds. Gerhard Bauchhenss and Günter Neumann, pp. 201–12. Köln, 1987.

—. "Who Are the Germanic People?" In *Proto-Indo-European: The Archaeology of a Linguistic Problem. Studies in Honor of Marija Gimbutas*, eds. Susan Nacer Skomal and Edgar C. Polomé, pp. 216–44. Washington, 1987.

Powell, Anton, ed. *Classical Sparta. Techniques Behind her Success*. Norman, 1989.

Powell, T.G.E. *The Celts*. London, 1958.

Provincialia. Festschrift für Fr. v. Zahn. Köln, 1968.

Puhvel, Jan, ed. *Myth and Law Among the Indo-Europeans. Studies in Indo-European Comparative Mythology*. Berkeley, 1970.

Rackham, H., ed. *Pliny. Natural History*. X vols. London, 1952.

Raddatz, Klaus. "Die germanische Bewaffnung der vorrömischen Eisenzeit". *Nachrichten der Akademie der Wissenschaften in Göttingen. Phil.-hist. Klasse* (1966) No. 11.

—. "Die Bewaffnung der Germanen in der jungeren romischen Kaiserzeit". *Nachrichten der Akademie der Wissenschaften in Göttingen. Phil.-hist. Klasse* (1967) No. 1.

—., W. Kimmig, B. Fischer, G. Ulbert, J. Garbsch, D.M. Wilson, H. Steuer, R. Grenz, R. Rolle, Gy. Laszlo, H. Jankuhn, R. Wenskus, P. Johanek, M. Last, H. Beck and P. Buchholz. "Bewaffnung". *Reallexikon* 2 (1976): 361–482.

Raftery, Barry. "The Island Celts". In *The Celts*, eds. Sabatino Moscati, Otto Hermann Frey, Venceslas Kruta, Barry Raftery and Miklós Szabó, pp. 555–72. New York, 1991.

Rahtz, P., T. Dickinson and L. Watts. *Anglo-Saxon Cemetaries 1979*. Oxford, 1980.

Rankin, H.D. *Celts and the Classical World*. Beckengham, 1987.

Rathje, Annette. "The Adoption of the Homeric Banquet in Central Europe in the Orientalizing Period". In Sympotica: A Symposium on the Symposion, ed. Oswyn Murray, pp. 279–88. Oxford, 1990.

Rau, Reinhold, ed. "Annales Bertiniani". In his *Quellen zur karolingischen Reichsgeschichte*

II, pp. 11–288. Darmstadt, 1980.

—., ed. "Anonymi Vita Hludowici Imperatoris". In his *Quellen zur karolingischen Reichsgeschichte* I, pp. 257–382. Darmstadt, 1980.

—., ed. "Thegani Vita Hludowici Imperatoris". In his *Quellen zur karolingischen Reichsgeschichte* I, pp. 215–54. Darmstadt, 1980.

—. *Quellen zur karolingischen Reichsgeschichte*. II vols. Darmstadt, 1980.

Rausing, Gad. "Barbarian Mercenaries or Roman Citizens?" *Fornvannen* 82 (1987): 126–31.

Reallexikon der germanischen Altertumskunde, begrundet von J. Hoops, 2. Vollig neu bearb. und stark erw. Aufl. unter Mitwirkung zahlreicher Fachgelehrter. Hg. von Heinrich Beck, Herbert Jankuhn, Hans Kurt Ranke, Reinhardt Wenskus. Berlin, 1973ff.

Redlich, Clara. "Germanische Gemeinschaftsformen in der Überlieferung des Tacitus". *Studien aus Alteuropa* II (1965): 186–94.

—. "Zur Trinkhornsitte bei den Germanen der älteren Kaiserzeit". PZ 52 (1977): 61–120.

—. "Politische und wirtschaftliche Bedeutung der Bronzegefässe an Unterelbe und Saale zur Zeit der Römerkriege". *Studien zur Sachsenforschung* 2 (1980): 329–74.

Redman, Charles L., ed. *Medieval Archaeology. Papers of the Seventh Annual Conference of the Center for Medieval and Early Renaissance Studies.* Binghamton, 1989.

Reece, Richard, ed. *Burial in the Roman World*. London, 1977.

Reichert, Hermann. "Zum Problem der rechtsrheinischen Germanen vor und um Christi Geburt: Wie kann die Namenkunde helfen, die Sprachzugehörigkeit der Namenträger zu bestimmen?" In *Festgabe für Otto Hofler zum 75. Geburtstag*, ed. Helmut Birkhan, pp. 557–76. Wein, 1976.

—. *Thesaurus Paleogermanicus: Lexikon der altgermanischen Namen*, Vol I. Wien, 1987.

Renior, Alan. "A Reading Context for *The Wife's Lament*". In *Anglo-Saxon Poetry: Essays in Appreciation for John C. McGalliard*, eds. Lewis E. Nicholson and Dolores Warwick Frese, pp. 224–41. Notre Dame, 1975.

Reuter, Timothy. "Plunder and Tribute in the Carolingian Empire". TRHS 35 (1985): 75–94.

Reydellet, Marc. *La royauté dans la littérature latine de Sidoine Apollinaire à Isidore de Séville*. Rome, 1981.

Riché, Pierre, ed. "La magie à l'époque carolingienne". *Comptes rendus des Académie des Inscriptions et Belles—Lettres* (1973): 127–38.

—. ed. *Dhuoda. Manuel pour mon fils*. Paris, 1975.

—. "Les representations du palais dans les textes litteraires du Haut Moyen Âge". In his *Instruction et vie religieuse dans le Haut Moyen Âge*, pp. 161–71.

—. *Instruction et vie religieuse dans le Haut Moyen Âge*. London, 1981.

Richards, John W. "The Celtic Social System". MQ 21 (1980): 71–95.

Richter, Michael. "Bede's *Angli*: Angles or English?" *Peritia* 3 (1984): 99–114.

—. "Kommunikationsprobleme im lateinischen Mittelalter". HZ 222 (1976): 43–80.

—. *Medieval Ireland: The Enduring Tradition*. Houndmills, 1988.

—. "Die Kelten im Mittelalter". HZ 246 (1988): 265–95.

—. *The Formation of the Medieval West. Studies in the Oral Culture of the Barbarians.* Dublin, 1994.

Ritzer, Korbinian. *Formen, Riten und religioses Brauchtum der Eheschliessung in den christlichen Kirchen des ersten Jahrtausends*. Münster, 1962.

Rivers, Theodore J. "Widow's Rights in Anglo-Saxon Law". *American Journal of Legal History* 19 (1975): 208–15.

Rivet, A.L.F. and Colin Smith. *The Place-Names of Roman Britain.* London, 1979.

Robinson, Fred C. "The Significance of Names in Old English Literature". *Anglia* 86 (1968): 14–58.

Rodwell, K. "Rome and the Trinovantes". In *Invasion and Response: The Case of Roman Britian*, eds. Barry Burnham and Helen Johnson, pp. 327–38. Oxford, 1979.

Roe, H. "Rome and the Early Germans: Some Sociolinguistic Observations". *Florilegium* 2 (1980): 102–20.

Roeder, Fritz. *Die Familie bei den Angelsächsen: Eine kultur-und literarhistorische Studie auf Grund gleichzeitiger Quellen.* Halle, 1899.

——. *Zur Deutung der angelsächsischen Glossierungen von 'paranymphus' und 'paranympha' ('pronuba'): Ein Beiträg zur Kenntnis des ags. Hochzeitsrituells: Nachrichten v. d. Köngl. Gesellschaft d. Wiss. zu Göttingen: Phil.-hist Kl..* Berlin, 1907.

Rolfe, John C., ed. *Ammianus Marcellinus.* III vols. London, 1964².

Ross, Anne. *Pagan Celtic Britain: Studies in Iconography and Tradition.* London, 1967.

——. *The Pagan Celts.* Totowa, 1986.

Ross, Margaret Clunies. "Style and Authorial Presence in Scaldic Mythological Poetry". SBVC 20 (1981): 276–304.

——. "Concubinage in Anglo-Saxon England". PP 108 (1985): 3–34.

——. "The Art of Poetry and Figure of the Poet in *Egil's saga*". In *Sagas of the Icelanders*, ed. John Tucker, pp. 126–45. New York, 1989.

Rouche, M. "Les repas de fête à l'époque carolingienne: Manger et boire au moyen âge". In *Actes du Colloque de Nice (15–17 Octobre 1982)* I, pp. 265–79. Nice, 1984.

——. "Des mariages païens au mariage chrétien. Sacre et sacrament". SSCI 33 (1987): 835–73.

Rowland, Jenny. "OE *Ealuscerwen/Meoduscerwen* and the Concept of 'Paying for Mead'". *Leeds Studies in English* 21 (1990): 1–12.

Roymans, Nico. "The North Belgic Tribes in the 1st Century BC: A Historical-Anthropoligical Perspective". In *Roman and Native in the Low Countries: Spheres of Interaction*, eds. Roel Brandt and Jan Slofstra, pp. 43–70. Oxford, 1984.

Rudolph, Kurt, Rolf Heller and Ernst Walter, eds. *Festschrift Walter Baetke.* Weimar, 1966.

Rüger, Christoph B. *Germania Inferior.* Köln, 1968.

——. "Gallisch-germanische Kurien". ES 9 (1972): 251–60.

——. "A Husband for the Mother Goddesses—Some Observations on the Matronae Aufaniae". In *Rome and Her Northern Provinces*, eds. Brian Hartley and John Wacher, pp. 210–19. London, 1983.

——. "Beobachtungen zu den epigraphischen Belegen der Muttergottheiten in den lateinischen Provinzen des Imperium Romanum". In *Matronen und verwandte Gottheiten*, eds. Gerhard Bauchhenss and Günter Neumann, pp. 1–30. Köln, 1987.

Russell, J.C. *Late Ancient and Medieval Population.* Philadelphia, 1958.

Russom, Geoffrey "A Germanic Concept of Nobility in *The Gifts of Men* and *Beowulf*". *Speculum* 53 (1978): 1–15.

——. "The Drink of Death in Old English and Germanic Literature". In *Germania. Comparative Studies in the Old Germanic Languages and Literatures*, eds. Daniel Calder and Craig Christy, pp. 175–90. Wolfeboro, 1988.

Ruttkay, Elizabeth. "Ein urgeschichtliches Kultgefäss vom Jennyberg bei Mödling/Niederösterreich". *Antike Welt* 5 (1974): 45–50.

Sahlins, Marshall. *Stone-Age Economics*. Chicago, 1972.

Sawyer, Birgit, Peter Sawyer and Ian Wood, eds. *The Christianization of Scandinavia*. Kungalb, 1987.

Sawyer, Peter, ed. *Medieval Settlement: Continuity and Change*. London, 1976.

——., ed. *Names, Words and Graves*. Leeds, 1979.

——. and Ian Wood, eds. *Early Medieval Kingship*. Leeds, 1979.

Sayers, William. "Conall's Welcome to Cet in the Old Irish *Scela Mucce Meic Datho*". *Florilegium* 4 (1982): 100–8.

——. "Martial Feats in the Old Irish Ulster Cycle". *Canadian Journal of Irish Studies* 9 (1983): 45–80.

——. "Old Irish *Fert* 'Tiepole', *Fertes* 'Swingletree' and the Seeress Fedelm". EC 21 (1984): 171–83.

——. "Warrior Initiation and Some Short Celtic Spears in the Irish and Learned Latin Tradition". SMRH II (1989): 89–108.

Scardigli, Piergiuseppe. "Das Problem der suebischen Kontinuität und die Runeninschrift von Neudingen/Baar". In *Germanenprobleme in heutiger Sicht*, ed. Heinrich Beck, pp. 344–57. Berlin, 1986.

Schach, Paul and Lee M. Hollander, trans. *Eyrbyggja Saga*. Lincoln, 1959.

Schach-Dörges, Helga. *Die Bodenfunde des 3. bis 6. Jahrhunderts nach Chr. zwischen unterer Elbe und Oder*. Neumünster, 1970.

Schauerte, Günther. "Darstellungen mutterlicher Gottheiten in den römischen Nordwestprovinzen". In *Matronen und verwandte Gottheiten*, eds. Gerhard Bauchhenss and Günter Neumann, pp. 55–102. Köln, 1987.

Scherer, Anton. "Die keltisch-germanischen Namengleichungen". In *Corolla Linguistica: Festschrift Ferdinand Sommer*, pp.199–210. Wiesbaden, 1955.

Schjødt, Jens Peter. "The 'fire ordeal' in the *Grimnismál*: Initiation or Annihilation?" MS 12 (1988): 29–43.

Schlabow, Kurt. *Textilfunde der Eisenzeit in Nord-deutschland*. Neumünster, 1976.

Schlesinger, Walter. "Herrschaft und Gefolgschaft in der germanisch-deutschen Verfassungsgeschichte". In his *Beiträge zur deutschen Verfassungsgeschichte des Mittelalters I: Germanen, Franken, Deutsche*, pp. 9–52.

——. "Uber germanisches Heerkönigtum". In his *Beiträge zur deutschen Verfassungsgeschichte des Mittelalters I: Germanen, Franken, Deutsche*, pp. 53–87.

——. "Randbemerkungen zu drei Aufsätzen uber Sippe, Gefolgschaft und Treue". In his *Beiträge zur deutschen Verfassungsgeschichte des Mittelalters I: Germanen, Franken, Deutsche*, pp. 286–334.

——. *Beiträge zur deutschen Verfassungsgeschichte des Mittelalters I: Germanen, Franken, Deutsche*. Göttingen, 1963.

Schlette, Friedrich und Dieter Kaufmann, eds. *Religion und Kult in ur-und Frühgeschichtlichen Zeit*. Berlin, 1989.

Schlosser, H.D. *Althochdeutsche Literatur*. Berlin, 1970.

Schmid, Karl. "Heirat, Familienfolge, Geschlechterbewusstsein". SSCI 24 (1977): 103–37.

Schmidt, Berthold. "Neue Reihengräberfelder im Saalegebiet". AF 1 (1956): 228–30.

——. "Opferplatz und Gräberfeld des 6. Jahrhunderts bei Oberwerschen, Kreis

Hohenmölsen". JmV 50 (1966): 275–86.

—. *Die späte Völkerwanderungszeit in Mitteldeutschland*. II vols. Berlin, 1970.

Schmidt, Karl Horst. "Keltisch-lateinische Sprachkontakte im römischen Gallien der Kaiserzeit". ANRW II, 29, 2 (1983): 988–1018.

—. "The Gaulish Inscription of Chamalières". BBCS 29 (1980): 256–68.

—. "Handwerk und handwerker im Keltischen und Germanischen. Beiträge zu einem historischen Vergleich". (1983): 265–85.

—. "The Celtic Languages in their European Context". In *Proceedings of the Seventh International Congress of Celtic Studies*, eds. D. Ellis Evans, John G. Griffith and E.M. Jope, pp. 199–221. Oxford, 1986.

—. "Keltisch-germanische Isoglossen und ihre sprachgeschichtlichen Implikationen". In *Germanenprobleme in heutiger Sicht*, ed. Heinrich Beck, pp. 231–47. Berlin, 1986.

—. "Die keltischen Matronenbeinamen". In *Matronen und verwandte Gottheiten*, eds. Gerhard Bauchhenss and Günter Neumann, pp. 133–54. Köln, 1987.

—. and Rolf Kodderitzsch. *Geschichte und Kultur der Kelten: Vorbereitungskonferenz 25–28 Oktober 1982 in Bonn*. Heidelberg, 1986.

Schmidt, Ludwig. *Geschichte der Deutschen Stämme bis zum Ausgang der Völkerwanderung. Die Westgermanen*. II vols. München, 1940².

Schmidt-Wiegand, Ruth. "*gens francorum inclita*: Zu Gestalt und Inhalt des langeren Prologs der *Lex Salica*". In *Festschrift für Adolf Hofmeister*, pp. 233–70. Halle,1955.

—. *Fränkische und fränkolateinische Bezeichnungen für soziale Schichten und Gruppen in der Lex Salica*. Göttingen, 1972.

—. "Frankisch *druht* und *druhten*: Zur historischen Terminologie im Bereich der Sozialgeschichte". In *Historische Forschungen für Walter Schlesinger*, ed. Helmut Beumann, pp. 524–35. Köln, 1974.

—, ed. *Wörter und Sachen im Lichte der Bezeichnungsforschung*. Berlin, 1981.

Schmitt, Rüdiger. *Dichtung und Dichtersprache in indogermanischer Zeit*. Wiesbaden, 1967.

—, ed. *Indogermanische Dichtersprache*. Darmstadt, 1968.

Schonfeld, Moritz. *Wörterbuch der altgermanischen Personen-und Völkernamen*. Heidelberg, 1911.

Schneider, Reinhard. *Königswahl und Königserhebung im Frühmittelalter: Untersuchungen zur Herrschernachfolge bei den Langobarden und Merowingern*. Stuttgart, 1972.

—. *Brüdergemeine und Schwurfreundschaft*. Lübeck, 1964.

Schrader, Richard L. *God's Handiwork: Images of Women in Early Germanic Literature*. Westport, 1983.

Schramm, Gottfried. *Namenschatz und Dichtersprache: Studien zu den zweigliedrigen Personennamen der Germanen*. Göttingen, 1957.

Schramm, Percy Ernst. *Herrschaftszeichen und Staatssymbolik*. III vols. Stuttgart, 1954–6.

Schrickel, Waldtraut. "Die Nordgrenze der Kelten im rechtsrheinischen Gebiet zur Spätlatènezeit". JRGZ II (1964): 138–53.

Schröder, Edward. "Walburg, die Sibylle". In his *Deutsche Namenkunde. Gesammelte Aufsätze zur Kunde deutscher Personen-und Ortsnamen*. Göttingen, 1944².

Schücking, Levin L. "Heldenstolz und Würde im Angelsächsischen". *Abhandlungen der sächsischen Akademie der Wissenschaften. Phil.-hist. Klasse* 42 (1933): 1–42.

Schücking, Walter. *Der Regierungsantritt: Eine rechtsgeschichtliche und staatsrechtliche Untersuchung.* Leipzig, 1898.

Schulten, Adolf. *Sertorius.* Leipzig, 1926.

Schultz, Herbert. *The Prehistory of Germanic Europe.* New Haven, 1983.

——. *The Romans in Central Europe.* New Haven, 1985.

Schultze, Alfred. "Zur Rechtsgeschichte der germanischen Brüdergemeinschaft". ZSSR (GA) 56 (1936): 264–348.

——. *Das Eherecht in den älteren angelsächsischen Königsgesetzen.* Leipzig, 1941.

——. *Über westgotisch-spanisches Eherecht.* Leipzig, 1944.

Schulze, Hans K. *Grundstrukturen der Verfassung im Mittelalter.* II vols. Stuttgart, 1985, 1986.

Schussler, Heinz Joachim. "Die fränkische Reichsteilung von Vieux-Poitiers (742) und die Reform der Kirche in den Teilreichen Karlmanns und Pippins. Zu den Grenzen der Wirksamkeit des Bonifatius". *Francia* 13 (1985): 47–112.

Schwarz, Ernst. *Germanische Stammeskunde.* Heidelberg, 1956.

Schwartz, Stephen P. *Poetry and Law in Germanic Myth.* Berkeley, 1973.

Schweitzerische Gesellschaft für Ur-und Frühgeschichte, *Ur und Frühgeschichtliche Archäologie der Schweiz: IV Die Eisenzeit.* Basel, 1975.

Scott, B.G. *Studies on Early Ireland: Essays in Honour of M.V. Duignan.* Galway, 1981.

Scott, Kenneth. "Merkur-Augustus und Horaz C. 12". *Hermes* 63 (1928): 15-33.

Searle, Eleanor. "Women and the Legitimization of Succession at the Norman Conquest". ANS 3 (1980): 159–70.

Sellevold, B.J., U.L. Hansen and J.B. Jörgensen, eds. *Iron Age Man in Denmark.* Copenhagen, 1984.

Sergent, Bernard. "Three Notes on the Trifunctional Indo- European Marriage". JIES 12 (1984): 179–91.

Service, Elman R. *Origins of the State and Civilization: The Process of Cultural Evolution.* New York, 1975.

Seibt, Ferdinand, ed. *Gesellschaftsgeschichte: Festschrift für Karl Bosl zum 80. Geburtstag.* II vols. München, 1988.

Sievers, Susanne et al. "Handicrafts". In *The Celts*, eds. Sabatino Moscati, Otto Hermann Frey, Venceslas Kruta, Barry Raftery and Miklós Szabó, pp. 436–50. New York, 1991.

Sharpe, Richard. "Hiberno-Latin *Laicus*, Irish *Láech* and the Devil's Men". *Ériu* 30 (1979): 75–92.

——. "Some Problems Concerning the Organization of the Church in Early Medieavl Ireland". *Peritia* 3 (1984): 230–70.

——. "Dispute Settlement in Medieval Ireland: A Preliminary Inquiry". In *The Settlement of Disputes in Early Medieval Europe*, eds. Wendy Davies and Paul Fouracre, pp. 169–89. Cambridge, 1986.

Sherwin-White, A. W. *Racial Prejudice in Imperial Rome.* Cambridge, 1970.

Shippey, T.A., ed and trans. *Poems of Wisdom and Learning in Old English.* Cambridge, 1976.

Simek, Rudolf. *Lexikon der germanischen Mythologie.* Stuttgart, 1984.

Simpson, Jacqueline. "A Note on the Word *Fridstoll*". SBVS 14 (1955): 200–10.

——. "Grimr the Good, a Magical Drinking Horn". EC 10 (1963): 489–515.

Sissa, Giulia. *Greek Virginity*. Cambridge, 1990.

Sjövold, Thorleif. *Der Oseberg-Fund und die anderen Wikingerschiffsfunde*. Oslo, 1958.

Sklute, Larry H. *"Freoðuwebbe* in Old English Poetry". NM 71 (1970): 534–41.

Skomal, Susan Nacer and Edgar C. Polomé, eds. *Proto-Indo-European: The Archaeology of a Linguistic Problem. Studies in Honor of Marija Gimbritas*. Washington, 1987

Smith, C.C. "Vulgar Latin in Roman Britain: Epigraphic and Other Evidence". ANRW II, 29, 2 (1983): 893–948.

Smyser, H.M. "Ibn Fadlan's Account of the Rus, with Some Commentary and Some Allusions to *Beowulf*". In *Franciplegius*, eds. J.B. Bessinger and R.P. Creed, pp. 92–119. New York, 1965.

Sochacki, Z. "The Radical-decorated Pottery Culture". In *The Neolithic in Poland*, ed. Tadensz Wislinski, pp. 296–332. Wroclaw, 1970.

Solberg, Bergljot. "Social Status in the Merovingian and Viking Periods in Norway from Archaeological and Historical Sources". NAR 18 (1985): 61–76.

Sörbom, P., ed. *Transport Technology and Social Change*. Stockholm, 1980.

Sörensen, Preben M. *The Unmanly Man: Concepts of Sexual Defamation in Early Norse Society*, trans. Joan Turville-Petre. Odense, 1983.

Spann, Philip O. *Quintus Sertorius and the Legacy of Sulla*. Fayetteville, 1987.

Sprigade, Klaus. *Die Einweisung ins Kloster und in den geistlichen Stand als politische Massnahme im frühen Mittelalter*. Heidelberg, 1964.

Stacey, Robin C. "Ties that Bind: Immunities in Irish and Welsh Law". CMCS 20 (1990): 39–60.

——. "Law and Order in the Very Old West: England and Ireland in the Early Middle Ages". In *Crossed Paths. Methodological Approaches to the Celtic Aspect of the European Middle Ages*, eds. B.T. Hudson and V. Ziegler, pp. 39–60. Lanham, 1988.

Stafford, Pauline. "The King's Wife in Wessex, 800–1066". PP 91 (1981): 3–27.

——. *Queens, Concubines and Dowagers: the King's Wife in the Early Middle Ages*. London, 1983.

Stead, I.M. "A La Tène III Burial at Welwyn Garden City". *Archaeologica* 101 (1967): 1–62.

——. "The Belgae in Britain". In *The Celts*, eds. Sabatino Moscati, Otto Hermann Frey, Venceslas Kruta, Barry Raftery and Miklós Szabó, pp. 591–5. New York, 1991.

Steblin-Kamenskij, M.I. "Valkyries and Heroes". ANF 97 (1982): 81–93.

Stein, Frauke. *Adelsgräber des achten Jahrhunderts in Deutschland*. Berlin, 1967.

Stephenson, Günther, ed. *Der Religionswandel unserer Zeit im Spiegel der Religionswissenschaft*. Darmstadt, 1976.

Steuer, Heiko. *Frühgeschichtliche Sozialstrukturen in Mitteleuropa: Eine Analyse der Auswertungsmethoden des archäologischen Quellenmaterials*. Göttingen, 1982.

——. "Schlüsselpaare in frühgeschichtlichen Gräbern—Zur Deutung einer Amulett—Beigabe". St. S 3 (1982): 185–247.

——. "Helm und Ringschwert: Prunkbewaffnung und Ringabzeichen germanischer Krieger. Eine Ubersicht". St. S 6 (1987): 189–236.

——. "Archaeology and History: Proposals on the Social Structure of the Merovingian Kingdom". In *The Birth of Europe. Archaeology and Social Development in the First Millenium AD*, ed. Klaus Randsborg, pp. 100–22. Rome, 1989.

——. "Interpretationsmöglichkeiten archäologischer Quellen zum Gefolgschaftsproblem". In *Beiträge zum Verständnis der Germania des Tacitus* II, eds. Günter Neumann and Henning Seemann, pp. 203–57. Göttingen, 1992.

Steven, C.E. "A Roman Inscription from Beltingham". *Archaeologia Aeliana* II (1934): 138–45.

Stibbe, Hildegard. *'Herr' und 'Frau' und verwandte Begriffe in ihren altenglischen Äquivalenten.* Heidelberg, 1935. Stjernquist, Berta. *Simris. On Cultural Connections of Scania in the Roman Iron Age.* Lund, 1955.

Stolte, B.H. "Die religiosen Verhältnisse in Niedergermanien". ANRW II, 18, 1 (1983): 591–671.

Stokes, Whitley. "The Bodlein Amra Choluimb Cille". RC 20 (1899): 30–55, 132–83, 248–89, 400–37.

Ström, Ake V. "Die Hauptriten des wikingerzeitlichen nordischen Opfers". In *Festschrift Walter Baetke*, eds. Kurt Rudolph, Rolf Heller and Ernst Walter, pp. 330–42. Weimar, 1966.

Ström, Folke. *Nid, Ergi and Old Norse Moral Attitudes.* London, 1973.

——. "Hieros-gamos-motivet i Hallfredr Ottarrssons Hákonardrápa och den nordnorska jarlavärdigheten". ANF 98 (1983): 67–79.

Studien zu den Militärgrenzen Roms II: Vorträge des 10. internationalen Limeskongress in der Germania inferior. Köln, 1977.

Sveinsson, Einar Ól., ed., *Brennu-Njáls saga.* Reykjavik, 1954.

Syme, Ronald. "Tacitus on Gaul". *Latomus* 12 (1953): 25–37.

——. *Tacitus.* II vols. Oxford, 1958.

Szabó, Miklós "The Celts and their Movements in the Third Century BC". In *The Celts*, eds. Sabatino Moscati, Otto Hermann Frey, Venceslas Kruta, Barry Raftery and Miklós Szabó, pp. 303–20. New York, 1991.

——. "Mercenary Activity". In *The Celts*, eds. Sabatino Moscati, Otto Hermann Frey, Venceslas Kruta, Barry Raftery and Miklós Szabó, pp. 333–36. New York, 1991.

Szarnach, P.E., ed. *Sources of Anglo-Saxon Culture.* Kalamazoo, 1986.

Tackenberg, Kurt. "Über die Schutzwaffen der Karolingerzeit und ihre Wiedergabe in Handschriften und auf Elfenbeinschnitzerein". FM St. 3 (1969): 277–88.

Talbot, C.H. *The Anglo-Saxon Missionaries in Germany.* New York, 1954.

Talley, Jeannine. "Runes, Mandrakes and Gallows". In *Myth in Indo-European Antiquity*. eds. Gerald James Larson, Scott Littleton and Jan Puhvel, pp. 157–68. Berkeley, 1974.

Tchernia, André. "Italian Wine in Gaul at the end of the Republic". In *Trade in the Ancient Economy*, eds. Peter Garnsey, Keith Hopkins, C.R. Whittaker, pp. 87–104. Berkeley, 1983

Tellenbach, Gerd. *The Investiture Contest.* trans. R.F. Bennett. Oxford, 1984.

Terry, Patricia, trans. *Poems of the Vikings. The Elder Edda.* Indianapolis, 1980.

Thénot, Andrée. *La civilization celtique dans l'est de la France. II vols.* Paris, 1982.

Thevénot, Émile. "Mars et Mercure en Gaule". *Latomus* 20 (1961): 535–40.

——. *Divinités et sanctuaires de la Gaule.* Paris, 1968.

Thomsen, Per O. "Die Goldblechfiguren ("guldgubber") der vierten Lundeborg-Grabung 1989". In *Der historische Horizent der Gotterbild-Amulette aus der Übergangsepoche von der Spätantike zum Frühmittelalter*, ed. Karl Hauck, pp. 512–17. Göttingen, 1992.

Thompson, E.A. *The Early Germans.* Oxford, 1965.

—. *The Visagoths in the Time of Ulfila.* Oxford, 1966.

—. *The Goths in Spain.* Oxford, 1969.

Thorpe, Benjamin, ed. *Beowulf Together with Widsith and the Fight at Finnesburg.* Great Neck, 1962².

Thorpe, Lewis, trans. *Gregory of Tours. The History of the Franks.* Harmondsworth, 1979².

Thurneysen, Rudolf. *Die irische Helden-und Königssage bis zum siebzehnten Jahrhundert.* Halle, 1921.

—. "Göttin Medb?" ZCP 8 (1929): 108–10.

Tierney, J.J. "The Celtic Ethnography of Posidonius". PRIA, C, 5 (1960): 189–275.

Timpe, Dieter. *Arminius-Studien.* Heidelberg, 1970.

—. "Der keltische Handel nach historischen Quellen". In *Untersuchungen zu Handel und Verkehr vor-und Frühgeschichtlichen Zeit im Mittel-und Nord Europa* I, eds. Klaus Düwel, Herbert Jankuhn, Harold Siems, Dieter Timpe, pp. 258–84. Göttingen, 1985.

—. "Ethnologische Begriffsbildung in der Antike". In *Germanenprobleme in heutiger Sicht*, ed. Heinrich Beck, pp. 22–40. Berlin, 1986.

—. "Die Absicht der Germania". In *Beiträge zum Verstandnis der Germania des Tacitus* I, eds. Herbert Jankuhn and Dieter Timpe, pp. 106–28. Göttingen, 1989.

—. "Entdeckungsgeschichte". *Reallexikon* 7 (1989): 307–89.

—. "Der Sueben-Begriff bei Tacitus". In *Beiträge zum Verständnis der Germania von Tacitus* II, eds. Günter Neumann and Henning Seemann, pp. 278–310. Göttingen, 1992.

Todd, Malcolm. *The Northern Barbarians. 100 BC–AD 300.* London, 1987².

—. "Germanic Burials in the Roman Iron Age". In *Burial in the Roman World*, ed. Richard Reese, pp 39–43. London, 1977.

Tolkien, J.R.R. "English and Welsh". In *Angles and Britons: The O'Donnell Lectures*, pp. 1–41. Cardiff, 1963.

Tovar, Antonio. *The Ancient Languages of Spain and Portugal.* New York, 1961.

—. "The God Lugus in Spain". BBCS 29 (1982): 591–9.

—. "The Celts in the Iberian Peninsula: Archaeology, History and Language". In *Geschichte und Kultur der Kelten: Vorbereitungskonferenz 25–28 Oktober 1982 in Bonn*, eds. Karl H. Schmidt and Rolf Kodderitzsch, pp. 68–101. Heidelburg, 1986.

Tristram, Hildegard L.C. "Early Modes of Insular Expression". In *Sages, Saints and Storytellers: Celtic Studies in Honour of Professor James Carney*, eds. Donnchadh O Córrain, Liam Breatnach and Kim Mc Cone, pp. 427–48. Naas, 1989.

Tucker, John, ed. *Sagas of the Icelanders.* New York, 1989.

Turville-Petre, E.O.G. and J.S. Martin. *Iceland and the Medieval World: Studies in Honour of Ian Maxwell.* Victoria, 1974.

—. *Myth and Religion of the North. The Religion of Ancient Scandinavia.* Westport, 1975².

—. *Scaldic Poetry.* Oxford, 1976.

Turville-Petre, Joan. "On Ynglingatal". MS II (1978–79): 48–67.

Uecker, Heiko, ed. *Studien zum Altgermanischen. Festechrift für Heinrich Beck.* Berlin, New York, 1994.

von Ungern-Sternberg, Jurgen and Hansjorg Reinau, eds. *Vergangenheit in mundlicher Überlieferung.* Stuttgart, 1988.

Untermann, J. "Die althispanischen Sprachen". ANRW II, 29, 2 (1983): 791–818.

Urban, Ralf. *Ur und frühgeschichtliche Archäologie der Schweiz IV. Die Eisenzeit*. Basel, 1984.

—. *Der "Bataveraufstand" und die Erhebung des Iulius Classicus*. Trier, 1985.

—. "Die Treverer in Caesars Bellum Gallicum". In *Labor omnibus unius. Gerold Walser zum 70. Geburtstag dargebracht von Freunden, Kollegen und Schülern*, eds. Heinz E. Herzig and Regula Frei-Stolba, pp. 244–56. Stuttgart, 1989.

—. "Aufbau, und Gedankengang der Germania des Tacitus". In *Beiträge zum Verstandnis der Germania des Tacitus* I, eds. Herbert Jankuhn and Dieter Timpe, pp. 80–105. Göttingen, 1989.

von Uslar, Rafael. *Die Germanen vom 1. bis 4. Jahrhundert nach Christus*. Stuttgart, 1980.

Van Hamel, A.G. "Odinn Hanging on the Tree". APS 7 (1932): 260–88.

Van Soesbergen, P.G. "The Phases of the Batavian Revolt". *Helinium* II (1971): 238–56.

Vatin, Claude. "Ex-voto de bois gallo-romains à Chamalièrs". RA (1969): 103–14.

—. "Wooden Sculpture From Gallo-Roman Auvergne". Antiquity 46 (1972): 39–42.

Vertet, H. "Remarques sur l'aspect et les attributs de Mercure gallo-romaine populaire dans le centre de la Gaule". In *Hommages à Albert Grenier* III, pp. 1606–16. Bruxelles, 1962.

Venclova, Natalie. "Das Grenzgebiet der Latènekultur in Nordwestböhmen". In *Frühe Volker in Mitteleuropa*, eds. Fritz Horst and Friedrich Schlette, pp. 121–8. Berlin, 1988.

Vendryes, J. "La racine *smer- en celtique". EC 2 (1937): 133–6.

Vierck, Hayo. "Religion, Rang und Herrschaft im Spiegel der Tracht". In *Sachsen und Angelsächsen. Ausstellung des Helms-Museums 18 November 1979 bis 28 Februar 1980. Hamburgisches Museum für Vor und Frühgeschichte*, ed. C. Ahrens, pp 271–83. Hamburg, 1980.

—. "Hallenfreunde: Ärchaologische Spuren Frühmittelalterliche Trinkgelage und mögliche Wege zu ihrer Deutung". In *Feste und Feiern im Mittelalter: Pederborner Symposion des Mediävistenverbandes*, pp. 115–22. Sigmaringen, 1990.

Vierneisel, Klaus and Bert Kaeser, eds. *Kunst der Schale-Kultur des Trinkens*. München, 1990.

Vigfusson, Gudbrand and F. York Powell. *Corpus Poeticum Boreale*. II vols. Oxford, 1883.

Vogelsang, Thilo. *Die Frau als Herrscherin: Studien zur 'consors regni' Formel im Mittelalter*. Göttingen, 1954.

Volkmann, Hans. *Germanische Seherinnen in römischen Diensten*. Krefeld, 1964.

Wagenvoort, Hendrick. "Nehalennia and the Souls of the Dead". *Mnemosyne* 24 (1971): 239–92.

—. "The Journey of the Souls of the Dead to the Isles of the Blessed". *Mnemosyne* 24 (1971): 113–61.

Wagner, Heinrich. *Studies in the Origins of the Celts and of Early Celtic Civilization*. Belfast, 1971.

—. "Old Irish FIR 'truth, oath'". In his *Studies in the Origins of the Celts and of Early Celtic Civilization*, pp. 1–45.

—. "Irish *fath*, Welsh *gwawd*, Old Icelandic *odr* 'poetry' and the Germanic god Wotan/Odinn". In his *Studies in the Origins of the Celts and of Early Celtic Civilization*, pp. 46–58.

—. "Der königliche Palast in keltischer Tradition". ZCP (1984): 6–14.

Wagner, Norbert. "Der völkerwanderungszeitliche Germanenbegriff". In *Germanenprobleme in heutiger Sicht*, ed. Heinrich Beck, pp. 130–54. Berlin, 1986.
—. "Ein neugefundener Wodansname". BJ 188 (1988): 238–39.
Wahle, Ernst, "Zur ethnischen Deutung frühgeschichtlicher Kulturprovinzen". *Sitzungsberichte der Heidelberger Akad. d. Wiss. Phil.- hist. Klasse* (1940/41) No. 2.
Wait, G.A., *Ritual and Religion in Iron Age Britain*. II vols. Oxford, 1985.
Wallace-Hadrill, James Michael, ed. *The Fourth Book of the Chronicle of Fredegar With its Continuations*. London, 1960.
—. *Early Germanic Kingship in England and on the Continent*. Oxford, 1971.
—. *The Frankish Church*. Oxford, 1984.
Waitz, Georg, ed. *Origo gentis Langobardorum*. MGH SS. rer. Lang. Hannoverae, 1878.
—., ed. *Pauli Historia Langobardorum*. MGH SS. rer. Germ. in usum scholarum. Hannoverae, 1878.
—., ed. *Vita Leobae*. MGH SS. 14. Hannoverae, 1887.
Walser, Gerold. "Veleda". PRCA VIII A, 1 (1955): 617-621.
—. *Rom, das Reich und die fremden Völker in der Geschichtsschreibung der frühen Kaiserzeit: Studien zur Glaubwürdigkeit des Tacitus*. Baden-Baden, 1951.
—. *Caesar und die Germanen: Studien zur politischen Tendenz römischer Feldzugsberichte*. Wiesbaden, 1956.
Wamers, Egon. "*Pyxides imaginatae*. Zur Ikonographie und Funktion karolingischer Silberbecher". *Germania* 69 (1991): 97–152.
Warner, Richard B. "The Archaeology of Early Historic Irish Kingship". In *Power and Politics in Early Medieval Britain and Ireland*, eds. Stephen T. Driscoll and Margaret R. Nieke, pp. 47–68. Edinburgh, 1988.
Watkins, Calvert. "Is Tre Fis Flathemon: Marginalia to Audacht Morainn". *Ériu* 30 (1979): 181–98.
Watt, Margarethe. "Sorte Muld. Hövdingesaede og kultcentrum fra Bornholms yngre jernalder". In *Fra Stamme til Stat i Danmark* II, pp. 89-107. Århus, 1990.
—. "Die Goldblechfiguren ("guldgubber") aus Sorte Muld". In *Der historische Horizent der Gotterbild-Amulette aus der Übergangsepoche von der Spätantike zum Frühmittelalter*, ed. Karl Hauck, pp. 195–227 Göttingen, 1992.
Webster, Graham, *Boudica and the British Revolt Against Rome AD 60*. London, 1978.
—. *Rome Against Caratacus. The Roman Campaigns in Britain AD 48–58*. Totowa, 1981.
—. *The British Celts and their Gods Under Rome*. London, 1986.
—. *Celtic Religion in Roman Britain*. Totowa, 1986.
—. "What the Romans Required From the Gods as Seen Through the Pairing of Roman and Celtic Deities and the Character of Votive Offerings". In *Pagan Gods and Shrines of the Roman Empire*, eds. Martin Henig and Anthony King, pp. 57–64. Oxford, 1986.
Weidemann, Margarete. *Kulturgeschichte der Merowingerzeit nach den Werken Gregors von Tours*. II vols. Bonn, 1982.
Weinstock, John, ed. *The Nordic Languages and Modern Linguistics 3. Proceedings of the Third International Conference of Nordic and General Linguistics*. Austin, 1978.
Weise, Judith. "The Meaning of the Name 'Hygd': Onomastic Contrast in *Beowulf*". *Names* 34 (1986): 1–9.
Weisgerber, J.H. *Die Namen der Ubier*. Köln, 1968.

Weisgerber, Leo. *Deutsch als Volksname: Ursprung und Bedeutung.* Stuttgart, 1954.

——. "Walhisk. Die geschichtliche Leistung des Wortes Welsch". In his *Deutsch als Volksname: Ursprung und Bedeutung*, pp. 155–232.

Weisweiler, Josef. "Die Stellung der Frau bei den Kelten und das Problem des 'Keltischen Mutterrechts'". ZcP 21 (1939): 205–79.

——. *Heimat und Herrschaft: Wirkung und Ursprung eines irischen Mythos.* Halle, 1943.

Wellesley, Kenneth. *The Long Year. AD 69.* Boulder, 1976.

Wells, C.M. *The German Policy of Augustus: An Examination of the Archaeological Evidence.* Oxford, 1972.

Wells, Peter S. *Culture Contact and Culture Change: Early Iron Age Central Europe and the Mediterranean World.* Cambridge, 1980.

——. "Mediterranean Trade and Culture Change in Early Iron Age Central Europe". In *Settlement and Society: Aspects of Western European Prehistory in the First Millenium BC*, eds. T.C. Champion and J.V.S. Megaw, pp. 69–90. New York, 1985.

Wemple, Suzanne Fonay. *Women in Frankish Society: Marriage and the Cloister 500–900.* Philadelphia, 1981.

Wenskus, Reinhard. *Stammesbildung und Verfassung: Das Werden der frühmittelalterlichen Gentes.* Köln, 1977².

——., H.R. Loyn and G. Blom. "Dienstmann". *Reallexikon* 5 (1984): 411–17.

——. and Dieter Timpe. "Clientes". *Reallexikon* 5 (1984) 20–30.

——. "Druht". *Reallexikon* 6 (1986): 202–3.

——. *Ausgewahlte Aufsätze zum frühen und preussischen Mittelalter.* Sigmaringen, 1986.

——. "Zum Problem der Ansippung". In his *Ausgewahlte Aufsätze zum frühen und preussischen Mittelalter*, pp. 85–95.

——. "Über die Möglichkeit eines allgemeinen interdisziplinären Germanenbegriffs". In *Germanenprobleme in heutiger Sicht*, ed. Heinrich Beck, pp. 1–21. Berlin, 1986.

——. "Die neuere Diskussion um gefolgschaft und Herrschaft in Tacitus' *Germania*". In *Beiträge zum Verständnis der Germania von Tacitus* II, eds. Günter Neumann and Henning Seemann, pp. 311–31. Göttingen, 1992.

Werlich, Egon. "Der westgermanische Skop: Der Ursprung des Sängerstandes in semasiologischer und etymologischer Sicht". ZdP 86 (1967): 352–74.

Werner, Joachim. "Römische Trinkgefässe in germanischen Gräbern der Kaiserzeit". In *Ur und Frühgeschichte als historische Wissenschaft*, pp. 168–76. Heidelberg, 1950.

——. "Leier und Harfe im germanischen Frühmittelalter". In *Aus Verfässungs—und Landesgeschichte* I, pp. 9–15. Lindau-Konstanz, 1954.

——. "Das Messerpaar aus dem Basel-Kleinhüningen Grab 126. Zu alamannisch-fränkischen Essbestecken". In *Provincialia. Festschrift für Fr. v. Zahn*, pp. 347–52. Köln, 1968.

——. "Danceny und Brangstrup: Unterschungen zur Cernjachov-Kultur zwischen Sereth und Dnestr und zu den 'Reichtumszentren' auf Fünen". BJ 188 (1988): 241–88.

Werner, Karl. "Die Nachkommen Karls des Grossen bis um das Jahr 1000". In *Karl der Grosse*, eds. Wolfgang Braunfels and Percy Ernst Schramm, pp. 403–79. Düsseldorf, 1967.

Wheeler, Mortimer. *Rome Beyond the Imperial Frontiers.* London, 1955.

White, Horace, ed. *Appian's Roman History*. IV vols. London, 1933².

White, Stephen D. "Kinship and Lordship in Early Medieval England: The Story of Cynewulf and Cyneheard". *Viator* 20 (1989): 1–18.

Whitelock, Dorothy. *The Audience of Beowulf*. Oxford, 1951.

——. *The Beginnings of English Society*. Harmondsworth, 1977².

——., M. Brett and C.N.L. Brooke. *Councils and Synods*, Vol I. Oxford, 1981.

Wightman, Edith Mary. *Roman Trier and the Treveri*. London, 1970.

——. "The Lingones: Lugdunensis, Belgica or Germania Superior?" In *Studien zu den Militärgrenzen Roms II: Vorträge des 10. internationalen Limeskongress in der Germania inferior*, pp. 207–17. Köln, 1977.

——. "Peasants and Potentates in Roman Gaul". AJAH 3 (1978): 43–63.

——. *Gallia Belgica*. London, 1985.

——. "Pagan Cults in the Province of Belgica". ANRW II, 18, 1 (1986): 542–89.

Will, Wolfgang. "Römisch 'Klientel-Randstaaten' am Rhein? Eine Bestandsaufnahme". BJ 187 (1987): 1–61.

Willems, William J.H. "Romans and Batavians: Regional Developments at the Imperial Frontier". In *Roman and Native in the Low Countries: Spheres of Interaction*, eds. Roel Brandt and Jan Slofstra, pp. 105–28. Oxford, 1984.

——. "Rome and its Frontiers in the North: The Role of the Periphery". (1991): pp, 33–45

Williams. J.E. Caerwyn. "The Court Poet in Medieval Ireland". PBA 57 (1971): 85–135.

——. "Posidonius' Celtic Parasites". *Studia Celtica* 15 (1980): 313–43.

——. "Celtic Literature: Origins". In *Geschichte und Kultur der Kelten: Vorbereitungskonferenz 25–28 Oktober 1982 in Bonn*, eds. Karl H. Schmidt and Rolf Kodderitzsch, pp. 123–44. Heidelberg, 1986.

Wittern, Susanne. "Frauen zwischen asketischem Ideal und weltlichem Leben. Zur Darstellung des christlichen Handels der merowingischen Königinnen Radegunde und Balthilde in den hagiographischen Lebensbeschreibungen des 6. und 7. Jahrhundert". In *Frauen in der Geschichte* VII, eds. Werner Affeldt and Annette Kuhn, pp. 272–94. Düsseldorf, 1986.

Wolf, Günther, ed. *Zum Kaisertum Karls des Grossen*. Darmstadt, 1972.

——. "Mittel der Herrschaftssicherung in den Germanenreichen des 6. und 7. Jahrhunderts". ZSSR (G.A.) 105 (1988): 214–38.

Wolfram, Herwig. *Intitulatio I: Lateinische Königs-und Fürstentitel bis zum ende des 8. Jahrhunderts*. Wien, 1967.

——. "Methodische Fragen zur Kritik am 'sakralen' Königtum germanischer Stämme". In *Festschrift für Otto Hofler* II, eds. Helmut Birkhan and Otto Gschwantler, pp. 473–90. Wien, 1968.

——. "The Shaping of the Early Medieval Kingdom". *Viator* 1 (1970): 1–20.

——. *Geschichte der Goten. Von den Anfängen bis zur Mitte des sechsten Jahrhunderts: Entwurf einer historischen Ethnographie*. München, 1980.

——. and Falco Daim, eds. *Die Völker an der mittleren und untern Donau im fünften und sechsten Jahrhundert*. Wien, 1980.

——. and Andreas Schwarcz, eds. *Die Bayern und ihre Nachbarn*, Vol I. Wien, 1985.

Wood, Ian N. *The Merovingian North Sea*. Alingsas, 1983.

Woolf, Rosemary. "The Ideal of Men Dying With Their Lord in the *Germania* and in *The Battle of Maldon*". ASE 4 (1976): 63–81.

Wormald, Patrick. "Bede, Beowulf and the Conversion of the Anglo-Saxon Aristocracy". In *Bede and Anglo-Saxon England*, ed. R.T. Farrell, pp. 32–95. Oxford, 1978.

—. *Bede and the Conversion of England: The Charter Evidence*. Newcastle upon Tyne, 1984.

—. "Celtic and Anglo-Saxon Kingship: Some Further Thoughts". In *Sources of Anglo-Saxon Culture*, ed. P.E. Szarnach, pp. 151–83. Kalamazoo, 1986.

Young, Bailey K. "Exemple aristocratique et mode funéraire dans la Gaule mérovingienne". AESC 41 (1986): 379–407.

—. "Le problème franc et l'apport des pratiques funéraires (III-Vᵉ siècles)". BLAFAM 3 (1980): 4–18.

Zeitler, W.M. "Zum Germanenbegriff Caesars: Der Germanenexkurs im sechsten Buch von Caesars Bellum Gallicum". In *Germanenprobleme in heutiger Sicht*, ed. Heinrich Beck, pp. 41–52. Berlin, 1986.

Zeller, Kurt W. "Kriegswesen und Bewaffnung der Kelten". In *Die Kelten in Mitteleuropa. Kultur-Kunst-Wirtschaft. Salzburger Landesausstellung Hallein*, pp. 111–32. Salzburg, 1980.

Zeumer, Karl, ed. *Leges Visigothorum*. MGH Leges nationum Germ, I. Hannoverae, 1902.

Zwicker, Ioannes. *Fontes historiae religionis celticae*. Berlin, 1934.

INDEX

Authors, classical, medieval and modern, are not included in the index.